JOHN DEWEY

Alan Ryan is also the author of:

The Philosophy of John Stuart Mill
The Philosophy of the Social Sciences
J. S. Mill
Property and Political Theory
Property
Bertrand Russell: A Political Life

and the editor of:

Social Explanation
Justice

JOHN DEWEY

And the High Tide of American Liberalism

BY

Alan Ryan

W · W · NORTON & COMPANY
NEW YORK · LONDON

FRONTISPIECE PHOTOGRAPH: Portrait of John Dewey by Edward B. Child.

First published as a Norton paperback 1997

The text of this book is composed in Galliard with the display set in Garamond and Bodoni. Composition and manufacturing by the Maple-Vail Book Manufacturing Group. Book design by Marjorie J. Flock.

Library of Congress Cataloging-in-Publication Data

Ryan, Alan.
John Dewey and the high tide of American liberalism / Alan Ryan.
p. cm.
Includes bibliographical references.
1. Dewey, John, 1859–1952. 2. Philosophy, American—20th century.
3. Liberalism. I. Title.
B945.D44R93 1995
191—dc20
[B] 94-36064

ISBN 0-393-03773-8
ISBN 0-393-31550-9 pbk.

W · W · Norton & Company, Inc., 500 Fifth Avenue, New York, N.Y. 10110
W · W · Norton & Company Ltd., 10 Coptic Street, London WC1A 1PU

1 2 3 4 5 6 7 8 9 0

To Kate and Sadie

Contents

Preface

The "death of the author" made so much of by literary critics is no news to authors. Few of us write a postcard from the beach with complete confidence that what appears on the card is what we originally had in mind. Books rarely end as the creatures they were conceived, and this one is no exception. I first thought of writing about John Dewey twenty years ago. I was puzzled by the way that Dewey and Bertrand Russell agreed so often in politics and never in philosophy. I was puzzled, too, by the way American students in Oxford to whom I suggested Dewey as a plausible topic for research would come back after a summer vacation hell-bent on studying Lukács, Marcuse, Adorno, or Habermas. They seemed to me to be missing something interesting, and I was curious to know what deterred them. When I moved to Princeton in 1988, it seemed a good moment to embark on discovering what it was. I had just finished a book on Russell's politics, and it seemed plausible to explore Dewey's place in a secular trinity of liberal intellectuals consisting of Mill, Russell, and him.

Hardly had I begun when two splendid new books on Dewey appeared. Robert Westbrook's *John Dewey and American Democracy*[1] has been justly praised as a distinguished intellectual biography of a seminal American thinker. More interesting to me was the book's political purpose. Westbrook was especially concerned to rescue Dewey for the New Left, to praise his defense of participatory democracy, and to hold him up as a critic of that New Left bugbear "corporate liberalism." At much the same time Steven Rockefeller published his *John Dewey*,[2] a less widely noticed book but one that I think is rather truer to Dewey's *philosophical* and religious concerns—in Dewey's own, broad sense of both terms. I am skeptical of the view that Dewey was a New Left "radical," though I am not in the least skeptical of the claim that he was a radical, just as I am skeptical of the claim that he was in the usual sense of the term a "religious" humanist, though I am not at all skeptical of the claim that he wished so to describe himself.

To add another volume to these large and distinguished works merely to quibble with their emphasis would have been overkill. But I found I wanted to say something unlike what had been said already. For one thing, writing out of a British background made all the difference to the way Dewey looks—"British" rather than "English," because the turn-of-the-century philosophers who wrote in the same Hegelian tradition as Dewey but on the other side of the Atlantic were Scots and Welsh as often as English; they were often "children of the manse," nonmetropolitan and nonconformist in rather the way Dewey was. The most famous of these British writers was Thomas Hill Green, whose career as philosophy tutor in Oxford in the 1870s was brief, but who inspired several generations of politicians, administrators, social reformers, and members of the churches with his own passion for public service. So powerful was his influence that he has often been described as the intellectual father of the British welfare state. During the years he taught at the University of Michigan the young Dewey was a great admirer of Green's and a surprisingly familiar figure to a British observer. Dewey was, and remained, a midwestern T. H. Green, more relaxed, more radical, less concerned with the ethics of a *class*-divided society, but otherwise not wholly altered.[3] These transatlantic likenesses undermined the cliché that Dewey was a quintessentially "American" thinker and made me wonder how Dewey's views—which were concerned with the predicament of "modern man" and "the modern world" rather than "Americans" or "the American world"—fed into his reception by Americans.

Seeing him in this transatlantic light made a great difference to what now seemed original and what seemed derivative in his philosophical, religious, educational, and political views. Seeing him as a "modern" and a "North Atlantic" figure more than an American one raised the question of what an *American* audience wanted from a public philosopher—from an intellectual figure whose credentials came from his academic standing as a philosopher but whose audience was so much wider than an academic one. So I continued, asking where Dewey fitted into the American radical tradition, how he was and was not like his transatlantic contemporaries, why he could for so long practice a form of philosophical inquiry that became unfashionable in Britain after 1914 at the latest.

Again, I write with a very different political slant from most of my American colleagues. Coming from a country which boasted the prewar Labour party whose absence from the United States Dewey lamented during the 1930s, I have none of Professor Westbrook's concern to demonstrate that Dewey was on my side. It is quite clear that Dewey would have been happy with the post-1945 Labour party and absolutely baffled by the ecstatic politics of the 1968 student uprisings, whether in Paris or in the United States. All the same, my interests are closer to Professor Westbrook's than to Professor Rockefeller's. It is true that Dewey was a philosopher rather than a publicist and that he espoused something one might call religious humanism. But unlike Professor Rockefeller, I think Dewey's "religious" outlook illuminates his politics very much more vividly than it does the philosophy of religion as ordinarily conceived. Professor Westbrook complains that "The secondary literature on Dewey is enormous, though much of it is not worth reading."[4] I, too, have been impressed by how thin, and how misleading, a lot of it is and how much the level has been raised by Westbrook and Rockefeller. I have indicated my debts to them in my notes and have pointed readers to them whenever I have thought I had little to add to their views. I have not tried to point out the innumerable occasions when "their" Dewey looks different from "mine."

Acknowledgments

I have accumulated many debts in writing this book. I was a Mellon Fellow at the Institute for Advanced Study in 1991–92 and greatly benefited from the encouragement of Michael Walzer and Albert Hirschman, from the skepticism of Clifford Geertz, and from Morton White's readiness to share his memories of Dewey; my fellow visitors were generous with their time and curiosity, too. The Center for Dewey Studies at Southern Illinois University, Carbondale kindly made papers and letters available; I am particularly grateful to Harriet Simon for her hospitality there. The Princeton University Center for Human Values enabled me to travel to Carbondale to use archival materials. The Conference for the Study of Political Thought, the Canadian Victorian Studies Society, the Doreen B. Townsend Center for the Humanities, the Columbia Legal Theory Workshop, The Greater Philadelphia Philosophy Consortium, and audiences at Bryn Mawr, SUNY Purchase, Princeton, Oxford, and McMaster University all enabled me to try out my ideas in a benign but critical setting. Benjamin Barber, Seyla Benhabib, Richard Bernstein, Michael Freeden, Elisabetta Galeotti, Casey Haskins, Jennifer Hochschild, Morris Kaplan, George Kateb, Margaret Macmillan, Pratap Mehta, Louis Menand, David Miller, Alexander Nehamas, Richard Shusterman, Avital Simchoni, and Cornel West at different times asked just the right questions. Roxanne Euben and Sadie Ryan were exemplary research assistants in successive summers. One debt I have no way of repaying; a few weeks before he died, Sidney Hook wrote to say that he was glad to see that I was working on Dewey but that the task was hopeless. No Englishman could make any sense of so American a figure, but he hoped I would persist and was sorry he would be dead before my work saw the light. I hope that what follows might have changed his mind about the interpretive skills of the English.

JOHN DEWEY

Overview

When John Dewey died in 1952, he was memorialized as America's most famous philosopher, revered by liberal educators and deplored by conservatives but universally acknowledged as his country's intellectual voice. "So faithfully did Dewey live up to his own philosophical creed that he became the guide, the mentor, and the conscience of the American people; it is scarcely an exaggeration to say that for a generation no issue was clarified until Dewey had spoken."[5] Henry Commager's *The American Mind* was published at the end of Dewey's life and perhaps had some of the poetic license proper to obituaries about it, but it was a fair estimate of Dewey's place in American intellectual life. Many things had conspired to give Dewey this extraordinary eminence. He was immensely long-lived and immensely prolific; he died in his ninety-third year, and his intellectual productivity hardly slackened until he was well into his eighties. The longest statement of his views on logic, epistemology, and the philosophy of science—*Logic: The Theory of Inquiry*—came out in 1938, when he was seventy-nine years old, and only the loss of the typescript during a summer holiday stopped him from giving the world his last thoughts on philosophical method at the age of ninety. His *Collected Works* fill thirty-seven substantial volumes and spell out Dewey's views on persons from Plato to Franklin Roosevelt and on subjects from immortality to the place of cooking in primary education. Mere productivity would not have been enough to secure attention. He wrote so much because he had an audience, both academic and lay, an audience for his philosophical outlook and for his political allegiances. He struck a chord with the public for the best part of sixty years.

He remained in tune with his times and with the spirit of his country from the last quarter of the nineteenth century to the second half of the twentieth. Young Dewey was a child of New England; he grew up in a devout Congregationalist household in Burlington, Vermont, attended a college whose president had been called from the pulpit, and until he was thirty-five years old wrote in a distinctively Christian idiom. Following the current of the time, he slipped gently out of orthodox Christianity into a secular faith in democracy, social reform, and, above all, education. But he was always happy to use a religious idiom in talking about politics and social reform; he talked readily about democracy's "faith in the common man," was glad to call his belief in democracy a "religious" belief, and wrote *A Common Faith*[6] to argue that he was as entitled as anyone else to talk of "God" when he talked about his deepest beliefs—even though his admirers wished he wouldn't.[7]

This readiness to use the language of traditional Christianity helped Dewey to communicate with a public that would have turned away from a more aggressively secular or skeptical writer. It was a surprising achievement, given that Dewey early on decided that the "supernatural" elements in traditional Christianity were superstitious, incredible, and outmoded. It was even more surprising that Dewey could so successfully use the language of religious belief in the process of arguing for a view of the world that is commonly thought to be squarely at odds with religion. Dewey called his mature philosophy experimentalism; he preferred "experimentalism" to "pragmatism" and "instrumentalism" as labels for his approach. What he meant was that the truth, or more broadly the value, of any belief or statement about the world is to be measured in experience. He was insistent that a thoroughgoing naturalism was the only intellectually respectable philosophy, the only approach to life, education, ethics, and politics that offered a hope of progress. He was thus part of the social and intellectual movement that subscribed to "scientific politics," the view that the world could afford neither old-fashioned conservatism nor violent revolution but must be governed by "intelligent action." Indeed, he was its major American propagandist, and his most famous political writings—*Liberalism and Social Action*,[8] for instance—were built around this simple, clear-cut message. A lesser man than Dewey would have been challenged much more sharply about the conflict between his emphasis on "the religious" and his emphasis on "science"; Dewey's critics often wished that he would make himself clearer, but they always thought he had something important and coherent to say.

Nor is it only the latent conflict between his views and everyday piety that makes his success surprising. Generations of readers have complained that Dewey was a terrible writer. This is not entirely fair. Justice Holmes's quip that Dewey wrote as God would have done if he had been terribly anxious to tell us something of great importance but had found himself temporarily at a loss for words catches the combination of deep seriousness and stylistic awkwardness that makes Dewey an engrossing read but a strenuous one. Dewey was not a dull writer; the problem was that he wrote all too exactly as his subject matter dictated. His short polemics were brisk and clear; the more complicated his subject, the more his prose wound around and about to follow it. It is not surprising that Justice Holmes's quip was sparked by reading *Experience and Nature* or that Holmes observed after reading the book that he felt as though he had for the first time seen the universe "from the inside."

Dewey had none of Bertrand Russell's skill at making complicated ideas accessible and entertaining. Nor was he adept at coining slogans. "Intelligent action!" is hardly on a level with "Liberty, equality, and fraternity" or "Workers of the world, unite!" Nonetheless, Dewey's stress on "intelligent action" served his rhetorical purposes well enough. It suggested (rightly) that Dewey's politics was radical, energetic, and innovative; it also suggested (rightly) that it was based on scientific investigation and the organized application of its results. However awkward the prose, this was quite clear. That brings us back to the puzzle of Dewey's success in preaching a contentious creed.

For those who doubted that "science" could tell us all we needed about politics, and who held that religion or ethics must fill the gap, Dewey had a consistent answer. The contrast between science and art, science and ethics, science and religion was illusory. Properly understood, the scientific attitude was continuous with the religious attitude; properly understood, what scientists do when they try to understand the world is not very different from what any of us do when we try to decide what to think and what to do; properly understood, the scientist's search for order is not so different from the artist's search for order.

Dewey softened the sharp contrasts in which philosophers, theologians, politicians, and writers on cultural issues generally have tended to trade. He was driven by more than the intellectual conviction that such contrasts misrepresented the way the world was. Dewey referred in later life to the "inward laceration" that his mother's puritanism caused his adolescent character. She had felt to the full the New England sense of the vast gulf between this world and the next, between God and sinner, between the selves we are and the selves we ought to be. Dewey's mature philosophy tried to overcome such dualisms, and in a world where many of his readers had had similar upbringings to his own and where many of his readers shared his sense that the world was in a critical but not a hopeless state, that neither standpat nor bloody revolution would do, his work was immensely popular. It spoke to a deeply felt need to believe that science would not undermine faith, that radicalism did not mean chaos, that a faith in individuals did not lead to wild individualism, and that a faith in community did not lead to an oppressive collectivism.

Dewey did not deny that there were *differences* between science and morality, between the religious and secular outlooks, between the demands of politics and the seductions of art. He insisted only that the experimental outlook could unify them. Since this leaves it less than crystal clear whether "science" is or is not the answer to all our problems, Dewey has always had two sorts of reader; one has seen him as trying to unite the religious conviction that the world is a *meaningful* unity with a secular twentieth-century faith in the scientific analysis of both nature and humanity, while the other has seen him as an aggressive rationalist, someone who expects "science" to drive out faith, and a contributor to the twentieth century's obsession with rational social management. Perhaps one ought to say that he has had four sorts of reader, since both sorts divide on the merits of the resulting system. I side with the first view and think he was very nearly successful.

This is a philosophical judgment and a contentious one. What is impressive is how wide the consensus once was that Dewey represented "thinking America" at its best. His ideas and cast of mind were distinctively American, but they were those of thoughtful America, as distinct from merely impetuous, or merely conservative, or merely pious America. It is impressive partly because the speed with which Dewey's reputation collapsed was impressive, too. By 1952 Dewey belonged to an outmoded philosophical tradition. He exemplified the "philosopher as sage," and by the 1950s that was old hat. Modern philosophers had become technically sophisticated about what they were doing and in the process had become reluctant to risk themselves over much of the philosophical landscape.[9] Moral philosophers did not talk about the philosophy of science, and philosophers of science did not talk about aesthetics; everyone went in fear of mathematical logicians, and everyone thought that "analysis" was the essential philosophical technique. There was nothing in the training of philosophers that entitled them to lecture the public on how to educate their children, whom to vote for, what to admire in modern art, and how to understand what they did in church. "Philosophical analysis" was, in the jargon of the day, "value-neutral."

Dewey was too old to be infected by these views, and when he noticed them, he condemned them. He agreed that it was not for philosophers to do the job of psychologists or physicists or to second-guess the activities of artists or politicians, nor for the matter of that, should they second-guess car mechanics and locomotive engineers. But the division of labor had no place within philosophy itself, and there were ways of appreciating and understanding the activities of scientists, artists, and politicians that did not amount to offering to do their jobs for them. The situation that paralyzed analytical philosophers liberated Dewey. Professional philosophers have for the past half century been made anxious by the fact that philosophy has no province of knowledge of its own, no techniques or theories peculiar to itself in the way that physics or psychology or even history and literature have. They have often said their technique is logical (or sometimes "conceptual") analysis; like other academics, they have often thought respectability demanded specialization: that we must specialize not just in moral philosophy but in the analysis of rights, not just in the history of philosophy but in John Stuart Mill and nobody else. Dewey drew an entirely opposite conclusion. He decided that philosophy had to be "cultural criticism" and take all human life as its province.

By the time he died, this was not a respectable view. Almost as soon as he died, he was therefore dismissed from the collective mind. He had a few disciples. Sidney Hook continued to insist that Dewey was the greatest philosopher of the twentieth century, but Hook admired Dewey because of his commitment to liberal democracy and because Dewey had been a great ally in

Hook's battles against the American Communist party in the 1930s and 1940s. Technically Hook's philosophy was closer to Russell's than to Dewey's, whatever Hook himself might say. Dewey's political virtues did not appeal to most philosophers; they thought philosophy was a technical subject, concerned to analyze concepts and not to take sides in politics. Of his later defenders, Richard Bernstein did most to put Dewey back in the philosophical mainstream.[10] Bernstein argued that Dewey's main ideas were not so very different from those that analytical philosophy had drawn from the later work of Ludwig Wittgenstein, and gave chapter and verse to show it. This comparison with one of the heroes of the day did much to rescue Dewey's reputation as a philosopher; it did less to arouse interest in him. To show that he was not much out of the mainstream suggested only that he had been competent in a recognized discipline; it did not suggest that modern philosophers would be using their time wisely if they were to go and read him for themselves.

Over the past twenty years the wheel has turned again, and Dewey has become fashionable. There are many reasons for this, most of which will only appear clearly in later chapters. One is that the 1970s and 1980s have been marked by a resurgence of "communitarian" moral and political thinking. Immensely popular sociological accounts of the morally lost and bewildered condition of the average American, such as *Habits of the Heart,* have ascribed his or her parlous condition to an overdose of "individualism," and in looking for a remedy, their authors have self-consciously appealed to John Dewey as the philosopher of "the Great Community,"[11] the American social thinker who above all insisted that individuals exist only as members of society and can find satisfaction only when society gives their lives "meaning" rather than mere consumer comforts.

Another and perhaps not unconnected reason is that Dewey seems to epitomize a time when intellectuals could talk to the public and could be listened to, understood, and appreciated, even if not always agreed with. It is not always noticed that Dewey was almost invariably on the losing side; one of the few times he voted for a winning presidential candidate was when he voted for Harry Truman in 1948. Although he voted for Woodrow Wilson in 1916, he had voted against Wilson and for Eugene Debs in 1912. He spent the 1930s criticizing Roosevelt's New Deal as a feeble, unimaginative, and inadequate attempt to prop up a dying economic and social system and always voted for Norman Thomas against Roosevelt. Yet Dewey commanded a hearing when he did not command assent, and he was taken seriously, even if that was a matter of being taken seriously enough to be disagreed with. That is something that contemporary academics miss. Political philosophy has, as Michael Walzer has complained, become a matter of professors' writing for professors, and contrary to appearances, many professors wish they were doing something more exciting.[12] Many of them wonder what Dewey did that they do not, and whether it can be done again, and whether Dewey can somehow be brought back to life for the purpose.

A third reason is that the 1990s are turning out to be astonishingly like the 1890s. Not in the sense that our technology is similar to that of the 1890s or in the sense that exactly the same anxieties strike us on exactly the same occasions. But Dewey was moved to write about individual unease and social and political failures in a context that resembles our own in crucial ways. Dewey's America was one in which the problems of the inner city were appalling. In the early 1890s homelessness in Chicago sometimes reached 20 percent; unemployment frequently hit one in four of the working population. Disease was rife, and medical services were out of the reach of the poor. Social conflict was everywhere: Strikes were physically fought out with a level of violence we have not seen for sixty years. The upper classes were apparently indifferent to the fate of the poor and even to the fate of the working near poor. In the cities the response of the better-off was to remove themselves to the suburbs, in state and local politics it was to send in the National Guard on the least provocation, in Congress it was to legislate to make it harder for the poor to organize, and in the courts it was to make it impossible for unions to strike.

Nor was it clear what any individual person should or could do about all this. The political parties of the day were networks of influence peddling, and local government was corrupt. The powers of the federal government over state and local affairs were unknown and untried, but nobody had much faith that Washington could formulate a coherent vision for the country's future and implement it throughout the sprawling and pluralistic nation that America had already become. Nor was anyone of a thoughtful disposition sure how to get a consensus on what needed doing, for whom, and how. The country was full of recently arrived foreign immigrants; there were many parts of many cities where English was hardly spoken. In Chicago, when Dewey got there in 1894, only one person in four had an American parent. In the country at large, there were hundreds of newspapers and magazines advocating the wildest possible politics in fifteen different languages. For many Americans "multiculturalism" was not an aspiration but a widely regretted fact.

Dewey's writings on every subject—philosophy, religion, politics, education, art, or whatever else—breathe this air of crisis. But it is important to see how insistent he was that the crisis was also an opportunity or, if you like, how insistent he was that opportunity was there if we were prepared to take it and that an activist philosophy was implicit in the American mind and desperately needed by a disordered American society. Modern readers react to all this in different ways. To those who think that a strain of mindless optimism about American potentiality underlies all his ideas, Dewey is painfully relevant—as an instance of the American habit of not looking deeply enough into the problems he addresses and papering over the cleavages and oppressions of American life.[13] To those who think that Dewey possessed not "the answer" but a way of thinking about how to reach some answers, he provides a model of engaged intellectual life. The chapters that follow steer between these positions. Dewey was a model of the engaged philosopher. He certainly had a vision of his own role in American culture, and to an astonishing degree he met the demands that role placed upon him. But he was also less willing than he ought to have been to confront the fact that not all good things can be had together, however "experimentally minded" we are in their pursuit.

Unkind critics have suggested that Dewey's vision of a world governed by "intelligent action" was self-interested. It was a vision of a world run by people like himself. In a country like the United States, where there had never been a traditional ruling class, the choice seemed to lie between old-fashioned and none-too-honest politicians, whose only talent was deal making; the tyranny of the captains of industry, whose only concern was to secure cheap government and a docile work force; and disinterested, public-spirited administration by a corps of experts trained in the new social sciences and animated by the sort of esprit de corps that this intellectual superiority would give them.[14]

In fact, Dewey was not the advocate of elitism in any form, and particularly not in this. To a degree his old colleague and sparring partner Walter Lippmann was. Lippmann's elegantly disillusioned essays *Public Opinion* and *The Phantom Public* explained to a wide audience in the 1920s why it was that democracy did not and could not work in the form that nineteenth-century democrats had hoped it would. Lippmann thought the public had no opinions by which politicians could be guided; the public had no time to acquire the information it needed—newspapers took too long to read, the public was busy doing other things, and the papers were anyway inaccurate—and no critical ability to sort out the information it did possess. If government was to operate in the public interest, it had to be supplemented by intelligence chosen for the purpose and placed above the hurly-burly of elections and deal making. Lippmann would have equipped American government with numerous committees of certified social scientists of nonpartisan views who would be required to approve or disapprove government decisions. How he could have thought that the American voter, let alone American politicians, would stand for any such thing is quite mysterious.

Dewey had a firmer grasp of reality than Lippmann on this particular point. More important, he was deeply, almost congenitally opposed to the elitism that Lippmann's proposals embodied. Dewey's defense of intelligence was intended to be wholly consistent with his defense of democracy. So far as Dewey was concerned, the problem was to make democracy in practice what it had the potential of being: not just a political system in which governments elected by majority vote made such decisions as they could but a society permeated by a certain kind of character, by a mutual regard of all citizens for all other citizens, and by an ambition to make society both a greater unity and one that reflected the full diversity of its members' talents and aptitudes.

The large question is whether this ambition has any political credibility. It is easy to conclude that it has none. The record of American democracy since Dewey's day is not one to encourage lighthearted optimism about the prospects of government based on intelligent action. Different observers will have different views about those things it has done that it ought not to have done and those things it has left undone that it ought to have done, but few observers will suggest that there has been no room for improvement. To take the issues that Dewey made his own, the state of public education remains at best a source of anxiety—even our best-educated students lag far behind their contemporaries in every other developed country—and is at worst a standing disgrace: The schools of many inner cities resemble nothing so much as holding pens where children who have not yet committed a crime are detained for a few years before being pitched onto the streets undisciplined, incapable of holding down a job, and unequipped with most of the skills that might induce an employer to hire them. Democracy appears to have a negative connection with intelligence, inasmuch as voters persistently underfund investment in their nation's future. Another of Dewey's obsessions was the meaninglessness of the working life. The size of the industrial work force has shrunk dramatically since Dewey's day, and many of the horrors of the manual laborer's life are a thing of the past; but work for most of the population remains a drab and uninteresting activity, a mere means to a wage. We are so anxious about finding work for all who need it that we have lost interest in what the work experience is like once work has been found. Dewey's claim that there is no democracy without industrial democracy is as important now and still as unlistened to now as it was in 1887, when he first uttered it.[15]

In one respect, we are clearly worse off than when Dewey wrote. He thought that the chief difficulty was to persuade government to take up its proper tasks and to perform them in an uncorrupt and efficient fashion. The "new liberalism" that he advocated in the 1930s was not simply collectivist, but it did imply, just as the "new liberalism" that British liberals had advocated twenty-five years before had done, that liberal governments must move beyond laissez-faire and that they could extend freedom by managing the economy more rationally than mere let-alone would do and by instituting the benefits of the twentieth-century welfare state. He was not systematically troubled by doubts about government competence but by doubts about government willingness to act. We appear to have lost faith in government in a more wholesale fashion than he would ever have anticipated.

The competence of modern governments to perform the tasks Dewey would have placed on them remains uncertain. Since 1945 the United States has escaped full-blown depression, and governments know how to ensure that nothing like the depression of the 1930s ever comes back. Globally matters are much less cheerful. We are no nearer understanding how to ensure prosperity for more than a small proportion of the world's inhabitants and no better at ensuring that the prosperity of the well-off countries is distributed with even minimal fairness. The record of the American economy is better than most yet deeply depressing. Since 1973 the real incomes of the worst-off one-third of the population have shrunk slightly, while since 1980 the incomes of the best-off one-tenth have increased substantially until the gap between the rank-and-file employee and the CEO is now as large as it has ever been. Nor can this redidistribution in favor of the well-off be explained as a reward for their imaginative entrepreneurship, for the economy as a whole has since 1973 grown at barely half the rate it managed in the first two decades after World War II. Dewey would hardly have thought this a triumph of organized intelligence.

He was not a theorist of public administration and policy studies, so it is impossible to guess what he might have said about the difficulties that beset the Great Society programs with which Lyndon Johnson hoped to end poverty once and for all, while closing also the gap between the housing, educational, and health prospects of the better- and worse-off. It is not hard to guess that Dewey would have sided with critics who have said that the effectiveness of such programs owes less to their design in the narrow sense than to their support by the public and their consistency with the social and political culture of the wider society and of the communities within which they are intended to work. A culture in which government programs are universally regarded as fair game for assorted forms of corruption, as they were during the administration of President Reagan, is one in which government works very badly. One in which they are seen as essential to our survival, as they were during World War II, is one where government works much better. Dewey understood the importance of public sentiment better than a lot of recent commentators who have thought to show how hard-nosed they were by assuming that exploitative motives are universal in politics.

In foreign affairs the United States has not had to fight a third world war, and this is no small achievement. Whether Dewey would have been more impressed by this fact than by the innumerable small wars in which his country has been engaged and has fought by proxy is anyone's guess. It is hard to know what he might have thought of the Vietnam War—he approved of the American intervention in Korea—but he would certainly have been depressed by the last forty-five years' failure to reduce the global level of fighting. His opposition to American entry into World War II right up to the Japanese attack on Pearl Harbor may have been idiosyncratic or misjudged, but it was not foolish to hope that democratic governments might find some way of preserving international peace other than by fighting wars. That we have thus far failed suggests the difficulty of the task, not the foolishness of the ambition.

The very fact that we are so much in the same plight as Dewey saw us in a century ago might be thought to make him intelligible only at the price of invalidating his ideas, especially his belief in progress. Dewey was often attacked for what his critics thought was a deeply implausible optimism about human nature and American society. If he was an optimist, then his country's subsequent history would surely have disappointed him. Human nature seems no less fallen than during his lifetime, and many Americans hanker after the soporific 1950s as for a lost golden age. In fact, Dewey's critics were chronically wrong about his views and exaggerated their differences with him.[16] He had anything but a sanguine view of progress, and rather than subscribe to a happy view of human nature, he tended, as the title of one of his best books, *Human Nature and Conduct,* might suggest, to dissolve the very idea of human nature into the question of how human beings behave in particular circumstances.

Dewey's main intellectual concept was that of a "problem." Individuals and societies alike are stirred into life by problems; an unproblematic world would be a world not so much at rest as unconscious. Such a world is unimaginable. Life is problematic; even when we are not thinking about our situation, our bodies are continuously solving endless problems of their own sustained existence. Problem solving is the condition of organic life. Societies, like individuals, solve problems and, like individuals, must do so by acting on the environment that causes the problem in the first place. Interaction with the environment alters the society or the individual that acts on the environment, with the result that new problems arise and demand new solutions. To the degree that this process gives the organism more control over itself and its environment, more ability to rethink its problems, and the potentiality for fruitful changes along the same lines, we may talk of progress. Dewey's preferred expression was always "growth."

Dewey would not have been surprised that life in the modern world remains unsatisfactory. He might have been surprised at our lack of confidence in our resources. He would certainly have been depressed by the estrangement of academic philosophy from issues of public interest. The rest of this book is a conversation between Dewey's aspirations and our doubts. That is not all it is, however. Reading Dewey is not just to engage with one of the great minds of the American twentieth century. It is to engage with America and the ways America has been conscious of itself in the past hundred years. There is little point in criticizing Dewey's thoughts about, say, the future of American religion unless we have some sense of what else we might say; the same is true of his ideas about education, democracy, war and peace, the prospects of socialism, the behavior of American Communists in the 1930s, and much else that he wrote and lectured on. No more than the rest of us did Dewey evolve his ideas in isolation like a spider spinning its web. More than most, indeed, he wrote in contradiction of what he found around him, and one hears echoes of Bellamy, Lippmann, Croly, the Niebuhrs, Trotsky, Russell, and lesser lights like Colonel Parker of the Chicago school board, or Earl Browder of the American Communist party, in his writing, just as one hears echoes of Dewey in much of their work. A dialogue between "us" and him is a many-way conversation between us and him and between both of us and his contemporaries. It must be said that this is not a task he makes easy; "From Absolutism to Experimentalism" tells us that "Upon the whole, the forces that have influenced me have come from persons and from situations more than from books . . ." but Dewey was a shy man who disapproved of personalities, and in everything but his shortest polemical essays he disguised all too effectively what situations and persons these were.[17]

As to the subject of that conversation, it is here organized conventionally.

I try to answer three questions: How did Dewey come to think as he did; what did he think; what can we now make of it? The turning point in Dewey's intellectual life—insofar as anything so untroubled could be a turning point—occurred quite early, in 1891, when he was barely thirty-two years old and a young assistant professor at the University of Michigan in Ann Arbor. Until that point he had been conventionally religious, taking Bible study groups with his students, contributing articles to the liberal Congregationalists' house magazine, the *Andover Review,* and sprinkling his writings on ethics, psychology, and social philosophy with references to Christ and Christianity. In 1891 he unobtrusively lost his faith; in 1894, when he moved to Chicago, he explicitly abandoned his church membership. Although, as I shall say more than once, Dewey's ideas in later life are remarkably continuous with his first thoughts on ethics and politics, it is still true that his early work was much more heavily impregnated with conventional Christian ideas than anything thereafter was. So I begin with the young man and the young man's intellectual formation and take the chance to say something about the way philosophers in the 1880s had to deal with the declining influence of religion on every field of American intellectual life.

Thereafter the chronology of Dewey's life coincides naturally with the pattern of his main interests, or to be more scrupulously honest, little is lost by a certain amount of stretching and compressing. So most of the discussion of his ideas on education coincides with my picture of the decade he spent in Chicago, when he wrote *The School and Society,* founded the Laboratory School, and became the acknowledged leader of a philosophical movement and an educational program. The next decade saw him at the height of his powers at Columbia University. Here, too, he wrote extensively on education, on the ethics of democracy, and on the new approach to philosophy that he sometimes called instrumentalism but on the whole preferred to call experimentalism. He was engaged in practical politics, but it was the politics of his profession, involving the creation of teachers' unions, for instance, and trying to secure a more professional status for the teachers who went out of Columbia Teachers College. For our purposes the crucial event of the decade came at the end of it in the fall of 1914 with the creation of the *New Republic* and Dewey's encounter with Progressivism.

It is in this context that his attitude to World War I and subsequently to the prospects of the League of Nations needs to be considered. Dewey had a bad war. He suffered from a sense that the United States ought to stay out of the war but ought nonetheless to do *something* significant about the war. This was not a stable position; there was practically nothing short of fighting that the United States could do, and Dewey had no very clear idea of what entry into the war would do to the country either. He sided with the United States' entry into the war, but halfheartedly and almost against his better judgment. In the event, he quarreled terminally with some friends, most notably with Randolph Bourne, and nearly wrecked his friendship with Jane Addams. The war and its aftermath were a terrible disappointment to Dewey, and he came very close to espousing simple isolationism thereafter.

Dewey was not personally an isolationist. He was vastly in demand as a lecturer on education, wanted by governments and universities as an adviser, and endlessly willing to help wherever he could. His 1920s lecture tours and spells of duty as an adviser in China, Mexico, Turkey, and Russia resulted in numerous books and essays on his experiences in those countries. In China he became something of an official sage; his philosophical and educational works were translated into Chinese and published in a collected edition that remained in print until the Communist take-over. He had a disinterested curiosity about the fate of China and had some good friends among progressive Chinese intellectuals and academics. This was rather different from the interest he took in the Soviet Union when many radicals were setting it up as a model for the United States. Dewey was quite sure it could not be a model of any kind, but he was so well disposed to the Russian educational experiments of the late 1920s that when he returned from a visit to the USSR, the American Communist party tried to recruit him; it discovered to its chagrin that he was staunchly anti-Soviet and anti-Communist. It was a mistake the party did not repeat, though many critics on the right did so.

Dewey's political activities and ideas in the 1920s and 1930s reflected this resistance to pressure. He was clear that the Soviet Union, even in the relatively benign years between the death of Lenin in 1924 and the rise to supreme power of Stalin in 1928 was no model for a vastly more developed country to follow. He did not have the instinctive hatred of the new Soviet state that many European liberals had felt for czarist Russia and had carried over to its Leninist successor; still, he was sure that violent and dictatorial one-party rule was horrible in itself and absurd when offered as a model for a developed democracy to emulate. On the other hand, the vigor of Russia's efforts at modernization impressed him. To someone who believed as strongly as he did that American capitalism was a dying social order, there was not much temptation to dwell on the contrast between American prosperity and Soviet austerity, even though he knew that the Russian worker was infinitely worse off than his American counterpart and likely to remain so for a very long time. In the 1920s it seemed to perfectly rational, even cautious observers that in Russia anyone who was willing to work would find work, shelter, and food, whereas mass unemployment was the most visible characteristic of capitalism in Europe and in the 1930s became so in the United States.

A more difficult question is what Dewey expected to be able to put in place of the American capitalism he disliked. He was not a straightforward socialist; he described himself as a liberal but spoke favorably of guild socialism, much as Bertrand Russell did. Dewey did not write about the need for and nature of a modern welfare state, though he was emphatic about the need for government to provide old-age pensions and unemployment relief and to take responsibility for securing full employment; Dewey never said what a "democracy of wealth" involved; he did not go into details about the public ownership he wanted in place of run-amok corporatism. He was emphatically not a simple collectivist; he was a "new individualist"; indeed, he never called himself a socialist but talked in terms of a renovated liberalism. What follows digs out much of what he was after, but I cannot say that I have found him clearer than my predecessors have. Unlike many of them, however, I have a generally sympathetic view of the matter. Dewey was not evasive, or muddled, or simply incapable of thinking about institutions. It was rather that he thought that detailed empirical analysis of institutions and their workings was a scientific task that others could tackle more effectively than he; his role was to give an account of the spirit in which the job had to be done. Nobody complains that the Gospels do not give immediate instruction on industrial organization, and to some degree at any rate, Dewey's work is better seen as a gospel for democrats than a handbook for institutional designers.

The clues to Dewey's political hopes are not to be found only in his set piece political writings. Nor are they only to be found in his newspaper polemics of the 1930s, interesting though these can be. They are to be found in three other places. The first is his philosophical treatment of social psychology, political culture, and their bearings on individual commitment. *Human Nature and Conduct,* which appeared in 1922, was both a textbook and a sort of lay Bible to innumerable teachers and students over the next quarter of a century. The politics of works like *Human Nature and Conduct* never got in the way of their acceptance as texts, partly because Dewey's politics were so much part of his philosophy that readers had no sense that he was launching a political campaign and partly because his politics were so broadly sketched that they plainly weren't part of a campaign.[18] The influence on American "political common sense" that his textbooks came to exercise may well have been profound, even though in the nature of the case it is unquantifiable.

The second place is his late writings on religion, especially *The Quest for Certainty* and *A Common Faith.* Here Dewey did many things that might have been calculated to enrage believers in biblical Christianity—biblical Judaism and koranic Islam, too—but always in the name of a communal faith that he sincerely thought capable of absorbing everything of value in particular religions and turning it to new uses. The other place is his writing on art. *Art as Experience* was the fruit of Dewey's many years as the educational guru of Albert Barnes's bizarre (even if also rather wonderful) museum and institute in Philadelphia, but whereas Barnes's desire to make modern art intellectually and physically accessible to ordinary working people was apparently motivated by hatred of the art establishment, Dewey's belief that a universal access to art was the culmination of the aspirations of a true democracy was all of a piece with his views on morals, politics, and religion. *Art as Experience* is mildly frustrating for a reader who comes to it expecting a treatise on aesthetics or an analysis of particular styles, artists, or works, but it is a perfectly splendid tract on the indispensable role that artistic creation and aesthetic enjoyment play in human life.

Dewey's most public decade was, astonishingly, the 1930s. I say "astonishingly," because he had turned seventy in October 1929, was already the author of a great many books, and in June 1930 retired from his professorial career. Nonetheless, it was then that he most energetically threw himself into the everyday political fray and fought for his brand of liberalism and democracy against the fury of Communists to his left and the sluggish indifference of the practitioners of politics as usual to his right. Still, this was the best part of seventy years ago, and the question obviously arises of whether this is all water under the bridge, whether the recent revival of interest in Dewey's work is only one more instance in which historians of ideas in search of a subject not yet studied to death coincide in their search.

To some extent it is that. It is at any rate not motivated by more romantic considerations. Dewey was a professor all his working life. He neither wrote the colorful prose of his contemporary Bertrand Russell nor lived Russell's colorful life. Nor does he offer the obvious attractions of his seniors in the pragmatist tradition: He lacked the capacity for irony that makes William James so engaging, and he had none of the rage for self-destruction that makes C. S. Peirce such an alarming and engrossing figure. Dewey's private life was, to all outward appearances, unremarkable. Only for a few months in 1918 did he fall illicitly in love, and little came of the affair besides some poetry on his side and some racy novels on the side of his inamorata. Though he sheltered Maxim Gorky, when the Bolshevik writer and his mistress came to New York before the First War and could find no hotel willing to give them room, Dewey wrote no autobiography to match Gorky's, or, for that matter, to match the autobiographies of Rousseau, Mill, and Russell. Nobody is likely to make *John Dewey the Movie*. His closest friends, who loved him dearly, remembered him as positively hostile to personal reminiscence.[19]

But professors in search of a topic not written to death are stirred by the spirit of their times. Though much of what they write amounts to "filling much needed gaps," they seize on writers because they think those writers exemplify something important—either importantly wicked or importantly positive. Dewey speaks to us for the reasons suggested above. "Aggressive atheism" of the sort Bertrand Russell practiced is out of fashion; we speak kindly of people's need to clothe their moral allegiances in the symbols of a religious vision and think it ill mannered or obtuse to press the believer on the details of her or his faith. That is the frame of mind of *A Common Faith*. Few doubt that democracy is the only acceptable political system for the late-twentieth-century world; the movement toward "democracy" is the most salient feature of world politics in the last decade. But we do not mean that American party politics is the last word in a humane and rational political order. Indeed, few people are particularly impressed by the actuality of American politics. What are we after then? Dewey had part of the answer when he claimed that "democracy" embraces a host of beliefs that go far beyond the organizational and constitutional details of the day. He had part of the answer in linking the attitude toward the world that we call "religious" with our "faith in the common man."

Again, we are in a strange mood about individualism and individuality. We do not hanker after any sort of collectivism; the sigh of relief when Eastern Europe threw off the tyranny of the past fifty years attests to that. But we are not sure that "rugged individualism" is useful in the electronic age; the qualities that help a man across the desert with a message hidden in his boots are not those of the age of the fax machine. Nor, on the moral level, are we sure where to draw the line between a necessary independence and simple bloody-mindedness, between legitimate aspiration and simple greed, and so indefinitely on. We have to some extent tried the politics of a return to a nineteenth-century ideal of individuality under the auspices of what is—significantly—called both neoconservatism and neoliberalism. But we neither made a wholehearted return nor liked the results of what we did. The recent interest in Dewey's work seems to me to be the result of a discontent with contemporary liberal democracy and with the efforts of contemporary philosophers to articulate its ideals and its workings. Is it possible that in Dewey's work there are clues to what other forms of a "new individualism" we might try?

There are. They are not always helpful, and they would not provide a base for a political campaign; but they are never indefensible, and they commonly light on ideas neglected in recent political philosophy, with its obsessive concentration on theories of rights and its neglect of questions about contemporary political culture. It is no objection that Dewey's ideas would not make a party platform.[20] Dewey would have been reluctant to give detailed advice to his contemporaries, let alone to the unpredictable world of six decades later. If it is a complaint against Dewey that some of these ideas are not exciting, it must be acknowledged that it was his intention to condemn the taste for excitement that he thought of as a rather corrupt intellectual influence on his contemporaries. One moral of Dewey's work was that we must not go overboard for simple and colorful ideas. Fascism and communism appealed to young people because they were simple and vivid; they were also disastrous. The same might be said of every psychological, literary, and political fad Dewey encountered.

Moderation is hard to defend with the vividness that comes easily to the expounders of immoderate visions. Plato the extremist is read with more pleasure than the cautious Aristotle, John Stuart Mill's *On Liberty* defends "one very simple principle" and finds a hundred readers to every one who consumes *Considerations on Representative Government,* with its careful balancing of arguments for and against different parliamentary and legal institutions, while Marx's *Communist Manifesto* has had readers—voluntary readers—in the millions who have found it impossible to struggle their way through *Capital.*

Dewey remains fascinating because his moderation in political and economic matters was not dictated by any such moderation in his ultimate philosophical ambitions. It was Dewey's purpose to reconcile modern man to the modern world; where Wordsworth had written glumly in his "Intimations" ode of "the light of common day" as a flat, dull light, Dewey thought that the light of common day cast a radiance sufficient to our purposes. It was true that everyday life was full of disappointments, small and large, that private and public lives were in innumerable ways disjointed, incoherent, and unsatisfying; but it was quite false that life was radically or cosmically flawed. The dominant tone of twentieth-century cultural criticism has been exactly at odds with Dewey's, therefore, and not only when it has taken the form of existentialist angst or a Nietzschean skepticism. Orthodox empiricist and analytical philosophy has assumed that the world is simply indifferent to our presence, and some of its most distinguished founders, Ludwig Wittgenstein and Bertrand Russell among them, displayed a disgust with everyday life that suggests they found the world not so much indifferent as hostile. Dewey was unique in the way he combined fierce criticism of the particulars of human existence with a resounding endorsement of the human project. Readers may therefore not be surprised that what follows ends on a note of enthusiasm for Dewey's work and almost unalloyed admiration for its author.

One

Starting Out

If we are to think seriously about our fate at the end of the twentieth century, one thing we must do—infinitely far from the only thing, but one thing—is to recapture the intellectual, emotional, and political mood in which a certain kind of American liberalism flourished in the first half of this century.[1] That is why John Dewey's attempt to provide his country with a philosophy by which its people could steer a more intelligent course in their individual and collective lives is more than material for intellectual history or antiquarian curiosity. Intellectual history and antiquarianism for its own sake are legitimate activities; done well, they are wonderfully interesting. If what follows gratifies such tastes, that is a bonus. My aim is rather to conjure up some half-remembered ideas to rethink and reevaluate them, to explain their initial staying power, their eclipse, and their revival over the past few years. Most of these ideas were not unique to John Dewey, but many were most famously articulated by him. What follows is less history or biography than a friendly but critical tour of the ideas that established Dewey's astonishing hold over the educated American public of his day.

These ideas were Dewey's "public philosophy."[2] They were not narrowly political or deeply metaphysical; they were supposed to appeal to readers of a wide variety of political allegiances and to be intelligible to anyone who took the time to think through them. They were what German writers have never minded calling a *Lebensphilosophie* but what American and British philosophers have for fifty years been shy about calling a "philosophy of life." Plato told his hearers that the question philosophers had to answer was: How shall we live? Dewey disagreed with Plato's answers to the question, but he was not embarrassed about asking it or about answering it in his own way.

Dewey addressed his public on the printed page and in the lecture room rather than on the soapbox or at political rallies, and this book is a critical guide to his more accessible books and essays. I evade technical questions about his logic and theory of truth, and focus on ethics, politics, art and religion, saying almost nothing about pedagogical blockbusters such as his textbook entitled *Ethics* and rather more about particular essays in journals like the *New Republic.* I put these ideas in context to show why he wrote what he did and why it was taken in the way it was; on occasion I suggest that he might have thought more fruitfully if he had thought differently, and I try to say how. I begin with a longish look at his early years. The society in which Dewey grew up is now so remote that readers cannot take on trust my claim that the revival of his popularity in the last few years owes much to the fact that so many of his ideas were calculated to soothe, or rather to answer to, anxieties that we in the 1990s share with Americans of the 1890s. Their anxieties about the collapse of religious faith, the horrors of inner-city destitution, the ineducability of the poor, and the instability of working-class employment were not *exactly* like our own, but they were *surprisingly* like our own. That, I think, does much to explain both Dewey's earlier popularity and the current revival of his reputation. The resurgence of a concern with community, both in the work of academic philosophers and in the programs of politicians is one instance; the debate over the benefits and dangers of multiculturalism in politics and education is another. The noisy and muddled discussion of the need for "foundations" for our moral and political allegiances is yet another. Often enough Dewey's name is invoked by the warring parties; even more often arguments are triumphantly produced that Dewey either advanced or demolished seventy years ago. But these are claims that must be proved, not only asserted.

The more obvious reason to begin at Dewey's own beginning is that to see how he came to be *the* philosopher of American liberalism in the first half of this century, we must understand how he built on the religious, political, and philosophical ideas he grew up with. Dewey was shy in person, unaggressive in argument, and awkward as a writer, and it is easy to underestimate the magnitude of what he did. Yet what he did was immensely difficult. He directed his defense of spiritual, artistic, and cultural modernity to an American society that has always impressed outsiders with its extreme cultural conservatism; he wrote against the unbridled capitalist search for profit for a society that has always been strikingly uninhibited in its search for a quick buck; he defended secular, scientific policy making in a society whose end of the twentieth-century attachment to traditional religion still astonishes sociological observers; and he defended a strong national government in a society whose localism is one of its most cherished legacies from colonial times. In arguing for these always unpopular and frequently lost causes, he never impaired his reputation as a decent, sober, serious, and thoughtful philosopher. With few exceptions, his intellectual enemies, who thought he was an inadvertent nihilist and an accidental destroyer of cultural traditions, dealt with his errors more in sorrow than in anger.[3]

He brought off this astonishing feat because he never broke *sharply* with the prejudices and proprieties of the intellectual world he grew up in. He belonged to the first generation of university teachers of philosophy who were not clergymen, but for the first ten years of his teaching career he wrote in theological journals, conducted Sunday schools, and gave little Sunday morning addresses to his students very much in the old manner. In due course his faith fell away from him, as did his faith in what he came to see as the various philosophical substitutes for Christian belief. He did not wake up one morning, decide that God was dead, and announce, as Nietzsche had done, that everything was therefore permitted.[4] He preserved the style of the lay preacher, while renovating those aspects of a religious view of the world that he could render consistent with the scientific world view. Other philosophers did something similar, but none with the same skill. Nor did they do it with his mixture of rhetorical calm and intellectual boldness. For the most part they found room for faith by limiting the reach of science. This was true of Dewey's own teachers, even the aggressive and go-getting G. S. Hall, who did more than any other one man to make experimental psychology a serious research subject.

Dewey was more intellectually interesting than this because he tried to show that there was no deep or serious conflict between science and religion. Science and religion were allies rather than enemies. They were equal partners in the search for the "meaning" of the experienced world. It followed that "supernaturalism" was a certain casualty of the modern world, but that a "religious" perspective on the world was not. Since most Americans think highly of a religious attitude to life and are uninterested in theology, Dewey struck the right chord. In Henry Steele Commager's words, "It is scarcely an exaggeration to say that during the nineteenth century and well into the twentieth, religion prospered while theology went slowly bankrupt."[5] Commager goes on to observe that the astonishing sectarian diversity of American religion did not produce elaborate philosophical justifications of these separate faiths. Dewey fed the American sense that faith was a good thing and that disputes about the details were unnecessary. Part of his success was less doctrinal than personal; his ideas and his life seemed all of a piece, and he himself seemed a natural embodiment of the democratic thoughtfulness he preached. That obviously raises the question of how he came to be the man he was. So I begin with an account of his early years, bringing the story up-to-date in subsequent chapters as the subject at hand demands.

Life and Thought

As an object of simple human interest, Dewey comes a long way behind his fellow pragmatists C. S. Peirce and William James, let alone his contemporary and rival Bertrand Russell or post-1945 intellectual superstars like Jean-Paul Sartre or Michel Foucault. Or perhaps it would be truer to say that he is a baffling figure just because the shyness and self-effacingness that were his most marked personal characteristics were so at odds with the almost reckless originality of his ideas. He was a striking example of the way that style and content can sometimes pull apart. His published work was impersonal, and as a correspondent he was almost equally reticent. Save for his brief and unconsummated affaire with the Polish-American novelist Anzia Yezierska, he was an undeviatingly faithful husband and a devoted but unselfconscious father. His personal papers reveal no very passionate *vie intérieure* and give the reader no sense that Dewey ever experienced any deep conflict between his private feelings and his public persona. This is not a complaint against him. C. S. Peirce was self-destructive; Bertrand Russell's duplicity caused himself and others needless pain; William James reached an urbane and cheerful middle age only after many years of misery and depression during which he resolved at one point to give himself one year to cheer up, at the end of which he would otherwise kill himself. (Happily he discovered that if he presented a cheerful appearance to everyone else, he would eventually come to present a cheerful appearance to himself, and he went on to a productive career.) If his friends are to be believed, Dewey was systematically silent about his youth and development. The recollections of Herbert Schneider, Dewey's colleague of many years at Columbia, are typical: "We tried to get him to reminisce. And it was very difficult. I think on principle Dewey wouldn't reminisce. He liked to look forward to the future, and he certainly liked to keep *au courant* with the present. But to get him to reminisce about his early days was very difficult."[6]

Dewey was conscious of the fact that he was not a *vivid* individual, either in speech or in writing. His prose was likened by Lewis Mumford—the architectural and cultural critic with whom Dewey quarreled in the 1920s—to the clanking of a subway train. This is unfair but not wholly unfair. A lot of Dewey's writing was wholly readable. What is not wholly readable is exasperating in the same way as its author; the underlying ideas are so interesting that the reader looks for an excitement and demonstrativeness in the writing that Dewey fastidiously refused to put there. It was, in an odd way, a democratic style. Dewey did not pretend to be entirely certain about what he thought and therefore would not paint his ideas in a deceptively confident style. He relied on intellectual content to engage the reader's attention and despised anything that smacked of flashiness.

Reports of his style as a lecturer suggest that he spoke much as he wrote. Sidney Hook admired Dewey only slightly this side of idolatry, but even his account suggests that being taught by Dewey was often hard work:

> As a teacher, Dewey seemed to me to violate his own pedagogical principles. He made no attempt to motivate or arouse the interest of his auditors, to relate problems to their own experiences, to use graphic, concrete illustrations in order to give point to abstract and abstruse positions. He rarely provoked a lively participation and response from students, in the absence of which it is difficult to determine whether genuine learning or even comprehension has taken place. . . . Dewey spoke in a husky monotone, and although there was a sheet of notes on the desk at which he was usually seated, he never seemed to consult it. He folded it into many creases as he slowly spoke. Occasionally he would read from a book to which he was making a critical reference. His discourse was far from fluent. There were pauses and sometimes long lapses as he gazed out of the window or above the heads of his audience. . . .[7]

Just as with his writing, this was partly a democratic gesture, Dewey's way of treating his students like colleagues. Part was an intense reluctance to project himself.

Reticent though he was, Dewey himself provided one argument for trying to connect the lives and concerns of philosophers to their philosophical views—not as an argument for racy philosophical biography but as a principle of philosophical and intellectual interpretation. One of Dewey's more famous claims about philosophy was that it was never in fact, though it had always been in aspiration, the revelation of an eternal truth that merely happened to require some particular human tongue or pen for its transmission to a human audience. Philosophers set out to tell their audience timeless truths about the ultimate reality of the world, but they necessarily failed. Every philosophical system expressed a particular personality and a particular culture located in a particular time and place. Philosophy answered to the needs and interests and talents of the author and to the needs and interests and resources of the society in which that author lived, and it was best understood in those terms. To see it as the product of a particular culture and a particular temperament was not to belittle it. "What is lost from the standpoint of would-be science is regained from the standpoint of humanity. Instead of the disputes of rivals about the nature of reality, we have the scene of human clash of social purpose and aspirations."[8]

Intellectual history was, for all that, not to be turned into simple biography. Dewey played down the quirks and peculiarities of individuals; he was more concerned with their character as representatives of their time, place, class, and political allegiance. He would have loathed psychobiography, just as he would have loathed the phenomenon of thinkers who set up as celebrities and the practice of writing celebrity biographies about them; still, he insisted on linking arguments to their authors and authors to their settings and hoped that we could explain those settings with the insights of history and social science. To do as much for him is to do him the kind of justice he sought.

Dewey had an acute sense of his own place in the history of the human intellect. He has always had a reputation as a thinker who turned his back on history—that is, on the past, on tradition, and on the intellectual discipline of history—but this is wrong. The reputation stems partly from Dewey's 1930s quarrel with Robert Hutchins, the president of the University of Chicago. Hutchins was a devotee of teaching students timeless truths in general and those uncovered by Thomas Aquinas in particular.[9] Dewey thought that there were no such truths to teach and that Hutchins would paralyze the minds of students by telling them that every serious thought about the human condition had been produced by the end of the thirteenth century. Hutchins thought Dewey wanted to throw the traditional humanities into the street and replace them with the modern and dubious social sciences. The minimal truth in the charge against Dewey is that he thought philosophers were too inclined to study questions passed down to them by academic tradition and not enough inclined to engage with "the problems of men" of their own day. Yet the charge of hostility to tradition as it is usually leveled against Dewey is false. All Dewey's work takes a distinctive view of the history of the modern world. He always wrote with particular philosophers, their particular doctrines, and their social and political allegiances in mind; they played the role of an imagined partner in a conversation that extended over millennia and continents rather than over the dinner table. A man who despised history could not have said that his favorite reading was Plato.

Though he would have been the last person to turn the history of philosophy into a kind of intellectual gossip—as Russell was prone to do in his *History of Western Philosophy*—Dewey was not devoid of a sense of individual style. When he writes about the individuals who occupy a central place in his own intellectual history, the pace of his prose picks up, and he reaches quite effortlessly for a more pictorial and more personal account of both them and their views. William James is the most obvious beneficiary of such essays, but A. N. Whitehead, C. S. Peirce, and George Sylvester Morris are handled with similar vivacity, and among political writers, Thomas Jefferson. Nor was it only writers he admired who benefited from his writing in this fashion: In his 1920s controversy with Walter Lippmann over international relations and American membership in the League of Nations, Dewey responded to Lippmann's vivid polemical style with a vigorously ad hominem approach of his own that cheered and surprised his allies.

Dewey's reasons for eschewing personalities were rooted in his philosophy as well as in his own character. He thought that our individuality resided in our biography, that individuals were more process than substance, that their substance was simply the process of their lives. These lives are more social than individual, or perhaps we ought to say that human beings are *individual* only because they are *social*. We are born as merely biological individuals, and only after the necessary period of education do we become ready to accept our personal share of the social, intellectual, moral, political, and artistic resources of the settings into which we are born and take our share of the responsibility for developing those resources. The life of the individual is not something separate from the life of the society in which he lives and works; an individual life is a facet of the life of the whole society, and society is the medium in which the individual thinks, feels, and lives. *Human Nature and Conduct* and *The Public and Its Problems* are built around this thought and were immensely attractive to readers looking for a lay version of religious uplift for just this reason. Dewey took that view of himself. He had an unusual combination of extreme diffidence and complete confidence in his own intellectual powers, and it seems plausible to suppose that part of that confidence came from his sense that all of us have an emotional and intellectual account with our own society that it is impossible to overdraw. Comparing himself later in life with the much more ebullient and visible figure of William James, he had no embarrassment about saying, "James cannot do what I can and I cannot do what he can. . . ." He felt on the pulses what his philosophy laid out analytically: that he had drawn on the resources of the intellectual traditions into which he had been born and had responded adequately to the demands they made of him. He could properly regard his own contribution with a degree of justified pride. Boastfulness would have been absurd; a decent gratitude to the society that gave him the resources he put to good use was required. A false modesty would have been preposterous and irrational, but so would any attempt to elevate himself in the eyes of others by pretending that his distinction was in some deep sense all his own work. He could afford to be self-effacing because he had such a strong sense that a man who felt himself to be an adequate representative of his society's aspirations ran no real risk of effacement.

Childhood and Youth[10]

John Dewey was born in Burlington, Vermont, on October 20, 1859. Both his mother and his father came from solidly established New England farming stock, who had farmed in the area for three generations. It made a substantial difference to his life that his mother's family—she was born Lucina Artemisia Rich—was much better off and more distinguished than his father's. Lucina's grandfather had been a member of the U.S. House of Representatives, and her father a member of the Vermont General Assembly. Unlike his father's family, they took a college education for granted, and the Riches were related by cousinhood, church membership, and long-standing acquaintance to most of Vermont's preachers and professors. Lucina continued the family tradition of public service in church charities rather than politics, but with the same uninhibited vigor. Unsurprisingly, she was long remembered as a social and moral leader of Burlington life. She was a person of enormous energy and devotion to duty. Besides her own three sons, she looked after the children of her widowed brother and in her middle years seems to have taken a particular interest in late-adolescent young men. It was in that role that she featured as the heroine of an improving work of fiction by a fellow townswoman. *Freshman and Senior* was published by the Congregational Sunday-School and Publishing Society, and there Lucina Dewey appears as Mrs. Carver, "the wise and understanding counselor of college youths, as solicitous of their moral and spiritual good as of their academic welfare."[11] Archibald Sprague Dewey, her husband, was almost twenty years older than she, and a good deal more easygoing, both in life and in business. "His energy was seldom directed toward advancing himself financially, and he was said to sell more goods and collect fewer bills than any other merchant in town."[12]

Archibald Dewey had broken with family tradition when he left the family farm and opened a grocery store in Burlington some twenty-five years before. He was on excellent terms with his family, but he may for all that have possessed a restless streak that made the nearby city attractive. At all events, when the Civil War broke out in 1861, Archibald, by now nearly fifty years old, volunteered for military service and spent the war as a quartermaster in the

Vermont cavalry, fighting with the Union forces in northern Virginia. When he came back from the war, he opened a cigar store. He won a small local reputation for his punning advertisements: "Hams and cigars, smoked and unsmoked" and of one brand of cigar, "A good excuse for a bad habit."[13] The thought that smoking was a vice but a necessary and harmless one was one that would not have come so easily to his wife.

The circumstances of John Dewey's birth were tragic. Soon after their marriage—Archibald was forty-four and Lucina in her early twenties—Dewey's parents had had two children. The younger of the two, Davis Rich Dewey, went on to become a distinguished economist who was for many years president of the American Economics Association. The older, John Archibald, was killed as a child in the sort of domestic accident that makes one wince to read of it even now; here is the local newspaper's report:

> Distressing Accident.—We learn, with pain, that our friend and townsman, A. S. Dewey, has lost his oldest child, by a most distressing casualty. The child, a fine little boy, between two and three years old, was fatally scalded last evening, by falling backward into a pail of hot water. The customary appliances of sweet oil and cotton batting was made, when, by some accident the cotton took fire, and burst into flames upon the person of the child. This last mishap added to the pain of the little sufferer, as well as to his parents' distress, and death resulted (from the scalding principally, as we understand,) about seven o'clock this morning. The afflicted parents have the sincere and tearful sympathy of the community, in their sudden and most painful bereavement. [*Daily Free Press,* January 18, 1859][14]

John Dewey was a replacement child, born almost nine months to the day after his brother's death. The effect of the death of his brother on his upbringing is a matter of speculation, but it is hard to believe that his mother's continuous attention to his moral and spiritual welfare had nothing to do with her guilt over the death of the first John Dewey as well as to the practical circumstance that for almost the entire duration of the Civil War she had the sole charge of two young children. The family was reunited in Virginia as the war drew to a close, but until then Lucina was in sole charge of the little household and doubtless had an anxious time of it. The third surviving brother, Charles Miner, was born in 1867, after the family had reassembled in Burlington.

A good deal of inaccurate legend has accumulated around Dewey's childhood. Dewey was physically just what we think of as a nineteenth-century New England countryman: robust, craggy, slow-spoken, a man of determined manner, but utterly unaggressive. Later admirers have thought that this meant that he was a typical Vermonter, a Yankee of the Yankees, and by the same token that his background must have been rural, slow-moving, and a repository of timeless New England values.[15] Dewey's lifelong devotion to the cause of democracy has often been credited to a rural background, even by friends and colleagues who knew him well, such as Irwin Edman, a professor of philosophy at the University of Columbia who worked alongside Dewey for years. The attraction of this myth, for myth it was, was that it sustained a simple account of Dewey's passion for democracy. An instinctive taste for democracy in social life as well as in politics has often been said to hang in the air of rural and small-town New England, and the implication is that all Dewey had to do was breathe it in. The leading inhabitants of Burlington in Dewey's own day claimed just that. "We claim for Burlington the prevalence of a social equality, as complete and untrammeled as can be found in the smallest country village anywhere in New England. Intelligence, virtue, and a reasonable degree of good manners, will at once admit a newcomer of any rank or occupation into any circle which he or she may choose to enter."[16]

In fact, Burlington had ceased to be what we think of as a typical New England country town two decades before. Though the population was not much over ten thousand, Burlington was a specimen of the rapidly industrializing and urbanizing places in which Dewey in fact spent his early years. It was a center of the lumber industry and the commercial and transportation center for the region, as well as the home of the University of Vermont. With its growth came the features that Dewey worried over in later life, such as the rapid and disturbing immigration of newcomers from French Canada and Ireland; a wide and widening gulf between the respectable and God-fearing middle class, on the one hand, and the rougher working class, on the other; and a sharp contrast between the conditions of life in the better residential areas and those in the slums along the waterfront of Lake Champlain.

It was not only the changing character of Burlington that should make us cautious about thinking of Dewey as a Yankee; the intellectual and cultural leaders of New England had, after all, mostly come from Boston, a much larger city than Burlington. Dewey himself had very mixed feelings about his background; he thought of New England as the home of an intrusive piety, a repressive and life-denying moralism that had been for him an "inward laceration of the spirit" and something he was glad to grow out of in the Midwest.[17] Far from being a natural home of democracy, the New England of his childhood later seemed to him to be the home of a very sharp divide between classes, one that was usually economic and always a divide of taste and morality.

It is significant that fifty years later Dewey listed *Looking Backward* as one of the most important books in his life.[18] Its author was the most famous American socialist of Dewey's day, Edward Bellamy. Bellamy himself was at pains to describe himself as a "nationalist" rather than a socialist; "socialism," he said, conjured up images of beards, atheism, and free love rather than the disciplined public service he had in mind. Yet if socialism involves the subordination of private property to public purposes and the attempt to press egalitarianism as far as it will go, Bellamy was a socialist, whatever he chose to call himself. Bellamy had grown up in Chicopee Falls, Massachusetts, a little country town close to Springfield. The whole region had been transformed much more suddenly and more completely than Burlington into a modern textile and manufacturing center, with all that that implied in the way of an influx of immigrants, the creation of slums, and a good deal of hostility and class resentment. It was this background, not a background of taken-for-granted social and political democracy, that prompted Bellamy to construct and publish his vision of an absolutely classless and egalitarian society. The appeal it made on its publication in 1888 to an astonishingly wide audience—it sold three hundred thousand copies in two years, and was the best-selling book of the decade—suggests its impact on readers from very varied backgrounds. Partly its appeal was doubtless that its science-fiction touches, such as music and lectures piped into every house and home delivery of shopping via a system of pneumatic tubes, caught readers' eyes; much more important was the picture it painted of a society in which poverty had been abolished and public spirit had triumphed, not after class warfare and bloody revolution but because people had seen how much they would prefer to cooperate rather than to compete. It is not without interest that one of Bellamy's admirers was John Dewey.[19] What provoked Dewey's passion for democracy was less the fact that it was taken for granted in his hometown than that it was under threat, as well as the fact that Burlington was economically and morally as hierarchical as Bellamy's Chicopee Falls. The society in which Dewey grew up may have been free of snobbery in the narrow or British sense, but it was neither easygoing nor naturally egalitarian.

The greatest oddity of Dewey's intellectual formation is that however he may or may not have been affected by the places he lived in while he was growing up, he left no recorded account of their impact on his intellectual life until he was in his late thirties. The intellectual passions that moved him in his teens and twenties were ones that might have preoccupied him in any town or village in the country. In later life he himself noted that it was a curious fact—to a would-be biographer it is a catastrophe—that while he was growing up in a rapidly changing Burlington, and while he taught high school in Oil City, Pennsylvania, a rough-and-tumble, new-built, and exceedingly raw oil town, what he was interested in was religion and philosophy, and not the world around him. The kind of philosophy he then practiced was usually known as intuitionism (or, as in an encyclopedia essay of Dewey's, as intuitionalism), and it was popular in the latter part of the nineteenth century largely because it seemed to support Christian belief on a philosophical rather than a scriptural basis. With its appeal to the supposed necessities of "the human mind" as such, it was not a philosophy calculated to encourage an interest in the biases of locality and nationality. Only later, when his political interests were a more salient part of his intellectual life, did Dewey relate his interests to his own background and upbringing and show more curiosity about the way they had affected him.

Even then he said nothing about the impact on him of the places he lived in, not even about the impact of Chicago or New York City, where he spent the last forty-eight years of his life. His silence about his physical surroundings is puzzling. His great book on aesthetics, *Art as Experience,* shows a real love for and knowledge of modern painting and a genuine affection for the modern urban landscape; moreover, Dewey read Whitman and Emerson and Wordsworth with pleasure and enjoyed the countryside enough to buy houses in the Adirondacks, on Long Island, and in Nova Scotia. Yet he either did not much notice the details of his physical environment or else found himself with little to say about them. This was true even in later years, when he traveled so widely to China, Japan, Russia, Turkey, and Mexico. It is perhaps this lack of a strong sense of place in his work that has allowed his admirers to construct their own rather sentimental picture of where he must have grown up and what it must have been like.

It is, on the other hand, not surprising that Dewey's early interests were religious or that he was well acquainted with the differences between life in the more and less respectable areas of Burlington. His mother's emotional and moral outlook focused on the church, and much of her energy was spent on its charitable work. That church was the Congregational First Church of Burlington. Lucina Dewey's piety was intense, personal, and uninstitutional. It might have been attached to almost any variety of Protestant faith, so long as it emphasized a personal connection with Christ. She was a Universalist until her late teens and lapsed into Congregationalism during a summer vacation, to the mild distress of her family. The earliest letter supposed to have been written by young John is the letter applying for membership in the First Church: "I think I love Christ and want to obey Him. I have thought for some time I should like to unite with the church. Now, I want to more, for it seems one way to confess Him, and I should like to remember Him at the Communion."[20] Signed by the eleven-year-old John, the letter is in his mother's handwriting and is identical to the letter she wrote for his older brother, Davis.

The First Church was a good choice for a budding philosopher. It was more intellectually stimulating and less morally repressive than most congregations of the day. Its pastor was Lewis Brastow, who subsequently became professor of pastoral theology at the liberal Yale Divinity School, and it was in the *Andover Review,* the house journal of the liberal theologians, that Dewey published many of his first essays on ethics and philosophy. Brastow's theology was liberal and evangelical. The God he offered his congregation was God the Son, Christ the messenger who brought good news, rather than the God of the Old Testament who would decide our fate at the Last Judgment. After he died, he was remembered as a minister whose reluctance to insist on the fine print of theological positions had made him particularly helpful to adolescents with dawning skeptical anxieties. He was one of several people who filled such a role in Dewey's life. It seems likely that Archibald Dewey found the congregation a congenial one; like Lucina, Archibald had been a Unitarian in his youth, and his theological tastes were much like those of both the congregation and its pastor.

Brastow's congregation valued good works and deep moral convictions more than theological subtlety, but it was devoted to keeping up high intellectual standards, as Brastow's translation to Yale suggests. President Matthew Buckham of the University of Vermont was a member of the congregation; so was H. A. P. Torrey, the professor of moral philosophy at the university who was to be Dewey's first serious teacher of philosophy and in some ways more influential on him than many later teachers and colleagues. So, too, was Buckham's predecessor as president of the University of Vermont, James Angell. Angell moved to Ann Arbor in 1871 to become president of the University of Michigan, in which position he subsequently became Dewey's first real employer when Dewey joined the Michigan department of philosophy as an instructor in 1884. (Dewey returned the compliment by employing the younger James Rowland Angell, who eventually became president of Yale.)

Lucina Dewey's allegiances matter so much because she exercised the dominating influence on Dewey's early years. Her piety was striking even in the eyes of her fellow congregationalists. She did not confine her efforts to her own son but earnestly inquired into the spiritual health of his schoolmates and friends, in a way that increasingly irritated and embarrassed Dewey—and no doubt them. Her inquiry "Are you right with Jesus?" seems to have been particularly irritating and to have caused that "inward laceration of spirit" that he complained of as the most predictable result of an excess of religion in childhood. "Are you right with Jesus?" may, as some Freud-inspired historians have thought, have been a covert inquiry into their adolescent sexuality and their commission of the sin of masturbation. Though that seems a gratuitous speculation, one wonders what undertone in the inquiry can have caused a lifetime of subsequent resentment. To call it a lifetime of resentment is no exaggeration. Dewey became angrier about his mother's piety as he got older. In his thirties he merely remarked in an address to a Students' Christian Association meeting that incessantly examining a child's convictions is as foolish as digging up a seed to see if it is growing. But the "autobiography" that his daughter Jane Dewey compiled when her father was eighty years old for inclusion in *The Philosophy of John Dewey* is much angrier, and ten years earlier it was in the little essay "From Absolutism to Experimentalism," written for the celebration of his seventieth birthday, that there occurred the "inward laceration" remark that all commentators have seized on.[21] His mother's efforts eventually alienated Dewey from all moralities that dealt in "sin" and guilt and by the same token from all understandings of religion that separated the believer from his God in the way traditional Calvinist Christianity did. A *deus absconditus*, or "hidden God," was intolerable to him. Mrs. Dewey's negative influence was a slow-ripening seed that matured in Dewey's transformation of traditional moral questions into topics in his own pragmatic theory of "practical adjustment."

Dewey's education began late. The family went to Virginia to join Archibald Dewey when he was serving with the Union Army of Northern Virginia; they were not properly settled in Burlington again until 1867, by which time John was nearly eight years old. His elementary school was as chaotic as schools of that period often were: Those in his entering class ranged in age from seven to nineteen, and he went through school with his older brother, Davis. He and his brother were energetic and intelligent boys, with voracious literary tastes, but school did not satisfy them. Dewey's daughter recorded of the entire experience, both elementary school and high school, that "school was a bore, not only to his companions, but to Davis and himself, who were interested in reading almost anything except their school books."[22] Nonetheless, Dewey was an apt student, perhaps because of the stimulus of his older brother, perhaps because of his mother's attention, perhaps out of some innate intellectual drive. He so made up for lost time that he went to high school at the age of twelve and got through the four-year high school curriculum in three years. In high school he took the college preparatory course; it was heavily biased toward the classics—four years of Latin and three of Greek—accompanied by some French, some mathematics, and a great deal of English literature. Dewey took the route to college under the influence of his mother. Archibald Dewey had no college education and saw little need for it,[23] but the Rich family had always taken it for granted that the boys would go to college. The Rich family was in any case related to the Buckhams; that meant the Dewey boys were friendly with the Buckham sons and took it for granted that a college education was theirs for the asking.

Dewey was not precocious; he showed no sign of the intellectual imagination that was to make him one of the greatest of twentieth-century philosophers. It may seem unnecessary to say so, but many philosophers, from Bishop Berkeley to John Stuart Mill, have been precocious metaphysicians, just as others have been the reverse. It seems curious in retrospect when we see the role that appeals to "science" played in his later work, that Dewey had so little high school science and so much English literature. The explanation is simple enough. The college education of the day was not expected to match the tastes of those who underwent it. It was influenced by the belief in the character-building quality of a classical education that influenced the British public schools and universities, and it is hardly surprising that the preparatory course for college should have resembled a junior version of the real thing.

What his Burlington contemporaries later remembered of the teenaged Dewey was how painfully shy he was. He could not talk with girls without blushing and stammering until well into his twenties.[24] This, too, he seemed in later life to think of as one of the ill effects of his mother's child-rearing practices. He was by no means a pathological case. He was a devoted reader, especially of the historical romances of Sir Walter Scott, but not in the conventional sense a bookworm, and he was regarded by his elders as a well-behaved boy but one who was not unwilling to join in whatever mischief his friends proposed. He and Davis were quiet but not excessively well behaved; if teachers were to be locked in the classroom, they were in on the scheme. Out of school Dewey used to the full the free time school gave him. He remembered all his life his adolescent adventures on Lake Champlain, where he canoed the length of the lake, and on one occasion took a longer journey into Canada, escorted by a French-speaking Indian guide. He worked for pocket money tallying timber in the lumberyards along the lake and paid extended summer visits to the Rich farm some twenty miles away. Dewey was not a sentimentalist about the vanished world of rural America, but his writings on education thirty or forty years afterward were full of references to the way in which everyday life in the countryside had once supplemented schoolwork with a training in practical skills and an understanding of the natural world in a way that everyday life in the city did not and in a way he thought had to be self-consciously re-created by urban public schools.[25]

He must have been conscious of the fact that his older brother, Davis, was socially more accomplished than he and that his much younger brother, Charles, had been born a *bon viveur* and raconteur. Nothing survives of what Dewey thought about this, only long-after-the-event recollections of Burlington people who had known John as a boy. His family letters begin only after his college years, and they are notably unrevealing; they are sturdily practical, devoted to the cost of board and lodging and the quality of the food at the various boardinghouses he lived in until he married. No doubt family life took place face-to-face and therefore not through the mail, but Dewey never got into the habit of letting himself go about just what he felt.[26] This is not to suggest that family life was anything but happy. It is hard not to wonder what the gap between Archibald Dewey and his wife in age and temperament meant for the emotional atmosphere in which Dewey grew up, but in the absence of evidence it is pointless to speculate.[27] Only when Dewey met and fell in love with Alice Chipman, his first wife, did he put his feelings on paper. The results are so extraordinarily unsophisticated that the reader can only suppose the writer of these—in their own way touching—love letters lacked practice in opening his heart to anyone.

University of Vermont

Dewey entered the University of Vermont in 1875. He was not quite sixteen years old; that strikes us as young, but it was not then unusual. The limited range of literary and mathematical studies needed for college entrance was not difficult to master by the age of sixteen. Endless rote-learned recitations were painfully boring—when considering how "progressive" Dewey's educational ideals were, we must always remember how much of the impetus behind them came from his hatred of the rote learning of his youth—but they were effective in instilling a basic knowledge of two or three literatures and some mathematics. Sixteen was late enough to abandon such a diet. When Dewey went to the University of Chicago in 1894, the first president of the brand-new university, William Rainey Harper, was only in his thirties and had gained his Ph.D. at eighteen. Before succumbing to astonishment, we must also recall that the late-nineteenth-century Ph.D. dissertation was not the laboriously constructed five-hundred-page monster that the modern graduate student undertakes. It was common to write a doctoral thesis in weeks rather than months; Dewey's own graduate education lasted only four semesters, culminating in a thesis that he wrote in the fourth semester. So far as his undergraduate years went, even to speak of the University of Vermont as a "university" may convey a misleading impression to modern readers. It was a very small college. Vermont was one of the oldest colleges in the country, founded in 1791. It was junior among the New England colleges only to Harvard, Yale, Brown, and Dartmouth; it had been at times a distinguished place. Nevertheless, by the standards of a later age it was tiny. Dewey's graduating class numbered eighteen, and although the college had merged with the state college of agriculture a decade before, the total student body was under a hundred. The faculty in arts and sciences numbered eight. The college's origins were, however, suitably philosophical—which in nineteenth-century terms is to say they were theological. Vermont's most distinguished professor had been the Reverend James Marsh, its fifth president, a disciple of Coleridge's, an influential contributor to American transcendentalism, and one of the men who had brought the philosophy of Kant—by way of Coleridge's theological speculations—to the United States, back in the 1820s.

James Marsh was, in a roundabout way, one of the most influential figures in nineteenth-century American intellectual life, partly because he introduced Ralph Waldo Emerson to the philosophy of Coleridge, and thus to Carlyle and German idealism, and thus to the main sources of American transcendentalism. As Dewey later recalled, "The University of Vermont rather prided itself upon its tradition in philosophy. One of its earliest teachers, Dr. Marsh, was almost the first person in the United States to venture upon the speculative and dubiously orthodox seas of German thinking—that of Kant, Schelling, and Hegel. The venture, to be sure, was made by way of Coleridge; Marsh edited an American edition of Coleridge's *Aids to Reflection*. Even this degree of speculative generalization, in its somewhat obvious tendency to rationalize the body of Christian theological doctrines, created a flutter in ecclesiastical dovecotes."[28] The immediate effect of Marsh's teaching was to bring to Vermont an intellectual liveliness as well as a metaphysical depth that must have made the contrast between his originality and the limited ambitions of his successors all too painful.[29]

The long-run effect was to dissolve the union of faith and philosophy, though this was the reverse of Marsh's intentions, or indeed Kant's. It was a history with an impact on Dewey's thinking, if only "negatively."[30] Kant claimed that what we could know to be literally true or false began and ended within human experience; claims about anything beyond that were not literally nonsensical, as a later generation of logical positivists was to argue, but they were and could only be expressions of faith, not assertions of fact. "Transcendentalism" was an awkward label for a philosophy whose critical aim was to insist on the gulf between claims made *within* experience and claims made *about* experience as a whole. The name suggests that it was a philosophy *of* the transcendental realm, but the transcendental was exactly what Kant claimed we knew nothing about and about which we could say nothing. What transcendentalism preserved was the thought that it was morally important that we should continue to believe that the world made the sense that traditional Christianity claimed for it. We could not *know* that the world had its unity and value bestowed on it by a creator, but we could certainly believe it. Such a philosophy made religious faith a matter of moral allegiance, not a question of truth in the sense of "true to the facts." It was therefore friendly to a "religious perspective" on the world but strongly suggested that no particular religion could claim a monopoly on the truth. We shall see the effect of this on Dewey's conception of "the religious" more than once in what in what follows. In the 1870s it was perilous stuff. Dewey's friends recalled his saying years later that reading James Marsh's edition of Coleridge's *Aids to Reflection* had "been our spiritual emancipation in Vermont." He went on to add, "Coleridge represents pretty much my religious views still, but I quit talking about them because nobody else is interested in them."[31]

What Dewey encountered in his philosophy classes, however, was not Kant in a pure form. Many of Kant's and Marsh's ideas had been absorbed into the intuitionism that had been the staple of American college philosophy since the 1860s. Intuitionism was an awkward mixture of Kant's transcendental idealism and Scottish "commonsense" philosophy. Intuitionists drew the same distinction as Kant between what could be known within experience—described as the "conditioned" by intuitionists—and what could not—the "unconditioned." Its origins in early-nineteenth-century Scotland were all too visible in its other claims. Thomas Reid had claimed commonsensically that we just *know* many things that philosophers had unsuccessfully struggled to demonstrate: that there is an external world, that mind is distinct from matter, that causes bring about their effects. Later critics wrote off the combination of Kantian idealism and Reid's commonsense realism as manifestly incoherent; that is harsh, but it was certainly an unstable mixture.[32] In the hands of its toughest English exponent, Henry Mansel, it was virtually a philosophy of nescience, but out of apparent nihilism Mansel contrived to rescue a biblical faith. Everything was so completely conditioned by the mind that nothing was better known than anything else, and so—Mansel was a dean of St. Paul's—belief in Christianity was as well founded as any other belief. In American hands, according to Dewey's later account, intuitionism did little more than affirm a trust that ideas accepted with a sufficient degree of unshakability must reflect reality.[33] "It is probably impossible to recover at this date the almost sacrosanct air that enveloped the idea of intuitions; but somehow the cause of all holy and valuable things was supposed to stand or fall with the validity of intuitionalism. . . ."[34]

The synthesis had been assembled by the Scottish philosopher Sir William Hamilton, and its chief American defender was President James McCosh of the College of New Jersey (now Princeton). In Britain it was thought that the publication in 1865 of John Stuart Mill's *Examination of Sir William Hamilton's Philosophy* had killed it stone dead; in America it flourished until the end of the century. McCosh had attacked Mill's *Examination* of the master in an acerbic little treatise, *An Examination of Mr. J. S. Mill's Philosophy,* whose general tone is easily inferred from its subtitle, *Being a Defence of Fundamental Truth.* Mill thought intuitionism was simply a way of propping up indefensible beliefs by ascribing them to the "intuitive" needs of the human mind; McCosh and his followers retorted in kind: Mill's empiricism was atheistic, materialist, and probably immoral. McCosh spent his days in Princeton writing *The Scottish Philosophy* to show how (some of) his countrymen had saved common sense and Christianity from the subversive ideas of David Hume and the two Mills, whose Scottishness had no doubt been diminished by their heresies. Dewey came to the conclusion that although Mill might be wrong on many of the issues, he was right in his main charge: Intuitionism was popular because it was comforting, not because it was intellectually persuasive. Dewey came to think that his teachers were intuitionists from cowardice rather than conviction, and he himself abandoned it a year or two after graduation.[35]

Vermont relied on its own resources rather than on McCosh's importations. James Marsh's *Remains* was a prescribed text for the moral philosophy course, and Dewey insisted sixty years later that it was still well worth reading.[36] More to the point, the professor of moral philosophy H. A. P. Torrey—inevitably known as Happy Torrey to his students—was the nephew of the Joseph Torrey who had been summoned to Vermont in the 1840s to rescue the college when it had been on the verge of collapse. There was thus a distinctive local tradition on which Dewey could draw, and in obscure ways it affected his thinking all his life. Dewey did not find his ideas about religion ready-made in Vermont, nor was he simply heir to "Congregationalism married to Kant." All the same, the concerns he grew up with and the intellectual resources he brought to them were a plausible starting point for his later ideas.

So much was Dewey a pillar of American philosophical life over a very long lifetime that it is easy to think that he must have entered college with his mind made up as to his future career. That would be a misreading of the situation. In the 1870s, when he entered the University of Vermont, there was scarcely such a creature in the English-speaking world as a professional philosopher. Scottish professors were to some extent an exception, but even they tended to conflate the teaching of philosophy with the tasks of instilling Christian ethics. John Stuart Mill, who had died in 1873, had earned his living as a senior administrator in the East India Company; Herbert Spencer had been a journalist and then a pensioner of Andrew Carnegie's. Professors of philosophy in American colleges were invariably clergymen, and their interests theological rather than abstractly philosophical. The first American journal to treat philosophical issues separately from theological or religious issues was W. T. Harris's *Journal of Speculative Philosophy,* founded in 1867; in Britain

Mind was founded a few years later, in 1875, but had to be refounded in 1892. The German universities were almost unique in sheltering what we should today describe as professional philosophers, whose careers were devoted to pure philosophical scholarship. The strength of the Germans' historical scholarship was such that much of their effort went into the history of philosophy—usually the sort of history in which the authors' positive doctrines were set out in the course of critical commentaries on their predecessors. Meanwhile, a good deal of their nonhistorical research lay in what later became experimental psychology rather than philosophy as the twentieth century conceives it. What the German universities offered was an image of the research career. Dewey's disaffection from the religious enthusiasms of his mother meant that whatever else he had in mind, he never contemplated ordination into the ministry. This meant that he could not look forward to a career as a college professor of philosophy.

The New England college was in any event not a plausible place for research. Americans wishing to pursue advanced scholarship went to Germany; many of Dewey's teachers had made the tour of Halle, Leipzig, Berlin, and Jena, to learn from historians of philosophy like F. A. Trendelenburg and psychologists like Wilhelm Wundt, who made Leipzig the leading center for physiological psychology. Some toured Britain to talk to the students and colleagues of T. H. Green, such as F. H. Bradley, Edward Caird, Henry Jones, and Bernard Bosanquet, all of them Oxford teachers of philosophy for varying periods after 1870, several of them subsequently the heads of colleges and universities and active spokesmen for higher education; but although American visitors admired the undergraduate syllabus of places like Oxford and Cambridge, they could not at that time have done anything resembling organized graduate studies in philosophy anywhere in Britain. Oxford and Cambridge college teachers were superior schoolteachers. They were distinguished by their possession of degrees in arts and divinity; they were frequently men of wide reading and some imagination, but outside the sciences they were not engaged in research as a later generation understood it.

For Dewey, who was always more at his ease in front of his typewriter than in front of another human being, a career as an old-fashioned philosophy teacher would have been a highly implausible choice. The way in which several philosophers of the time moved in and out of the pulpit and public administration—William Torrey Harris was the editor of the very first American journal of philosophy; he led the unlikely group of midwestern philosophers who have come down to history as the St. Louis Hegelians; he was superintendent of schools in St. Louis, a considerable polemicist on behalf of high intellectual standards in schools, and finally the first federal commissioner for education—attested to the amateur nature of the discipline. "Amateur" is not a term of abuse; Harris and his friends were genuinely learned men. They were amateurs in the sense that thinking about philosophical problems was an avocation practiced in their leisure for disinterested reasons, not a profession for which they were rewarded financially. It was only with the opening of Johns Hopkins University in 1876 that the modern research university opened its doors in the United States, and even there, as we shall see, its energetic president, Daniel Coit Gilman, had no wish to promote research in philosophy in particular.

Dewey's Teachers: Their Style and Beliefs

Dewey's account of his college days suggests he took little interest in the prescribed courses he had to attend in his first three years. He claimed that his real education came from reading the English periodicals that the college library subscribed to, magazines such as the *Nineteenth Century*, the *Fortnightly Review*, and the *Contemporary Review*. The 1870s were the heyday of these heavyweight intellectual journals. They were not as magisterial in tone or as expansive in their contents as their forerunners, the *Edinburgh Review* and its radical rivals, the *Westminster* and the *London and Westminster Review*. But what was lost when Macaulay was no longer writing reviews of a hundred closely packed pages had been made up for by the greater vivacity and pugnacity of the new generation. In the *Fortnightly*, for instance, James Fitzjames Stephen had in earlier days written reviews of such ferocity that even his friends winced for his victims' sensibilities when they nicknamed Stephen the Gruffian. They were the sparring grounds of advanced thought, whether they were Liberal or Conservative in political allegiance, and they gave space to writers who enjoyed a degree of freedom that academic writers a century later would not know how to employ if they had it. T. H. Huxley savaged the opponents of evolutionary theory as he performed his role as "Darwin's bulldog," Walter Bagehot expressed his anxieties about the narrowness of the line between stagnant conservatism and mere chaos in essays on *Physics and Politics*, while G. H. Lewes—the companion of George Eliot—acted as a go-between interpreting Continental philosophical currents to his insular British readers; there was a great deal of popular scientific speculation from writers such as Sir John Tyndall and much thoughtful, agnostic brooding on the Victorian crisis of faith from all of these, from positivists like Frederic Harrison, and in Mill's posthumous essays on religion.

It is infinitely far from the truth that Dewey simply swallowed these writers and their ideas and turned everything he received to his own uses, but it is certainly true that the greatest intellectual influence he acknowledged from that time was not a philosopher, and not one of his teachers, but T. H. Huxley, physiologist, evolutionist, agnostic, and reformer. Recalling his reading of Huxley's *Elements of Physiology*, Dewey remarked that it was there that he had found the model of intellectual activity that had animated his own subsequent career. Dewey remarked at the age of seventy:

> It is difficult to speak with exactitude about what happened to me intellectually so many years ago, but I have an impression that there was derived from that study a sense of

interdependence and interrelated unity that gave form to intellectual stirrings that had been previously inchoate, and created a type or model of a view of things to which material in any field ought to conform. Subconsciously, at least, I was led to desire a world and a life that would have the same properties as had the human organism in the picture of it derived from study of Huxley's treatment. At all events, I got great stimulation from the study, more than from anything I had had contact with before; and as no desire was awakened in me to continue that particular branch of learning, I date from this time the awakening of a distinctive philosophic interest.[37]

Dewey's teachers were learned, sympathetic, and in their treatment of the books they taught not uncritical, but they were in Dewey's eyes too inhibited by their prior commitments to be what he needed and wanted. During the first three years of his undergraduate work he essentially did more of what he had already done enough of in high school: classical literature and language, ancient history and historians, some mathematics, some English. The only novelty was biology. He may well have been bored by much of the work; in later life he attacked the old-fashioned college syllabus as essentially futile. It was excessively historical, retrospective, and pious even when the subject matter was far removed from religion. As we shall see, it is questionable how far Dewey enjoyed historical studies for their own sake. Although his was not a vulgar pragmatism, he found it hard to resist asking what help a knowledge of the past would be in dealings with the problems of the present. In his recollections of those days he observed that the battle between intuitionism and empiricism "aided in generating a sense of the value of the history of philosophy; some of the claims made for this as a sole avenue of approach to the study of philosophic problems seem to me misguided and injurious. But its value in giving perspective and a sense of proportion to immediate contemporary issues can hardly be overestimated."[38] In more formal, syllabus-centered terms, his complaint was not with the discipline of history or with a simple curiosity about the past—both of which were entirely acceptable—but with the underlying assumptions of the classical studies of his youth. It seemed to be assumed that there was a sharp break between the concerns of the present and those of the "classical" past and that those of the past were superior to those of the present, implying always that it was the task of the present to emulate the literary and philosophical achievements of the classics. However hard Dewey tried not to believe in the inevitability of "progress," it would have been beyond the youthful (or even the elderly) Dewey to think that education was essentially retrospective and that liberal education amounted to an induction into a body of truths that newcomers were to have no hand in shaping.

His last undergraduate year was a great improvement on what went before. American colleges of the time followed the practice of taking all their students through a course of moral philosophy, usually taught by the president of the college. Vermont had an unusually liberal understanding of the course. It was conceived by Buckham and Torrey as a chance to civilize their charges by exposing them to philosophy, though its content was a good deal wider than that suggests. President Buckham's course in political and social philosophy was more nearly a course in what we should now call social theory and practice. Students read Mill's economics as well as Guizot's *History of Civilization in Europe* and learned as much constitutional law as they did political theory. Buckham's radicalism stopped with his reading list and his attachment to Socratic methods in the classroom. He did not think that radical reform was needed to solve the evils of the day; rather, he said, society needed to develop the principles already inherent in existing practice. Oddly, this—though understood very differently—was just the thought Dewey himself later put forward to justify his radicalism. It was because society was making such a bad job of living up to its own principles that Dewey felt compelled to recall it to its own better nature. Dewey construed those principles as the principles of modern liberal democracy, implying a positive affection for novelty and innovation. Buckham's conservatism rested on the belief that the first principles of American society were those of undogmatic Christianity. This implied a certain political quietism: What mattered in the end was the individual's salvation, and radicalism would not help in that department. That was a thought that did not survive into Dewey's mature thinking.

Dewey's view of his teachers emerges more strongly from his reflections on H. A. P. Torrey than from anything we know of his view of Matthew Buckham. His relations with Torrey were very close. Torrey taught him the usual intuitionist repertoire; but Torrey was a good Kant scholar, and the introduction to Kant that Dewey got from Torrey was something for which he was lastingly grateful. Dewey's letters to Torrey from Johns Hopkins may be deliberately flattering, but Dewey told his former teacher that he had learned enough Kant in Vermont to find what he was taught at Johns Hopkins rather elementary and uninspiring. Their friendship lasted beyond Dewey's undergraduate career. After Dewey had graduated from Vermont, but before he went on to Johns Hopkins, he learned philosophical German with Torrey, well enough to be able to offer to translate portions of Hegel into German for W. T. Harris. Intellectually, however, his ultimate judgment of Torrey was severe:

> Mr. H. A. P. Torrey was a man of genuinely sensitive and cultivated mind, with marked esthetic interest and taste, which in a more congenial atmosphere than that of northern New England in those days, would have achieved something significant. He was, however, constitutionally timid, and never really let his mind go. I recall that in a conversation I had with him a few years after graduation, he said: "Undoubtedly pantheism is the most satisfactory form of metaphysics intellectually, but it goes counter to religious faith." I fancy that remark told of an inner conflict that prevented his native capacity from coming to full fruition.[39]

Whether Torrey was as timid as Dewey suggests, it is hard to tell. Dewey may have mistaken Torrey's unwillingness to pretend to a certainty he did not feel for intellectual timidity. On the other hand, Torrey would undoubtedly have irritated Dewey—retrospectively—by his intuitionism.

Although Dewey and Mill denounced intuitionism as pure wishful thinking, they were not entirely just. They exaggerated one feature of intuitionism—the view that the world corresponds to our deepest feelings about it—and neglected what intuitionism borrowed from Kant: the idea that our mind is active rather than passive, that it shapes experience, and that what we call experience is a reflection of the mental structures that have shaped it. Everything hinges on the way we understand weasel words like "necessary." To hold that a belief in God, freedom, and immortality—Kant's three great topics of metaphysical inquiry—is "necessary" as a starting point for all other inquiry may be a way of smuggling belief back into our philosophy after acknowledging that it cannot respectably be done; but Kant did not do so. Kant sharply distinguished between two orders of belief; one is genuinely necessary for human experience to have the orderly character it does—causality, personal identity, that objects are distinct in space and events are distinct in time—while the other consists of the ideas that provide us with guidelines by which to make sense of experience in general rather than explain any particular portion of it. The existence or otherwise of God, freedom, and immortality makes no difference to our ability to navigate our way around everyday life, but our convictions about them will make every difference to what we believe the purpose of that navigation to be. Just as a scientist must *believe* but cannot *know* that every event has some kind of physical explanation, so we must *believe* though we cannot *know* that human life is not confined to the years we spend here on earth. In the first case, our belief that a failure to find the explanation of what we are investigating is a failure in us rather than the world makes us keep looking for explanations when we might otherwise give up; in the second case, our belief that we shall see the results of our this-worldly projects after our earthly life is over inspires us to take those projects seriously when we otherwise might not. Were such a belief truly essential for life to have any point or purpose or meaning for us, one might well call it necessary. One might even see in this account of necessity an element of the pragmatist's instrumental account of belief. Still, Dewey was surely right to fear the dishonesty implicit in conflating what is arguably a metaphysical necessity with what is at best a practical necessity.

Dewey ended his career at the University of Vermont by being graduated second in his class. His grades in his last year were better than in previous years and much better than the average, but his record over the whole four years was not astonishingly good. He was still very young, barely nineteen years old, and as shy and awkward and unsure of himself as he could well be. He was at a loss about his future career, and the obvious course, schoolteaching, must have looked unpromising both to him and to anyone who wondered how on earth he was to keep order in the classroom. Something must have stirred in his mind, since it was less than two years later that he wrote his first published essay in philosophy, "The Metaphysical Assumptions of Materialism," written in the winter and spring of 1881 and published in the *Journal of Speculative Philosophy* in April 1882.

Oil City and After

This was some way ahead. Dewey spent an anxious summer after graduation searching for work and finding none. Finally a cousin who kept a school in Oil City, Pennsylvania, stepped in and offered him a job as a teacher. It paid four hundred dollars a year, and Dewey gratefully accepted it. Astonishingly there is no record of what he thought of Oil City or of what anyone there thought of him. One would have thought that the Dewey who in later life took an active part in national and international politics, who wrote for the *New Republic,* presided over a "trial" to hear the charges that Stalin's government had leveled at Leon Trotsky, and was the very model of an engaged intellectual must have reacted to the rawness and vigor of the extraordinary place he now found himself in. Apparently he did not, unless we are to count his continuing passion for metaphysics as a reaction to the all too physical squalor of his surroundings.

Oil City was the product of the first United States oil boom. The first "strike" had been made a few miles away at Titusville, Pennsylvania, and as the oil industry grew, Oil City had grown from a hamlet of a few dozen inhabitants in the early 1860s to a town of seven or eight thousand in Dewey's time. Its position at the junction of Oil Creek and the Allegheny River gave it an obvious role as a transshipment point for crude oil coming down the creek from the wells in the hinterland on its way to the refineries at Pittsburgh. That role, in turn, provided a basis for the establishment of a commodity exchange, brokerage firms, and other adjuncts to the oil business. Oil City presented the paradoxical picture that other boomtowns have presented in their time, that of being a home to the extreme ends of the social and economic spectrum. Dewey is said to have turned down an offer of cheap shares in Standard Oil, but the story sounds too like something made up after the event to emphasize his unworldliness. Large fortunes were indeed made and lost on the exchange, though not usually by the teamsters and dock workers who manhandled oil barrels into barges or assembled barge convoys for the trip to Pittsburgh. The landscape by the docks was as lurid as usual in such places, with migrant workers crowded into insanitary shanties, hugger-mugger with saloons and brothels. The streets were not much better than swamps during much of the winter and spring; but the febrile prosperity of the oil boom supported an opera house, and the growing number of children had led to the building of a high school a few years before Dewey arrived there.

This was the school that his cousin Affia Wilson looked after, where Dewey taught his charges algebra, Latin, and some science. One would have expected a nineteen-year-old metaphysician to have had some difficulty controlling classes whose students were much of an age with himself; a couple of years later he had a dreadful time dealing with obstreperous students at another school nearer home. In Oil City things went smoothly. A handful of Dewey's pupils were interviewed in the 1950s; they reported that "contrary to notions popular in Oil City school circles long after Dewey had left . . . Dewey was well-liked and respected by his students, who took no more liberties with him than with the other two teachers."[40] The main event of this time that Dewey later recalled was as unlikely as one could well imagine in Oil City. This was his one and only "mystical" experience. Since the only report of its occurrence comes in an article written sixty years later by Max Eastman, who was a student of Dewey's at Columbia in the early 1900s before going on to a long career as a poet, editor, Trotskyite, and eventual anti-Communist pillar of *Reader's Digest,* it should probably be taken be taken with a pinch of salt, especially since Eastman was the only source for the story that Dewey had turned down the chance to make a fortune in Standard Oil. Eastman was such a glamorous figure and had such a rackety youth himself that he probably found it impossible not to embroider a little. Dewey, as reported by Eastman, said that he had brooded on the question "whether he meant business" when he prayed; then he found himself overtaken by a "supremely blissful feeling that his worries were over." The oddity of this account is that it appears to explain both a loss of faith and a revival of faith: "I've never had any doubts since then, nor any beliefs. To me faith means not worrying. . . . I claim I've got religion, and I got it that night in Oil City."[41] One reason for wondering whether the event occurred, whether Dewey told the story in quite that form to Max Eastman, and whether it had quite the significance Eastman gave it is that Dewey carried on going to church and teaching Sunday school until he left the University of Michigan in 1894, more than a dozen years later. Then he stopped.

After two years of Oil City Dewey took one more teaching job. This was a really miserable experience. The school was in Charlotte, a village a few miles south of Burlington. The job allowed him to continue reading philosophy and German with Henry Torrey; otherwise it was a dreadful business. The village of Charlotte had only intermittently possessed a school. The school in which Dewey was to teach had burned down some years before; it had been restored, reorganized, and reopened in the previous year. What it lacked was pupils who could do high school work. Since the students ranged in age from thirteen to twenty, they would have been a handful under any conditions; with Dewey they were impossible. Dykhuizen quotes a former pupil as recalling only two things about Dewey's time there: "how terribly the boys behaved, and how long and fervent was the prayer with which he opened each school day."[42] Dewey's future was about to be settled, however. Before he left Oil City, he sent his first essay in philosophy to W. T. Harris, for possible publication in Harris's *Journal of Speculative Philosophy.* "The Metaphysical Assumptions of Materialism" is unreadable 110 years later; there were innumerable nineteenth-century attempts to demonstrate that the doctrine that there was nothing in the world except matter in motion was self-contradictory; Dewey's is no more and no less accomplished than many others. More interesting was the letter Dewey sent with the essay. He asked Harris whether he supposed Dewey had enough philosophical ability to make it worth his while continuing to study it: "I suppose you must be troubled with many inquiries of this sort, yet if it would not be too much to ask, I should be glad to know your opinion on it, even if you make no use of it. An opinion as to whether you considered it to show ability enough of any kind to warrant my putting much of my time on that sort of subject would be thankfully received, and, as I am a young man in doubt as to how to employ my reading hours, might be of much advantage. I do not wish to ask too much of your time and attention, however."[43] The tone is diffident, but Dewey must have had more confidence in his ability than the letter suggests. Few American graduate students at the end of the twentieth century send essays to learned journals before their twenty-first birthdays.

Harris took several months to acknowledge the essay and say that he was going to use it; in the meantime, Dewey wrote the second piece to appear in Harris's *Journal,* a short essay titled "The Pantheism of Spinoza." This made the sensible, if not very original, observation that Spinoza's claim that everything was an aspect of one Substance or God did not do what Spinoza had intended—that is, show how everyday events and objects shared in the being of something timeless, eternal, and perfect. Dewey identified a problem that most readers have felt in an inarticulate fashion: that Spinoza offered no explanation of why everyday events and objects *seemed* so thoroughly unpermeated by the divine.

The puzzle has some philosophical interest, if only because it was just the sort of puzzle Dewey's later philosophy pushed aside. It is the kind of problem that shows why philosophy is a cousin of theology and why the relationship causes trouble. One standing problem for Christianity is the "problem of evil," the problem of reconciling the belief that the world is the creation of a good God with the pain, misery, and other evils it contains. Philosophically the puzzle is to see a good God in a bad world. The Judeo-Christian myth of the Fall and Redemption suggests that all Creation shared the Fall and that the transitoriness, fragility, ugliness, and other deficiencies of the world—mosquitoes, viruses, cancer cells, and phenomena of the sort give substance to the notion that the world is "defective"—are part of Creation's separation from God. Before the Fall and after Redemption, all was and will be well, even if it is in a fashion we now have no inkling of. Skeptics think the unimaginability of a perfect world shows that religious faith is nonsense; philosophers who believe that *something* in conventional religion survives such skepticism must show what the rational core of the traditional religious story may be. If they are as "God-intoxicated" as Spinoza but do not invoke a supernatural deity as an external and none-too-intelligible cause of the world of experience, pantheism is attractive. Pantheism says that the world is identical with God or is permeated by the divine principle; when we look at the world of experience in the right light, what we see is God. Dewey's second published essay argued that it was hard to hold on to both sides of the equation. Either the everyday world gets its full weight as an everyday, ordinarily experienced world, and the ascent to God is impossible; or it is given its full weight as a God-permeated and perfect world, and the return to its ordinariness and everydayness is impossible.

It would not be worth dwelling on this essay but for one thing. Spinoza's problem remained Dewey's problem. Pragmatism, as Dewey explained it, held that the only world there is is the world of experience *and* that it is meaningful and coherent in ways we do not *impose* on it but *find* in it. It was this that allowed Dewey to be so confident that there was no ultimate clash between science and religion and that a religious outlook could survive any amount of scientific investigation of the world. Dewey's friends, colleagues, and students were absolutely not of one mind about what he really believed. Some thought he had a naturally pious mind, some thought the reverse; some wished he would avoid all talk of God, some were glad that he went halfway to meet the conventionally religious. I say a good deal more about this in due course. For now it is enough to note that even before he became a graduate student at Johns Hopkins, Dewey's interests were so thoroughly set. It would be absurd to say that Dewey's purpose in life was simply to reaffirm the comforts of faith in a scientific universe, but it would not at all absurd to suggest that this was one of the goals he set himself. St. Paul offered some memorable comfort to beleaguered followers of Christ when he said that nothing could separate us from the love of God; at various times Dewey looked to the Hegelian Absolute Idea, to T. H. Green's eternal self, and finally to "social intelligence" for that reassurance. Whether or not he ever had the mystical experience in Oil City that Max Eastman claimed Dewey told him about, "not having to worry" is not a bad summary of Deweyan faith. Dewey expected to worry about where to get a job, where to find lodgings, how to support his family, and so on and so forth; but *cosmic* anxiety could properly be shrugged off.

Two

Pastors and Masters

Nobody is entirely a product of other people's contriving, but all of us are to a degree the fruits of the labors of our parents and teachers, and intellectuals especially so. Dewey carried with him all his life both the positive and the negative marks of his graduate work at Johns Hopkins. This is not to say that he was always exposed to famous (or distinguished) teachers there. The teacher who had most impact on him—G. S. Morris, the idealist philosopher—is remembered largely because he taught Dewey at Hopkins and gave him his first job at the University of Michigan. It was Dewey's good fortune to encounter at Hopkins two teachers whose minds were of the first rank: Charles Sanders Peirce, the first pragmatist and perhaps the most original philosopher the United States has ever produced, and G. Stanley Hall, trained as a philosopher but, more important, as one of the two or three creators of United States experimental psychology. It was Dewey's great misfortune to learn at the time nothing from the first and to be disliked by the second.

Perhaps for this reason Dewey was touchy about his own intellectual formation. When people remarked on the Hegelian residues in his work, he became prickly, as if he resented the marks left by Morris and Hall. In an autobiographical essay he got in a preemptive blow: "I should never think of ignoring, much less denying, what an astute critic occasionally refers to as a novel discovery—that acquaintance with Hegel has left a permanent deposit in my thinking."[1] Yet Dewey is interesting just because his intellectual evolution was so steady. Unlike Bertrand Russell's philosophical development, which Russell used to joke about as a case of leaping from the Hegelian view that the world was a bowl of treacle to the atomist view that the world was a heap of lead shot, Dewey's development was marked by no sharp reversals and violent changes of mind. To the end of his life, the style, concerns, and even some of the intellectual techniques of his youth remained visible in his work. The sixty-, seventy-, or eighty-year-old Dewey was very much the child of his twenty-year-old self.

Dewey graduated from Vermont with a strong sense that philosophy ought to save the world. But if he was to show how the world could escape meaninglessness, and life escape futility, he had to become a much more accomplished scholar and practitioner than he yet was. In the light of Dewey's complaints about Henry Torrey's intellectual timidity and unwillingness to "let his mind go," it is surprising that it was Torrey who encouraged him to think of taking up philosophy as a professional career and so to pursue graduate study. Neither Dewey's autobiographical sketches nor any of his commentators' accounts are entirely clear why he decided to attend Johns Hopkins. The reason may have been financial; the alternative to graduate work at Hopkins would have been to have gone to Germany to sit at the feet of the great psychologists and logicians of the day, Wilhelm Wundt and R. H. Lotze, and that would have strained the family's resources impossibly. Local piety may have played a role; both G. S. Morris and G. S. Hall—two of the three philosophers at Hopkins—were Vermonters. As it was, money turned out to be a problem after all. Daniel Coit Gilman, the president of Johns Hopkins, had a clear ambition for his new university. It was to practice science. Considering the almost universal association of philosophy and theology, this meant that he preferred experimental psychology to the philosophy of mind, political science to political philosophy, and anthropology to ethics. He had no wish to waste his scarce resources on aspirant students of neo-Hegelianism. Dewey applied for a five-hundred-dollar fellowship and was turned down; he applied for a three-hundred-dollar scholarship and was turned down. Battered but unbowed, he accepted an aunt's offer of a loan of five hundred dollars for his first year of work, put in an application for admission, was accepted, and in the fall of 1882 enrolled in the program in philosophy and psychology.

Hopkins, 1882–84

To do justice to the first years of Johns Hopkins would take a book rather than a paragraph; it would also involve a long excursion into the dangerous subject of the effect upon American higher education of American educators deciding to copy the German university rather than the English or Scots university.[2] The results are with us still, and the evaluation of those results is a vexed business. The long-term effects of persuading university teachers that research matters more than teaching, that graduate students are more interesting than undergraduate students, and that academic respectability is a function of specialization have been endlessly debated. It is enough to notice that Johns Hopkins was something very new in American higher education when it opened in 1876, six years before Dewey went there. It was the first university to give priority to the training of graduate researchers as distinct from the general cultural polishing that liberal arts colleges gave their undergraduates. Its teaching methods also were new to the United States; laboratory instruction in the sciences and small seminars led by distinguished faculty in all subjects replaced "recitations." Its vision of the role of a professor was new to the United States, as was its vision of the role of graduate students. It was the first American university to measure a professorial career by the weight of published material and the first to associate graduate students closely with the research work of their senior teachers.

For the first few generations of graduate students it was wonderful. Josiah Royce, the Harvard philosopher who had been there at the very beginning, borrowed Wordsworth's description of the first days of the French Revolution and wrote of the dawn wherein 'twas bliss to be alive. Dewey cast a less than rosy light on his undergraduate career at the University of Vermont when he later told a Michigan audience about the pleasures of graduate work at Johns Hopkins: "The student is treated not as a bucket for the reception of lectures, nor as a mill to grind out the due daily grist of prepared text-book for recitation, but as being in search of truth, which he is to discover for himself, the proper encouragement and advice as to means and methods being furnished by his instructor."[3] One wonders what the undergraduate teaching offered by Matthew Buckham and Henry Torrey had really been like after all. Dewey was too loyal to complain directly, but it may well have been dull until he was of an age to go for educational walks with Torrey. Classes were called recitations for a good reason: Students were expected to learn passages of set texts by heart and recite their lessons on demand. In Oxford twenty years earlier an undergraduate tutorial would have had half a dozen young men parsing a prescribed text in a way we flinch at seeing in a secondary school, and Dewey's implicit criticism of Vermont as a place where students were treated as "buckets" may have been accurate enough, and the contrast with Johns Hopkins as striking as he said. Gilman thought little of philosophy and could not imagine that anyone might seriously embark on a career as a teacher of the subject; his first kindly act was to try to persuade Dewey to embrace some other discipline. Beneath his shyness, however, Dewey was tough. He had enough of the Puritan in him to think that philosophy was his "calling" and that not to listen to his calling was sinning against the light. In any case, Henry Torrey had commended him to the care of George Sylvester Morris, and it was to Morris's courses that Dewey therefore took himself.

Peirce, Hall, and Morris

The department of philosophy and psychology was tiny. Moreover, in the eyes of history, Dewey's estimate of the merits of his teachers was exactly wrong. When he was there, the instructors were G. S. Morris, G. S. Hall, and C. S. Peirce; Dewey ranked them thus, but subsequent philosophers and psychologists have always thought that Peirce was the most original and imaginative philosopher ever to have been born in the United States, while Hall, though boastful, self-important, by no means as imaginative as his colleague Peirce, and not in the same league as a psychologist as his contemporary and teacher William James, was the most influential figure in establishing experimental psychology as a university discipline in the United States. In this company Morris was outclassed. Peirce and Hall were representatives of the future; Morris had backed a philosophical world view that was about to become obsolete. It made no odds whether one went down the empirical psychological track espoused by Hall or the pragmatist track espoused by Peirce, James, and Dewey; within forty years idealism in all its varieties—excluding Marxism as a bastard offspring of Hegelianism that rejected its parent with a violence in proportion to its intellectual debts, and pragmatism as a liberal version born in the same stable as Marxism—lay on the beach of historical oddities like a stranded whale.

Nonetheless, Morris was a learned and serious man, and Dewey encountered him at a time when he had struggled through great miseries and hardships to arrive at an intellectual safe harbor. Morris's books of the 1880s are aggressively written and meanspirited in their assessment of everyone who did not share his "dynamic idealism," but they are brisk, confident, and tolerably clear. They are also by late-twentieth-century standards almost entirely devoid of argument as distinct from bald assertion.[4] One can imagine the diffident Dewey's taking some time to throw off such an influence. Morris had an interesting upbringing. He was born in 1840, the youngest of eight children; his father, Sylvester Morris, was a well-known abolitionist from the Vermont town of Norwich. Norwich was a bare mile or two over the Connecticut River from Hanover, the site of Dartmouth College, and it was to Dartmouth that Morris duly went at the age of seventeen. There he distinguished himself but suffered the slights he attracted throughout his life as predictably as a church steeple attracts lightning. He was by far the best student of his year, and if his classmates had had their way, he would have been valedictorian when he graduated in 1861. The honor was instead given to a faculty member's son; Morris's class had to content themselves with cheering Morris's speech and receiving that of the chosen student in stony silence.[5] After a year of teaching high school and a year of Civil War service with the Second Vermont Brigade—he fought in the later stages of the Battle of Gettysburg—Morris went on to train for the ministry at Union Theological Seminary in New York City.

Morris found the low intellectual level of the instruction intolerable, experienced religious doubts, and had a nervous breakdown. A benefactor gave him the chance to escape by giving him the money to go to Germany for three years. Without quite admitting that he was about to abandon the ministry for philosophy, Morris went to Germany and worked with F. A. Trendelenburg, the most important of the nineteenth-century German historians of philosophy after Friedrich Überweg. Trendelenburg was a biographer of Hegel's who rejected Hegel's philosophy, though sympathetically, and espoused a modernized Aristotelianism. This in due course had enough of an effect on Dewey for many casual critics to describe him as an Aristotelian, and in many ways a better effect than it had on Morris. It enabled Dewey to absorb what he wanted from Hegel and then to go on to produce a naturalistic and utterly empirical philosophy. Morris, on the contrary, got no further than dynamic idealism and Fichte and mostly seems to have acquired from his German teachers a wholesale contempt for British empiricism.[6] It says much for Dewey's sweetness of character that he unswervingly followed Morris in repudiating the dualism and materialism of the British tradition but never caught the embittered tone of his teacher.

Morris's career got on to a satisfactory footing only in the last few years of his life. When he died in 1889, in his forty-ninth year, he was a successful teacher and the well-liked head of the department of philosophy at the University of Michigan in Ann Arbor, but he had held that position for only five years. On his return from Germany in 1868, his future looked grim: In his absence his mother had died, his fiancée had decided that his character and his religious opinions had changed for the worse and had abandoned him, and there was no obvious channel of employment. He found a position as a private tutor with the Seligmans, a well-to-do New York banking family, and settled down to translate Überweg's *History of Philosophy*. The translation was recognised as a serious scholarly achievement, but it did not secure Morris a post in philosophy. It landed him a professorship, but not the one he wanted. Nonetheless, the professorship in modern languages that the University of Michigan offered him was at least an improvement on private tutoring, and to Ann Arbor he went. He was successful in establishing the modern languages department in a university that had been severely shaken by administrative quarrels over the previous decade, but he was far from happy. The dourness of his manner and his sense that he was doing hackwork alienated him from both his colleagues and his pupils. The kindest thing that was said of him by his students was that "the transparent honesty of his character serv[ed] to chasten pupils, even when it did not fully win upon them."[7] It cannot have added to his happiness that the chair of philosophy had been bestowed on a man described as a "Methodist preacher whose formal schooling had ended at age thirteen but who was a gifted speaker and a person of great moral earnestness."[8] The Methodist preacher and ex-accountant was an improvement on his predecessor, whom, according to Morris's biographer, "tradition says, a certain church became tired of, and palmed off on the University, because it could not get rid of him in any other way."[9]

The excessively serious Morris, struggling with doubt, Überweg, and a job he regarded as a poor second best, was regarded as an unhappy loner. Professors were expected to deliver uplifting addresses to students and colleagues, a task that Dewey later performed with immense skill; getting Morris to perform was like extracting teeth. In his first decade he did this small duty only three times. Matters slowly got better. He joined the Episcopal Church, married, and was finally invited to lecture at Johns Hopkins. His lectures were a success, and he had hopes of becoming Johns Hopkins's first professor of philosophy. Before these hopes were dashed, his situation at Michigan improved. The American tradition whereby universities recognize the merits of their faculty only when they are in danger of leaving for another employer had already been established, and Michigan let Morris step down from the chair of modern languages and become professor of ethics, philosophy, and logic in 1881.

What Morris wanted by then, however, was the chair of philosophy at Johns Hopkins. In this he was frustrated by two things, one the doubts of President Gilman, the other the ambitions of G. Stanley Hall. Gilman was a double obstacle. In the first instance, his conception of research was narrowly scientific, and in the second, he was determined that his faculty should cause him no trouble by showing doubts about the Christian religion. Morris's doubts were all too well known. The circle within which philosophers moved was very small, and anyone who cared to could discover that ever since his days at Union Theological Seminary, Morris had been beset by doubt. At this distance in time it is difficult to discover quite what Johns Hopkins's official standards were.[10] It appears that silent agnosticism and outward conformity would serve perfectly well in most disciplines other than philosophy, but professors in philosophy were still expected to provide "uplift" and thus to speak with a proper show of conviction about the spiritual benefits of Christianity. Morris suffered the ill effects of a transparent character: He could not say what he did not sincerely believe, and the misery this caused him made him seem aloof, austere, and uncaring to everyone else.

Morris's loathing for John Stuart Mill, and by extension for the entire British philosophical tradition, had a lot to do with these miseries. Mill was the representative figure of high-minded agnosticism and the preeminent philosopher of science in the middle of the nineteenth century. He recorded in his *Autobiography* that he felt himself to be unusual among his contemporaries in never having passed through a crisis of faith, though he rather undermined that claim by devoting a long and revealing chapter to "A Crisis in My Mental Life." It detailed the long period of unhappiness Mill endured in his early twenties when he could find no reason to take any of his father's or any of his own ideals seriously, and it explained how he had resolved the crisis through the healing power of Wordsworth's poetry and the inspiration of Goethe. What Mill never experienced was a loss of an orthodox Christian faith. He had been brought up as an agnostic and in his last essays on religion suggested that the furthest that reason could take us was toward the idea that the universe might be governed by an intelligence of some kind but one that was plainly not omnipotent.[11] Bertrand Russell recorded that it took one reading of Mill's *Autobiography* to destroy his faith, and reading Mill has always been likelier to fortify skeptics in their skepticism than to show them the road back to the faith. This was not what Morris wanted. If Dewey is to be trusted, Morris hoped that Mill would explain how the everyday world of experience is intelligible, explicable, and, in spite of its obvious unsatisfactoriness, one where we can realize our ideals of a better world. Morris had hoped that Mill would give him the courage to live in this world without the transcendental comforts of religion or metaphysics. Mill's tight-lipped agnosticism was insufficient.

Writing about Morris many years later, Dewey struck this note:

> I cannot but feel that a genuinely typical significance attaches to his judgment of John Stuart Mill. The personality and the intention of Mill had a great attraction for Morris; I like to think it was because of a real kinship between the characters of the two men. But Mill's standpoint and achievement in philosophy, judged from the standpoint of the idealism so dear to Morris, repelled him. I have a feeling that his lectures betrayed the fact that he never quite forgave the English empiricists, "externalists," and mechanical philosophers for having, for a time, led him astray. The tone of his judgments seems colored by his own conversion from allegiance to English philosophy. However that may be, I cannot refrain from quoting the words to which I have referred as genuinely typical: "I conclude that J. S. Mill's greatest personal misfortune was that he was born the son of James Mill, and not of Johann Gottlieb Fichte." The spiritual kinship which I am confident Morris felt between Mill's intention and his own thought, an intention frustrate in Mill, he found achieved in the ethical idealism of Fichte.[12]

It was not Morris's hostility to British empiricism that stood in the way of the Johns Hopkins chair; although undergraduates were eager consumers of Mill and Spencer, their elders were not. Success at Johns Hopkins was snatched away by a man whom Morris had befriended and who had for several years revered Morris as a scholar and thinker of great learning and deep seriousness. This was the egregious G. Stanley Hall.[13]

Hall was another New Englander, born in 1844 into a fiercely Puritan western Massachusetts farming family; he was ill taught as a boy but began to show signs of unusual ability at Williams College, whither he went in 1862. Although a perfect higher education has famously been defined as "Mark Hopkins at one end of a log and a student at the other," President Hopkins was nearing the end of his reign by the time Hall encountered him. Whether Mark Hopkins was beginning to flag or the religiosity of Williams alienated the young Hall is not clear, but certainly Hall got more from other professors than he did from the president's high-altitude surveys of human existence. A first reading of Mill stimulated an interest in psychology, but Hall was not otherwise precocious in his intellectual interests; American psychology did not spring full born from his eighteen-year-old brow. Ambition did, perhaps stirred up by the sneers he had suffered from fellow students who had treated him as a yokel when they discovered his farming background.

What came next was Union Theological Seminary, where Hall first encountered Morris. Like Morris, he discovered that he did not want to be a minister. In his case it was less a matter of doubt's seeping in and undermining his faith than of youthful energy and adventurousness's finding itself cabined, cribbed, and confined by the "safety first" outlook of the seminary professors. He hankered after a broader vision, and having by an extraordinary fluke managed to borrow the necessary funds, he set out on the same journey as Morris, to sit at the feet of Trendelenburg in Berlin. He also encountered Karl Michelet, one of the few remaining followers of Hegel's, and came back to the United States intoxicated by the combination of Trendelenburg's updated Aristotle and his own first encounter with Hegel. But back home he was trapped in the same way as Morris: He had no wish to become a minister, but what else was he to do? Morris again showed him the way. When Morris left for Michigan, he recommended Hall to the Seligmans. Hall spent two years in the job, then found himself a college professorship that he later described as less like a chair than "a whole settee," the professorship of English, French, and German language and literature at Antioch College in what Hall felt to be the wilds of Ohio. He was not oppressed as Morris was at Ann Arbor, but he was very bored. He was taken up by W. T. Harris and the St. Louis Hegelians, but their relations rapidly soured. Hall's arrogance appears to have been the problem. Hall wished to be top dog in whatever he did. He was careful not to make this too obvious when dealing with established figures like William James, but he was less discreet in St. Louis.

W. T. Harris, then superintendent of schools in St. Louis and the entrepreneurial leader of the St. Louis Hegelians, was not impressed with what Hall had picked up in Germany or by what he had worked out for himself. After this encounter Hall's enthusiasm for Hegel waned. He visited Morris in Michigan and was depressed by the size of Morris's library and by the fact that Morris was intimately acquainted with every book he possessed. The Midwest was not the promised land after all. Indeed, Hall soon came to loathe it. One of the many attractions of the Johns Hopkins appointment when it eventually came was that it fulfilled his heartfelt prayer that fate would not "send me west" again.[14]

How he came to discover his destiny as an empirical psychologist is mysterious. In his autobiography he claimed that he read the German Wilhelm Wundt's treatise *Physiological Psychology* when it reached the United States and forthwith set out for Germany to learn from Wundt at first hand. That leaves out a good deal. Hall had his sights on a job at Johns Hopkins from the day it opened its doors, long before his conversion out of philosophy and into experimental psychology. He wrote ingratiating letters to Gilman suggesting himself for posts in philosophy and psychology and got nowhere. Progress toward Johns Hopkins was painfully slow, indeed. Hall first went to Harvard, where he worked with William James, did some work in the medical school, and obtained the first Ph.D. in psychology granted by any American university. This was a doubly distinguished achievement since Harvard had only recently started awarding graduate degrees, and Hall's doctorate was the first the philosophy department had given anyone. Only then did Hall go to Germany for a year's further study at Leipzig.

There he was both disillusioned and inspired. He was disillusioned by discovering that Wundt, as Hall now perceived the matter, absorbed simple facts from the English, wrapped them in impenetrable German metaphysics, and sent the by now unintelligible results back into the world. But he was enthusiastic enough about Helmholtz's seminars on perception to remain unbothered by the conflict between his own theories of vision and Helmholtz's, and he became even more enthusiastic about the growth of the new sciences and about the success of physics and physiology in underpinning the results of psychological investigation. He was well on the way to holding the view that Hegel's philosophy was merely obscurantist and an obstacle to clear thinking and scientific progress. The visit had other useful features. He attended lectures in educational psychology, a subject in which Germany was years ahead of the United States and one which was in due course to provide Hall the entrée into the world he so desired to join. He spent some time in the Berlin psychiatric hospital La Charité, and this was another omen for the future: In 1909 it was Hall, by then the president of Clark University and a great man in American psychology, who brought Freud and Jung to the United States and secured for both the first academic recognition they had yet received. A last achievement meant more for his future happiness than any other: He remet an acquaintance from his days at Antioch College and married her.

All the same, when Hall returned at the end of 1879, he was still without a job. His letters to Gilman, even backed by William James's recommendations, went unheeded. It is easy to see why they might have done so; they are an unattractive combination of supplication and boasting. Nor did Hall have any sense of how to endear himself to the wider academic community. His last gesture, as he left for Germany at the beginning of 1879, had been to publish an essay titled "Philosophy in the United States." It was doubly offensive: In the first place, he published it in Britain, in the English journal *Mind;* in the second place, it damned everything that went under the general heading of philosophy in America. Excepting Harvard and Johns Hopkins, and speaking more or less well of his old mentor at Williams, President Mark Hopkins, Hall complained that philosophy was subordinated to the tyranny of theology, taught by ignoramuses and taught at a level infinitely below that of Britain, let alone Germany. Though there was some truth in this picture, it was not calculated to make him friends. He may have known this. When he returned from Germany, he put together a collection of his occasional articles, entitled *Aspects of German Culture,* which he dedicated to Mark Hopkins and from which he omitted his offensive account of America's philosophical shortcomings.

Hall's lack of tact was personal rather than doctrinal. Publicly he was committed to showing that science and religion had nothing to fear from each other, a lifelong theme in Dewey's work, too; but it is now impossible to decide with any certainty how sincere Hall was about the project. Commentators take very different positions.[15] It is possible that Hall was hiding a deeper skepticism than he thought it politic to reveal, and it is possible that he was more attracted toward a purely empiricist view of science than he ever admitted and that his habit of preaching in a local, though rather unorthodox, church was pure bluff. It seems unlikely, however. He taught one philosophy course a year all his life and continued to do so during the thirty years in which he was president of Clark University. It was a course with a strong element of moral uplift. As a famously autocratic head of the university in an age when autocracy was taken for granted, and as the leading representative of the most popular of all the new sciences, he had no need to kowtow either to his trustees or to public opinion. At all events, when Dewey was a graduate student at Johns Hopkins, he took a course in "speculative psychology" from Hall, and the course title was sufficiently morally loaded to satisfy anyone: "Psychological and Ethical Theories."[16] Hall always wanted, even if in a slightly confused fashion, to show that psychology could help sustain morality in a skeptical age. Even if the science in science came first, so to speak, he found it easier to practice his science in the confidence that it was an essentially moral discipline.

This did not mean that he approved of teaching scientific ethics to the young before they were ready for it. He was radical only in his skepticism about academic philosophy. In educational terms he was a conservative. In a discussion of high school education he harped on the dangers of teaching philosophy to high school students. Raising questions about the meaning of life and the validity of our claims to knowledge would demoralize young people rather than enlighten them. This repressiveness somehow coexisted with the view for which he is most famous: that adolescence, with its sexual awakening and its uncertainty about our characters and ambitions, was the best period of human life and ought to be prolonged as far as possible. Initially neither bold démarches nor efforts at reconciliation did Hall's career much good. In 1880 he was in doubt as to how he could keep body and soul together in a more literal sense than that raised by his work on psychology; with a wife and two small children, his unemployed or half-employed condition was frightening. Friends spoke of finding him so hard up that he was genuinely—physically—hungry.

In the fall of 1880 he was rescued by a savior who arrived on horseback. "As Hall liked to remember the event, President Eliot of Harvard rode out to his home one day in the Fall of 1880, appearing suddenly as a knight on a charger, and offered him lecturerships in pedagogy and the history of philosophy."[17] Eliot had little interest or faith in pedagogy. Indeed, Hall was as much struck by the fact that Eliot was so uninterested in his mission that he never dismounted as by the fact that he appeared on horseback in the first place. The success of Hall's *Aspects of German Culture* must have suggested him to Eliot as a plausible candidate to give public lectures in that field (reviewers described the book as a uniquely lively and well-informed guide to the German intellectual scene from socialism to Schleiermacher); in the event the lectures on pedagogy were a smashing success. Educational theory was in the air. The lectures were given in Boston rather than Cambridge, and they were given on Saturday mornings so that teachers could attend. Then as now teachers knew that the road to promotion and reputation was through educational theory, and the lectures were packed. Hall repeated the series twice. Harvard was tempted to start a school of education. Hall recruited teachers to collect data on child development and so launched his later career in child study. An industry was born.[18]

By now Gilman was ready to appoint someone to head his department of philosophy and psychology, but he was still unsure whom he might contrive to attract. In 1881 he invited Hall to give a set of lectures the following spring. These went well enough for Gilman to appoint Hall as a part-time lecturer on a three-year contract. For fifteen hundred dollars a year, Hall was to teach one semester of philosophy and psychology each year. His progress to headship of the department and a full professorship was now rapid. Gilman had always worried about C. S. Peirce's reputation for agnosticism and sexual unreliability, and when he discovered that Peirce was living with a woman to whom he was not married, he sacked him. (In fact, he sacked all the assistant professors and rehired the whole lot except for Peirce.) This happened in the spring of 1884. Gilman now had to choose between Hall and Morris. It was no contest. One is tempted to think that Hall must have schemed and planned and lobbied for the job, but even though he undoubtedly did a certain amount of just that—he had been pestering Gilman for the better part of a decade already—Morris's character played the larger part in losing him the chance. Gilman noted in his diary that Morris had become livelier and happier and more productive only on Hall's arrival. Morris needed Hall to bring him to life, but Hall did not need Morris to energize him; Hall, not Morris, would be a leader.[19]

Hall was not a success as head of department. He was frightened of men of his own intellectual weight. He refused to appoint Dewey to a lecturership when the department needed a social and moral philosopher, and he drove the cleverest of his graduate students away by first refusing them fellowships and then lying about his reasons for so doing.[20] So although he was, in a manner of speaking, successful in making Johns Hopkins the first place in the country to set up a psychology laboratory and give adequate graduate instruction in experimental psychology, he built nothing that would outlast himself; when he left at the end of the decade, the department of psychology itself collapsed, and philosophy was hardly revived until the arrival of Arthur Lovejoy in the next century. By that time Dewey was elsewhere and flourishing.

What Dewey Learned

Dewey's two years at Johns Hopkins were only moderately satisfactory. The smallness of the department meant that the range of courses offered was narrow; in fact, they were agreed on all hands to be barely sufficient to justify students' taking a major in philosophy at all. The pleasures of the work lay in the way the subject was taught. To teach, as Dewey put it, *seminarisch,* was a real novelty and implied a degree of intellectual equality between student and professor that American higher education had never before contemplated. It also implied a common interest in what Dewey's generation had not yet learned to describe as "cutting-edge" research. Still, there was not much of it. Morris taught in the fall, Hall in the spring, so Dewey began with "a seminar in Science of Knowledge, History of Philosophy in Great Britain, and Hegel's

Philosophy of History." In the second year he got a seminar on Spinoza's *Ethics* and a course on German philosophy from Kant to Hegel.[21]

The great disappointment for Dewey was Peirce. Or rather, what has disappointed everyone since Peirce's abilities were at last universally appreciated was Dewey's uncomprehending response to Peirce's courses in mathematical logic and the philosophy of science. Until Dewey worked out Peirce's ideas for himself, some twenty years later, he could not see them in Peirce's work; Peirce never thought much of Dewey, in 1882 or twenty years later. The difficulty was that Peirce was fascinated by mathematics and formal logic, and Dewey, like most enthusiasts for Hegel, was hostile to formalism. A post-1945 analytical philosopher, taking it for granted that logic *is* formal logic and that "philosophical logic" is philosophy, would leave it at that. A post-1945 analytical philosopher would relish the mental gymnastics provided by formal logic and would use as much or as little of the formal apparatus he had mastered as seemed useful.

Dewey's generation could not agree to leave formal logic to logicians and discuss informal logic as "conceptual analysis" or just "philosophy." They hankered after a different logic, one that would be modeled on Hegel's *Science of Logic* and would capture the way concepts changed and developed as they became more adequate to the purposes for which we used them. This was the project of creating a "real logic." Dewey acquired the ambition to develop a "real logic" from working with Morris, and like many other ambitions thus acquired, he did not wholly give it up even when he changed his first conception of what it involved. Eventually Dewey split the difference between Hegel and formal logic; he abandoned the Hegelian attempt to chart the inner life of the concept and produced an informal account of intelligent problem solving or "inquiry." "Morris was given to contrasting what he called 'real' logic and associated with Aristotle and Hegel, with formal logic of which he had a low opinion. Dewey, in his years of association with Morris in Ann Arbor, developed the idea that there was an intermediate kind of logic that was neither merely formal nor a logic of inherent 'truth' in the constitution of things; a logic of the processes by which knowledge is reached. Mill's logic seemed to him an effort in this direction, but an effort that was disastrously blocked and deflected by Mill's acceptance of a sensationalistic and particularistic psychology."[22] That account—Dewey's own—makes one even more unhappy at his failure to understand what Peirce was about; if he had understood Peirce's investigations into scientific method, he would have seen how close they were to what he needed.

Dewey's struggle went on for sixty-odd years. His last published attempt to produce such a logic appeared when he was eighty. The book that embodies it, *Logic: The Theory of Inquiry,* is very long, very dense, and very difficult. It was unappreciated in Dewey's lifetime, and unlike his ethics, his politics, and his metaphysics, it has not gained new admirers in the past decade and a half. Even so, the project was not a complete failure. Earlier essays, such as *How We Think* of 1910, were much liked and remain highly readable; they were essays in what one might properly call "informal" logic, essays describing how we *do* think, with the object of making us think better. They were essays in the mode of the 1930s English philosopher Susan Stebbing's best-selling *Straight and Crooked Thinking,* and *How We Think* was for years a staple in the diet of progressive teacher training colleges. It was said that contrary to the whole point of the book itself, student teachers were required to memorize whole pages for recitation in class.

Dewey's thoughts about logic in the narrow sense were uninspiring; an essay on the law of the excluded middle, written in the early 1930s, for instance, labors to make the point that we do not always treat "A or not-A" as a logical truth. Frequently the terms we use do not lend themselves to sharp dichotomies. If you ask whether my tea is hot, and I say, "Well, not exactly hot or exactly cold, you know, sort of lukewarm?" I do not violate the law of excluded middle but convey a more useful and more informative picture than I otherwise would.[23] The point that Dewey raises has general applicability; it is dotty to insist that my thought of Esmeralda either does weigh two ounces or does not, because weight is not a property of thoughts, and we cannot make any true statement about how much thoughts weigh. "My thoughts of Esmeralda never weigh as much as two ounces" is very peculiar, while "My letters to Esmeralda never weigh two ounces" makes perfect sense, since it is false if I persistently address screeds of romantic verse to her, but true if I always send her postcards. In post-1945 "ordinary language" philosophy, attempts to understand the usefulness and limitations of logical formality were the common coin of philosophical discussion. These attempts came easily to philosophers who had once thought that the world must be analyzed with the aid of formal logic and had then come to believe that a looser and more flexible logic was needed. Dewey, educated in the Hegelian mode, had a harder time explaining such matters; the old Hegelian wish for a logic that would display the real movement of the concept infected his argument. Later thinkers, never having thought that there was such a *logic,* had an easier time.

The other source of difficulty with Peirce was grounded in an ambition that persisted more fruitfully throughout Dewey's work. Dewey remarked in one of his rare autobiographical excursions:

> [A]s my study and thinking progressed, I became more and more troubled by the intellectual scandal that seemed to me involved in the current (and traditional) dualism in logical standpoint and method between something called "science" on the one hand and something called "morals" on the other. I have long felt that the construction of a logic, that is a method of effective inquiry, which would apply without abrupt breach of continuity to the fields designated by both of these words, is at once our needed theoretical solvent and the supply of our greatest practical want. This belief has had much more to do with the development of what I termed, for lack of a better word, "instrumentalism," than have most of the reasons that have been assigned.[24]

This was an ambition that Hegelianism to some extent fostered, as did the Aristotelianism that G. S. Morris combined with his idealism. Peirce had a distinctive ethical position that was after a fashion continuous with his views on scientific inquiry, but it was not something Dewey could have encountered in Peirce's class.[25]

Dewey wrote a discouraged letter to Henry Torrey, telling him, "I am not taking the course in Logic. The course is very mathematical, & by Logic, Mr. Peirce means only an account of the methods of physical sciences, put in mathematical form as far as possible. It's more of a scientific, than philosophical course. In fact, I think Mr. Peirce don't [*sic*] think there is any Phil. outside the generalizations of physical science."[26] He wrote in much the same terms to W. T. Harris, saying that "the lectures appeal more strongly to the mathematical students than to the philosophical."[27] Peirce had already published the two seminal essays, "The Fixation of Belief" and "How to Make Our Ideas Clear," that historians of philosophy generally reckon to be the founding documents of pragmatism, but Dewey appears not to have read them until the 1890s. It is easy to believe that Peirce's enthusiasm for probabilistic reasoning and his imaginative attempts to uncover forms of inference other than deduction and induction might have baffled a student whose mathematics had ended with elementary algebra and whose philosophical preferences were still as piously idealist as Dewey's.

In later life Dewey hardly mentioned the fact of his having worked with G. S. Hall. Conversely, Hall was always acerbic about his former student's work. When in 1886 Dewey published his *Psychology*—an introductory text designed for his Michigan students—Hall abused it as a futile attempt to glue Hegelian ideas onto facts that Dewey had to misrepresent for the purpose, and later, when Dewey's ideas about primary school education had become vastly popular, Hall speculated that the reason for Dewey's success (and thus for his own relative lack of it in this field) was that Dewey was essentially conservative. Readers found him comforting rather than disturbing; Dewey might have *meant* in books such as *The School and Society* to say that schoolchildren were to be brought up to be good citizens of a much-improved society and critics of the one around them, but Dewey's readers could plausibly misread him as saying that children were to be brought up as integrated, cooperative, and compliant members of the world their parents had created. There is something in this besides an undeniable element of sour grapes.

At Johns Hopkins, Dewey's encounter with Hall left him puzzled as to the connection between psychology and philosophy. He worked out (or perhaps simply borrowed) a view very like that which Hall professed in public, but one that was rather farther from the view Hall was moving toward. Dewey argued that empirical psychology proved the truth of the Hegelian system or, if not the Hegelian system in particular, at least some idealist picture of the world. The study of the individual psyche showed, he thought, that the World was Mind and reality in essence mental. The arrogant treatment of writers like David Hume and J. S. Mill in the essay titled "The New Psychology," which Dewey read to the Metaphysical Club in his second spring at Hopkins and then published in the *Andover Review,* is shocking to a fastidious mind but was doubtless something he had caught from Morris. Dewey was to perpetrate worse in two essays, entitled "Philosophy as Psychology" a few years later, and the kindest thing one can say about all three is that they were more the fault of Hall and Morris than of their author.

All three pieces were sparked off by Hall's own inaugural lecture, "The New Psychology," on which Dewey's thoughts are unashamedly parasitic.[28] They were motivated by the desire to square faith and science that animated the lecture. Hall denied that psychology was materialistic, even where it drew on the resources of physiology; the way the human body and human mind functioned as one differentiated unity was an image of the unity implicit in the whole of nature; the contemplation and explanation of this unity were not merely the object of science but the object of religion. How this got one from the psychology lab to Christianity was left obscure, left in an obscurity not acknowledged but covered by uplifting rhetoric. Dewey made the same case as Hall and employed the same rhetoric. Dewey's latent agnosticism was perhaps revealed by the way he evaded the crucial question whether the God toward which the argument moved was the Christian God, some more generic deity, or a nonpersonal divine principle, but to a later age it is his eagerness to get from science to religion that is the most striking feature of these essays. In Dewey's view, the ability of psychology to draw on physiology, biology, and other sciences of the functioning organism showed how impossible it was for science to proceed on the basis of merely empirical, merely mechanical, or merely mathematical principles. The logic of the organism was teleology. That is, the thoughts, feelings, and sensations of the individual person formed a unity, and that unity reflected larger social, intellectual, and spiritual unities into which the individual fitted.

The new psychology, wrote Dewey:

> insists upon the unity and solidarity of psychical life against abstract theories which would break it up into atomic elements or independent powers. It lays large stress upon the will; not as an abstract power of unmotivated choice, nor as an executive power to obey the behests of the understanding, the legislative branch of the psychical government, but as a living bond connecting and conditioning *all* mental activity. It emphasizes the teleological element, not in any mechanical or external sense, but regarding life as an organism in which immanent ideas or purposes are realizing themselves through the development of experience. Thus modern psychology is intensely ethical in its tendencies. . . . As it goes into the depths of man's nature, it finds as stone of its foundation, blood of its life, the instinctive tendencies of devotion, sacrifice, faith, and idealism which are the eternal substructure of all the struggles of all the nations upon the altar stairs which slope up to God. It finds no insuperable obstacle in the relations of faith and reason, for it can discover in its investigations no reason which is not based upon faith, and no faith which is not rational in its origin and tendency.[29]

In one form or another Dewey never abandoned this view, but by the time he looked back upon these early effusions, all he recalled was that they had been much easier to write than what replaced them: They were imitative and mechanical exercises in the conventional thinking of the day that stretched neither his mind nor his expository resources.

What justified his time at Johns Hopkins so far as Dewey was concerned was the time he spent with Morris and the ideas he acquired from him. Morris had by now read widely in the English disciples of Hegel, especially in the work of T. H. Green; some of Dewey's arguments for supposing that the study of psychology leads inexorably to a belief in metaphysical idealism could have been drawn from Green's essay "Can There Be a Natural Science of Man?"[30] and perhaps they were. The belief that the human mind is essentially communal and that the individual mind therefore amounts to the individual's share of a resource that is in essence social and national—and ultimately divine—rather than individual was very Greenian, and Morris's confidence in the obsolescence of the entire British empiricist tradition may have owed something to the long and devastating introduction that Green and his collaborator T. H. Grose attached to their edition of Hume's *A Treatise on Human Nature*.[31]

Dewey's retrospective account of his intellectual development during this period is stronger on emotional tone than on intellectual detail, but it is illuminating for just that reason. Of Morris, he wrote, "I have never known a more single-hearted and whole-souled man—a man of a single piece all the way through; while I have long since deviated from his philosophic faith, I should be happy to believe that the influence of the spirit of his teaching has been an enduring influence."[32] Jane Dewey's sketch of her father's biography adds:

> The singular and sensitive purity, the whole-souled and single-minded personality of his teacher undoubtedly contributed, but the effect of this appeal is understandable only if the New England background of the pupil is kept in mind. He had nominally accepted the religious teachings in which he was brought up and had joined the White Street Congregational Church at an early age. He had tried, without being aware of the effort this required of him, to believe in the doctrines of the church, but his belief was never whole-hearted enough to satisfy his emotional need. From the idealism of Hegel, as interpreted by Morris, he obtained in his late adolescence that fusion of emotions and intellect for which he had sought unsuccessfully in his boyhood religious experience.[33]

There might have been some tremors in Dewey's mind at the ideas he was encountering; it was an old charge against Hegel that his system was "pantheistic" and therefore atheistic or at any rate un-Christian. Dewey was ready with an indignant rebuttal of the narrow-mindedness that led to such complaints, and by now he had heard Henry Torrey himself admitting that it was only faith that told us that monotheism was true, that Christianity is a revealed religion, consistent with what philosophy discovers, but not limited by philosophy. In any case, Dewey hankered after a larger idealism, and Morris provided it.[34]

At a more mundane level Morris began even at Johns Hopkins to launch Dewey on his career. In his second semester Dewey was asked to look after the undergraduate course in the history of philosophy while Morris was teaching back in Ann Arbor. Dewey's ability to turn his hand to almost anything is suggested by the way he observed: "There will only be about 30 recitations on the whole of modern phil. so of course it can't go in very deeply."[35] For a shy young man teaching his first course, this was tolerably confident talk; then again, he had only seven students, and their obligations in the course mostly amounted to reading Überweg's *History* and memorizing parts of it. Looking after them may have required little preparation, and more patience than cleverness. The class went well, and Morris wanted to give Dewey a teaching fellowship for his second year. President Gilman had some residual doubts about Dewey's ability to project himself to an audience and addressed himself to Dewey's former teachers Matthew Buckham and Henry Torrey for reassurance. They responded favorably; Buckham suggested that Dewey might lack something of "the amount of dogmatism that a teacher ought to have," but both he and Torrey said, sensibly enough, that confidence would develop with practice, and Dewey was given his fellowship.[36] At the end of the second academic year he submitted a thesis titled "Kant's Psychology," now lost; he gave an impressive oral defense of his thesis and was duly graduated Doctor of Philosophy.

University of Michigan

The greater service that Morris rendered Dewey came the next year. When Hall was appointed to the chair at Johns Hopkins, Morris went back to Ann Arbor for good. As his two years at Johns Hopkins ended, Dewey was without a job for the next year; Hall resisted any idea that he stay on and lecture at Johns Hopkins, and it looked for a moment as though he would be at the same sort of loose end as when he had left college five years earlier. All ended well; Morris wanted to appoint Dewey at Ann Arbor, the president, James Angell, formerly of Burlington and a friend of the family's, was more than happy, and in July the letter of appointment came. In September 1884 Dewey started on a teaching career that ended officially only in 1930 with his retirement from Columbia and unofficially only with his death in 1952.

Dewey's teaching obligations at Michigan covered whatever Morris did not teach. Morris taught the history of philosophy and "real logic," while Dewey took on topics in psychology and gratified student demands for more attention to British ideas by lecturing on Herbert Spencer and John Stuart Mill. Students liked Dewey but did not like the extent to which even after the departure of the Reverend B. F. Crocker, philosophy remained the handmaiden of theology. A little before Dewey's arrival they had suggested none too discreetly that the reason behind the neglect of modern empiricism was not only its tendency to encourage agnosticism in religion but the incapacity of their professors to take on and defeat the arguments of their opponents. "[W]hen young men see the philosophy of these persons, whom they have been taught to respect in science, rather contemptuously left unnoticed, an idea that perhaps it is a disinclination to grapple with them on the part of the professors, is liable to take possession of their minds."[37] That was unfair to Morris, who was better known for his *British Thinkers* than for anything other than his translation of Überweg's history. Still, it was not entirely unfair. Dewey described Morris's course on British philosophy at Johns Hopkins as a general and critical account of his victims; this suggests rather strongly that Morris did not want to reenter the spirit of their work and "grapple" with it, but rather to denounce it at a safe distance.

Although Dewey taught what passed for psychology, the articles he published at that time, as well as the textbook he wrote for his students, indicate that it was heavily Hegelianized psychology and that the object was as much to demonstrate that the empirical study of human nature drove one irresistibly into the arms of the Absolute as to teach students what was known about perception, memory, attention, and learning. In retrospect, this turned out to be less of a problem for Dewey's intellectual development than it may have been for the undergraduates who sat and listened to him. Because he began with a prejudice in favor of a holistic, communitarian, antidualist psychology, Dewey was able to shed his Hegelian commitments without shedding the prejudices that his Hegelianism justified. His own account of all this rings true enough to be credible in spite of his habit of imposing more retrospective order on his intellectual growth than he can possibly have experienced at the time:

> Hegel's idea of cultural institutions as an "objective mind" upon which individuals were dependent in the formation of their mental life fell in with the influence of Comte and Condorcet and Bacon. The metaphysical idea that an absolute mind is manifested in social institutions dropped out; the idea, upon an empirical basis, of the power exercised by cultural environment in shaping the ideas, beliefs, and intellectual attitudes of individuals remained. It was a factor in producing my belief that the not uncommon assumption in both psychology and philosophy of a ready-made mind over against a physical world as an object has no empirical support. It was a factor in producing my belief that the only possible psychology, as distinct from a biological account of behavior, is a social psychology.[38]

What he came to see in the next ten or a dozen years was that his beliefs did better on their own two feet than standing on a Hegelian cloud.

During the ten years from 1884 to 1894 Dewey went from being a new instructor to the grand position of professor and head of department. He was astonishingly productive, and his personal diffidence invariably vanished the moment he sat down to write. The Michigan students had not been keen on the philosophy department's offerings before Dewey arrived. That began to change with his arrival. Unlike Morris, Dewey was perfectly ready to advertise his and the department's wares, to talk to the Student Christian Association about issues in the philosophy of religion, ethics, and social philosophy, and to establish ties with the local schoolteachers' association so that they could discuss general issues in education. His interests were indeed broad. Michigan had become coeducational as early as 1872, and among the subjects Dewey wrote on in those early years was whether higher education was bad for women's mental and physical health, not to mention their reproductive capacity. Dewey did not take the high ground and argue that women who wanted to go to college should do so even if it wrecked their health, nor did he denounce the anxiety about its impact on their health as the superstitious rubbish it surely was. He judiciously concluded that all empirical evidence suggested that aside from perhaps inducing some greater than ordinary level of anxiety in the women who attended college, education seemed to have no effect on their health one way or the other.[39]

Dewey's superiority to most of his peers made his promotion rapid. Within a couple of years Morris had become head of department, and Dewey was then made assistant professor and his pay increased to sixteen hundred dollars a year. But in 1888, when he was still under thirty, the University of Minnesota lured him away from Ann Arbor with the chair of philosophy; it was true that he was head of a department consisting of himself, but the compliment to so young a professor was hard to resist, as was the 50 percent jump in his pay. The Minnesota excursion was very brief. In Dewey's absence, Morris suddenly died at the early age of forty-nine, and the Michigan trustees overcame their anxieties about Dewey's youth and asked him back as the chair and head of the department.

Finding mileposts in Dewey's life is a dubious pastime, because on the one hand, there were so many of them, and on the other, his career was curiously seamless. But this was a crucial moment; he was already an infinitely more original and interesting philosopher than Morris, and as head of the department he was able to appoint junior faculty who shared his own tastes and interests and were constrained by neither religious anxieties nor loyalties to any particular philosophical creed. His first step was to appoint James Tufts, with whom he was later to write the stunningly successful textbook, *Ethics*, that was a staple of university courses for four decades after its publication in 1908. Tufts left a couple of years later to do graduate work in Germany, and Dewey hired another assistant, who was to become a close colleague and, until his death in 1931, Dewey's closest friend. This was George Herbert Mead, whose work on "the I and the Me" laid the foundations of modern American social psychology in the areas of role theory and symbolic interaction and was, Dewey later reported, so persuasive that Dewey was thereafter content to abandon psychology as a subject in which he might himself work and simply use Mead's work where he needed to. The third new appointment he made was A. H. Lloyd, whose tastes were also more empirical and psychological at this point and with whom Dewey again worked in Chicago after they all had left Michigan for John D. Rockefeller's new creation.

Dewey's turns toward ethics and social philosophy and away from empirical psychology were clear in the changes in what he taught. With Morris's death, Dewey took over the advanced courses in Kant and Hegel and in addition taught the courses in ethics, political philosophy, and the history of political thought, as well as a seminar in applied ethics. The confidence in his own interests and abilities that this seems to show had one other source. When Dewey arrived at Michigan in 1884, he met a student, Alice Chipman, who was in her junior year but was in fact a few months older than him. She came from the Michigan town of Fenton, forty miles from Ann Arbor; she had been orphaned when a young girl and brought up by two very sprightly grandparents, Fred and Evelina Riggs. Fred in particular was an adventurous sort; in his youth he had made himself unpopular with the first white settlers in Michigan by making friends with the local Chippewa and consistently standing up for the rights of Indians against the newcomers, while in his seventies he explored Colorado with a view to making his fortune in gold or silver mining. Much of Dewey's surviving family correspondence is concerned with Fred's problems with a mine that might or might not eventually yield a profit. The mine was probably a dud; but it was impossible to tell at a distance, and it was not easy for the elderly Riggs and the busy young professor to go out into the hinterland and inspect it up close.

Alice boarded at the same rooming house as Dewey and took three of his courses in his first year at Michigan. He was smitten, and so was she; sadly none of her letters to him survives, so we have little idea of the speed with which the affair progressed on her side. Dewey's letters to her are entirely inarticulate. He seems to have found that being in love deprived him of the power of articulate speech to about the degree that being struck by a freight train might have done.[40] They had to wait to marry until Alice was graduated in June 1886, by which time Dewey had been promoted to assistant professor and his salary doubled. Their first son, Frederick Archibald, was born in 1887, their daughter Evelyn in 1889, and their second son, Morris, named for Dewey's mentor, in 1893. Alice brought Dewey three things he needed. The first was an entire fearlessness about the ideas and opinions of the rest of the world. In later years Mrs. Dewey increasingly felt that her abilities had not been used and that she had been boxed into a domestic existence that was less interesting and less valuable than, for instance, her work as the principal of the Lab School in Chicago. When Dewey met her, she was just what Dewey needed to counteract the effect of his mother. The second liberation was emancipation from the constraints of organized religion. Dewey was a member of the local Congregational Church, but after his marriage an increasingly notional member, and when he left for Chicago in 1894, he did not resume church membership in his new home. Alice Chipman strengthened Dewey's belief that institutionalized religion was on the whole an enemy to true faith. The third liberation she brought him was a more down-to-earth understanding of what the true faith might be concerned with. Grandfather Riggs had a fierce sense of justice. What led him to take the side of Native Americans in their conflicts with the settlers of thirty years before led his granddaughter to take the side of the poor, the working class, women forced into menial work or into prostitution, and many other groups she thought unjustly treated by society.

It was this last that Dewey particularly needed. Because he wrote so much about practical politics, because his reputation for so many years was that of "educator," and because "pragmatism" is rightly associated with the view that ideas get their value from the way they are used in assorted forms of human practical activity, commentators have always been tempted to think of Dewey as somehow naturally or innately attracted to practical issues and concrete subject matters. Nothing could be further from the truth. Dewey knew himself better than that. "I imagine," he wrote in "From Absolutism to Experimentalism," "that my development has been controlled largely by a struggle between a native inclination towards the schematic and formally logical, and those incidents of experience that compelled me to take account of actual material." After speculating that many writers have tried hard to write *against* the grain of inclination, he went on: "Anyway, a case might be made out for the proposition that the emphasis upon the concrete, empirical, and 'practical' in my later writings is partly due to considerations of this nature. It was a reaction against what was more natural, and it served as a protest and protection against something in myself which, in the pressure of the weight of actual experiences, I knew to be a weakness."[41] Dewey is interesting just because he succeeded so well in balancing these two pressures in the hope of providing a world view that a modern industrial society can use to understand itself, reform itself, and reconcile itself to itself. To say, as I shall, that Dewey did not abandon philosophy, turn it into a branch of social science, or confuse philosophy with social punditry is not to say that he carried on all his life doing what he would have called philosophy at the age of twenty-five. The idea that philosophy was "cultural criticism" or "the criticism of criticism" was one he came to quite slowly. All the same, the only way to make sense of Dewey's simultaneous emphasis on "the problems of men" and "the techniques of philosophy" is to remember that he never abandoned Morris's project of finding a way of thinking that allowed each of the issues studied to reveal itself in its own distinctive fashion yet to show all of them in relation to one another. The danger of any such project is that it inevitably drifts toward the abstract and the general, the chronically fuzzy and the indistinct; the virtue of it is that it constantly reminds us that we must be alive to the way our ideas about one subject—child welfare, say—have implications for many others—government intervention in the location of industry, perhaps—and that specialization is not always the path of intellectual progress. Alice Chipman forced John Dewey to keep asking the pragmatist question, What was the "cash value" of his philosophical speculation? She did him and intellectual life in the United States a great favor by making him focus on the unsatisfactory, unjust, and thoroughly disorganized here and now, rather than the realm of the ideal.

This is to look ahead. Until the last few years of his time at Michigan, Dewey's work had a decidedly Victorian air. The first glimmerings of his new ideas on ethics, on democracy, and on the need for philosophy to come down from the mountain peaks and explore the everyday world emerged in the early 1890s after his return from Minnesota and his promotion to the headship of his department. The fact that he was essentially a moralist was apparent in his essays on psychology and throughout his *Psychology* textbook. William James disliked that aspect of the book a good deal, and so we may guess did Hall, even though the latter concentrated most of his fire on its Hegelianism, and the former concentrated his on the overall implausibility of the project. Nor could anyone have guessed from Dewey's first talk to Michigan students that he was becoming an agnostic in religion and a radical in politics. Entitled "The Obligation to the Knowledge of God," it takes a stern line. We might think that Christian charity should incline us to pity the agnostic. Somebody who failed to know that there was a God and who therefore failed to live his life in accordance with the Scriptures was just unlucky. Dewey considered the thought only to reject it on the basis of scriptural authority. "We treat skeptics not as those who have failed to meet a duty, but as unfortunates whose peculiar mental constitution is depriving them of God's presence. Many skeptics declare that their greatest sorrow is that they live as orphans in an orphaned world, without the Divine Father, and that the greatest joy would be knowledge of Him. But the statements of Christ and his immediate followers are explicit. To fail to get knowledge in these matters is not an intellectual, but a moral defect."[42]

The philosophical reasons Dewey gave for accepting this stern saying are more interesting than the bare fact that he accepted it. The one doctrine that Dewey preserved intact from intuitionism, from Hegelianism, and throughout his experimentalism was that the mind was essentially *active,* and knowledge a matter of *doing.* The mind was not a passive reflector; we do not confront the world as a sort of recording device picking up "facts." Rather, we act upon the world, giving it sense, exploring its meaning, and working out as we go how best to think about it. The "world" in Dewey's work was always a generic label for "what we interact with," and so here the gently liberal—if we speak theologically—young instructor, can assert without embarrassment that we do indeed have a duty to know God, just because it is wholly and always up to us to adopt a God-centered understanding of the world. That the argument is riddled with holes, Dewey would a little later have been the first to admit. There must, after all, be failed experiments, and there is a vast gulf between what one might concede to be a duty to give the God hypothesis a chance and what nobody in his right mind could possibly claim to be a duty to agree that the God hypothesis had been confirmed. The one essay written in these early days that broaches the view of the world that we associate with the later Dewey is a critical review of Sir Henry Maine's *Popular Government*, written in 1888 for a departmental collection of essays. But since this essay marks the beginnings of Dewey's concern with theories of democracy, with political philosophy, education, and economic justice, we shall do better to launch into the next chapter and the 1890s with it.

By 1890 Dewey was an established figure. He was married and the father of two children. Though young, he was in a worldly sense safe. He had finished growing up. His intellectual *style* would not change greatly, though the content of his philosophy was utterly transformed over the next decade. From being an unambiguous philosophical idealist he became a much more ambiguous naturalist, instrumentalist, and experimentalist. Or rather, he tried to escape the tyranny of "isms." In particular, his naturalism was not a form of materialism. Where idealism substituted "consciousness" for God and said the world exists only for and in consciousness, Dewey's pragmatism went a long way toward asserting that the world exists only for, and as far as it is known by, the community of intellectually active human beings. The element of continuity was as great as the element of radical departure from the ideas of his youth. The ambitions of the new philosophy remained the same as those of the old, save to the extent that they could not be *exactly* the same once they put on new philosophical clothing. In idealism the Christian desire for union with God had been transformed into the reassuring claim that the human organism was in indissoluble moral and intellectual union with the larger organic whole of reality; in Dewey's pragmatism the idealists' claim would be once more transformed and complicated. The new sustaining thought was that the unity aspired to in religion could be achieved by an intelligently self-conscious commitment to the human community. Morally and psychologically this reassuring doctrine offered something like what believers claim to be their trust that "underneath are the everlasting arms."

As I have already suggested, much of the attraction of Dewey's ideas stems from the way they combined a thoroughly down-to-earth attention to the ills of twentieth-century America with the consolations of faith. From now on I shall say less and less about Dewey's life and more about his books, his times, and the ideas he ought to have taken more seriously than he did. If we may borrow Dewey's own imagery, these first two chapters have aimed to give a picture of the growing organism in its first environment—its drives and its capacities and the impact of those other organisms Dewey's parents, teachers, friends and colleagues. Now it is time to turn the perspective around and consider the organism's output.

Three

Finding a Voice

Dewey was always described as a sturdy, steady, somewhat slow-moving man and thinker, but he abandoned his Congregationalist origins, intuitionalist philosophy, and early apolitical concern with the individual's spiritual development with some briskness. This chapter picks up that process. Many of the ideas Dewey adopted in the early 1890s run throughout his life and work; some became important only somewhat later.[1] I begin with Dewey's views on ethics, since this was the time when he first began to turn moral arguments into sociological and psychological ones. He also turned them into historical arguments and into arguments about the chances of the average person leading a satisfactory individual life in a modern democratic society. It was Randolph Bourne in 1916 who looked forward to his countrymen's leading the life of "developed personality in the Beloved Community," and the concept of the "Beloved Community" was drawn from the Harvard philosopher Josiah Royce; but Bourne drew the thought that this was the guiding ideal of a democratic society from Dewey, and it was certainly a very Deweyan thought.[2] Some extraordinary features of Dewey's work appeared very early, if not as prominently as later. Two that were important ever after were his urge to close the gap between what we desire for ourselves and what we want for other people and, secondly his wish to abolish any sharp distinction between the demands of morality and the demands of "intelligent action" in general. To my eye, the second feature is a move in the right direction, but the first contains more wishful thinking than is decent in a philosophical theory. I follow Dewey in thinking that "moral" considerations are not special or marked off by appealing to "non-natural" values,[3] but I resist the thought that a better understanding of morality will much reduce occasions of conflict between one person and another. That notable advocate of the disabused moral vision Friedrich Nietzsche argued that with increased clarity would come increased, but healthier, conflict. Dewey's account of morality as the intelligent management of life in society rightly implies that morality is not concerned *only* with conflicts between the claims of one person and another, but that leaves a great many conflicts to be thought out and fought out. It is slightly unfair to Dewey to leave the matter there. He was a good Darwinian and thought progress was provoked by the conflict between our desires and the environment's niggardliness; he was also enough of a romantic to think that we develop our personalities by experiencing conflicts among our goals and learning how to resolve them. Still, one might well think that he hoped for an implausible harmony both within the individual and among individuals.

Dewey's Debts

To understand what Dewey thought and what he renounced, we must dig into the ideas of T. H. Green and his master, Hegel.[4] I have suggested that what links Dewey in the 1890s and us in the 1990s is our shared anxieties; a second link is the debt of liberals late in both centuries to an obscure and difficult German philosopher of doubtfully liberal credentials, who had died in Berlin in 1831. A famous explanation of why Germany fell in love with extreme political visions was that Germans were intellectually tyrannized over by the Greeks.[5] "Germany felt a desperate longing for the absolute." German thinkers were desperate to recapture the unity of purpose and harmony of spirit that the Greeks had possessed in the youthful innocence of the human race and that individualist, rationalist, modern man had lost. Dewey's ideas in the 1890s and recent—1980s and 1990s—social and political philosophy display a different tyranny: the tyranny of Hegel over the Anglo-Saxons. Hegel had resisted the romantic urge to return to the unity and simplicity of Greek life as imagined by Schiller and others; he agreed that the modern world was fractured and uncertain of itself, but he offered to show how we might have *both* the spiritual and moral unity of classical Greece and the concern for individuality that is typical of the modern world. The young John Dewey eagerly consumed that message and made it his own.

I do not mean that Dewey took over Hegel lock, stock, and barrel or that T. H. Green had done so. Green was as much indebted to Kant and Fichte as to Hegel. Moreover, there was one aspect of Hegel's work that is intrinsically pretty unattractive but that we may regret that Green did not come to terms with. This was Hegel's bloody-minded insistence that moral progress was parasitic on general cultural progress, that cultures need states to shelter them, and that states are inevitably plural, defended by military force, and, however rationally governed, sustained in the last resort by their citizens' willingness to die on their behalf. Hegel declared in the introduction to his *Philosophy of History* that history was a "slaughter bench at which the happiness of peoples, the wisdom of States, and the virtue of individuals have been victimized"; human life was emotionally and intellectually engaging only because all good sprang from evil. Among the evils from which good often sprang, war was one. Philosophy must therefore not flinch from the rough spectacle of war and death.[6] On the whole, Green did flinch from it; more so did Dewey. Both were at ease in describing the virtues of a liberal society at peace with itself and other societies. It is not that Dewey *refused* to acknowledge a fruitful role for conflict—given the importance he attached to problem solving in life and thought, he insisted on it—but individual, cultural, and national self-assertion were forces he found hard to understand and come to grips with, and thirty-odd years later, when he came to write about the political possibilities that World War I opened up, his critics unanimously complained that he had no feel for the passions that the war had actually unleashed.[7]

The second feature of Dewey's work with which we must embroil ourselves is closely related. This is his first engagement with the theory of democracy; this was the start of an extraordinary development in which Dewey came to think that every aspect of philosophy was an aspect of understanding a modern democratic society. That ethics should have turned into an account of the mutual adjustment of individual and society and thus into a sort of applied sociology shocks many philosophers who think ethics is concerned with the analysis of proximate and ultimate ends and with their justification. Dewey did not deny that view of the tasks of moral philosophy, but he rejected the implication that it involved something other than an analysis of the condition of man in modern society. Dewey could understand this as an aspect of thinking about democracy because he thought of democracy in a sense much wider—and perhaps deeper—than as a set of political arrangements. Dewey did two things that nobody else tried to do in quite the same way: He defended modernity against its detractors, and he defended democracy as the modern, secular realization of the kingdom of God on earth.[8] Everything then hinged on the question of how far talk of the kingdom of God was a metaphor, how far deity was compromised by secularization, and whether such volatile new wine in old bottles posed a significant danger of explosion and spillage. The view I press is that Dewey put together an astonishing combination of old hankerings and new understandings and that it is a fascinating and still-open question what parts give under pressure.

In a democracy understood as Dewey understood it—not only a system of majority rule, not only a system that allows popular pressure to sway legislation, not domesticated class warfare but deep and rich "communication" between citizens and "intelligent action" on the strength of that communication—the role of the intellectual becomes problematic, not for the first time but in a new way. It was clear enough that professors, publicists, and social critics were to inherit the mantle of the clergy; it was less clear what their authority was to rest on. Dewey complicated matters by appealing to the need to draw on the findings of "science," as though it were not so much intellectuals as technicians he had in mind, and this has suggested to critics that for all his talk of democracy Dewey had it in mind that an elite of philosophers and social scientists should reconstruct society behind the public's back. In fact, he never was guilty of the charge that Christopher Lasch leveled at him: that his talk of "intelligent action" and his constant appeal to a "scientific" approach to social issues reveal a concern to make people more amenable to social control and to encourage intellectuals to become social engineers and psychological manipulators.[9] If that were so, all the talk of democracy would be a sham, and it plainly is not.

It is perhaps arguable that Dewey *ought* to have been guilty of the charge, that if he had had a clearer and more definite view of the social sciences and the administrative and organizational techniques they could sustain, he would have held such a manipulative view. He had a great respect for particular skills and expertises, perhaps because he was himself not very deft, perhaps because his father had said that he did not much care whether his sons went to college but did hope that one of them might become a competent mechanic. More likely, Dewey was groping for an answer to a very old question, What gives philosophers any right to speak about issues in ethics and politics? The authority of philosophers had been questioned for twenty-four centuries; like Plato, Dewey was puzzled to know what philosophers could do that others could not. We do not ask philosophers to fix cars, unblock toilets, or do brain surgery; what can they do? If Dewey had held a simple view of the omnipotence of science, he might well have said that philosophers should contemplate ideal ends and then get social scientists to engineer ways of putting those ends into practice. He did not.

Dewey spent much of his life explaining why this view of social engineering and this view of philosophy would not do. He never quite made himself clear, and one can sympathize with Christopher Lasch's exasperation: "Dewey cannot be blamed for the perversion of his doctrines. It is curious, however, that although he repeatedly complained that his ideas were being distorted, the evident ease with which they were distorted did not cause him to reexamine the ideas themselves. He might at least have reflected on the possibility that they contained ambiguities which made them peculiarly susceptible to misinterpretation, if misinterpretation was in fact what was taking place."[10] Dewey's answer was that philosophers could help everyone to think his or her way through puzzles and obscurities that were not in the first instance *technical* puzzles and obscurities. This was what using the techniques of philosophy to deal with the problems of men amounted to. It was a slow business and did not lend itself to snappy arguments so much as elaborate descriptions of how people in fact manage their lives, whether these are the lives of plumbers or rocket scientists, elementary school teachers, or migrant workers. The thought that animated Dewey was that if he kept doing this, other people could see where they had got stuck in their thinking and become unstuck. Not that he would tell them what to think next; he would tell them what he thought, since that was part of his work as a citizen and a philosopher, but he would not tell them what to think, since this was not a situation where expertise meant much. Like most people who have held such views, he operated in practice at several different levels, according to whether he was fighting off the criticisms of other philosophers, writing books for the general reader, nagging President Roosevelt over the inadequacies of the New Deal, nagging recalcitrant school boards over their philistinism, or nagging misguided union leaders over their susceptibility to Communist propaganda in the 1930s. As a public intellectual he felt a duty to communicate with a wide public and became strikingly good at doing so.

Dewey's first attempts in this direction, however, were faintly comic; they form the third topic of this chapter. In 1891 Dewey briefly fell under the spell of a New York newspaperman, Franklin Ford. Ford had been a successful financial journalist but had become disillusioned with everyday journalism and had devised a scheme for publishing a paper to be called *Thought News,* the editor of which was to be Dewey. The scheme fell through, but not before Dewey spent an deeply emotional summer embroiled with Ford, when they walked, swam, talked incessantly, and planned to wake up the world by broadsheet philosophizing. Ford believed that Dewey backed out of the scheme through cowardice and lack of real radical inclinations. In later life Dewey was reticent about the affair and seems to have written Ford off as a con man. Horace Kallen, who knew Dewey in New York during World War I and after, wrote, "There was this man, Franklin Ford—in Michigan—to whom he was intellectually indebted; and I once raised a question about him; and all that John would say was, 'He turned out to be a scoundrel.' "[11] The event provides a convenient moment, however, to speculate briefly about Dewey's relationship to the radicalisms he encountered in the early 1890s.

American industrial relations were at their most violent and embittered; the great influx of immigration from eastern and southern Europe brought with it anarchists, radical socialists, Marxists, and other revolutionaries, all in variations by race, creed, and ethnicity; it is a fascinating, if unanswerable, question how far to the left Dewey was pulled. There is no problem in locating him squarely among the anticonservative forces of the nineteenth- and twentieth-century United States; the puzzle is to locate him on the liberal-socialist spectrum. My view, defended throughout this book, is that Dewey's political views were those of what in Britain was called advanced liberalism—politically radical, attached to the rights of women, attached to a secular state, siding with labor against capital, but not confiscatory, not "impossibilist," not insurrectionary, and in the last resort not particularly socialist if by "socialist" we mean attaching great importance to public ownership and the abolition of private property in the means of production. Dewey's views would have been familiar in the Fabian Society and at the London School of Economics, but they were colored by American concerns that British thinkers of the same persuasion did not particularly share, especially that of integrating immigrants into American society without suppressing their distinctiveness or abandoning the project of creating a distinctive American culture.[12] To understand how he found his own center, we need to see where else he might have strayed. In the next chapter, when we follow Dewey to the University of Chicago, we can see how much more naturally he embraced such activities as the settlement house movement than he was ever likely to embrace any more radical political movement. At the end of this chapter we leave him poised to leave Michigan for Chicago and his first triumphs.

T. H. Green and His Impact

T. H. Green was an English premonition of Dewey; like Dewey, he exerted an extraordinary influence in his day, one no less extraordinary for being hard to describe exactly. Just as a diluted pragmatism became the operating theory of American lawyers, judges, and politicians in the 1920s and 1930s, so Green's idealism, duly diluted, became the operating theory of bishops, social workers, and a surprising number of politicians in Britain. British cabinets and the American Supreme Court never became full of idealists and pragmatists respectively, nor did their members neglect normal business to discuss Kant and Hegel, or Peirce, James, and Dewey, but it surely made a difference that Woodrow Wilson was a professor and that Britain had one distinguished philosopher as prime minister and another as lord chancellor.[13] A certain way of talking and thinking about large social, legal, political, and cultural issues became current and remained current for a long time. "Professional" philosophy was in both countries more various and more changeable than this "public" philosophical style, but for public purposes a particular idiom and style of thinking and writing "took." The style had many advantages. One was the extent to which it talked—*they* talked, for Deweyan pragmatism carried on where Greenian idealism left off—the language of the *via media*.[14] Intellectuals owed a debt to Hegel, but talk of a middle way between collectivism and unbridled capitalism, between an established church and complete secularism, between a rigid moral conservatism and "anything goes" was not essentially intellectuals' talk. The ordinary man and woman shared in a common life of culture, ethics, and politics that was there to be used intelligently by them, and the middle way was natural to him and her. Yet it was intellectuals' talk, too; the common man's grasp of how the common culture fitted together was not strong, and even though the common man's moral inclinations were to be respected, the world might pose problems and difficulties that could not be dealt with by common sense alone.

Green came by his astonishing influence for personal reasons as much as intellectual ones. He was a person of great purity of manner, without a flicker of arrogance or self-conceit.[15] He died in 1881 at the early age of forty-six, and his entire career was spent teaching philosophy. But because he was placed at the center of English higher education, he exerted an enormous influence. Through his tutorials at Balliol College in Oxford there passed future archbishops, prime ministers, and judges, heads of colleges and presidents of universities, both those who confined themselves to Britain and those who spent much of their lives seeing to the intellectual and moral welfare of the empire. Green's philosophy appealed especially to the sons of the manse and to nonconformists from the Celtic fringes, and for much the same reasons that it appealed to Dewey. He taught a nonflashy, nonmetropolitan picture of a decent human life, and this emotional affinity between Dewey and Green was perhaps even stronger than the intellectual. Dewey's first published discussion of Green's work borrows and endorses the observation of Green's biographer Edward Caird that "one of the main features of Green's character was the distinction with which he lived by conviction, not by impulse. It was the belief, the profound belief, that action should spring from conviction, not any love of abstract and abstruse speculations, that made him a philosopher. He saw in what is called philosophy only a systematic search for a justification of the conviction by which man should live."[16] The language in which Dewey expressed that conception of philosophy changed: it became folksier and less highbrow. The idea did not change in the least.

Even though his disciples were drawn to Green by admiration of his character and a shared moral sensibility, it was the intellectual apparatus that he had put together that they wanted to teach their students. Like the young Dewey, Green wrote as a critic of the empiricist and utilitarian theories of Jeremy Bentham and John Stuart Mill, but in those days Green had rather more sense than Dewey of the real progress that Bentham and Mill represented. Green thought that what was wrong with utilitarianism was its hedonistic theory of motivation rather than its deeper allegiances. He agreed with the utilitarians that ethics was concerned with the common good, but he denied that individuals were led to promote the common good by getting pleasure in doing so, and he denied that the proper understanding of the common good was that it consisted in the "greatest happiness" of humanity, understood as a maximum of pleasure. As a pragmatist Dewey argued just this, and it is easy to see why. The virtue of utilitarianism was to place at the center of ethical theory a regard for consequences and a willingness to think about how to promote desirable consequences and escape undesired consequences. Compared with the blind acceptance of tradition, compared with appeals to individual conscience in the absence of an interpersonal standard for assessing the insights of the individual conscience, and compared with appeals to the deliverance of moral intuition, the insistence on assessing consequences that was the essence of utilitarian ethics was indeed progress.

The crux lay elsewhere. Critics of utilitarianism attacked it by complaining of its emphasis on pleasure; Carlyle famously characterized it as a "pig philosophy." But this was to attack it at its strongest point. As Mill retorted to Carlyle, it would have been a pig philosophy only if men's pleasures were the same as pigs' pleasures. "[T]he Epicureans have always answered that it is not they, but their accusers, who represent human nature in a degrading light; since the accusation supposes human beings to be capable of no pleasures except those of which swine are capable. . . . The comparison of the Epicurean life to that of beasts is felt as degrading, precisely because a beast's pleasures do not satisfy a human being's conception of happiness. Human beings have faculties more elevated than the animal appetites, and when once made conscious of them, do not regard anything as happiness that does not include their gratification."[17] If mankind were capable of pursuing truth, beauty, perfection of character, and the well-being of others—which for Mill implied that they took pleasure in the idea of such things' being achieved—utilitarianism was as capable as any other doctrine of recommending them. A subtler objection was that utilitarianism was impossibly demanding. If it saw individuals as creatures bound by their very nature to pursue their own pleasure and avoid their own pain, yet asked them to pursue the general good rather than their own, it must either set up an intolerable tension between self-interest and the general interest or provide some device for obliterating each person's individuality. Green's ethical theory provided an answer to the question of how to square the good of a creature's pursuing his or her own good with the moral demand that we should pursue the good of a whole community. Part of the answer was to throw overboard any idea that individuals are forced by nature to pursue their own pleasure. What they pursue is *satisfaction*. To talk of satisfaction is to talk of the satisfaction of a persisting self, so a second idea in old-fashioned utilitarianism that also had to be rejected was the suggestion that an individual life is a sequence of psychic states, for "hedonism" was the doctrine that what counted as success for an individual was a maximum of pleasurable psychic states.

Green pointed out something that recent writers have emphasized.[18] This is that we often do not want to have our wants satisfied; if I am a drug addict, I hope to be rid of my wants, not to satisfy them. The wants I want to satisfy are those with which I "identify" myself over the long run. By the same token, the pleasures I seek are those with which I "identify." I have to know what to value, with what to identify myself, before I can decide which pleasures to pursue or, better, what to take pleasure in. Characteristically the wants with which I identify have as their object states of the world rather than narrow states of myself. I want my child to prosper and be happy in her career, not as a means to my own happiness but because I think it is objectively a good thing that she does. If my child flourishes, I shall be happy, but I do not want her to flourish *because* it will make me happy. We could not want anything unless its occurrence pleased us rather than the reverse, but that is a truth that hedonism makes too much of.

Green, and for a while and following him Dewey, argued that we aim at "self-satisfaction"—in absolutely the reverse sense of the everyday sense of "self-satisfied." We try to set our desires in a context where we can satisfy more of them without self-reproach, where we can, so to speak, side with more of them and regret fewer of them. Green, Dewey, and much modern philosophy concur in the view that we can do this only if our selves are not separate, atomic, isolated, and impenetrably *other* to the selves of everyone else. Recent philosophy hesitates before the conclusion that Green went on to draw; Green claimed that our ultimate aim is to be part of a universal self, since only in this universal self is complete satisfaction to be had. Dewey briefly subscribed to that conclusion, but vestiges remain in his later insistence that individuals could achieve complete self-fulfillment only in a wholly satisfactory community.

Such a fulfillment is not something that moral philosophy most emphasizes, however. Moral philosophy concentrates on the analysis of less than ideal situations, where *duty* and *obligation* tie us to what we *must* do. For visions of a fusion between ourselves and the world, we characteristically turn to poetry rather than ethics, and Dewey reminded his readers that Green had come to idealism not so much by finding the apparent conflict between science and ethics intolerable as by finding himself puzzled by the contrast between science and *poetry*.[19] In his *Prolegomena to Ethics* Green pointed out that people hugged poetic insights to themselves, as if they could protect the poetry against the corrosive effect of a purely factual and scientific analysis of the world and as if it would protect them in return. People used poetry as a comfort and a prop to emotions they did not want to give up, but they resisted any suggestion that they should try to understand the place of these feelings and to justify their intuitive sense of their importance. Neither Green nor Dewey said it in this context, but Dewey later went on to say that one of the thoughts that poetry gives expression to is that at any given moment our present thoughts and actions are set in a vast but indefinite framework on which they draw for their sense and importance. If this idea lies behind the significance of poetry, making sense of ethics and making sense of poetry are closely related.

This was Green's conclusion, one that Dewey seconded. What Green went on to provide in the *Prolegomena*—Dewey's summary of that large and baggy book is accurate but overstates the closeness of Green's views to orthodox religious ethics and understates the extent to which Green insisted that they could stand on their own secular footing—was an explanation not only of why science was not a threat to ethical and poetic insight but of how the existence of science showed the validity of the intuitions of poetry. Green's argument was a variation on one that Kant had used against earlier kinds of empiricism. People can experience the world only if they are much more than devices that react to strings of experience. They need memory and expectation; they need to relate experiences to one another. That implies a framework within which they can be related. Green's view was that this framework was essentially an intelligence. Since we suppose that what we explain and analyze is experienced by other people in the same way we experience it, allowances being made for the differences of standpoint, understanding, and sensitivity that distinguish us from one another, we must suppose that we are working in a framework supplied by a universal intelligence, not just by our own individual intelligence. It is an argument that simultaneously appalls the reader by its sheer badness and remains tempting because it points out something we cannot deny. Its badness is the result of the equivocation between the perfectly proper thought that things are related within any given person's consciousness and the thought that all relations between things are contained in some larger consciousness. It is true that it takes a consciousness to *recognize* relatedness, but that does not imply that relations so recognized are themselves relations *within* some consciousness or other. The simpleminded view that we *recognize* relations that are not themselves relations within a consciousness implies that the world contains minds as well as whatever minds encounter; it does not suggest that everything we encounter is mental. The attractive side of Green's argument is just that it emphasizes what later writers have called the holistic quality of experience; we fit our experiences and our beliefs into a holistic system of explanation and understanding. I stress this because it is one more thing that survived into Dewey's mature thinking after being cut loose from its moorings in traditional metaphysics.

These large matters do not immediately seem to bear on ethics. Yet they must. They must because the motivation of Green's moral philosophy is to close the gap between the "is" and the "ought," between fact and value, science and morality. I am skeptical of this project and shall not offer an elaborate account of the argument that is supposed to effect the juncture. In a cowardly fashion I shall also hide behind the fact that Dewey does not offer anything very persuasive either and within a year or two had himself come to think that Green opened a chasm rather than close it.[20] Dewey short-circuits all discussion by claiming that the universal intelligence within which the world is intelligible is a *divine* intelligence. "[E]experience comes to us in successive moments, but that which is brought by experience neither comes nor goes,—it is the permanent divine intelligence. Science is simple *orderly* experience. It is the working out of the relations, the laws, implied in experience, but not visible upon its surface. It is a more adequate reproduction of the relations by which the eternal self-consciousness constitutes both nature and our understandings."[21] The thought is not unintelligible even if it is not persuasive. The aim of science is to gratify our understanding of the world by bringing more and more of experience under wide regulatory principles; the aim of ethical life is to bring more and more of life under a similar control. "Having found that in respect to his knowledge man is not a child of nature, but holds from a spiritual source, there is reason to apprehend that this spiritual principle may find expression in action: in consciousness of a moral ideal, and in the determination of action by it."[22] We find ourselves acted upon by the world—that is, experiencing its effects on our sensory capacities—and make sense of what is happening by scientific inquiry; in the same way we find ourselves acting upon the world and make sense of our actions by ethical reflection.

The ethical theory that Green created was an interesting mixture of English liberal individualism and something more Hegelian and communitarian. It provided a template for Dewey's first lectures and courses on ethics in the late 1880s and early 1890s, and much of it was continuous with his later pragmatist ethics. Dewey picked out four elements in Green's argument to emphasize;

they were well chosen, and they illuminate Dewey's ideas as much as they illuminate Green's. The first is the bare contrast between what we want and what we think we *ought* to want. The second is what fills out that bare contrast between mere wants and wants for something we approve of; Green argued that our true good is the full development of personality and that this development can occur only in a society of like personalities. Generations of students have complained of the vagueness and formality of such thoughts, and not without reason. Dewey acknowledged that more was needed, and he spelled it out with the third thought he extracted from Green—that the existing content of the ideal of personal development is found in the way society has developed and progressed since earlier times—and with what he extracted as Green's fourth claim: that the good man or woman is the person who combines a dutiful observance of the community's existing standards with his or her own individual efforts to push the community toward ideals that its current condition gestures toward but that its behavior does not yet embody.[23]

To see anything enlightening in this, it was necessary, and for Green's readers it was easy, to see what an approach like Green's rules out. A rapid-fire list includes the following: Our duties could not in the first instance be duties to the whole of humanity as such but must be learned and practiced in some particular society or group; so the utilitarian goal of maximizing the welfare of *all* sentient creatures was ruled out, but so was a bare reliance on conscience, religious inspiration, or purely individual ideals. Our duties were not fixed in stone or revealed once and for all; they grew and diminished over time, as humanity became capable of profiting from different ways of life and different ideals of human existence. This historicist perspective denied what many religious moralities have claimed about their own codes; in the late twentieth century it is perhaps more interesting that it also rules out the attempts of sociobiologists to extract a moral code from the demands of a fixed "human nature."[24] Again, in Green's view, there was no simple opposition of self-interest and morality; since our deepest desire was to be treated as a person by others, we wanted to live among our fellow creatures not out of a biological *instinct* of sociability but because that is the only way we can complete our natures. That ruled out the idea that morality is based on some form of social contract, for instance, the Hobbesian view of ethics as a set of terms to govern the common affairs of selfish individuals. Among late-twentieth-century political theorists, John Rawls has given a famous account of justice in a liberal democracy which he explicates in terms of the outcome of a "hypothetical contract"—that is to say, he asks his readers to think whether their intuitive ideas about justice are ones that we *would* come up with if we had to contract with other people about the rules that should govern our dealings with one another.[25] It is not entirely clear how far this more sophisticated appeal to contractual ideas falls foul of Green's insistence on the social roots of morality, but recent "communitarian" critics of Rawls have certainly attacked him in much the same terms.[26] It is also true that Rawls takes the central problem of ethics to be the reconciliation of conflicting interests, which is just what Green and after him Dewey dispute.

In his own time the most radical implications of Green's ideas were threefold. Against his fellow idealist F. H. Bradley, who held that morality demanded above all an attachment to "my station and its duties," Green argued that morality demanded the ability to go beyond that; Bradley thought that a desire to do more than was conventionally required was to "verge on immorality," but Green thought this was a cripplingly conservative view.[27] It was also imprudent, since persons who set their sights on so limited an end would fall short even of it, let alone of anything more demanding. In the second place, against the excessively pious and the overly secular, Green's philosophy steered a delicate middle path; moral thinking revealed our duty and motivated us to do it without revelation, but an appreciation of our moral nature must lead us toward a religious view of the world and even to an understanding of God—a point that Dewey made much of in characterizing Green for the liberal Congregationalist readers of the *Andover Review*. Lastly, Green's ethics contained elements of internationalism and a broad humanitarianism that were notably lacking in the work of Hegel.

We shall take up this last point again, especially when we encounter Dewey's ambivalent response to the World War I and the American part in it. Since I have already complained that Green was too easily convinced that the rule of law would soon replace the law of force, justice demands that we acknowledge the way intellectual history influenced him. Hegel's philosophy was only some two-thirds known to Green's generation or Dewey's. Their Hegel was the Hegel of the *Science of Logic,* and they read his social and political philosophy in the *Philosophy of Right,* which he wrote in middle age, essentially as a textbook for his Berlin students. They did not read his *Phenomenology of Spirit,* the wild and romantic volume in which he roamed from Antigone to the French Revolution, from elementary self-assertion to high spirituality, casting off brilliant and half-finished thoughts on the subjects to which he later devoted volumes. In the *Phenomenology* Hegel insisted on the need for individual self-assertion; in a long section variously translated as "the Master-Slave Dialectic" or "the Dialectic of Lordship and Bondage," he argued that human beings wish to dominate the world, to impose their wills upon it, to give it what value it has, and to demonstrate in so doing that without them the world would have no value of its own. When we encounter other human beings, our first thought it to treat them in the same way as anything else in the world. We want to turn them into components of our world, to demonstrate by controlling them that they have no value of their own and that such value as they do have is what we give them. Two creatures so inclined must fight, and the fight is likely to be a fight to the death. Hegel imagines the fight's ending when one party decides that he would rather be defeated than dead and so yields. At this point the victor enslaves the loser, and human culture begins. The loser now spends his time working for the winner, and something resembling ancient society begins to form.[28]

The details are not here important; the fact of the argument is. Hegel wanted a more dramatic world than Green's good-natured and cooperative society of liberal-minded progressives. War was an unmixed evil in Green's ethics, but an expected consequence of the human need for self-assertion in Hegel's. In his *Philosophy of Right* Hegel was more at peace with the modern world than he was in the *Phenomenology;* the *bon bourgeois* holding down a respectable job and looking after his family is (to the extent that anyone so well intentioned can be such) the "hero" of the story. Nonetheless, respectable people leading respectable lives do not justify the existence of the world, do not give history the shape it must have if it is to be the "march of God in the world." The state is more than an umbrella of law and security beneath which we lead safe middle-class lives. It exists to shelter cultures whose history is world history. These cultures must conflict with one another, and when they do, there will be war. Into everyday life "the gleaming sabers of the hussars" bring a meaning beyond what our individual projects give it. We are swept into the current of the world's career, and whether we live or perish, we experience something that mankind cannot do without.[29] This is a much rougher and fiercer vision of social life and the forces of change than Green took from Hegel and Dewey took from Green. James understood the psychological demands to which Hegel was responding when he wrote his famous essay on the need for a "moral equivalent of war."

One wonders what Dewey made of Hegel's views on war when he taught Hegel's *Philosophy of Right* in his history of political philosophy course at Michigan.[30] His account of his course follows Hegel and Green in seamlessly moving from individual conscience to membership in society and thence to the state. "The function of the state is defined as the guaranteeing, defining, and extending of rights. This necessitates a discussion of the nature of rights, which really forms the backbone of the course. The basis of rights, the theory of 'natural' and 'positive' rights, the various forms of rights, are taken up. This gives occasion for consideration of questions relating to property, punishment, war, etc., which are discussed at some length."[31] It would be good to know what Morris had taught Dewey, and what Dewey's own line was, but we have no firsthand account of the course. My guess is that Hegel was "Americanized"—that is to say, that his discussions of rights was emphasized and his admiring noises about the hussars and their sabers were buried—but this may do an injustice to Morris's combative spirit and his ability to pass on to Dewey something of his Civil War experience in the Union army.

Dewey was not an uncritical follower of Green or Hegel. Little by little he came to see that what he had gained from them could survive the repudiation of their metaphysics.[32] Before he reached that conclusion, he came to see a divergence between them that he thought told in Hegel's favor, though many readers might think the opposite. Green came closer than Hegel to endorsing the everyday faith of the Christian nonconformists among whom he and many of his students had grown up, and he was never as accepting of the world and its evils as Hegel. Although Green argued that each individual intelligence was an aspect of the divine intelligence doing its work of giving the world an order and a sense, he insisted that the degree to which the divine intelligence was realized in any of us was extremely limited. Green thus preserved a sharp distinction between the individual self and the universal self, between the way the world looks to each of us and the way we hope it looks to God. In the same way, the gap between our own achievements and what we take to be perfection of character remained wide. Hence the role of Christ in Green's ethics. Green's ethics were launched from a secular basis, but some such figure as Christ was required to provide reassurance that it was possible to be perfect. It was this that Dewey steadily came to reject. The separation of our imperfect selves from this image of what they might become reintroduced the lacerating separation of flesh and spirit, the actual and the ideal, that Dewey wanted to overcome.

He rejected both the idealist emphasis on the will and the transcendental character of the better or higher self by reference to which we judge our actions. He was influenced by reading William James's *Principles of Psychology* in 1891; Dewey briefly tried to out-James James and throw out the whole idea of a will that was responsible for our knowing and doing. James, Dewey observed in a footnote, had bravely thrown out the "owner" of the "stream of consciousness" and decided that the stream of consciousness was self-managing and self-criticizing and therefore not in the need of an ego to manage it; if he could go so far, why not go the whole hog and throw out the will as a separate entity, too? (The explanation, perhaps, is that even James thought that some entity had the job of imposing order on our mental lives; if our minds did not simply "mirror" the way the world was, then our wills had to determine how we would think of it.) Dewey argued that parallel to the stream of consciousness was the stream of activity. Ethical theory must be a theory of satisfactory activity, not a theory of how the empirical self can identify with the eternal or divine self.

From then on Dewey increasingly wanted to say something novel and difficult about ethics, and it was from about this time that he got into the habit of thinking out loud. That is, he would increasingly throw out half-formed suggestions, putting on the reader the onus of deciding how far to take the suggestions set in front of him. Dewey's reflections on James raise the obvious question of whether Dewey really intended to deny the existence of the will. The answer is that he did not but that he did want to say something quite complicated. James did not entirely deny that *we* think, and Dewey did not entirely deny that *we* act; but both believed that thoughts do initially "happen" to us and that only when we reflect on our thoughts and take responsibility for them is there an "I" thinking. This "I" is not an ego in the sense in which Kant had claimed that there must be a unitary ego to give coherence to experience;

it was simply the human person. The same analysis holds for action. It is William James and John Dewey who think, William James and John Dewey who act, not a self or a will housed in James and Dewey. When we hold John Smith responsible for what he did, it is the person John Smith whom we hold responsible. Dewey rightly flinched from saying that there was simply no such thing as the human will in any way that might suggest he had made a surprising empirical discovery. He therefore searched for a way of saying that while the phenomena of wanting, wishing, choosing, desiring, and so on are exactly what they turn out on investigation to be, they are not to be explained in terms of the operations of some mysterious faculty or property inherent in ordinary persons. It is not an easy view to spell out clearly, and Dewey never believed he had said it quite as he hoped.[33]

Dewey's longest work in ethics before the great textbook of 1908 came in the form of two textbooks primarily designed for use at Michigan and adopted elsewhere on a small scale. *A Critical Outline of Ethics* and *Ethics, a Syllabus* were largely devoted to surveying the landscape and not much to pressing Dewey's own views. But both strike a note that Dewey struck all his life, and it is one that is worth emphasizing, considering the usual picture of Dewey as an ahistorical philosopher. The Greeks get the credit for being the first people to *think* about ethics, and moral philosophy must begin with their thoughts. In one sense it is an implausible claim. It seems farfetched to suggest that there was no ethical thinking before classical Athens, the rise of democracy, the birth of philosophy, and the argumentative views to which the Athenians were addicted. There were dilemmas, struggles between individuals, and conflicts between one goal and another, none of which could have occurred to creatures without the human capacity for reflection. Yet there is also something plausible about the claim that in Athens people for the first time took *argument* seriously, that they explored their ideas to see whether they were well founded or ill founded, coherent or contradictory. Dewey treated the Greek contribution to philosophy with a nice mixture of admiration and wariness. The basis of the admiration needs no explanation; the wariness sprang from Dewey's view that philosophy was always in danger of valuing mind above matter, thought above action. A society in which the grinding hard work was done by slaves, or by a lower class excluded from politics, was always in danger of associating thinking with high status and doing with low status and thus of projecting its own snobberies into the universe and receiving them back as metaphysics.

What the little textbooks emphasized, and what Dewey felt keenly, was the awkward position of moral philosophy in relation to everyday life. Dewey's view of moral theory emphasized its similarity to scientific theory. Neither science nor ethics can tell us *what to do*. Because we look to both of them for advice, we naturally look for something like a rule book; then we complain because we have not found one, even though we know quite well that if we were given one, it would need to be applied to cases it did not obviously cover, it would require good independent judgment in interpreting the rules, and so endlessly on. What does science do? On Dewey's account, it offers us resources to be exploited in action. The science of metals does not tell us whether to build a bridge, and more surprisingly, it does not tell us how; it gives us resources with which to work out what we need if we are to build the Brooklyn Bridge. Geology does not tell us where to site the Brooklyn Bridge, but it gives us the resources from which to work out where to lay the foundations of the piers that must support it. An adequate ethical theory, Dewey suggests, has just that quality. It is not a set of instructions but an account of the things we need to take into account when deciding what to do.

Democracy

Among the things said about T. H. Green, the most famous was the obituary judgment that he was above all things a democrat. This may seem a strained judgment when we consider that during his lifetime Britain was far from entertaining universal suffrage even for men. Full universal suffrage reached Britain only in 1928, when both men and women were entitled to vote on reaching their twenty-first birthdays; women of thirty had received the vote in 1918. At the time Green died, men were entitled to vote under a "householder franchise"—that is, on the basis of a property qualification. Conservative and Liberal politicians had for fifty years been anxious about the rise of democracy, fearing the incursion into politics of irrational mobs or ignorant crowds following socialists or populists with their eyes on the property of the wealthy. Both Liberals and Conservatives in fact managed the transition rather effectively, setting up the first national party organizations to build on local political clubs and turning the newly enfranchised working class into docile voters of impeccably—even disappointingly—middle-of-the-road opinions. From the outset the Conservative party managed to secure some 30 percent of the working-class vote and has, if anything, done better in the twentieth century under universal suffrage than it did in the nineteenth.

Green would not have been impressed by this smooth transition to mass politics. His democratic leanings were not essentially political, and they were not closely tied to electoral politics in particular. It is true enough that it would be hard to imagine Green as a member of the Conservative party—he had none of the raucous bonhomie that working-class Toryism traded in, and he was an ideological progressive of a sort that that no upper-class Tory could tolerate—but Green's vision of democracy was moral rather than political. All the same, he had a strong sense of the importance of economics in framing the moral possibilities. He offended enthusiasts for laissez-faire by saying, as Mill had done before him, that the modern industrial worker had little more liberty than an Athenian slave. Mill had said that the hard-up worker had no choice of whom to work for or on what terms and that freedom of contract was an absurdity with such disparity of bargaining power as existed between owners and workers. Green believed this and added the more morally elevated observation that it was absurd to regard workers as self-governing beings when they lived cramped, ignorant lives, surrounded by grogshops, and bereft of the amenities of civilized life. Mill would have agreed with most but not all of that: Green was a temperance reformer, and Mill a savage critic of the temperance movement.

Green wanted a world where the Kantian idea that human beings are equal members of a Kingdom of Ends would be brought down to earth and made actual in the institutions of modern society. This was just what Dewey had in mind. One of the most extraordinary essays Dewey wrote on that subject was "Christianity and Democracy." Here he argued that democracy was the agency of religious truth and that the church as a separate institution and a separate vehicle of divine revelation would in due course be folded back into society at large as simply one aspect of a democratic society. "Democracy thus appears as the means by which the revelation of truth is carried on. It is in democracy, the community of ideas and interest through community of action, that the incarnation of God in man (man, that is to say, as organ of universal truth) becomes a living present thing, having its ordinary and natural sense. This truth is brought down to life; its segregation removed; it is made a common truth enacted in all departments of action, not in one isolated sphere called religious."[34] This was not a Christian defense of democracy, for all that it imbued the democratic project with a religious meaning. It looked even less Christian when Dewey adduced the role of science in promoting democracy.

It was "no accident that the growing organization of democracy coincides with the rise of science, including the machinery of telegraph and locomotive for distributing truth."[35] In other idioms, other philosophers have said something not dissimilar about the democratic quality of scientific inquiry. Just as democratic politics hinges on those with ideas about policies and programs being ready to stand up and persuade their fellow citizens to subscribe to their vision, so science hinges on those with hypotheses, theories about the workings of nature, being ready to stand up and persuade their fellow investigators of the fruitfulness, truth, scientific adequacy of their hypotheses.[36]

Karl Popper's defense of the "open society" is famous for treating the scientific community, the community of theorists and inquirers as the paradigm of that "open society."[37] Since it has largely established the framework for subsequent discussion of just what makes science *credible,* Popper's account is important in many respects. What matters for us is Popper's conviction that the reason for admiring science has nothing to do with its ability to sustain technology, or with its ability to pile up more and more information about the world, and almost everything to do with the fact that it is a free construction of the human spirit. The goal is to find a view that other people can accept, work with, and explore for themselves. This is why for Popper the object of science is the relentless criticism of hypotheses and why any hypothesis is acceptable only in the degree that it has stood up to tough scrutiny. Dewey's idea of democracy as embodying the scientific, experimental view of the world is very much in the same spirit. It is not quite identical because Dewey's communitarianism stresses the *communicative* and collective aspects of science whereas Popper displays a more individualist concern with the inventiveness, boldness, and determination of the person who launches the hypothesis into the world. After the remark quoted above, Dewey went on to say, "There is but one fact—the more complete movement of man to his unity with his fellows through realizing this truth of life."[38] Democratic self-government, like scientific inquiry, is a self-disciplined exercise in freedom that uncovers a truth that is never fully attained but is progressively achieved.

In 1891 it was less these anticipations of philosophical and political views that would only become clear after 1945 in someone else's work that was so striking than the break with orthodox Christian ideas. Dewey obviously drew on some distinctively American resources in this bold move. The thought that what matters is not the church but faith is an old one, and one that the conditions of American life made plausible in ways that set the United States apart from Britain and Europe. For one thing, no church ever had established status throughout the colonies; for another, the restless westward push of the colonists and the vast expansion of that process after independence made it impossible for churches to exercise the discipline over their pastors and their members that European churches had been able to exercise. Most American preachers beyond those who preached to the congregations of the older churches in the northeastern states were pretty uneducated and therefore uninhibited by theological qualms about standing up and ventilating their feelings.[39] Dewey was thus working in an American idiom in thinking that institutional forms mattered less than their animating spirit and that "attitude," rather than dogma, ritual, or authority, was what counted. It is a view with obvious attractions and less obvious drawbacks. The obvious attractions are ones Americans have always felt, and they account for the fact that Americans are the most churchgoing people in the world, that there is a greater variety of churches in the United States than in any dozen countries elsewhere, and that American television screens are filled with evangelists promising worldly success, sexual contentment, and safety in the hereafter for the price of a telephone call and a small annual donation. Even at Williams College and Dartmouth College when G. S. Hall and G. S. Morris attended the one and the other in the 1850s, the "spring revival," when freshmen "got religion," was a central feature of the emotional landscape.

The drawbacks are simple to list and complicated to elaborate. One is that in subordinating religious thought to religious attitudes, we risk encouraging a weak-minded romanticism at best and a raging anti-intellectualism at worst.[40] This charge cannot be laid at Dewey's door, even though he occasionally wrote things that might provoke the accusation. He was clear enough that if we would do better not to spend our time in theological speculation, we certainly should not give in to whatever sentiments we were struck with instead. Given the extent to which American anti-intellectualism has focused on a hostility to the theory of evolution, an enthusiastic intolerance in race relations, and a pressure for authoritarianism in education, Dewey was the last person to give comfort to the enemy, and he actually gave none. A more delicate objection is that Dewey chronically failed to see the value of church membership, ritual, the liturgy, and the like. The argument is that we cannot have a religious world view in general but need to see the world through the medium of some particular "vocabulary" of observance and belief. It may be that what Catholicism and Reform Judaism have in common is what is most valuable in them, but we cannot grasp it except through the practices and narratives of the particular faiths. The objection would then be that Dewey's discussion of the relations of individual and society is too often conducted as though it were obvious what the reference of "society" is. But it is not.

There is certainly something to the complaint that Dewey was a pluralist who knew full well that we actually belong to societ*ies* rather than "society" but that he was not enough of an anthropologist to go on to say anything very illuminating about any of them other than the school and the teachers' union. Dewey had found church membership a source of strain rather than support, so he had all the less incentive to make it a topic of analysis. In any case, he swam with the American tide in discounting ritual and the liturgy and would have needed a positive reason to swim against it. A much more devastating objection, to which we must return when we consider *A Common Faith,* is that Dewey was simply wrong about the nature of the religious attitude, all issues of institutionalization aside. So eager was he—this objection runs—to escape from the judgmental God of his Puritan ancestors that he threw out all the more serious features of traditional religious belief: the sense of human finitude; awe in the face of the vastness of the Creation; James's famous "oceanic feeling"; the proper self-doubt that the doctrine of original sin picks up (and maybe traduces). Dewey thought of the "religious" attitude as a matter of finding nature hospitable to our moral and political ideals; this omitted entirely the fear that both human and nonhuman nature might be drastically flawed. This was the reaction Dewey provoked in Reinhold Niebuhr in the 1930s, at a time when Niebuhr's politics were much like his own but when Niebuhr's bleakly Protestant vision of fallen humanity was very much not.[41]

These are anxieties about the conception of religion that Dewey went on to develop in the 1920s and 1930s. They are not anxieties about the conception of democracy for whose sake he explored these fields. So far as that goes, "Christianity and Democracy" remains a dazzling and a dazzlingly brave piece of work. It displays a really inventive and imaginative intelligence ready to take risks and contemplate ideas that would certainly startle their hearers. Dewey wrote several essays at much the same time in defense of modernity, democracy, and the quotidian life. Almost his earliest thoughts about democracy came in an essay, "The Ethics of Democracy," of 1888, criticizing Henry Sumner Maine's *Popular Government.* Although Dewey did not say so, it seems likely that he would have particularly disliked Maine's book because Maine shared Dewey's evolutionary perspective on social and political institutions; his *Ancient Law* is often cited not only as a monument to the comparative method but as a founding document in the attempt to explain institutional change in evolutionary and naturalistic terms. To turn so savagely against democracy was to repudiate the thought that evolution was on the whole progress. From the perspective of someone less committed to democracy than Dewey, Maine's apostasy would have been neither surprising nor alarming (nor justified, but that is another issue). Maine's famous slogan "From status to contract" always contained the seeds of his later conservatism. Indeed, to call his fears of democracy conservative is not quite right; what Maine wished to conserve was a liberal achievement that he thought was under pressure from below. The achievement was the Victorian laissez-faire state of the mid-nineteenth century. In Maine's account of the matter, humanity had made its way from societies in which everyone had fixed social roles to play and a fixed social status to go with them, with which property, occupation, marriage partners, and everything else were associated, to societies in which we got a bundle of resources and bargained our way through life as best we could. This was what Maine wanted to hang on to. Bright working-class boys like Maine could make their way up through the system from charity school to Cambridge and on to a Regius professorship and worldly honors. Less bright boys might well think that a less contract-oriented society would suit them better. There was nothing to stop history from being the record of "from status to contract and back again," and more than one commentator since Maine has thought that the natural condition of mankind is feudal rather than capitalist or liberal. Late in the twentieth century the thought has even struck Western business commentators that capitalism itself may be better supported by a more feudal, less liberal social order. Japan and Singapore have experienced tremendous economic growth with few of the social disruptions common in the United States, and China may be doing so; in all these cases it has been claimed that a "Confucian" emphasis on the individual's duty to society and family should receive much of the credit.[42]

Dewey's reaction was to defend something different from what Maine attacked. Maine tried, sensibly enough, to define democracy in terms that would not beg the question for or against it. It was, he claimed, only a form of government, and its definition picked out its only differentiating feature: It was government by numbers, not by merit. Dewey's response was to denounce this as purblind; it implies that society is just an aggregate, a heap, and "the theory which makes of democratic society a mere mass, makes, on the other, the democratic citizen a mere minced morsel of this mass, a disorganized fragment."[43] This crude view of the world, said Dewey, was by now out-of-date. Society is organic, not aggregative, and "if, however, society be truly described as organic, the citizen is a member of the organism, and just in proportion to the perfection of the organism, has concentrated within himself its intelligence and will. Disguise it as we will, this theory can have but one result, that of the sovereignty of the citizen."[44] The elegance of this response is that it saves undignified scuffling over the question of the intrinsic radicalism or conservatism of "the masses," a question endlessly debated and never resolved, and empirically an ill-formed question. Another nice feature of it is that it takes arguments over democracy out of the realm of moral dispute, or better, it takes the moral arguments over the merits of democracy out of a moral framework that suggests that these are pure moral choices and places them in a framework in which we have to consider what makes modern societies *modern*.

This is the ground Dewey occupies when turning the young Ernest Renan against his later self. In two essays, "Two Phases of Renan's Life" and "Renan's Loss of Faith in Science,"[45] Dewey goes back to Renan's 1848 defense of science as a comprehensive system of knowledge from *the standpoint of humanity as a whole*. What he admires in it is Renan's admission that if science is to be comprehensive, it must become reconciled to the resources we use in other areas of life, especially with poetry. How this reconciliation is to be effected is something Dewey never quite says, either then or later. He seems to suppose that once we understand the sense in which both science and poetry are *practical*—even when in obvious ways they are not—the reconciliation will have occurred. In a way this is perhaps as far as the argument can go; for a given individual, the smoothness with which he turns from one interest to another may possibly be an adequate measure of integration. Beyond that Dewey was always bound to find himself somewhat stuck, since he could not deny that the interest poetry takes in the world is not on all fours with the interest science takes. He did all anyone could by way of showing that there was no necessary incompatibility between the one thing and the other—the meteorologist has no business replying no when Shakespeare asks whether he should compare his love to a summer's day—yet Dewey plainly thought more might be achieved, that some philosophical synthesis could show that within science there was a place for poetry. A commencement address delivered at Smith College strikes the same note; it is largely devoted to contrasting Matthew Arnold's glum agnosticism with Robert Browning's celebration of springtime and hope—the "long, withdrawing roar" as Arnold's faith ebbs versus "God's in his heaven—All's right with the world" of Browning's springtime. But the underlying thought is that "We must bridge this gap of poetry from science. We must heal this unnatural wound. We must in the cold, reflective way of critical system, justify and organize the truth which poetry, with its quick, naive contacts, has already felt and reported. The same movement of the spirit, bringing man and man, man and nature, into wider and closer unity, which has found expression by anticipation in poetry, must find expression by retrospection in philosophy. Thus will be hastened the day in which our sons and daughters shall prophecy, our young men shall see visions and our old men shall dream dreams."[46] Renan had became disillusioned after 1848 and had come to believe that science simply couldn't be spread among the whole population without such dilution that it ceased to have any enlightening effect at all. One could have extensive knowledge or intensive knowledge but not both. Dewey does not suggest any practical way of getting around Renan's problems; rather he insists that we must not give up the hope that there is a scientific vision of our condition that will show us how to live now and how to move forward.

It is striking how much less tough-minded Dewey is than the writers he criticizes and the writers from whom he learns so much. The ratio of exhortation to self-examination is high. Dewey's essays display an optimism that contrasts sharply with the interior tension that had marked the work of Mill, for instance. In the essay *On Liberty* Mill was acutely aware of the difficulty of reconciling all the various aims that he had in mind. *On Liberty* tries to persuade its readers that society ought to be governed by a self-restraining principle according to which nobody ought to be made to do what he would not otherwise choose to do except in self-defense. Essentially the principle is that collective coercion is permitted only to frustrate individual coercion. While there are problems about working out just what stopping people from "harming others" is to include, the point of Mill's principle is obvious, and its libertarian status undeniable. Among other things, the principle says we may *not* coerce people into being more virtuous, religiously enlightened, or sexually chaste or in general into adopting the moral values of the majority. Mill put it forward because he wanted individuals to search for perfection in their own lives, and he thought they could not do so unless they lived in a society that was strenuously open-minded, critical, and freethinking. He thus left himself open to nasty questions: Fitzjames Stephen's *Liberty, Equality, Fraternity* pointedly asked why we mightn't beat people into good behavior if it would work; Maine's *Popular Government* held that unrestrained ordinary people would naturally gravitate toward a regime of boring conformity. Mill knew that he was vulnerable to critics, and his long treatment of democracy in *Representative Government* was meant in part to fend off such criticisms. But the reader has in addition a strong sense of Mill's arguing in part against himself, which gives his work a tension not found in Dewey's early work. One might say it is unfair to contrast Dewey with Mill, one of the enemy and a despised empiricist; since Mill's views were condemned as erroneous, they would naturally exhibit tensions that more adequate views would not. But even Hegel's emphasis on conflict, tension, and the unresolved problems faced by the modern world was at odds with Dewey's blithe optimism about the ability of the modern social organism to resolve its problems.

It is not that Dewey was not a bold thinker. His dazzling vision of the impending collapse of the separate churches into the bosom of a secular democracy is brave and original. Compared with the thin gruel offered by most of his fellow academics, Dewey's philosophy of democracy was robust and energetic. But it was not and it never became fully seized of the nastiness of political dilemmas or the intricacy of public policy making. Two reasons external to Dewey's philosophy do something to explain this. One is that until he went to Chicago, Dewey lived in a very small world. When he lived in Oil City and Baltimore, his mind was entirely focused on issues in metaphysics and psychology; Ann Arbor was a little college town, and the university a school of only 1,150 students. Unlike Hegel, who wrote to Goethe that he felt that reading the morning papers was his secular morning prayer, Dewey was concerned to square ethics and theology, to show that the world depended on a "spiritual principle," and that philosophy provided the "uplift" expected of it by college presidents. James Angell was a liberal Congregationalist, but he expected the faculty of the University of Michigan to provide a distinctively Christian higher education, and he was famous for the depth of his piety.[47]

The second is that Dewey's audience was no wider than his academic colleagues and the students of the Students' Christian Association. Neil Coughlan's *Young John Dewey* makes a great deal of this fact, contrasting Dewey's upbringing and early professional life with those of his British peers: They would have gone to Oxford or Cambridge; they would have known one another through personal contact; they lived in a society centralized in its intellectual and cultural life, habituated to easy exchange between dons and politicians and newspapermen, a world in which a man like Dewey would have encountered an intellectual class of his own fighting weight and one in which a great diversity of views was always current.[48] It is hard to know how much weight to give this contrast. It is true that Henry Carter Adams and Dewey's wife, Alice, were Dewey's only radical peers at Michigan, but Dewey did not feel isolated, and as a man more at ease with his typewriter than with flesh-and-blood people, he may have felt no great loss at not being part of the larger world; on the other hand, the enthusiasm with which he joined the great world when he got the chance suggests that something had been stirring in Ann Arbor. As he steadily shed his Congregationalist piety and then shed piecemeal the Hegelian metaphysics that had sustained that piety and had made it intellectually respectable, he began to see that what ethics and political philosophy were about to become in his hands was social criticism. Social criticism was not something to be confined to a small audience; once the image of the philosopher as a dealer in saving truths had gone, and the image of the philosopher as cultural critic had replaced it, the question of what audience he was to address became more pressing. He was, as he kept on saying after the mid 1880s, a democrat; it followed that talking to a wide public about its problems—to borrow the title of one of his most famous works—was the social duty of the new breed of philosopher. He was groping for new ways of expressing new thoughts, and it was never going to be easy to get them across. Oliver Wendell Holmes's famous wisecrack hit the mark exactly. Dewey's first attempt at broadcasting his views to a wider audience was not just unsuccessful but a fiasco.

Thought News

All of Dewey's biographers dwell on the tragicomedy of Dewey's involvement with Franklin Ford and the abortive attempt to put out a journal to be entitled *Thought News*.[49] The outlines of the story are easily told. Franklin Ford was a financial journalist; he worked for some years for Bradstreet's but became disillusioned when he discovered that even a paper purporting to give financial advice to would-be investors possessed no solid information about the prospects of different regions of the country or different industries and businesses. He tried to persuade his employers to set up a research bureau, but they saw no need for it. He then resigned. How he turned up in Ann Arbor and on Dewey's metaphorical doorstep is obscure in the extreme. At all events, he did so in 1888, and did more than anyone other than Alice Dewey to steer Dewey's thoughts in the direction of politics and social reform.[50]

The reason for Franklin Ford's effectiveness is not far to seek. He wrote in a curious private jargon and in retrospect looks like a first-class crank. The underlying thought that he pressed on Dewey, however, was one that Dewey had entertained already and entertained all his life in a variety of guises. Like Dewey, Ford believed in the magic of the word "organic"; once society's organic quality was thoroughly understood, appropriate political reforms would drop into place. But America in the 1880s was a very rough place; it was a decade in which the assault on the social and political system by the Vanderbilts, Fricks, Goulds, Astors, Rockefellers, and Morgans and all their allies on the one side and by workers ready to resist them by violence on the other was in full swing.

Chicago, the metropolis of the Midwest, had been particularly violent in the previous decade. It was the home of the International Working People's Association, the "anarchist international," whose members were few but whose following swelled every time there was an economic downturn. In 1886 the battles between anarchists and their supporters on the one side and the police and employers on the other had reached a crescendo when a bomb was thrown during a demonstration in Haymarket Square, and seven police and an undetermined number of civilians had died. Four anarchists—none of whom had had anything to do with the bomb—had been hanged in 1887.[51] That act of state terrorism had destroyed the anarchist movement, but it had not much lowered the level of industrial violence. Almost every strike was met by injunctions, Pinkerton agents, state militias, and vigilante mobs. Any dispassionate observer might think that the organic nature of society was manifesting itself in a pretty peculiar fashion.

The Ford brothers—in 1894, after the dust had settled, Franklin's brother, Corydon, wrote the only firsthand but hardly unbiased account of their relations with Dewey—shared a view that would inevitably appeal to a philosopher far from the battle.[52] What was wrong with society was a failure of intelligence and information. Society was an organism whose members were themselves organisms, persons whose lives were steered by their own understandings. If the results of their self-steering was chaos, bloodshed, and battles between strikers and Pinkertons, did it not follow that they were much misinformed or at any rate uninformed about the workings of the social organism? A few years earlier the eccentric libertarian anarchist Stephen Pearl Andrews had devoted himself to the creation of a grand integrated science of everything and had published *The Basic Outline of Universology* to reveal its results to date; in such a climate the idea that the format of a newspaper might be employed for the synthesizing purposes of philosophy seemed anything but absurd.

With no resources and few ideas about how to obtain them, the Ford brothers seem initially to have envisaged publishing a series of trade journals conveying information of concern to particular professions and branches of commerce. How they moved from this particularistic vision to the idea of a philosophical newspaper is unclear, but the paper that Franklin persuaded Dewey to lend his name to was *Thought News*. All his life Dewey suffered from the habit of simultaneously over- and underestimating the conservative pressures of the status quo. The generally low state of social understanding he ascribed to the manipulations of vested interests, but vested interests would be routed if they were exposed. *Thought News* would expose them. He wrote enthusiastically to Henry Carter Adams: "Ford says the municipal question is essentially a publicity question. No paper can afford now to tell the truth about the actual conduct of the city's business. But to have a newspaper whose *business*, i.e., whose livelihood, was to sell intelligence, and it couldn't afford to do anything else, any more than a genuine business can afford to sell spurious goods."[53] A hundred years of sad experience later and one wonders whether to boggle more at Dewey's naïveté about newspaper financing and distribution than at his naïveté about the interest in municipal politics that most inhabitants of most cities actually take or about the ease with which "facts" when uncovered would be accepted as facts.

What was *Thought News* to contribute to the triumph of enlightened intelligence? In the spring of 1892 Dewey issued a circular that cast a flood of darkness on the matter. He called the forthcoming journal a newspaper but envisaged its appearing irregularly, at any rate, not less often than once a month and on the usual basis of a monthly—that is, twelve issues to a volume. It was to be small: twelve to sixteen quarto pages per issue. It was to be moderately priced by the standards of the day, $1.50 for an annual subscription. It was also to be a journal

> which shall not go beyond the fact; which shall report thought rather than dress it up in the garments of the past; which, instead of dwelling at length upon the merely individual processes that accompany the facts, shall set forth the facts themselves; which shall not discuss philosophic ideas per se but use them as tools in interpreting the movements of thought; which shall treat questions of science, letters, state, school and church as parts of the one moving life of man and hence common interest, and not relegate them to separate documents of merely technical interest; which shall report

new investigations and discoveries in their new outcome and not in their overloaded gross bulk; which shall note new contributions to thought, whether by book or magazine, from the standpoint of the news in them, and not from that of patron or censor.[54]

How all this was to be achieved in twelve to sixteen quarto pages, with the slender resources of the three-person Michigan philosophy department was a question many asked and nobody answered.

Thought News never appeared. Mocking editorials appeared in the Detroit papers, and Dewey took flight. Grumpily insisting that the paper had never been intended to take over the entire newspaper world, only to show that philosophy was of some use to everyday political life, he backed away. It might be said that he did not back away as far as a more empirically minded thinker would have. He told a skeptical reporter who tackled him on the topic that "it can be seen, for example, that Walt Whitman's poetry, the great development of short stories at present, the centralizing tendencies in the railroads and the introduction of business methods into charity organizations, are all parts of one organic social movement" and that the revelation of their interconnection was the work of philosophy.[55] Skeptics might retort that the claim that they were all parts of "one organic social movement" was exactly what needed to be proved. Apart from anything else, reformers like Dewey had every reason to hope that many of the things to which they were attending were not *too* deeply implicated in the social organism, since they wanted to change them fairly dramatically. Skeptics have always believed that the great weakness of appeals to the "organic" quality of social life is just that the writer making the appeal is likely to attach the things he approves of *to* the social organism and detach the things he disapproves of *from* the social organism, without much empirical grounding beyond his own hopes and fears.

The collapse of the *Thought News* project saw a rift with the Fords that Dewey nowhere discussed; after it Franklin Ford vanishes from the record. The contretemps raises an urgent question that has lurked in what I have thus far written and ought now to be brought into the open and answered—at least for the first time around, since it is not a question that can be laid to rest in 1890. Dewey's philosophy was what many people have described as "naturalized Hegelianism." Its chief attraction is obvious: It reconciles the oppositions that make social theorists anxious. So, for instance, it is communitarian rather than aggressively individualist, but it is individualist rather than aggressively collectivist. It achieves this by asserting that individuals are products, or even facets, of the life of the community and then going on to insist that the community itself exists only in the life of associated individuals. One can play the same theme for history: We are created by our history, but we shape it by reacting to it and by building new futures on the pasts that we inherit.

This suggests why the *via media* was such a prop to reformism. Institutions cannot remain wholly unaltered, no matter what. Even if institutions do not change their outward form, they come to mean something different to us over time. The standpat conservative is thus literally illogical, but so is the revolutionary. The revolutionary cannot start from zero and must in spite of himself choose among portions of his inheritance however hard he tries to reject it. Thus much we have seen by now. Dewey borrowed much of the apparatus from others. He did with it what nobody else had quite dared to do and almost at once threw out the idealist concern to show that the world was ultimately "idea" or "spirit." He did not say instead that the world was ultimately matter or mere stuff; rather he decided that the goal was to live without talking in such terms, and he said James's and Peirce's pragmatism showed how to do it. But neither James nor Peirce had much to say about social and political matters, while Dewey wanted to write about them more than about anything else.

The question then arises of what he learned from all these sources, whether he learned it well or ill, whether he ought to have learned something entirely else. The question is one about the 1890s, but it matters for the 1990s. The revival of interest in Dewey and the competing accounts of what we are supposed to learn from him make an account of *his* politics a contribution to the argument about what ought to be *our* politics. Whether Dewey learned anything useful from Franklin Ford over and above the need to take an interest in the empirical realities around him is an open question. That raises a prior question: whether the *Thought News* project made any sense in the first place. Robert Westbrook takes Franklin Ford's side against Dewey and accepts Corydon Ford's accusation that Dewey backed away from *Thought News* only because he was frightened of losing his job if he became a political activist and a public figure. Westbrook wishes that Dewey had been an activist professor in the fashion of the late 1960s and is disappointed by his refusal of the role.

One might hope that it was not cowardice but good sense that had broken out and that Dewey had finally seen how hopelessly naïve the project was. Corydon Ford's denunciation of Dewey's backtracking is a wonderful piece of high-Hegelian outrage, but not persuasive. "He could not give the Supreme Court at Lansing the revolution of its concept or Detroit the remedy for the disorder of its city government; he could not put the cross upon President Angell who stood against progress on the Campus; neither might he denounce as a Judas his earnest pastor falsifying Christ. Clogged of the dead institution, he could not move; his salary meant that he was to keep quiet as to the overturning concepts."[56] The belief that an announcement of "the overturning concepts" was all that was needed to transform the world was just the delusion that Marx had accused the Young Hegelians of suffering from in the 1840s. Here it was fifty years later in the American Midwest. Hegel had suggested in his *Philosophy of History* that the Concept would make its way westward and find new expressions in the New World, but it was doubtful whether he had this dottiness in mind. If one holds the view I have been suggesting—that Franklin Ford was spectacularly confused, and the whole project half baked from beginning to end—the episode raises interesting questions about Dewey's gullibility.[57] It does not suggest that Dewey was a likely recruit for a

1960s style of radicalism. It also thrusts upon us the question of what else Dewey had around him that he might have subscribed to.

Other Radicalisms, Available and Unavailable

We have to begin by disabusing ourselves of the thought that Dewey might have been an enthusiast for socialist projects of any sort. There were perhaps three sorts of socialist possibility in the 1880s and 1890s, plus an anarchist movement that I do not rule out of the socialist canon but would push to the extreme edge of Dewey's vision. They are worth a rapid glance here for several reasons, some of which have been broadly hinted at already. Eugene Debs, for whom Dewey voted in 1912 and who has no rival for the title of the best-loved American socialist,[58] did not become a socialist until 1894. It was then that the federal government sent him to jail for his part in the Pullman strike. Debs's offense was to organize railroad workers to boycott trains containing Pullman cars as a way of exerting pressure on George Pullman at a time when the Pullman company was locked in conflict with its workers in Chicago. It is a nice coincidence that Dewey arrived in Chicago to take up his new chair at the height of the strike, and we know from his letters to Alice that he was firmly on the side of the workers and, like many others, even more firmly against their employers.[59] Before 1894, however, there was no such thing as "Debsian socialism." It was not an option for Dewey in 1890.

After 1894 it is an open question quite what Debsian socialism was, but one unmissable feature is enough to put Debs and Dewey in separate camps. Debs held a semi-insurrectionary view of the class struggle and valued trade unionism for its political potential as much as for any immediate good it would do for union members. He was not an "impossibilist"—that is, he was not committed to the idea that animated Georges Sorel: that the workers should make demands that they knew could not possibly be met in order to provoke a final showdown between capital and labor in the shape of the "revolutionary general strike."[60] But Debs was not a reformist; he referred to the reform-minded members of the Socialist party of America, founded in 1899, as "slow-cialists," he took it for granted that capitalism was sustained by the sheer brute force that the employers and their servant the capitalist state could bring to bear against the workers, and he looked to a workers' state, a proletarian democracy in some form, as the only ultimate goal. Above all, he was not, in the Leninist jargon, simply an "economist"; he did not hold Samuel Gompers's belief that the point of unionism was jam today and more jam tomorrow, did not think unions should limit themselves to securing a greater share of the proceeds of their industry.

In the end, of course, Gompers's vision won, Debs's lost. The American Federation of Labor took the measure of the American worker more accurately than Debs did. We need not decide whether Debsian socialism was a good thing or a bad thing; it appears to me self-evident that it was exciting but doomed and that Debs's supporters would have done better to spend their energies inside the AFL pushing Gompers to the left. That is beside the point. The point is that when Dewey was beginning to abandon Hegel for democracy, there was no Debsian socialism to subscribe to and that if there had been, he would not have subscribed to it. Dewey deplored the inegalitarianism of his own society and insisted that "democracy is not in reality what it is in name until it is industrial as well as civil and political."[61] The gloss he put on his talk of a democracy of wealth led not toward class warfare but toward something akin to British "new liberalism" or perhaps toward a form of guild socialism. Dewey, too, was not an "economist" and thought that it was the authority relations between owners and workers, not just the size of workers' wage packets, that needed reshaping. What he sought, however, was to democratize work, not to socialize the means of production. Or rather, the sense in which Dewey *did* want to socialize the means of production had nothing to do with expropriating the expropriators in the Marxist sense; owners and workers alike had to gain a sense that work was social service.

The thought is an important one, and mildly expressed though it is, it is enough to set writers like Dewey in the United States and new liberals such as L. T. Hobhouse and J. A. Hobson in Britain squarely at odds with the defenders of the rights of property. Neither a social Darwinist picture of the economy as a realm in which competition sorted out who was fit to survive nor a Lockean picture in which owners could stand pat on their right to do what they chose with what was lawfully theirs cut any ice with Dewey. The operations of the economy were always subordinate to public morality, and modern public morality was a democratic morality in which the law of the jungle had given way to the law of individual development—for everyone. Once upon a time, observed Dewey, Aristotle could distinguish between persons who were necessary conditions of the life of the polis and those who were truly members of it, citizens.

> It was necessary that there should be some who should give themselves to that which is purely material, the industrial, in order that others might have the leisure to give themselves to the social and political, the ethical. We have, nominally at least, given up the idea that a certain body of men are to be set aside for the doing of this necessary work; but we still think of this work, and of the relations pertaining to it, as if they were outside of the ethical realm and wholly in the natural. We admit, nay at times we claim, that ethical rules are to be *applied* to this industrial sphere, but we think of it as an external application. That the economic and industrial life is *in itself* ethical, that it is to be made contributory to the realization of personality through the formation of a higher and more complete unity among men, this is what we do not recognize; but such is the meaning of the statement that democracy must become industrial.[62]

This is the language of Émile Durkheim's *Civic Morals and Professional Ethics* and of Fabian socialism; it is not the language of a man who was a class warrior.

Dewey's philosophy ended by setting a Hegelian vision of the world atop a flatly empirical, nonmetaphysical base. The competitor to a liberal vision of this sort is Marxism. It, too, is a naturalized Hegelianism, and if more of Hegel's system-building passion survived in Marx's work than Marx was aware of, and if Marx was firmly in the grip of an antimetaphysical metaphysics of his own, much the same could be said of Dewey. The peculiarities of American political culture meant that Dewey's pragmatism faced less intellectual and political competition from Marxism than it would have done elsewhere, even during the 1930s, when Dewey was savagely attacked from the Marxian left, but Dewey's antipathy to class war accounts of politics would have made him deaf to the attractions of Marxism no matter what. Another reason why he would have flinched if he had encountered Marx in the 1880s was Marx's antipathy to religion in all its varieties. Dewey deplored "aggressive atheism," and Marx's atheism was nothing if not aggressive. But the odds against Dewey's encountering any of this were formidable. Unusually among his teachers and colleagues, Dewey never went to Germany; where Hall came back with some understanding of Ludwig Feuerbach, the left-Hegelian humanist socialist and critic of the historical veracity of the Gospels, while G. H. Mead acquired a taste for Marx's competitor for the allegiance of the German working class, the brilliant orator and agitator Ferdinand Lassalle, Dewey's knowledge of German intellectual life was a knowledge of the successive twists and turns of German idealism.

Of native American Marxists, there was was a drought. Daniel De Leon, the solitary American socialist whose understanding of Marxism was on a level with that of his European contemporaries, had yet to write a word on the subject. He was on his way from an enthusiasm for Henry George by way of an equal enthusiasm for Edward Bellamy to his final Marxist faith, but he had not yet arrived at it. There were handfuls of Marxists all over the United States, and the First International had spent its last days in New York when Marx moved its headquarters from the Old World to the New to keep it out of the hands of Bakunin's supporters. But there was none whom Dewey could have expected to read or encounter. The American Workers' party, for instance, had a membership of about fifteen hundred, almost none of whom spoke English; until the late 1890s the presence of Marxist social democrats inside the American labor movement was hard to detect.

A third variety of socialism Dewey knew well. It was, however, a socialism that dared not speak its name. This was the utopian socialism of Edward Bellamy's novel *Looking Backward*. The plot of *Looking Backward* is of the simplest, not to say the most boringly transparent, but the book itself is fascinating. The hero of *Looking Backward* is deeply unhappy, hates the poverty and squalor of life in the Boston of 1888, and intermittently gets on badly with his fiancée, who cannot understand why he holds such radical views; one night he retires to an underground room he has had built in order to sleep more peacefully, has himself mesmerized in order to fall asleep, and awakens in Boston in the year 2000. In this Boston poverty has been abolished, and absolute equality established. Bellamy takes the reader on a guided tour of the new Boston, and his host, the omniscient Dr. Leete, explains what is not readily apparent. Crucially, in the new world, there is no politics, no money, no free market, and no social disorder. William Morris, who loathed the book, called it a "cockney utopia," because it contained no account of the pleasures of work, artistic creation, and sociability, only of isolated, individual consumption.

This is unfair to the cockney vision. "The land of Cockaigne" is the place where "cakes and ale" flow in abundance, and its uninhibited character is very different from the repressed Boston of Dr. Leete. *Looking Backward* presents a *tidy* world, one where a very formal financial equality reigns and a glacial managerial efficiency has replaced politics. I say its equality is "formal" because the crucial feature of the new world is that each person receives an identical annual income; it comes as a kind of credit card, from which the various concerns that the consumer deals with deduct the cost of the goods and services he or she buys. Since everyone gets the same income, hours of work are adjusted to square supply and demand, and if there is any sort of employment that nobody will undertake no matter what, then the goods or services that it would produce are forgone.

Looking Backward is a chilling book. It is so because it is driven by fear rather than hope. It is instructively chilling, however. Dr. Leete explains the industrial system and explains that the head of the country is the head of the productive system. "Engine" Charlie Wilson's famous quip that what's good for General Motors is good for America is the organizing principle of Bellamy's society; as the corporations of late-nineteenth-century America expanded, it became clear that organization must triumph over competition and that once that had happened, the distinction between government and management vanished. Everyone had a job to do, everyone was content in his job—since people could change jobs when they wished, they had no need to do anything that they did not on the whole like—and the rank and file knew better than to question the wisdom of the oligarchy that administered the society. In short, *Looking Backward* is collectivist, hierarchical, and a very strange mixture of individualist and anti-individualist notions. It is also very American. Dr. Leete emphasizes the fact that the change from bad old world to brave new world has happened without revolution. It is a triumph of good sense, not of an insurrectionary army.

Bellamy refused to call his view socialist on the reasonable ground that in polite society socialism evoked thoughts of free love and beards. He called it nationalism. For a few years after the book's appearance, there were numbers of Bellamy Clubs all over the country, in which earnest middle-class lecturers talked of the need to establish the new order. The idea had a strong appeal to veterans of the Civil War, which is no surprise; it also appealed to the clientele of unitarian and universalist reading circles in the Northeast, again not very surprising. In 1935 Dewey, along with Charles Beard and Edward Weeks of the *Atlantic Monthly,* drew up a list of the most influential books of the last fifty years; all three lists had *Looking Backward* second only to Marx's *Capital*. It sold vast numbers of copies; it seems to have been runner-up to *Uncle Tom's Cabin* among nineteenth-century best sellers, and it sold more than two hundred thousand copies in the first two years of its life. But it was not a plausible basis for a social movement since its message was that politics was essentially ugly and disruptive. People who believe that are unlikely to make effective organizers.

Among other utopian or semiutopian visions of the time, one that Dewey admired and defended all his life, was Henry George's famous proposal for the "single tax." George's *Progress and Poverty* was a more robust work than anything Bellamy wrote, and George was briefly an effective political campaigner; he ran an effective campaign for mayor of New York in 1896, and even though he lost, he beat Theodore Roosevelt into third place.[63] Mostly he suffered the usual reformer's fate of constant poverty and intermittent employment. But *Progress and Poverty* gained innumerable adherents when it was published and has kept a good many to this day. Bertrand Russell, who knew a good deal about economics, having been a student of Henry Sidgwick's and a friend of John Maynard Keynes's, thought there was more sense in George than in Marx. In fact, many people think that a broad interpretation of George's views makes perfect sense, and that his attack on monopoly remains as valid as ever.

To broaden his views does some violence to their begetter. George was obsessed with landlords. Land is a fixed quantity—some allowance being made for the diligence of the Dutch—and its owners therefore have a natural monopoly. The rent they get for their land reflects little more than this monopoly; they get their rent whether or not they have done anything to make their land more valuable. If all taxation were to fall upon imputed rents, it would have two good effects. One would be to make the owners of land use their land as efficiently as possible: they would have to pay tax on the *imputed* income they would get from such a use and would therefore have a monetary incentive to use it so. The other would be to redistribute income away from people who had done nothing to deserve it. Proposals for "site value taxation" are a variant on this thought. If my land becomes valuable because a railroad has just been built next to it, so that I *could* develop it for industry, the added value has nothing to do with my efforts; I have made none. If I am taxed on the new value of the site, I shall get it developed, but I shall not forgo anything to which I am truly entitled. Society gets the benefit of social changes in value. Like most people with a good idea, George thought it was the only idea anyone needed, but the search for nondistorting taxes and doubts about the legitimacy of landlord ownership have continued to this day, for good reason.[64]

Dewey could have become a *follower* neither of George nor of Bellamy. Against Bellamy's vision of the world, with its talk of an "industrial army," Dewey's passionate commitment to democracy and his interest in the details of work and the working life were an absolute barrier. One could imagine

Dewey as a disciple of Ruskin and Morris, but not of Bellamy. Indeed, *Art as Experience* forty years later showed just how far Dewey could go toward an aesthetic socialism and toward a view of art that linked art and everyday work in the same way that Morris had done. Against George's attempt to reduce everything to the wickedness of the system of landownership, Dewey's sense of the intricacy of social life and its unamenability to any single solution was one barrier; more to the point, nothing in George's recipe promised an insight into the nature of industrial democracy.

What Dewey wanted was more nearly what was offered in the next century by G. D. H. Cole and guild socialism.[65] An enthusiasm for guild socialism was something he shared with Bertrand Russell. One of the innumerable agreeable paradoxes in which intellectual history abounds is the way Russell and Dewey could not stand each other's philosophical opinions—Russell thought Dewey's view of truth was *wicked,* not just inept, while Dewey thought Russell was concerned to score debating points, rather than to understand him—but generally shared each other's political and institutional allegiances. The superiority of Dewey to Russell as a *social* theorist rather than a logician lies largely in the fact that Dewey's philosophy led up to and underpinned his social and political ideals, while Russell's philosophy was irrelevant to his politics or at odds with it.

The historian of American socialism who has any taste for the human spectacle—and it would be hard to write the history of such complete and continuous failure without such a taste—will always find the anarchists of the period between 1880 and the end of World War I fascinating and engaging.[66] One way that Dewey's rather sturdy common sense simultaneously sustained him and limited his imagination is that he never hankered after any kind of anarchism. In *Young John Dewey,* Neil Coughlan talks of Dewey's coming to embrace a form of syndicalism, but it was not the anarcho-syndicalism of Sorel or of the Spanish syndicalists.[67] Westbrook quotes letters to Alice in which Dewey refers to their views as "anarchist," but it is clear that all Dewey means is that John D. Rockefeller would have thought them such.[68]

As a good Hegelian, and a good ex-Hegelian, Dewey spoke naturally and easily of the role of the state; indeed, the fact that he so domesticated Hegel's bloodthirsty insights into the state's role in world history and the struggle of competing cultures made it easier for him to speak of the state as a benign coordinating mechanism, or not even a mechanism so much as a benign structure of law and morality that allows us to live a common life as equal citizens and equally valuable members of the great community. Dewey was not a political romantic. Bertrand Russell thought anarcho-syndicalism was attractive but impracticable; the mere fact that it would not work did not mean that it was irrational to feel attracted to it. We might settle for something else—guild socialism was the solution on which both Russell and Dewey agreed—but we could properly *yearn* for the wilder shores of anarchism.[69] Dewey would have thought such an attitude light-minded and self-destructive. He wanted more from the existing state of affairs than a reluctant compromise; he wanted to give a wholehearted loyalty to things as they are. He also wanted a tidier world than Russell did; he wanted institutions and ideas to fit together. That is, one may suspect, why he did not react to Bellamy with the same outrage as William Morris had done. The Dewey who left Michigan for Chicago in 1894 was a great deal more radical, more down-to-earth, and more interesting than the young man who had left Johns Hopkins for Michigan ten years before. He was not a fire-eating leftist, and he never became one.

Four

The Pedagogue as Prophet

Dewey left the University of Michigan for Chicago in 1894. Ten years later he left Chicago for his final academic position, at Columbia University in New York. Ten years after that World War I broke out in Europe. The twenty years between Dewey's arrival in Chicago in 1894 and the outbreak of the war were the high point of his philosophical career. In those years he became well known in the public arena and became the guru of progressive educators.[1] Philosophically this was, above all, the time when Dewey's brand of pragmatism was worked out in his own mind, published under the names of Dewey and his colleagues at the University of Chicago, and hailed by William James as a the founding doctrine of a "new school." James wrote of the collection of essays by members of Dewey's department *Studies in Logical Theory:* "[I]t is splendid stuff, and Dewey is a hero. A real school and real thought. At Harvard we have plenty of thought, but not school. At Yale and Cornell, the other way about."[2] Recognition was not acceptance. "The volume," wrote Jane Dewey on her father's behalf, "would probably have attracted little attention even among university teachers of philosophy had it not received a cordial greeting from William James, whose review hailed the birth of a 'Chicago School' of thought, working along lines sympathetic to his pragmatism. This secured for it a certain recognition, for the most part hostile." It was, however, an indisputable landmark. Jane Dewey went on to record that Dewey's introduction to the essays "marks a final and complete break with his early Hegelian idealism and launches his instrumental theory of reflective thought."[3]

High Tide

The twenty years were philosophically all of a piece. It was in Chicago that Dewey finally created his own kind of pragmatism, so much so that most of what he published during his first ten years in New York was a working out of what he had projected in Chicago. It was not only his philosophical work in the narrow sense that flowered in Chicago. His applied psychological work flowered, too, and some of his most accessible essays were written in that period. The most famous of them at the time was the lecture *Interest in Relation to the Training of the Will,* delivered to the National Herbartian Society in 1896. In conjunction with Dewey's personal impact on colleagues at Teachers College, a decade later, the essay weaned his colleagues off traditional ideas about the importance of rewards and punishments and affected the educational theory, if not the educational practice, of a large percentage of the nation's leading teachers and administrators. In the years at Chicago Dewey rose to prominence as the nation's leading philosopher of education, a position he occupied until his death a half century later. He wrote innumerable essays on the application of psychological and anthropological theory to education, along with two of the books that spelled out what his philosophy entailed for the first few years of a child's education: *The School and Society* and *The Child and the Curriculum.* He also did most of the drafting for *How We Think.* The first of these was the most widely read of all his works and was translated into dozens of foreign languages, including Chinese and Japanese, and the third, published only some years after he had left Chicago, became a textbook that had a life of some twenty-five years.

In Chicago Dewey and J. H. Tufts created Dewey's most famous textbook, *Ethics,* also published after Dewey had left for Columbia, a book that remained in print for the next forty years and introduced tens of thousands of students to as much moral philosophy as they ever read. On politics in the usual sense, Dewey wrote little in those years. Outside the realm of teacher training and childhood education it was much later that he wrote his best-known, best-liked, and most influential work for a wider audience. Only in 1914, by which time he had been established in New York for a decade, did Dewey begin to write on large political issues in the pages of the newly founded *New Republic.* The high tide of that second career as secular preacher and lay saint to the Republic came during and after World War I with *Democracy and Education, Reconstruction in Philosophy, Human Nature and Conduct, Experience and Nature, The Public and Its Problems,* and *The Quest for Certainty,* to be followed by the more polemical and directly political essays in *Individualism Old and New, Liberalism and Social Action,* and finally *Freedom and Culture,* with *A Common Faith* and *Art as Experience* as explications of where his experimentalism stood on the ultimate goods of art and religion. This post-1914 career was multiply surprising. Dewey was almost sixty when the war ended, an age when most of us become less radical and less energetic. Moreover, he had been much chastened by the war, and the account of social, moral, and intellectual progress cheerfully proclaimed before 1914 had not come through the war unscathed.[4] To pick himself up and defend the intellectual and political radicalisms that he did was an astonishing feat.

This was far in the future when Dewey went to Chicago. During his years at the University of Chicago his energy went of necessity to the practical business of managing his department, getting the Laboratory School started and operating, finding it money and pupils, and ensuring that the teachers knew what they were doing. It was not an unmixed success. The dispiriting correspondence Dewey carried on with the president of the newly refounded University of Chicago over the decade from 1894 to 1904 strongly suggests that Dewey was not a good administrator and would not have been a good one even under the best of circumstances. The circumstances were anything but the best. Dewey and his president, William Rainey Harper, had never sorted out exactly what the duties of Dewey's chair of "pedagogy" were. As the name Laboratory School suggests, the school with which Dewey's name is indissolubly linked was supposed to serve the function of a social psychology laboratory. Funds had been set aside for a laboratory in physiological psychology, but there was no need for it; accordingly, the funds were devoted to the experimental school. In the event, the school became a sort of site for pedagogical demonstration; visitors could see Dewey's ideas about elementary education in operation. The improper but familiar label of "the Dewey school" suggests the extent to which its laboratory functions were diverted in favor of its operations simply as a school. It also provided an excellent, if unintended, base for training elementary school teachers. In this it very much resembled the schools associated with Teachers College in New York.[5]

This confusion of aims did not matter while the university was not engaged in teacher training, but in 1901 the university acquired the Chicago Institute of Education complete with its own training school. At this point the unclarity of the relationship between Dewey's chair of pedagogy and the orthodox teacher training program rapidly made all parties—Harper, Dewey, Mrs. Dewey, who became the principal of the University Elementary School, her teachers, and the faculty of the institute—as irritable and unhappy as they could well be.

Dewey was a tremendous success as the theorist of, and the publicist for, a new approach to education, but he was in the familiar position of the prophet without honor in his own land, receiving and sending off endless querulous memorandums on the administration of the department, the Lab School, the institute, and the rest. The Lab School itself was a constant source of financial anxiety because it had no endowment and only a small subvention from the university. The school was expensive. Personal care was lavished on the students, and this required a generous ratio of teachers to pupils; creating a suitable environment for small children meant specially made chairs and tables and apparatus for the children to play on. For much of the decade the school was on the brink of extinction for purely economic reasons, rescued several times by Anita Blaine, the heiress of the McCormick agricultural machinery fortune, a friend and ally of Colonel Parker's, and an enthusiast for educational innovation. As a colleague and chairman Dewey was surprisingly prickly, though it is only fair to admit that he was much provoked. Harper was habitually duplicitous in his dealings with his faculty, partly because he was autocratic by nature, partly because he was always looking over his shoulder at the reactions of the university's chief benefactor, John D. Rockefeller, and partly because he wanted to experiment and could not afford to tell his faculty that their experiments might be declared failures. Dewey was right to complain that decisions against the interests of himself, Mrs. Dewey, or the Lab School were often taken behind his back, but he underestimated the pressures under which Harper worked.[6]

When Dewey went to Columbia in 1904, he was neither an official member of the faculty of Teachers College nor a holder of a chair in education, and after his ten years as head in Chicago, he chaired the Columbia philosophy department only for a couple of interim stints when a colleague was on leave. Dewey's administrative problems possess some intellectual and biographical interest. Dewey's political philosophy gave an important role to the administrative virtues; the politics of "problem solving" could hardly do anything else. By the same token, his philosophy gave a central place in intellectual life to cooperative discussion and the hammering out of agreed views. Not only do Dewey's querulous letters about his department and his duties suggest that his practice was at odds with his theory, but in a note to his junior colleague A. W. Moore Dewey admitted rather wryly that his intellectual practice, too, was at odds with his professed theory. He worked as a loner. His style was to go off and work out what he thought by seeing how it looked when it came off the typewriter. Nothing very much follows from this. Dewey was perfectly happy to expose his ideas to criticism by other people, and to the degree that what counts is not how we come by our ideas but how we respond to criticism, there is little to flinch at in the fact that he was a solitary worker.[7] It may, however, indicate a certain gap in his official doctrine and suggest that Dewey's pragmatism, perhaps as opposed to James's, was vulnerable to Santayana's complaint that Dewey had little understanding of the extent to which thinking demands withdrawal, a retreat into an inner self, and a distancing of oneself from the world.[8] His emphasis on practical, engaged thought understated the need for impractical and disengaged thinking. We ought not to ascribe too much to the flawed logic of pragmatism; much of the petulance Dewey displayed as head of department sprang from the unadmitted difficulties of his domestic life. But even in an irritation largely caused by extraneous factors one might see an unresolved tension between Dewey's official belief that the wholly engaged thinker doing his duty as teacher and administrator will find complete fulfillment in his tasks and the realities of a life in which there is never time enough to do any one job properly, let alone all of them together.

Chicago

Dewey's call to Chicago was not the recognition of a triumphant young man's indispensability to John D. Rockefeller's proud new university. The university had just been refounded; its doors opened in the fall of 1892. Its predecessor had gone bankrupt a little beforehand, and Rockefeller was eager that no such disaster should befall his new creation. Rockefeller appointed William Rainey Harper, a wunderkind of thirty-four when appointed to head the university in 1890, and gave him enough money to hire away from his existing employer anyone willing to head out to the yellow mud of a raw and undigested and explosively growing Chicago. Dewey was too young and too obscure to be the object of an elaborate campaign of wooing and bribery. His appointment was faute de mieux. Harper wanted grander people than Dewey but failed to lure them; he tried G. H. Palmer at Harvard, Jacob Schurman at Cornell, and Benjamin Andrews at Brown; William James suggested he should hire Peirce, but the respectable ganged up to prevent it.[9] Dewey's name was suggested to Harper by Dewey's former assistant professor from Michigan, James H. Tufts, who had returned to Chicago after his time in Germany. Harper was unenthusiastic but finally thought he had better settle for what he could get. He had spent three years looking for someone famous to head the department, and had only landed two assistant professors. An indicator of Dewey's lowly standing was the salary he was offered; at four thousand dollars a year, it was hardly more than half the seventy-five hundred dollars that the grander recruits were getting. He knew this and begrudged it. Harper made promises of rapid improvement as and when the budget permitted and as a sweetener threw in an extra quarter's leave of absence so that the Deweys could have an extended break between Michigan and Chicago.[10]

During this leave occurred the first of the two catastrophes that did so much to destroy Dewey's domestic happiness. By now the Deweys had three children. The youngest, Morris, was a charming, bright, and beautiful little boy, loved and admired by everyone who met him. Alice Dewey and two of the children went to Europe; Dewey and Morris followed some months later. In Europe Morris caught diphtheria and died. Jane Dewey simply says: "His death of diphtheria in Milan, Italy, at the age of two and a half, was a blow from which neither of his parents ever fully recovered."[11] There was more to Alice's unhappiness than this. Reading between the lines of Dewey's letters to Alice when she was in Europe, one gets the impression that she was already chafing at the constraints of domestic life and finding motherhood an inadequate outlet for the energy and the political enthusiasms that had attracted Dewey in the first place. In the absence of Alice's side of the correspondence one can only guess what her letters to Dewey were like, but the apologetic tone of his to her suggests that she believed her talents and energies were underused in the role of wife and mother. He sympathized in principle but had little idea how to mend matters; once the Lab School was opened, it provided an outlet for Alice Dewey's enthusiasms—or would have done so if she had not turned out to be a poor manager and an overcritical head.

One of the greatest bonuses of life in Chicago for Dewey was his friendship with Jane Addams, and the chance to see Hull House in action. His relations with Jane Addams and his work for Hull House deserve a discussion in their own right and receive it at the end of this chapter. But Dewey's life in Chicago was a great deal livelier and more interesting than it had been at Ann Arbor for many reasons besides his friendship with Miss Addams and her allies. Not all of them had much to do with Chicago, at any rate geographically. When Dewey became more prosperous, he built a house in the Adirondacks at Mount Hurricane, where he spent every summer with his family. Mount Hurricane was something of an intellectual center, and during his vacations Dewey made friends with Felix Adler of the Society for Ethical Culture, finally met William James in person, and was drawn partway into the circle that gathered around Thomas Davidson's summer school. Dewey's old mentor and correspondent W. T. Harris was to be found there, too. There, too, Dewey was not a great "joiner." Adler's Society for Ethical Culture, for instance, might seem to be the kind of venture Dewey would approve. It provided a forum for ethical discussion and conducted meetings with a mildly Congregationalist flavor; although the society's central belief was the futility of debating ultimate metaphysical issues, it essentially offered the social comfort of church membership without the theological discomfort of formal religious commitment. Dewey seems not to have wanted these comforts and took no particular interest in the society, nor did he make close friends with Adler when they later became colleagues at Columbia.

The University of Chicago itself gave Dewey a great deal. Intellectually Dewey got more from G. H. Mead than from anyone, and he took over Mead's account of the formation of the self and the nature of reflective thinking lock, stock, and barrel. Mead's emphasis on the way the "I" is formed in social interaction became a sociological cliché only after his death in 1931, but it was tailor-made for Dewey's purposes, as he saw at once. The Meads became the Deweys' closest friends, but the other great stimuli of Dewey's educational work were Colonel Francis Parker, whom we have met before in Boston and who was by now the head of the Cook County Normal School, where he remained until he moved to head the Chicago Institute, and Ella Flagg Young, the district superintendent, the first woman in the nation to hold such a position. It was she who encouraged Dewey to think out the curricular implications of his philosophy of education and she who was the recipient of an astonishing letter he wrote in 1895 before the opening of the Lab School, in which he sketched the educational program he had in mind. It linked cooking to chemistry, food preparation to meteorology, to the passage of the seasons, and the rhythms of working life in a series of circular diagrams that Hegel himself would have admired.[12] Anyone who thinks of pragmatism as a down-to-earth and drearily realistic philosophy ought to recall the emotions that fueled Dewey's work. Dewey was driven by a passion for the spiritual wholeness and psychological integration that the romantic poets had celebrated, and that yearning bursts out in the oddest places in Dewey's sober prose. "Experimentalism"—Dewey's preferred label for his philosophy—suggests a somewhat cool and clinical approach to philosophy, but the thirty-five-year-old Dewey was anything but cool and clinical. He was in the grip of an intellectual fever.

Invention of Experimentalism

The decisive step in Dewey's intellectual development not marked was by a large book or the unveiling of a brand-new synthesis, but by a short article, "The Reflex Arc Concept in Psychology," which appeared in the *Psychological Review* in 1896.[13] The article criticized the use of the concepts of stimulus and response by physiological psychologists, and in a way that only Dewey ever fully mastered, it attacked contemporary psychology from a reactionary and a progressive position simultaneously.[14] Dewey maintained that his attack was launched entirely from the progressive position; the observer who is not committed to Dewey's position might be forgiven for thinking that the great attraction of his view was that it yielded the "organic" conception of thought and action that Dewey refused to give up, while it avoided any further detours through Hegel or Green and exempted Dewey from having to provide a metaphysical demonstration of the permeation of the world by thought.[15]

"The Reflex Arc Concept" is a lively essay and was much admired when it was published, but its bearing on Dewey's development may be a little obscure after a hundred years. Simply put, many writers hoped to employ stimulus-response connections as the atomic building blocks of an empirical psychology and to construct models of elaborate forms of human behavior by putting together increasingly complicated skeins of simple, more or less mechanical stimulus-response connections. This was not a program that Dewey's arguments laid to rest. Within his own department there was resistance; the leader of the behaviorist movement, J. B. Watson, was a graduate student at Chicago. Watson gained his Ph.D. in 1903, working with James Rowland Angell. He left soon after for Johns Hopkins, supposedly because he thought Angell's approach was too "mentalistic," and the resolutely antimentalist work on conditioning responses associated with the behaviorist movement remained prominent in empirical psychology between 1920 and 1970, long after Dewey had lost interest in empirical psychology. Dewey's argument was really tangential to arguments between mentalists and behaviorists; Dewey was himself a behaviorist. What Dewey defended was a holistic against a narrowly analytic approach to psychology. The bearing of his essay on orthodox learning theory was not a simple opposition to laboratory work on conditioning responses but a demand for much greater subtlety in interpeting the results.

Dewey's argument was simple. He took the standard illustration of a stimulus-response connection, famously employed by William James in his *Principles of Psychology:* A child attracted by the light reaches toward a candle flame, grasps it, is burned, and flinches away from it. The child with the candle became as much a staple of Dewey's psychology as the streetcar conductor contemplating whether to join a strike became of Dewey's ethics after his first appearance in *A Critical Outline of Ethics* in 1891.[16] "Antimentalists" might be reassured by the reflection that Dewey does not need even a child to make his point; any organism capable of learning from experience would do. Dewey makes two points amid a lot of surrounding comment. The first and main point is that nature does not come cut up into discrete stimulus events and discrete response events wearing their statuses on their faces. The distinction is one we impose for analytical purposes; Dewey insists throughout that stimuli are only stimuli *for* an organism that is, so to speak, primed to receive them as such.

In the second place, everything hangs on what Dewey calls the value of the stimulus, by which he means its meaning to the creature stimulated to act. The response the child emits is not an unanalyzed flinching away, a mere bodily reaction. It is not a considered and thought-out response, but it is also not a mechanical reflex. It is a reaction whose *point* is to avoid the "candle as something burning." Once the child can use a candle to provide light, he is not torn between avoidance of and attraction to the candle; he lights the candle to provide himself with light and keeps his hand away from the flame to avoid being burned. Where we are hesitant about how to approach a situation, Dewey denies that one and the same stimulus produces different responses and says that uncertainty lies "in the stimulus." The conclusion is that forms of behavior as simple as the child's avoidance of the flame are still too complicated for the mechanical stimulus-response explanation. The response side of a stimulus-response arc is a response to a "complex"—to a whole state of affairs with a meaning. What the stimulus means is in turn not something that fits easily into either an "objective" or a "subjective" framework. The child flinches from the candle as from "something burning"; the *meaning* of the candle lies in its capacity to burn the child. The mistake we are prone to make is to pack all the meaning into one side of the equation, either to demand that the situation should have a meaning regardless of the interpreting organism that encounters it or to insist that the organism just projects a meaning onto the world. Later learning theorists have increasingly found themselves employing similar ideas—that is, for anything other than the conditioning of reflexes not under voluntary control, explanations in terms of the desires, plans, and interpretations of the situation by the responsive creature appear to be inescapable. The cleavage between the mental and the physical is not the point so much as the inescapability of a vocabulary invoking ideas of the meaning of the "stimulus" to the stimulated organism.

Dewey argued against the stimulus-response theorists from both sides. He preserved the idea that action involves teleological explanation and would not be action otherwise, but he did so while refusing any old-fashioned split between the physical and the mental, between a physical stimulus and a psychic response. *If* Dewey's account were going to fall onto one side or other of any divide, it would be by siding with those who say that we *impose* meaning and that teleological concepts are a methodological convenience, not what he calls "existences."[17] The reason "The Reflex Arc Concept" mattered so much is that the central idea of Dewey's pragmatism was that organisms bring meaning into the world. Dewey's new, pragmatist conception of "meaning" in fact formed a kind of bridge between the Hegelianism he now rejected and the empiricism he would never accept. It was no longer necessary to suppose that an Absolute or a Divine Intelligence filled the world with meaning; in dealing with the world, we fill it with meaning. Curiously enough, this brought Dewey into a closer relationship with a thinker who is otherwise his polar opposite. This was the eighteenth-century Scots empiricist David Hume.

Years later Dewey described *Human Nature and Conduct* as "continuing the tradition of David Hume" in its analysis of the relations between habitual and reflective behavior in everyday life and at moments of moral crisis.[18] At first sight, this is an odd description; Dewey's hostility to empiricism was unyielding, and Hume was an archempiricist. On inspection, it turns out that Dewey's relationship to Hume was ambiguous. Dewey wished to undertake a naturalistic inquiry into human behavior in its habitat, and that was what Hume had done. Like Hume, Dewey wanted to dispense with metaphysics in the process of doing so. But it is doubtful that he was tempted by Hume's view that everything meaningful is brought into the world by ourselves, with its obvious implication that the world "in itself" has no meaning. Hume wrote of the human mind's disposition to "spread itself" upon the world and thus to color the world with what was strictly its contribution rather than the world's. This was part of a campaign to eliminate from the world whatever could readily be accounted for as the product of the mind. Because of his behaviorist approach, Dewey was often accused of a similar reductionism, but he always resisted the charge.

Dewey would not allow himself to be recruited for reductionism. He evaded the question of what the world might or might not contain in itself. The world we talk about, and live in, is the world of experience. In the experienced world there is meaning. Organisms live in a world of meaning. That was where everything must start. Questions about meaning in the absence of an organism were not exactly meaningless, but they were idle. A meaning-filled world is a world filled with meaning for an appropriately "tuned" or receptive creature acting in that world. Since we are such creatures, we shall in fact discover such meanings in the world when we look for them. The question of whether *we* provide all the meaningfulness that the world contains or whether the world provides it is unanswerable and therefore uninteresting and a distraction from the task of chronicling the meanings it does contain.

At this point we have the heart of Deweyan pragmatism. It altered somewhat between the 1890s and the 1920s and 1930s. *Human Nature and Conduct,* for instance, is more sociological in its approach to the meaningfulness of the world than "The Reflex Arc Concept." That is, it shares with the sociology of Émile Durkheim a disposition to credit human society with the establishment of meaning in the world, while the earlier, psychological essays simply follow the insight that Dewey said he got from his undergraduate reading of T. H. Huxley: the thought that the individual organism is an organized whole the behavioral elements of which can be understood only by reference to its economy as an organism. What is common to all of Dewey's work is the link between his pragmatism and the Hegelian idealism that Dewey grew out of. This was his refusal to be intimidated by the success of the physical sciences into believing that analytical, decompositive methods were the only legitimate way of making sense of the world. Like Hegel, Dewey insisted that the world was a world of meaning, not just a world of flatly unintelligible cause and effect connections. Cause and effect connections depend on the prior meaningfulness of the world. *We* attribute effects to causes and look for the causes of effects. That is not to say that causes do *not* cause their effects or that there are no causes and no effects other than the ones we uncover; it is to say that the concept of a cause and effect connection is part of the sense-making and meaning-giving apparatus that acting and interpreting organisms bring to the world. Cause and effect connections are part of the interpretive schema by which we organize the world.

Josiah Royce, who refused to abandon Hegelian Idealism for the new pragmatism, said that pragmatism was itself a form of idealism, and up to a point he was right—but only up to a point. The point where idealism and pragmatism diverge is clear enough. Both idealism and pragmatism insisted that we live in a world replete with meaning, a world with an organic unity of some kind; but idealism went on to give an account, couched in terms of the Absolute, of how the world came to be replete with meaning, while pragmatism went on to say that no such account was needed or possible.[19] Either the Absolute to which idealists appealed was a different kind of consciousness from our own or it was not; to the degree that it was different, we could only "project" onto it our own capacity for finding a meaning in the world, for the Absolute's capacity for finding meanings must be unknown to us. To the degree that it was no different from ourselves, it must see in the world only what we see in the world. Either way, it is we who are doing all the intellectual work, and an appeal to the Absolute is redundant.

The rock-bottom and irreducible status of the fact that the world is a meaningful unity is matched by one other thing that links Dewey's pragmatism to its Hegelian ancestry. This is Dewey's emphasis on activity, on the organism's nature as explorer, maker, and creator. The organism makes sense *of* the world for the sake of acting productively *on* the world. One reason why Dewey was never able to accept the orthodox account of stimulus-response was the fact that it made the organism whose behavior was supposed to be built up out of endless stimulus-response circuits too passive, too spectatorial, and too much a creature of the environment. Dewey did not deny that we were in part creatures of the environment; nobody who spent so much energy preaching the virtues of educational reform could have thought that we were *immune* to the environment. But he was concerned to add that it shaped us because we acted on it; we learned about it only by acting on it, doing things to it and with it.

We act on the world because we have needs and the world sets us the problem of satisfying them. The centrality to Dewey's philosophy of the idea of a *problem* dates from this period. An organism that had no needs, and therefore experienced no tension between what it was after and what it had, would be an organism with no knowledge of its environment at all, hardly distinguishable from its surroundings. Dewey's vision of the situation that all organisms found themselves in, and human beings more than any other, was that of making demands on an environment, being constantly checked, thrown back on themselves, forced to rethink their approach to the environment, and then trying again. It was no wonder that he was tempted by the term "instrumentalism" to describe his philosophical views; all thought was for the sake of action, and often enough it sounded as though he believed that all thought was a form of action. Such a view has some obviously exposed flanks: In avoiding a spectatorial view of the world so thoroughly, it is open to the complaint that sometimes we do want just to look at the world, that there are passive, non-problem-solving enjoyments and thoughts that we cherish. Poetry, art, and religion do not fit easily into an activist perspective. What the "action" is that is involved in thinking through a mathematical puzzle is obscure. Dewey came to prefer "experimentalism" as a label partly for this reason and devoted a great deal of thought to "consummatory" experiences later in life, trying to show how thought might be instrumental to something other than an end yet to be achieved.[20] His critics were not wholly convinced.

Talk of the "meaning" of events is parasitic on our understanding of the meaning of speech and writing. The world is not, of course, *literally* a text to be read, but just as we need to understand a language and its written forms if we are to see a page of writing *as* a page of writing, so we must learn to "read" the world around us in increasing depth. About meaning in the narrower sense of the meaning of words and propositions, Dewey held the orthodox pragmatist view that meaning was a matter of use. Like James, he said that statements meant what James had called their "cash value"—what it takes to get us to believe them or reject them—while words mean what they do in virtue of their place in statements. This sounds like the "verificationist" account of meaning associated with the logical positivists of the late 1920s Vienna Circle that dominated positivist philosophies from the late 1920s onward. In fact, there are many differences, three of which stand out. Logical positivism construed verification as "truth to fact," establishing a point-to-point correspondence between what we say and how the world is. Many logical positivists believed that there existed "atomic propositions" that matched the elements of thought to the elements of fact and formed the basis of our ordinary beliefs and statements. Others did not.

Dewey thought those who did were utterly wrong. When Otto Neurath, a founder of the Vienna Circle and in the late thirties a refugee from Nazi Austria, approached Dewey to get him to write a short monograph on the theory of value for the *International Encyclopedia of Unified Science,* Dewey demurred on the grounds that the positivists believed in atomic facts and he did not. Neurath brought the discussion to an end only by holding up his hand and declaring with great solemnity—he was an enormous man of great sweetness of nature and a sense of humor that led him to sign his letters with little cartoons of an elephant—"I *swear* that we do not believe in atomic propositions." At that Dewey relented, agreed to write, and poured memorably stiff drinks for all the participants in the negotiation, including the teetotal Neurath.[21]

Dewey believed neither in correspondence nor in atomic facts, nor that "truth to fact" was the only truth there was. Indeed, by the end of his life he had replaced the concept of truth by the notion of "warranted assertibility" and was well on the way to suggesting that even warranted assertibility was rather too rigid a standard to which to hold what we say; to call a statement "true" was no more than to say that it was good to steer our practice by. The second difference between Dewey's ideas about verification and the positivists' runs in harness with this. For Dewey, but not for the logical positivists, systems of ideas, scientific or aesthetic theories, religious and other organized sets of beliefs about the world live and die holistically. They may die by attrition, losing weaker members one by one until the whole edifice collapses, but they are themselves more than aggregates of statements that we hope are true. They are essentially—though this is a very un-Deweyan word—*systems* of belief. Accordingly, we verify not one thought or hypothesis at a time but an entire approach to the world.

The third great difference—and again it runs in harness with the first two—is that for all his emphasis on the virtues of the scientific method and for all his appeals to "science" in his educational and other writings, Dewey did not make the physical sciences the touchstone of intellectual respectability. Logical positivism suggested, and particular positivists said, that the only respectable understanding of the world is found in the heart of modern physics; everything else is reputable to the extent that it could be reduced to modern physics. Dewey saw matters the other way around. Science was sophisticated common sense; it was special in various ways—it underpinned modern technology; its practice when it lived up to its own standards was one of the high achievements of Western society; it allowed us to form new and surprising views about the world—but it did not shut out other sorts of understanding of the world. The project that Dewey inherited from George Sylvester Morris, of showing that religion and science could not merely coexist but could do so on terms of real friendship, was one he thought pragmatism fulfilled. Science and religion had in the last analysis the same aim, to render the world more deeply intelligible, to show its organic character more perspicuously, and thus to make us more thoroughly at home in the world. The contrast with A. J.

Ayer's memorable chapter on the elimination of theology and metaphysics in his iconoclastic *Language, Truth, and Logic* could hardly be greater. Ayer's book was a very pure representative of the logical positivist dismissal of everything not compatible with a simple account of "the scientific world view." Dewey's whole career was a protest against that kind of simplicity.

From Hegel to Darwin

One last reason why Dewey was content to say that we could dispense with metaphysical supports for our ethics, our science, and our politics was his faith that Darwin had not ejected us from a cozy man-centered universe, as so many philosophers of his day had thought. It is hard today to recapture the sentiments of philosophers who thought that everything sacred was threatened by Darwin, but it is clear that in the United States particularly, antievolutionary thought was immensely powerful. Dewey believed that evolutionary theory, adequately understood, showed not only why we possess the sensory capacities we do, and why we can use them to make our lives run more or less smoothly, but also where we should look for progress. It is hard to recapture exactly the mood in which Dewey wrote about evolutionary ethics and the place of evolutionary considerations in philosophy generally.[22] It is especially hard if one is as skeptical as I am about the capacity of the theory of evolution to do the philosophical work Dewey wanted it to do. Dewey and others were plainly right to think that many of our abilities and many of our desires are more or less "built in" to us for survival-oriented reasons. What is less easy to see is how many desires and abilities and how much knowledge can be so accounted for. Thus the mere fact that human beings exist at all shows that some degree of self-love must be "wired in" to us; if human beings had not cared whether they lived or died, the species would by now have died out. Again, some willingness to sacrifice ourselves for our children seems to be "wired in" as well; if it were not, adult human beings would have not have bothered to rear their defenseless offspring, and the race would have come to a rapid end. Among factual beliefs, the ability to distinguish dangerous objects, to avoid poisonous substances, and to see, secure, and use things useful to us all seem to be capacities that evolution would give us. Without such survival-enhancing capacities and beliefs, we would not be here in the first place. But this takes us only a little way. It says nothing about the grounds for preferring Einstein to Newton, Beethoven to Bach, or the life of an ascetic to the life of a Wall Street banker. The evolution of complex ideas, moral ideals, and aesthetic tastes is so unlike the evolution of animal species that it is hard to believe that the second illuminates the first.[23]

Dewey was deaf to such doubts. A striking piece of testimony is a lecture he gave in Chicago entitled "Evolution and Ethics"; it was a reply to T. H. Huxley's famous Romanes Lecture of the same name. In literary style and rhetorical force Huxley wins. Argumentatively it is less easy to declare a winner. Dewey was distressed by Huxley's lecture; Huxley had declared that the theory of evolution could not offer any moral advice. "The survival of the fittest" in evolutionary theory referred only to the survival of those able to outbreed their competitors. It told one nothing about the *moral* desirability of whatever was "fittest" by such a standard. Huxley appealed to the metaphor of a garden. Left to itself, the garden degenerates into a riot of weeds. In a competition to grow and reproduce, weeds beat flowers hands down. This shows that human beings have to decide what sorts of plants they *want* to grow; they cannot ask evolution to decide. Applied to society, it meant that Herbert Spencer's attempt to preach social Darwinism was nonsense and that societies had to decide for themselves what values to promote, then organize themselves to promote them. This was written at the height of the American enthusiasm for social Darwinism, and Huxley's lecture was rightly understood to be a deadly blow to the social Darwinist sociologist William Graham Sumner and the entire tribe of laissez-faire political economists.[24] It was no part of Huxley's purpose to assail anyone beyond Herbert Spencer; indeed, it is doubtful whether he had much idea of or interest in the ravages of American social Darwinism. His American readers did, of course. Sumner was professor of sociology at Yale and the first professional sociologist in the United States. In works such as *What Social Classes Owe to Each Other,* he insisted that what the capitalist did *not* owe the working class was the creation of a welfare state; the economy was properly red in tooth and claw, and the price of allowing the unfit to survive was misery for all.[25] Sumner relied a good deal on Spencer's evolutionary sociology for this familiar view.

But Dewey, too, felt Huxley's lecture to be a threat. This was not because he shared the views of Sumner and the devotees of the free market. Chicago sociology as practiced by Dewey's friend Albion Small was a running critique of the social Darwinists' optimism, and Michigan sociology, as represented by Charles Horton Cooley, was committed to an anti-Spencerian view of the social organism that Cooley had acquired in Dewey's political philosophy lectures.[26] Dewey had no liking for laissez-faire, then or ever; he had worked out for himself Huxley's devastating riposte to Spencer's laissez-faire manifesto *The Man versus the State:* that on Spencer's own principle of evolution, according to which complexity and coordination increase together, the tendency of modern society should be toward cooperativism and socialism rather than laissez-faire and government inaction. Spencer held that differentiation of function went along with greater central coordination. The only possible political moral was that progress meant centralization, not laissez-faire.

However, Dewey wanted evolution to be on the side of ethics and regarded Huxley's lecture as a departure from the true faith. Dewey's underlying motive for rescuing evolutionary ethics is stated without embarrassment at the end of his own lecture: "I question whether the spiritual life does not get its surest and most ample guarantees when it is learned that the laws and conditions of righteousness are implicated in the working processes of the universe;

when it is found that man in his conscious struggles, in his doubts, temptations and defeats, in his aspirations and successes, is moved on and buoyed up by the forces which have developed nature; and that in this moral struggle he acts not as a mere individual but as an organ in maintaining and carrying forward the universal process."[27] Dewey's later rhetorical style was homelier than that, but it was a thought he never let go of and one that underlies *A Common Faith* and *Art as Experience*.

All the same, it is one thing to *want* the universe to endorse our moral values and another to think that it does so. Dewey's criticisms of Huxley are deft, but they have one common characteristic—namely, that they tinker more or less drastically with the notion of the environment in which survival is to occur or not occur. Huxley had compared society with a garden that, left to itself, would rapidly become clogged with weeds and that flourishes as a place of beauty only because of constant intelligent intervention; this observation, claimed Dewey, though it was true enough, did not have the consequence Huxley supposed. Weeds are *not* the "fittest" in a world of human gardeners, just as brute strength and blind ignorance are *not* sources of fitness in an environment that includes other people with highly developed intelligences and the capacity for social organization to quell the violent and the murderous. Philosophically, there are two things to say. The first is that Dewey's argument is mere cheating; it is indecent to rescue the evolutionary perspective by packing human wishes and moral values into the "environment" in which the struggle for survival is to take place. Secondly, it is a point of real intellectual interest and importance to observe that the concept of an "environment" is inherently ambiguous.

The lecture on Huxley has one impressive feature in common with "The Reflex Arc Concept." In "The Reflex Arc Concept" Dewey absorbed the stimulus-response account of human behavior into his own holistic and teleological account. In "Ethics and Evolution" he absorbed the opposition between the natural and the cultural environment on which Huxley depended into a wider organic scheme. Culture is not opposed to nature but is part of nature and itself forms the natural environment for human behavior. Because the cultural environment is a moral environment, it favors the kind of fitness for survival that decent moral attitudes give their possessors. A school run on Deweyan lines is not a "blackboard jungle," but it is an evolutionary environment. Anyone who thinks that arguments about the contributions to our fully socialized characters made by nature and by culture respectively can be conducted only if we draw sharp analytical lines between the environment provided by nature and that provided by culture will think Dewey is cheating; anyone who sees an ill-defined but engrossing issue lurking here—roughly, how far the "second nature" of human custom, of what Durkheim called the conscience collective, really is a "nature"—will stifle her doubts, until she sees what Dewey can do with the framework he works within. One thing it surely aided him in doing was finessing many of the usual anxieties that beset theorists of education.

The Faith of a Pedagogue

Dewey had always been interested in the processes of education. From his earliest days at Ann Arbor he had lectured on issues in education, had given little impromptu addresses on the value of college education, had cooperated with the association of Michigan high school teachers, and had lectured quite widely on the impact of the "new psychology" on teaching practices. There was much more to his concern with "pedagogy" than that, however. Dewey's aims as a teacher of teachers or perhaps one might better say as a provider of moral and intellectual frameworks for teachers were pitched at a higher level than curriculum reform or bringing much-needed life to the curriculum. The continuity of purpose and even of idiom between his Sunday morning talks to the students at Ann Arbor and his new addresses to teachers is striking. Dewey's first famous statement of his educational convictions, "My Pedagogic Creed," which he wrote in 1896 for the *School Journal,*[28] is so replete with striking statements of the religious character of all true education, as well as with equally striking statements of the centrality of the school to social progress and the centrality of the educational experience to all social understanding, that anyone writing about him must be sorely tempted to give up and let him do the job for himself.[29] It is also so briskly written that it makes one wish that Dewey could more often have brought himself to shoot from the hip as he does here. After explaining the place of the school in rationally organized social change, elegantly rebutting the forced contrast between an individualism that lets the child run amok and a collectivism that stifles him, Dewey ends with the declaration "I believe that in this way the teacher always is the prophet of the true God and ushers in the true kingdom of God."[30] As Lawrence Cremin mildly observed, "Little wonder that American educators came to view this quiet little man with the dark mustache as a Moses who would eventually lead them toward the pedagogic promised land!"[31]

The "uplift" offered by Dewey's conclusion was one aspect of the continuity of interests between his younger, more straightforwardly religious self and his secular, liberal, and pragmatist self. Another, and it is closely connected to the first, is the way education becomes a central case for a view of the world that smoothed away sharp oppositions and allowed readers a strikingly optimistic view of the future. Education was thus redefined as "the art of giving shape to human powers and adapting them to social service" and, as so defined, was "the supreme art." To suppose that *this* was what education did was to suppose that children came into the world not as tabulae rasae upon which teachers might write whatever they chose or as limbs of Satan, whose wills must be curbed to make them "apt for society," as Hobbes once put it, but as bundles of intellectual, emotional, and moral potential naturally ready to turn into useful and happy adults. As he did later in *Democracy and Education,* Dewey took the chance to display his vision of the way individual and society might mesh. He asserted his belief that:

> the individual who is to be educated is a social individual, and that society is an organic union of individuals. If we eliminate the social factor from the child we are left only with an abstraction; if we eliminate the individual factor from society, we are left only with an inert and lifeless mass. Education, therefore, must begin with a psychological insight into the child's capacities, interests, and habits. It must be controlled at every point by reference to these same considerations. These powers, interests, and habits must be continually interpreted—we must know what they mean. They must be translated into terms of their social equivalents—into terms of what they are capable of in the way of social service.[32]

This was the educational creed of a progressive, but not altogether the creed of a "progressive educator." That is, to the extent that progressive education came to be a label for an educational theory that *over*emphasized the importance of teaching what interested the child, that *over*emphasized the child's responsibility for what went on at school, what rules governed the school's activities, and what he was or was not supposed to learn, Dewey was utterly hostile to progressive education so described. He said endlessly that he believed that his emphasis on the need to take the child's abilities and interests seriously had been taken by some people as a license to abandon teaching, that "child-centered" had come to mean that it was unimportant what the teacher did, and for any such view he had complete contempt. His position was decidedly a progressive one in every other sense. It made sense as an educational doctrine only if one supposed that the school was an engine of social progress; anyone who believed that the engine of social progress was the marketplace and that schools simply produced a supply of more or less trained labor would have found Dewey's views absurdly romantic. By the same token, anyone less optimistic about social progress would have thought him naïve; Bertrand Russell once observed that nobody who did not have a profound sense of the reality of original sin ought to teach. Dewey could make no sense of such a view. He took it for granted that even in the best-run school there would be a need for a minimal amount of repressive discipline; but he did not say so loudly, and it did not bulk large in his views. It might be necessary to protect the social environment in which learning took place, but it had no place in the learning process itself. His thoughts on evolution suggested that the integrated child is a happy child, that virtue is both its own reward *and* the path to true happiness, and that a well-run school will thus be working with the grain of infant nature and not against it.

In a more cynical or merely more anxious age, this seems unduly optimistic, but one aspect of Dewey's progressivism has lost none of its point in the intervening hundred years. A democratic society must be a restless society; it must be an innovative society. Even in 1896 Dewey insisted that "it is impossible to foretell definitely just what civilization will be twenty years from now. Hence it is impossible to prepare the child for any precise set of conditions."[33] The lesson was that every pupil must be put "in complete possession of all his powers." Only by making children the masters both of what is already part of "the funded capital" of society and of the aptitude to acquire what will unpredictably added to it in the future do we prepare them for the world after school. In a general way, this is plainly *the* liberal view of education; that it should seem banal to many of us is only a sign of how far we have moved from a belief in the virtues of producing factory fodder or instilling simple political acquiescence in a lower class whose destiny is to take orders and do the world's work.

At the University of Chicago Dewey had a chance to put all this into practice. The "Dewey School," otherwise the Laboratory School, was supposed to be what its name suggested: a laboratory. It was not a teacher training institution or primarily intended to provide a dazzling different elementary education for its students. In practice it became a test bed where Dewey's ideas about how to teach children were put into practice. A hundred years later Dewey's school seems less astonishing than it did to his contemporaries. It was obviously a wonderful school. It was also wonderful in ways that strike a modern reader as utterly unsurprising—until we reflect that the school was intended to break with the practice of elementary schools generally and to provide an intellectually and logically coherent education rather than a mere infusion of factual information. Its resemblance to the better sort of elementary school in post-1945 Britain and the United States is not an indictment of it but a tribute to its success. By the time the Laboratory School was founded, Friedrich Froebel's experiments in kindergarten teaching were sixty years old. Froebel's pedagogical practice was not unlike Dewey's; it emphasized cooperative play and manual training and was imaginative in its use of wooden blocks and rings for teaching arithmetic.[34] Compared with Dewey, however, Froebel was a mystic, while his vision of the child's innate drive for creative self-expression credited the child's "nature" with a good deal more than Dewey was inclined to do and led to a corresponding rigidity in his pedagogy. The observer of a late-twentieth-century elementary school sees what one might call the precipitate of sensitive teaching through creative play that has been left behind when the philosophical soup in which it first existed has been boiled off.

In something of the same way we do not see the differences between Dewey's practice and that of Maria Montessori that so agitated the young William Kilpatrick in 1914. But Mme. Montessori believed that children's development took place according to fixed principles and at fixed stages; her techniques and the apparatus she invented for children to play with and learn from could be, as they were with her, treated as sacrosanct. Dewey's experimentalism was at odds with that attitude, just as his interactive view of the way the child developed almost as a *part* of the environment was at odds with any idea that everything was "innate." His emphasis on the development of the child's sociability was also at odds with Montessori's emphasis on more narrowly intellectual development; she was famous for insisting that when children drew trees, they must color them green, not red.[35] It is because Montessori's methods and equipment were so readily usable by teachers who had little sympathy with her early intellectualism or her later mysticism that one would today be hard pressed to guess the philosophical affiliations of most elementary schools.

Dewey's school lasted only seven and a half years; it was closed by being wholly merged with the training school at the institute when Dewey left for Columbia. With adequate financing there was no reason why it could not have gone on forever. Its educational results were entirely satisfactory, as everyone from the most to the least committed agreed.[36] It was in this quite unlike more radical and freewheeling undertakings, such as the school at Beacon Hill that Dora and Bertrand Russell ran in the 1920s and A. S. Neill's Summerhill.[37] Their results were much less impressive.

It would have been surprising if the Dewey School had been anything other than a success. It was an object of admiration and enthusiasm to some of Dewey's most distinguished colleagues, including the sociologists Albion Small and W. I. Thomas, the geologist Thomas Chamberlin, and the physicist Albert Michelson, all of whom lectured to the children. One of the engaging features of the University of Chicago was the way in which it was set up to take an intelligent interest in the city around it and in the social and intellectual development of its inhabitants. Dewey and Albion Small discussed pedagogical and sociological theory in the context of the school, and it was very much in the minds of Dewey's junior colleagues Mead, Tufts, and Jim Angell. With devoted teachers able to call for help and occasional lectures from people with such a passion for their own disciplines, it would have been surprising if the children had failed to learn a great deal. Nonetheless, the reader of Dewey's work is invariably surprised by the minor place that the details of the curriculum occupy in his account of the school and its purpose. Even when Dewey writes *The School and Society,* what he writes about is the place of the school in a democracy and the role of the school as an agent of social progress—not down-to-earth issues like the kind of mathematics to teach eight-year-olds. There are barely a dozen pages of curricular matter in the hundred-odd-page discussion of educational principle and description of the Lab School.

Dewey's opening discussion is one that he repeated, if not endlessly, at any rate very frequently; it is in itself enough to give the lie to anyone who supposes that his ideas were "child-centered." He observes that in the fairly recent past education took place at home because life was lived mostly around the home. In the countryside the connection between getting a living and everyday life was everywhere intimate, visible, and immediate. Children were inevitably socialized into becoming useful participants in the household and village economy. "There was always something which really needed to be done, and a real necessity that each member of the household should do his own part faithfully and in cooperation with others."[38] The modern city has broken that simple bond between child, his upbringing, and his finding a useful place in society. As always, Dewey was fastidious about not giving a one-sided account. "We must recognize our compensations—the increase in toleration, in breadth of social judgment, the larger acquaintance with human nature, the sharper alertness in reading signs of character and interpreting social situations, greater accuracy of adaptation to differing personalities, contact with greater commercial activities. These considerations mean much to the city-bred child of today."[39]

It left a large question: "[H]ow shall we retain these advantages and yet introduce into the school something representing the other side of life-occupations which exact personal responsibilities and which train the child in relation to the physical realities of life?"[40] On this there are several things to be said. One is how important it was from the very beginning that Dewey saw elementary education—education up to the age of thirteen—as moral training rather than purely intellectual training. Indeed, "purely intellectual" would have been a term of abuse. There are two extremes from which Dewey has always been attacked, on the one side as someone who has an inadequate view of the need for discipline, order, and instilled habit, and on the other as a theorist of the manipulation of children into docile membership of the corporate order.[41] If one were forced to choose sides, the latter complaint is nearer the mark than the first. Both, however, are infinitely far from the truth. The place the skeptic must start from is not Dewey's desire that the powers of the child should find their natural fulfillment in life in a democratic society but his belief that there is such a natural harmony to be had. Though Dewey claimed to have thrown out metaphysics as a basis for social and political thinking, there is a broad sense of "metaphysical" in which it remained true that what separated him from more skeptical liberals was his metaphysical assumption of a harmony to be realized by intelligent action as against their belief that at the very best we were never going to be *wholly* at ease with one another in a modern society.[42]

The second thing to notice is the light that Dewey's starting point casts on his concern with "manual training." Another traditional complaint against Dewey is that his emphasis on learning by doing amounts to a recipe for preparing children to go on to vocational schools. Since American schools, like British and other schools, often put the perceived brightest children into academic streams and the perceived less bright into vocational streams and thus made it more likely that the bright children would go on to be prosperous and well-rounded members of the managing classes while the less bright would be variably but certainly less prosperous members of the managed nonelite, all discussion of manual training tends to raise the unlovely specter of an educational system that takes the existing division between managerial and manual work and reproduces it in the classroom. Dewey's position defies simple categorization. He admitted that *if* there were an adequate system of trade schools, there would be something to be said for manual training in the elementary school as a way of getting children to acquire the dexterity, discipline, and work habits that such trade schools could then turn into the skills needed for wives and mothers, on the one hand, and manual workers, on the other. But he promptly abandoned that ground. To think of practical training in this way was "unnecessarily narrow. We must conceive of work in wood and metal, of weaving, sewing and cooking, as methods of living and learning, not as distinct studies."[43]

Agricultural societies focused on farm and village showed the child the entire process by which life went on; there was no turning a switch and having electric light, but an elaborate process of killing animals, rendering tallow, making candles, and so on and so forth. What the school needs to do is show children the complexity of the modern world. Dewey did not think that it could be done by just telling them about the way industry and commerce worked; swamping children with elaborate information in their early years was hopeless: They would get the habit of superficial understanding, probably be bored, never learn to concentrate on one topic or activity. What they had to do was work their way through some such activity from beginning to end; at the Lab School the children grew wheat in a corner of the schoolyard, ground it, learned to make bread, and so on. When slightly older, they learned about metal smelting and built their own furnace. To learn chemistry, they cooked, and to cook, they learned chemistry. This was what one might genuinely call acquiring a hands-on understanding of the world. The striking thing about it is not that it was commercially driven but that it was so visibly driven by moral and philosophical preconceptions. Among the many ways in which it was unobtrusively ahead of its time, there was no distinction in the work done by boys and girls. Dewey was not a particularly radical feminist, but he was an intransigent egalitarian.

A third feature of Dewey's discussion was that it was predicated on a view of the need for the educational process to make adequate ties with every aspect of the life around it that Dewey felt with some passion but whose intellectual as distinct from its emotional point is not easy to discern. In the chapter "Waste in Education"—itself a slightly odd location for what he actually discussed—Dewey leaped in one bound from the concept of waste to that of organization and then spread his wings on the topic of just what organization meant for the school. Producing several charts, he read his audience a sermon on the theme that "All waste is due to isolation. Organization is nothing but getting things into connection with one another so that they work easily, flexibly and fully."[44] The details of his picture of the integrated school do not matter very much, but the frame of mind that it evidenced does. For "organization" took on a decidedly supermanagerial tone in the argument. The school was a spiritual rather than a physical entity; as one might expect from a philosopher who so stressed the way we react to the "meaning" of events, Dewey emphasized that the school was a network of meanings rather than merely a collection of spaces in which children read, cooked, played, painted, and whatever. The "organization" Dewey had in mind was a kind of balancing of the school's ties to the entire social environment; cooking in the school kitchen linked the child both to home, where such activities went on, and to the countryside, where food was grown, and thus to the school's own physical environment, while sewing in the textile room tied the school both to the home, where such things went on, too, and then out to the world of business and industry.[45]

The School and Society was vastly popular; its popularity may have been a function of the curious combination of the great clarity of its general orientation and the great openness of its argumentative texture. As the above discussion suggests, Dewey insisted over and over that school was itself part of life, not just a preparation for it, that the child had to bring into play at school all of his or her energies, not just intellectual ones and not just manual skills; that something of vast importance was happening in the school, since this was where the next generation was growing, and everyone knew that it was vastly easier to form children adequately than to have to reform them when they were teenage delinquents. All this was good news, but it did not yield very obvious conclusions about just what to teach and just how to teach it. There, too, of course, Dewey had headed off his critics in advance; the distinction between how to teach and what to teach was another of the isolations and separations that he deplored. Form and content, style and matter were to be adjusted to each other as we more fully understood what successful elementary teaching was all about. We knew that it was not about handing over slabs of undigested fact, we knew that it was a mistake to send the young out into the world primed with information but with no skills of processing and evaluating it; beyond that, *experientia docet* was the motto: People must experiment, report on their experiments, and hope to agree on good practice. Dewey himself was thus ready to do things recommended by theories and perspectives that he did not accept as an adequate guide to education in general.

So, for instance, he told an amusing story of a visitor asking to see the kindergarten section of the Lab School and being told there was none. Then the visitor "asked if there were not singing, drawing, manual training, plays and dramatizations, and attention to the children's social relations. When her questions were answered in the affirmative, she remarked, both triumphantly and indignantly, that that was what she understood by a kindergarten, and that she did not know what was meant by saying that the school had no kindergarten."[46] Dewey observed that there was a sense in which everything the school did for children between the ages of four and thirteen was intended to "carry into effect certain principles which Froebel was perhaps the first consciously to set forth."[47] But Dewey would not have passed himself off as a disciple of Froebel's, nor did he associate himself with the Froebel movement in America. One reason is particularly interesting: Dewey thought Froebel had been unable to give a direct and sensible account of the value of play in early education because he lived in an authoritarian society to which such playful activities were anathema.[48] In Dewey's view of Froebel's plight, Froebel had to give elaborate metaphysical justifications of the symbolic values of childish playacting, and to do so, he had to detach school activities from the outside world, to protect the child against the everyday world.[49] The American child had an inalienable right to the pursuit of happiness, and his activities at school needed no elaborate symbolic defenses. They were ways of integrating his everyday desire for play into the process of leading him gently toward adult life. Froebel's kindergarten methods could be employed, usefully detached from his philosophy.

The same attitude of not quite acceptance and not quite rejection marked his approach to the influence of Johann Herbart. Herbart was best known for the slogan "Ontogeny recapitulates phylogeny"—a misleading and distracting slogan in biology and much worse in its effect on the social sciences. What it means literally is that the growth of the individual takes place in stages that mirror the development of the species. What it meant in schools was that the curriculum was supposed to be governed by the individual child's gradual movement from an infancy in which he or she mimicked the mental and social relations of primitive peoples to an adult life in which he or she was a full member of a fully civilized community. Dewey wrote several papers disputing this as a picture of child development.[50] Yet the curriculum of the Lab School took something like it as a model; as a critic noticed, "in the ordered progression of theme activities from preliterate man to modern society there were patent vestiges of the very recapitulation theory Dewey had attacked before the National Herbart Society."[51]

In Dewey's mind, teaching children about the growth of human culture in an evolutionary fashion and sophisticating the children's grasp of increasingly abstract material did not rest on any such theory as Herbart's. Dewey's guiding thought was much more nearly that children were gradually weaned from their homes and the emotional and intellectual stimuli that home provided and onto a more abstract, more impersonal intellectual and social diet. It would doubtless have been possible to each children history and social studies by starting with modern society and working backward, but it takes little imagination to think of some reasons why we prefer them to learn a little about Neolithic man and a lot about the contemporary world rather than a little about New York and a great deal of paleontology.

On the broad issue of the plausibility of Dewey's picture of child development, opinions have always varied. Nonacademically minded infant teachers might think that Dewey always had his eye too much on where children were going next and not enough on the joys of the particular stage they had reached. Academically minded readers by contrast may well flinch at Dewey's account of how long it was before the children of the Lab School were supposed to settle down and learn some of the three Rs. What cannot be denied, however, is that the gradual shift from what others would have denoted as play to what others would have denoted as real work—neither of which Dewey would have so labeled at any point—was always controlled by a clear idea of the child's destination. It was not nostalgia for a vanishing rural past that made Dewey start the six-year-olds on small-scale farming, harvesting, and cooking the results of their labors, but his belief that these were the basic activities of human existence, ones that children already understood some part of by the time they reached school.

Letters to friends describing the first days of the school show the children always being propelled toward adult competence: On their first morning they made boxes to hold their pencils; then they saw how to measure them and learned some basic geometry. Play in the sandbox turned mathematical almost immediately, too. The homeliness of Dewey's manner, and the homeliness of his examples, are misleading as to the real intellectual thrust of the syllabus he suggested. It was not that he thought that all knowledge is applied knowledge or that he thought all learning was somehow to be assimilated to farming or washing the dishes; it was rather that he believed so passionately that ideas made sense only as solutions to problems and that educationalists had chronically neglected this fact that he saw his own contribution as suggesting ways of putting children into situations where they would grasp the problems to which increasingly sophisticated ideas were solutions and for which sophisticated academic skills of a familiar skills were increasingly needed. Dewey always tried to steer a delicate path between simpler but wrongheaded views that were not *wholly* wrong but that in his eyes missed the point. When he started writing about education, two opposed positions much in the public eye were the Herbartian emphasis on *interest* and the emphasis of his old mentor W. T. Harris on *effort*. Dewey thought the Herbartian's emphasis came to no more than sugaring the pill of a set curriculum, while Harris's emphasis on effort without interest would create students who were either excessively passive or merely rebellious. The point of Dewey's complicated argument about setting children *problems* and teaching them to *think* was that he believed that under those conditions they would be interested as the Herbartians wished them to be and would make the effort that Harris and his colleagues rightly stressed.[52]

All these arguments are, so to speak, "precurricular," and Dewey's little pamphlet *The Child and the Curriculum* is in the same way not a discussion of the curriculum but another plea for the abolition of sharp separations in methods of teaching where there ought to be none in the process of learning. The slogans of "Discipline" and "Interest" that opposed sides hurled at each other, one thinking to defend "the subject," the other thinking to defend "the child," reflected an analytical distinction that had been inflated into a false vision of the world. Of course, children must learn something in particular, of course, there was a particular direction in which they needed to be led, so of course, they needed to master the disciplines of learning; but to master anything in such a way as to have really been educated by it was a matter of absorbing it and turning it to one's own purposes, and this was a matter of our own interest. The only discipline worth having was self-discipline, and the only interest worth gratifying was an interest capable of being sustained over a long enough run to enable us to learn a subject matter thoroughly.

How We Think

This is the lesson spelled out for two hundred pages in *How We Think*.[53] *How We Think* was a characteristic exercise in Dewey's mature idiom. It was published in 1910, six years after Dewey left Chicago, but like much else published during that time, it is essentially a "Chicago" work. It remains eighty years later an astonishingly sensible book, and it offers exactly what Dewey proposes to offer—namely, a guide for teachers who are puzzled to know what counts as intellectual progress on the part of their students and when they are in its presence. All the same, it contains a good deal of philosophical provocation. The observation that "Primarily, naturally, it is not *we* who think in any actively responsible sense; thinking is rather something that happens in us" is both true and shocking; the further suggestion that to say "*I* think" is to announce an achievement is in the same vein.[54] The whole book is a good example of the strengths and weaknesses of the kind of philosophy that Dewey came to practice. On the debit side, a lot of what Dewey says can appear too obvious to be worth elaborate statement, and the steadiness of Dewey's treatment of his subject makes it hard for the reader to know when sudden illumination will strike. An unkind paraphrase of the book's argument might be that we think in order to reach answers, that we need answers because we have questions, and that good thinking is thinking that is well tailored to produce good answers. By the same token, his view of teachers' tendencies to divide children into bright and dull is fair enough but not unusually insightful: "A boy dull in geometry may prove quick on the uptake when he takes up the subject in manual training; the girl who seems inaccessible to historical facts may respond promptly when it is a question of judging the character and deeds of people of her acquaintance or of fiction."[55]

Nothing is gained by denying features of Dewey's work that readers have complained of for eighty years. There are two things to be said on the other side, and they are of great importance. The first is that Dewey was addressing himself to teachers who found themselves bombarded on all sides with panaceas; he refused to add to their number. He made good sense philosophically credible and morally uplifting, and that is an achievement not to be sneered at. In that spirit he refused to accept that teaching was to be left either to muddling through or to the flair or lack of flair of the individual teacher. There really was a problem—catching the child's attention, providing materials for thought, getting the child to think consecutively, coherently, organizedly, self-propelledly, and relevantly, and watching always for how this contributed to what was to come next—and this problem was not soluble simply or by some trick;

but it was not soluble at all by people who failed to identify it. Or as he put it, the problem was to find "the forms of activity (a) which are most congenial, best adapted, to the immature stage of development; (b) which have the most ulterior promise as preparation for the social responsibilities of adult life; and (c) which, *at the same time,* have the maximum of influence in forming habits of acute observation and of consecutive inference."[56] Once we set up the issue like that, scientific education must look tremendously attractive, the more so to the extent that children themselves devise their own experiments, build their equipment, cooperate in designing and running their own projects, but answer to someone else for the results. Yet even the reader who thinks Dewey has loaded the scales in favor of his view that good education is permeated with the scientific outlook must admit that the contrast between lugubrious modern discussions in which scientific education is assumed to have the one and only purpose of assisting the country in international trade and Dewey's vision of a training simultaneously moral, social, and intellectual is all in Dewey's favor.

A question we must return to but may properly duck for the moment is whether Dewey's approach does not slight training in the humanities. As we have seen several times, Dewey's stress on problem solving, on the social basis of knowledge, and on education as a form of social training looks as though it will make science central to the content of education, will turn history and geography into applied social science, as the study of how societies conceived as problem-solving organizations adapt to their environment by adjusting themselves to its opportunities and demands and adjusting it to their needs and techniques. Where in this is a love of poetry, art, or music for its own sake? Where is the cultivation of the eye and ear and a sense of rhythmic aptness? Dewey in fact thought that human beings had a natural urge to celebrate, commemorate, dance, play, sing, and paint and had no difficulty in encouraging these as school activities. The difficulty lay in giving an account of their developed state, accommodating the thought that Mozart's operas are not "good for" society but that their creation justifies society's existence. The fact that unlike both his old teachers G. S. Morris and G. Stanley Hall—the latter of whom had hankered after a career as a concert pianist—Dewey was tone-deaf and had no interest in or liking for music may explain the comparative feebleness of his remarks about this side of school life. Throughout the 1930s he defended art education in elementary schools as an essential, not a frill, and he knew what he was in favor of. The question of how it fitted into the schema he offered teachers was another matter.

The second point to be made in Dewey's favor is that he was writing against many current practices but with a swelling tide. *We* see as common sense ideas that came to be common sense because liberal educators like Dewey made them common sense. *How We Think* was addressed to working teachers; a large part of the teacher's trade at the turn of the century was conducting recitations, sessions when, as the name suggests, children had to "recite their lessons" and the teachers "heard" them. Dewey felt that unless they were conducted very well, they were diseducative: "To re-cite is to cite again, to tell over and over. If we were to call this period *reiteration*, the designation would hardly bring out more clearly than does the word *recitation* the complete domination of instruction by rehearsing of second-hand information, by memorizing for the sake of producing correct replies at the proper time."[57] When visitors to the United States encounter multiple-choice tests for the first time, they usually share Dewey's sentiments.

When Dewey was writing, the better-trained teachers were accustomed to drawing up lesson plans along lines laid down by Johann Herbart. Herbart had claimed, in Dewey's presentation at any rate, that "there is a single 'general method' uniformly followed by the mind in an effective attack upon any subject. Whether it be a first-grade child mastering the rudiments of number, a grammar-school pupil studying history, or a college student dealing with philology, in each case the first step is preparation, the second presentation, followed in turn by comparison and generalization, ending in the application of the generalizations to new and specific instances."[58]

Suppose the lesson was to be a lesson on rivers, to take Dewey's example. As "preparation," we would begin by getting the children to talk about streams and rivers they had seen, or about water flowing in gutters, and explain the purpose of the lesson; "presentation" would then involve the formal viewing of films, photographs, models, perhaps a visit to look at rivers. Comparison and generalization are the stages by which the *in*essential features of the phenomenon are stripped way, so that a solid sense of what we are supposed to know about rivers is left. Finally this knowledge would be anchored by being applied to new cases, so that children who knew about the Thames, say, would go on to write about the Hudson. Dewey was in something of a rhetorical dilemma vis-à-vis this Herbartian orthodoxy. He did not want to say that teachers should walk into class and play it by ear, but he did want to say that the five-stage schema was too pat, too neat, and in crucial ways misleading. He did not want to exaggerate the difference between his own view and the Herbartian. Still, he did want to insist that the Herbartian schema suggested that imparting concepts and information *for their own sake* was the sum total of instruction. What was lacking was any sense of the purpose of instruction; it left out the whole purpose of acquiring knowledge—namely, the need to solve a problem.

This emerged by contrast with Dewey's own five-stage schema, one that he cheerfully admitted was never followed in all its steps and was very much elicited from our thinking rather than dreamed up a priori. Dewey's five stages of what he called "the complete act of thought" were "*(i)* a felt difficulty; *(ii)* its location and definition; *(iii)* suggestion of a possible solution; *(iv)* development by reasoning of the bearings of the suggestion; *(v)* further observation and experiment leading to its acceptance or rejection; that is, the conclusion of belief or disbelief."[59] The examples Dewey gives show how far he refused to draw a line between method in factual subjects and methods for making decisions. The first example is that of a man who realizes he is pressed for time to get to an appointment and wonders whether to take the subway or the elevated railroad; the second is that of seeing a long white pole with a gold ball at the tip projecting from the prow of a ferry and wondering what its purpose is; the third is more nearly a scientific puzzle: discovering what accounts for the phenomenon of bubbles forming around the rims of newly washed glasses stood upside down to drain. For Dewey, they are illuminated by the same structural analysis. The analysis he offers is informal but interesting because it suggests how difficult it is to map the process that he so plausibly describes by a formal logical analysis. The fourth step, in particular, which consists of converting a hypothesis into a suggested explanation whose relevance to the phenomena to be explained is articulated and made obvious, is exceedingly hard to formalize, though logicians have labored to create a "relevance logic" for many years. In the context of Dewey's long career, the analysis occupies a central place because it is the structure of all scientific (and therefore of all fully articulated) thinking. In the context of this morality tale for teachers, however, it serves a slightly different purpose.

Considering that he wanted to praise the Herbartian scheme, while suggesting it was inadequate, and that he wanted to offer a structure for teaching without cramping the teacher or the child, what Dewey had to do—and what he rather successfully did—was show that his five-stage scheme overlapped the established scheme but brought out more clearly and more aptly something central to the educational process. The crucial difference comes at the very beginning. Dewey's children begin with a problem; the objects of the Herbartian schema begin with a teacher's lesson plan and the goals that the teacher was supposed to announce to the class before she started the lesson. Dewey's children acquire information on their way to solving a problem; information is assimilated in the process of thinking their way through to a solution. As Dewey says, the Herbartian scheme does not, so to speak, exclude the idea that we think about what we learn, but it does strongly suggest that thought is incidental to information acquisition, while Dewey insists that acquiring information is incidental to thinking as problem solving. Not emphasizing this sufficiently made the Herbartian scheme misleading.

In light of the attacks on Dewey and progressive education that came after his death, it is amusing to see him launching preemptive strikes against the degeneration of his ideas that perhaps did occur with his supposed disciple William H. Kilpatrick at Columbia Teachers College.[60] *How We Think* makes thinking an active business, but it is unremittingly hostile to any attempt to reduce education to undisciplined activities meant to keep the children interested. Such an attempt, Dewey thought, was doubly doomed: The children would get bored, and they would learn nothing. Deweyan education involved gaining a capacity to act intelligently—that is, to formulate plans, to take relevant facts into account, to do what he regarded as particularly difficult:

namely, to suspend judgment, hold on to doubt, rethink problems, but never lose sight of the ultimate end in view. Activity for activity's sake was neither here nor there, and Kilpatrick's enthusiastic advocacy of the "project" system was something that Dewey accepted only so long as there was a very clear view of what purposes the projects were to serve and a great deal of dispassionate reflection on how at every stage of the child's intellectual growth the projects now undertaken would propel him or her to the next stage of growth.

Estimating the effect Dewey actually had on American education is extremely difficult. On the whole, his defenders suggest that he had rather little effect; one might parody their argument as the claim that since public education is still absolutely terrible, Dewey cannot have had much effect. His detractors have sometimes suggested that he single-handedly debauched a previously fine system; since he first wrote about education at a time when no more than 7 percent of the population had a high school education and less than half got as many as five years of schooling, this is perhaps an exaggeration. The one example of a school system supposedly devoted to running all its schools on Deweyan lines, the school system at Gary, Indiana, directed by Superintendent William Wirt between 1909 and 1920, evaporates on closer inspection. Wirt's ideas about running a school system were extremely clever. He thought it should be possible to double the use of a given set of school buildings by carefully planning the school day and by designing the schools in such a way that two shifts of children could use the buildings in succession. He organized the schools on what was described as a "platoon system," where half the children would be using the classrooms while the other half were using the facilities for manual training, so that the whole school would be in constant use. He was also an educational radical and in his account of the Gary system appealed to Dewey's ideas about education in support of his own. Yet Wirt's schools were not run on the lines of the Lab School, and from the beginning many of Wirt's critics complained that the only radical thought he possessed was about how to make schools radically cheaper.

This is probably too severe. *Schools of Tomorrow,* jointly written by Dewey and his daughter Evelyn, praised the Gary schools as an exercise in educating children for democracy, and Randolph Bourne's *The Gary Schools* also answered the question I posed earlier by arguing that Wirt had shown that Dewey's ideas were capable of implementation on a mass scale.[61] One may still wonder whether this was true. Wirt himself seemed always much prouder of the fact that his schoolchildren were competent to rebuild their own schools from scratch if the occasion were to arise than of anything more "Deweyan." Dewey himself never seemed to be quite sure which of his ideas were capable of large-scale implementation in the American public school system and which might be hard to implement outside the setting of the Lab School. The Lab School taught classes of eight and ten, while most public schools had classes of forty and often more. *Schools of Tomorrow* praises the Gary schools—Dewey never saw them firsthand, but his daughter Evelyn did so—more for the role they played in the community and their adaptability to different needs than for their espousal of his own view of child development. This communitarian passion sustained all his writings on education. As we shall see below, Dewey's desire that the school should not be an "apart institution" led him to set great store by the educational side of ventures like Jane Addams's Hull House, and it was this facet of the Gary schools that he admired. The idea of the school in the Gary system was that it should be open all the year-round, that it should be a community center as well as a school, narrowly considered, that it should offer courses on a variety of bases and for a variety of ages.[62] It was thus the product of the same frame of mind that produced in Britain in the 1930s and 1940s "village colleges" that housed the local school, together with meeting rooms, and very often space for child welfare clinics and other social services. It would be easy to approve of such initiatives for any number of different reasons, from the efficiency of housing as many activities as possible in one place for maximum utilization of the buildings to the virtues of using the place to which parents had anyway to bring their children as the place where they could also get useful information, use recreational facilities for themselves, and be tempted to undertake adult education. Such reasons might very well suggest Dewey's desire that the school should both *be* a community and be *of* its community.

Among the reasons why Dewey's influence was never likely to be as great as critics and defenders have claimed, three stand out. They are obvious, but they are conclusive. One is that Dewey schools would be expensive; they need small classes, a lot of equipment, and elaborate internal administrative arrangements so that teachers can spend time and attention rethinking what they are doing. Dewey's vision of the school as a place of experiment was, it must be remembered, not a vision of an "experimental school" in the sense of a place where eccentric, novel, or surprising things went on, but the vision of a place permeated by the experimental spirit. It could only be run by teachers who were able to get together to discuss their goals, their techniques, their successes and failures, and prospects for change. Second, Dewey schools are appallingly demanding of their teachers. Dewey may have assured teachers that they were doing God's work, but God's work is hard work. Since Dewey's educational philosophy was so determinedly teleological—at every stage the child was seen as a creature about to embark on the *next* stage of growth—the teacher could not concentrate only on the child's current attainments and interests. Every encounter with a child was an occasion to see how the moment might be turned to advantage in giving him or her a grasp of arithmetic, languages, physics, chemistry, biology, geography, history, and whatever other skills we wish them to acquire. There never were many teachers' colleges capable of turning out teachers with that range of skills, and considering the rates of pay for primary teachers, it was unlikely that many people with the ability to learn what this demanded were going to volunteer to become teachers. The third reason is that it is simply unclear just what a "Deweyan" school is like. Dewey was a philosopher. He was not an administrator, as William Wirt was, and he was not a teacher of teachers, as William Kilpatrick was. His writings were chronically described as impenetrably difficult. Indeed, readers today would often be hard put to it to decide just what their implications are for the organization of schools and the content of their syllabi. Anyone defending Dewey against his critics has a much easier time showing what he does *not* believe about the purpose of education than in giving a concrete account of what his views entail for school reform.[63] That is not altogether a complaint against Dewey; just as a "Christian" education, for example, might take many forms but would always be recognizably unlike a secular education, so a "Deweyan" school might take many different forms but would be recognizably unlike the main alternatives: It would be secular, self-conscious, friendly to science, hostile to standardized tests and academic examinations, and a good deal more besides. But under that general umbrella a good many alternatives might plausibly shelter.

When critics complain of progressive education, they have in mind a host of different grievances, not all of which fit together smoothly. For instance, critics of progressivism in education sometimes complain that students learn too little about serious academic subjects and sometimes that they learn nothing practical and useful for earning a living. The first complaint would clearly be met by insisting on four years of Latin and Greek, but it would do little for the second; the second would be met by universal computer literacy, but it would do little to meet the first complaint. Again, critics commonly complain that progressive educationalists underestimate the need for discipline and allow schools to turn into disorganized playgrounds, but they also complain that schools turn out children who have too little initiative, which is not ordinarily produced by rigid discipline. Assessing Dewey's progressivism is made difficult by the absence of a single clear alternative.

All the same, in defending Dewey against the usual complaints, one must not lose sight of his real vulnerability. He was, in general, more interested in making children competent members of their society than in encouraging the very cleverest to scale the highest intellectual peaks. He emphasized the importance of tradition, but only as something to *use,* and there is certainly one form of intellectual conservatism that sees tradition as something which we immerse ourselves in and test ourselves by rather than as a mere stock of useful resources. The introspective nonjoiner gets rather short shrift in Dewey's universe; no doubt many such children are alienated and isolated and ought to be encouraged to be more sociable, but many more are imaginative, quirky, original, and simply working out their own intellectual salvation. Bertrand Russell's grandmother gave him a Bible, inscribed with her favorite moral admonition: "Thou shalt not follow a multitude to do evil." That ethical individualism, that ability to stand out against the crowd, is something Dewey never sufficiently emphasized in his educational writings. It is as though he thought the main hazard that children faced was that of estrangement from their surroundings—and in 1890s Chicago and pre-1914 New York he had every reason to do so—but forgot that one of the resources we want children to acquire from their education is the ability to put up with estrangement from their fellows when sufficient intellectual or moral reasons demand it.

Schools and Settlements: Dewey and Jane Addams

Having argued throughout this chapter that Dewey's educational theory was in the ordinary sense of the term less a theory of education and more a theory of the place of education in the politics of modern society, I must say some last things about Dewey's politics during his Chicago years and about one of the radicalizing influences on him, that of Jane Addams. When Dewey arrived in Chicago, Jane Addams was already well known for her work at Hull House, the Chicago settlement house that she had founded in 1889. Addams founded Hull House on her return from a European tour during which she had spent some time at Toynbee Hall in London, the settlement house founded in 1883 in memory of the young economist Arnold Toynbee.[64] The politics of the settlement house movement are an intriguing part of the politics of the late nineteenth century, in both Britain and America. The British experience is better chronicled than the American, but the interesting thing is how far the sentiments behind the movement were the same on both sides of the Atlantic and how far the same kinds of people became involved for the same kinds of reasons.[65]

In England the memory of T. H. Green was much invoked, and he was something of a lay patron saint to the movement; but it was essentially fueled by a more orthodox Christian sense of the charitable imperative. The "gospel of service" that featured so largely in the social thought of the 1880s and 1890s, whether among those who preached the Social Gospel in the form that Walter Rauschenbusch later made famous or who preached the subordination of economic values to the value of service as Richard T. Ely did, led readily to the thought that social work was a moral commandment to the comfortable. Ely and Rauschenbusch were the American counterparts to Canon Barnett, the radical Church of England clergyman who was at the center of the social work movement in the East End of London. Jane Addams's ambitions were not fueled by the distinctively Christian socialist ideals of the English art historian and cultural critic John Ruskin and his ally the London economist F. D. Maurice that had inspired many of her English counterparts. Nonetheless, she had read Ruskin and Carlyle, her ally and companion Ellen Starr was a convinced Christian socialist, and her own conception of democracy as an ethical brotherhood was in the same vein.

The democratic side of the movement was very important to Jane Addams, and to Dewey, of course. Like her English counterparts, Jane Addams was fiercely insistent that the settlement movement was not a matter of going among the poor as a Lady Bountiful. The good she proposed to do was not done *for* the poor or *to* the poor. Indeed, one aim of the settlements was to provide for the moral health of those who financed them and worked in them. By sharing the lives of the poor and by opening to them intellectual and cultural opportunities they could not otherwise find, the givers would be as enriched as the receivers.

Hull House was thus very much in the spirit of the university settlement houses that were established in the East End of London and those founded elsewhere in the United States, such as the Henry Street Settlement in New York, which Lillian Wald had set up a few years before Hull House opened its doors. The English founders had aimed to re-create the setting of an Oxford or Cambridge college in the middle of the slums, not with a view to running anything so out of place as an undergraduate college in poverty-stricken terrain but to create a sense of fellowship and community that would then spread downward and outward through the lives of parents, children, young people at risk of turning into juvenile delinquents, and, in the American case especially, new immigrants, who needed to be taught English and the rudiments of civics.

When it was a matter of the tough- and practical-minded Jane Addams, things did not remain on the level of widening intellectual and moral horizons. The discovery of the extent of municipal corruption in Chicago fired her with indignation, and she waged a long and strenuous battle against the diversion of public funds to the pockets of politicians and their supporters. How much good it did is hard to estimate; she did not dislodge the bosses and the ward heelers from city government, but she may well have forced them to attend more diligently to the needs of their constituents. Addams understood better than most reformers how it was that the boss system could flourish in a society of immigrants, that it was a matter not just of wickedness on the part of politicians but of large and otherwise unmet needs on the part of the immigrants. By the time writers like Robert Merton explained the functions of the boss system as filling a gap left by the missing welfare state, this was old hat, but Miss Addams had understood the point some fifty years before.[66] She also waged a long and equally untriumphant battle to rescue prostitutes from their customers and "protectors" and introduced Dewey to Chicago by taking him on a tour of the red-light district.

Other residents of Hull House, of whom Florence Kelley was the most famous, fought for labor legislation to reduce the hours of work for everyone and for health and safety legislation to safeguard children and women in particular. During the long-drawn-out depression that gripped the American economy for much of the 1890s, Addams ran a feeding program to keep alive as many as she could of the unemployed and destitute. Her memoirs, *Twenty Years at Hull-House*, give a vivid impression of a place that was whatever need dictated: a maternity hospital when a single mother went into labor and could get no help from the stalwart Irish matrons who thought she deserved all she got; a terminal ward when one of the regulars died of consumption; a refuge for battered wives; a manual training shop for immigrant boys; a library; a self-help probation service; and so on. From the beginning it added an art gallery, meeting rooms, a hostel for working girls, and a nursery, and over forty years it grew to occupy an entire large city block on Halsted Street and to offer many of the resources of a city's education department and most of its social services. The distinctive side of what Addams did was what happened at Hull House itself, for it was there that the lectures and concerts and discussions took place that enlivened its members' and visitors' existences.

Addams and Dewey became close friends. He was one of the most admired lecturers in Hull House history, and he served on the board of trustees until Jane Addams died. She in turn taught him much he might not otherwise have noticed about the politics of a big city; those of his readers who think that Dewey was astonishingly naïve about the workings of the political system and about the real causes of the irrationality and inefficiency of most modern societies may be grateful that he had Jane Addams to take him on guided tours of the red-light district and to teach him about the meat-packing factories and the insanitoriness of the food that emerged from those hideous places. His second daughter, Jane Mary, was named Jane after Jane Addams, and Mary after Jane Addams's great friend and ally Mary Smith, and Dewey's friendship with Addams survived even his flat-footed and silly attacks on pacifism during the First World War.

Settlement house politics were very much on Dewey's emotional and moral wavelength. Hull House was intended, in Jane Addams's words, to be "a good neighbor" to the poverty-stricken people round about, and Dewey's concern for the politics of the local community fitted perfectly into this ambition. Dewey and Addams saw eye to eye on the iniquities of plutocrats, such as the railroad magnate George Pullman, and Dewey greatly admired her savage account of the Pullman strike of 1894 in "A Modern Lear." Addams was not a socialist, even though she sheltered many socialists under her roof. She was an enthusiastic supporter of trade unions, whose organizers she aided with money, places to meet, help with creating and distributing circulars, and an education in the rudiments of industrial sociology, but always from a reformist point of view. Like Dewey, she wanted to raise the esteem in which working people of all sorts were held, not to launch proletarian revolution. Like him, she was mostly reviled by persons to her right, but not infrequently from the left. Before the Pullman strike of 1894, for instance, she had been a friend of George Pullman's; during the strike she had believed that somehow she could speak to both sides. By the end of the strike she thought that it was terrible that unionists resorted to violence and that discussion went by the board but that the blame lay with Pullman in particular and with the employing classes in general. "A Modern Lear" went much beyond this general disillusionment. The theme was that just as King Lear found out the hard way that loving his daughters only as dependent and weak creatures was not enough to secure their affection, so George Pullman's paternalistic treatment of his workers denied their standing as free and self-governing citizens. It was therefore absurd for him to feel affronted by what he saw as the workers' ingratitude.[67] This was very much Dewey's line.

Characteristically Dewey celebrated the settlement as essentially a place of education. In "The School as Social Centre," a lecture to the National Council for Education, he struck a very 1990s note and argued for the work of the settlement in doing what community colleges and similar institutions have tried to do in the past forty years or so. He stressed the decline of traditional authority and deplored the growth of juvenile delinquency of mild and less mild kinds. Aptly in the setting of turn-of-the-century Chicago, but he could have said as much today, he emphasized the way immigrant households are broken up by the strains of migration: "[W]ise observers in New York and Chicago have recently sounded a note of alarm. They call attention to the fact that in some respect the children are too rapidly, I will not say Americanized, but too rapidly de-nationalized."[68] Like many of his contemporaries, he thought that the United States was highly effective in *de*racinating new arrivals but perfectly hopeless at *re*racinating them.

This was a thought Jane Addams had already embraced. She was very depressed by the way immigrants lost touch with the culture of their old country and found themselves adrift in their new environment. Hull House was devoted to the delicate task of showing its clients how to adjust to America without losing their attachment to the Old World. This was a novel task. The British had thought of themselves as establishing their own culture in a new place and had no pangs of *cultural* adjustment. By and large, Scandinavians and Protestant Germans had scarcely more trouble; they were for the most part literate and perfectly capable of establishing new communities where they felt at home. Migrants from southern and eastern Europe, Catholics, and Jews faced a much more hostile environment than even their Irish predecessors had done, and many of them had few intellectual resources even in their native languages. Addams devoted herself to the double task of instilling in them a knowledge of, and a pride in, their ancestral culture along with the language and other skills they needed in their new home.

As he had done before, Dewey stressed the extent to which American society was a mobile, swiftly changing society, in which old skills became out-of-date almost as soon as they were acquired. This gave places like Hull House a particular social function; adults needed to be kept abreast of the skills and the learning they needed to keep up with a changing world. Even more, they needed not to be left to molder in an intellectual, cultural, and emotional ghetto. Here, again, was where Hull House's theatrical performances, poetry readings, literature classes, and the like were appropriate to the needs Dewey perceived. In effect, the moral of the lecture was that Hull House was a wonderful school and that schools ought, so far as it lay within them, to aspire to the condition of Hull House. Before I move on to the moment at which Dewey's liberalism was tested to breaking point by the stresses of the First

World War, and his friendship with Jane Addams nearly so, one last point is worth making. Addams briefly leaned toward a Tolstoyan view of the world, until an encounter with Tolstoy himself sent her back to the practical good works of Hull House; still, she was one of nature's pacifists and, by the same token, a person who could not really see why mankind divided itself into nation-states that then set out to fight one another. Dewey could never move into the Tolstoyan camp.

Dewey's capacity for occupying the middle of the road is nicely illustrated by his relations with Jane Addams. At their first meeting they had a long conversation that Dewey reported to his wife. Jane Addams went on at length about the wickedness of conflict; he was, he said, half convinced while talking to her, but not on reflection.[69] Once he had begun to think in evolutionary terms, he could hardly flinch from Darwin's emphasis on progress through struggle. Yet, as I have already said, he did not endorse class conflict, personal antagonism, or nationalistic self-assertion. Compared with Hegel, Dewey was not an aggressive nationalist, but he was a nationalist of sorts. His emphasis on education and on the education of the immigrant was unabashedly an emphasis on the Americanization of newcomers. It was not a simple "melting pot" theory that he held, but Dewey wanted to see newcomers both *made* to learn English and *helped* to learn English by being given free classes at convenient times. He was less ready than Miss Addams to serve people as he found them; he also wanted to turn them into good Americans, public-spirited citizens, and members of the "great community." These things are all matters of nuance, but it is worth recalling that Dewey's communitarianism is more than a communitarianism of the neighborhood. He was a benign, mild, and good-natured nationalist, but he was a nationalist.

Five

Pragmatism at War

Dewey was at the peak of his intellectual powers during his years at Chicago. His intellectual fertility and his capacity for sustained hard thought were at their greatest in that decade, and Dewey lived for the next several decades on the philosophical resources he accumulated in Chicago. Nevertheless, the manner of his leaving the University of Chicago was distressing to all concerned. In April 1904 Dewey abruptly resigned when he decided that he could bear no more conflicts with Harper over the running of the School of Education. An impartial observer would think almost everyone behaved badly during the two years before Dewey left, but Dewey worse than anyone. In 1901 he appointed Alice principal of the Lab School, and in 1903 principal of the new school formed by combining the Dewey School with the elementary school of the former Chicago Institute (now the School) of Education. Dewey consulted no one and was unable to see how this laid him open to charges of nepotism.

Nor could he see that Mrs. Dewey was a bad boss who was much too hard on her teachers. In addition, Dewey squabbled with Wilbur Jackman, who ran the School of Education until Parker's death in 1902 and was Dewey's second-in-command thereafter. Dewey slighted the faculty of the School of Education as mere trainers of teachers, and they complained to President Harper. Harper behaved badly, too. He never made it clear to Alice Dewey that her appointment was improper and thoroughly alienated both Deweys by first seeming to approve her appointment and then going on to insist it was only a temporary expedient for the first year of the merger. Dewey was eventually so annoyed that he resigned from Chicago without bothering to find another post to go to. He wrote to William James, and Harvard nibbled; but nothing came of it. He also wrote to James McKeen Cattell, the head of the department of philosophy and psychology at Columbia. He became mildly anxious about his prospects, but Columbia soon came up with a satisfactory offer. His salary was initially less than it had been at Chicago; but with the addition of a one-semester lecturership at Teachers College, an adequate salary was stitched together, and the Deweys arrived in New York, never to leave.

In New York Dewey played a more active role in public affairs than he had in Chicago. He was instrumental in setting up the city teachers' union and was for a long time its president. He wrote more widely than before on the needs of the teaching profession, as well as on issues of school organization and the politics of teaching. Intellectually he operated with the ideas he had developed in Chicago. As we saw in the last chapter, *How We Think* was only accidentally a New York book, and *Ethics* even more so. Even *Human Nature and Conduct*, published after the war and based on lectures delivered at Stanford in 1918, was in many respects an abbreviation and popularization of the themes of his *Ethics* and thus a recapitulation of themes from Dewey's Chicago graduate seminars of the late 1890s.

This is not to belittle Dewey's later work. It is merely to say that his search for a satisfactory philosophical position had come to an end by 1900 and was only reopened during the search for an adequate account of experience that began with *Experience and Nature* in 1925. Dewey had discovered that the world did not need to be sustained by the Hegelian Concept any more than it needed to be sustained by the Christian God. The tasks of describing how we think and of suggesting ways in which we might think better were still to be performed, but not with a view to finding transcendental guarantees that we think well.

If his intellectual life had thus reached a stable state, his domestic life became less happy. Once again Dewey and the family set out for Europe for a long break between jobs, and again disaster struck. They had had three more children in Chicago, Gordon, Lucy, and Jane. This time their eight-year-old son, Gordon, caught typhoid fever on the boat over, seemed to have got better, then relapsed and died. Alice and the other children continued their tour of Europe, and she and John characteristically chose to restore their family by adopting an eight-year-old Italian boy, Sabino. Oddly enough, Sabino was the only one who followed in his adoptive father's footsteps: He became a teacher and then a very successful designer of school equipment.[1] Brave though Sabino's adoption was, it could not disguise the fact that this second blow was really more than Alice Dewey could bear. From then until her death in 1927 she became increasingly tired, withdrawn, and querulous. The hypercritical style that had upset her assistant teachers at the Laboratory School led several of Dewey's colleagues and students at Columbia to marvel at the saintly way he endured her ill temper. Ninety years later it is easier to sympathize with her and to regret that her own voice has been muffled; she insisted on having her papers and letters destroyed on her death. She was an original, radical, and energetic woman who found too few outlets for that energy, and Dewey's saintliness may well have been more of an irritant than a consolation. Toward the end of her life Alice was troubled by heart problems, which must have exacerbated her anxieties and these in turn her heart troubles.

Dewey's public life thrived even while his private life did not.[2] Needless to say, he never mentioned his private distresses to outsiders, never complained, left no record of them, and only once late in the war strayed even slightly from the path of strict marital virtue. Although the view of human existence that we get in Dewey's ethics made it slightly mysterious that human beings have private lives, private ambitions, and private miseries at all—so thoroughly did Dewey explain our inner selves as reflections of outward social training—that view of the world seems to have helped him to subordinate private misery to public-spirited work and to have given him an enviable easiness about his own temperament and intelligence. It is no wonder that when Bertrand Russell met him for the first time in 1914, he observed in a letter to Ottoline Morrell that of all the American philosophers, the only one he liked was Dewey. "He has a large slow-moving mind, very empirical and candid, with something of the impassivity and impartiality of a natural force."[3]

Dewey spent slightly over a quarter of a century on the regular faculty of Columbia University. He was appointed in 1904 and retired in 1930; the next decade he spent as an emeritus but active professor, drawing a full salary and continuing to teach graduate students. It has been observed that Dewey's active participation in politics of one sort and another increased dramatically once he got to New York.[4] The connection with New York seems largely accidental. Dewey did not take up a chair at Columbia in order to free himself for political activism, but he was freed of the burdens of the Lab School and the institute, had none of the duties of the chairman of a department, taught exactly what he chose, and was very much his own master. He was already a hero to schoolteachers, and until the outbreak of World War I it was they who occupied most of his political attention.

Dewey's larger political engagements reached their high and low points in and after World War I. American military involvement in the conflict lasted only nineteen months, from April 1917 until the armistice of November 1918. Yet it is not too much to say that between 1915 and 1925 the war and its meaning for his vision of the world were constantly on Dewey's mind. Indeed, Dewey's espousal of near isolationism during the 1930s tempts one to say that the war was on his mind from 1915 until he died thirty-seven years later. Although this chapter ranges over many other issues besides Dewey's attitude to World War I, the war and its impact on Dewey's thinking are the intellectual crux. Vocational education, academic freedom, the nature and virtues of democracy were subjects he dealt with at greater length, and with more poise, but the war shook both Dewey and his ideas to their foundations.

Dewey played a more visible and publicly influential role in American politics in the 1930s than during World War I; the importance of his support for American intervention in 1917 is certainly not that Dewey supplied an intellectual backing for intervention in whose absence American troops might never have left home. They would have been sent even if the American intelligentsia, such as it was, had been entirely opposed to their going. Once the United States had decided to defend the freedom of the high seas against Germany, but not against Britain, it was only a matter of time before war occurred. But Dewey was one of the prowar intellectual elite, and at odds with many of his usual allies and former students as a result. He was not a very important member of that elite. Dewey was part of the influential group of progressive intellectuals centered on the *New Republic,* whose support Woodrow Wilson certainly cherished, but he had much less influence than the editor Herbert Croly or the much younger and more energetic Walter Lippmann.[5] They were close to the policy makers, and Dewey was not.

If Dewey was not especially important to the war, the war was overwhelmingly important to Dewey. The intellectual importance of the war was that Dewey's political philosophy found in it a test case designed by fate to place his instrumentalism in the worst possible light. The test was not of Dewey's choosing and was one he would have given much not to confront. War in general, and America's role in World War I in particular, raised intellectually and emotionally baffling questions about pragmatism's ability to find something to say about events that were not easily explained as intelligent problem solving. The war raised the question whether pragmatism was incurably emotionally shallow: Was it light-minded about death and violence and about ethnic and national passions; was pragmatism a doctrine only for people facing issues less urgent than life and death and with plenty of time to resolve them intelligently?[6] The verdict of the disillusioned Randolph Bourne was that instrumentalism failed all along the line.[7] Though Bourne's objections to pragmatism were not *philosophically* compelling in all respects, there was something persuasive in the thought that Dewey's pragmatism was essentially a peacetime doctrine and credible only in a society that was in most respects harmonious, prosperous, and morally at ease with itself.

This was a shaft more easily aimed at Dewey than at others. William James had died in 1910, and if he had still been alive, he would not have been vulnerable to such complaints. James's sense of the irreducible plurality of human passions and his interest in the quirkiness and peculiarity of individual lives—not to mention the fact that his father had raised a regiment of infantry in the Civil War—made James much readier than Dewey could ever be to appreciate the furious emotions that led people into war and the yet more furious emotions that war stirred up. James's famous essay on the need to find a "moral equivalent of war" testified to his unwillingness to write the wilder and more aggressive passions out of the human psyche and to his sense that they needed to be given some nonlethal form of exercise if life was not to become intolerably gray and boring. Though he supported American involvement in World War I and wrote critical essays on the pacifists who opposed it, Dewey was himself essentially a pacifist, and his emotional reach did not extend so far as James's.

In this Dewey was like his master T. H. Green and unlike their common master Hegel. He was, for that matter, unlike his teacher G. S. Morris, who had served in the northern armies in the Civil War, and unlike his Chicago friend and colleague Thorstein Veblen. Veblen was a very curious mixture of the tough cynic and passionate scientist, whose wholesale contempt for the debased intellectual standards of American colleges and universities was finally ventilated in 1918 in *The Higher Learning in America* and whose great fear during World War I was for European learning. As his *Theory of the Leisure Class* made clear, he did not care for the excesses of the warrior impulse, but he understood what they sprang from, and he refused to reproach the barbarian spirit.[8] Moreover, when Veblen defended the war against Germany, he did it with gusto. Dewey understood well enough that there were worse evils than war but had little sense of how to talk about either the evils of war or the evils that war might avert, and he found it impossible to sound a convincing note. Early in the war, before American involvement, he wrote rather as though the United States ought to do something, so long as that something did not involve joining in a European war; then, as events began to push the United States toward involvement on the side of Britain and France, he seemed to have little to say other than to urge his countrymen to swim with the tide. In this he was pretty much at one with them. From the sinking of the *Lusitania* in the spring of 1915 onward, Woodrow Wilson found himself in the difficult position of trying to appease a public that wanted him to stand firm but not to fight. As a commentator observed at the time, "How both these desires can be satisfied, it is difficult to see."[9]

World War I was an unnecessary war, and its hideous consequences were all too undeniable. To that extent, being uninvolved was better than being involved. The narrower question of what the United States ought to have done once the war had dragged on into 1917 is harder to answer. The Allies were—in spite of the presence of czarist Russia in the alliance—the more liberal and democratic force, and they very much needed American assistance at the moment the United States intervened. As in World War II, the presence of the United States on one side settled the question of which side would win and brought an end to an interminable conflict. The Allies' need was obvious. Russia was close to military and political collapse by the time the United States was ready to join; America's entry into the war in April 1917 came soon after the Russian Revolution of March 1917 had deposed the czar and installed a provisional government that was itself soon to be ousted by Lenin and Trotsky in the October Revolution. By 1917 the French Army had been weakened by mutinies and by the previous year's horrors at Verdun; the British Army had suffered terrible casualties in the 1916 offensives on the Somme. Neither the French nor the British were capable of decisive offensive action. If America was to rescue democracy, this was the moment.

There was, on the other hand, much to be said for the view that the United States should take advantage of the exhausted condition of all sides to bully them into making a nonpunitive peace. How plausible an American role as uninvited arbitrator could have been has been debated ever since. American neutrality was far from impartial as between the warring parties, and Germany, Austria-Hungary, and Turkey would have had to have been in a very bad way to accept American arbitration. The history of arbitration throughout the war had been that both sides made conciliatory gestures only when they feared military defeat; whenever one side suggested a readiness to negotiate, the other became more intransigent and redoubled its efforts on the battlefield.

If there was to be military intervention, it could be only on one side. France and Britain were halfhearted democracies, inasmuch as neither yet had female suffrage (nor did the United States), and France was not to adopt universal adult suffrage until 1945. They were more ostentatiously class-based societies and less committed to equality of opportunity than the United States. They were nonetheless ruled by liberal, constitutional governments, and they allowed the common people a substantial voice in their own affairs. However partial these achievements, they marked a substantial difference between the guiding principles of the French and British governments and those of the absolutist, militarist monarchies of Germany and Austria-Hungary. In 1917 Dewey signed up for the war to end all wars and the war to make the world safe for democracy. Four years later he believed that he had been taken for a ride and that gullible Americans had been duped by the imperialist ruling classes of Britain and France.

Even while he was writing in support of the war, he was being savaged by his former friends and admirers. The two epic confrontations of Dewey's career—epic because both parties were writing at the top of their form, were fully engaged, and understood exactly what they were replying to—were those with Randolph Bourne in 1917 and 1918 and with Walter Lippmann in the 1920s. It was no accident that the confrontations concerned democracy and war, though Bourne and Dewey fell out only over the war, while he and Lippmann were first of one mind over the war and then at odds over postwar democracy and the possibility of "outlawing" war. Dewey had many other arguments with many other critics. Those on purely philosophical matters were often marked by a sharpness surprising in the mild-mannered Dewey (his critics complained that he never said what he meant clearly enough for them to get a grip on it, and Dewey felt he had not been given sufficient credit for at least trying), but these professional disputes were at least in intention collegial in tone.[10] Bourne and Lippmann were of Dewey's own intellectual weight and on most matters close enough allies for their criticisms to matter deeply.

The Last of the Peace

We need to locate Dewey in context before we plunge into his war work. By 1914 he had been living in New York for ten years. To the external observer, domestic life seemed cheerful but unsettled; the family moved house every year or so. Mrs. Dewey was not easy to please in this or most other matters, but Dewey himself seems to have been pretty restless to judge by his frequent moves after Alice's death.[11] Dewey was privately under a good deal of strain. Max Eastman, who was a student of Dewey's at Columbia, remarked that anyone other than Dewey would have found Alice intolerable.[12] This seems to have made little difference to the children. Although their mother never recovered her former energy and enthusiasm for life after Gordon's death, family life appears to have gone on happily enough for them, if less so for their father. Sidney Hook suggests that Dewey's children were oddly unappreciative of their father's intellectual reputation and that with the exception of Evelyn, who wrote *Schools of Tomorrow* with him, oddly uninterested in what he most cared for. A friendlier rendering might be that Dewey was a wonderfully affectionate parent, if not always fully present in either body or mind, and the children attended to that and not to his remote, adult concerns. All the same, they, too, could be lost from sight. Entertaining tales were told of Dewey's forgetfulness about the children. On one occasion Dewey was deep in conversation with a colleague when a small boy accosted him and asked for money. Dewey handed over a nickel and complained mildly, " 'The trouble with boys in this city is that they're always asking you for money.' The friend looked astonished, and said, 'Well, Professor Dewey, isn't that *your* son?' John looked and said, 'Why, yes, I guess it is.' "[13]

He was a cheerful and unauthoritarian father. Another Columbia story suggests the style. Returning from work with a friend, he found his children had flooded the bathroom. For a moment he was at a loss, but one of the children cried out, "Don't stand there like a fool, John. Get a broom and help!"[14] Eastman remembered Dewey as perfectly happy to work amid any degree of childish noise and disorder. This was an enduring characteristic: Dewey and his second wife adopted two young Belgian refugees in 1946, when he was very nearly eighty-seven years old, and he happily resumed the habit of typing away while the chair he sat on and the desk he sat at were festooned with children.

Political life became lively and interesting almost immediately on his arrival at Columbia. Even before the New York teachers had decided to form a union in 1913, urged on by Dewey more cogently than by anyone else, he spent a good deal of time addressing them on issues of school management as well as education more narrowly conceived; between 1912 and 1913 he urged the formation of a union, and in 1915 he encouraged his colleagues in the newly formed union to join the American Federation of Labor. In 1906 he became briefly notorious when Maxim Gorky and his mistress, the actress Mme. Andreeva, visited the United States. They were put up at Hull House by Jane Addams, who was immediately accused of being herself a raging "Red." When they came to New York, no hotel would accommodate them, for reasons of sexual propriety rather than for political reasons. Mrs. Dewey was ready to accept whatever damage to the Deweys' reputation was involved in taking them in, and the Deweys duly did so. It is said that the furor over this incident was so great that Dewey stood in some danger of losing his job, but Alice Dewey declared that she would see her husband and children starve before she saw them abandon their principles. Max Eastman, the source of this tale, may have been embroidering a bit, but the remark imputed to Alice Dewey was certainly in character.[15]

Migration from Chicago did not mean that Dewey lost touch with the settlement house movement. The most famous of the New York settlement houses had been established at Henry Street on the Lower East Side by Lillian Wald, and Dewey was soon recruited to lecture there. The Henry Street Settlement was interested in a practical project close to Dewey's heart, the vocational training of poor city children. One of the subjects this chapter shortly takes up is Dewey's views on vocational education; we have already seen his emphasis on linking the practical management of existence to education through teaching children to cook, showing them how to construct simple mechanical and other sorts of apparatus, and so on. For half a dozen years from about 1910 onward, he was increasingly embroiled in the heated arguments that set the defenders of a system of separate industrial training schools against those who thought that such schools would involve an expensive duplication of facilities—among them William Wirt in Gary, Indiana—and those who thought that it was educationally undesirable to hive off manual training because it would stigmatize "nonacademic" education and exaggerate the already exaggerated class bias of education. Dewey was a member of both these oppositions. Henry Street's efforts to provide some basic training and to inform the settlement's students where they could find the best vocational training afterward, on the other hand, were just the sort of thing he approved of.[16] As Dewey observed in his introduction to Henry Street's directory of training courses in the city, it had been the settlement house movement that had led the way *negatively* by pressing for child labor laws to keep children in school and out of the workplace until they were old enough to work full-time without damage to their health and intelligence, and now Henry Street was leading *positively* by providing training and pressing for a more organized public system.

The influence of strong-minded women at home and in the settlement house naturally led Dewey in the direction of the women's suffrage movement, and he was an active supporter of the New York campaign for votes for women. One of the better-known stories about Dewey in his guise of "absent-minded professor" is that he was getting ready to march in one parade, picked up the banner that was thrust into his hands, and was mildly surprised by the number of amused grins he attracted as the column marched down the street. Only at the end did he look to see what he had been carrying: "Men Can Vote; Why Can't I?"[17] Here, too, he was prominent in the movement only as a distinguished intellectual supporter, not as an organizer or an original thinker. His reasons for supporting female suffrage were traditional "new liberal" reasons. It was not just that women had distinct interests which they needed to be able to promote through the ballot box, though up to a point he thought that there were some—conditions of work for women, family issues generally, and the opening of professions for women—that fell into that category; it was rather that only those with a vote had an incentive to take an informed interest in the political and social world around them. A person who was only half aware of what was going on around her was only half a person; the extension of the ballot to women would be an extension of full participation in the modern world. It is hard not to warm to Dewey when reading his reply to a questionnaire on votes for women. Asked whether an educational qualification ought to be required, he observed that it would be time to worry about the intelligence of women once men had themselves got educated. In later years, too, he did his bit for planned parenthood by chairing Margaret Sanger's meetings in New York and so providing her with some respectable backing at a time when she was much under attack for her advocacy of birth control, companionate marriage, and a more enlightened attitude toward sexual matters generally.

Columbia and Its Pleasures

In spite of having no official relationship with Teachers College, Dewey took an increasing interest in its activities, particularly after 1914 when the college began to do research work in earnest, and Dewey was one of the seven professors who constituted the department of educational research. In 1909 his great admirer and disciple William H. Kilpatrick joined the Teachers College faculty; as the longtime head of the foundations of education department he imparted a decidedly Deweyan stamp to the compulsory courses in the philosophy and sociology of education that his department offered the students. Kilpatrick was a more flamboyant figure than Dewey and readier to take ideas to extremes than his hero. Nonetheless, the three basic themes that he clung to through thick and thin were Deweyan enough: "that everything about the schools should prepare the child for a preferred kind of social living; that method should always involve purposeful activity; and that the curriculum should consist of what is useful in the present rather than what is to be used in the future."[18] One might demur at the third point, seeing how strongly Dewey emphasized the need for a constant awareness of what was to come next in the child's development, but construed as a refusal to adopt the old-fashioned practice of telling children that they would "eventually" see the point of the Latin pluperfect subjunctive and other rebarbative items, it was something Dewey would have concurred in. The younger people who came in during the 1920s had views of their own, but the so-called Kilpatrick Discussion Group, which met for the first time in 1928 and disbanded on Kilpatrick's retirement a decade later, counted Dewey among its members for a while and established "John Dewey's Page" in the journal *Social Frontier,* which it put out from 1934 onward.[19]

Teachers College altogether got the reputation of being a "Deweyan" school.[20] This understated the diversity of views that the institution actually contained. The faculty who taught in the departments concerned with curriculum design and the relationship between subject matter and techniques of instruction were almost as a matter of institutional logic hostile to the pretensions of the foundations department, something to be borne in mind when one tries to guess how much impact Dewey's ideas had on the college's students as opposed to its faculty. Some indication of the gulf between the faculty's taste for philosophical speculation and the exigencies of the teachers' world is provided by the history of the college's schools. None was a laboratory for Deweyan experimentation; none was especially unorthodox, though all were progressive. The Horace Mann schools were very good, expensive, fee-paying schools that sent almost all their students to good colleges; the Lincoln School was more experimental, but it experimented in the reverse of a Deweyan direction. It was set up on the urging of Abraham Flexner to meet what he thought was needed—discipline and high academic standards. Even more of the Lincoln School's pupils went on to college. Against the demands of parents and the entrance requirements of colleges, imagination has always had an uphill struggle. Even if the college's schools had been much more radical than they were in fact, their impact on the rest of American education might well have been slight. One reason why Teachers College had been established in the first place was the experience of American liberals who had gone to Germany; they found German educationalists imaginative, open-minded, and kindly and German schools old-fashioned, rigid, and brutal.

Among the college faculty who took an interest in the philosophy of education, there was by no means unanimity. The dean, William F. Russell, was pleased by the amount of argument that Kilpatrick and his friends generated but thought their social and philosophical views more or less silly. From the beginning William C. Bagley had complained that Dewey and Kilpatrick overemphasized the problem of making children think, to the detriment of providing them with something to think about, and in later years Isaac Kandel argued rather persuasively that experimentalism was morally null. "Experimental" was not a term of moral approbation, and a practice's experimental standing said nothing about its value. Kandel complained that the totalitarian experiment might, qua experiment, be as plausible as the democratic experiment. Not for the first or the last time he and his allies said that in the United States experimentalism bred a self-defeating skepticism and anti-intellectualism. The conflict was long, and the writing voluminous. The conservatives called the progressive softies, while the progressives replied with the epithet "fogies." Kilpatrick argued that progressive education was democratic, and Bagley replied that the progressives' goals could be achieved only if children were taught real subjects, such as English, history, and mathematics.[21] I have always thought that Bagley got the best of the argument, but I was taught English and history by teachers of something like genius and might have sighed for a project-driven education if they had not been.

Not only Teachers College but the department of philosophy came to be thought of as "Dewey's department." Once more this was not entirely accurate. The philosophy department was much more nearly F. J. E. Woodbridge's department. When Dewey arrived, the head of the department of philosophy and psychology was James McKeen Cattell; he was succeeded in 1911 by Woodbridge, who was an administrator of genius and ran both the department and the graduate faculty with great skill and good nature. Whether Dewey was thought to be a poor manager is moot; it was at any rate clear that he had come to Columbia to get on with his own life and ideas and not to be embroiled in administration. The standard history of the Columbia philosophy department sets the tone: "He performed all his academic duties conscientiously, as a matter of course, when he remembered them, or Mrs. Dewey reminded him. But he took little part in the planning or the administration of the Department. Under Woodbridge, and later Coss, that seemed to be in good hands; when consulted on major matters, or appointments, he approved. But he certainly attempted no educational program of his own. Weary of battles with Harper at Chicago, he was content to be let alone. Butler's laisser-faire policy of University administration worked splendidly with him."[22] Randall somewhat slyly adds, "He used to advise the young instructors to get the reputation of being a poor man on a committee."[23]

Nobody at Columbia became a friend to the Deweys in quite the way the Meads had become friends in Chicago, but Dewey's departmental colleagues were intellectually congenial and all the more so because they were friendly but persistent critics of his work. Dewey had to stay intellectually alert to fend off the assaults of Woodbridge in particular. Woodbridge was a dozen years younger than he but had arrived at Columbia two years earlier. He was an effective and useful antagonist; like Dewey, Woodbridge espoused a form of naturalism, but unlike Dewey, he defended a kind of realism about the objectivity of the world itself and the objective truth and falsity of statements about the world that cast a glaring light on Dewey's unwillingness to split the experiencing self off from the experienced world, or the thoughts that we have about the world from the world about which they were thoughts.

The argument between Dewey and Woodbridge centered on the nature of truth. Dewey's account of truth was hard to grasp because he wanted both to say that what we believe is "about" the world and to deny that the world was separate from our experience of it. The claim that caused the greatest offense, however, was the claim that what a statement meant was to be explained by how we verify it. Woodbridge, like most of Dewey's critics, insisted that claims about the world were true or false in virtue of the facts of the case. Their truth was one thing; whether or not we could ever find out if they were true or false was another. We can never find out whether the number of small pebbles never observed by human beings is a prime, but presumably it either is or it is not.

Dewey did not want to deny that, but he did want to say that such claims are somehow pointless, useless, or futile because they cannot enter into any conceivable problem-solving activity. To someone who went on to say that useless, pointless, and futile though they were, they were nonetheless true or false, though we could never know which, Dewey had several replies ready. One was to observe that for the peculiar purposes of mathematics and formal logic it might be necessary to adopt a concept of truth that treated every grammatically acceptable statement as true or false, but that was no guide to the way we should think of truth and falsity in other fields. Nor was it evidence that the logicians' concept of truth was in any way superior to the ordinary person's. It was different because it was useful in a different context. Among the very many ways in which Dewey was not in tune with the mainstream of twentieth-century Anglo-American philosophy, his refusal to grant any single account of the world priority over all others was one of the most important. Where Russell and Wittgenstein had once believed that formal logic revealed the inner workings of both thought and reality, Dewey thought there were no such workings to be revealed. Formal logic was, like the rest of language, a tool to be employed in the tasks it helped in. It had no claim to exercise an imperial authority over the rest of our thinking.

Dewey was already more than halfway to his final view in which the idea that statements either are or are not "true to fact" had been thrown out in favor of talk about their "warranted assertability." Woodbridge's robust realism was good for Dewey because it forced him constantly to rethink just what he wanted to say about the relationship between the mind and the nonmental world that makes our thoughts about the world true or false. If this refining process did not result in a great clarification of Dewey's ideas, it resulted during the 1920s in some exceedingly interesting elaborations of them in *Experience and Nature* and *The Quest for Certainty*. Randall suggests that we owe those books to Woodbridge's provocations: "Woodbridge made a profound impact. He encouraged Dewey to cut loose from the remaining idealistic formulations in his philosophy of experience, to think and talk more naturalistically, and to develop an empirical metaphysics as the ontological implication of his conception of human life and culture. *Experience and Nature,* the fundamental statement of his later experimental naturalism, and the book of his that is likely to wear best, is the one that most clearly reveals Woodbridge's influence, and tries consciously to come to terms with his thought."[24]

Of Dewey's other colleagues in the philosophy department, Felix Adler was so busy with the Society for Ethical Culture that he came into the department only on Friday afternoons and thus made less difference to Dewey than one might have expected him to. Dewey gave talks to Adler's congregation at the society's building on Central Park West, but he seems not to have felt philosophically or emotionally close to him, even though he knew him from summers in the Adirondacks.[25] Of all Dewey's colleagues, W. P. Montague was perhaps the most intellectually energetic, if not the most self-critical. He, too, was a self-described realist, and as unaccepting of Dewey's work as Woodbridge, and he might have been as useful a critic as Woodbridge—for all one can see eighty years later—had he not been deeply engaged with undergraduate teaching at Barnard College and therefore not part of the circle of faculty and graduate students in which Dewey thrashed out his ideas. This is not to say they had nothing to say to each other: Randall suggests that it was from Montague as much as from Woodbridge that Dewey caught the habit of arguing for his own views by arguing against those of Plato.

All the same, it was Woodbridge that Dewey remembered as the more useful antagonist, especially in the early years before Woodbridge was buried under the duties of the dean of the Graduate School.[26] Woodbridge was more nearly a Gladstonian liberal than Dewey—Randall describes him more than once as very "British" in both his intellectual and his political style—but he saw eye to eye with Dewey on educational and other matters, and this lent their philosophical disputes a particularly congenial quality. Oddly enough, Sidney Hook, who idolized Dewey, had little good to say about the department. This could hardly be because it was either snobbish or anti-Semitic; Adler's father had been the rabbi of Temple Emanu-El, and Adler was meant to succeed him. Hook's proffered grounds were that the students spent too much time wondering whether they had Dewey and Woodbridge on their side and that the faculty spent too little time arguing out their views with one another. But Hook also disliked what Randall and others praised, which was the department's interest in the history of philosophy; Hook held that it was more important to know whether an idea was right or wrong than to understand what persuaded its holders to put it forward, a view that most historically minded philosophers would have felt was hopelessly crude.[27]

The benefits of the Columbia environment were not narrowly, and perhaps not mainly, to be had in the philosophy department. Since Dewey's philosophy was decidedly more capacious, both in the degree that it drew on and in the degree that it reached out to other disciplines, than philosophy as traditionally conceived, it was not surprising that he made the most of the presence of some astonishingly distinguished colleagues in other departments. This was a time when Columbia, Chicago, and Johns Hopkins dominated advanced work in the social sciences and history, and a good many of Dewey's colleagues at Columbia had passed through Chicago during his time there.[28] His friendship with Charles Beard in political science, James Harvey Robinson in history, Veblen's disciple Wesley Mitchell in economics, Franz Boas, the anthropologist, and R. M. MacIver in sociology meant that Dewey was always surrounded by people whose natural mode of thinking was much like his own: politically progressive, friendly to science, skeptical of appeals to fixed and eternal truths or fixed and eternal values, biased toward cultural analyses rather than the abstract analytical categories of classical and neoclassical economics, and generally unwilling to see the university as an ivory tower remote from the life of the city.[29]

Franz Boas appears to have exerted the greatest intellectual influence on Dewey. The reason was fairly predictable. One natural destination of a lapsed Hegelian is cultural anthropology; Boas was the greatest cultural anthropologist of his day, and his influence would have been reinforced by that of his younger colleague Ruth Benedict, who later became famous for her work on Japan and whose book *The Sword and the Chrysanthemum* had an incalculable effect in persuading Americans that Japan was all but unintelligibly different. Boas held views that Dewey would have found congenial; when many, perhaps most, of his colleagues thought innate racial differences were at the root of the differences between "primitive" and "advanced" societies, Boas thought the effects of biology were swamped by the effects of history and culture. This may have owed something to the fact that he had been brought up in Germany, where historical and cultural analysis had a long and reputable history. Boas's impact on American social science was not confined to students of anthropology; he persuaded sociologists and political scientists, too, to take contemporary American culture as their subject matter, and works such as the Lynds' *Middletown* study of Muncie, Indiana, in the early 1930s testified to the fruitfulness of the inspiration. It is doubtful whether Dewey's philosophy would have taken the cultural turn it took in the 1920s without the stimulus of this encounter with Boas's anthropology. The impact in the reverse direction is harder to say anything about, though once more several of Dewey's friends thought he had made no impact on Boas at all. When Dewey attended Boas's seminar, it is said that he spoke only once and then to say he agreed with everything Boas said.[30]

All commentators agree that in some sense or other Dewey was the "philosophical spokesman" of these figures, but the phrase covers a multitude of possibilities from their merely liking what they read of his philosophical work to their finding real methodological and other insights in it that then influenced their own research. My sense is that Dewey's impact fell somewhere between these extremes. I doubt the possibility of tracing in any detail a "Deweyan" strand in their empirical work, but I do not doubt that his ideas genuinely reinforced the confidence with which they held their own views. In the argument between "legal realists" and their critics in the twenties and thirties, the leading legal philosophers of the day, Roscoe Pound and Karl Llewellyn, assumed an implicit alliance among Beard, Veblen, Holmes, and Dewey, with no attempt to give chapter and verse for agreement on particular points, but clearly expecting to carry conviction as a gesture toward a shared world view, shared political allegiances, and a common methodology.[31] Morton White's account of Dewey's place in the "anti-formalist revolt" in *Social Thought in America* rests on much the same appeal to political and intellectual affinities and mutual quotation—especially in their writings in the 1920s for a wider and nonacademic public—rather than on the demonstration of a point-to-point doctrinal influence, and that is perhaps as far as the story can be taken.[32]

Dewey's twenty-five years at Columbia coincided with the period of its greatest growth in numbers and prestige. Until the university moved out of its midtown location in 1897 and set up on Morningside Heights, there was neither space nor money for expansion, and not much of an intellectual base on which to build either. Under Seth Low the momentous move from Madison Avenue to the Upper West Side took place. After the arrival of Nicholas Murray Butler as the new president in 1901 the university grew at the same hectic pace as the city around it. From a university of rather under five thousand students in 1905, when Dewey arrived, it grew to one with more than thirty thousand full- and part-time academic and professional students by the time he retired twenty-five years later, while the full-time faculty grew from some five hundred at the time Dewey arrived to eighteen hundred by the time he left. Nicholas Murray Butler's presidency was not uncontentious; in spite of a deserved reputation as an enthusiast for liberal education, for educational reform and generally liberal politics, he was autocratic in administrative style and had no hesitation in using the arbitrary power that the trustees of private universities and colleges enjoyed at the turn of the century and for many years thereafter.

As at Chicago, Dewey said nothing about the managerial style of his employers until very much provoked. His actions off campus spoke louder than any words uttered on campus; Dewey was one of the founders of the American Association of University Professors in January 1915, having served on the organizing committee that had brooded for the previous two years on how to bring it to life. He was its president for the first year of its existence—1915—and never hid the fact that the association's raison d'être was to resist autocratic presidents and trustees, in order to get some control over the intellectual content of university life into the hands of the professors and out of the hands of presidents and trustees. Then, as now, academics were inclined to resist the proletarian overtones of trade unionization, but Dewey took the sensible view that the association's main task was to gain a voice in university policy making for the teachers and researchers, who should be treated as something other than factory hands producing a product that could be left to the management to decide on. If in the process they improved their economic position, that was not to be sniffed at either. To any non-American observer, the fragility of academic freedom in the United States has always been a surprising and alarming feature of a generally liberal country; commitment to the university as a place of contending unorthodoxies has always been weak, whether on the part of the trustees of private institutions or the legislatures that supervised public ones.

Dewey was slower to see the illiberalism around him than he might ideally have been. There is no comment in his letters or his published writings on the dismissal of the economist Edward Bemis from the University of Chicago and no inkling that this was brought about at the direct instigation of John D. Rockefeller's secretary; Thorstein Veblen was eased out of Chicago a little after Dewey left, but his improprieties were sexual rather than political, and most institutions then or now would have had some difficulty coping with him. Once Dewey noticed official wickedness, or, as with the cases of Scott Nearing at the University of Pennsylvania, who was dismissed for his socialism and hostility to World War I in 1915, and James Cattell and Henry Dana at Columbia, who were dismissed in 1917 for their hostility to the war, once they were obtruded upon him, Dewey was brave enough in sticking up for academic liberty. At the end of the war he helped found the New School for Social Research, opened in 1919, an institution whose first purpose was to give a home and students to the victims of the purges that universities had launched against critics of America's involvement in the war, and in the next year he was one of a group of some fifty influential intellectuals and academics who founded the American Civil Liberties Union. At the New School he lectured and gave seminars and was a prominent, though far from dominating, figure. The New School was, of course, much more closely associated with its director, the Cornell-trained economist Alvin Johnson; its leading philosopher was Horace Kallen, a German Jew who had written eloquent attacks on Americanization during the war and was to continue in the same vein until 1970. In the ACLU, too, Dewey was not a prominent figure, though he was a member of the National Committee and took part in the battles of the 1930s, when liberals like him tried to resist the take-over of the union by the Communist party and resigned when they failed.

The Philosopher of War and the Philosopher of Education

Although it is convenient or, rather, an inescapable necessity, it is misleading to separate out Dewey's continuing defense of liberal education from what he later wrote about the war. One of the most striking (though not strikingly persuasive) books Dewey ever wrote—*German Philosophy and Politics*—is both a wartime tract and an essay on the impact of philosophical views on the political culture of Germany.[33] It is a treatise on education as well as a somewhat indirect tract on the war. Conversely, many of Dewey's interventions in the public discussion of education from 1915 onward were sparked off by the prospect of war and preparation for war. They were concerned to protect the values of a liberal education from the corrosive effects of political manipulation. Dewey was an American nationalist—not a phrase I use in criticism—but as an American nationalist he was very emphatic that the American nation was unlike other nations in its commitment to pluralism, federalism, and localism and in its belief that community bubbled naturally upward from small-scale interactions and was not to be imposed from above. How the schools might serve the nation's interest in time of conflict was thus a topic that had to be handled with extreme delicacy. Again, and conversely, when the war came closer, Dewey treated it in the spirit in which his philosophy forced him to treat it: as part of experience and so as something that had to be made the most of—that is, that the nation must find the experience of war educative rather than diseducative.

One might unkindly think that the war taught all sorts of lessons that Dewey was incapable of learning. This was the view that Randolph Bourne publicly and loudly, and Jane Addams more privately and quietly, came to. With no unkindness at all, one might still think that the whole thing was "no end of a lesson" in the unmanageability of human affairs and that Dewey was a slow learner. Still, such conclusions are, if justified at all, justified only as conclusions—that is, after we have seen what there is to be said in Dewey's defense. Nonetheless, the very fact that one is tempted to talk in terms of war as education suggests the way Dewey's invocation of a startling admixture of educational, philosophical, and political considerations worked.

From a pragmatist perspective, war fitted squarely but awkwardly in pragmatism's problem-solving framework. To find oneself in a world war was surely to find oneself in a deeply problematic situation; if anything could be a stimulus to thought for the entire social organism, this was surely it. But just what the nature of the problem might be and what it was to solve it were harder to seek. Dewey provided about as plausible an answer as one could expect. He thought that the war would be justified as an experience for American society if, but only if, it taught the American people deep and permanent lessons about how to work together as one people, though a people made up of *peoples*. It might be justified if it showed that the absolute right of the owners of private property to do as they chose with their "own" was no such thing but must be subordinated to national need. It might be justified if it taught all parties that law, not violence, must rule in international affairs. It might be justified if it showed everyone that international organization must be grafted onto national organization. It might teach all these lessons at much too high a price, and it might thus be a disaster even when all the balancing possible had been done; but in principle Dewey's pragmatism set out what argument humane liberals had to reach for in defending the war and what results would force them to admit that the war was a disaster.

None of the arguments Dewey considered as justifying involvement in the war were ones that old-fashioned patriots, xenophobes, militarists, and others might put up. National pride was not a reason to get into the war or a reason to be happy with victory. Considerations of pride, indeed, struck no chord with Dewey. Bertrand Russell, violently hostile to the war and thus on the opposite side of the fence from Dewey, always saw the war as the effect of pride, and himself appealed to national pride as a reason to keep the peace.[34] Russell thought the British should have conciliated the Germans, out of a sense of the superiority of British values to German ones. The Germans did, but the British did not, need to acquire colonies and strut about on the world stage as a prop to their self-respect. This is just the kind of thought Dewey did not have and did not admit into the discussion. Woodrow Wilson, curiously enough, came closer to Russell's view early in the war, suggesting that the United States might with good reason be too proud to join in the struggle. "There is such a thing as a man being too proud to fight. There is such a thing as a nation being so right that it does not need to convince others that it is right."[35]

The "educative" issues posed by the war thus had two distinct aspects for

Dewey. When he took "education" in the narrow sense of what goes on in schools and colleges, Dewey's subject was how to prevent the warlike passions damaging whatever progress was being made in the American educational system. When he took "education" in the wide sense of the way organisms make fruitful use of experience, his subject was how the war could be part of America's education rather than of its diseducation. Dewey had by this time come to believe that philosophy was in essence the theory of education. It is thus easy enough to see that we might conclude either that Dewey's view of the world during these years wonderfully integrated his philosophical, educational, and political interests or that Dewey got into a terrible intellectual and emotional tangle because he found it impossible to discuss any one issue without bringing in all the rest.

I incline to the second view. I believe Dewey would have been more persuasive if he had been less "holistic." At any rate, I begin my account of his intellectual development during the decade from 1910 to 1920 by following up the discussion begun in the last chapter about Dewey's contribution to the argument over vocational training schools. Since one of his arguments against most current (then and now, one might add) proposals for "industrial training" had to do with their class-biased and undemocratic character, I then take up *Democracy and Education*—the book that Dewey maintained came as close as anything he wrote to giving a complete guide to his philosophy—to answer the naïve question of what Dewey supposed the connection between democracy and education actually was.[36] Finally I cast back to the beginning of the war years and follow Dewey's developing views on the war.

One important issue at least remains elusive even after this brutal imposition of some structure on the discussion. The period from about 1890 to 1920 was one in which the late-twentieth-century argument over multiculturalism received one of its periodic airings, and as intellectually strenuous an airing as it has ever had. It was by no means a uniquely American argument. As in the United States, so in Britain there was intense fear of an influx of "aliens," a fear exacerbated by the fact that immigrants so often clustered together in slums, took poorly paid jobs in sweatshops, and had very different tastes from their new compatriots in cooking, hygiene, religion, and much else. Britain mostly experienced immigration from eastern Europe, and resentment was mostly directed against newly arrived Jews. In the United States Jewish immigration was only one fraction of the human tide that had been variously swept into motion by the expulsive force of pogroms, and agricultural depression, and the attractive force of American prosperity in an age of cheap and reliable transportation. As each new nationality and ethnicity arrived, the prophets of doom declared that at last the United States had reached the limits of its ability to assimilate newcomers and would fall to the forces of racial degeneration, religious fanaticism, political corruption, and much else. The right feared national disintegration, the left the competition of immigrants ready to work for ever lower wages and ready to be drafted as strikebreakers and blacklegs.

After the war, bloody-minded xenophobia won out decisively, and multicultural voices fell silent. Xenophobia only rather slowly eroded thereafter—anti-immigrant, antiblack, and anti-Semitic voices were loud all through the thirties—and more rapidly eroded only after the horrors of nazism and Stalinism had reminded even the most obtuse of what xenophobia leads to. The post-1945 argument over the "melting pot" was first articulated in those exact terms only after 1908, the year in which the play of that title was a New York hit. (*The Melting Pot* was written by an Englishman, Israel Zangwill, for the New York Society of Emigrants; it was widely performed in Yiddish, and its message was all in favor of the melting pot.) But Randolph Bourne, Horace Kallen, and Dewey himself all contributed to the argument for multiculturalism during the war.

Dewey is interesting because he was a theorist neither of the melting pot nor of multiculturalism in its later guises. He believed in a genuinely national culture. It really was possible, he thought, to have a national culture, built on a common faith in a democratic society; since democracy was for him more a matter of culture than of politics, faith in a democratic society must be a faith in a common culture. It was, however, to be a novel and unique culture—open, innovative, pluralistic, and thus in a sense a culture of many cultures. Dewey was not, therefore, straightforwardly a theorist of "hyphenated Americanism." This was the right-wing anti-immigrant term that Horace Kallen turned around for his own use; Kallen suggested that immigrants might properly have a social, religious, ethnic culture "brought with them" from wherever they originated and a political allegiance that they acquired upon arrival. What made Americans *American* was their political culture, not their private, familial, local resources. Hyphenation was thus a matter of having strong emotional roots in their native culture, but cool political heads breathing the American liberal air.[37] Dewey wanted greater assimilation than this. For Kallen, a German-American was culturally German and politically American, and that was entirely acceptable; in Dewey's eyes, such a person was getting less than he might out of the experience of the New World. But the culture Dewey wanted him to absorb was to be more mosaic than melting pot.

Alas for such ambitions, once the United States entered the war, spasms of nativist passion swept the country, and throughout the entire country a policy of forced Americanization was put in place. One obvious target of Americanization was the schools. But because the program was driven by war fever and a hysterical terror of foreigners, especially Germans and eastern Europeans, it was much more repressive than educative, aiming to stop children from speaking their native languages, forbidding the teaching of German literature and the playing of German music. This was just what Dewey did not wish to foster. He therefore had to pick his way through an emotional and intellectual minefield, and as one might expect, he did it by being more inclined to accept liberal immigrant cultures and less inclined to accept their conservative branches. One illustration of Dewey's attitude to immigrant communities and their integration in American social and political life was the report he helped write on the political allegiances of the Polish community in Philadelphia in the last months of the war. The project was almost entirely propagandist in purpose, the purpose being to persuade the American government to support the liberal faction rather than the conservative faction among the Poles who were hoping to get a new Poland out of the Versailles Treaty. The translator for the group was Anzia Yezierska, and the sponsor of the research was Albert Barnes, the millionaire inventor of the antiseptic Argyrol, later famous as a collector of modern art and the founder of the Barnes Foundation.

Vocational Education

Dewey was anxious to inject a large practical component into primary education because he feared that in the conditions of modern city life children would lose touch with the realities of how life was sustained. It is important to recognise this basic motivation since it sets Dewey apart from everyone else who wrote about industrial education. Dewey's obsession with the experiential world's cycle of building, using, rebuilding, and reusing was one theme, and his sense that there was in the countryside a natural or organic connection between life and its supports was another. The latter suggests that some kind of nostalgia for a lost rural world had been provoked by the aggressively urban quality of Chicago and New York life, and Dewey's life as well as his writings tends to confirm this. After the war he gave up the cabin in the Adirondacks and bought a farm on Long Island. Many of his neighbors never realized that he was a distinguished philosopher; they took him to be what he seemed, an elderly neighbor who sold them eggs and peaches from his farm. "My goodness, it's the egg-man," a neighbor is said to have exclaimed in some alarm when the distinguished philosopher she had invited to her party showed up at the door. Dewey may well have thought there was a deep value involved not only in owning a farm but in working it for a profit, though he may equally have believed only that with Alice increasingly unwell and himself increasingly lonely, it was a comfort to engage in the tasks by which his family had for generations made their livings in Vermont.

Nostalgia for life on the farm would not provide much of a basis for industrial education. The boys and girls he saw in the training schools at Chicago and Columbia and the children of the hard-up streets around Hull House and Henry Street were not going to become farmers. What they needed was the training that would make them skilled workers with more reliable employment prospects than those of casual manual workers; since such skills were likely to become obsolete with time and were likely to be rendered obsolete by the progress of automation, what they needed even more than simple training was some idea of how to get further educated and perhaps some chance of future promotion into the supervisory or managerial ranks. Dewey understood that well enough, even though neither of his basic obsessions bore very directly on the subject.

They bore on it indirectly. Dewey's emphasis on the role of practical training in the first years of primary school was directed toward the socialization of young children into cooperative activities of all sorts. It was not enough to give a single child a vision of the process by which a grain of wheat is planted, grows, produces more grain, is ground, turned into flour, and cooked into bread; that you could teach any halfway adept child by giving him or her a picture book. Getting down to it themselves, children had to do it in company. They had to work with other children; they had to learn what difference their behavior made to the success and failure of the group, how to control the urge to take the nicest and easiest jobs for themselves and leave others to do the boring or tedious ones. For Dewey, this was an element in training them to live in a democracy. It had obvious practical uses. Knowing how to play one's part in cooperative undertakings would be useful in no matter what future occupation a child might eventually find for himself. The emphasis on cooperation and the acceptance of such practical goals were features of Dewey's argument that set him most sharply apart from other progressive writers with whom one would have expected him to be in considerable sympathy. Though he reviewed Bertrand Russell's educational writings with some enthusiasm, he noticeably praised the spirit rather than anything more definite and approved of Russell mostly because he shared Russell's anxiety about the society outside the school rather than anything distinctive in Russell's view of the child.[38] There is a good reason. Russell never denied that children needed to learn to live with one another and to acquire the arts of cooperation. He did, however, write as though the object of the exercise were to cultivate each child as a sort of specimen of well-nurtured humanity, as though teachers gardened children rather than in the Lab School, where children gardened wheat.

It seems at first sight a surprising fact that Mme. Montessori, whom Russell vastly admired, got no sympathy from Dewey's admirers and that her work was dismissed as rigid, unscientific, superstitiously (and expensively) attached to her "apparatus"—familiar nowadays as the climbing frames possessed by every kindergarten—and not in the same league as Dewey's.[39] It is less surprising on second thoughts, for Montessori violated two distinct prejudices, both of which Dewey tended to reinforce. In the first place, her belief that children's development followed a fixed pattern was thought by critics to be hard on the children, allowing them too short a period for "childlike" activity; in the second, she was an archetypical individualist: As with Russell, she did not at all suppose that children should be allowed to do exactly as they chose, but she wrote as if each child were the repository of some special spark that had to be cultivated into a bright glow.

Dewey's opposition to this way of thinking did not mean that he thought teachers should aim to produce large numbers of "average" children. As a devout believer in progress he was less concerned with the average than that the "average" level of attainment should rise dramatically. But this was not the way he framed the matter. Nor did he think of it as many democratically minded educators have done, as a question of doing one's best for the many as opposed to an elitist concentration on the outstanding few. He knew that children were very different from one another and that anyone who enjoys teaching enjoys teaching distinct individuals. He knew as well, though he made little of it, that as regards aptitude for almost any given subject of study, children vary widely. The point is rather different. Dewey's conception of education was so deeply rooted in the thought that education was above all a process of socializing the young person into the culture of his or her own society, and therefore in modern America a process of socializing the young person into a democratic culture, that the individualism that came naturally to Russell and Mme. Montessori was inconceivable for Dewey. They wanted to protect the child from the stultifying and deadening impact of the quotidian world until sufficient such children had been created to turn that world into something less stultifying; Dewey wanted to strengthen the child's ties to the best in that society. Characteristically this makes him difficult to place among radical educationalists; he was not much more attached to the empirical reality around him than Russell was, but he was more inclined to think that the ideals that should guide education must be found in that reality or nowhere.

One route to achieve what he was after was industrial training. Before 1914 few children stayed at school beyond the age of twelve or fourteen. Many of those who left at the age of fourteen had acquired nothing more than a rote-learned acquaintance with the three Rs and whatever miscellaneous and useless information their teachers had managed to make them memorize. Sending them out to work at that age either with or without some elementary practical skills would do them no good. "There are nineteen chances out of twenty that any work they can get into will prove a blind alley both industrially and economically."[40] Their academic skills were of no use to them in their future employment, and the standard complaint, then as today, was that ill-educated youths simply drifted from one job to another, making no progress in skill, income, or anything else.

William Wirt's schools in Gary, Indiana, were intended to be emphatically unlike this; in *Schools of Tomorrow,* Dewey's daughter Evelyn printed several photographs of students at Gary's schools working in what amounted to a small factory within the school. Wirt aimed to produce genuinely skilled workers. He claimed, and the photographs suggest he was not boasting, that the Gary schools could be built, furnished, cleaned, repaired, and wholly maintained by the students working in the school workshops. One of the merits he claimed for this state of affairs was that it would make schooling very cheap. We may have mixed feelings about the commercial aspects of these claims; what is more striking is how incidental Wirt's aims were to anything Dewey had in mind. What Dewey and his daughter admired in the Gary schools was "the social and community idea" behind them. Wirt's schools were themselves to be working communities, and they were to be both in and of the larger community—the idea that connected Dewey's admiration for the Gary schools with his admiration of the educational achievements of Hull House and Henry Street.[41]

Dewey's view, whatever the reality may have been, was that in the Gary schools this social idea dictated both the syllabus and the way the school was organized; a key element of it was that it broke away from the usual divisions between lower and upper schools, so that the children should spend their entire school career in the one school community.[42] Nor did Dewey and his daughter praise the industrial training students got in the Gary schools for its utilitarian benefits. At the risk of repeating the point ad nauseam, we may recall how firmly they insisted that "[t]he industrial features of his [Wirt's] schools . . . were not instituted to turn out good workers for the steel company, nor to save the factories the expense of training their own workers, but for the educational value of the work involved."[43]

Eighty years afterward it is hard not to smile at this unconcern with the economic benefits of a well-organized system of vocational training. It seems at least unnecessarily fastidious. If it were true that the steel industry could benefit by having its work force trained at school rather than in the steel plant, it would be rational to do the training at school and to recoup the cost to the public by getting U.S. Steel to pay for the benefits received. If it was a good bargain, U.S. Steel could not complain, and if it was a bargain for neither U.S. Steel nor the students, it would not be worth doing in the first place. Again, it would surely have been a good idea in the early 1900s and at any time since then to integrate schools and work with an apprenticeship system of the kind that Germany and the Scandinavian countries operate today. Germany and Sweden are models of a sensible approach to creating a highly skilled work force, just as Britain and the United States have long been notorious for neglecting such integrated training. To shrug these considerations aside as merely utilitarian is less a matter of political or philosophical virtue than a lamentable neglect of practicality.[44]

In 1914 Dewey could perhaps afford to turn up his nose at the German example, but it is interesting to see what a variety of dismissive epithets he produced when he discussed German vocational training in the course of defending his own plans for America. It was, he thought, "extraordinarily irrelevant to American conditions." Its purpose was "frankly nationalistic," it had done nothing to raise the wages of skilled workers, it was part of a policy of assisting industry to beat off foreign competition, and its justification was always in terms of the "well-being of the state as a moral entity."[45] In an American context he feared that the German example would be used merely to allow employers to shift the burden of training their workers onto the taxpaying public. "It is natural that employers should be desirous of shifting the burden of this preparation to the public tax-levy. There is every reason why the community should not permit them to do so."

The reason offered is very Deweyan, and it suggests one reason why Dewey later found it so easy to support American entry into the war. Germany was a peculiarly undemocratic society, but the United States was the natural embodiment of democracy and therefore should beware of copying German industrial education for fear of copying German social and economic attitudes. "Class against class, there is no reason why the community should be more interested in the laboring class than in the employing class, save the important reason that the former constitutes a larger part of itself. But every ground of public policy protests against any use of the public school system which takes for granted the perpetuity of the existing industrial régime, and whose inevitable effect is to perpetuate it with all its antagonisms of employer and employed, producer and consumer."[46]

Dewey's contribution to the debate over industrial education mostly came in articles and lectures written during the years from 1913 to 1915, and a few sporadically over the next thirty years. These essays were inevitably repetitive; Dewey had a well-articulated view and was not lightly going to abandon it, while there were all sorts of groups and organizations that wanted him to lend his prestige to their campaigns against "dual control." Dewey's view was that vocational education was, if done properly, absolutely basic to the role of the public schools in a democracy. This is a feature of Dewey's views that otherwise deft critics like Christopher Lasch somehow get absurdly wrong. Lasch sees, quite correctly, that Dewey's view of industrial society criticizes it from what one might loosely call a corporatist direction, but he misunderstands the consequences; *loosely* is of the essence, for Dewey's critique has nothing at all to do with the defense of a corporatist state or with the defense of the modern business corporation.

Dewey disliked the modern business corporation in almost all its manifestations—its bureaucratic and hierarchical structure, its routinized working practices on the shop floor and in the offices of the white-collar staff, its divorce of management and real labor, and its remoteness from the interface of man and nature. He did not follow other Progressives—Herbert Croly, for instance—in thinking that the capitalist corporation was an inchoate but genuine anticipation of a "national" rather than a disorganizedly capitalist and competitive economy. The way in which and the extent to which Dewey was a corporatist were just what we ought to expect from someone with Dewey's residually Hegelian view of the world. Industrial life was significant for its place in our culture, as a way of life, as the expression in work of a scientific society's success in organizing itself to keep itself fed, clothed, and sheltered. Work was admirable when imbued with an understanding of this, but it was mere drudgery when not so imbued. Modern capitalism was thus chronically at odds with its own deeper meaning, and class division was not so much a brute fact about the capitalist order as a wrong turning in the evolutionary process.

Christopher Lasch, like several other critics of Dewey, supposes that this "corporatist" perspective means that the point of industrial training was to produce a docile work force adapted to the needs of capitalist employers.[47]

And of course, this is exactly wrong. A simpler and more telling complaint that may underlie Lasch's objections to Dewey is that Dewey's talk of adjustment and adaptation and reorganization leaves it unclear how dramatically different from existing society a better-adapted and more acceptably organized society will be. So much does Dewey want to train children for a society that has realized its immanent potential that one might be tempted to see him not as a corporatist but as a near Marxist who holds that the potentially fulfilling life of work and enjoyment that modern industry makes available to us, and whose outlines we can dimly see in our current practice, will be liberated only after a cataclysmic collapse of the old order, followed by its revolutionary overthrow and reconstitution on a democratic basis.[48]

That revolutionary view is not there either. The ground Dewey occupies is squarely in the center of the alternatives. Even in the 1930s, when he had become convinced that capitalism was dead or at best a semiambulant corpse, he refused the revolutionary route. So far from seeing Marx as an ally, he would not let Sidney Hook or Max Eastman persuade him that Marx had any merits at all. Dewey had the moralist's rather than the organization theorist's vision of his subject. Although Dewey seemed to have turned ethics into sociology, it was a sociology of a peculiarly moral kind. In other words, just as was the case when he was discussing teaching small children their place in the world via gardening and cooking in kindergarten, so when he discussed vocational education for fourteen- to eighteen-year-olds, it was always in the framework of what would help them take a full part in democratic society.

Lasch wrote critically of Dewey's project because he thought Dewey passed off a system of social control for the sake of the owners of industry as "democracy," and such duplicity would indeed have been reprehensible. Nor is the charge intrinsically absurd. We have seen Bellamy's fantastic projection into a socialist future of the hierarchical and bureaucratic organization creeping into industry in his own day. Dewey could have been tempted in that direction. A related route that might in principle have tempted him would have been the Comtist route. Among the infinitely various responses of the nineteenth century to the startling changes in technology and the economy that took place between the 1780s and the 1880s, one of the most persuasive was offered by Henri de Saint-Simon and Auguste Comte. They started from the thought that what "industrial society"—a label they coined—most needed was a new principle of organization. The journal of the Saint-Simonians was aptly titled *L'Organisateur*. This new organization was to be supported on a new religion, the religion of humanity, and the new order was to be one in which a spiritual attachment to a harmonious social order was to be inculcated by a *pouvoir spirituel*, or secular priesthood. Economic life itself was to be governed by committees of financiers and scientists. It was, though it was considered very ill mannered to say so, an attempt to mimic the supposed qualities of the medieval Roman Catholic Church, on the basis of a scientific philosophy or "positivism." Herbert Croly, the author of *The Promise of Ameri-*

can Life, the leading theorist of Progressivism, the leading figure in founding the *New Republic,* and briefly an infinitely more influential publicist than Dewey ever was, had been brought up on a diet of Comte and the Positivist Church, and one can see traces of it in his work.[49]

Dewey as an undergraduate had been interested in Comte, but only as a stepping-stone to Hegel. He had read Harriet Martineau's translation and abridgment of Comte in college but had not been much moved. Indeed, his philosophical training might almost have been designed as an inoculation against Comtist tendencies. Anyone who had had prolonged exposure to Hegel would have believed, as Marx famously did, that Comte was philosophically not in the same league as Hegel and that his endless treatises on how to organize society on Comtist lines were utopian in the most abusive sense of that term, as well as expressive of a temperament far gone in megalomania and self-delusion. Dewey was inherently unlikely to sign up for anything that smacked of an ideological-cum-industrial dictatorship, and in fact, he did not.

He did what he always did. He raised the stakes of the argument. He announced that the "question of industrial education is fraught with consequences for democracy. Its right development will do more to make public education truly democratic than any other one agency now under consideration. Its wrong treatment will as surely accentuate all undemocratic tendencies in our present situation, by fostering and strengthening class divisions in school and out."[50] To critics who thought that almost any training scheme and almost any system of training would be an improvement on the present state of affairs, he replied that it would be "better to suffer a while longer from the ills of our present lack of system until the truly democratic lines of advance become apparent, rather than separate industrial education sharply from general education, and thereby use it to mark off to the interests of employers a separate class of laborers."[51]

How far we should go in approving of this stand is a very vexed issue. If all that is at stake is the extent to which Dewey's enthusiasm for a form of participatory democracy extended to his concern for industrial democracy, we may cheerfully agree that his preferred industrial order would have been something like the guild socialism of which the British philosopher and political theorist G. D. H. Cole was the chief begetter and proponent and after which Dewey still hankered many years later. Such a socialism does not rest in any very strenuous way on what Marx described as the expropriation of the expropriators and neatly finesses the question of existing and future property rights in the means of production. That is, the standard, or Marxist, view of capitalism and socialism stresses the fact that employers exercise power over workers because they, the employers, monopolize access to the means of making a living. The corollary would seem to be that the workers must seize the property of their masters in order to emancipate themselves. Chronically Marxists stopped short at this point and failed to say anything very persuasive about what quasi-property rights over the means of production there would be after the revolution, by whom they would be exercised, or by what mechanism they would be enforced. The history of post-1945 socialism in the Soviet bloc and elsewhere is in large part the history of a failure to sort out such questions in a way that makes the efficiency and social justice at which socialism aims even remotely likely.

In a rough-and-ready way, nineteenth-century American history was a testimony to the plausibility of Marx's thought that it was the capitalist's monopoly of the means of livelihood that was the basis of class conflict. American exceptionalism is a many-splendored thing, but one feature of it was the absence of class conflict during the period of European class warfare on the grand scale. Until the late nineteenth century the United States was unique in the ease with which laborers could set up in business on their own or, even more strikingly, go out and settle public lands west of the existing settlements. Dewey himself subscribed to the myth of the frontier—that is, to the view that America had escaped the horrors of European class conflict in the eighteenth and nineteenth centuries because the open frontier allowed capitalists and laborers to strike out for new pastures rather than fight to the death in the cities of the East Coast. Conversely, when Frederick Jackson Turner announced in 1893 that trouble loomed as a result of the closing of the frontier, Dewey believed him.

However, Dewey never thought class conflict was simply a matter of property rights; conversely, he never thought the distasteful features of a class-divided society could be overcome by turning a class monopoly of access to work and life into a state monopoly. The evils of class division were many and had as much to do with differences of morality, snobbishness, and, above all, managerial power as with questions about who got the larger share of the social cake. Guild socialism as a form of industrial democracy in which emphasis was switched from the issue of *ownership* to the issue of *government* was just what Dewey was looking for. There would be no need to expropriate the expropriators, merely to replace boards of directors chosen entirely by the owners by boards of directors answerable to a combination of worker and community interests.[52] Once this was achieved, it would become easier, though surely not easy, to devise new ways of managing the enterprise so as to give every worker in it a strong sense of membership.

With this as the eventual target, it is clear that no system of industrial training could by itself do very much to foster it. As we saw with Dewey's views on childhood education, the understanding he brings to industrial education is very much a combination of philosophical imagination and a social psychologist's assumptions—in this case assumptions about how to work on the motivation of individual children and teenagers. At this point our judgment of his achievement is likely to be somewhat ambivalent, since on the one hand, this is a strikingly imaginative and farsighted view of the purpose of education, and on the other, it is a long way from the gritty issues of just what we are going to teach our fourteen- and sixteen-year-olds when they come for vocational education. It is hard to resist Dewey's claims for the moral purpose he has in mind—fewer people than he often suggested have ever wanted hierarchy for its own sake or have thought boring repetitive work was just what the working class ought to do as a matter of principle—but hard to know quite what follows. As so often, there is an alarming lack of concrete illustration, either of the more democratic industries into which the trained young people would be going or of the democracy-enhancing work that they would be doing in training.

Democracy and Education

The place where one might expect to find answers yields rather few. This is *Democracy and Education,* the book that Dewey described upon his retirement as being "for many years that in which my philosophy, such as it is, was most fully expounded."[53] It is puzzling that he should have so described it since by then he had published *Experience and Nature* and *The Quest for Certainty,* either or both of which might plausibly be offered as a definitive statement of his vision of the world.[54] On the other hand, *Democracy and Education* was a striking work, sold handsomely, was translated into a dozen languages, and was the book of which Dewey was fondest. There is a substantial discussion of vocational education in the book, but when Sidney Hook exempted "some elements of the chapter on 'Vocational Aspects of Education' " from his claim that *Democracy and Education* remained "a classic in the philosophy of education and in the related fields of social, political, and moral philosophy" sixty years after its first publication, it was precisely because the chapter failed to answer crucial questions about the way society and the school would have to be integrated to give vocational education the point Dewey wished it to have.[55] By the time Hook came to make this criticism, his attachment to democratic socialism, though not to the memory of Dewey, had become diluted; nonetheless, the questions Hook raises are ones that anyone looking to Dewey for something more than complaints against the existing order is surely bound to raise.

One is the question of whether we can guarantee that there will be jobs for the people so trained and particularly whether we can guarantee that there will be *satisfying* jobs for them. Something far more ambitious than the liberal welfare state would be needed to achieve that. Some jobs appear to be intrinsically so tedious that the best we can manage is to mechanize them out of existence or to compensate the people who do them by high pay; Dewey is unwilling to trade off monetary compensation and job satisfaction but gives no clear account of what else is possible. In general, as Hook observes, there is a nagging question about what price we are willing to pay in diminished efficiency for an attempt to make work more interesting.

One ought not to give ground to these anxieties too swiftly. Hook writes as though the argument could have only one outcome, and there he may be wrong and Dewey right. Consider unemployment. In any society there will be some need for a pool of labor that is ready to work but cannot presently be used. If the unemployed are left to hang out on street corners, they become demoralized and work-shy; moreover, they have to be kept alive by welfare payments that are visibly administered by government officials and visibly appropriated out of tax revenues. This may be an unnecessary source of inefficiency as well as a needless source of social friction. If industry was obliged to find employment for such people or if there were public service jobs that they could do usefully, though not in the usual sense profitably, they may very well be less demoralized, and the total cost to society be less than the cost imposed through the tax and welfare system. It would have been open to Dewey to argue along these lines, as also to suggest that the conceptions of efficiency prevalent in orthodox economics were not adequate to measure the "overall" effectiveness of a social and economic system. Hook's claim that there is a risk of "socializing hunger" if we sacrifice "efficiency and the price and profit system" to whatever socialist objectives we may have is fair enough, but it is neither conclusive in itself nor necessarily very apt in the context of the United States.[56] To believe that at any given moment the American economy is as efficient as it can be is a utopian view however much it may be sustained by orthodox economic analysis.

Dewey's vagueness about vocational education in *Democracy and Education* was one more way in which he sacrificed concreteness to "uplift." Dewey still wrote in a way that suggested that the schoolteacher was engaged in God's work, though by this stage in his career he did not talk in such terms. Rather he emphasized the importance of education by insisting that the philosophy of education was not just a branch of philosophy or a specialism within philosophy but was central to philosophy as such. Indeed, he said, he could not understand how anyone could call himself a philosopher yet fail to be passionately interested in education. This view equivocates somewhat over just what we are going to count as "education." It would obviously be less plausible to suggest that all philosophers should take an interest in the technicalities of teaching elementary arithmetic to five-year-olds than that they should take an interest in how the natural world and human culture combine to shape our minds and personalities and the cultural settings in which we live. It was education in this larger sense that Dewey was most concerned with, but it was to teachers who were engaged in education in the "apart" sense that he addressed his book. Naturally, philosophers were inclined to think it was not for them. Dewey, however, thought it was only their usual snobbishness that led professional philosophers to ignore *Democracy and Education*.[57]

Reviewers of the book were mostly very taken with it. More than one thought that it was the third member of a distinguished trio of books whose other two members were Plato's *Republic* and Rousseau's *Émile*. Like Dewey's other writings on education, however, *Democracy and Education* was much more concerned with the social bearings of school education than with the details of the curriculum, though it came down to earth at least to the extent of discussing the place in the syllabus of particular subjects such as history, geography, and natural science. Just as in *How We Think,* the thrust of the argument is always toward asking how a given subject's *methodology* will develop a particular facet of the child's mind. As we saw both there and in *School and Society,* that question in turn is just one aspect of the larger question of how education enables the child to become a full member of society. The emphasis on the *social* quality of all thought is striking. Just as in more technical philosophical works, Dewey argued that even what we tend to think of as most distinctively *ours*—that is, our own minds—is essentially a social rather than an individual possession. Most of what human beings do, they do without anything describable as articulate thought; most of what we do is intelligent behavior but it is *behavior:* We drive through crowded streets, type letters, dismantle automobile engines, and we do these things intelligently, but without the benefit of articulated internal plans or commentary. Only when we pause do we articulate to ourselves what we are doing, how we have organized the doing of it, and what it is that has caused us to stop. And what we draw on in doing that is the language in which we deal with other people as part of the world we inhabit. Dewey never quite said that the mind was a product of language or that all thought is done in language; to have said that would have been too close to the reductionism he deplored in others. Still, he thought it more illuminating to explain private thinking as the internal aspect of public speech than the other way about.

Democracy and Education was intended as a textbook, and one reason for its popularity was the excellence of the summaries with which Dewey ended most of the chapters; a deft but idle student could extract the essence of the book in thirty pages or so. For our purposes, the book's main interest is what led Dewey to describe it as the place in which he had fully spelled out his philosophy. It links boldly, if not entirely convincingly, his ideas about the history of intellectual life, about the connections between individual growth and formal education, about the individual and social psychology of education, and about the inescapability of democracy—at least in America. The central chapter "The Democratic Conception in Education" encapsulates almost all these themes, and it has always been seen as a privileged statement of Dewey's understanding of both democracy and education.

In particular, it does much to spell out the place of leadership in the classroom and beyond. As all his admirers have said, Dewey did not believe in "child-centered education" in any sense that implied a slighting of the role of the teacher; children did not grow by the light of nature but were shaped by the creative efforts of their teachers. By the same token, he did not propose to rely on children's existing interests to motivate them to get on and learn, but as usual he had something up his sleeve to avoid admitting the necessity for "external" disciplinary measures. It is in the nature of organisms like ourselves to approach the environment in an energetic and effortful manner; we are, so to speak, preshaped to accept useful forms of discipline and self-discipline, and the conflict traditional teachers saw between letting children follow their interests and forcing them to make an effort with what they did not want to do was a false dilemma. The skill we needed to learn was that of creating an environment in which we built on the existing interests of children in order to give them new interests and new capacities for self-control and sustained effort.

Dewey thought Plato and Rousseau would have agreed with him on this point. It was not only his more enthusiastic reviewers who compared him with the great figures in intellectual history; Dewey was often reviled for not taking the history of philosophy seriously, but this was always a misdirected complaint. Like most philosophers, he thought most easily by "triangulation"—that is, discovering where he was by seeing where he stood in relation to other writers and thinkers. As an educational theorist he used Kant almost more happily than Rousseau as one of his triangulation marks, but his method of working was essentially genetic, evolutionary, cultural, and historical. Having prayed Plato and Rousseau in support, he then had to distance himself from them by arguing for a peculiarly democratic conception of education. In effect, he took two steps to this conclusion: The first was to stress the social quality of education, and the second to stress the democratic essence of social life. To make the first point persuasive, he reminded his readers that "Society is one word but many things."[58]

Society is an association of associations; each person belongs to many different groups for different activities, and it may seem that they have "nothing in common except that they are modes of associated life." Picturesquely he observed that there are "political parties with differing aims, social sets, cliques, gangs, corporations, partnerships, groups bound closely together by ties of blood, and in endless variety," and in addition, they may well be attached to "varying languages, religions, moral codes and traditions."[59] Education in the broad sense is socialization into a plurality of groups.

Looking for some criterion for deciding whether the "social" aspect of education could yield some evaluative standard by which to decide what sort of society we should try to foster, Dewey noted rather more sharply than one might have anticipated that "society," like "community," was a term more often used eulogistically than descriptively. "Society is conceived as one by its very nature. The qualities which accompany this unity, praiseworthy community of purpose and welfare, loyalty to public ends, mutuality of sympathy, are emphasized. But when we look at the facts that the term *denotes* instead of confining our attention to its intrinsic *connotation,* we find, not unity, but a plurality of societies good and bad. Men banded together in a criminal conspiracy, business aggregations that prey upon the public while serving it, political machines held together by the interest of plunder, are included."[60] To find a criterion for good social groupings, Dewey argues that we must elicit it from what makes all groups groups and then see whether it picks out "anti-social"

social groups from desirable ones. The criterion he finds is given by the answer to two questions: "How numerous and varied are the interests which are consciously shared? How full and free is the interplay with other forms of association?"[61] A band of muggers scores badly on both scores: The basis of association is narrow, and they are obliged to be at odds with other groups, whether their rivals in crime or the citizenry and its agents the police.

Democracy is then rather obviously the most attractive form of society because it is the one in which society is most essentially itself. Moreover, this form of democracy is obliged by its own nature to be internationalist and cosmopolitan in outlook; since its own legitimacy rests on its scoring high marks on the question of openness to other forms of association, democracy thus understood is committed to something like the cosmopolitanism of Kant's educational philosophy. The extent to which Dewey's educational writings are tracts in political theory comes out very clearly when he says:

> It is not enough to teach the horrors of war and to avoid everything which would stimulate international jealousy and animosity. The emphasis must be put upon whatever binds people together in cooperative human pursuits and results, apart from geographical limitation. The secondary and provisional character of national sovereignty in respect to the fuller, freer, and more fruitful association and intercourse of all human beings with one another must be instilled as a working disposition of mind. If these applications seem to be remote from a consideration of the philosophy of education, the impression shows that the meaning of the idea of education previously developed has not been adequately grasped.[62]

On all this there are three brief things to be said, before we consider how the cosmopolitan educationalist turned so swiftly into the defender of America at war. The first is that the smoothness with which Dewey moves from society to democracy to internationalism did nothing to deceive conservative and nationalist critics who thought progressive education was inclined to subvert patriotism. Conservative and nationalist parents might well have thought that a school run according to Dewey's views would be a school in which their children would be indoctrinated in excessively liberal and internationalist opinions that they did not share. Dewey would not have been distressed by such a reaction. Unlike the liberalism of recent years in which demands for the political and moral "neutrality" of schools have predominated, Dewey's liberalism was unflinchingly political and not in the least neutral. This did not mean that schools were supposed to indoctrinate their students, but Dewey thought that the superior intellectual standing of his liberalism meant that it would always prevail in an open discussion.

A second thing to observe is that Dewey's argument was persuasive partly because he picked his enemies with some skill. Hegel's argument that we could not expect people to feel the same loyalty toward humanity in the abstract that they feel toward smaller groupings and thus that we should cherish national identity rather than throw it aside in favor of a cosmopolitan identity was not refuted but drowned out by references to the way German education was conscripted for national purposes. This was in keeping with Dewey's lectures entitled *German Philosophy and Politics,* delivered the year before *Democracy and Education* was published. In these lectures it was Kant rather than Hegel or Nietzsche who was supposed to have turned the Germans in a nationalist direction—not deliberately, since it was undeniable that Kant was a cosmopolitan and no nationalist, but indirectly by persuading his countrymen that ultimate moral values were disembodied and transcendent and in the process leaving them to adopt national efficiency as their main earthly end.[63] The argument relied rather too heavily on Friedrich von Bernhardi's *Germany and the Next War* to suggest that German policy was somehow dictated by the dualistic determination to impose ethical principle on a recalcitrant world, and it is not surprising that even the loyal Sidney Hook thought it was unpersuasive. Dewey was strangely unrepentant. His failure to see how vulnerable his account was shows, if nothing else, just how far he saw dualism as the root of all evil. He also took the more common view in which Hegel's enthusiasm for the state as an aspect of the divine was a good deal disapproved of. Germany was the country where the state was the ethical end and nationalistic goals ruled. *That* sort of nationalism had only be mentioned to be deplored.

Dewey's argument throughout *Democracy and Education* benefited by his having Plato and Rousseau / Kant as the only sparring partners allowed into the gymnasium. Plato was obviously right in thinking of education as a social matter and of its purpose as the creation and maintenance of the highest possible form of society. To our eyes, however, he was quite wrong to sacrifice individuals to the ends of the whole society and wrong to confine education for citizenship to a narrow class. Conversely, Rousseau was right to emphasize the needs of the individual but remiss in having so little to say about how one might sustain such an education as his *Émile* sets out. "Nature" is not an answer to the question of what makes a Rousseauean education work, but an evasion. The absence of a serious answer left the door open for Hegel and his successors to insist that it was the state that dictated what we should teach, how it should be taught, and to whom. Once those alternatives were clearly visible, Dewey's own vision of an education that was public but not indoctrination by a national state, that was politically relevant but not aimed at a governing elite, that helped children prepare for adult life but was not a narrowly class-based vocational education won in a walkover.

The third thing to observe, however, is how very sensible almost all of *Democracy and Education* is. It is no wonder that William H. Kilpatrick employed it as the bible of the Columbia Teachers College. I have complained that Dewey often strays toward the utopianism that consists in not asking hard questions about how we can organize ourselves *politically* to achieve the goals we set ourselves. I shall make the same complaint against *The Public and Its Problems* and much of Dewey's polemical work in the 1930s, so it is the more important to remind ourselves how often Dewey was on target as a theorist of the classroom. There is a pious quality to his constant invocation of the social, and that quality was not wholly dispelled by his reminder that a gang of bandits is no less "social" than a respectable family. In the classroom setting what he wrote made continuous good sense. His stress on task-oriented and cooperative learning remains the basis of good elementary school teaching today—indeed, not only there but all the way up to graduate school.

To the extent that countries such as Britain practice it more effectively at the primary level than does the United States, and Japan and China all the way through the educational system, the loss is not Dewey's but the present generation of schoolchildren. By the same token, Dewey's task-oriented approach to teaching was light-years away from contemporary concerns for the child's "self-esteem" but infinitely more likely to produce an abiding sense of self-worth as tasks were accomplished, as well as a capacity for social cooperation as they were accomplished by working in teams. There are few subsequent books in the field that can hold a candle to *Democracy and Education* for sustained good sense of this sort.

Philosophy Embattled

Among the many aspects of Dewey's intellectual career that defy rational reconstruction, the years just before and during the American involvement in World War I perhaps come at the top of the list. Over a period of three years he wrote the best-selling *Democracy and Education,* put together a collection of essays by his allies he entitled *Creative Intelligence* with a long introductory essay of his own that later turned into *Reconstruction in Philosophy,* and wrote endlessly on education, on the war, and especially on the interaction of the two. It was a time of such emotional and intellectual turmoil for Dewey that he might decently have gone quiet; instead he wrote faster than ever and for a wider readership. The notion of a midlife crisis is so hackneyed, and Dewey's robustness so remarkable, that one flinches at suggesting he ever went through such a thing. Yet he plainly did, and so did his ideas. By 1916 he was, though not old, decidedly middle-aged. He had always had weak eyes, and they were deteriorating; he had always sat awkwardly at his desk, and he now developed neck aches, headaches, blurred vision, and all the common signs of middle-aged stress.

Mrs. Dewey was getting old faster than he; she had not yet begun to suffer the heart ailments that killed her a decade later, but she had become something of an invalid, more for psychological than for physiological reasons. The bodily ailments from which Dewey was suffering he set to rights by following the ideas of F. M. Alexander, the inventor of the so-called Alexander Technique. Although Dewey rather fell for Alexander's ideas, and was called "superstitious" by Ernest Nagel for so doing, he did not quite swallow whole the "scheme of universal salvation" that Alexander offered.[64] Alexander was, as Dewey was not, a reductionist; he thought that *all* the troubles of modern civilization could be traced to bad posture. Human beings had been equipped by nature with a body decently adapted to a vigorous, if rather short, existence. The upright posture and a sedentary life simply did not suit it. Alexander invented a set of exercises that corrected the set of the neck, and they largely did the trick for Dewey.

The emotional stresses may have been alleviated or alternatively exacerbated by Dewey's involvement with Anzia Yezierska.[65] Yezierska was a strikingly good-looking Polish woman of great energy and a good deal of ill-organized literary and philosophical talent. She was some twenty years younger than Dewey but was no mere girl. She had married young and had become intolerably bored and depressed as a housewife married to an orthodox husband whose expectations of marriage did not include a wife who wanted a life of her own. She left him, attended Columbia as a mature student, and sat in on Dewey's lectures. Since Dewey destroyed their correspondence, it took some rather extraordinary detective work by the editor of Dewey's *Collected Works* to bring to light the fact that Mrs. Levitas—her married name and the name under which she worked as the secretary and translator for Dewey and Barnes's commission of inquiry into the social and political allegiances of Polish immigrants—was not only Dewey's helper in this investigation but his inamorata for some ten months of 1918.

The affair never came to anything and was naturally never mentioned by Dewey. Anzia Yezierska's life was genuinely tragic, however many of her troubles she may have brought upon herself. Her husband hung on to their children and intermittently punished her by refusing to let her see them, and her own family sided with him rather than her. She lived until 1970—she was ninety when she died—but had only a modest literary success. She was a best-selling novelist for a couple of years in the 1920s, never quite made it into screenwriting, and fell out of fashion. She had only one subject—herself and the problems she faced in emancipating herself from the Polish Jewish background she came from—and even the touching biography recently published by her daughter is more persuasive of her mother's personal engagingness than of her literary talents.[66]

From our point of view, the relationship is only indirectly important. During this time Dewey wrote a lot of (to my eye, not very good) poetry; he seems to have crumpled it up after writing it and then to have stuffed it into his desk. Waldo Frank, the editor of the *Seven Arts* during the war, knew at the time that Dewey wrote poetry but never saw any of it, and it seems clear that Dewey had no wish to show it to anyone. The poems came to light because one of Dewey's junior colleagues in the philosophy department, Herbert Schneider, inherited Dewey's office and desk, investigated the drawers, and so found and hung on to the poems. Milton Halsey Thomas, the Columbia librarian, acquired some other poems independently: He explored Dewey's wastebasket and got the janitor to do so, too.

After Dewey's death the poems were recovered from Columbia by Dewey's widow, Roberta, and they have been wonderfully well edited by the editor of Dewey's *Collected Works*. They offer some fairly simple insights into Dewey's frame of mind in his late fifties: He felt some familiar pangs about the discrepancy between his elderly appearance and his sexual drives ("loins of fire and head of grey") and allowed himself to admit that he found marriage a burden but an inescapable one. There is also a good deal of nature poetry that suggests the continuing impact of Wordsworth and Emerson. In light of Dewey's extreme evasiveness about his inner life, it is tempting to try to extract more, but I am not persuaded that much more is there. The intellectual interest of his verse is that it provides simple but conclusive evidence of the genuineness of the poetic urge that underlay his later writings on religion.[67]

Dewey always insisted that poetry told us about the real world, just as science did, even though its "rules" for speaking about the world of human experience were not those of the physical sciences. Just as he was anxious not to allow science to drive out a religious perspective on the world, so he was anxious not to admit any idea that the scientific view of the world should drive out the poetic. This is both one of the reasons why it mattered so much to him that pragmatism did not accord one way of talking about the world a philosophical and logical respectability that other ways lacked and one of the motives for holding that view. Neither his poetry nor his involvement with Anzia Yezierska tells us much about the most difficult aspects of his intellectual life from 1917 to 1919. During that time Dewey was embroiled in ferocious debates about the American role in the war, and to these arguments the relationship with Yezierska contributed nothing.

The question of American involvement in the First World War was a difficult one for Dewey. From the beginning of its existence he had been associated with the *New Republic,* founded in November 1914, and most of his social commentary appeared there. He was also associated with the *Dial,* and his disciple and subsequent nemesis Randolph Bourne also wrote for both, as well as for the *Seven Arts.* The *New Republic* had begun at the tail end of its editors' enthusiasm for Theodore Roosevelt's Progressivism; in 1912 they had supported the breakaway Bull Moose movement that cost the Republicans the presidency and put Woodrow Wilson in the White House. Little by little they gravitated toward Wilson, even though they covered their defection by insisting that it was because he represented the same values as Roosevelt; by the time of Wilson's reelection in 1916, they were firmly in the camp of reform Democratic politics. Of the three first editors—Herbert Croly, Walter Weyl, and Walter Lippmann—the last was the most eager to be close to where power was exercised, and in 1917 he left the periodical to work for Colonel House and in Wilson's information office. He played a large part in drafting the famous Fourteen Points; he was disappointed by the small part he played in the Paris Peace Conference after the war and soon returned to the world of high-level newspaper commentary in which he occupied such an astonishing place thereafter.[68]

Croly and Weyl were not ambitious for direct, hands-on power; they had a vision of the modernization and democratization of American life through education, the creation of a welfare state, government intervention to build a transport and urban services infrastructure, and the like, and saw themselves as propagandists for the program, not administrators. This was the program of Croly's *Promise of American Life*. As Wilson moved away from a backward-looking hostility to new industrial and business practices and began to support—it is hard to believe that he did so with very much conviction—more egalitarian, welfare-minded, and internationalist politics, the *New Republic* found it easy to support him. The editors hoped until the last moment that the United States could stay out of the war;[69] like everyone else, they supported Wilson in 1916 as the man who would keep the United States out of the conflict. Since Theodore Roosevelt was uninhibitedly in favor of wading into the fight—as into *any* fight—as soon as a good excuse could be found, they found it all the easier to abandon their old allegiances.

Dewey was not wholly at ease in this environment. He brought to the *New Republic* his prestige as a reformer and the best-known pedagogical thinker in the country. It was less obvious that an uncoerced poll of his peers would have chosen him as the country's most distinguished philosopher; but after the death of James and in the absence of Peirce, it was Dewey, Royce, and Santayana who would plausibly have been thought to be the leading three, and Dewey was certainly the most public-spirited of them. All the same, he was not entirely a *New Republic* "natural." Dewey had voted for Eugene Debs in 1912 and was much less enamored of political power in any shape than were the editors of the *New Republic*. He was more nearly a lay preacher looking for a public forum than an amateur politician looking for a government to infiltrate. Indeed, it is plausible that he was of all of them the one most influenced by H. J. Laski's arrival from Britain to work on the *New Republic;* Laski came bearing the news that the "state" was neither the most important of institutions nor the one most deserving of our loyalty, a pluralist view that was congenial both to Dewey's communitarianism and to his guild socialism.

Dewey's thoughts on the war were not distinctive. They were those to which almost any "new liberal" might have come; they could have been articulated by a much less distinguished philosopher than Dewey. This is not to say that his views were anything but intelligently argued, deeply felt, and within limits persuasive—more persuasive in most respects than Dewey's postwar attacks on the League of Nations and his advocacy of the "outlawry of war." But almost everyone of a liberal persuasion would have assented to the need to replace war with a system of international arbitration, to the hope that if America was forced to fight, national unity might be achieved without invoking hysterical nationalism and encouraging xenophobia and that the war would be justified, if at all, by its success in expanding the rule of law, not by its success in enlarging the colonial territories of France, Britain, and the United States. Opposition to the war once it began was very much a minority option. Eugene Debs saw the American socialist movement split apart as he led opposition to the war and found allies such as Victor Berger leading the majority in support of it; Randolph Bourne found his usual places of employment successively closed to him as his former friends and editors closed ranks in favor of the war.[70] Dewey, for instance, responded to Bourne's—admittedly pretty savage—criticism by blackmailing the editors of the *New Republic* into closing its pages to Bourne and getting him thrown off the editorial board of the *Dial*.[71]

Congress responded to even the mild dissent that existed by passing ferocious legislation to suppress it; magazines hostile to the war were bankrupted because they could not use the U.S. mails, and courts invoked expansive readings of the Sedition Act to jail antiwar demonstrators and speakers. At the very end of the war Eugene Debs was jailed for ten years under the Sedition Act. Justice Holmes was one of the Supreme Court majority that upheld the sentence; Holmes's "clear and present danger" test for curtailing the First Amendment right to free speech would have benefited a few small fry if the other justices on the Court had accepted it, but in Holmes's view, it did not benefit Debs.[72] Jane Addams found herself and Hull House constantly under attack from local politicians and to a degree in danger from loyal mobs. Dewey, in other words, was not on this occasion on the side of an oppressed minority or on the side of the unrepresented view. He was never in the least danger of turning into a gung ho militarist or xenophobe, but he was very much a "national purpose" liberal.

German Philosophy and Politics

Dewey slid toward supporting the war, just as the editors of the *New Republic* did and as critics of the war, like Jane Addams, Randolph Bourne, and Max Eastman, did not. The first stage of the slide was his 1915 lectures *German Philosophy and Politics*, criticized by Max Eastman as a contribution to the war effort rather than to philosophy. In fact, they may decently be regarded as both. Dewey's argument was as much a piece of special pleading on behalf of pragmatism as a critique of German nationalism. In essence, he claimed that what lay behind German nationalism was Kant's dualism of fact and value, Kant's division of reality into matters to be understood in terms of cause and effect and scientific control and matters hived off to a transcendental realm of ends in themselves. This allowed two things to happen, exemplified to some extent in Kant's own career indeed: one the relegation of everyday life to a mere matter of efficiency and the other the elevation of individual values to a self-centered and apolitical concern with the purity of one's soul.

Add to this the deep doubts about ordinary human nature that we find in Kant, and the way is open for a regime of rigid discipline linked to efficiency at the level of the state and politics and a concern with a high, nonutilitarian *Kultur* as the justification of human existence in general.[73] This is in the end what links Kant's ability to remain a loyal servant of an absolute monarch, Nietzsche's impact on his disciples, and—though Dewey was in no position to know it—Max Weber's defense of Germany's First World War attempt to impose its *Kultur* on the world. Dewey never denied that Kant himself was a cosmopolitan and never denied that Hegel's talk of the state as the "march of God on earth"[74] was a much more plausible foundation for nationalism and state worship than anything actually to be found in Kant. Nor did he spare Nietzsche's role in promoting the vulgar conception of the "will to power" as the will to push everyone else around in the name of one's own transvaluing value. Dewey could be a very sharp critic, and in *German Philosophy and Politics* he nailed this curious combination of nationalism and snobbishness quite decisively. "When Nietzsche says, 'Man does not desire happiness; only the Englishman does that,' we laugh at the fair hit. But persons who profess no regard for happiness as a test of action have an unfortunate way of living up to their principles by making others *un* happy."[75]

If Nietzsche and Hegel defended power politics and state worship, it was Kant's dualism of fact and value, science and morality, cause and effect on the one hand and a knowledge of ends on the other that left a gaping hole into which German nationalism could rush. What the war showed was clear enough: first, that nationalism was a disaster, and second, that only a naturalistic, experimental, sociologically and psychologically informed approach to ethics and politics was viable. With readers thus lined up behind pragmatism, Dewey could attack Hegel head-on. For Hegel, the state was the work of reason; for Americans, government was the product of experiment. "Psychologists talk about learning by the method of trial and error or success. Our social organization commits us to this philosophy of life. Our working principle is to try: to find out by trying, and to measure the worth of the ideas and theories tried by the success with which they meet the test of application in practice." As Dewey cheerfully agreed, this approach was itself to be tested by experience. "From the standpoint of *apriorism,* it is hopelessly anarchic; it is doomed, *a priori,* to failure. From its own standpoint, it is itself a theory to be tested by experience."[76] Dewey's hostility to absolutisms was thoroughgoing, and he knew better than to make pragmatism's commitment to experiment an absolute. Even though there is something faintly mad about the suggestion that experiment could lead us to abandon experimentation in general, it certainly could do so in particular fields.

Behind all this argument lay one further conviction: that the "present situation presents the spectacle of the breakdown of the whole philosophy of Nationalism, political, racial and cultural."[77] America was faintly schizophrenic, attached to "the older philosophy of isolated national sovereignty" in its relations with other states, while in its "internal constitution" it was "actually interracial and international." The reason the war was a disaster, in this view, was not just that it was a disturbance of the peace—there were many things worse than disturbing the peace—but that it violated the search for what *Democracy and Education* the following year set out as the principles of social growth—namely, an ability to accommodate a wider and wider membership and a wider and wider range of interactions among them. This was the true cosmopolitanism to which Dewey was committed and which—if only by the accident of its situation—the United States was uniquely placed to promote.

On this issue, Dewey was of one mind with Horace Kallen and Randolph Bourne. Bourne's essay "Transnational America"[78] and Kallen's parallel discussion in "Democracy versus the Melting Pot" defended the idea that America was to be a nation of nations; its uniqueness was to lie not merely in its federal governmental structure, with all that that implied about religious, ethnic, and economic pluralism, but in its ability to sustain a democratic culture in which immigrants achieved the kind of freedom that they could have only when complete and unfettered access to the political life of their society was joined to complete freedom to sustain their original cultural and religious attachments. Dewey thought that the ideal of the melting pot was an ugly one: "The theory of the Melting Pot always gave me rather a pang. To maintain that all the constituent elements, geographical, racial and cultural of the United States should be put in the same pot and turned into a uniform and unchanging product is distasteful."[79] Bourne thought it had proved to be a failure because it did not work. All three thought that conservative fear of "hyphenated Americans" was nativist scaremongering and beneath contempt.

Kallen indeed turned the scare around and defended the thought that what made America unique was just this ability to incorporate many cultures within one political order. After the war he retreated from this, but the retreat was a matter of expediency rather than a change of heart. In effect he came to think that the kind of tolerance and acceptance of diversity that a "mosaic" rather than a "melting point" required was not going to be got in a hurry. Seventy-five years later the jury is still out, but from any other perspective than a highly idealistic one, the United States has lived up to the "transnational" idea better than any other country in history, with the possible exception of the Roman Empire in its most flourishing phase.

Lurking beneath their agreement, however, there were differences of emphasis between Dewey and Bourne. Dewey's liberal pluralism was always justified on instrumental grounds. He found it easier to subscribe to the mosaic picture of the United States because he had little sympathy with the cultural and national aspirations that nationalism fed on. Passionate national grievance did not move him. Ireland's claims to independent nationhood, for instance, he simply shrugged aside. Since economic and political trends led in the direction of larger rather than smaller units, small nation-states were anachronistic, and his arguments for cultural diversity had at least some flavor of a faute de mieux, a consolation of a cultural kind for a missing political cosmopolitanism. Bourne and Kallen took pluralism as a value in its own right. They took an almost aesthetic pleasure in the spectacle of a multicultural America, and

Bourne's vision of the "Beloved Community" comes at the end of an account of "the incalculable possibilities of so novel a union of men."[80] By the same token, Bourne was more gloomy than Dewey about the actual impact of migration on the migrant. Americanization had created "hordes of men and women without a spiritual country, cultural outlaws, without taste, without standards but those of the mob."[81]

Bourne was a critic of mass society ahead of his time; Dewey could never be one, partly because Bourne was spiritually rather less of a democrat than Dewey. Dewey would have found it impossible to talk of his fellow countrymen as having only the standards of "the mob." He might have felt a similar despair as Bourne at the spectacle of uprooted migrants who had lost one country and not yet found another, but he would not have allowed such a brutal statement to emerge on paper. Partly this was a matter of age. Bourne was tremendously conscious of the need for his thirty-year-old generation to speak out in favor of vividness, adventurousness, uninhibitedness in sex, politics, poetry, and everything else. Dewey had no such aspirations and no such sense of spearheading Young America. He was at best a middle-aged fellow traveler of such a movement. The other aspect of this near agreement that held the seeds of a later parting of the ways is that Bourne was, and Dewey was not, an emotional Europhile. Bourne disliked England and English stuffiness but admired Germany and German culture, even though he recognized the militarist and authoritarian aspects of German politics for what they were. For Bourne a war between Anglo-America and German-Europe, however those lines were blurred by the participation of France and Russia on the Anglo-American side, was a tragedy in a deeper sense than any Dewey was fully aware of. Dewey's Germany was the home of the Absolute and untenable philosophical dualisms, rather than the poetry of Goethe, Heine, and Rilke and the music of Bach, Mozart, and Beethoven.

Even so, Dewey fought a rearguard action against the idiocies of the Americanization campaigns and against attempts to turn schools into training camps for soldiers. He testified against compulsory military training before a Senate committee in 1916, wrote a string of essays on the general theme of education and national preparedness, and in all of them argued against trying to conscript intelligence and the curriculum for narrowly political, nationalistic goals. What he could not do, and what nearly cost him the friendship of many old friends, was understand pacifist objections to the war. Two essays in particular, "Force, Violence. and Law" and "The Future of Pacifism," simply belittled the pacifist case.[82] Critics who think Dewey was wrong about the war have suggested that he cheated in his discussion of the use of force in social and political life and that Bourne and the critics of Dewey were truer to Dewey's own pragmatism than he was. Both these claims seem farfetched. The defect, if it is one, went all the way down.

Dewey held that "force" was the same thing as power in general. Social life uses different kinds and degrees of force the entire time. We constantly make people do what they otherwise would not, and for anyone to object to the use of force as such is more or less to renounce the desire to have any social organization at all. For a pragmatist, the desire *not* to have an effect on the world is close to unintelligible, and it seems clear enough that Dewey had no understanding at all of this kind of Tolstoyan refusal to act. But the thought that "force" was inescapable is not, as is sometimes said, a willful confusion of force and violence, of persuasion and social pressure with clubs and guns. The broad category really is "force," and Dewey in effect challenges his opponents to answer a simple question: *What* means to getting others to do what they otherwise would not do are they prepared to employ, and what means are they not prepared to employ? Most people draw a sharp line between threats of violence, on the one hand, and mere nagging, persuading, entreating, and at a pinch withdrawal of cooperation, on the other. But this line can be blurred. Is the factory owner who waits until striking workers are driven back to work by starvation using a legitimate form of force or not? Dewey's pacifist critics would mostly have agreed with him that the fact that the factory owner got his way without guns and clubs did not make much difference. By the same token, Dewey was inclined to think that once the United States started down the slippery slope of embargoes and blockades, there was not much difference between that and war.

What shook Dewey's critics and the targets of his attacks was not the rift with pragmatism that his support of the war required but the brutality of the pragmatist position once it was spelled out. For Dewey, the issue was simple in logic though complicated in fact. Could the American involvement in the war yield consequences that outweighed the losses involved? This was not a utilitarian calculation; who could measure the pleasures forgone and given by anything as uncontrolled as a war? It was a rough-and-ready estimate of whether the principles of sociability set out in *Democracy and Education* would be damaged or enhanced by war. On the face of it, Dewey had given his answer: War was intrinsically the antithesis of sociality. It was the opposite extreme of extending our sympathies and incorporating a wider range of people into our activities and widening those activities in the process. It meant taking sides, separating people into friend and foe, ally and enemy; more than that, it meant reducing what "we" and "they" did to a brutally simple and narrow set of tasks: kill to avoid being killed. Until the war was on him, this was in fact Dewey's position, and even in the essay he wrote on the brink, "In a Time of National Hesitation," he took this line.[83]

Once events had gone too far for such reflections, however, a new question was raised: What are we fighting for? Dewey wrote several essays on that theme, and they all say much the same thing. The war will be warranted if it spreads the principles of democracy and not otherwise; America is not fighting for land, empire, national pride, or American *Kultur,* but to safeguard the principle of democracy. What that involves is not a matter of bullying every other country into some facile "one man, one vote" political scheme. It involves an attempt to substitute intelligence for violence in the affairs of the world. Dewey argued for the Fourteen Points: no reparations, no attempt to make the losers pay the costs of the war, no dismemberment of existing states. When the war was over, more effective international institutions should be set up to secure the peace. As liberals had been arguing since the 1860s on the other side of the Atlantic, a league of nations had to be established, to secure a more effective role for international law and international mediation and establish collective rather than national security. Dewey was even more concerned about the effect of the war on the United States itself.

The war would not be an economic disaster; it would not consume a great deal of the country's financial or human resources. The greatest danger was to American habits of toleration and the acceptance of dissent; the greatest benefit the country might reap was the acknowledgment that a greater degree of social organization was required. Old-fashioned appeals to laissez-faire and the sanctity of property were now visibly a drag on the war effort, and progressive Americans would count the war a good bargain if, but only if, it accelerated the process of strengthening internal economic, social, and political organization. Herbert Croly had suggested in passing in *The Promise of American Life* that a good war might help to "nationalize" American politics. This was too crude for Dewey and too much in the spirit of the rough-riding Theodore Roosevelt, but it was not altogether out of line with his wishes. Randolph Bourne complained in "The Twilight of the Idols" that Dewey's support of the war revealed pragmatism as essentially bankrupt. It had always been bankrupt, but Bourne saw it only when the war revealed it. For pragmatism was a theory about means, not about ends. "Instrumentalism" told us to judge ideas, institutions, and actions as "instruments," but in the absence of a convincing account of what they were instruments for, we might do almost anything. The temptation, one to which Dewey had succumbed, was to pick up our goals from the most powerful institutions around us. In times of peace, and as preached by good-natured philosophers who had received the standard middle-class Christian education that Dewey had received, pragmatism was harmless. It encouraged mild reform and took its goals from benign rather than malign forces. When the times that try men's souls came around, pragmatism had nothing to say.

Philosophically this was not a well-aimed blow. Dewey's various ethical writings, culminating in the great textbook *Ethics,* of 1908 and 1932, had a lot to say about how a pragmatist looked for the ends of life. Dewey knew as well as the next person that a means is in logic a means to an end and that a pragmatist ethics must have a stopping point in what he later called "consummatory experience," those states of ourselves and the world that we think are good in themselves and that our ideas and actions, theories and institutions are instrumental in creating and enhancing. Dewey wanted to blur the distinction between means and ends, wanted to emphasize that there was no class of things that somehow could only be ends and never means, wanted to emphasize that ends change and that we very often value the process of achieving what we want rather than the end result as something separate and distinct from that process. It was these emphases that made pragmatist ethics distinctive. But that is a long way from suggesting that pragmatism had no account of ends and how we choose them. Its distinctiveness was to insist that we discover our goals in experience and not by the favored procedures of past philosophers such as Plato, Kant, or Mill.

Bourne clearly struck home with the thought that Dewey's ideas were ill adapted to a time of war. Dewey claimed that his opponents were in the grip of moral absolutes and that they were more interested in keeping their hands clean than in doing anything to bring about a better peace. It ought to be said in his defense that this was not a prelude to encouraging the authorities to round them up and jail them. Dewey insisted throughout the American involvement in the war that there should be *no* attempt to impose uniformity of thought or outlook over the war, and he always said that the country had far more to fear from intolerance than from whatever inconvenience protesters, conscientious objectors, and any other opponents of the war might pose. Still, he was obtuse about his opponents. For one thing, it was highly debatable whether his opponents were absolutists in any intellectually serious sense. Many of them—Bourne included—thought that there were worse things in the world than war but insisted that the First World War did great evil for no corresponding good and that it was thus wrong. In this, Bourne was very like Bertrand Russell, who always maintained that *some* wars were justified, but not this one.

Many critics thought, just as Dewey later came to think, that the war was none of America's business. For another thing, it was not obvious why Dewey believed that a degree of absolutism was always wrong. There is something to be said for the view that many rights and prohibitions are couched in absolute terms because we do not want people calculating whether to change them. We might think that freedom of religion is ultimately justified by the fact that it achieves a rational attitude toward serious matters, and still agree that on any given occasion people ought to be free to believe and practice whatever religion they wish, regardless of the rationality of their views. One might in the same way think that people who were utterly committed to nonviolence would do better over the long run than people who calculated whether to drop that policy every time the question came up. The last thing one might want to say in complaint is that Dewey's habitual mode of thought was simply ill adapted to the pressures of war. Nobody can write sensibly about war who does not understand that war has a tendency to run away with those who engage in it and that what may begin as a controlled use of force for clearly defined ends frequently masters those who wage it and turns into something else entirely, driven apparently by its own malign logic. Democracies are especially vulnerable to this. Democracies cannot fight unless public opinion is mobilized, but when it is mobilized, it is prone to swallow absolutist slogans; this means that democracies are bad at fighting limited wars. The Civil War was recent enough for Dewey to have no excuse for failing to understand this. The Civil War had begun as an old-fashioned war and had turned into something close to total war. What had begun as a war for the defense of the Union had ended as a war to abolish slavery and reconstruct the South. What had begun as a rather primitive military exercise in 1861 had gone on to be the first mechanized war and a harbinger of the horrors of World War I.

Dewey's reactions to events as they unfolded suggests that he was by no means happy even with his own views. At Columbia, President Butler had set up a committee to consider whether anyone on the faculty opposed the war in such a way that he could be considered "disloyal" enough to warrant dismissal. When the first case came up, he ignored the committee and dismissed the distinguished psychologist James McKeen Cattell, who had been more responsible than anyone else for bringing Dewey to Columbia; he then dismissed Henry Wadsworth Dana, the literary critic, again without summoning the committee. Dewey had begun by treating such intolerance as he had observed as something of a joke, a sort of puppyish overexcitement natural in a country not used to such excitements; now in an article entitled "In Explanation of Our Lapse," he admitted that he had simply been wrong.[84] Even so, he did not lash out at Butler in the same way that Bourne did, and he did not follow Charles Beard in resigning from the university. As Dykhuizen says, "he cancelled his classes for the day." The cases went to the AAUP, which duly censured Butler, who duly took no notice and went on in his autocratic ways for another twenty-eight years, collecting a Nobel Peace Prize on the way. But the case stimulated the efforts of Dewey, Beard, Croly and others to establish the New School for Social Research as the first university-level institution that practiced absolute freedom of inquiry and academic self-government.

Polish Politics and Albert Barnes

Dewey's liberalism in time of war is illuminated a little further by the commission of inquiry that he served on in the summer and fall of 1918 at the fag end of the war. This was set up and paid for by Albert Barnes, more famous as an art collector and for his bad temper than as a sponsor of social science research. He had attended Dewey's classes at the same time as Anzia Yezierska and had fallen for Dewey's ideas with the same passion that he brought to collecting modern art. The research Barnes wanted to sponsor was into the political allegiances of the Polish community of Philadelphia, and the aim he had in mind was to swing the Poles behind Deweyan democracy as the guiding principle of the postwar Polish state. The Polish community in America was divided in its allegiances between those who supported the conservative Polish National Committee and those who supported the liberal and mildly socialist Committee of National Defense; both organizations were primarily based in Europe, and both wished to exercise a dominating influence on the makeup of an independent postwar Poland. The famous pianist Jan Paderewski was the American spokesman of the conservatives and was a good friend of both Wilson and his assistant Colonel House. He also enjoyed the overwhelming support of the Polish community.

Commentators have written anxiously and disapprovingly of the way Dewey, egged on by Barnes, turned the research into propaganda and the basis of an attempt to combat the manipulations of the conservative National Committee and its offshoots in America.[85] It is a particular indictment that Dewey was ready to use whatever influence he could gain with House and the American negotiators in Paris to throw American support behind the liberals and against the conservatives even though the majority of American Poles would not have been of the same mind as he. This seems altogether too squeamish. On the one hand, Dewey did not set out to manipulate government opinion by underhand means; he thought that the American government got distorted advice and information from reporters associated with the Polish National Committee, and he put his hopes in getting other information into the government's hands. On the other hand, he was faced with a situation in which the United States government in conjunction with the European allies was about to be responsible for drawing up new borders and recognizing new regimes. The thought that he ought to have sat on his hands and not argued for his own opinion seems faintly bizarre.

That is no more than to say that Dewey's instrumentalism was instrumentalist. He never flinched from the thought that governments ought to govern, that people with strong political views ought to organize to get those views implemented as policy, and that philosophers who wanted to have an effect on the world ought not to mind getting their hands dirty. To pull back fastidiously from making a difference just because it involved making a difference would be a very strange policy for a pragmatist. One can complain that Dewey never realized the limits of the power of opinion, that he never took the full measure of the boundless cynicism of politicians—after all, it took three years of close contact with them before Walter Lippmann learned that lesson—and that he shared in the characteristic self-deceptions of most politically engaged intellectuals. That, however, is a very different accusation from any suggestion that his liberalism was not genuine liberalism or that his democratic goals were not democratic. He was a liberal, and a democrat, and anxious to make a difference. By the standards of anything less than twenty-twenty hindsight, Dewey did better than most of his contemporaries, both in the United States and in Europe.

Six

Political Narrowness and Philosophical Breadth

In the 1920s Dewey's politics and philosophy went in opposite directions; his hopes for both American and international politics were much diminished, while his philosophical imagination took wings. One might guess that the two things were connected, that as American democracy in its grubby actuality disappointed him, he turned to the contemplation of the ideal community in which we might enjoy rich and uninhibited communication with one another and with nature itself. If any such thing did underlie Dewey's postwar career, it was very much against his own will and judgment. To the extent that Dewey held any ideal as an absolute, he was absolutely committed to not abandoning his fellow citizens as irredeemably irrational, gullible, and shortsighted and absolutely committed to not using philosophy as a consolation.

This chapter frequently focuses on Dewey's politics in the down-to-earth sense: his view of the failure of American policy during and after the war, his anxieties about the prospects for democracy in the age of mass communication, his fears of the masses' reactions to the ravings of demagogues, and his thoughts on the prospects for exporting American liberalism and of underdeveloped countries' developing their own brand of modernity on the other. This is not the chapter's only concern, however. The most common complaint against pragmatism, during the war and forever after, was that it had nothing to say about ultimate goods. Catholic critics contrasted Thomas Aquinas's account of the *summum bonum* and the *finis ultima*—our highest good and our final end—with Dewey's emphasis on the "instrumental," but it was also the standard complaint of leftish critics such as Randolph Bourne and Lewis Mumford. The complaint is simple: Pragmatism explains everything in terms of "instrumental" considerations; but instruments are only means, and what we want from philosophers is an account of how we select the ends or goals for whose sake we employ these means. One may suspect that sensitivity to this charge was one reason why Dewey came to call himself an experimentalist rather than an instrumentalist.

The Not-So-Roaring Twenties

During the 1920s Dewey responded to his critics—generally with no suggestion that he was doing so—by writing increasingly freely about his "ultimate" beliefs. I put "ultimate" in quotation marks to acknowledge that Dewey did not accept the conventional division between proximate and ultimate goals. Though he acknowledged an obligation to say something to those who had misunderstood pragmatism as a theory that emphasized only immediate goals and narrowly practical considerations, he was no more inclined than he had been to accept the conventional distinction between means and ends.[1] The really imaginative move that Dewey made was to introduce the idea of "consummatory experience" into the argument: experiences that we not only pursue for their own sake but that crystallize the meaning of our lives and especially of our experience of poetry, painting, and nature. These are the proper subject matter of art and religion. I defer an account and criticism of Dewey's views on art and religion until the next chapter, and I leave to two chapters ahead his own popularizations of his ideas in the 1930s, but in giving an account of the philosophical underpinnings of his politics during the twenties, I cannot wholly evade these subjects.

Between 1920 and 1940—that is, between his early sixties and his early eighties—Dewey produced a flood of work for a wider audience. Of his *Collected Works,* half were written after 1924, when he was already sixty-five, and of the one thousand published essays, books, etc. that the *Collected Works* contain, some three hundred were written after Dewey retired at the age of seventy. Even a fiercely selective look at this must ignore a great deal and range too widely for intellectual comfort. I begin with a sketch of Dewey's busy life in the 1920s, which began with an extended tour of the Far East and ended with his retirement from active duty at Columbia, and then go on to discuss his turn toward an essentially isolationist view of foreign affairs. This brought him into head-on disagreement with two impressive thinkers, Arthur Lovejoy, who had rescued the philosophical reputation of Johns Hopkins and was Dewey's peer in philosophical and historical matters, and Walter Lippmann, who was a former collaborator on the *New Republic* and was now plowing his own furrow as twentieth-century America's most distinguished journalist and political commentator.

It was Lippmann again who wrote two scathing accounts of the failure of democracy in his *Public Opinion* and *The Phantom Public* and so provoked Dewey's attempt to provide a more elaborated account of democracy than he had hitherto produced. *The Public and Its Problems* is a work that Dewey's admirers particularly cherish, as did Dewey.[2] There have been critics who have thought it more successful in describing the public's problems than in suggesting any solution, and I am very much on their side; but it can certainly be said that *The Public and Its Problems* was Dewey's longest and most considered theoretical account of what he thought democracy entailed, and his account surely explained why democracy was so hard to practice.

I then turn to Dewey's overseas tours. These have a more than merely biographical interest. Since Dewey has so often been described as the most American of American thinkers, the obvious question is how far he believed his ideas were capable of global application and how far they were more narrowly directed, to early-twentieth-century America alone. There is no simple answer, but Dewey's attempt to think his way through it is impressive and oddly moving. The spectacle of this very self-consciously middle-class Middle American coming to grips with utterly foreign social structures and political mores is all the more engrossing for its determinedly plainspoken and antiromantic expression. So I follow him to the Far East, Turkey, and Russia, though I say nothing of his brief lecture tour of Mexico, largely because this was a visit in which he lectured on philosophy to a largely academic audience at a time when he was anyway preoccupied with Alice Dewey's rapidly worsening health. Finally I turn to the philosophical foundations on which this extraordinary bustle was built.

The 1920s saw Dewey publish what in most ways was the most satisfactory account of his own ideas—clear, accessible, and full of wide-ranging suggestions about the implications for political and social life of his pragmatist position. In *Reconstruction in Philosophy, Human Nature and Conduct, Experience and Nature,* and *The Quest for Certainty,* Dewey repeated his basic convictions: the need to start with everyday experience; the dangers of any philosophy that made thought superior to work, that elevated the timeless over the transitory and shunted ideals off to a realm of the eternally inaccessible; and, as always, the perils of separating in thought what was not separated in life, dividing art from science, morality from self-interest, everyday work from creative satisfaction. Dewey insisted that all experience is saturated with *meaning* and that the philosopher's task was to reflect on what meanings experience contained and how they fitted together. Poets and artists revealed the meaning latent in everyday experience, but scientists did so too; a religious attitude to the world did so, though formalized and dogmatic religion obscured the meaning of the world rather than revealed it. These books were the product of Dewey's endless labors at the lecturer's podium. They are repetitive and fuzzy-edged, they are sometimes labored, and they alternate passages of real nobility with passages of clumsy and long-winded groping after an elusive point. They are also wonderfully thought-provoking, imaginative, and original, and like nothing else in twentieth-century philosophy. It is hard to imagine anyone of even very mildly developed philosophical curiosity who would not find them both enchanting and infuriating.

Getting Over the War

The First World War severely damaged Dewey's intellectual and political poise. Our image of Dewey as a sturdy and benign force for free speech and unforced communication must be a little damaged by the spectacle of Dewey forcing the editors of the *New Republic* to close their pages to Randolph Bourne and browbeating the editors of the *Dial* to force him off the editorial board.[3] On the other hand, there is no evidence that Dewey himself felt any pangs about his own conduct. We might suppose that he had behaved badly because he was none too secure in the views he put forward, but it is not clear that he himself believed then or ever afterward that he had behaved badly. As when he felt himself under attack in his last years at Chicago, Dewey was both self-righteous in self-defense and pretty uninhibited about standing up for himself. Indeed, by most people's lights, he had at worst been boorish and slightly obtuse about Jane Addams and thoroughly in the wrong only about Randolph Bourne. Dewey would not talk about Randolph Bourne after the latter's death in the flu epidemic of November 1918, and when friends later pressed him on the subject, all they got was a vague suggestion that Bourne had lacked substance.[4] It seems at least possible that this later reaction, some twenty years after the event, reflected Dewey's later disputes with Bourne's allies. Dewey reviewed Lewis Mumford's *The Golden Day* in hostile terms and took the chance to get his revenge for Mumford's complaint that pragmatism was a theory of "acquiescence" in whatever the holders of power in the United States might get up to by accusing Mumford of a self-indulgent retreat to the ivory tower.[5]

The conclusion of the war and its aftermath in the Paris Peace Conference came as a shattering disappointment to Dewey. He had subscribed wholeheartedly to Wilson's Fourteen Points and had embraced the war as a war to make the world safe for democracy. Like many others who had signed on in the same cause, he discovered that the war had largely been fought to make it easier for Britain and France to carve up the Middle East and to appropriate former German colonies in Africa. The League of Nations that emerged from the war was nothing like the League of Nations he hoped would replace international conflict. He had wanted a magnanimous peace and a league that replaced international anarchy with international law. What he got was a vindictive peace and a league of the victorious powers that excluded the losers and left out the newly established Soviet state. The vindictiveness of the treaty was typified by a reparations policies, insisted on by France and to a lesser extent by Britain, that aimed at making Germany pay the war expenses of the Allies. A shattered German economy plainly could not meet the cost, and it was hard to escape the thought that the policy's purpose was less to compensate the Allies than to make Germany suffer.

Allied policies thus contradicted everything Dewey had thought America had been fighting for, and the peace that emerged from the Paris Conference was exactly the scheme for the legalized plundering of the defeated that Dewey believed American intervention had aimed to prevent.[6] Dewey took some time to despair. Although he had wanted a much more dramatic transformation of international relations than was ever likely to come out of the war and was therefore anxious about the outcome of the postwar settlement from early 1918 onward, he encouraged support for Wilson and the League until it was quite clear that the peace conference was a disaster for his cause. Once the terms of the Treaty of Versailles became known, he jumped ship and never changed his mind again.

Dewey's views were squarely in line with those of the *New Republic* and initially with those of Walter Lippmann.[7] Lippmann came back from playing a humble and dispiriting role in the preparations for the peace conference, still ready to swallow a bad peace for the sake of getting a League, only to decide as the provisions of the peace treaty were revealed that it was too bad to be borne and the League not worth having in its projected shape. Lippmann, but not Dewey, changed his mind one more time. Lippmann was more willing to make the best of a bad job, less willing to see the United States retreat from the mess left by the war, and more sympathetic than Dewey toward the plight of Germany, the Soviet Union, and the inheritors of the Austro-Hungarian Empire. By the time the outlawry of war movement had become a major force in American foreign relations, largely through the support of Senator William Borah of Idaho, the chairman of the Senate Foreign Relations Committee, Lippmann was in favor of renewing the American entanglement with Europe and deeply contemptuous of the line taken by the outlawry of war movement. Borah—and Dewey, too—argued that war should be made illegal but went on to argue that the United States should not be part of the World Court that any "outlawry" seemed to depend on.[8] Lippmann wrote some wonderfully scathing criticisms of this policy, and Dewey was perhaps the only defender of it who could put together a halfway adequate response.

Japan and China

Dewey was not in the United States to feel the full force of the *New Republic*'s disappointment with Versailles; when he returned from a long tour of China and Japan in 1921, he took up the isolationist and outlawry of war banner and stood by the views he then expressed until the Japanese attack on Pearl Harbor on December 7, 1941, rendered them irrelevant.[9] While the Paris Peace Conference was in progress during the first half of 1919, he was elsewhere. He had sabbatical leave for 1918–19 and spent the fall of 1918 living on the West Coast. He had been invited to lecture in Japan and in January 1919 embarked on what became a two-year tour of the Far East. He delivered a series of lectures that eventually turned into *Reconstruction in Philosophy* in Japan; while there, he was invited to give a further set of lectures at the National University in

Beijing, to run from June 1919 to March 1920. His stay in Beijing coincided with that of Bertrand Russell, there with his young mistress, Dora Black. Although Russell had met Dewey in 1914 and had liked him a good deal, this was their first close encounter.

Russell was under an official cloud, actually under several dense layers of official cloud: His opposition to the war had not endeared him to the British diplomatic service, and British diplomats in Peking made themselves as unpleasant as they could. Nor did his attitude to the postwar behavior of the Western powers toward China improve matters. Russell wanted America and Britain to rescind the treaties that gave them a humiliating degree of power over the Chinese in such port cities as Shanghai and to renounce their various monopolies over Chinese exports and imports; he also insisted they should repay the profits they had made from their lopsided trading relations with China and return the Boxer indemnity, the money extorted years before after the Boxer Rebellion. The fact that Russell was there with a woman to whom he was not married affronted the respectable expatriate community. Russell was accepted everywhere, but his secretary and mistress, Dora Black, was not. As she had earlier done with Maxim Gorky, Mrs. Dewey refused to side with the respectable. The Deweys' house was one of the few that was open to the two of them without hesitation.[10]

While Dewey was in Beijing, Russell nearly died of pneumonia. Dewey was a frequent visitor to Russell's bedside, though he seems not to have been the intermediary who got a new serum from the American hospital and so saved Russell's life. Newspaper reports at the time claimed that Dewey took down Russell's last will and testament; Dewey himself did not record that fact if it was one. Russell's eccentric assistant Ralph Schoenman later gave an elaborately embroidered account of animated conversations between Russell and Dewey, suggesting that they had a tremendous impact on Dewey.[11] Nothing that Dewey wrote then or later confirms this tale; indeed, during the 1920s the two of them began to write increasingly irritable and dismissive accounts of each other's works. Dewey's "Pragmatic America," for instance, appeared in the *New Republic* in 1922; it is not only an interesting essay on the question of how far pragmatism is a distinctively American philosophy but a highly effective demolition of Russell's casual and silly claim that he found the "love of truth obscured in America by commercialism of which pragmatism is the philosophical expression. . . ." It was William James who excoriated "the moral flabbiness born of the exclusive worship of the bitch-goddess SUCCESS," and Charles Peirce was so far dedicated to truth and individuality that he nearly starved in consequence.[12] Irritation was a more likely result of a prolonged encounter between Dewey and Russell than mutual admiration.

Dewey's lectures in Japan were not very successful; his boring delivery made for a dwindling audience, and his unflinching allegiance to democracy made him unwelcome to the authorities. In China he became a celebrity, and his views on education passed into the intellectual repertoire of Chinese reformers, especially those associated with the May Fourth Movement. The May Fourth Movement had been sparked off by the Chinese government's abject capitulation to Japanese demands for something very like a veto over Chinese economic and political policy. On May 4, 1919, a few days after Dewey's arrival and a month before he was due to start lecturing, students at Beijing University had staged a demonstration against the government's policy and had gone on to demand a boycott of Japanese goods. The movement spread through the entire country, forcing the government to backtrack on its appeasement of Japan and inspiring Chinese intellectuals with new hopes for a policy of cultural modernization. It was all utterly fascinating not only to Dewey but to Mrs. Dewey and their daughters Lucy and Evelyn who accompanied them on the tour.

The contrasting reception of Dewey's work in Japan and China had an ironic result. In China Dewey's success meant that thirty years later he became an object of suspicion and obloquy during the most ideologically narrow-minded periods of Maoist rule, and his translators and disciples were forced to recant their enthusiasm for his word and denounce the "poison" of pragmatism. In Japan, on the other hand, his relatively unfriendly reception meant that the seeds were sown for the widespread acceptance of his ideas about elementary education only when they were brought back with General MacArthur's army of occupation in 1945. In neither country did "pure" philosophers take pragmatism seriously as a philosophical doctrine, but in both countries Dewey's educational theory was congenial to teachers and those involved in teacher training. In Japan, however, the illiberalism of the regime made progress impossible; in China the inability of the government to impose any particular creed gave Dewey's followers more room for maneuver.

Dewey was, moreover, more easily assimilated by a Chinese audience than was Russell. Dewey's liberalism was holistic; it stressed community values, emphasized the child's ties to his or her local culture and community, and saw the school as a natural extension of the family. To an audience brought up on Confucian ideals of family and community loyalty, Dewey's liberalism was much more attractive than the fiercely individualistic liberalism of someone like Russell, who struck his Chinese and Japanese hosts as a very distinguished creature from another planet entirely.[13] In the Far East, just as in America, Dewey brought off the delicate rhetorical trick of investing his views with the mystique of modernity and science at the same time that he persuaded his hearers that they were firmly linked to tradition and the ways of everyday common sense.

Dewey was prevailed on to stay in China for a second year, Columbia cheerfully giving him an extra year's leave of absence even though his colleagues constantly wrote to assure him how much they missed him. He returned from China in 1921 and took up the familiar round. He revised the lectures he had delivered in Stanford in 1918, and they appeared as *Human Nature and Conduct;* in 1922 he gave three Carus Lectures to the American

Philosophical Association, and these, much revised and extended, came out in 1925 as *Experience and Nature*. The two books together give as clear and persuasive an account as Dewey ever gave of his ethics and metaphysics. What *Human Nature and Conduct* lacks in elaboration compared with *Ethics,* it more than makes up for with its verve and briskness. On the political front Dewey wrote a string of essays attacking the postwar settlement, approving of America's decision not to sign the Treaty of Versailles or join the League of Nations, and supporting the work of the New York Committee for the Outlawry of War. While the country turned sharply conservative after the war, Dewey swam as hard as he could against the tide. When the League for Industrial Democracy was established in 1921, he immediately joined; he became a member of its national committee and subsequently a vice-president, in 1939 was elected president for a two-year stint, and thereafter was honorary president for life. His politics in the orthodox, or electoral, sense remained as nonpartisan as ever. In 1924 he joined the La Follette third-party campaign and spent the next fifteen years vainly looking for a third-party alliance of progressives that might somehow extricate the country from the mess into which postwar conservatism had plunged it.

Experience and Nature bears the signs of another of Dewey's postwar passions. Besides Anzia Yezierska, his classes of 1917–18 had contained Albert Barnes, the inventor of Argyrol.[14] Barnes's presence in the classes has been variously described. Although others said that Barnes invariably fell fast asleep as soon as the class began, Dewey described him as the sharpest student he ever had. Barnes's devotion to Dewey's educational theories was not diminished by his experience of Dewey's educational practice, their friendship was cemented by their joint work on the commission of inquiry into the Polish immigrants of Philadelphia, and when Barnes established the Barnes Foundation in 1922, to bring the blessings of his extraordinary collection of Renoirs, Matisses, Monets, and Degases before the students he thought should see them, Dewey was appointed the foundation's educational adviser.[15] Dewey was the only person of any independent intellectual or social standing who did not quarrel with Barnes, a fact that Sidney Hook later described as the only serious failing that Dewey ever exhibited.[16]

It is on the face of it strange that Dewey, who was in thought and deed a democrat through and through, could have tolerated the autocratic, changeable, and wildly aggressive Barnes. However, Dewey had a taste for the company of oddballs of all sorts, and the seeming gullibility of which his friends complained may have been less a real failure of judgment than a policy of giving possible charlatans the benefit of the doubt. At all events, Dewey appears to have found Barnes more entertaining than disagreeable. Whatever Dewey's judgment of Barnes, it cannot be denied that (in addition to a good deal of money over the years) what Barnes gave Dewey was of enormous value. The great complaint against pragmatism, reiterated over and over by its critics, was that it had nothing interesting to say about *ultimate* values; the most effective rhetorical counterstroke was to give an account of some of these ultimate values from a pragmatist perspective. The values displayed in art were plainly one of the best places to do so. It was not until 1934 with the publication of *Art as Experience* that Dewey did this at length, but *Experience and Nature* sketched what was needed and showed the impact of Barnes's generosity in exposing Dewey to the masterpieces of late impressionism and postimpressionism.[17]

The International Sage

The 1920s were the Indian summer of Dewey's academic career—not his career as an intellectual appealing to the public at large but his career as a professor and teacher. Between his work in the philosophy department at Columbia and his influence on Kilpatrick's Teachers College, he was universally respected as a progressive guru. It was not surprising that in 1924 the Turkish government called on him to advise it about the reform of education in its newly modernizing state; in the summer of 1926 he was invited to lecture in Mexico City, and in 1928 he went on a private initiative along with some thirty others to investigate the educational system of the Soviet Union. His account of Soviet education in that brief moment before the darkness of Stalinism fell on the country was sufficiently favorable to hang the reputation of fellow traveling around his neck for many years and to make the American Communist party briefly hopeful that it might somehow use him for its own purposes. Needless to say, it failed rather dramatically; during the 1930s and indeed until his death Dewey was a fierce and persistent critic of everything to do with Soviet totalitarianism and the American sympathizers with the Soviet system.

The sense of a career's winding down must have been strong in Dewey's mind in the last few years of the twenties, however. On their visit to Mexico City Alice Dewey fell ill with heart trouble and became steadily more ill through the following fall and winter. Finally, in July 1927, she had a series of attacks that killed her. Dewey adopted the Puritan recipe for dealing with grief—which is to say, he carried on working more energetically than ever and writing even more for even wider audiences. In 1928 he gave the Gifford Lectures at the University of Edinburgh; these were, and indeed still are, intended under the terms of Lord Gifford's endowment to be devoted to topics connected with "natural theology," a charge that most lecturers nowadays ignore without making much of it.[18] Whether it is quite right to say that Dewey also evaded it is debatable. At all events, *The Quest for Certainty,* appearing in 1929, dismayed more than a few readers because of its dismissive account of the consolations of religion. It forms an apt third member of the trio of books that marked the decade. One might say that *Human Nature and Conduct* turns ethics into social psychology and sociology and the investigation of when habit is fruitful and when it must be abandoned, *Experience and*

Nature provides a pragmatist metaphysics by showing that experience is its own guide, its own support, and its own critic and neither needs nor could be given the kind of metaphysical underpinnings that philosophers have often tried to supply, while *The Quest for Certainty* drew the obvious, if alarming, conclusion that we neither could have a supernatural guarantee of our everyday natural grasp of the world nor would know what to do with it if we had it; it would be tainted by our natural understanding of it or else unintelligible. One might imagine that Dewey's readers, having seen so much of the traditional philosophical enterprise thus leveled with the ground, would conclude that the book that began the sequence, *Reconstruction in Philosophy,* might have been better called "destruction of philosophy prior to reconstruction in everyday life." That was, after all, the upshot of the view that we must turn away from the problems of philosophers to use the skills of philosophers in analyzing the problems of men.[19]

As though it were not enough to scandalize the religiously and philosophically orthodox, Dewey turned on a former ally when he took up the cudgels against Walter Lippmann. One occasion for controversy was provided by the outlawry of war movement, attacked by Lippmann and defended by Dewey in what was thought to be the most effective exchange of polemics the movement ever sparked off. The outlawry of war national committee collected Dewey's responses together in a little book, *The Outlawry of War: What It Is and What It Is Not,* of which some twenty thousand copies were distributed. Lippmann had also turned his attention to the role of the public in democratic government and had come perilously close to the conclusion that it could have none. In *Public Opinion* and *The Phantom Public* he argued that public affairs were beyond the comprehension of the average man and woman and that good government could be had only by allowing disinterested experts to exercise a preponderant power over government. Accountability to an uninformed mass was useless. Dewey replied in *The Public and Its Problems,* a polemically shrewd assault on Lippmann's increasingly elitist view of politics.

At the end of the decade Dewey was seventy and about to retire from active teaching at Columbia. He retired in June 1930. The celebration of his long and fruitful career went on for two days and provoked his one essay in autobiography, "From Absolutism to Experimentalism." At the celebrations he made some extemporary remarks about the need to defend a modern and more adequate form of individuality than had been dreamed of in traditional liberalism, and this was the theme of a series of articles in the *New Republic* that was later turned into a short book, *Individualism Old and New.* Its natural place is with *Liberalism and Social Action,* and discussion of it can decently be left until then; but it marked the beginnings of what became clearer in the 1930s, a developing sense that Dewey had perhaps exaggerated the social element in human life or at least might have left openings through which unacceptable forms of collectivism might creep.

A Bad Peace

There is by now universal agreement that the peace treaty forced on the defeated Germany and Austria-Hungary after 1918 was entirely unsatisfactory. The nature of the unsatisfactoriness is more open to dispute. Broadly the attempt to exact reparations was misguided and was likely to lead to disasters such as the great inflation of 1922–23, when the German currency collapsed, the savings of the middle classes were wiped out, and the way was paved for the rise of the Nazi party. Whether a League of Nations with the United States playing a full and active role from the beginning might have made a system of collective security possible and might therefore have curbed the dictators before they ran amok is hard to tell. In any case, it is hard to see how the United States could have played any such role. The effect of the war was to reinforce isolationist tendencies rather than to encourage a taste for humanitarian intervention in the affairs of Europe.

It was not only isolationist tendencies that had been sparked off by the war. The fact that so many of the members of radical organizations of one kind or another opposed to the war had been German or eastern European or Russian had sent the country into paroxysms of fear of the Red Menace. The first few years after the war saw the roundup and deportation of large numbers of resident aliens who had often been living in the United States for twenty or thirty years. The energetic role of the Democratic Attorney General A. Mitchell Palmer in organizing raids on these foreigners led to the title of the "Palmer Raids" being bestowed on this episode in the "Red Scare."

It was not only against socialists and foreigners that these nativist assaults were directed. In the southern states the Ku Klux Klan revived its old campaigns against blacks who tried to break free of the informal servitude in which they were held and against any white sympathizers. The conservative backlash played much the largest part in Dewey's isolationism. Dewey feared the effect of any future war on the American social fabric much more than he feared the physical destructiveness of war itself. He may have had some distant memory of the ravaged region of northern Virginia when he and his family lived there for a couple of years at the end of the Civil War, but since he was only five or six at the time, he may well not. The physical devastation of war was not something he dwelt on, and it may not have been something he felt imaginatively. The destruction of American tolerance and mutual acceptance was another matter entirely. The horror at "apartness" and "sharp dualisms" that gives his philosophical writings their flavor was a psychological trait of great force independently of its intellectual basis. "No more war" was the response.

Dewey's thoughts on the need for a League in the first place were very characteristic of liberals in both Britain and America before 1914. In a series of articles in the *Dial* and the *New Republic* in mid-1918, Dewey deployed the pragmatist approach to ethics to argue that replacing force by morality in international relations was essentially a question of organization. "Individuals have to be moral because they can be. They can be because they are partakers in modes of associated life which confer powers and confer responsibilities upon them. States are non-moral in their activities just because of the absence of an inclusive society which defines and establishes rights. . . . The distance which separates the code of intrigue and conquest permissible to nations from the code exacted of persons measures the significance for morals of social organization."[20] As always, the thought was that people *use* moral standards for practical purposes that arise naturally out of everyday living together. Since states existed in a "state of nature" rather than in a social state, they had too few common purposes and too few common tasks to force a regard for ethical standards upon them. This then meant that a League of Nations must be very much more than the "League to Enforce Peace" that was how the League was initially envisaged. It had to be an organization devoted to many more and many broader tasks, especially to the achievement of international economic and social cooperation. The same arguments that Dewey had leveled against laissez-faire economics in domestic matters applied in international economic affairs as well.

He made one especially shrewd point. He observed that apart from the major powers such as Britain, the United States, and France, smaller countries had always managed their international affairs by becoming clients to more powerful states. The danger that faced the powers that proposed to set up the League was that they would destroy these old arrangements, bad as they were, and put in place nothing to replace the good things these bad old arrangements had achieved. A League that looked to most of the world like a device to make it easier for the victorious Allies to engage in the economic exploitation of the rest of the world was unlikely to succeed and indeed did not deserve to.

Dewey was lecturing in Asia while the Versailles Treaty was being hammered out in 1919 and returned to the United States only in 1921. The debate over the League had been fought and won by the anti-League forces the year before. For the most part Dewey sent the *New Republic* short essays on Chinese affairs during the years of his absence, but he wrote a certain amount on American attitudes to international politics. The first announcement of his own disillusionment came in "The Discrediting of Idealism" in the summer of 1919. Rather wickedly Dewey found it impossible to admit that he himself had held too simple a view of the passions and interests at stake in the war. He tried to blame the pacifists and antiwar activists for the fact that "[t]he ideals of the United States have been defeated in the settlement because we took into the war our sentimentalism, our attachment to moral sentiments as efficacious powers, our pious optimism as to the inevitable victory of the 'right,' our childish belief that physical energy can do the work that only intelligence can do, our evangelical hypocrisy that morals and 'ideals' have a self-propelling and self-executing force."[21] This was a strange complaint against people who had been trying to stop the United States from taking either its virtues or its vices anywhere at all.

Still, Dewey's reaction against the war and then against postwar policies was not itself simple. As he had done before the war broke upon him, he argued for the inescapability of doing something rather than nothing and for the importance of combining a readiness to go to all lengths with the careful investigation of what lengths those should be. It was not mere passivity or a "back to normalcy" campaign that he backed. As with the war itself, he found himself advocating an energetic approach to nonintervention. A little piece, "Our National Dilemma," written a year later, sums up his difficulties all too exactly. It starts with the declaration that "a policy of isolation and nonparticipation is impossible" and ends with the injunction "not to engage too much or too readily" with other countries, unless cast-iron guarantees can be had that "we shall not make themselves and ourselves worse rather than better, by what is called sharing the common burdens of the world, whether it be through the means of a League of Nations or some special alliance."[22] Much the same tension exists between his assurance that "[w]e are not holier than other nations" and his claim that it was out of a deep democratic instinct that the United States had rejected the treaty and the League. For a philosopher who was so critical of "apart" thinking, he found it all too easy to separate his view of America as the home of democracy when he wanted to praise the country's rejection of the League and his view of America as the home of bigotry, class war, and primitive thinking when he wished to complain of the Red Scare and the unthinking hostility to ideas of industrial democracy on the part of politicians and popular newspapers.

The outlawry of war movement grew stronger later in the decade and even achieved a sort of success when sixty-odd states became signatories to the Pact of Paris in 1928, better known as the Kellogg-Briand Pact. The limits of that success may be guessed from the fact that Dewey himself thought the pact pretty much beneath contempt. The pact remains an item of international law, one more world war and an infinity of lesser struggles later. The price of its passage was utter toothlessness; the signatory states agreed to renounce war except for matters that seriously affected their national interest, and the only effect of a signatory's going to war was that other signatory states were then free to decide what attitude to take toward the breach—if it was one. Walter Lippmann observed that it was an agreement not to fight wars that the signatory states had no intention of fighting anyway, and he commented very tartly on the oddity that enthusiasts for the pact were the very same people who had voted against American involvement in a World Court that could have provided some kind of tribunal to hear accusations of "illegal" war making. Dewey was not one of Lippmann's initial targets, since he was merely a prominent intellectual backer of the people Lippmann really thought at fault: Salmon O. Levinson, who had been campaigning for the outlawry of war since before 1914, and, above all, Senator William Borah, whose maverick isolationism Lippmann had earlier supported but had come to regard as self-indulgent silliness. Dewey had known Levinson for many years, however, since Levinson was a well-to-do Chicago lawyer, and their acquaintance went back to Dewey's years in that city.[23]

Lippmann was savage about the history of the outlawry of law program, and it is hard not to sympathize with him. Like everyone else, Levinson had begun by thinking of the League as a league to keep the peace by making war on aggressor nations but had then backed away from the actual League. This was not unreasonable given the composition of the League as it existed, but when the Court of International Justice was set up, Borah and Levinson, like Dewey, decided that it was not what was needed either. They thus seemed to be in the position of advocating a form of outlawry of war which committed nobody to anything and in particular lacked any sort of mechanism to bring the outlaws to justice. Theodore Roosevelt ten years earlier had suggested that the only rational approach was via collective security: Nonaggressor nations should form a posse comitatus and go after the bad guys. Summing up the history of the Borah-Levinson view, Lippmann commented on the outlawry of war: "We find then that the phrase was first employed to strengthen a League, before there was a League. It was used to defeat the League after there was a League, and to advocate an international court before there was a Court. Now that the Court has been created, it is being used to defeat the Court, and to advocate another court which does not exist."[24] Although he was not the target of this devastating quip, Dewey felt himself morally obliged to defend the outlawry of war movement against Lippmann's charges. This was in fact the one passage of Lippmann's essay that Dewey quoted verbatim; Dewey saw clearly enough that if he could not fend off those accusations, all the world would think him vacillating and light-minded.

Dewey defended himself against the accusation of self-contradiction in several places, but his argument with Lippmann was entangled in another with Arthur Lovejoy. Lovejoy was a thorn in Dewey's flesh in philosophical issues both pure and applied. He was a scathing critic of Dewey's views on truth; he was also a scathing critic of Dewey's views on the League of Nations. By 1923 the League had been established for three years, and there was a continuous undercurrent of pressure in the United States in favor of a change of direction in U.S. foreign policy and a commitment to some form of membership. At the same time, the Hague Court of International Justice had been strengthened at least to the extent that it had been constituted as a genuine court rather than as a panel of arbitrators. Its jurisdiction was obscure, and it could act only when states in dispute with each other invited it to do so. Nor could its judgments be enforced without the concurrence of the unsuccessful party.

It was, for all that, a going concern, as it has been ever since. All the same, the opponents of the League were not merely being captious when they opposed the Hague Court as well. Although the two institutions were separate and had no formal connections with each other, many defenders of the court wanted its judgments to have more weight than a simple expression of international disapproval. The only plausible extra weight would have implied some system of collective security. This did not have to be a military form of collective security, but it would have to be a system with some sanctions, such as trade embargoes or diplomatic isolation, and any step in that direction would have to go through the League of Nations. To that extent the League and the court stood and fell together as institutions worth supporting.

Dewey opened the argument in 1923 with an essay called "Ethics and International Relations." It was a characteristic production, especially in the way Dewey suddenly switched from a long and unexciting account of why the law "of nature and of nations" that Grotius described in the seventeenth century had ceased to be credible in the nineteenth century to a defense of the outlawry of war movement. Dewey's argument was simple. Just as he had earlier argued, he said now that morality was effective—that is, it would guide men's conduct—only if there was an objective situation that pressed moral considerations upon them. Appealing for a change of heart without thinking about how to change the objective situation was silly. Lippmann and Lovejoy were unlikely to demur at that observation. They wanted to change the objective situation by encouraging a system of collective security. Indeed, it was Dewey who appeared to be trying to change the world by mere exhortation, for he went on to say, "I do not see how anybody who faces the situation can do otherwise than be convinced that the legality of war constitutes the greatest anomaly that now anywhere exists in morals."[25] This begged many questions, among them that of what the force was of saying that war was "legal" and what would be meant by declaring it illegal. The peculiarity of Dewey's position was that in this case, but in no other, he held that a declaration unattached to institutional consequences would be enough to make a great difference.

Unsurprisingly his critics thought this was nonsense. Lovejoy attacked a contemporaneous essay entitled "Shall We Join the League?"[26] in which Dewey went out of his way to argue against doing anything institutionally effective to enforce international law. As he usually did in polemics of this kind, Dewey painted his opponents as simple naïfs who thought that America had only to join the League for universal peace and goodwill to break out. Alternatively, they suffered from a "boastful self-esteem" that was irked by the United States' being "out of things, quiescent when things are happening."[27] The tone of these accusations is curious; they turn against Dewey's opponents the very same complaints that Randolph Bourne had directed against Dewey and the *New Republic* activists half a dozen years earlier. It was Dewey's own desire "to be busy, to be in things, to be virile and red-blooded" that had then come under attack, and one might well imagine it gave Dewey some pleasure to be able to throw the charge back at his critics now. Still, it was bluster. Lovejoy retorted that nobody in his right mind supposed that the League of Nations was a surefire success, that America had only to join for universal goodwill to replace universal spite, and that Dewey was attacking straw men. All the League's defenders argued was that some forum for international cooperation and debate was better than none and that it was hard to improve institutions by boycotting them.

Dewey's replies to Lovejoy and later in the year to Lippmann are skillful ad hominem retorts to opponents with well-honed rhetorical skills. They are not impressive contributions to the morality and jurisprudence of international affairs. Dewey's "What the Outlawry of War Is Not" was an effective response to Lippmann's exaggerations. Lippmann had claimed that the outlawry enthusiasts had slighted the uses of diplomacy and offered outlawry as a single all-purpose panacea; Dewey replied that they had done nothing of the sort. They had simply urged that diplomacy should take place against a background in which war had been declared illegal, and a court stood ready to adjudicate disputes when diplomacy failed. As to Dewey's positive views, two main points emerge. The first is that he thought the European powers that set up the League were imperialist powers that had no intention of changing their spots; this might or might not have been true, but it was an argument for isolationism based on just the "holier than thou" position that Dewey disavowed. The second was that the defenders of outlawry rejected the Court of International Justice because it lacked the powers that courts enjoy within any given nation-state and was therefore not really a court at all. A full reply to that observation would take us very far afield and into some difficult analytical terrain. The question of whether international law is really law at all has been endlessly debated, and the world continues to divide between those who think that it is sufficiently like domestic law to be law and those who think that the fact that sovereign states are bound only if they choose to be means that it is not law at all.

Dewey's position was elusive, for he seemed to hold two utterly opposed views simultaneously. The first was that declaring war illegal would make a great difference to the way the citizens of potentially belligerent states thought of war. The word "illegal" would carry all the connotations of contrariety to law and all the sentiments that "illegality" evokes in domestic matters. The second view was that existing institutions were fatally flawed by being unable to make their view of the justice or injustice of a given state's behavior prevail in a way that would modify that state's actions. The second position cancels out the first, while the first makes the second irrelevant. The entire argument was one that pragmatists ordinarily took care to avoid. Dewey's "sociological" reinterpretation of ethics and jurisprudence implied that the *word* "law"—like "legal" and "illegal"—was not what mattered, but the behavior of individuals and states. Dewey seemed to be arguing that the Court of International Justice at The Hague was useless because when states went to war to protect what they considered their vital interests, war was not itself a crime in international law, whereas once war had been declared a crime in international law, a court indiscernibly different from the present court would be valuable, legitimate, and effective. It was not surprising that the other side thought this was isolationism hiding behind a few shreds of bad argument.

Looking for the Public

The more famous confrontation between Lippmann and Dewey came as Lippmann slowly abandoned the radicalism of his youth and became increasingly unhappy with the chaotic and unstable state of American policy making both domestic and foreign. Two books recorded Lippmann's increasing disillusionment with American democracy as actually practiced, *Public Opinion* in 1922 and *The Phantom Public* in 1925. They are detailed, sober, and alarming essays and were rightly very famous in their day. Oddly, it is the less dramatic of them, *Public Opinion,* that has gone on being read, perhaps because it is less completely nihilistic than *The Phantom Public.* The basic argument is simple, however, and the same in both books. To the extent that American democracy is supposed to be government in response to a coherent public opinion, in which the public at large forms a view of the good of the country, and politicians are kept up to the mark by the public's ability to have that view enforced, American democracy is a wholesale failure.

There are two arguments going on simultaneously in both books. They both rest on the observation that ordinary people simply cannot cope with the quantity of information that they would have to cope with in order to render a rational judgment on the performance of their governors. The first argument was that there was no process of coherent opinion formation, and therefore no public, since the average citizen is just too busy working, going to the movies, looking after the family, and otherwise engaging in some nonpolitical activity that takes up all the time that might be spent on becoming politically informed. In any case, the multiplicity of interests, tastes, ideologies, and commitments that would have to be amalgamated to form a view of the public interest is far too great for any ordinary person to manage the process. Lippmann, it should be noticed, was not, early in the 1920s, taking the view that there was no such thing as the public interest, no such thing as the good of the country, to be aimed at. This skeptical position had been put forward by A. F. Bentley as long before as 1908 in *The Process of Government,* and it later became one of the conventional wisdoms of American political science.[28] It was not Lippmann's position.

Lippmann's position emerged more clearly when the second argument was unveiled. If the public was either inept or nonexistent, things were not very much better with the politician. Lippmann was thus not entirely like the most famous of the later theorists of "democratic elitism," Joseph Schumpeter.[29] For Schumpeter, the great divide lay between professional politicians and the laity. It was up to politicians to create a public for their policies, just as it was up to manufacturers by means of advertising to create a public for their goods. Nobody had known he wanted a Model T Ford before Henry Ford created it and sold it to him; what was true of consumers in their economic role was true of voters in their political role. They said yes or no to what politicians offered them. Lippmann was not so skeptical. He thought that there was some tolerably clear difference between policies that were in the public interest and policies that were not and that this was a good deal more than the difference between those policies that people liked and those that they did not like. So he fretted that politicians were as irrational, as volatile, as ignorant, and as generally unreliable as the voters to whom they were answerable. Whether there was a plausible remedy was not clear. He suggested in *Public Opinion* that the executive branch should appoint committees of social science experts to guide it in its administrative work and in its dealings with the legislature, but he must have known this would not be accepted by a public so deeply skeptical of expertise and superior learning as the American. And he suggested in *The Phantom Public* that since politicians could create publics—essentially in the plural—that there were moments, in the nature of the case fairly rare moments, when the public or *a* public would properly be called upon by one group of politicians or by some other group of would-be wielders of power to rally behind them and against their opponents in defense of a policy clearly in the public interest and against one that was clearly not. The drift of Lippmann's ideas was toward a hope that everyday government might fall into the hands of a disinterested elite who would enjoy the acquiescence, if not the intelligent support, of a public whose lives were at least smoothly and benignly managed. The role of the public in all this was then to act as a sort of latent presence ready to push its betters back to the strait and narrow if they strayed.[30]

This, of course, was exactly what Dewey was against. Whatever "Deweyan democracy" might be—and it was an elusive thing to describe in positive terms—it must involve the active and interested participation of every American on terms of free, open, and equal communication. The difficulty for readers of *The Public and Its Problems,* the book Dewey published in 1927, after two brief squarings of accounts with Lippmann in short reviews of his two books, is that Dewey accepted most of Lippmann's complaints against the existing order of things. Dewey could hardly have done anything else; given that one of his many arguments against America's joining the League was the fact that American politics was ignorant, passionate, and all too often dominated by ideologues and zealots, he could hardly complain when Lippmann observed that the findings of recent psychology showed that most people were governed by motives of an unconscious and not infrequently a disreputable sort. Dewey was not concerned to argue that American democracy was in good shape but that it could be got into good shape.

He did, however, claim that the public was not, even now, quite hopeless. Dewey thought that Lippmann's criticisms of contemporary democracy were those of a disappointed idealist, and part of Dewey's response was that the public often did the kind of job Lippmann wanted doing, and did it not too badly. Just *who* the "theorists of democracy" were who were supposed to have offered an unconvincing ideal of the American citizen's continuous involvement in the affairs of his polity was never clear in such discussions, but some composite Locke-Rousseau figure is what everyone appears to have in mind. Dewey, however, took matters back to first principles and began again. Eschewing utopian theorizing, he started by trying to persuade his hearers—the book began as lectures at Kenyon College in the fall of 1925—that the way to proceed was to clear our ideas of what constitutes a "public" and so discover what tasks publics could and could not perform. Dewey's definition has never satisfied anyone, but it served his purpose fairly well. "The public consists of all those who are affected by the indirect consequences of transactions to such an extent that it is deemed necessary to have those consequences systematically cared for. Officials are those who look out for the public and take care of the interests thus affected."[31] How this was supposed to illuminate the distinction he had drawn a little earlier between private paths and public highways, private and public schools, and the like is mysterious.

The thought behind it is entirely rational, however. Dewey wanted to get away from Aristotle and talk of man as a "political animal," with all that suggested about some kind of instinctual drive toward political association; he wanted to get away from theories of the social contract, and he wanted to get away from utilitarian theories about the need to organize ourselves to maximize the general welfare. Approaching public life in the spirit of a disinterested naturalist, one might well believe that one could discern two realms. In one, people deal with their own self-set goals with others whom they encounter in person or at least in some direct and chosen fashion, but there will be spillovers affecting other people, who will also be doing things that have spillover effects on others, and so endlessly on. When these spillovers are serious enough, common action is called for and up to a point is usually forthcoming. Dewey's picture of the role and purpose of government makes it essentially an enterprise for mopping up the negative consequences that our voluntary actions may have for strangers and facilitating our avoidance of bad side effects that we may not have noticed and that will cause us trouble in future. The state is not the march of God on earth, nor is it a utility-maximizing machine; it is a collection of officials whose individual tasks vary enormously but whose raison d'être is to enable the infinitely various private projects of the citizenry to flourish alongside and in interaction with one another.

A democratic state was simply one in which absolutely everyone's interests in this enterprise is taken into account on a free and equal basis. But democracy is a historical phenomenon, and Dewey's concern was with the fact that "the democratic public is still largely inchoate and unorganized."[32] The thought was the reverse of what John Stuart Mill had argued a hundred years before in *On Liberty*. Mill had thought that democracy had sprung up first as a movement of resistance to monarchs and aristocrats, essentially on a defensive basis. Then it had triumphed, and the sense that the public is always right—*vox populi vox Dei*—that was useful as a slogan of resistance became dangerous. Once public opinion was omnipotent, what was needed was some way of curbing its intrusion into matters that did not concern it. Dewey mostly accepted Mill's view of the origin of democracy, but he also believed that modern society has become so amorphous, so sprawling, so generally unmanageable and incomprehensible to its individual members that they are simply lost. At the same time, new aristocracies unknown to Mill had sprung up in the place of the old. The bankers and the captains of industry did not simply control the state—they, too, were not so well organized as that—but they were the most potent and most organized of contemporary social forces.[33] Then, too, the fact that most ordinary people earn their daily bread in vast impersonal organizations meant they were subject to forms of power over which they had no control and which there were no institutional means to remedy. Industrial capitalism and mass society make life hard for democratic government at the same time that they render it impossible to govern decently in anything but a democratic fashion.

The *ideal* underlying modern democracy was one we could not escape, however badly we might live up to it. That ideal was summed up in a slogan that means less today than it would have meant to Dewey's readers; indeed, to a modern reader it is likely to mean nothing at all. The ideal was to transform the great society into the great community. The concept of "the great society" was devised by the English sociologist and political theorist Graham Wallas; Wallas was a friend of Justice Holmes's, and of Lippmann's, and he had taught at Harvard as well as at the London School of Economics, where his chair was located. Wallas's notion was that modern industrial societies were increasingly abstract and impersonal and increasingly deprived their members of the sort of understanding of one another that they had in face-to-face interaction in small-scale communities. Dewey's response was to insist that democracy must be committed to re-creating in an industrial society the mutual comprehension and appreciation that we experience in "face-to-face" communities.[34]

The "problems" of the public turn out to be problems in the way of establishing meaningful interaction with one another. At this distance in time it is easy to have simultaneously two entirely contradictory reactions to Dewey's account of the problem. On the one hand, Dewey's views, allowing for the difference in terminology that the intervening decades have produced, are strikingly like those of contemporary thinkers of a broadly hermeneutic persuasion.[35] The difficulty of squaring instrumental rationality in the management of public affairs with the affective and emotional commitments and needs of individuals and groups in a modern society is a common theme, as is the search for a kind of "intelligence" in self-government that does not boil down to economic, cost-benefit calculation on the one hand, or float up toward an appeal to a Hegelian or Platonic Reason on the other. This is a large subject, and one I take up in the final chapter of this book. One may also have the diametrically opposite reaction; Herbert Spencer long ago observed that society is not a family writ large—in other words, that we must not look to form intimate relationships in the anonymous, arm's length encounters of economic and political life. It is hard to repress the thought that Dewey may simply have been asking too much of democratic politics and that a moderate degree of alienation from one another is the price we pay for a liberal society and its virtues of privacy and diversity.

Advice to an Anxious World

Dewey practiced philosophy in the traditional manner; one could not readily get from his work a clear view whether one ought to take up or give up a job, a marriage or any other particular undertaking. What one would always get was an account of what kinds of considerations to bear in mind and in what frame of mind it was proper to proceed. There was much to be said for this way of carrying on. Philosophers know less about bicycles than bike mechanics, and less about cooking than chefs; they have some competence in sketching a picture of how the advice we receive from experts is to be put together and what sort of advice we ought to look for in the first place. Yet Dewey lived on a day-to-day basis like the rest of us, and as we have seen, he had decided opinions on many policy issues of the day. It was the sense that he knew how to buckle everyday life to high metaphysical principle that made him so attractive to audiences all over the world. He was a poor lecturer, unable to look his audience in the eye, unequipped with rhetorical tricks, and cursed with a dull, drawling delivery. Audiences subjected themselves to all this because they were conscious of being in the presence of a great man. In the 1920s he spoke to a wider audience than the American, and a brief detour through his views on China, Japan, Turkey, Mexico, and the Soviet Union has more than curiosity value. From these foreign places he sent reports—"pot-boilers" he called them—to the *New Republic* and *Dial* and other familiar outlets, and their concreteness is a nice foil to the abstraction of his philosophy.

Dewey's first port of call in 1919 was Japan; the Japanese were, as they had long been, at odds with the American government over the anti-immigration policy of the latter. On the East Coast this was directed at Poles, Russians, and other eastern Europeans, while on the West Coast it was directed at the Chinese and Japanese. Moreover, Japan and the United States were perennially at odds over the exploitation of China. The Japanese were readier than the United States to emulate prewar Western governments and invade China whenever it seemed necessary to enforce a point, but they were already convinced, as they were for the next two decades, that American disapproval of Japanese militarism was duplicitous and a screen for the American penetration of China by peaceful methods.

This is touched on in Dewey's articles on Japan.[36] His first impression of Japan was that the success of the United States in the recent war and the concomitant collapse of Germany had made a vast difference to public opinion. "Patriotism" was still the overriding value of Japanese public life, but being patriotic was no longer a matter of espousing a Prussian image of Japanese success. For many modernizers, the United States had become the model to emulate, even though for many people the very success of the United States in gearing up for war had also been a source of alarm. "There is also a natural reaction in the face of the surprising exhibition of patriotism and power, military as well as economic, manifest by the United States. There is a revulsion of combined suspicion and dread not unlike that which in the United States followed after Japan's victory over Russia. The result was desired but it seemed unnecessarily demonstrative."[37] It was, he thought, all the more necessary that Americans should support the League of Nations and a peace settlement that recognized Japan's stake in the postwar settlement. "The Americans at home who have advertised opposition to the League of Nations have assumed a heavy responsibility. They have made many intelligent foreigners, previously sympathetic with America, open to the impression, fostered by inadequate news service, that Wilson's professed aims were a cloak. They have done America an ill turn by spreading the conviction that in truth America cares at home only for her supremacy in South America and abroad only for such power as will increase trade."[38]

This was early in 1919, before Dewey had become disillusioned with the peace treaty and thus with the League of Nations. The enemy at this point was still the isolationists and doubters, and Dewey's vision of what the United States had to do was still focused on bringing the allies of the war—Japan and China both had sided with Britain, France, and Russia and against Germany—into the postwar regime of peaceful cooperation. By the time he wrote his second short essay on Japan a few weeks later, he had more doubts about both Japanese and American attitudes. In particular, he had begun to reckon with the Japanese sentiment that the accords leading to the establishment of the League ought to have done something to curb the racialism of American immigration policy and that American negotiators had been obtuse in failing to appreciate that *some* concessions to Japanese feelings were essential, even if only for the sake of preserving Japanese face.

Dewey held a view that most philosophers and sociologists have until recently held as an article of faith: "[N]o nation can enduringly live a double life. . . ."[39] But Japan had embraced Western industrialism while trying to resist Western social, moral, and political attitudes. Even if this was "an impossible experiment," it was one that was still in progress, and Dewey understood just how obstinately Japan proposed to confront the twentieth century.[40] Japan was engaged in modernization with a feudal face: "With extraordinary toughness and tenacity it has managed somehow to conserve the feudal and even barbarian morale and politics of the warrior, while it has borrowed wholesale the entire scientific and industrial technique of the world."[41] This could not go on indefinitely; even though schools from the lowest to the highest level were a system of indoctrination in militarism and patriotism of the worst sort—"the most incredibly reactionary system of primary education the world has ever known."[42]—liberal ideas were bound to seep in. On this claim there are two things to be said. The first is that it is empirically only partly plausible; if we leave aside the example of the United States, which presently combines the world's highest standards of productivity with utterly reactionary attitudes toward criminal justice, social welfare, and the possibilities of a secular morality, the German reversion to barbarism under Hitler did little damage to German industrial and scientific work, though it destroyed many intellectual and cultural activities, while the Japanese to this day appear to combine a flair for industrial production with social and cultural attitudes unlike anything in the Western world. There is something to be said for the view that the technological tide erodes traditional attitudes in societies affected by industrial modernization, but not much for the idea that the erosion ends in a liberal democratic social and political order on the American model.[43]

The second is that Dewey's pluralism and his hostility to what William James had denounced as the "block universe" should have made him more suspicious of the idea that individual minds, let alone entire societies, must reduce their ideas and affections to such coherence. Twenty-five years before the American Navy had to deal with kamikaze pilots who combined a belief in the divinity of their emperor with sufficient technical competence to find their targets, evade their antiaircraft fire, and crash upon their decks, it was harder to believe that one mind or one society could harbor such opposite outlooks. Nonetheless, Dewey's philosophy in particular was supposed to open our minds to such diversity; his appeals to a "logic of consequences" as opposed to the familiar formal logic was supposed to remind us that the bonds of logical entailment and deductive implication were of less significance to us than whether our schemes of belief and attitude "worked" as a whole.

Dewey's views on China were deeper, more elaborate, and better informed than his views on Japan. He was there for the better part of two years rather than a few weeks. He also found China more visible than Japan; the very chaos that reduced the Chinese government to ineffectiveness meant that it could do nothing to stifle dissent. "Intellectually China has the advantage of a weak and corrupt government. Publicity regarding the country's evils, domestic and international, flourishes."[44] Dewey also found the Chinese temperament less reserved than the Japanese, so that discussion was easier and more wide-ranging, and his interlocutors suffered less from the inhibitions of "patriotism." His Chinese host was the philosopher Hu Shih, who had studied at Columbia before the war; he went on to play a distinguished role in Chinese politics and, by the time Dewey went to China, was already more interested in reforming China than reforming philosophy. What this may have meant by way of limiting Dewey's philosophical impact on his hosts was more than compensated for by the opportunities it gave him to explore the possibilities of Chinese liberalism.

China had been the largely unresisting prey of competing European, American, and Japanese mercantile interests for the previous forty years or so; any hope that the war to make the world safe for democracy was going to improve matters in this regard dissolved after the Paris Peace Conference. The

Japanese hoped to replace Germany in the treaty ports previously subject to German exploitation and were none too delicate in the methods they employed to secure that position; the British and American governments took up their prewar competition for commercial and political advantage where they had left off. Dewey was less susceptible to the simple charm of Chinese life than his fellow visitor Bertrand Russell; Russell's *The Problem of China*—reviewed by Dewey in the *Dial*—was a curious piece of work because Russell seemed to think of China, at any rate for the better-off, as a sort of eighteenth-century Whig paradise and was more eager that the Western powers should leave China alone than interested in what they might do to help modernization along. To the extent that Russell raised that issue, it was largely from a concern that China should not provide a casus belli for another round of imperialist war making. Dewey rightly objected that this was to see China from a very Western perspective and not from that of the would-be liberalizing Chinese with whom he lived and talked.[45] It is hard to imagine Russell's being moved by the objection.

The long series of essays that Dewey contributed to the *New Republic* and elsewhere deal with many momentarily important issues that now interest only the historian of international relations. Some of them touch more relevantly on Dewey's ideas about the possibilities of exporting liberalism to vastly different societies, however, and these pieces remain of more interest. Indeed, some seventy years after they were written, the question of whether China and the West will ever share a common culture is livelier than it has been for the past fifty years of Communist rule. As economic liberalization makes increasing headway, the question of whether cultural liberalization is bound to follow is once again on the agenda. Dewey's views are very persuasive, if only because they are so cautious and so sensitive to the difficulties of the West's providing anything more than encouragement. "Chinese National Sentiment,"[46] for instance, dwells on the Chinese antipathy to direct government pressure of most kinds. Dewey notes: "According to literary records, the following verse is the oldest poem in the language—a song put into the mouth of a farmer":

> Dig your well and drink its water;
> Plow your fields and eat the harvest;
> What has the Emperor's might to do with me?[47]

The moral was faintly depressing but plausible enough: Few Chinese relationships were quite what they seemed at first glance, and what passed for politics in China was not what passed for politics in the West. Trying to take part in the life of China would stretch the imagination of the most benevolent Westerner. Dewey and Russell in fact agreed on the largest conclusion to be drawn: There was little that outsiders could do for China beyond keeping their hands off. The political problem of the day and for the next twenty years was essentially the problem of trying to persuade interested parties to agree to a hands-off policy. What made that so difficult was that each party rightly suspected that every other country would take advantage of any unilateral concessions by one country in order to advance its own positions.

Dewey went further in his doubts about how change might be effected. The orthodox view, one that Dewey often seems to share, is that industrial modernization leads to cultural and intellectual change, so that anyone looking for the liberalization of China would think of economic change as the first order of business. To the degree that he looked at the sociological basis of intellectual change, Russell was of the same camp, non-Marxist, but mildly materialist or mildly economic determinist. Dewey was more nearly a member of a group of one, thinking that everything hung together so intricately that there was no single causal factor on which a wise person would rely. So far as the influence of America went, it had already exerted more influence over the educational system than any other power had and had exerted more influence over education than over anything else. The subsequent rise of the militaristic and nationalistic Kuomintang movement of Chiang Kai-shek meant that America got few returns from this investment of effort, but Dewey placed his hopes in its long-run effect.

It was not the mere fact of industry that would count; the Chinese could turn into the low-paid serfs of the worldwide division of labor if industrialization was all that took place. What counted was the growth of scientific and reformist habits of mind. A process in which Chinese officialdom sold the cheap labor of their subjects to foreign capitalists, while keeping the bribes they took for their services in their own pockets and using them for their own purposes or for purely military expenditure, would do no good at all. It was Western, reformist, individualist, liberal habits of mind that were needed. One way in which one might think that Dewey's liberalism was rather narrowly directed toward American realities was that he never suggested, as Russell did, that the Chinese had their own indigenous resources for a distinctively Chinese kind of liberalism. Russell's liking for what he saw as a Chinese eighteenth-century skepticism allowed him to think the Chinese might move in such a direction. Dewey was more impressed by the impact of four thousand years of farming; he saw the Chinese farmer as collectivist and conservative—a combination that seemed more paradoxical then than it does now—and as anything but potentially liberal.

The farmer cooperated with others in self-defense rather than from cooperative inclinations, and he was conservative because most change had been for the worse and he expected future change to be so, too. *Political* liberalism was, in any case, not a possibility at present or something that Dewey was especially interested in. China, as he said many times, was, in any event, not a nation-state in the modern sense.[48] Somewhat like the United States, it was more nearly a continent than a country, more like Europe than like France, say. One might have guessed that Dewey would have thought that somewhat as in the American case, the country needed first to become a nation, then a liberal nation. While it is true that he thought that the continental scale of China and the great diversity of peoples and cultures within the country ought to make it more intelligible to Americans than to most outsiders, Dewey did not, on the whole, take the line that the natural progression runs from the establishment of effective government to the establishment of parliamentary procedures for installing governments and thence to the rule of law, civil rights, and the full apparatus of liberal politics with which we are familiar.[49]

There was a philosophical reason behind this, as well as shrewd observation. Always his liberalism was social liberalism, built around the notion of the exploitation of social intelligence for the fullest development of the individual. Chinese liberalism, should such a thing come into existence, was thus not to be expected as a gift of the state in a country that scarcely had such a thing. It was or might be the gift of a frame of mind that would be a long time in the cultivating. The one thing one can surely say in Dewey's favor in this context is that he avoided all kinds of ethnocentrism; he neither praised China for being so different from America nor regretted the fact. This comes out very nicely in the review of Russell's *The Problem of China;* Russell, said Dewey, had gone to China utterly disillusioned with Europe and had therefore seen in China the mirror image of what he left behind. He praised the patience, the calm, the slowness of Chinese life; all this was fair enough, but it left out the enormous social costs that these imposed on the Chinese themselves.[50] True to his own view that societies are problem-solving organisms that create problems as they solve problems, Dewey rightly reproached Russell for the way he slid over the miseries of Chinese family life, political corruption, and economic stagnation. Dewey spent a great deal of his adult life explaining that "pragmatic" did not mean "practical" in a merely utilitarian and down-to-earth sense, but sometimes just such a down-to-earth and practical outlook was needed. His discussions of China consistently displayed it.

Liberalism in Turkey and New Schools in Russia

It was, however, as an educator that Dewey was best known. It was as such that the newly modernizing government of Turkey called on his services in 1924. So far as anyone can tell, it appears to have been out of a pure regard for Dewey's eminence that the Turkish government asked him rather than anyone else. What was wanted was a report on the state of Turkish education in general, and Dewey obliged with two reports, a preliminary one setting out some first thoughts and a brief final report making recommendations. The editor of the volume of Dewey's *Collected Works* in which they have been reprinted for the first time since they were presented to the Turkish government praises them as an exemplary piece of investigation and advice, and this seems right.[51] They are much more concrete, brisk, and decisive than most of Dewey's writings, and one wishes he had done more of such work. Their description of the need for efficient administration and well-trained teachers ought to be borne in mind when one thinks of Dewey's difficulties at Chicago.

Dewey was not a deft administrator himself, but it was not because he did not know what was needed. His final report opened with a brisk statement of what one might call standard mature Deweyan principle:

Fortunately, there is no difficulty in stating the main end to be secured by the educational system of Turkey. It is the development of Turkey as a vital, free, independent, and lay republic in the circle of civilized states. To achieve this end the schools must (1) form proper political habits and ideas; (2) foster the various forms of economic and commercial skill and ability; and (3) develop the traits and dispositions of character, intellectual and moral, which fit men and women for self-government, economic self-support and industrial progress; namely, initiative and inventiveness, independence of judgment, ability to think scientifically and cooperate for common purposes socially. To realize these ends, the mass of citizens must be educated for intellectual participation in the political, economic, and cultural growth of the country, and not simply certain leaders."[52]

Dewey showed no anxiety about transplanting Western liberal ideas into new terrain. Kemal Atatürk's revolution of 1920 had been a revolution intended to promote a Westernizing and modernizing regime, and Dewey was entirely content to help a government that was intent on creating a "vital, free, independent, and lay" republic. What he thought in Turkey was much what he had thought in Chicago in 1894 and had written in *The School and Society* and was to go on to write a dozen years later in *Education and Experience*. There is little to be said about the specific recommendations Dewey came up with, other than to notice how neatly he adjusted his standing principles to a different culture. Schools ought to be models of hygiene and cleanliness, especially in rural districts, and teachers ought to be housed in similarly model conditions; schools ought also to include a local health clinic. The schools should combine their schoolwork with useful scientific research and research into the local causes of illness and how to cure them: "[S]tudents should, in malarial districts, take part in locating the breeding grounds of mosquitoes, in draining, covering with oil etc., and demonstrating to the community the possibility of doing away with the disease."[53]

Nor was this all developed a priori: Dewey suggested that Turkish investigators should go and look at the way the schools in Denmark had been integrated into the rural economy. The civil servants who ran the schools should remember that unity was needed but uniformity was not; the teachers should be better paid, to prevent the constant loss of teachers looking for better-paid work; and their teaching should become more flexible, with less rigid division of subject matter and more attention to the possibilities of integrating mathematics and science, geography and history, languages and their use in particular disciplines. One would more quickly call it a splendid piece of well-honed common sense if it were not so painfully true that most of what Dewey urged on the Turks in 1924 is far from being the usual practice in the United States seventy years later. It was not instantly Turkish practice either; Turkish translations of the report were republished in 1939 and 1952. Perhaps one should call it well-honed *un*common sense.

The visit that got Dewey into most subsequent trouble was his brief tour of the Soviet Union in 1928. He went privately, as one of a group of thirty interested Americans. The difficulties it later caused him stemmed from the fact that on the whole he was favorably impressed by what he saw of Soviet schools, museums, art galleries, and much of everyday life. On the one hand, this meant that he was regarded as a fellow traveler by the American Communist party, which therefore tried to inveigle him into supporting its causes, while on the other, he was denounced by conservatives as a dupe of the Bolsheviks. Dewey's attitude was not unpredictable; when he arrived, he promptly wrote an article in the *New Republic* that said how much he wished that people would stop fighting a propaganda war over bolshevism and concentrate on what it meant to make a revolution.

It was a low blow. Dewey himself never explored the idea of revolution in anything other than intellectual matters. Copernican, Newtonian, and Galilean revolutions were well within his range, but political revolution much less so. It is odd because he had all the resources he needed—not only his Hegelian background with its emphasis on the way cumulative change can suddenly produce a discontinuous leap into a different condition of things but his pragmatist understanding of the way genuine novelty emerged from its underlying base. When human beings acquired language and therefore minds, this produced a real novelty in the world. By the same token, scientific thought and self-consciousness were emergent novelties and were therefore revolutionary arrivals on the human, social, and natural scene. It did not follow that they had to be brought into existence by violence and upheaval. Dewey's politics were, as we have seen, reformist and utopian but not revolutionary, so it is all the more interesting that what he wanted to know about Russia was what the revolution had *meant*.

The answer was wonderfully un-Marxist. Or, to be a little more temperate, it was wonderfully at odds with anything that a vulgar materialist might have said. What Dewey was interested in was not the effects of the revolutionary appropriation of the means of production but the effort to create a new civilization. In this he thought Russia had been extremely successful, and in some respects a model to the West. "Perhaps the most significant thing in Russia, after all, is not the effort at economic transformation, but the will to use an economic change as the means of developing a popular cultivation, especially an esthetic one, such as the world has never known."[54] What he had seen was something that has always impressed foreign visitors to Soviet museums such as the Hermitage—namely, the "groups of peasants, working men, grown men and women much more than youth, who came in bands of from thirty to fifty, each with a leader eager and alert."[55] As he observed, it was all very different from Chicago and New York.

Dewey's interest lay in Russian schools, and he visited several and talked to several educators, even including Lenin's widow, Krupskaya. Nonetheless, he said rather little about their organization or syllabi. He contented himself with praising the Soviet approach to industrial education for being polytechnical and concerned to create a broad competence and with suggesting that the Soviets took a more serious approach to practical work than the United States. In the Soviet view, too many educational projects in the United States were trivial and badly designed and taught no significant lessons. As we read Dewey's impressions, it is indeed easy to think that he was unduly friendly to the Soviet experiment. There are several things to bear in mind before we accept that conclusion. In the first place, Dewey was at great pains to distance himself from the capitalist dogmatists, on the one hand—he cited the future American president Herbert Hoover as an example—who knew a priori that the Soviet experiment would collapse in starvation and disorder, and from the Communist dogmatists, on the other, who knew that the Communist utopia was inscribed in history.

Dewey saw the Soviet system as a fascinating experiment that might go well or badly but would certainly not go where the dogmatists guessed. He admitted rather wryly that he was grateful that somewhere other than his home country was running the experiment, but he was also glad that it was being run. As for the obvious tyrannical features of Soviet political life, he had two observations, the first the familiar point that Russians were not comparing bolshevism with democracy but with centuries of czarist autocracy, the other the less familiar point that the real menace posed by the Soviet Union lay in its leaders' readiness to stir the pot of international civil war. An American reader would not have been mollified by this, since the implication was that *all* politicians who continued to think of war as a possible means of foreign policy were just about as bad as one another. The Soviets were worse than most inasmuch as the Third International would try to add the horrors of civil war to any future international conflict, but this was wickedness at the margin.

Remarkable though his travels and reports were, even more remarkable was the energy with which Dewey continued to fight the pragmatist fight in philosophical matters. The twenties saw the creation of four extraordinary books, the most ambitious of which, *Experience and Nature,* is like nothing else in twentieth-century philosophy. They were not written to be parts of a system, but they form a unity, one with decided political and social implications. They yield, of course, innumerable other pleasures for philosophers, historians of ideas, and historians of American culture in the twentieth century, and what I take from them here is a fraction of what they have to offer. Still, it is astonishing enough that in the decade that gave the world its first knowledge of Ludwig Wittgenstein's *Tractatus Logico-philosophicus* and that saw the foundation of the Vienna Circle and logical positivism, Dewey could unabashedly say in *Experience and Nature* that one of the questions of the day was whether nature was hospitable to democracy. To analytical philosophers such a question is utterly without meaning, or a symptom of a theological hangover, or just sentimental. One of the pleasures of reading Dewey is discovering that it may in part be a hangover from theology, but how much more there is to it than that.

Reconstruction in Philosophy, the first of the group, was the published version of the lectures Dewey gave in Japan in 1919; it had been presaged by an essay, "The Need for a Recovery of Philosophy," that he wrote in 1917 as an introduction to a collection entitled *Essays in Experimental Logic.* It marked the most public declaration of something that Dewey had believed for some time but that he was slow to set out. Philosophy was a subject without a subject matter. Or better, it was a subject that did not "solve" problems but "got over" them. This has ceased to be a heretical doctrine; the 1950s Oxford philosopher John Austin compared philosophy with the solar system in its gaseous state: As disciplines cooled down, they became stable, separate, and manageable and were labeled mathematics, physics, psychology, and so on. Philosophy itself was the generator of puzzles that became manageable only when they ceased to be philosophical. Dewey held a not dissimilar view. More to the point, however, he thought that philosophy was primarily driven by moral disquiet rather than idle curiosity, though idle curiosity was not something he dismissed as of no importance in the history of science. The need for a "reconstruction" in philosophy was made more acute by the war but was not primarily a reaction to the war. It was rather that what Dewey took to be the "classical" stance in philosophy was so tied into the "spectatorial" conception of knowledge and so imbued with the idea that the paradigm of knowledge was the tidily atomic understanding of the world achieved in Newtonian physics that it had become unhelpful in understanding human life.

Something more Darwinian, historicist, and biological had to provide the intellectual model; here we find what we have seen before brought to a self-conscious and almost propagandizing pitch. Only by one's looking at human beings as organisms in an environment that is both natural and cultural can the dead ends of classical philosophy be escaped. These dead ends are familiar to every undergraduate student of the subject: determinism versus free will; the problems of mind and body; the existence of the self and the problem of personal identity. Every student is familiar with the fact that what they all have in common is that they seem to be insoluble. Dewey thought they were insoluble, but it was not so much because they were difficult issues as that they were badly posed, or posed in a way that presupposed starting points for inquiry that we do not in fact occupy. If we think of the mind as a nonspatial, nonphysical entity, the owner of which has direct access to its contents, we instantly make it impossible to understand how such a "thing" could have an effect on the material, public, objective world. If we separate the experience of a supposedly detached observer from what the experience is experience of, we can never put them together again in such a way that the observer really knows what is going on in the world.

Here we can only explore the implications of Dewey's thoroughgoing naturalism on his social and political thinking. The first question we may ask is whether it had *any* implications for Dewey's social and political ideas. Dewey's most passionate disciple and admirer, Sidney Hook, was embarrassed by the existence of both *Experience and Nature* and *A Common Faith;* they seemed to give too many hostages to the religious and the traditionally philosophically minded.[56] So far as Hook was concerned, the man who wrote *Democracy and Education* and *Freedom and Culture* had no need to write *Experience and Nature* as well.[57]

This is very wrong. It is easy to see that someone as politically minded as Sidney Hook would want Dewey's social and political ideas to be divorced from a metaphysics and theory of religion that were too accommodating of traditional religion. Hook had been a student of Morris Cohen's at City College in New York before he worked with Dewey; Cohen was a fierce critic of Dewey's work from what one might call the "tough-minded" direction, more analytically minded, more respectful of the insights of the new logic, less persuaded that philosophy could do much more for the lay public than teach it to think a bit more clearly. Hook became a devoted admirer of Dewey's philosophy, but he continued to admire Cohen and Bertrand Russell, too, during all the time he worked with Dewey. Their skeptical and analytical stand, much more nearly empiricist in the traditional sense that stemmed from Locke, Hume, and Mill, was congenial to Hook.

In fact, the whole relationship between Hook and Dewey was full of paradoxes. Hook was a Jew from the Williamsburg area of Brooklyn, a street-smart socialist before he left high school, founder and member of innumerable Marxist and *marxisant* attempts to recruit the American worker for libertarian socialism. He was trigger-happy and aggressive and never saw a fight he didn't want to take part in. It would be easy to think that he wanted to exploit Dewey as a liberal front man in the internecine struggles of American Communists, socialists, Stalinists, Trotskyites, and the rest of it, but it would be wrong. Hook wanted to exploit Dewey's pragmatism for some genuinely interesting intellectual purposes; among other things, he saw that pragmatism provided a much-needed intellectual basis for the critical humanism of the young Marx. Although Hook had lost much of this youthful enthusiasm by the time he came to give his last thoughts on it all, enough remained to ensure that his distaste for Dewey's readiness to accommodate the religious was intact.

Hook's wish that Dewey would *not* talk about ultimate issues was never going to be fulfilled. Dewey's pragmatism was so much of a piece that Dewey had to give some account of just how he thought experimentalism escaped the dead ends and false dilemmas of traditional philosophy. Nor is it easy to see such a sharp dividing line between Dewey's social and political theory and his metaphysics as would have allowed him to evade the issues Hook wished him to evade. In one sense, Dewey's social philosophy swallows up his metaphysics since "mind" is a cultural phenomenon rather than an individual one, and experience is a collective possession of language using beings rather than something like a private movie show in individual heads; in another sense, his metaphysics swallows up his social and political philosophy since social and political problems are to be understood as rifts and discrepancies and oppositions within the natural-cum-cultural world of experience. Without the rest of his world view, Dewey would scarcely have held just the social and political views he did, and it is hard to imagine anyone holding just those social and political views who did not wish to embrace much of the rest of his philosophy.

The argument of his naturalism is that philosophy must learn to live with the approach to the world that the natural sciences have developed. There are several aspects of this thought, none of them including the idea that "scientists know best" or that we can abandon philosophy in favor of science. What he meant, and it is a constant refrain of *Reconstruction*, is that philosophy is still addicted to the idea that the realm of ideals is fixed, eternal, static, the realm of Being, or the One, presided over by the unmoved mover.[58] Science has freed itself from this addiction; science is an experimental activity, in which we manipulate things and instruments and theories in order to comprehend nature better. From this more than anything else stems the fact that science has made an enormous difference to the technical facility with which we control our environment, while ethics has made no such progress.

Dewey complained that we contrast science and morals, thinking that the latter, the realm of ideals and goods, is a realm of the fixed, the unbending, and the absolute. It this intellectual error that accounts for the great difference between our mastery of the physical world and our disorganization in social and political and psychological affairs. "Not only has the improvement in the method of knowing remained so far mainly limited to technical and economic matters, but this progress has brought with it serious new moral disturbances. I need only cite the late war, the problem of capital and labor, the relation of economic classes, the fact that while the new science has achieved wonders in medicine and surgery, it has also produced occasions for diseases and weaknesses. These considerations indicate to us how undeveloped are our politics, how crude and primitive our education, how passive and inert our morals."[59] If we could see our moral and political attitudes as equally experimental, we might make more progress than we do.

The ambitiousness of Dewey's philosophical stand can be measured by the rhetorical question he goes on to ask: "Is there not reason for believing that the release of philosophy from its burden of sterile metaphysics and sterile epistemology instead of depriving philosophy of problems and subject-matter would open a way to questions of the most perplexing and most significant sort?"[60] Just as science has left the realm of fixed theoretical frameworks and entered that of experimental hypotheses, so ethics has left the realm of fixed eternal principles and rules and entered that of rules of thumb, situationally sensitive thinking, and attention to the peculiarity of particular contexts. Philosophy is part of this movement. Modern moral philosophy does not offer to give us large and general rules; it is going to encourage us in the sensitive exploration of contextual problems. Yet Dewey himself makes some large and general claims. He says, for instance, "Surely there is no more significant question before the world than this question of the possibility and method of reconciliation of the attitudes of practical science and contemplative esthetic appreciation. Without the former, man will be the sport and victim of natural forces which he cannot use or control. Without the latter, mankind might become a race of economic monsters, restlessly driving hard bargains with nature and one another, bored with leisure or capable of putting it to use only in ostentatious display and extravagant dissipation."[61] There is no real contradiction here, of course, for it is not logically incoherent to claim, first, that *what* we ought to do in each particular case has to be decided case by case with the aid of rules of thumb and, second, that just as the individual can become healthy only by eating well, exercising moderately, and taking care of himself situation by situation, so there is such a thing as social health, describable in general terms as the proper balance of material and spiritual activity, the balance to be maintained case by case and occasion by occasion.

If there is no logical contradiction, there is some rhetorical tension between the largeness of the claims about what is at stake in the well-being of an entire civilization and the methodological injunction to look at each case in its own right. What one misses is what Dewey's hero Francis Bacon called axiomata media, middle-range principles that connect the large concern and the particular case. It is all rather reminiscent of a certain preaching style in which the preacher, not wishing to prescribe too minutely for his flock, reminds them to bear in mind the distinction between the sheep and the goats and sends them out of church with no more than the thought that one becomes a sheep or a goat action by action and instance by instance.

Still, Dewey distinctly did *not* do many things that other philosophers, pundits, and preachers did and do. He did not elaborate a fixed scheme of neatly organized principles in the manner of Kant or, lately, of John Rawls.[62] He emphasized the place of ethical considerations not as trumps in deliberation but as the outgrowth of our intelligent attempts to discover what we really want and how we hope to live together. *Human Nature and Conduct* spelled out a good deal of what this implies. Quite what discipline it belongs to has always been disputed; it is "about" social psychology, but not a treatise in that discipline; it is certainly about ethics, but again in a somewhat arm's-length fashion. Fundamentally it is Dewey's elaboration of William James's old observation that the formation of habit was the most important feature of human life in the context of C. S. Peirce's claim that thinking—in the sense of articulate and conscious thought—arises when habits fail and we are checked in our problem solving.

The lectures in *Human Nature and Conduct* had been delivered at Stanford University in 1918 and ought, according to the contract between Dewey and Stanford, to have been published within two years. The extended tour of Japan and China held that up, so the book appeared after *Reconstruction;* they are part of one project, however, and breathe the same spirit. *Human Nature and Conduct* is more narrowly focused on Dewey's favorite topic of "intelligent conduct" and has none of the historical sweep of *Reconstruction,* but the upshot is identical. It is fixity and inflexibility that we must avoid; we must not confuse steadfast adherence to our moral values with adherence to standards that we suppose to be graven on stone. If *Reconstruction* turns to issues of social philosophy only at the end of the book, its outcome is not dissimilar: The individual can only flourish as an individual by being a fully participant member of a healthy society; there is no difference between *moral* decision making and decision making in general, save to the degree that when we ask moral questions, we are asking questions about what ultimate good our actions will serve.

Human Nature and Conduct is sometimes said to be a difficult book to read, but that is quite untrue. Its briskness and enthusiasm carry the reader along without difficulty. The difficulty one faces is not the readability of the book but the credibility of the views that Dewey wanted to persuade his readers to accept; as he often said, he was trying to say something for which there was no obvious and readily available vocabulary. Dewey later provided a crucial thread in the foreword he added to the 1930 edition of the book; "Were it not for one consideration, the volume might be said to be an essay in continuing the tradition of David Hume." The "one consideration" that separates them is that most readers thought of Hume as simply a philosophical skeptic. Dewey did not. He had no interest, then or ever, in skepticism, and he was interested in Hume as a precursor of his own naturalistic philosophy. What Dewey wanted to write was a constructive, descriptive treatise on how human beings living together created—not consciously, of course—language, morality, and the intellectual arts. As he put it, Hume's "constructive idea is that a knowledge of human nature provides a map or chart of all humane and social subjects, and that with that chart in our possession we can find our way intelligently about through all the complexities of the phenomena of economics, politics, religious beliefs, etc. Indeed, he went further, and held that human nature gives also the key to the sciences of the physical world, since when all is said and done they are also the workings of the human mind. It is likely that in his enthusiasm for a new idea, Hume carried it too far. But there is to my mind an inexpugnable element of truth in his teachings."[63] The "too far" was, I suspect, that Hume put too much to the credit of the individual psyche and too little to the provocation of *what* we experienced, but the key to understanding Dewey is that he is trying to provide, as Hume had done, a natural history of belief, desire, and morality.

As to what it yields, Dewey said some striking things. Against those who thought that reason had to curb passion, he insisted that we needed *more* passions rather than fewer; we needed the imaginatively sparked passions that would curb the misguided passions and foster the productive ones. Dewey was not hostile to some features of notoriously rationalist views such as Kant's, but he wanted to reinterpret them. Kant's demand that we test the morality of a decision by asking whether it would pass the test of being generalized as a universal law for all rational creatures is not best understood as an attempt to curb passion by reason, since no such thing is possible. It was better construed as a way of emphasizing the need to take broad consequences into account, not to make self-interested exceptions, and to think impartially.[64] To be committed to this degree of impartiality, we had to yoke imagination and desire together, to understand the impact of habits of behavior, and to react adequately to what our imagination yielded.

Dewey's critics have spent enormous amounts of energy complaining that he committed the fallacy of reducing "the desirable" to "the desired." It is worth remembering at every point that Dewey tied the ends of action not just to what we desire but to what we desire to desire—that is, to what we can endorse ourselves desiring. *Reflective* desire is what ethical judgment comes down to. The results that Dewey is eager to insist on are not very surprising to readers of Hume but would have been mildly alarming to listeners in 1918, when philosophy was still largely the preserve of clergymen or at least of the conventionally religious; morality was natural and social, not primarily individual or based on supernatural sanctions. Human freedom was a matter of intelligence, not will, but this was not to be understood in the sense of classical rationalism, that by reason we could emancipate ourselves from desire and its disappointment. It was to be understood as an effect of intelligence, by means of which we can bring a considered view of the future to modify the present and thus the future, too. The more we understood of ourselves, our social situation, and the possibilities they presented, the freer we would be.

Dewey makes, however, one concession to the classical rationalist view that freedom was the ability to govern ourselves by reason, and that reason was inscribed in the workings of the universe. He acknowledged that the theory took a moral weight off our shoulders. We are not left opposing our moral values to a universe governed by blind physical forces. One of the attractions of Hegelianism was its offer of what James cheerfully described as a "moral holiday"; such an arm's-length appreciation was beyond Dewey, but the comfort so described was not to be sniffed at. Dewey put his hopes on the thought that what morality demanded was the fullest possible appreciation of the *meaning* of our action. Nor did Deweyan ethics limit itself to the usual subject matter of moral argument. One thing we had to reflect on was how deeply we were immersed in the world and how completely we might be at home in it. This was the territory of the artist and the poet and the religious thinker rather than the scientist and the philosopher, but it was the task of the philosopher to acknowledge the importance of these sentiments and to show their rationale. It was not so much that after ethics came aesthetics as that aesthetics completed ethics.

The deeply communitarian turn of Dewey's moral thinking emerges when he appeals to the importance of this immersion in the ideal, acknowledges its affinity with the concerns of the religious life, but stresses its true connection not with conventional religion but with social membership. "Infinite relationships of man with his fellows and with nature already exist. The ideal means, as we have seen, a sense of these encompassing continuities with their infinite reach. This meaning even now attaches to present activities because they are set in a whole to which they belong and which belongs to them. Even in the midst of conflict, struggle and defeat a consciousness is possible of the enduring and comprehending whole."[65]

Dewey promptly reads another lesson against apart thinking. Society needs ritual, ceremony, and celebration to strengthen this connection of all of us with each of us, but they have been parceled out into a special and set-apart activity. "Consciousness of the whole has been connected with reverences, affections, and loyalties which are communal. But special ways of expressing the communal sense have been established. They have been limited to a select social group; they have hardened into obligatory rites and been imposed as conditions of salvation. Religion has lost itself in cults, dogmas and myths. Consequently the office of religion as sense of community and one's place in it has been lost."[66] What kinds of civic rituals might do better, it is not easy to guess, but it is striking how far Dewey echoes ideas that one associates with Durkheim's writings on our need to worship society under the guise of God. It is also striking how deep Dewey's hatred of orthodox religion goes; he took pains not to indulge in "aggressive atheism" and never set out to offend the orthodox in the way Russell constantly did, but his antipathy to the faith of his mother is pretty savage. "Instead of marking the freedom and peace of the individual as a member of an infinite whole, it has been petrified into a slavery of thought and sentiment, an intolerant superiority on the part of the few and intolerable burden on the part of the many."[67] Yet as St. Paul remarked so eloquently, nothing can separate us from the love of God, and in Dewey's eyes, nothing can separate us from human sociability. "Within the flickering inconsequential acts of separate selves dwells a sense of the whole which claims and dignifies them. In its presence we put off mortality and live in the universal. The life of the community in which we live and have our being is the fit symbol of this relationship. The acts in which we express our perception of the ties which bind us to others are its only rites and ceremonies."[68]

The thought this leaves us with is that what sustains moral thinking must in some fashion transcend it. But this is not a thought we can feel entirely comfortable with in the presence of Dewey, who thought that notions such as transcendence are at best misleading and at worst entirely disastrous. All the same, we need some way of expressing the thought that morality rests on a sense of the way the world hangs together with our hopes and fears that is in the end the province of art—and of a sufficiently sanitized religion that expresses itself in poetry and fine art rather than dogma. One's sense of the extraordinary consistency of Dewey's ideas over a period of almost fifty years is very much strengthened by the thought that *Human Nature and Conduct* developed themes that Dewey first developed in the 1890s in Chicago but opened up others that he took as the themes of *Experience and Nature, Art as Experience,* and *A Common Faith.*

Experience and Nature was not the very first place in which Dewey broached the thought that "art perfects nature," human nature included therein. Indeed, even in *Experience and Nature* it is not set out in quite that form. From the middle of World War I onward, Dewey had increasingly come to claim that the ultimate standards by which we assessed the satisfactoriness of the world were those of art. But *Experience and Nature* was the most extended account he ever gave of his conviction that nature was itself replete with the materials of esthetic satisfaction and that the task we had to set ourselves was to find ways of attuning ourselves to its content. The most important consequence of Dewey's refusal to open a gap between experience and nature is that nature is not more truly or more grasped in the form in which it appears to science than it is in art and poetry or religion. *Every* form of experience can make mistakes about the world, and this is true of art and poetry as much as it is of religion and science; but no form of encountering the world can claim a priority over all the others that then sets them the impossible task of justifying themselves in its terms.

Art is not failed physics, and the world is not more truly the world of the physicist than the world of the artist. Blake's fear that Newton had taken all the color out of the world was not exactly unjustified, for if men thought it had happened, it would have happened. Still, it was not true that it had to happen, not true that there was a competition for the same territory between the physicist and the poet. This truth—if it is one—is a large part of what recent enthusiasts for Dewey have been saying. To send a rocket to the moon, we call upon our engineers, and they in turn upon our chemists, physicists, computer scientists and so on; to send a billet-doux to our beloved, we call on the painters and poets, and most of us are more interested in ingratiating ourselves with our beloveds than in going to the moon.

In *Experience and Nature* Dewey places the discussion of "experience, nature, and art" just before the last chapter in the book, "experience, value, and criticism." The logic of the book is simple enough: We move gently from considerations bearing on our practical concerns with controlling the world and therefore with understanding it through an elaborate account of the cultural basis of mind, and the social nature of consciousness, and thus to the question that Dewey could never help asking: How does it all hang together, and how do we know what it's all for? Dewey never stopped and asked the question in quite such a vulgar form; rather he set out to show that we can find a satisfaction in experience that is in essentials an answer to that question. Moreover, the answer is latent in the modern world itself and in the modern mind's grasp of the world. "Scientific humanism" is not in the end a bad label for Dewey's philosophy, so long as it is always remembered that this does not mean, as it did in the hands of vulgar Marxists who took the label for themselves, that science boils down to the technology of producing an ever-higher standard of living. In Dewey it means that the mental outlook of modern science holds the key to appreciating the unity and beauty of the world and its ultimate fitness to be a home for humanity. We must see:

> that science is an art, that art is practice, and that the only distinction worth drawing is not between practice and theory, but between those modes of practice that are not intelligent, not inherently and immediately enjoyable, and those which are full of enjoyed meanings. When this perception dawns, it will be a commonplace that art—the mode of activity that is charged with meanings capable of immediately enjoyed possession—is the complete culmination of nature, and that "science" is properly a handmaiden that conducts natural events to this happy issue. Thus would disappear the separations that trouble present thinking: division of everything into nature *and* experience, of experience into practice *and* theory, art *and* science, or art into useful *and* fine, menial *and* free.[69]

Although this sounds rather wonderful, talk of the "culmination of nature" rings alarm bells in the modern mind. We know that one of the effects of the Copernican revolution and the work of Galileo and Newton was to abolish teleology from the natural world; we do not think that plants have the shape and appearance they do because these are the "signature" of the good they can do us as medicinal herbs, nor do we think that the eye is useful for vision because God so designed it. We therefore panic in the face of suggestions that there can be a "culmination" of nature since it seems to reintroduce the teleology expelled over the past several centuries.

Dewey's reply is that mankind still has to think in terms of tendencies; we cannot steer our way through the world unless we can visualize the outcomes of tendencies. We always look for an order in the world that is sometimes there in a completed form, but that is mostly in the making. Much of the time *we* produce such an order because we work on the materials we can lay our hands on to turn them to some use or other, narrower and more immediate or wider and more nearly ultimate. This means that there is no simple cleavage between science as a cataloging of cause-and-effect connections in the world and art as a *creative* process of making objects that persons of taste and refinement can then admire in a special way. Dewey borrows from Veblen's account of the way conspicuous consumption attests to the pecuniary reliability of those who indulge in it to abuse the kind of taste that leads us to collect objects that "remind others that their owner has achieved an economic standard which makes possible cultivation and decoration of leisure."[70] How art should be judged is a story we shall turn to in the next chapter.

What is worth noticing here, however, is the extent to which Dewey's views on art and its relations to ethics have both a positive and a negative dimension. The positive dimension is what eventually led him to spell out his views at length in *Art as Experience*, but it is easy to see how he was driven by his negative feelings, especially by indignation at the horrors of everyday industrial work. His sharpness as a critic is easy to miss, but it is crucial in explaining something that is otherwise inexplicable. Nothing that Dewey wrote about art lined up with philosophical aesthetics in the usual or classroom sense; he did not accept or reject "expressivist" theories, had little to say about formalism, and in general kept the discussion moving at an angle to the tradition of philosophical aesthetics that runs back to Aristotle and in the modern world back to Burke and Kant. He always asked where art was to belong in social life, what its social function was, though *not* in a way that suggested we might use it for propagandist or "socialist realist" purposes, since its function seemed rather often to act as a sort of reproach against the ugliness of what we produce and consume and even more against the ugliness of the lives we lead in so doing.

To do this, he had to make one dazzling move. It is easy to suggest that we live the way we do because we are engaged in instrumental activities: We drive on clogged highways not for its own sake but to get to work, we work in a dreary law firm not for its own sake but to earn enough to feed our family and keep a roof over its head. Dewey denied that the ugliness of life and work was the result of a conflict between instrumental goods and ideal ends, as if handsome train stations and clean streets that give us pleasure as we walk them were a vain hope; it was rather a failure to think hard enough about enough of the consequences.

Lastly, then, why might we believe any of this? In the final chapter of *Experience and Nature,* Dewey relaxed entirely. He observed that if philosophers insist on evacuating all meaning from the world, they have no resources available to pump it back in, from which it follows that we would do better not to start down that philosophical track. "Recent philosophy has witnessed the rise of a theory of value. Value as it usually figures in this discussion marks a desperate attempt to combine the obvious empirical fact that objects are qualified with good and bad, with philosophic deliverances which, in isolating man from nature, qualitative individualities from the world, render this fact anomalous." If the philosopher denies that "Poignancy, humor, zest, tragedy, beauty, prosperity, and bafflement . . ." are features of experience, he speaks at odds with his own behavior, since he steers himself through the world precisely by ascribing such qualities to it; if he divides the world into mere mechanical stuff that has no such value-laden qualities and a realm of value, he then has the familiar but impossible task of trying to explain how the world of fact and the world of value are connected.[71]

Dewey dismisses all such accounts as "arbitrary." Moreover, philosophy has no special standing in the matter of our acceptance of the values we find in our experience. It cannot claim the role of a lawyer who makes sure that all claims to truth are valid, and in any case the realm of value is wider than the realm of "true-and-false meanings."[72]

When the claim of meanings to truth enters in, then truth is indeed pre-eminent. But this fact is often confused with the idea that truth has a claim to enter everywhere; that is had a monopolistic jurisdiction. Poetic meanings, moral meanings, a large part of the goods of life are matters of richness and freedom of meanings, rather than of truth; a large part of our life is carried on in a realm of meanings to which truth and falsity as such are irrelevant. And the claim of philosophy to rival or displace science as a purveyor of science seems to be mostly a compensatory gesture for failure to perform its proper task of liberating and clarifying meanings, including those scientifically authenticated.[73]

As Dewey says, if truth were the only thing at stake, we should hardly go on reading Plato and Aristotle, Locke and Spinoza. What this implies for Dewey's own philosophy seems to be that we should treat his views in the experimental spirit in which they were offered. We should try looking at the world the way Dewey did and see whether we get on better with life if we do.

Experience and Nature was often thought to be Dewey's greatest book. It was of it that Justice Holmes said it had shown him God's creation from the inside. It was wide open to attack from philosophers who did not wish to give up their dualisms, and it was duly attacked. Those attacks are irrelevant here. Here all that is relevant is the way in which Dewey's most "metaphysical" work still contrived to be so thoroughly a piece of social and political criticism. After *Reconstruction in Philosophy* had argued that philosophy arises as a response to social problems that defy ordinary solutions, *Experience and Nature* self-consciously offered itself as a response to the splits, antipathies, antagonisms, and vague unhappiness of the modern world. It is a *response,* not a solution; Dewey never suggested that all problems have solutions. Indeed, he rather suggested that most problems have evasions rather than solutions and that intelligence largely consists in finding ways around difficulties rather than over them.

The last of this quartet of bold presentations of the pragmatist position was *The Quest for Certainty*. The lectures were something of a sensation in Edinburgh in the spring of 1929 because Dewey so firmly put his agnosticism on the line. The essential argument of the lectures was not very different from what it had been since the late 1890s. We are engaged in the quest of the title; up to a point we must be, since all thinking is for the sake of action, and action can occur only when an indeterminate situation is made determinate. Certainty is relative to context; we generally act on "good enough" and very rarely on "absolutely right." Even those occasions that seem to be cases of "absolutely right" have a nasty tendency to appear in retrospect as something else entirely.

Once again, philosophers are told off for encouraging people to hanker after fixed and absolute conceptions of the world and for not having adjusted to the realities of modern intellectual life. The realities of modern intellectual life can be inferred from the behavior of scientists; they do not sit down and try to evolve a fixed picture of the universe from within their own heads but seize upon whatever means prove fruitful in experimental investigation. By this time Dewey had been reinforced in his instrumentalism by P. W. Bridgman's instrumentalist account of the role of theories in physics. What was later known as operationalism rested on the thought that the meaning of concepts lies in the procedures by which we assess the truth and falsity of the claims we use the concepts to make. Thus the entities that modern physics uses—electrons, quarks, bosons, or whatever—are not to be scrutinized for their resemblance or lack of it to the medium-sized dry goods of everyday experience; rather what an electron is is whatever it is that aids the exploration of subatomic physics and produces the predicted results of the physical theories that refer to electrons. If the theories work too badly, we say there aren't really any such things as electrons; if they work well enough, we say that there are.

To get stuck on the issue of whether there are "really" such things as electrons is a mistake, since there is no such condition as that of really existing in the abstract. It is unsurprising that Dewey entitled only one of his lectures "The Supremacy of Method," for that was the operating idea behind his account of the purpose of education, and it is the operating idea behind the emphasis in *Experience and Nature* on "intelligent action." It was the scientific method rather than any of the particular results of modern science that Dewey appealed to. Indeed, Dewey seemed not to be particularly interested in the dramatic advances made by modern physics and chemistry, and he was too austere in his personal tastes to be much impressed by the technological wonders and new consumer goods that modern science had provided. Unlike people who were more impressed by these achievements, Dewey was infinitely far from proposing a tyranny of scientific administrators who would look after the welfare of all the incompetent others of us. All of us are supposed to approach life with the self-conscious purpose of getting it into an adequate shape, and the role of science in Dewey's argument is mostly to illustrate the most successful modern form of encounter and control.

We must focus on what he has to say about ethics and social life. The task of philosophy is once more laid out as the re-creation of a unity in experience and in our associated life. "The problem of restoring integration and cooperation between man's beliefs about the world in which he lives and his beliefs about the values and purposes that should direct his conduct is the deepest problem of modern life. It is the problem of any philosophy that is not isolated from that life."[74] I said earlier in this chapter that *Human Nature and Conduct* and *Experience and Nature* were, in effect, Dewey's most accessible accounts of his "ethics" and "metaphysics" respectively. It is clear that this is one more observation that must be qualified by noting that Dewey's refusal of divisions within philosophy, as within the rest of life, means that *all* philosophy is moral philosophy and that all moral philosophy is—given the level of abstraction at which it must operate—an account of method, not a list of precepts. Dewey's naturalism means that now, as previously, he insists that values are tied into our enjoyment of the world. This he always recognized as the one element of truth in utilitarianism.

This is in the broadest sense a question about how to educate our tastes. "Instead of there being no disputing about tastes, they are the one thing worth disputing about, if by "dispute" is signified discussion involving reflecting inquiry."[75] A person's character is most completely revealed by his tastes—that is, by what he thinks desirable or enjoyable—and the cultivation of excellence of character is in this view one with the formation of intelligent tastes. As he had before, Dewey took judgments of value to be judgments about the long-run and widest consequences of the things whose value we were assessing. "*Judgments about values are judgments about the conditions and results of experienced objects; judgments about that which should regulate the formation of our desires, affections and enjoyments*. For whatever decides their formation will decide the main course of our conduct, personal and social."[76]

Once again Dewey argued that we can escape many of the ills that this appeal to a scientific approach to ethics seems to threaten; we can, for instance, attend to what it takes to make ourselves more adequate moral agents without this degenerating into a morbid self-obsession, since we can ask not how to be "better" in some ideal sense but how to be a more effective source of good in the world in a pretty down-to-earth fashion.[77] Moreover, the importance of the down-to-earth elements of social life is itself something in need of rescue: "[W]e can hardly expect a moral system which ignores economic conditions to be other than remote and empty."[78]

The office of philosophy in achieving all this is not obvious. Dewey belonged to the current of twentieth-century thought that saw it as a major task of present-day philosophy to overcome the errors and illusions of previous philosophy, whence the recent tendency to write of Dewey in the same breath as Wittgenstein and Heidegger. In other respects, he was quite unlike them; he never said, as Wittgenstein did, that philosophy leaves everything just as it is, and he would not have remained a philosopher had he believed it. Philosophy was a form of public service; it was the heir of traditional religion and could not escape the obligations that this imposed upon it. Its task was to expose the sources of breaches and lesions in experience and in society and to illustrate the ways in which they might be cured. The "Copernican Revolution" that Dewey calls for in the final chapter of *The Quest for Certainty* amounts to asking his readers to turn away from the desire for certainty and accept that they can have security in the midst of uncertainty instead; and this will give them as much as traditional faith ever offered.

> Religious faith which attaches itself to the possibilities of nature and associated living would, with its devotion to the ideal, manifest piety towards the actual. It would not be querulous with respect to the defects and hardships of the latter. . . . Nature and society include within themselves projection of ideal possibilities and contain the operations by which they are actualized. Nature may not be worshiped as divine even in the sense of the intellectual love of Spinoza. But nature, including humanity, with all its defects and imperfections, may evoke heartfelt piety as the sources of ideals, of possibilities, of aspiration in their behalf, and as the eventual abode of all attained goods and excellences.[79]

I shall delay trying to settle accounts with this vision. I want to emphasize here the extent to which Dewey took on just about every ancestral piety in *Quest* and its predecessors. The God of Christianity was not so much dead as institutionally superseded; whatever the historical value of the Christian Church, its current standing as the guardian of a religion separated out from everyday life was inimical to social progress and individual moral excellence. It is a commonplace to say that Dewey's philosophy was a twentieth-century naturalization of his youthful Congregationalist faith. But it is not true; Dewey's own intention was to rescue religious life from his youthful faith. In something of the same way, the understanding of Hegel that Dewey had first encountered was repudiated with equal vigor. Though it is true, as I have emphasized, that Dewey preserved Hegel's passion for finding the truth in the whole rather than the parts and for seeing every phenomenon reflected in the other phenomena to which it was related, what Dewey thought Hegel had given him in his youth was reassurance that the empirical world was only a manifestation of the Absolute. This was as much as to say that the world possessed only as much reality as was conferred on it by a universal mind standing in for God, and Dewey would have none of it.

The Quest for Certainty set out to justify the world as a self-sufficient, adequate world, a home for the human spirit and the human mind as well as for the human body and our material life. It was atheism that Dewey preached, though he did so decorously, and *all* gods were felled by it. Yet it was an atheism that worked in the interest of taking the world religiously—Dewey did not mind talking of piety—and one of the many ways in which Dewey's assertion that his favorite reading was Plato ought to be taken seriously is by acknowledging that as much as many Greek thinkers, Dewey combined disbelief in a personal deity with piety toward our world. Sixty-odd years later it is a less alien basis for social and political philosophy than it has been for most of the intervening time. But it is time to end this account of Dewey's shorter remarks on the subject and to turn to his extended account of "consummatory experience."

Seven

God, Beauty, and the Higher Learning

In 1929 Dewey reached the age of seventy, and he retired from Columbia at the end of the 1929–30 academic year. It was a good deal less than a genuine retirement inasmuch as he was appointed "Emeritus Professor in Residence," so that he could retain his full salary and his office at Morningside Heights, from which he continued to supervise the dissertations of graduate students in the department of philosophy and join in the department's work. The generosity of the treatment he received was a striking testimony to the value his employers set on him and to the value that Nicholas Murray Butler set on the study of philosophy: The American economy was about to plunge into the Great Depression of the thirties, not to emerge until the outbreak of war in 1939 created the demand for military hardware and the means to transport it that brought the economy back to life. Indeed, at the end of the thirties Columbia found itself so strapped for money that Dewey was told that the previous arrangements could not go on—he was almost eighty by now—and that he would have to manage on his ordinary pension.[1]

Retirement

Cutbacks were not called for. Albert Barnes was as prosperous as ever and had long been minded to pay Dewey a retainer of five thousand dollars a year for life in recognition of his value to the Barnes Foundation and to Barnes's own educational efforts. So Dewey continued to enjoy an affluent old age in various apartments in the East and West Eighties and finally in a large flat at 1138 Fifth Avenue overlooking Central Park. There he was cared for by his daughters and after 1939 by Roberta Lowitz Grant, the daughter of old friends from Pennsylvania.[2] The shy and retiring Dewey became a more sociable figure during the last quarter century of his life. Now that Alice had died and their children had gone their own ways, he was less enclosed within the family and freer to make friends as and where he liked; retirement widened that freedom. His political involvements brought him the company of all sorts of anti-Communist figures; one comrade in these battles was the novelist James Farrell.

Farrell was multiply congenial: He had also studied philosophy with Mead at Chicago, and in turn Farrell remembered Dewey for his almost unique ability to make Edgar Lee Masters feel liked. Dewey was regarded with affection by innumerable people in the literary and political world from Agnes Meyer, wife of the owner of the *Washington Post* and a participant in her own right in anti-Stalinist politics, to the colorful Carlo Tresca, a radical who opposed Stalin and Mussolini with equal vigor and was murdered in 1943 by gunmen whose employers were never uncovered, but who might have been Fascists, Stalinists, or mafiosi.[3] Through Albert Barnes, Dewey met large numbers of artists as well as collaborators of Barnes's in his various educational projects; there is minimal evidence of these encounters in Dewey's writings, but Barnes's enthusiasm for black art and culture and for the spontaneous achievements of the black American community in dance and theater is one influence that comes through distinctly.

In 1946 Dewey married Roberta Lowitz Grant, to the dismay of his children—other than the adopted Sabino, who seems to have found the ebullient and sociable Roberta a perfectly acceptable stepmother. Dewey's second marriage cost him a good deal of money. Alice Dewey's will had left him only a life interest in the income from her estate, and capital and income alike would go to the children if Dewey remarried. Some friends thought the children should not have taken the money, but Roberta was comfortably off, so was Dewey, and it was not a blow that Dewey himself resented. The second marriage distressed Sidney Hook, too, though he was uncharacteristically tight-lipped about his reasons. It is not hard to imagine that Hook must have felt displaced in Dewey's affections. He had been close to Dewey ever since he had begun work with him in 1926 as a graduate at Columbia, had been nominated by Dewey himself as the standard-bearer of pragmatism, and had fought alongside Dewey in all manner of hearts-and-minds campaigns for the allegiance of the radical center—the non-Communist social democrats of the 1930s and 1940s. Most of Dewey's political battles were ones that Hook either dragged him into or brought to his notice in the hope that Dewey would join in of his own accord. It was through Hook that Dewey met the members of the innumerable committees that flowered in the thirties for the defense or repudiation of this, that, and the other victim and injustice. Hook knew the way the Communist party of the USA tried to make use of distinguished people without their full knowledge, but while he was careful to protect Dewey from the party, he saw no reason why he should not persuade Dewey to fight for the anti-Stalinist left instead.[4]

During the 1930s Dewey was more active in politics than at any time in his life. Much of that activity, and its intellectual defense, are the subject of the next chapter. A very brief outline of some of it is needed now, however, since it bears so directly on his views on religion, aesthetics, and education. Dewey's activities in the People's Lobby and his work for the League for Independent Political Action belong most naturally with his defense of aggressive reformism in *Liberalism and Social Action* and *Freedom and Culture* and were "political" in a narrow sense. Much else was all of a piece with a lifetime of defending teachers against their conservative employers and defending liberal teachers' unions against subversion by the left. The endless articles, speeches, and lectures that this involved fill a substantial part of the later volumes of the *Collected Works*. Their intellectual interest lies in the way they were part of the long war over the nature of progressive education; Dewey turned very readily from polemics against school boards and Communists to popularizations of his own educational views in such works as *Experience and Education* and to his acerbic little battle with Robert Hutchins over the tasks of higher education. This was what we have come to call cultural politics, and it was conducted in much the same acerbic tones in the 1930s as in the 1980s.

Dewey was not a "party man." He had no sense of the positive value of party systems in modern democracies and not much "feel" for the realities of political life. It is tempting to say that this is no cause for complaint; he was a professional philosopher, not a professional activist. More interestingly, Dewey's philosophy was almost in principle antipathetic to the adversarial system in politics. The reason lay in Dewey's assimilation of political decision making and scientific inquiry. The idea that politics, like science, involved a cooperative and intelligent search for solutions to consensually defined problems consorts badly with the politics of "winners and losers" that the party struggle involves. It is not exactly *impossible* to give a defense of party politics in a Deweyan framework, even if we visualize politics as something like science, and science as something like politics, and both as essentially experimental activities.[5] We may think of the different parties in a democracy as offering competing hypotheses about what lines of reform and "adaptation" will be most fruitful, just as we may think of the upholders of different theories in science as members of intellectual parties trying to persuade scientific investigators to stake their careers on one view of the world rather than another.[6] But this emphasis on conflict is at least rhetorically difficult to square with Dewey's emphasis on seeing society as a whole as one problem-solving organism.

Dewey's view was more naturally hospitable to an old-fashioned radicalism that divided the political world into the upholders of the partial interests of particular social groups and the upholders of the interests of "the people." Dewey did not espouse a backward-looking populism or hanker after agrarian radicalism; he was a forward-looking, modernizing populist. In spite of plausible arguments to the contrary, I do not think that he much hankered after the simplicities of rural life and small-town America. He did do all he could to suggest that politics separated the believers in "intelligence" and the public interest from assorted practitioners of the politics of self-interest, class warfare, and blind adherence to tradition; though it is couched in the language of intelligence rather than virtue, it is a populist vision. Because he could not attach much value to party politics as ordinarily practiced, Dewey underestimated the difficulties of organizing a third party in the face of the electoral system that the United States shares with Britain—a simple plurality system that penalizes splitting—and underestimated also the extent to which the American political system was already a multiparty system, or a system of a multiplicity of local two-party systems.

Neither his isolationist hero William Borah nor the progressive Republican senator from Nebraska George Norris would play ball when appealed to to lead a third party. Dewey had been misled by the maverick behavior that they both indulged in into thinking that they wished to lead a new party rather than enjoy the luxury of dissidence inside the Republican party. Dewey also overestimated the extent to which either of them was persuaded of the necessity of the kind of socialist measures that he thought the slump required. In November 1930 Dewey's open letter to Norris on behalf of the League for Independent Political Action, asking him to resign from the Republicans and take up the radical mantle the league had offered him secured wide publicity, though little support, perhaps because Dewey wrote over the Christmas holiday and assured Norris that his acceptance would be a Christmas gift to the nation.

Norris replied that he was a "good Republican" and that what was needed was not a new party but a constitutional amendment to abolish the electoral college and recognize the reality of the president's answerability to the whole of the American people. Newspaper comment sided with Norris and against Dewey. Subsequent opinion has mostly done so, too.[7] Since Norris went on to become one of the key figures in establishing the Tenessee Valley Authority and a major supporter of Roosevelt's New Deal—as an independent, since by this time the Republican party had thrown him out—it is hard to regret his refusal as much as Dewey did.

Dewey's position during the 1930s was one that a British observer would have found easier to understand than most American observers might. He was a reformer rather than a revolutionary, but he nonetheless opposed Roosevelt's New Deal throughout. The position he occupied was roughly that of the British Labour party, as he himself said on more than one occasion.[8] He thought that the capitalist order had been irreparably damaged by the postwar boom and slump, by the depression of the 1930s, and by the protectionist trade policies that governments had increasingly introduced to protect their own markets. Like most noneconomists and all rational people, he thought a system that allowed food to rot while people were starving and threw a quarter of the working population on the streets while there was manifestly plenty for them to do was quite mad. Since the American economic system seemed to have run out of the self-correcting capacity that economists appealed to to explain why capitalism flourished in spite of its occasional absurdities, Dewey thought it doomed. Roosevelt's measures were better than Hoover's total inaction, but quite inadequate to the crisis they were dealing with. They were "messing about—a bit of this and a bit of that," rather than the bold experimentation the situation called for.

On the other hand, the far left's demands for insurrection and a revolutionary make-over of the United States were in all respects misguided; they were morally obtuse because they underestimated the horrors of violent social transformation, and they were technically obtuse because they had no plausible account of how to marry democracy and a planned economy. As we shall see in the next chapter, Dewey introduced the rather deft thought that what socialists should aim at was not the planned economy but the "planning" society; indeed, a fair estimate of his credibility as a social theorist hangs on whether he had much idea of what that slogan committed him to. It would certainly involve more government intervention than Roosevelt wanted in principle, and it needed a long-term, not just an emergency, exercise of political authority in economic matters. Some mixture of nationalization, price and wage controls, technical and manpower planning would have to be a permanent fixture.

As president of the People's Lobby Dewey kept up a constant nagging campaign from this position. The lobby made no difference to the history of the New Deal, and Dewey's editorials and letters to the press amounted to a very minor sideshow.[9] The People's Lobby is an interesting symptom of center-left dissatisfaction with Roosevelt but no more. Dewey's defense of unionized teachers against conservative hysteria over the political loyalty of teachers and his campaigns against Communists' attempts to manipulate teachers in the interests of the party may well have made more difference to the lives of those he was working for, at least in New York City.

Dewey's most prominent role in the struggles between the left and the farther left came at the end of the 1930s, when he went to Mexico City to chair a commission of inquiry into the charges against Trotsky that had featured in the Moscow show trials of 1936–37. Trotsky had been accused of trying to organize the assassination of Stalin and other leading members of the Soviet government; he had also been accused of organizing wreckers and saboteurs to undermine the Soviet economy. The charges were intrinsically incredible; since his expulsion from the Soviet Union, Trotsky had been in almost constant motion, pushed out of one country after another by governments anxious not to offend the Soviet Union and fearful of Trotsky's potential for radicalizing their own working classes. Nonetheless, the accusations were widely believed, or half believed, and in the United States it was an axiom in many quarters that *expressed* doubts about the Moscow trials would destroy the anti-Fascist unity of the popular front.

Dewey's family were all opposed to his going; supposedly liberal periodicals such as the *New Republic* and the *Nation* were quick to denounce the inquiry as a Trotskyite plot against the Communists, who had by now been told by Moscow to abandon their campaign to destroy the moderate left and had begun a popular front campaign. Trotsky himself had been anxious about the terms on which Dewey would agree to serve and almost equally afraid that at the age of seventy-eight Dewey was simply "past it." Only Sidney Hook was unequivocally in favor of Dewey's taking part. Even he agreed that Dewey was rather elderly for such adventures and left it up to Dewey to decide what he wanted to do. It was, paradoxically, the efforts of his former colleagues on the *New Republic* to persuade him not to rock the popular front boat that made up Dewey's mind.[10] The one thing calculated to make him furious was the suggestion that he had been manipulated by the Trotskyites and did not understand what he was doing. The affair marked the end of his quarter of a century's association with the *New Republic.* All the same, Dewey went with a genuinely open mind. On the train ride down to Mexico he told James Farrell that he was inclined to believe Stalin's charge that Trotsky had conspired to assassinate him. The "trial" was in fact a vindication of Trotsky's innocence of Stalin's charges; it was at the same time a triumph for Dewey and a total rout for the American Communist party and its fellow-traveling allies. I embroil us more deeply in all this in the next chapter.

Pragmatism and the Ends of Life

Here I turn to a topic that presents some difficulty for the pragmatist of a Deweyan stripe. This is the realm of "ultimate values." One difficulty it presented for Dewey it also presents for any commentator: the problem of finding any kind of neutral vocabulary in which to talk about the differences between Dewey's ideas and more orthodox ethical, theological, art-historical, and art-critical traditions. Another, or perhaps the same in a different guise, is the way Dewey displaced the traditional subject matter of much of philosophy. As we have seen, ethics seemed to become a branch of social psychology, but this was because social psychology had itself taken on the task of assessing the "satisfactoriness" of the human organism's "adjustment" to its surroundings (including therein the adjustment of those surroundings to the organism). Now we find that Dewey's aesthetics does not tackle the usual conundrums of the subject—the relation of subject matter to artistic form, the relevance of the medium to the effect it produces, whether traditional divisions between the various arts make sense—at least not head-on.

Modern philosophers have been fascinated by such puzzles as the *identity* of Beethoven's Ninth Symphony. The symphony is not to be identified with its score, or with any particular performance of itself, but we seem to understand what we mean when we say that the orchestra has just played Beethoven's Ninth, and we can walk into a music bookstore and ask for "Beethoven's Ninth" in the expectation of getting a score. Dewey seems to have been utterly uninterested in such puzzles. He was to some degree interested in what they spring from, which is an ambiguity in the way we talk about works of art, which points in its turn to something puzzling about the way we experience them: what we pay attention to and how. He was not interested in the stuff of postwar analytical aesthetics. He may have been right or wrong, and I do not want to beg that question, merely to observe that *Art as Experience* may be harder to read for a reader with some training in recent aesthetic theory than for a reader with none. Just as *The School and Society* was concerned with the social value of education rather than the curriculum, so *Art as Experience* could have been called "Art and Society," so much is it concerned with the social role of art rather than with criteria for judging the merits of what we see and hear and read.

Matters are not nearly as difficult when it comes to Dewey's discussion of religion in *A Common Faith,* if only because that is a short essay, casual in manner and expression, one that got Dewey into such unwelcome hot water that he swore off writing on the subject again. There, too, however, Dewey writes at an angle to the philosophy of religion as generally practiced. He does not settle down to discuss the concept of the numinous or to unravel Aquinas's Five Ways to knowledge of the existence of God. He diverts the discussion from the traditional issues in natural theology—God's existence, the problem of evil, squaring divine foreknowledge and human freedom, and so on—and focuses on the social value of a "religious" perspective on the world. The conventionally religious at the time, who wished to know whether Professor Dewey believed in God or not, were variously irritated, baffled, and angered. Art, on the other hand, was for Dewey religion under another label; his claim that his religion was Coleridge's at least implied that the religious sensibility found in the world the same unity as a source of value and a support for value that we find in great art.[11]

What that involves is hard to say, but it was Dewey's view. His approach to the subject was, as usual, both distinctive and indirect. Art and religion are the stuff of discussions of "ultimate values," but a good pragmatist will go to all lengths not to talk of "ultimate values" in just those terms. The language of higher and lower, immediate and ultimate was what Dewey always tried to escape. This is an implication of his naturalistic and psychological approach to valuation.[12] A glass of water, for instance, may in Dewey's universe possess ultimate value. If you are thirsty, and a glass of cold water is exactly what you need, want, and hanker after, that glass of water will quench your thirst, satisfy your needs, and gratify your hankering. The circle of thirst, desire for a drink, the drink itself is complete and self-sufficient and not in need of further justification or explanation.

Our desire may itself become an object of further reflection; we may brood on the sad fact that several large beers would taste even better than several glasses of cold water but would leave us with a hangover or unfit to drive, but that reflection arises only when we are checked in our action in just the sort of way Dewey endlessly discussed, say, when we first want a large beer, then think of the ill consequences of gratifying the desire, then turn to rethinking our situation and perhaps settling for lemonade. The simple cycle of want and satisfaction is, so to speak, complete in itself. Thirsty people want something refreshing; when they get it, the want is extinguished by being satisfied. In that sense, this glass of water is an ultimate good. Its goodness is not derivative, not a matter of its leading to anything other than the satisfaction that it provides, even though there is much to be said about why creatures like ourselves *find* ourselves thirsty and then satisfied. Life is thus full of ultimate values of a very humble kind.

Nonetheless, pragmatists also recognized some form of a hierarchy of values. Often this is commonplace: We do one thing for the sake of another—we go on a diet for six weeks to look elegant at the beach, say—where the former is a means to the latter as an end. Relative to the diet, the hoped-for elegance is the ultimate end, the diet's value merely that of a means. If we are lucky, we shall enjoy the diet, and then the two do not stand in quite the same relationship as a means that gets *all* its value from the end it serves, or one whose disvalue is offset by the value of the end it promotes. Dewey did not deny any of this, but he took it for so much for granted that he tended to bury the point in a discussion of something much less commonplace. This is that even a means which is disagreeable in itself—suppose it involves four tablespoons of oat bran every morning and a spoonful of cod-liver oil—may become for us an occasion to demonstrate our intelligence, determination, farsightedness, and bravery in triumphing over the disagreeableness of cod-liver oil first thing in the morning. Now, it becomes quite hard to say what is a means to what and what carries the value. It is only because the diet is a diet-carrying-the-promise-of-elegance that we bother with it; we would not eat oat bran and cod-liver oil for fun or even to demonstrate our self-control. Considering that we *are* bothering, however, dieting itself becomes an object of value as an occasion for demonstrating our various virtues of persistence and good sense. It could not do that if we found it straightforwardly agreeable, and it could not do it if it was pointless—because then we would merely be suffering pain for its own sake, which would not deserve praise but a good talking-to. Only by virtue of the diet's having both the consequences it does and the character it does can it have this double aspect.

Why is it worth emphasizing such cases? Only because there are in real life many important situations with just this character, such as the kind of work we do to put our family's bread on the table. I choose the example deliberately. Dewey's socialist inclinations are hard to describe, but one thing that they very much involved was his wish to see work invested with its proper value and reorganized in such a way as to provide meaning in people's lives. Everyday work was the major activity that Dewey complained that moral philosophers dismissed as not worth thinking about because it was "only a means to an end." A 1960s study of the relatively well-off workers who worked in the British motor industry concluded that one reason why the "affluent workers" of the study's title were not inclined to political radicalism was that they expected nothing from their jobs except a fat pay packet at the end of the week.

They were instrumentalists who thought of work as a matter of selling as little of their time as they had to for as much money as they could get.

The work they did was boring, and they knew it; but they did not mind. They did not like its being boring, but they were not inclined to protest it. They did not protest because the available work was either boring and badly paid or boring and well paid, and faced with that choice, they sensibly chose the second. Whether work *had* to be boring was not a question they let themselves ask themselves, and it was not one that they were encouraged to ask by their management, their trade unions, or anybody else. Moreover, to the degree that they did ask such questions, they were—since they were decent people, good family men for the most part, and sober in their expectations of what they were entitled to demand—keenly aware that they could take money home for their wives and children and spend it on food, clothing, holidays, and the home but that they could not take "job satisfaction" home in the same way.[13]

Dewey understood all this perfectly well. He did not accept it as an immovable obstacle to the transformation of American society, however. Much of *Art as Experience* is reminiscent of the work of John Ruskin, who also wanted to emphasize the continuity between good work in an everyday, humdrum context and the so-called fine arts. Dewey was concerned to close the gap between work done for purely instrumental reasons, work that he thought resulted in ugly objects built down to a price rather than up to a quality, and work whose character was soul-destroying rather than life-enhancing. If this was to happen, he thought, people needed to think rather differently about activities that were undertaken for instrumental purposes in order that they were not devalued by being thought of too instrumentally. Like the mythical diet I offered as a joking example, work ought to be valued for expressive and intrinsic reasons as well as for the sake of the goods it produced and the money it paid. If it were, there would be no *one* ultimate value that it promoted since what counted as its ultimate point would depend upon where one stood. Since good and interesting work is one of modern man's greatest needs, it would have an ultimate value as good and interesting work, but since modern man also needs to get to work in comfort, needs to eat, clothe himself, live in tolerable comfort, and care for his dependents, it would be instrumentally useful, too. The one value would not rule out the other or be subordinate to it.

It is, then, a third difficulty of Dewey's account of ultimate values that he both accepts the usual account of the need to justify the ends for whose sake we concern ourselves with means to achieve them and criticizes it because he is so anxious that we should stop and remind ourselves that many means are also capable of being valued as ends, that they may be given attention as experiences with a "consummatory" value of their own. Lastly, and to pick up my observation about the way in which a glass of water can function as an ultimate but low-level value, it is worth remembering that Dewey wanted to do two not quite contradictory things at once in the discussion of ultimates.

He wanted to remind his readers that "ultimate" did not always mean highfalutin; humble ultimate values exist. He was also very willing to agree that he owed the world an account of the experimentalist's vision of the great goods, an account of when and how we could see the world making sense and having a value that illuminated everything else in life. It was up to poets, playwrights, painters, architects to catch that light for us, but each individual had some spark of creativity that could be brought out and employed. This was the realm of consummatory experience.

"Consummatory experience" was not a label for a distinct form of experience in the sense in which a tickle is different from an itch. Indeed, Dewey stands in an awkward relationship to twentieth-century philosophers who have tried to give an account of experience *as* experienced. Dewey's analysis of experience employs a phenomenological approach to the world-as-experienced, but Dewey was himself dismissive of the German phenomenologists who turned up at the New School, where Alvin Johnson's "University in Exile" had started up in the mid-1930s to receive the victims of Hitler's purge of German higher education. He saw them as German idealists who had failed to acclimatize to their new American environment. The reason he saw so little in their work was that he was not concerned to *characterize* the experience we have when we encounter artistic creations of one or another sort. Rather he wanted to emphasize that experience can be approached *as* consummatory. The distinction between the humdrum and the aesthetically engaging is partly a matter of the content of art objects, but in Dewey's eyes, it was, more important, a question of the way we engage with them.

To understate the importance of the objects themselves would be entirely misguided; some objects would appear trite and boring on prolonged inspection and would not repay the attention that the appreciation of a work of art demands. Some objects have the depth and complexity that preserve our interest indefinitely; the idea of a work of art as a "completed infinity" is one that Dewey is happy to employ when he needs it. As always, however, Dewey emphasizes the active participation of the audience in an aesthetic as much as in a scientific context. Since Dewey thus implies that works of art must be seen *as* works of art to be appreciated as such, the question of how people can be got to look at their environment, their work, and deliberately created art objects in the right way and with the right interests is inescapable, and we find ourselves once again in Dewey's philosophy of education. How do we "read" a work of art; how do we "read" nature as divine; does Dewey have any thoughts about how education in the conventional sense can teach us how to "read"? The remainder of this chapter advances from art to Robert Hutchins by way of the religious attitude.

The Point of Art

Dewey said little about his own tastes in matters of art. Readers of his poetry can see that Wordsworth and Whitman played a large part in his literary formation; but there is nothing very distinctive in the use he makes of them, and nothing suggests he had any interest in experimentation with metrical or other techniques. He was a contemporary of modernist poets like T. S. Eliot and Ezra Pound but took no interest in their work. His prose was deliberately unstylish, not because he could not recognize elegance, verve, or novelty when he saw it but because he was interested only in one thing: getting some complicated and novel thoughts across. He was perfectly capable of coining aphorisms that would stick in his readers' minds, and contrary to popular belief, there is such a volume as *The Wit and Wisdom of John Dewey.*[14] Mostly he was ruthless about subordinating such flashes of high spirits to the main task. The form and content of his verse suggest that it was an outlet for emotions he had no way of talking about and nobody to talk about them to, rather than for reasons that a literary theorist would find interesting.

This has implications for Dewey's account of art. If his aesthetic theory had to be put in any of the standard categories of twentieth-century art theory, it would have to be bracketed with "expressivist" theories of the art object. The most famous philosopher of art in the 1930s was the Italian historicist and neo-Hegelian Benedetto Croce, and Croce observed almost fifteen years later that it was puzzling that he and Dewey should so largely agree in their view that art objects were interesting as expressions of the aesthetic intention of their creators.[15] Croce was, in fact, not only puzzled by the seeming resemblance but annoyed that Dewey acknowledged no debt to him and felt no sympathy for Crocean idealism. As we shall see, the similarity is only a surface similarity; the expressivist aspects of Dewey's theory are embedded in a different theory, an essentially communicative one.

In any case, Dewey was not intent on producing a general theory of art, let alone a historical theory of art forms. Among other deficiencies that he knew disqualified him from such a task, his uninterest in music was pretty conclusive. What he had was an eye for the paintings that Albert Barnes collected and for the painters whom Barnes admired. He also shared Barnes's belief in the aesthetic value of many things that had not been constructed for aesthetic reasons. Visitors to the Barnes Collection will remember that Barnes had his paintings arranged in a very particular, not to say very unorthodox, fashion. They are displayed so as to produce a whole wall of color and mood, and paintings are balanced against one another to enhance the pattern of the wall rather than to facilitate the inspection of each painting singly. In the same spirit, no details of the painting are given beyond the bare fact of the painter's name; dates of composition and information that might assist a viewer in speculating about what the painter was trying to do are scrupulously omitted. Displayed among the paintings are two other sorts of object: Hinges and keys are set out flat on the wall, and small items of furniture—wooden sea chests, little tables, and the like—as well as spindles for spinning cotton and wool stand against the walls.[16]

Like many other writers and critics, and painters themselves, in the first thirty years of the century, Dewey shared the urge to bring into the light of modern critical interest many things that had not been thought of as anything more than anthropologically interesting curios: Benin bronzes; Oceanic carvings; "primitive" art generally. Among the painters whose works Barnes collected, Picasso and Rouault paid overt homage to such influences, and this is reflected in *Art as Experience*'s photographs of Bushman rock paintings and Scythian jewelry as well as in the way Dewey happily invokes African sculpture along with the work of Jacob Epstein to make a point about the importance of the physical form of art objects. Much of the material Dewey discussed was more predictable: items from the Barnes Collection, especially Cézanne still lifes and Matisse semifigurative works such as his *Joie de vivre*. When Dewey stretches back to write of El Greco, it is easy to feel, as one does in the Barnes Collection itself, that El Greco is there to make a point about the modern masters. At all events, there is no doubt that the combination of constant access to Barnes's collection of pictures and the constant flow of enthusiasm from Barnes himself meant that Dewey got very genuine pleasure from the late impressionists and early modernists that Barnes collected in such quantities.

It is perhaps worth observing that Dewey followed Barnes in one important feature of the way Barnes approached paintings. The epitome of Barnes's view of art was "The painting is on the canvas, not behind it." In other words, from an aesthetic point of view, a painting was to be engaged with as an experienced object, not primarily to be thought about as a social or historical product; knowing about its status as those things could be helpful in trying to engage with it, but it need not be, and it was only occasionally indispensable. One needed to know a good deal about what an artist might be aiming to do, but the end result was the experience of the spectator. Thus Dewey starts *Art as Experience* by observing: "By common consent, the Parthenon is a great work of art. Yet it has aesthetic standing only as the work becomes an experience for a human being."[17] This suggests that we may get *pleasure* from it in a wholly untutored fashion.

Yet the suggestion is hardly made before it is at least somewhat undermined. For it is clear that what we cannot get in an untutored fashion is *understanding*. "[I]f one is to go beyond personal enjoyment into the formation of a theory about that large republic of art of which the building is a member, one has to be willing at some point in his reflections to turn from it to the bustling, arguing, acutely sensitive Athenian citizens, with civic sense identified with a civic religion, of whose experience the temple was an expression, and who built it not as a work of art but as a civic commemoration."[18] Something Dewey never quite explains is the relationship between understanding and enjoyment and about how understanding features in what one might call developed enjoyment; it is, however, plausible to suppose that it is enjoyment that takes priority and that understanding is its handmaiden.

Discussing the way in which art objects have become the prey of collectors, removed from public life and shut up in museums, Dewey elaborated on the relative irrelevance of historical background by adding, "My purpose, however, is not to engage in an economic interpretation of the history of the arts, much less to argue that economic conditions are either invariably or indirectly relevant to interpretation of individual works of art."[19] Plainly the thought was that the point of art theory was to enhance and assist experience, whereas the point of art is just to be the object of that experience; what sort of theory enhanced experience was an experimental question, and Dewey was quite sure that some theories reflected the conditions of modern collecting rather than anything very germane to the encounter with the art object itself. It was this encounter that we had to concentrate on.

Dewey's friends and family were impressed with the way he would stand for a very long time in front of a single painting, chewing over his reactions and the painting's possibilities for as long as he needed. In spite of this, the reader might think that *Art as Experience* is more concerned with art as seen from the artist's perspective than as seen from the spectator's; in a sense, Dewey's target is to reconstruct what the creator does when he creates rather than what the spectator does when he experiences that creation. Of course, Dewey thought these were two sides of the same coin; the effect the painting has on the spectator is bound up with the way the creator creates it, and it would be a mistake to separate too sharply what Dewey was at pains to run together.

It remains of some interest that one way in which Dewey's emphasis on the social implications of art and his hostility to the separation of the fine arts and the practical arts come out in his aesthetics is by leading him to start from the side of creation rather than reception. Having said which, we ought to remember also that he accepted enough of the idealist conception of art to have written: "A new poem is created by every one who reads poetically—not that its *raw* material is original for, after all, we live in the same old world, but that every individual brings with him, when he exercises his individuality, a way of seeing and feeling that in its interaction with old material creates something new, something previously not existing in experience."[20] What is true of poetry is true of every art medium. "As a piece of parchment, or marble, of canvas, it remains (subject to the ravages of time) self-identical throughout the ages. But as a work of art, it is recreated every time it is aesthetically experienced."[21] Creation may be the central concept here, but the spectator is a party to the act of creation, and the artist needs an audience for the creative task to be accomplished.

To see how Dewey put aesthetic experience and artistic creation back in the street, one can begin where he begins. "In order to *understand* the aesthetic in its ultimate and approved forms, one must begin with it in the raw; in the events and scenes that hold the attentive eye and ear of man, arousing his interest and affording him enjoyment as he looks and listens: the sights that hold the crowd—the fire-engine rushing by, the machines excavating enormous holes in the earth; the human-fly climbing the steeple-side; the men perched high in air on girders, throwing and catching red-hot bolts."[22] If we could not be absorbed in the pleasures of experiencing the world, engrossed by its colors and sounds, there would be no place for art in our lives. The "aesthetic" exists in everyday life and would exist in more abundance in a more intelligently organized society than ours. Conversely, the "artistic" exists in just the same way: "The intelligent mechanic engaged in his job, interested in doing well and finding satisfaction in his handiwork, caring for his materials and tools with genuine affection, is artistically engaged. The difference between such a worker and the inept and careless bungler is as great in the shop as it is in the studio."[23]

Given that Dewey sets himself the task of elucidating aesthetic experience, we might guess that he would do what we have seen him do everywhere else: that he would provide a genetic and social psychological account of how the more complex and elaborate experience of taking an educated pleasure in Matisse grows out of our everyday enjoyment of the engaging experiences he mentions, such as the rushing fire engine or the steeplejacks at work in the girders. *Art as Experience* does so. But Dewey sees his task as something other than elaborating another aesthetic theory to go with all the others. The difference he sees between his own concerns and his predecessors' is that he treats our interest in art as something we can look at in much the way he looked at social habit in *Human Nature and Conduct:*

> Theory is concerned with discovering the nature of the production of works of art and of their enjoyment in perception. How is it that the everyday making of things grows into that form of making which is genuinely artistic? How is it that our everyday enjoyment of scenes and situations develops into the peculiar satisfaction that attends the experience which is emphatically aesthetic? These are the questions theory must answer. The answers cannot be found unless we are willing to find the germs and roots in matters of experience that we do not currently regard as aesthetic. Having discovered these active seeds, we may follow the course of their growth into the highest forms of finished and refined art.[24]

The need for such a theory is all the greater because what we denominate as "art" has been split off from everyday life to such a degree that the popular contempt for the artist and the artist's contempt for the populace are only to be expected. Dewey observes in passing that "the forces at work are those that have removed religion as well as fine art from the common or community life"; the thought is scarcely a surprising one from Dewey.[25]

To say that Dewey's efforts go into the social and political analysis of the distorting and alienating effects of the misuse of categories of appreciation runs the risk of suggesting that he does not have an aesthetic theory at all. This would be false. He does. It is not easy to summarize because he was eager to emphasize how many *different* things art meant to us and how many different qualities we could look for and enjoy in the objects of art. Another difficulty is that *Art as Experience* is not a very consecutive book even by Dewey's relaxed standards. It possess a loose genetic logic, but little more. Readers may well think that the book moves backward and forward between issues that lie well within traditional aesthetics—form and content, expression and its bearer, what *kind* of unity we look for in a work of art—and a historical and sociological and psychological commentary on why such questions arise, how answering them is made difficult by such social conditions as the association of art and connoisseurship, or the role of art in certifying the pecuniary reputation of its owners. All the while, of course, there is an underlying educational or pedagogical thrust to the argument since all the while Dewey is concerned to answer the question of what use *Art as Experience* might be to someone who habitually does (or does not) look at paintings, read poetry and fiction, listen to music, and observe his natural and man-made surroundings attentively.

The argument starts with the thought that the roots of aesthetic enjoyment and artistic fulfillment start well below the level of rational, self-conscious human reflection.[26] The animal stalking its prey or building its nest moves with a grace and facility that we envy, and we envy it because it is such a pure example of an action moving smoothly and undistractedly toward its proper consummation. Indeed, Dewey harks back to Coleridge and even beyond when he observes: "There is in nature even below the level of life something more than mere flux and change. Form is arrived at whenever a stable even though moving equilibrium is reached. Changes interlock and sustain one another. Wherever there is this coherence there is endurance. Order is not imposed from without but is made out of the relations of harmonious interactions that energies bear to one another. . . . Order cannot but be admirable in a world constantly threatened with disorder. . . ."[27] For all his objections to Kant's ethics and metaphysics, Dewey sounds a thoroughly Kantian note in insisting on the irresistibility of the human urge to find a meaning in the order of nature and in tracing that urge to the fact of our own existence in a world that is always threatening disorder, death, and dissatisfaction at the same time that it promotes order, life, and fulfillment if properly and adequately used for those ends.

Art as Experience is parasitic on the account of experience that Dewey gave years before in *Experience and Nature;* one way that emerges, and nicely calculated to give offense to the analytically and logically minded, is in Dewey's observation that aesthetics takes priority over logic. What that startling reflection amounts to is the thought that a person who is thinking may be guided only by the most random chain of thought, where ideas flit in and out of the mind according to no coherent scheme at all, while a person who is thinking to some purpose controls the process for the sake of an intellectual coherence that has the same order that we take aesthetic pleasure in when we find it in nature. The point is again to remind the reader that however "high" high art may be, it is rooted in everyday experience, and the rhetorical force of the claim that even abstract thought is similarly rooted and the two of them connected in their origins is obvious enough.

Dewey steadily presses on through an account of experience, expression, and the crystallization of experience in permanent objects. Essentially the argument is that *having* an experience is a distinctive and creative achievement, one that needs concentration, attention, and memory to give it its full value. Dewey moves easily between the commonplace and the powerful. He offers as instance of an experience in this fully realized sense what we might feel as we cross the Atlantic in a ship that runs through a powerful storm. We might reflect on it by saying, "*That* was a storm," attending to our encounter with something that is fully and thoroughly itself—both that storm and at the same time a thoroughly convincing example of what storms can be. Reinforcing this point, he invokes the famous letter in which Keats pointed out the way a quarrel in the street may be *fine* even though the motives and occasion may be vile.

It then becomes simple for Dewey to claim that what the artist puts into a work of art and what the spectator therefore gets out of it is a particular realization of the artist's experience, in which the spectator can then participate. This is why I said earlier that in the conventional account of aesthetic theories, Dewey's would count as an "expressive" theory, though only because he was putting forward a communicative theory, in which the artist's expressive purposes form one-half of the whole story. The expressive theory of art made several points that Dewey acknowledged in passing. It was worth recalling that a poem *expresses* what a psychological account of my state of mind would not express but merely *describe;* it was also worth recalling that the detachability of what is expressed from the way it is expressed is much diminished in art compared with science and everyday description. "I am tired" and "*Sono stanco*" mean "the same thing," and I can use either to state the fact that I am tired, though I would do well to use the former to an English speaker and the latter to an Italian speaker. Monet's paintings of Rouen Cathedral, on the other hand, are infinitely far from meaning nothing, but *what* they express seems impossible to detach from *how* they express it. Dewey knew that critics were tempted to say that for this reason paintings did not mean anything or express anything, but provided a stimulus to the spectator's imagination and reveries. Dewey resisted any such argument.

Although he did not mention them, he might have been mindful of some conclusive counterexamples to any theory that reduces paintings to something like Rorschach blots. A series of canvases painted to commemorate a dynastic marriage can do so only if their representational qualities line up with such meanings as "France and Spain are now allies rather than enemies" or "The hope of the contracting parties is that this alliance will yield heirs to the thrones of France and Spain and general prosperity to the humble inhabitants of both countries." Much else makes such paintings "proselike": We can ask detailed questions about the way particular scenes and particular figures convey the message they do, we can easily detach these meanings from their representation, and we can ask questions about the sincerity or insincerity of the painter of the sentiments. Even if neither side expected the alliance to last six months, we can agree that what the paintings *say* is "Let us hope the alliance lasts forever." Interestingly, however, the more we can ascribe a clear meaning to the painting, the less that meaning has to do with its aesthetic assessment.

One way to see this divergence between meaning and aesthetic viability is to ask the familiar and contentious question whether the supposed insincerity—or uninterest in his employer's sincerity—that we ascribe to the artist does any damage to the aesthetic qualities of the art. Dewey insisted that the artist's integrity is essential to the success of the painting as a work of art, but there is much to be said for caution in applying that view to court painters like Rubens and Van Dyck. There must be a certain wholeheartedness about the painting and a kind of conviction about it—nymphs and satyrs must gambol enthusiastically if they are to be symbols of political celebration—but they may well be enjoyed for their own sake, and their shape, texture, and coloring appreciated while all the time we are perfectly aware that this is a *pièce d'occasion*, turned out with tremendous skill by people whose unillusioned grasp of the politics of the day might make our blood run cold. We can positively wallow in enjoyment of the technique while bracketing away the sincerity of the artist.

Dewey could have answered such doubts, but he did not. And we may wonder whether it would have been worth his time to do so. Dewey could readily enough have rearranged his argument so as to say that *what* we enjoy in art is what it is that is wholeheartedly expressed and done with the proper conviction. If this means that we enjoy different things in Rubens, Piero della Francesca, and Picasso, that is no great surprise. Dewey might, however, have done better to have taken a self-consciously modern, but not altogether modernist, stand and have held that what *we* nowadays value in art is the communication of the artist's experience and then have taken his chances on what this implied for twentieth-century tastes in seventeenth-century painting.

Historicizing the value of art in this way is a contentious tactic, but it would allow someone of a Deweyan persuasion to agree that we get a lot of pleasure from the court paintings of the seventeenth century as well as from late impressionism and then go on to distinguish those different pleasures from one another and from the pleasure we get from Cézanne's paintings of Mont Ste.-Victoire. It would also be a first move in admitting the importance of historical knowledge in aesthetic appreciation, something Dewey acknowledges in passing but does not discuss at length. It would hardly have been inconsistent with Dewey's approach to experience to acknowledge that we, the heirs of romanticism and its ideas about how we encounter nature and what we derive from the encounter, will find the rendition of the natural world in impressionism and postimpressionism immediately engrossing in a way we cannot find the work of Rubens engrossing without all sorts of historical, mythological, and technical information about what he painted, when he painted, for whom he worked, and why.

Dewey himself observed, "An English Protestant of the seventeenth century who savored to the full the theme of Milton's epic may have been so out of sympathy with the topic and setting of Dante's *Divine Comedy* as to be unable to appreciate the latter's artistic quality. Today an 'unbeliever' may be the one who is most sensitive aesthetically to such poems, just because of indifference to their subject matter. On the other hand, many an observer of pictures is now unable to do full justice to the painting of Poussin in its intrinsic plastic qualities because its classical themes are so alien."[28] That was Dewey's way of acknowledging that the literal meaning of a painting might well obstruct our aesthetic appreciation of it.

The reference to "intrinsic plastic qualities" suggests that Dewey was tempted by a more formalistic account of aesthetic value than can readily be squared with his obsession with communication. He was less tempted by what formalist accounts find it easy to acknowledge, the element of sheer playfulness in art. Dewey's official theory, with its insistence on expression and communication as the heart of artistic creation and its sympathetic response as the heart of aesthetic perception, suggests a degree of engagement and a strenuous and active approach to art of all kinds that are not always called for. The element of play that Schiller stressed in his *Letters on the Aesthetic Education of Mankind* often seems to be missing in Dewey's account. He had nothing illuminating to say about surrealism or about abstract art, and one gropes for what he might have tried to say about, say, the work of Piet Mondrian. Where not missing, play is always explained as protowork, a kind of rehearsal for serious engagement with the world, and that seems not to be right.

To say that he was trapped by his communicative account is not wholly adequate. He was somewhat trapped, but it was by several other ideas as well. Dewey was enough a child of his times and enough in debt to Albert Barnes to have been influenced, as Barnes was, by the early-twentieth-century British critic Roger Fry and his insistence on the formal properties of art. Hence the reference to "intrinsic plastic qualities" and the suggestion that there are qualities unrelated to content, history, artist's intention, and the work's literal or representative meaning that give a work its aesthetic quality. How Dewey thought he had squared this with his emphasis on the artistic role of the creator is not easy to understand.

Early in *Art as Experience* he wrote emphatically that the human origins of an art object are essential to its artistic standing. Were it to emerge that something we had previously valued as "a finely wrought object, one whose texture and proportions are highly pleasing" and had believed to be "a product of some primitive people," was after all a happenstance freak of nature, its standing would entirely change. "[A]t once it ceases to be a work of art and becomes a natural 'curiosity.' It now belongs in a museum of natural history, not in a museum of art."[29] Neither sociologically nor in Dewey's own scheme of things is this true. It would not, as matter of dreary social fact, be implausible to encounter it in an art gallery; someone might have picked the thing up on the beach and decided it belonged in an art museum as an *objet trouvé*. Nor is it clear why Dewey, with his general antipathy to putting things in museums in the first place, is so quick to identify its categorical destiny with its geographical one. All that can also be pushed to one side; we might agree that *works of art* had by convention to be man-made and go on to observe that some naturally occurring objects were in other ways aesthetically admirable, seeing that we do after all find mountains and waterfalls and sunsets sublime and enjoy the "playful" aspects of nature revealed in crystals and plant forms in something of the same way that we enjoy the work of Mondrian. When all that has been done, Dewey's urge to keep the artistic and the aesthetic together cannot entirely be squared with his readiness to recognize that not everything the spectator finds in an art object was put there by the artist—at any rate, not as part of the artist's intention—whereas the artist's intention would always be crucial if the theory rested entirely on expression and communication. Form, therefore, matters as a more or less independent matter.

Dewey gave an account of the place of formal considerations in art; it was entirely characteristic, and it is generally persuasive. "The Natural History of Form" is the title of one of the chapters devoted to the topic, and Dewey tackled the subject in the same genetic fashion as the origins of artistic creation and aesthetic enjoyment in general. As usual, he was more interested in emphasizing the social roots and the social value of art as an activity than in crossing swords with other theorists of art. Thus he denied that there was an absolute distinction between form and content, denied that they were related as intellect to sense or reason to emotion, and always and everywhere returned to the claim—which I disputed above—that the "formal" properties of a work of art are of interest to the extent that they allow the fullest and most adequate expression and communication of the artist's experience. What Dewey meant by "form" was, as in most discussions of this very vexed subject, defined in contradistinction both to subject matter and to "formlessness," and his examples were adjusted accordingly.

To illustrate the "subject matter versus form," distinction, he used Max Eastman's reflections on the different ways a traveler on the Hudson ferry might see Manhattan, and to illustrate the avoidance of "formlessness," he cited Matisse's explanation of the way he placed different colors in relation to one another on a canvas. The traveler on the ferry may identify buildings one by one, may be curious about the height of the buildings, think of their cost and the state of the real estate market, and much else besides. "He may go on to think of the planlessness of arrangement as evidence of the chaos of a society organized on the basis of conflict rather than cooperation. Finally the scene formed by the buildings may be looked at as colored and lighted volumes in relation to one another, to the sky, and to the river. He is now seeing aesthetically, as a painter might see."[30] This was the form versus content contrast at work; the form versus formlessness opposition underlies the way Matisse's reminder that "[i]t is necessary that the different tones I use be balanced in such a way that they do not destroy one another" leads to Dewey's conclusion that the alternative is "confusion-confusion, that is, *in perception*. Vision cannot then complete itself."[31] The classical idea that *ars naturam perfecit*—art completes or perfects nature—is given a pragmatist twist. All perception is a striving to order the world, and so we find that "[f]orm is a character of every experience that is *an* experience. Art in its specific sense enacts more deliberately and fully the conditions that effect this unity. *Form may then be defined as the operation of forces that carry the experience of an event, object, scene, and situation to its own integral fulfillment.*"[32]

It hardly needs further demonstration that *Art as Experience* emphasized Dewey's familiar themes of the values of wholeness and unity in experience, though wholeness and unity are valuable only when they are *won* out of the fragmentary and constantly unraveling encounters we have with both nature and our made surroundings. It is perhaps worth ending this account of Dewey's aesthetics with three last ideas, ones that we should expect him to stress but that are brought out in *Art as Experience* with a clarity and a passion that give the lie to the thought that Dewey was incapable of eloquence. In the abstract these ideas may seem commonplace. It is not news that for *us* at least art has become a medium of communication of a peculiarly important kind, that for *us* at least the separation of the work we do to earn our bread and the chances we find to express our creative interests is often painful, and that for *us* at least the relationship of man to nature and man to culture has become a problem for art as well as for science.

The uncommonplace side of Dewey was his readiness to tie this back to his politics, to announce that to make art in practice play in our lives the role it can play in theory, we must reconstruct the industrial and economic system on which the modern world is based. We could have more experiences worth communicating if we lived differently; we could appreciate what is conventionally called art and located in galleries if we lived differently and produced new forms of art that we did not lock away in galleries. We would learn to hold in a proper balance the tension and serenity that we find in art objects and come to understand that what we enjoy is neither timeless nor merely transitory. This is closer to Oscar Wilde's discussion of the soul of the man under socialism than one would ever expect to find in Dewey. On the other hand, there is something of this to be found in the work of Roger Fry, and it seems likely that the filiation of this enthusiasm, or this expression of very pure and passionate Dewey, runs from Fry to Dewey via Barnes.

At all events, Dewey insisted that "[s]ince art is the most universal form of language, since it is constituted, even apart from literature, by the common qualities of the public world, it is the most universal and freest form of communication. Every intense experience of friendship and affection communicates itself artistically. . . . That art weds man and nature is a familiar fact. Art also renders men aware of their union with one another in origin and destiny."[33] These are not claims to be scrutinized in a carping frame of mind; one might equally well observe that art distances man from nature and so allows him to think reflectively, for instance, but that would hardly be a great objection since it could be accommodated without difficulty and might be seen fairly cheerfully as an alternative perspective, valid in its own way for the range of experiences it illuminates. The point rather is to see that Dewey's claims are part of his insistence that pragmatism has its own account of the ultimate goods of human life—those experiences that we value for their own sake, as conferring meaning on the rest—and that their explication involves no appeal to transcendental values, to "the spiritual," or to qualities of perception that only the highly educated or the upper classes can possess. Equally, it is part of an insistence that when we feel most intensely ourselves, we are not cut off from the experiences of others but most deeply and thoroughly in touch with them.

As to the relation between work and art, Dewey speaks with the accents of John Ruskin and William Morris; for the matter of that, he speaks with the accents of the youthful Marx. This makes one wonder yet again why he was so resistant to Hook and Eastman when they tried to persuade him that a proper interpretation of Marx—Marx as social critic as much as materialist social scientist—was consistent with pragmatism and would serve his own critical purposes very well. Presumably Dewey thought that Marx had been too thoroughly appropriated by the Communists of the Soviet Union and their allies to be saved for liberalism, and he must in any case have believed that there was no reason why he in particular should make Marx respectable when he needed no philosophical instruction or social insight from that source. But Dewey's commitment to the reunification of everyday work and artistic creation was never in doubt.

All the same, comparisons with Ruskin—even with Morris—must be taken cautiously. Ruskin at least was hostile to machinery and industrial civilization more or less in their own right; Morris was not in principle hostile, but it is very noticeable that his wonderful utopian essay *News from Nowhere* relies on a mysterious "Force" to provide clean, quiet power to drive factories and ships and that his workers are somehow working happily offstage while the characters in his story are walking along a towpath by the Thames and end up at a harvest supper in Morris's Kelmscott deep in rural Gloucestershire. Dewey, on the other hand, insisted that urban civilization was breeding its own aesthetic, and he stood up for the functionalism of the 1930s quite unabashedly. "If one compares the commercial products of the present with those of even twenty years ago, one is struck by the great gain in form and color. The change from the old wooden Pullman cars with their silly encumbering ornamentations to the steel cars of the present is typical of what I mean."[34]

What Dewey objected to was the real and inescapable hideousness of the surroundings industrial societies had built in recent years and the work that most of the working class spent their lives on. Dewey observed:

> [T]he organism hungers naturally for satisfaction in the material of experience, and since the surroundings which man has made, under the influence of modern industry, afford less fulfillment and more repulsion than at any previous time, there is only too evidently a problem that is left unsolved. . . . The labor and employment problem of which we are so acutely aware cannot be solved by mere changes in wages, hours of work and sanitary conditions. No permanent solution is possible save in a radical social alteration, which affects the degree and kind of participation the worker has in the production and social distribution of the wares he produces. Only such a change will seriously modify the content of experience into which creation of objects made for use enters. And this modification of the nature of experience is the finally determining element in the aesthetic quality of the experience of things produced.[35]

The Soviet enthusiasm for "proletarian art" cut no ice with Dewey; nor did Marxist critics' simpleminded equation of an interest in the materials of a painting—a Tintoretto, say—with a reductionist account of it as an ideological artifact produced to enhance the power and wealth of the people who bought it.

The role of art in rendering nature an object of the right kind of interest has already been sufficiently discussed. It remains only to mention in passing—since we shall now turn to it directly—that Dewey's understanding of the role of art in reconciling us to nature and in revealing nature's nurturing and sustaining possibilities was part of his assault on the pretensions of religion to fulfill that role exclusively. Although the merely natural cannot be appreciated as *art,* it can be appreciated aesthetically; it possesses formal and plastic qualities that we can enjoy in the same way as when they are created for the purpose. Dewey's uninterest in the traditional puzzles of aesthetics means that he does not do what his eighteenth-century precursors did and distinguish between the beautiful in art and the sublime in nature. Rather he was interested in seizing the territory for his own social, moral, and political philosophy, thus keeping it safe from snobs, spiritualists, and the merely pious. Some writers, of course, have made the move from art to religion by arguing that the beauty of the natural world leads irresistibly to the thought of a creator; Dewey always took the opposite tack. The beauty of nature, which *would* be a triumph for the deity's artistic capacity if there were a deity to create it, is by itself and without other props beauty enough. We do not *need* a divine creator to make the world beautiful; the fact that we wish there were a God who appreciated it as we do tends, if anything, to show how unnecessary a supernatural support is. So both the nature that man has not much touched and the second nature that is our built environment offer materials for appreciation and a terrain onto which we can project our hopes and values. Since that is a public terrain, we come again full circle; Wordsworth's daffodils may flash in memory upon our inner eye, but even that private pleasure is not merely publicly communicable—as witness the poem—but makes sense to us only because the natural world is also a human world.

Art as Experience is a curious work even after several readings; since Dewey never analyzed a painting or a poem at length, one has little sense of exactly how he would have set about it. He appealed to many paintings, poems and passages of prose from his favorite writers—W. D. Hudson, Goethe, Wordsworth—and beat off the demands of writers like T. S. Eliot for "great subjects." He constantly mentioned Cézanne, Renoir, Matisse, and other favorite painters. He unabashedly defended modernity in the pictorial arts but said nothing to depreciate the classical tradition; by the same token, he applauded Greek sculpture but praised African sculpture as well as the work of modern sculptors like Jacob Epstein. What we do not get much idea of is whether there is, was, or could be a distinctively Deweyan form of art criticism. My guess is not. The reason is that in the last resort Dewey was trying to give a reasoned account of why art matters rather than how we can decide whether a given work is more or less successful—a task he thought one often had to undertake but not the main task of the book. It is this that allowed him to offer views that in a lesser writer might quite properly be condemned as contradictory and this that explains the preacherly tone of some of his perorations.

God Reinterpreted

Dewey knew better than to say too bluntly that art could do for modern man what Christianity had done for his ancestors, even though that is in some ways the upshot of *Art as Experience*. The incessant dwelling on "experience" meant that just as he submerged familiar critical issues in an account of the creative experience on the one side and the receptive experience on the other, so he could properly and nonduplicitously duck such questions as Does God exist? in favor of a discussion of the religious experience. Dewey was never very explicit about the route by which he had deserted the Congregationalism of his youth. All that is clear is that he stopped giving little talks to the Students Christian Association when he left Michigan for Chicago in 1894 and did not join another church in his new home. His early writings, as we have seen, were full of a somewhat generalized Christian piety, and such early pieces as his talk entitled "The Duty to Knowledge of God" take a fiercely traditional line about the moral obligation to cultivate sincere and solid belief. This became diluted during his Hegelian discipleship, both because "God" is a rather ambiguous and shadowy presence in Hegelianism and because what was initially an attraction of Hegelianism—that it allowed us to ascend from matter to mind and thus to God—soon came to seem a redundancy.

Dewey's characteristic movement in such matters was to suggest that our knowledge of what it was that we wanted supported was more solid than our understanding of *what* provided the support and of *how* it provided it. We might have nameless longings for a coherence and finishedness in experience that the world as we encountered it did not provide, but any account of how "God," conceived as a supernatural support for the natural, could provide that coherence and finishedness raised the same problems as provoked the thought of his existence. Between 1898 and the late 1920s Dewey said almost nothing one way or another about religion. During the 1920s, however, the tone of his writing changed quite markedly.

Experience and Nature and *The Quest for Certainty* are not in any extended way concerned with religion, but they are about topics that march with it. *Experience and Nature,* for instance, excludes God as a supernatural support for the natural and any supernatural presence in the world, and it does it by insisting so continuously that everything we know of lies within experience.[36] *The Quest for Certainty* pushed traditional religion out of the room by pushing traditional metaphysics out of the room. The quest for *certainty* was not to be equated with the quest for *security;* in a world that was genuinely open-ended and indeterminate, security must come from learning to live with doubt and the suspension of the craving for certainty. This was a defense of epistemological modernism, not a defense of secularism, but its implications were hostile to traditional religious conceptions of the world. Dewey's insistence on the singleness of the experienced world, and his account of the growth of knowledge as a matter of improving the fallible maps with which we navigated around this world, left nothing outside experience.

If there was to be religious experience, it was in the same sense that there was aesthetic, poetic, scientific, and everyday experience, and this meant that although religious experience need no more compete with science, art and everyday enjoyment of the world than they needed to compete with one another, the traditional ontological claims made in such familiar parts of the Christian liturgy as the Nicene Creed were ruled out. Dewey, with his instrumentalist preconceptions, may well have failed to see why his opponents minded so much about their credal claims for the ontological priority of God to his creation; he certainly got irritated with them when they maintained that he identified the world with God and God with the world.[37] At all events, *A Common Faith* is built upon a thought that Dewey expressed a few months earlier when replying to Henry Weiman, Carl Otto, and the other authors of *Is There a God? A Conversation* following his review of their book in the *Christian Century.*[38]

> Separating the matter of religious experience from the question of the existence of God (as for example, those as far apart from one another as the Buddhists and the Comtean Positivists have done), I have found—and there are many who will corroborate my experience by their own—that all of the things which traditional religions prize and which they connect exclusively with their own conception of God can be had equally well in the ordinary course of human experience in our relations to the natural world and to one another as human beings related in the family, friendship, industry, art, science, and citizenship. *Either then the concept of God can be dropped out as far as genuinely religious experience is concerned or it must be framed wholly in terms of natural and human relationship involved in our straightaway human experience.*[39]

Dewey had acknowledged in his retirement essay "From Absolutism to Experimentalism" that he had not discussed the philosophy of religion and had not gone out of his way to make his religious outlook clear, but he had not elaborated on the point. Or, rather, he had said a good deal about the way in which the punitive and judicial aspects of Congregationalist Christianity had grated on him as a boy, and he had referred darkly to "a trying personal crisis" of which there is no other record.[40] But he also said there that that his difficulties with Christianity had not moved him to think about theological and metaphysical issues so much as to persuade him to think about the social issues with which religion had commonly been concerned. It seems odd nonetheless that he remained so reticent, especially when contemporaries like Josiah Royce and George Santayana were anything but reticent and William James was passionately interested in the phenomena of religious experience.

One may guess that the reason was contained in the unlikelihood that most of his readers would share the outlook encapsulated in the sentence italicized above. Persuading readers who firmly believed that the validity of religious experience stood or fell with the existence or otherwise of the Christian God that this was absolutely not the case would be a pointless and uphill struggle. It then becomes, and unfortunately remains, somewhat mysterious that he turned his attention to religion four years afterward in *A Common Faith*. It is less surprising that as soon as he done so and had replied to assorted reviewers and critics, he decided to leave the subject alone once more. His critics wanted him to answer yes or no to the question, Do you believe that there really is a God? while he wanted to dissolve that question. It is clear enough that he had an answer of a not very complicated kind, even so. In essence, it was that while it was not logically impossible that there existed "a personal will which is causative and directive of the universe and which is devoted to the promotion of moral ends," he himself did not believe in it.[41] But he believed that "the important thing is the fact, the reality, namely, that objective forces, of a great variety of kinds, actually promote human wellbeing, the efficacy of these forces is increased by human attention to and care for the working of these forces, so that if Mr. Weiman or any one else gets contentment and energy by naming them God as they function to promote welfare, let him do so. . . ."[42] His autobiographical essay suggested, too, that he had some doubts about the motives of those who might have debated the issue with him. "It seems to me that the great solicitude of many persons, professing belief in the universality of the need for religion, about the present and future of religion proves that in fact they are moved more by partisan interest in a particular religion than by interest in religious experience."[43]

A Common Faith is a short book, scarcely more than an extended pamphlet. Nor does it break new ground. Its interest in regard to Dewey's own development in fact lies less in its subject matter than in demonstrating at the most fundamental level Dewey's conviction that everything a reasonable person might want could be had within experience or perhaps his conviction that the pragmatist conception of experience was wide enough to encompass truth, beauty and goodness, art, and the ultimate meaning of the world. The importance of *A Common Faith* in the history of American religious thinking is another matter. It is a representative and significant example of the phenomenon that Commager so vividly described: "It is scarcely an exaggeration to say that during the nineteenth century and well into the twentieth, religion prospered while theology slowly went bankrupt."[44] Nothing could be further than *A Common Faith* from an insistence that there is no salvation outside the one true church or from the marriage of logical and doctrinal zeal that had animated, say, Jonathan Edwards and his New England predecessors.

A Common Faith is *almost* equally distant from the fundamentalist Christianity that insists that every important truth is in the Bible and that no interpreter of the words of the Bible need come between the Christian and his book. I say *almost* because such a fundamentalism is itself antitheological, and while Christian fundamentalism is certainly at the opposite pole from anything Dewey could have embraced in its obsessive concern with *one* book and a personal relation with only *one* ideal type of human existence as revealed in Christ, it has its own kind of insistence on the self-certifying character of the religious experience. The antirationalism of American fundamentalism and its association for the most part with right-wing politics are equally at odds with Dewey's emphasis on intelligent liberalism, but its insistence that faith must be a practical faith and its repudiation of any idea that religion ought to be kept out of everyday life appeal to something of the spirit that animated him. Dewey's atheism was a Protestant atheism and an American world-affirming atheism.

The bare bones of *A Common Faith* are simply described. As elsewhere, Dewey began with a sharp contrast between religion and the religious attitude; his first chapter was aggressively headed "Religion versus the Religious." Several targets clustered under that one heading. Firstly, the idea that there was such a thing as "religion" was demolished; religion is not one but many, and most dead or superseded religions are regarded by adherents of their successors as variously wicked or disgusting.[45] Dewey ignored the fact that the same might be said of the attitude of later scientists to earlier and exploded scientific theories, without anyone's saying that science is importantly multiple rather than singular. The point he wanted to make had little to do with singularity and plurality. His aim was to persuade his readers to bear in mind the historicity of religious faith. If old creeds have been superseded and overthrown in the past, our own creeds may not be the last word in religious thought.

The other rhetorical move Dewey was engaging in was to prevent anyone from moving from a definition of religion to a defense of some particular religion; starting with the *Oxford English Dictionary* definition of religion as "Recognition on the part of man of some unseen higher power, as having control of his destiny and as being entitled to obedience, reverence and worship,"[46] Dewey has no difficulty showing that "unseen powers" have been thought of in innumerable different and inconsistent ways, that "reverence" has taken some very curious forms, and worship has involved "the worship of animals, of ghosts, of ancestors, phallic worship, as well as of a Being of dread power and of love and wisdom. Reverence has been expressed in the human sacrifices of the Peruvians and Aztecs; the sexual orgies of some Oriental religions; exorcisms and ablutions; the offering of the humble and contrite mind of the Hebrew prophet, the elaborate rituals of the Greek and Roman churches."[47] Nor did Dewey give much credit to the cant claims for the moral utility of religious belief. Religions as they have historically existed have appealed to an almost unimaginably wide range of moral hopes and fears: "fear of lasting torture, hope of enduring bliss in which sexual enjoyment has sometimes been a conspicuous element; mortification of the flesh and extreme asceticism; prostitution and chastity; wars to extirpate the unbeliever; persecution to convert or punish the unbeliever and philanthropic zeal; servile acceptance of imposed dogma, along with brotherly love and aspiration for a reign of justice among men."[48] The moral Dewey drew was that asking for a revival of "religion" was therefore silly; there was no one thing, no discernible essence, to be resurrected or revitalized.

The stronger conclusion was that many people have religious experiences to which traditional religions do no justice. They are not "religious" in the conventional sense of being signed-up members of a denomination or sect; they may never go near a church or a meetinghouse. All the same, they have the sensibilities and are attached to the experiences that Dewey thought of as "religious," and their disaffection from the conventional forms of religion might well owe a lot to their feeling that conventional forms are "encumbrances that now smother or limit it."[49] Dewey's campaign aimed to emancipate religious experience from its institutional forms. Curiously enough, this once again puts Dewey into surprisingly close proximity to Bertrand Russell. Ordinarily they were almost as far apart on religion as they were on logic; Dewey deplored "aggressive atheism" and deplored Russell's excursions into a sort of lachrymose defiance of all the world might do—the attitude of "A Free Man's Worship." Yet Russell's *Principles of Social Reconstruction,* written to show the "spark of the divine in each of us," contained a lengthy chapter on religion, and its tone was very close to that of *A Common Faith.* As Dewey's review of Russell's *Religion and Science* a couple of years later showed plainly enough, Dewey thought that Russell's old-fashioned empiricism led him to think that perception was private and ethics subjective, so that both science and morality were somehow withdrawn from the realm of public discussion where Dewey wanted to keep them; still, even there he readily admitted that most of Russell's conclusions were ones he wanted to embrace, especially Russell's emphasis on the dangers of the new forms of political irrationalism that drew their strength from the same sources as the old authoritarian religions they were replacing.[50]

One of the many ways in which Dewey's allegiances were not narrowly American was in their affinity with the views of Edwardian new liberals, Fabians, and even the Bloomsbury Group on the other side of the Atlantic. Their passion for art, their unwillingness to separate art, religion, and ethics had their counterpart in his work. Much like some of them, Dewey wanted to insist that his philosophy provided a better foundation for these convictions than any alternative. But like many of them—Russell, Keynes, and Leonard Woolf among them—he was ready to agree that his liberal allies might reach their liberal commitments by quite other routes than he.

A Common Faith, then, sought to emancipate the religious attitude from traditional institutional constraints on the one hand and from ontological questions about the existence of God on the other. Matters did not rest there, however. Dewey also proposed to emancipate the religious attitude from any suggestion that there was some one and distinctive quality that all religious experience shared. By this stage of his intellectual career Dewey was shedding fixities as soon as they became inconvenient. Even a humble color property such as "red" had lost its universality; we called things red for whatever purposes of comparison and contrast it helped us so to call them. No two red objects were exactly alike even in their color, and there was no point at which we could stop and declare that some object was so exactly red that no further discrimination would make sense.

We might have any number of reasons for establishing a standard red by convention, just as we established the standard yard and the standard meter and the standard imperial gallon, but these conventions did not pick out (or create) a universal quality either, and were not intended to. How much less did "religious" pick out a quality always and everywhere present in religious experience. At best "religiousness" was a secondary or tertiary quality of experience. Indeed, Dewey went on to add several more qualifications to his account. One was that the "religious" element in many experiences lay in the effect produced rather than in some narrowly described feature of the experience that produced it. He took up an otherwise unidentified writer who claimed that he encountered God when, after agonizing about the meaning of life, he had "resolved to stop drawing upon myself so continuously and draw upon God. I determined to set apart a quiet time every day in which I could relate my life to its Ultimate Source, regain the consciousness that in God I live, move, and have my being. That was thirty years ago. Since then I have literally had not one hour of darkness or despair."[51] To this Dewey replied, "The actual religious quality in the experience described is the *effect* produced, the better adjustment to life and its conditions, not the manner and cause of its production." To the obvious objection that this misplaces the relationship of cause and effect that the writer believed he was describing—divine assistance was the cause of his reassurance rather than a name for it—Dewey replied, "If the reorientation actually occurs, it, and the sense of security and stability accompanying it, are forces on their own account."[52] It is hard to believe that many people would think this quite met the case.

In the same spirit Dewey went on to stress the creative and productive role of the imagination in religious experience. Here is one place where we can see him tying his thoughts on art to his view of religion. Just as a successful encounter with an art object demands an active response from the audience for it—as Dewey says, the *object* only becomes a *work* by being set to work by the imagination of the beholder—so experience can only be encountered religiously if we are co-workers with the raw materials of nature and social life. Lest this sound too much as though we were being encouraged to imagine the world as permeated by God in any way that gratifies us, Dewey was at pains to emphasize the extent to which the imagination was involved in seeing almost anything in the world as a unity. "The connection between imagination and the harmonization of the self is closer than is usually thought. The idea of a whole, whether of the whole personal being, or of the world, is an imaginative, not a literal, idea. The limited world of our observation and reflection becomes the Universe only through imaginative extension."[53] The idealist stress on the active powers of the mind was a resource that Dewey had never let go of when he abandoned Hegelianism, and here, as everywhere else, he happily appealed to the mind's capacity to achieve something that would be misdescribed either as simply finding unity in the variety of the world or as simply imposing it. The thought, rather, was that the mind ordered experience, but in a fashion that the world cooperated with or was suited to; the world's capacity to yield religious experience is thus a fact about it, in much the same way that the capacity of a work of art to yield aesthetic delight is a fact about it.

To the best of my knowledge, Dewey never carried his analysis of religious experience to the same level as his analysis of aesthetic and artistic experience, nor did he dive into the fascinating and troubled waters of the question of whether some kinds of religious experience are unavailable to us today, or merely less available, and just how. On the face of it the answer ought to be that what holds for the experience of art holds for religious experience, too, a thought that is reinforced by the readiness with which he followed George Santayana in identifying the religious and the poetic imaginations. If some kinds of poetic representation are simply unusable in the late twentieth century, it seems plausible that some kinds of religious vision are unavailable in much the same way. Nor is this a thought that unduly disturbs modernist theologians, however much it unsettles the laity.

With the assimilation of religion and poetry, we are in the territory of Matthew Arnold and Coleridge; neither is discussed at any length, but their presence broods over Dewey's discussion. Dewey does quote Arnold's famous definition of religion as "morality tinged by emotion" (just as he later mentions Arnold's definition of God as that "power not ourselves that makes for righteousness"[54], and whatever may be said against this as a definition, it catches the point that what is common to religious experiences in Dewey's account of them is their confirmation that nature is "on our side," implicated in our projects, friendly rather than hostile to our ideals. Once *Experience and Nature* had broached the question whether nature was on the side of our ideals, Dewey was committed to saying something about why we might decently answer yes.[55] So it is no surprise to find that the discussion of the religious quality of religious experience ends in an appeal to the "moral and practical import" of belief.[56] Dewey wanted to steer a somewhat tricky course; he had to deny that the ideal is *already* embodied in the world, but he had also to insist that our ideals are in some fashion part of the powers of the world. The argument runs rapidly and none too securely from the thought that religion originally "meant being bound by vows to a particular way of life" via the claim that "the religious attitude signifies something that is bound through imagination to a *general* attitude"—that is, to something wider than a moral outlook alone—such as is displayed in "art, science and good citizenship."[57]

What holds all this together is something whose centrality to religion would be very hard to deny, the thought that what gives sense to the world gives sense to the individual life. Put thus, it may sound like something that philosophers and intellectuals hanker after, but this is the reverse of Dewey's thought. It may take a philosopher to *analyze* this route to the integration of individual with individual and humanity with nature, but it is something that anyone can experience. "Any activity pursued in behalf of an ideal end against obstacles and in spite of threats of personal loss because of conviction of its general and enduring value is religious in quality. Many a person, inquirer, artist, philanthropist, citizen, men and women in the humblest walks of life, have achieved, without presumption and without display, such unification of themselves and of their relations to the conditions of existence. It remains to extend their spirit and inspiration to ever wider numbers."[58] One might hear in this paragraph echoes not only of Green and Hegel but of the thinker who stood behind them, Baruch Spinoza. After all, Dewey's first philosophy teacher, H. A. P. Torrey, had admitted that in purely philosophical terms pantheism was the only possible resting place—that is, that the universe was not the fallen creation of an "apart" deity but was itself divine.

Intellectually it was the first chapter of *A Common Faith* that made the boldest strokes; in spite of occasional conciliatory observations, Dewey's purpose was aggressive. Just as the rest of his philosophy emphasized the need for modes of thought appropriate to the modern world, and by implication slighted intellectual traditionalism and any attitude of reverence toward the classics, so his thoughts on religion demanded religious attitudes apt to the modern world and emancipated from the authoritarianism of traditional faiths.[59] It cannot be said that he gave much ground in subsequent chapters; when Dewey turned to discuss "Faith and Its Objects," he largely evaded the need to give a positive account of what the objects of the positive faith of the nonsupernaturally religious were.

Instead he spent most of the chapter condemning "supernaturalism" in all its guises. To the nonbeliever's eye, one of the most interesting features of the discussion is the way Dewey abuses modern, liberal theologians even more heartily than their medieval predecessors. Unlike some later critics, such as Antony Flew, who observed that liberal theologians subjected faith to death by a thousand cuts as they gradually gave up one discredited doctrine after another, Dewey took the bolder line that liberal theologians were just wrong in principle to think that they could do better than their forebears. The crucial question was too simple to be fudged: Were science and religion in conflict or not? If they were not, all matters of fact had to be agreed in principle to lie within the competence of science, and there was an end to supernaturalism. If they were, supernaturalism was equally vulnerable. The private experience of God, and inner conviction of all sorts, were no more likely to resist the advance of psychology than the miraculousness of eclipses had resisted the advance of astronomy.

No sooner had Dewey evicted God and all his works from the scene, in favor of the familiar combination of scientific analysis and poetic synthesis that we have seen him invoking in so many contexts, than he changed tack—to the dismay of Sidney Hook and the confusion of his critics.[60] He declared that it was entirely proper to talk of God in the context of our deepest ideals and encouraged his readers not to give up the habit of so talking if it strengthened their convictions. "One reason why personally I think it fitting to use the word 'God' to denote that uniting of the ideal and actual which I have spoken of, lies in the fact that aggressive atheism seems to me to have something in common with traditional supernaturalism."[61] What Dewey went on to say after that lends color to the thought that it was Russell's hostility to Christianity that he had in mind. If so, it was a nicely judged shot. For Russell's loathing of pragmatism had much, or rather almost everything, to do with a desire to protect "truth" from the merely practical affairs of everyday life, and Russell himself admitted that once Wittgenstein had persuaded him that logic was not a key to the ultimate truth about the universe but simply a device for ordering our thoughts, he lost interest in it. One might, if one were Dewey, feel tempted to say that Russell had had an essentially religious view of logic and had reacted against its hegemonic pretensions much as he had reacted against his grandmother's puritanism and piety.

Dewey's practical objection to "aggressive atheism" was that its negativism meant that it gave no positive direction to the human mind; this was because like supernaturalism, it was excessively individualistic and concentrated too hard on "man in isolation." Supernaturalism placed the earth "at the moral centre of the universe" and placed "man at the apex of the whole scheme of things." Obsessed with the drama of sin and redemption, it thus made the inner conflicts of individuals its main preoccupation, which isolated them one from another and from their own nature and external nature alike. "Militant atheism is also affected by lack of natural piety. The ties binding man to nature that poets have always celebrated are passed over lightly. The attitude taken is that of man living in an indifferent and hostile world and issuing blasts of defiance. A religious attitude, however, needs the sense of a connection of man, in the way of both dependence and support, with the enveloping world that the imagination feels is a universe. Use of the words 'God' or *[sic]* 'divine' to convey the union of actual with ideal may protect man from a sense of isolation and from consequent despair or defiance."[62]

It is an interesting and unanswerable question whether Russell suffered from a lack of "natural piety" toward the natural world. There is at least something engaging in the fact that Russell accused Dewey of "cosmic impiety" for reducing objective, pristine truth to warranted assertability. In later life Russell was savage about the American proposal to place nuclear missile launchers on the moon, regarding it as a contamination of untouched nature by the puerile squabbles of humanity. On the one hand, one might regard this as an expression of piety toward the nonhuman world; on the other hand, one might think it an example of exactly what Dewey complained of, the outlook that itself dragged nature into human moralizing in a way that lacked true natural piety. Russell certainly loved the sea, the mountains, and the stars, but to the extent that they entered his moral universe, it was their coldness and remoteness from human affairs that he loved, and to that degree Dewey was surely right about the results of at least one form of aggressive atheism. All of which is far from answering the question of whether Dewey was persuasive of the virtues of his own outlook; there is perhaps something too *briskly* pragmatic about his endorsement of the utility of talking about "God."

As myself an aggressive atheist, I am not persuaded that the *usefulness* of such ways of talking has much bearing on their *truthfulness;* to put it unkindly, one might complain that Dewey wants the social value of religious belief without being willing to pay the epistemological price for it. To put it less unkindly, we may wonder whether in fact, it is possible to have the *use* of religious vocabulary without the accretion of supernaturalist beliefs that Dewey wishes to slough off. What holds for belief might be thought to hold for institutions. That is, if the religious attitude is to be inculcated as a generalized social sentiment of cosmic confidence, we can inquire whether special institutions, rites, liturgies, and rituals are plausible expressions of that confidence and whether some are particularly effective in strengthening that outlook. Hegel wrote to Goethe to say that he thought of reading the newspapers as a secular morning prayer, but the apt little joke makes the sense it does only because there were organized churches in which morning prayer was said in traditional form.

Since Dewey had no enthusiasm for established churches of any sort, it is a large question what institutions he thought were needed. He produced an answer in a characteristically indirect fashion. In most human societies people did not belong to religious organizations at all; they were simply members of their society, and the society was permeated by whatever local faith it accepted.

Even in Christian Europe this was for a very long time the state of affairs; one was born, lived, and died in the faith of one's fathers. Not so in the modern world: "There are a few persons, especially those brought up in Jewish communities in Russia, who can understand without the use of imagination what a religion means socially when it permeates all the customs and activities of group life. To most of us in the United States such a situation is only a remote historical episode."[63] Dewey offered a quick historical sketch of the natural history of organized belief:

> In the first stage, human relationships were thought to be so infected with the evils of corrupt human nature as to require redemption from external and supernatural sources. In the next stage, what is significant in these relations is going to be akin to values esteemed distinctively religious. This is the point now reached by liberal theologians. The third stage would realize that in fact the values prized in those religions that have ideal elements are idealizations of things characteristic of natural association, which have been projected into a supernatural realm for safe-keeping and sanction. Note the role of such terms as Father, Son, Bride, Fellowship and Communion in the vocabulary of Christianity, and note also the tendency, even if a somewhat inchoate one, of terms that express the more intimate phases of association to replace those of legal, political origin: King, Judge, and Lord of Hosts.[64]

To reach the third stage safely is in effect to see all sorts of social affiliations as capable of sustaining the religious sentiments and grounding religious experience. Insofar as we pursue ideals through such association, we are pursuing a religious quest, and doing so in a way that has escaped from the old dualism of sacred and secular forms of association. Disgruntled churchgoers who object to the way Dewey appears to be advocating the abolition of the church may be a little appeased when they reflect that in an article in the *New York Times* the previous year—"Dewey Outlines Utopian Schools"—he had begun by announcing: "The most Utopian thing in Utopia is that there are no schools at all. Education is carried on without anything in the nature of schools, or if this idea is so extreme that we cannot conceive of it as educational at all, then we may say nothing of the sort at present we know as schools. Children, however, are gathered together in association with older and more mature people who direct their activity."[65]

Nobody can accuse Dewey of hostility to schools or education, and we may imagine that his understanding of how religious life would operate in the absence of what we currently call churches was much like his understanding of how education would proceed in the absence of what we now call schools. People would doubtless gather to explore their religious intimations, perhaps acknowledging the superior spiritual insight of some or one of their number, and something very like the evangelical Catholicism practiced at present by people who find God more readily revealed in their kitchens and sitting rooms than in churches and cathedrals would seem quite likely to flourish.

The upshot is political rather than doctrinal. Dewey was sensitive to the religious conflicts that went on in 1930s America—especially the attempt of the Roman Catholic Church to hang on to an absolute spiritual and moral authority over all its members and the agonies that beset Protestant churches as they tried simultaneously to be "socially relevant" by saying something practical and down-to-earth about the economic and political crises of the day and to be spiritually authoritative by insisting that they spoke in the name of a God who voted for no particular party and had no particular economic ax to grind. But if he was sensitive to them, he was not sympathetic to the plight of the churches. Christianity was in too many ways intrinsically antidemocratic: Mankind was divided into the sheep and the goats, the saved and the damned; there was an aristocracy of the elect or the spiritually enlightened; and one way or another hierarchy rather than equality was encouraged. So the fact that democracy rested on a common faith, that is, a faith in the capacities of the common man, did not mean that democracy rested on Christianity or even on that looser amalgam "the Judeo-Christian tradition." It was the other way about: Christianity and the Judeo-Christian tradition, were entitled to as much respect as they could get by embracing democratic institutions, dropping any claim to supernatural authority, and working to sustain the common faith of a modern liberal, democratic society.

Dewey's essay *A Common Faith* ends in much the same place as his 1893 essay "Christianity and Democracy." Whereas in the old days he had begun by thinking that science led to mind and then to God, he now thought that science practiced piously led to an affection for the universe as a whole and for oneself as a part of it, but in neither case did he believe that the conflict of science and religion—the *historical* reality of which he accepted as brute fact—was a conflict of their essential natures. Since all inquiry is for the sake of revealing the meaning of experience, science and religion are in the same business, but in different branches of it: Science looks for more local sorts of order, religion for more global sorts of order; science detaches itself from our emotional and affective needs the better to analyze the mechanisms that animate nature, while religion embraces those needs, the better to enrich and illuminate experience. The broad mind or, better still, the widely affectionate heart will not wish to squabble over boundaries.

Liberal Education Rethought

The last subject this chapter must tackle is Dewey's later reflections on education. It is somewhat artificial to separate Dewey's political battles in the New York teachers union and elsewhere from his principled defenses of a (moderately) progressive philosophy of education, but it is impossible to preserve order otherwise. There were two set piece engagements between Dewey and his opponents that allow us to come to grips with the considered views he held after years of debate. The first took place in his review of Robert M. Hutchins's *The Higher Learning in America* and his short, ill-natured retort to Hutchins's response to the review, though the argument rumbled on for a decade and more and was rehashed after Dewey's death in Mortimer Adler's surprisingly evenhanded little book of 1953 *The Revolution in Education*. The second was the slight volume on *Experience and Education* that Dewey published in 1938 as a retort to all those who accused him of bringing American education to its knees.

We must leave a final reckoning with the impact of Dewey's educational ideas until later, but *Experience and Education* goes such a long way toward dissociating Dewey from the wilder and more startling ideas of progressive educators that it cannot but reraise the question of whether Dewey had any distinctive view of his own at all. Defenders of Dewey's ideas are always in something of a cleft stick, since too successful an attempt to make everything he wrote come out sensible can leave him looking entirely unoriginal, while anything less cautious exposes him to some obvious assaults.[66] My view is that Dewey's originality lay in his obsessive concern with using elementary education to re-create social ties that might otherwise be lost and to help the child to experience the world as a meaningful rather than a merely mechanical entity. Since Dewey had little to say about syllabuses, much more to say about who ought to exercise authority over the schools, and an enormous amount to say about the place of education in social life, and since in the turbulent 1930s in particular he had a great deal to say about the role of education in social reform, I am surprised that this view is not by now commonplace.

One explanation of its not being so might be that the attacks on the graduates and faculty of Columbia's Teachers College from assorted antiprogressives from H. L. Mencken downward naturally invite the response that Kilpatrick's faculty were teaching their charges sensible pedagogical techniques and sensible ideas about syllabuses. This is mostly true, though one of Kilpatrick's successors as president of Teachers College has observed that Kilpatrick translated Dewey's passion for activity into an enthusiasm for teaching through "projects" without much thought about the intellectual content of the projects involved. My account of the matter shifts the argument from that terrain; just as Dewey's politics have overtones of "religious"—in his sense—revivalism, and his account of religion a decidedly political cast, so his politics have educational overtones, and his educational philosophy is essentially political. It was not a matter of what went on in the classroom so much as a matter of how we were to approach what went on in the classroom.

The other thing to bear in mind is the extent to which Dewey's interest in "experience" dominated everything else. *Experience and Education* begins with the kind of discussion of traditional and progressive education that Dewey had by now been writing for forty years but promptly moves to a chapter entitled "The Need for a Theory of Experience." Because experience is to a high degree *social* experience, it is not quite true that Dewey's earlier obsession with socializing children into being competent users of their society's stock of intellectual, moral, religious, and aesthetic resources had given way to an obsession with experience and its enhancement, but it is certainly true that the stress now fell on the capacity of education to enrich our experience of the world. The point of education is to enhance our experience and our capacity for experience, and since the concept of experience is not exactly transparent, Dewey could not hope to give an account of education without a good deal of philosophical commentary. Indeed, one of the more bizarre features of the encounter between Dewey and his critics was that so many of them thought him the advocate of a narrowly vocational and wholly practical education, geared to narrowly utilitarian ends, while he spent his time elaborating a philosophical account of the nature of education that might with perfect justice have been called "metaphysical" rather than narrowly practical. The argument he and Robert Maynard Hutchins engaged in over higher education was a nice illustration of this misunderstanding.

The brisk little spat between Dewey and Robert Maynard Hutchins was inscribed in their stars. Hutchins had gone to Chicago in 1929, chosen to be president at the age of twenty-nine; one would marvel at the confidence the Chicago trustees placed in such an untried young man if Hutchins had not already served two years as dean of Yale Law School with great success. His tenure at Chicago is impossible to characterize briefly; he spent a great deal of time and energy fighting battles with his faculty that he could not possibly win, but in the process he established some astonishingly innovative educational programs in the undergraduate college—or at any rate presided over other people's efforts in that direction. Hutchins started his tenure of the presidency with a full-scale fight with the philosophy department. He had taken up the young Mortimer Adler, a bumptious graduate of Columbia who as a student had taken as his great intellectual project the demolition of Dewey's pragmatism and had pursued it with so little grace that he had to take his graduate work in psychology rather than philosophy.[67]

By the time Hutchins encountered him, Adler had become convinced that the modern world was in a bad way because it had lost faith in the metaphysical ideas of medieval Christendom, particularly those of St. Thomas Aquinas. Hutchins proposed Adler for a full professorship, at a higher salary than anyone except the most senior philosophers. The department rebelled, and Adler ended up with a nondepartment position. The affair drove G. H. Mead into retirement, and although there is no reason to suppose that it had anything to do with his dying immediately afterward, the coincidence of the death of his closest friend and the arrival of Adler must have struck Dewey disagreeably.

Although Hutchins was the standard-bearer of the "back to the classics" movement, he knew no philosophy; he seems to have read only what Adler suggested and to have got his ideas about modern philosophy at second hand. When he gave the Storrs Lectures of 1936, which were published as *The Higher Learning in America,* the results were stronger on rhetoric and intellectual dazzle than on content; Hutchins had a wonderfully rapid and clever style and a good ear for the bon mot. Much of the book that resulted is about issues that could not in a hundred years have provided a casus belli with Dewey; Hutchins's jokes against the effects of alumni loyalty, football, and conservative businessmen were extremely funny and quite unlooked for from a university president. Much else in the lectures was tangential to anything that separated them; Hutchins was obsessed with the way in which general education competed for resources with the research tasks of the true research university. What he sought was a revised pattern of higher education; he more or less preinvented the junior college, with the intention of providing a general education for students in the last two years of high school and the first two years of tertiary education. Most students, he thought, need not then go on to university since they had neither an interest in nor a capacity for real research and specialization. In a way he was right. His complaints about the feebleness of American education at every stage from the elementary school to the graduate school suggest that if Hutchins had got his way, any intelligent student could have had a B.A. at seventeen, if he had not had a nervous breakdown first. That was general education, however, not research training, bringing the young up to the level of existing scholarship rather than training them to push on into uncharted territory. Like Thorstein Veblen and Abraham Flexner, Hutchins seemed to believe that a true university would have scarcely a student in the place. Unlike them, he thought seriously about what would benefit the student in the undergraduate college that he had now carved out of the true university.

It was in the setting of the general education of non-research-oriented undergraduates that Hutchins set down the views for which he became famous and which provoked the fight with Dewey. Hutchins was distressed by the absence of any kind of rationale for the various studies that both the university and the college undertook. To provide such a rationale, he thought, they must look to some kind of metaphysical foundation. In a famous and exceedingly incendiary phrase, Hutchins declared, "Education implies teaching. Teaching implies knowledge. Knowledge is truth. The truth is everywhere the same. Hence education should be everywhere the same."[68] Pouring oil on the flames, he went on to add that "the heart of any course of study designed for the whole people will be, if education is rightly understood, the same at any time, in any place, under any political, social, or economic conditions. . . . If education is rightly understood, it will be understood as the cultivation of the intellect. The cultivation of the intellect is the same good for all men in all societies."[69] Since he had already denounced schools of education, medicine, and law as incompatible with education, it is easy enough to see how sure Hutchins was to give grave offense to Dewey. The School of Education over which Dewey had briefly presided had already been closed, and now Hutchins was announcing that there was no progress in our knowledge of the ends of life, that there was no room for intellectual novelties in education, and that the only route to making education morally useful was to feed college students a diet of great books, particularly the great books of Plato, Aristotle, and Aquinas.

Dewey's response was surprisingly measured. He wrote two fairly gentle accounts of Hutchins's book in the journal *Social Frontier* and a much more tart reply to Hutchins's response to the reviews. Dewey was ready to agree with Hutchins that higher education, like all education, was in a state of near crisis, though Dewey would have put much more weight on the way the depression was destroying school budgets, cutting into teachers' wages, and impoverishing the child's experience in the classroom. What he would not accept for one moment was exactly what Hutchins most minded about. Dewey's whole life had been spent combating Hutchins's insistence that higher intellectual life must be protected from the contamination of practical life. This is one of the places where Dewey's views must be set out with some caution, for although he was deeply hostile to the whole outlook embodied in Hutchins's lectures, it was not because he had any great sympathy for professional schools as such. All his life Dewey had given an account of vocational education as hostile as Hutchins's own to the demands of immediate utility and the needs of the students' next employers. The only professional schools that Dewey ever taught in were the Institute of Education at Chicago and Teachers College at Columbia, and it was only because Dewey thought that teachers were engaged in "God's work" that he was ready to engage in teacher training.

Similarly, it was only because Dewey held a somewhat exalted view of the nature and function of law that his account of the place of the law school in a university was not the contemptuous view expressed by ex-Dean Hutchins. Mere practicality was not what Dewey was after. Social engagement and social commitment, on the other hand, were what he was after. Any suggestion that higher education would remain "higher" only if universities and colleges drew the hems of their skirts away from the mud of the public streets irritated him. It might be necessary to balance immersion and distance in a delicate fashion, but in principle the object was to reinforce the connections between college or university and the public and political world.

Hutchins's view of the relations between the world of learning and the world of business and politics was squarely opposed to Dewey's. Dewey did not want higher education to be the hired help of big business, but he did want higher education to be the servant of social progress. Hutchins disbelieved in the very idea of progress. That was to reject the central concept of Dewey's philosophy. Dewey's lifework was provoked by the scandal of the fact that science manifestly makes progress while philosophy, ethics, and art do so dubiously, if at all. Why else would Dewey have spent so much energy appealing not to the *results* of science but to its method and spirit if not because that method and spirit could create philosophical progress, too? Dewey did not in fact *argue* against Hutchins's defense of an education built around unchanging and eternal truths; he treated him as three parts deranged.

Dewey never broached the thought that we are faced with a cultural choice between two different educational and intellectual styles and there may be nothing decisive to be said about which one to choose. Hutchins argued for an education that emphasized what one may call the passive intellectual virtues: receptivity to existing truth and existing achievement, a desire for adjustment in the *un*-Deweyan sense of a desire to bend our minds and tastes to tradition or to existing forms of intellectual and religious authority. Hutchins could not express this in any way that Dewey could embrace. Hutchins drew a sharp contrast between the work of the intellect and mere experience and naturally argued that the task of education was to develop the intellect. Since Dewey used the concept of experience to embrace all our encounters with the world, Hutchins's contrast between intellect and experience seemed grossly mistaken.

The truth was that neither could make sense of the other's point of view. Dewey seemed to Hutchins to be the sponsor of quick fixes and the sacrifice of intellectual values to the immediate demands of politicians, while Hutchins seemed to Dewey to be merely reactionary. Oddly enough, Mortimer Adler, who was in many ways the cause of all the trouble, came closer to getting the warring sides right when he wrote *The Revolution in Education* some years after the war. There Adler laid out a tolerably sympathetic picture of Dewey's "modernist" views and made it at any rate intelligible that the two camps might differ over the weight to be given to great books versus modern science, social science, philosophy, and literature without either's being just wrong—even though Adler's own views were so firmly in the great books camp.[70] Adler struck some shrewder blows than Hutchins by pointing out that Dewey's emphasis on active education could be a fudge; as he noticed, the fact that we talk of "doing" mathematics does not mean that studying Fermat's Last Theorem is interestingly or illuminatingly described as learning by doing.

Dewey ended his encounter with Hutchins by suggesting that Hutchins had not been entirely serious in the Storrs Lectures, and there is something in that thought. They were flashy, designed to start controversy, spectacularly uninformed about anything other than the relations between the president of the University of Chicago and his trustees and alumni and in taking as their title the title that Veblen had employed for his own ironic reflections on American education, plainly challenging comparison with his gadfly predecessor.

Dewey did not leave the subject, though he left Hutchins's name out of his further reflections; a year later *Experience and Education* summed up his view of the contrast between "traditional" and "progressive" education. We may be fairly brisk with this last full-dress account of his views, well received though it was by his readers. The book largely recapitulated the striking good sense of *The Child and the Curriculum* of thirty-six years before. The main difference between Dewey's first and later thoughts was terminological; the former essay's contrast between "old" and "new" has turned into a contrast between "traditional" and "progressive." Reading the two books together also reveals a more elusive contrast. Thirty-six years earlier Dewey was still content to write of the acquisition of "habits" and to think of education as a matter of inculcating deft intellectual habits; his turn to the investigation of "experience" did not make a *great* difference, but it made some difference to the later book's content and more to its emotional flavor.

Old or traditional education is characterized in familiar terms:

> The main purpose or objective is to prepare the young for future responsibilities and for success in life by means of acquisition of organized bodies of information and prepared forms of skill which comprehend the material of instruction. Since the subject matter as well as standards of proper conduct are handed down from the past, the attitude of pupils must on the whole be one of docility, receptivity, and obedience. Books, especially textbooks, are the chief representatives of the lore and wisdom of the past, while teachers are the organs through which pupils are brought into effective contact with the material. Teachers are the agents through which knowledge and skills are communicated and rules of conduct enforced.[71]

It is often suggested that Dewey was not so much a progressive in education as a critic of the boring, rigid, hidebound, and authoritarian modes of teaching prevalent when he was young. Horror stories, such as that of New York classrooms where students had to look rigidly to the front all period long, make it easy to credit such a view.[72] In fact, it is not quite right, and Dewey would have repudiated it with some vigor.

Dewey himself argued that it was not enough to repudiate traditional education. As he had remarked of the relationship between atheism and traditional religion, the trouble with mere opposition is that we are excessively influenced by what we negate. It was not enough for progressive teachers to throw out everything the old schools had done, to replace discipline by chaos, a rigid syllabus with no syllabus. And Dewey was inclined to think that many schools had done exactly that and had used his name to justify it. The difficulty was to give an account of the educational experience that would elicit a kind of discipline, an approach to the syllabus and to the authority of the teacher in the classroom that would grow out of experience itself. This, too, needed some further analysis. Not every experience was educational; many experiences had bad effects on those who had them: They might make pupils dislike intellectual work; they might make them less attentive rather than more.

What was needed was a criterion of growth-promoting experience, and Dewey found it where he had found it in 1916: in the concept of democracy. Old or traditional education was essentially aristocratic, and when done well, it was good aristocratic education, capable of producing a disciplined and trained elite. New education had to ask those questions that Dewey had broached in *Democracy and Education* twenty-odd years before. How were we to acquire and hand on a capacity for wider, deeper, more organic experience and the capacity to communicate it? Not by letting children run amok or by letting them wander through a syllabus in their own sweet time. Nor, on the other hand, by an enforced and artificial discipline.

Against an overemphasis on *activity,* Dewey sets the requirement that it be *intelligent* activity, that it strengthens the child's ability to plan his activities, organize his dealings with the world. As he dryly observes, a man who buys a house wants one that will stay up and do its job, and there is more to building than being active in the presence of a pile of materials. Against the old emphasis on rigid stages in presenting educative material, Dewey insists that there is no essential quality of most of the work one does at school that picks it out as fifth-grade work or ninth-grade work, but at the same time he insists that there is a logic to learning most subjects and that children need to be allowed to absorb information and skill in a progressive sequence. Social control is essential, and so is freedom, and in a fashion reminiscent of the Hegelianism of his youth, he reminds the reader that a discipline stemming from the task in hand is not an external constraint but an aid to freedom. There is more to freedom than mere lack of control. The argument is, in short, an unabashed defense of the educational *via media,* modernist but not avant-garde, not a forerunner of the deschooling movement—and interesting because its middle-of-the-road quality is not the result of a compromise, not a matter of splicing a bit of traditional education onto a bit of progressive education in an attempt to appease all parties. Dewey thought in 1938, as he had since he encountered T. H. Green more than fifty years earlier, that experience itself demanded this sturdy equilibrium position; stagnation was death, but the alternative was not lunatic frenzy but self-sustaining, healthy life. Readers of Dewey who thought they were getting middle-of-the-road liberalism found it dull; his admirers knew they were getting something deeper and grander. Fifty-five years later it is clear the admirers were right.

Eight

Liberal Politics in Theory and in Practice

At an age when most men pause from their labors to reflect on the account of themselves they propose to offer the recording angel hereafter, Dewey threw himself into a postretirement career as a political activist, propagandist, pamphleteer, and gadfly to the New Deal with an energy that would have been astonishing in a man half his age. This career led to an extraordinary widening of his social circle, so that by the end of the 1930s his friends ranged from the wife of the owner of the *Washington Post* to innumerable now-forgotten members of committees to protect art education in the public schools, to defend teachers against dismissal for political reasons, and much else besides.

The mystery of Dewey's thirty-seven volume *Collected Works* is not only that he wrote so much that one wonders how he found time to talk to his friends but that his evenings seem to have been so consumed by acting as chairman to an endless round of meetings that one wonders when he ate and slept.[1] To some extent it was less that he threw himself into this whirl, more that he was dragged in by the irrepressible Sidney Hook. This is not to suggest that Dewey was a passive instrument of Hook's purposes. Hook's view of Dewey's usefulness was that Dewey was both a bulwark against the misdeeds of the Communist left and a substantial intellectual resource for the non-Communist social democrats. It was not so much exploitation as an offshoot of hero worship. Hook thought Dewey had supplied Marxism with the epistemology and social philosophy that Marx had half seen for himself and had half sketched out in his early works but had never adequately spelled out in his maturity. Marx had been an active revolutionary and had had less time for such foundational work than Dewey. Dewey thus supplied the intellectual weapons for a decently social democratic, nontotalitarian Marxism. One of many ways in which Dewey kept a certain distance from his disciple was that Dewey never said this was nonsense (and in fact, it is not), but he made it clear that he was not interested in the role of posthumous underlaborer in Marx's vineyard.

Dewey was very much his own man, and while he relied on Hook for his information about what the enemy was up to, his political activities were continuous with his antiwar, anti-League, and mildly socialist writings in the 1920s. He changed the direction of his attention to some extent. In the 1920s American domestic politics was not constantly on his mind; he denounced the judicial murders of Sacco and Vanzetti[2] and wrote plaintively about the febrile and unsatisfying quality of the years of prosperity, but when his eyes were not focused on philosophy, they were focused on American foreign policy and on the need to avoid doing anything that might involve the United States in a second world war. With the depression and the horrors of the 1930s Dewey broadened his scope. He remained a semi-isolationist until the end, arguing that the United States should support anti-Fascist forces but avoid direct military involvement in the affairs of Europe and the Far East.[3] Mostly, however, he wrote about American domestic politics, about the need for drastic measures of public ownership and public control to pull the country out of the depression, about the obsolescence of laissez-faire, about the fatally damaged condition of American capitalism, and about the need for a new radical party to put in place the policies of public ownership he thought were needed. For several years he did all this in a semiofficial capacity as president of the People's Lobby or chairman of the League for Independent Political Action—there was no conflict between the aims of these bodies—and many of his interventions in the politics of education were undertaken as chairman of committees of inquiry or as a member of the executive committee of his teachers' union local. The most widely read of his essays and short books were, however, written in no official capacity, the product of Dewey's indefatigable urge to do whatever the good citizen could do during hard times.

Third-Party Politics

The League for Independent Political Action was established in December 1928. It was bent on encouraging the formation of a third party whose policies should be along the lines of those of the British Labour party, but as its name suggests, its self-image was nonpartisan. In a fashion rather oddly reminiscent of the origins of the Labour party itself, many of its members hoped that the league might model itself on the Fabian Society, which had begun life as a nonparty group dedicated to the "permeation" of British politics with Fabian ideas without taking sides in party politics.[4] The Fabian Society had eventually and rather reluctantly affiliated itself with the nascent Labour party, but the LIPA was less bashful. Ten months after its creation came the Wall Street crash of October 1929; the LIPA response was to demand the creation of a new party committed to the standard program of a European welfare state–

oriented social democratic party: unemployment insurance, pensions and health insurance, and substantial disarmament. The executive was distinguished: Dewey as chairman; W. E. B. Du Bois; Oswald Villard, the editor of the *Nation;* Norman Thomas; Harry Laidler, of the League for Industrial Democracy; and Reinhold Niebuhr among other members.

The LIPA's chances of getting anywhere with the creation of a third party were not good, nor were they improved by the conflict of aims between those, like Dewey, who wanted a *new* third party, marching under a populist banner, and the allies of Norman Thomas, who thought their Socialist party was already filling that need. Dewey held the same sad view that Edward Bellamy had held forty years before when he adopted the "nationalist" label: Middle-class Americans were scared off by the word "socialist." The Socialist party would not do. Socialist policies needed a party without the word "socialist" on its banner. Dewey's attempt to enlist Senator George Norris of Nebraska as the leader of an insurgent people's party went off at half cock. It cannot be said that it deserved to do better. Dewey's enthusiasm for Norris owed more to Norris's espousal of the Dewey-Levinson nostrum of the outlawry of war than to Norris's vision of domestic politics. Nor was the idea of building a party around Norris very sensible. Other considerations aside, it was foolish to ask a man to embrace a third party simply because his dislike of *all* parties had led him to bolt the Republican whip on many occasions in the past.

Skittishness is not a political virtue. The British Labour party survived its many years in the wilderness because of the passion of the "brothers" for solidarity; *partinost* was not an English word, but the notion that there was no political salvation outside the party was an English thought. Dewey understood none of this. Indeed, his dislike of the old parties appears to have been much stronger than any sense of just what the third party would be for or how it would be organized. In a phrase that the *New York Times* remembered in his obituary, Dewey went on the radio in mid-October 1929 to denounce the major parties as "bag-carriers for big business" and as essentially out-of-date. While social life had been changed by "the radio, the railway, telephone, telegraph, the flying machine and mass production," there had been no comparable modernization of the political parties, which continued to "mouth the old phrases and flaunt the old slogans" in front of a wholly skeptical public.[5] The illustrations of modernity that Dewey employed here were anchored in the definition of democracy he had offered in *Democracy and Education;* they are, above all, means of *communication.* Still, the connection between one of Dewey's favorite half dozen concepts and the demands of party organization is not as close as he thought. Indeed, late in the twentieth century, after several further "communications revolutions," it is possible to see that mass communication may produce greater partisanship, as audiences listen only to those messages they find congenial, and wholesale fragmentation of public opinion, as new delivery systems enable advertisers, politicians, and religious hucksters of all sorts to target audiences that will listen to their pitches and screen out anything that conflicts with them.

Fourteen months later Dewey wrote an open letter to George Norris urging him to lead a party that would break with the "rugged individualism" of his Republican leaders and promote the "social planning and social control" that Norris believed in.[6] Norris would do nothing of the sort; Dewey's belief that the third party might win the presidency by 1940 was not news an incumbent senator (Norris had been in the Senate for more than two decades already) was likely to greet with pleasure in 1930. As a British prime minister observed, "a week is a long time in politics"; a decade is longer. Norris's reply was courteous but firm: Dewey should support Norris's demand for a constitutional amendment abolishing the electoral college in order to encourage independents to run for president. I have found no evidence of Dewey's views on that suggestion; he ought to have disapproved a good deal since he shared—if not immediately, certainly in the next few years—the general anxiety that the depression would encourage people to look for a strong leader and that some form of fascism was a distinct danger for the United States. Making life easier for insurgent leaders was not an obvious route to follow. Quite what he thought is impossible to guess. Among the lacunae in Dewey's discussions of democracy, one particularly large omission is the role of leadership. On the face of it *The Public and Its Problems* leaves room for an imaginative leader to create an intelligent public in a way that sustains rather than threatens democracy, but it is not an idea Dewey embraced. Dewey never reconciled himself to Roosevelt and never suggested that Roosevelt had achieved the feat of building a "public" in Dewey's sense, as political scientists and historians who have written admiringly of the way Roosevelt put together the New Deal coalition have done. By the mid-1930s Dewey at least came to see that Roosevelt and his New Deal policies did not threaten American democracy, while Stalin and Hitler were liberticide autocrats of the most repulsive sort, and in the 1940s he admired Roosevelt's wartime leadership. Further than that he would not go.

Norris replied to Dewey that "experience has shown that the people will not respond to a demand for a new party except in case of a great emergency, when there is practically a political revolution."[7] Dewey was urging not a revolution but an "adaptation"; it might be a dramatic adaptation, but the language of revolution was one that never came naturally to Dewey. The immediate result of Dewey's appeal to Norris was that Norman Thomas and the other socialists left the LIPA; with his usual lack of rancor, Dewey voted for Thomas and the Socialist party in the 1932 elections. Any thought that this was a particularly magnanimous gesture must be tempered by the reflection that when Dewey was offered a choice between Roosevelt and Hoover, he found it easy to choose Thomas. Dewey was unabashed by the debacle of his appeal to Norris. In 1931 he wrote a series of four articles in the *New Republic* arguing once again the need for a new party.

It is hard to escape the feeling that Dewey missed the point. In most societies there is a crying need for a third party—not to say a fourth and anything up to a twenty-fifth—if we mean only that imaginative and creative policies are chronically required and chronically in short supply. The question that it takes a distinctively political intelligence to answer is whether the policy deficit we have identified can be met by any group available for the purpose, whether it could gain enough public support to govern, and whether it could build a durable constituency. Considering the extent to which the American party system is a system of rather loose coalitions of vested interests, it is easy to see why so many American intellectuals always hanker after the creation either of a labor party built on the union movement or a committedly social democratic party—and why they are not likely to get their wish. Had Dewey been more astute, he might have seen that pressure from the labor movement would push Roosevelt and the Democratic party toward a nonideological social democratic line and that the Republicans would see the danger of encouraging their propertied supporters in resistance to the point of civil war. Dewey understood that Americans were hostile to the word "socialism." Bellamy's old joke that the word conjured up images of bearded bomb throwers and advocates of free love was as valid as ever; whether he should have thought it was possible to create a party that advocated—mildly—socialist policies so long as it eschewed the label "socialist" was another matter. Electorates do behave inscrutably. The British electorate has long disapproved of "nationalization" while approving of "public ownership," and it is just possible that the American electorate of the 1930s would have applauded "social control" while fleeing "socialism" like the plague. They might for the matter of that have more readily accepted such policies from the Democratic party than from any new party, and if so, Dewey's argument was once more undercut.

In his *New Republic* articles Dewey reiterated his familiar view. Both major parties were in the pay of big business. The Republicans had flourished in the twenties by persuading the public that if they let the rich flourish, their prosperity would trickle down to the less well-off; the Democrats saw the Republicans prosper and concluded that they had better adopt a policy of "us, too." Democrats were so eager to reassure business that the Democrats were "safe"—something Dewey found particularly nauseating—that they failed to oppose Republican policies and had no policies of their own. That was why a third party was needed. Dewey added some new wrinkles that suggested that he had been listening to Sidney Hook and his Marxist friends even while he had been refusing to take them quite seriously. He argued that the American political system inevitably favored producers over consumers, the controllers of industry rather than the users of their products; he even put the point in Marxist-sounding terms: Attacking Secretary of the Treasury Andrew Mellon's proposal to restore prosperity by giving tax breaks to the rich, he observed that "Mr. Mellon's solicitude for the incomes of those in the higher brackets was openly an anxiety concerning the forces of production."[8] The

Marxist appearance is somewhat deceptive. The point that Dewey was making is an old—and still valid—point about the operation of the American political system—namely, that it is open to manipulation by special interests, and until the rise of trade unions and modern techniques of lobbying, the pressure groups with the most clout were those of the owners of businesses.

In general, it is true for fairly obvious reasons that groups with specific common interests, in constant communication with one another in the course of their everyday business, find it easier to organize than diffuse and dispersed consumer groups with little in common and few channels of communication.[9] "Special privilege entrenches itself at the cost of consumption. Transportation and the mechanism of distribution are connected with production and they have been constantly fostered with no regard for the standard of living. Our land system, our forests, and now our water power have, when politics have touched them, fallen under control of ownership by the 'producer.' "[10] One of the most striking examples of the producer interests' ability to get their own way in spite of the damage they did to workers and consumers was the tariff legislation that Congress passed at the end of the 1920s; it did much to embitter international relations, started a trade war, reduced international trade, and threw American workers out of work. All these evils were predicted; nonetheless, Hawley-Smoot passed.

Dewey rejected the thought that the Socialist or Communist party might provide what was needed. His view of the Communists was simply scornful: "Not much need be said about joining the Communists. As a party, they are directly governed from Moscow, and foreign control is simply out of the question for any party in the United States that means to be a going concern. And, aside from the fact that the Communist party does not speak the American idiom or think in terms relevant to the American situation, it is identified with a fanatical and doctrinaire inflexibility."[11] It was in thinking of the Socialist party's possible future that he argued in the fashion outlined a little earlier: "I think a new party will have to adopt many measures which are now labelled socialistic—measures which are discounted because of that tag. But while support for such measures in the concrete, when they are adapted to actual situations, will win support from American people, I cannot imagine the American people supporting them on the ground of Socialism, or any other sweeping ism, laid down in advance."[12] The idea that moderate social democrats like Norman Thomas were pressing for socialist measures as "elements in an *ism*" was, of course, quite absurd. Dewey was carried away by his own rhetoric and by the disputes within the LIPA. Since he voted for the Democratic candidate Al Smith in 1928 only on the ground of practicality and invariably supported Norman Thomas (whom he had preferred to Smith in 1928) against Roosevelt thereafter, it is hard to see quite what he thought he was doing.

Still, Dewey made a shrewd point about the audience for a new party. In an American context there was no point in demanding a labor party on a narrow working-class base. America was a middle-class country, reform movements had always been built on the radical middle class, and they had to be so now. "In spite of the disparaging tone in which 'bourgeois' is spoken, this is a bourgeois country; and an American appeal couched in the language which the American people understand must start from this fact."[13] "Bourgeois" was something of a joke; in the European sense of the term the United States has never had a bourgeoisie. What it has almost always had is the diffusion of middle-class comfort and middle-class aspirations through a wider portion of the population than European observers were used to. This was the news that Tocqueville took back to Europe in the 1830s, and it led John Stuart Mill to anticipate late-twentieth-century Americans by declaring that in the United States there was none but a middle class. Dewey did not believe that. He thought there was a large working class, both urban and rural. He explicitly left industrial laborers and farm workers out of his list of the target audience. Their interests were as important as anyone else's, and a radical party would self-evidently look after them; the point was that a party based on working-class interests alone was a nonstarter. Dewey thought the radicals must appeal "to professional people, including, of course, teachers, the average retail merchant, the fairly well-to-do householder, the struggling white-collar worker, including his feminine counterpart, and the farmer—even the farmer who has not as yet reached the ragged edge of despair."[14] The aim should be to "protect and render secure the standard of living enjoyed by the middle class and to extend the advantages of this standard, in both its cultural and economic aspects, to those who do not enjoy it."

The middle class was not to be sacrificed to the workers, but the better-off were to pay their way for a change: "This should be accompanied with whatever leveling down of the idle, luxurious and predatory group such a goal necessitates." The model Dewey had in mind was "the Progressive movement of 1912" and "the La Follette insurgency of 1924" rather than the British Labour party. The policies Dewey thought necessary were those of the British Labour party, but an American labor party was an implausible goal. "[W]e should not be misled by a supposed analogy with British conditions. There are three factors in the growth of the British Labor Party which do not exist here. The racial homogeneity of Great Britain is lacking here; the new party in Great Britain had the aggressive support of organized trade unions. The American Federation of Labor is officially no more than lukewarm to political action. And the British Labor Party had an organized cooperative movement of producers and consumers to rely upon. There is no corresponding body in this country."[15] In spite of all this, Dewey added a list of things that must be done for labor: the abolition of yellow-dog contracts, curbing the abusive use of injunctions against union activities, countering unemployment and "the general absence of security and stability," providing health care and old-age pensions—in short, setting up the welfare state apparatus that European countries had begun to invent from the 1880s and that the United States began to create four years later, when Roosevelt had taken the measure of the country's problems. It was in 1935 that the Social Security Act instituted old-age and unemployment benefits, together with schemes such as Aid to Dependent Children (renamed Aid to Families with Dependent Children in 1950) in a system that has remained more or less the same in the sixty years since.

Dewey's account of the policies of the third party remained vague. This was not the result of an incapacity for detail; Dewey's editorials and news releases for the People's Lobby were invariably devoted to specific issues, attacking Congress for propping up Cuban sugar prices at the expense of consumers, attacking Roosevelt when he was still governor of New York for failing to push up tax rates on the New York rich, arguing for the expenditure of five billion dollars on public works, and so on. What Dewey was incapable of visualizing was a party platform. He settled for the Henry George recipe of taxation of land values to fight one source of monopoly power, appealed in a general way for public ownership as a counter to private manipulation, and demanded the regulation of the securities markets and banking to make sure bankers and stockbrokers did not ruin the economy while lining their pockets. In international affairs, he linked the curbing of the activities of profiteers to the curbing of imperialist enthusiasms. The characteristic note, however, was his remark that "[t]here are many matters not mentioned which are incidents of general policy. They will almost take care of themselves as the general movement gathers momentum."[16] The history of progressive parties in power suggests the trouble this casual attitude can cause. The only safe outlook for a politician is that *nothing* will almost take care of itself.

The LIPA was not Dewey's only passion in the early thirties. The People's Lobby, of which he became president in 1929, had a prehistory as a "Georgist" organization, the Anti-Monopoly League; it changed its name to accommodate Dewey's wishes, and until 1936 he wrote on its behalf a stream of press releases for the *New York Times* and little articles for the *People's Lobby Bulletin*. The lobby's position was what one might imagine: Before the 1932 election and the installation of Roosevelt as president, it demanded aid for farmers and unemployment relief, urged Congress to pass legislation promoting birth control, asked for funds to be made available for child welfare, and nagged at Governor Roosevelt for failing to make the rich pay their share for measures needed to alleviate the miseries of the depression in New York. After Roosevelt was elected in 1932, it nagged at President Roosevelt from the left. Dewey's line from beginning to end was the same. It was too late in the day to rescue capitalism; the system was doomed, and palliatives were putting Band-Aids on a severed artery. In 1928 Dewey had voted for Al Smith, in spite of his cleaning lady's complaint that a professor had no business voting for an ill-educated candidate. In 1932, and again in 1936, he voted for Norman Thomas; it was a protest vote he could indulge in, knowing that Roosevelt would win. In 1932 he wrote dryly to his outlawry of war ally Salmon Levinson that he feared that Herbert Hoover's increasingly angry and desperate response to his impending electoral defeat had reduced Norman Thomas's vote by persuading more voters to stick with Roosevelt to be sure of getting rid of Hoover. Dewey had himself voted for Al Smith in just that frame of mind.

Dewey and the New Deal

It is hard to assess Dewey's response to Roosevelt. He was right to think that Roosevelt wanted to rescue the capitalists who had run the old order into the ground, though not because he felt any affection for them. Roosevelt was not a revolutionary and had no desire to change the United States more than necessary to restore it to prosperity. On the other hand, he was unusually untrammeled by fixed views of what measures might or might not work, and he surely subscribed to what John Locke had laid down as the touchstone of political virtue: *Salus populi suprema lex esto* (the welfare of the people is the highest law). Nothing was sacrosanct, and the greatest achievement of the New Deal was its sheer inventiveness; Roosevelt's technique was essentially to secure the services of clever, imaginative, ambitious, and energetic men and let them have their heads. Whether it "worked" remains unclear even after sixty years. Politically it worked wonderfully well; Roosevelt was reelected with overwhelming majorities and served four terms, though his final term lasted only a few months before his death in April 1945. It is not insignificant that it was a political success. For most of the everyday purposes of twentieth-century government, the American presidency is one of the worst-designed executive institutions in human history; it puts vast responsibilities in the hands of one man, gives him far too little guaranteed support from the legislature, makes him far too independent of his cabinet, and leaves him poorly supported by his own staff in the formulation of policy. If so much of everyday life were not in the hands of state and local governments, the system would have collapsed long ago. If the president is to overcome the handicaps the system imposes on him, he must either have overwhelming public opinion at his back or possess a Machiavellian talent for securing party support in Congress by whatever mixture of threats and caresses it takes. Roosevelt was rich in both resources, and it is hard to see how the United States could have got through the 1930s and World War II with so little damage to its essential character and institutions if it had not been led by someone with his skills and resources.

Dewey had no sense of the exigencies of the job Roosevelt had undertaken and the institutional difficulties of carrying it out at all, let alone carrying it out well. Dewey was unpersuaded of Roosevelt's economic competence, and here the justice of Dewey's doubts is particularly difficult to assess. The American economy improved steadily after Roosevelt's election in 1932, but long before there had been enough growth to restore full employment, the economy dipped back into recession in 1938. It climbed out again only under the impetus of rearmament. There is no evidence that Roosevelt wholly understood what he had done right and what had gone wrong. In particular, the view that

Roosevelt hit on Keynesian countercyclical methods by a stroke of intuitive genius and that the New Deal was a first success for Keynes's *General Theory* is nice but unbelievable.[17] Much as in Britain, in fact, the 1930s were not an unalloyed disaster. For anyone who had remained employed or had a steady income of any kind, life got steadily better, since the prices of most commodities dropped, and a stream of new consumer goods came onto the market to make life more agreeable. For anyone not so situated, they were grim years. Dewey's view of Roosevelt's personality was more favorable than his view of Roosevelt's policies. As between Roosevelt and Herbert Hoover, Dewey shared the universal view that Hoover was at best a cold fish. At worst he was simply callous. Hoover's reaction to the depression was typified by General MacArthur's notorious charge on the tented encampment that unemployed veterans had set up in Washington, D.C., an affair that ruined Hoover's reputation in Dewey's eyes, as in the eyes of most Americans. Roosevelt was a warm and sympathetic person, genuinely moved by the plight of ordinary Americans. This did not alter Dewey's attitude toward the policies he expected Roosevelt to pursue. Dewey stuck to the LIPA / People's Lobby view that Roosevelt would engage in half measures and that half measures were not enough.

This was the message of the most succinct of Dewey's declarations on the subject in November 1934. "There is no half-way house for America. Invoking the profit motive to provide employment is a confession of impotency, since the quest for profits—as rent, interest, and gains on invested capital—is the cause of unemployment and poverty. There is no way out for America, except to recognize that labor has prior claims upon production which take precedence of current return upon property, even when property ownership is due to investment of savings from income." As economics this does not score highly, but no matter. Dewey went on to argue: "We cannot achieve a decent standard of living for more than a fraction of the American people, by any other method than that to which the British Labor Party and the Social Democratic Parties of Europe are committed—the socialization of all natural resources and natural monopolies, of ground rent, and of basic industries." This was mild, but his conclusion verged on the apocalyptic: "Only elimination of profits through socialization will prevent eventual chaos."[18] He never publicly recanted this view, but he had plainly given it up by the end of the Second World War. He turned out to be wrong about the impossibility of resuscitating capitalism, though less wrong about the impossibility of resuscitating old-fashioned, freebooting, laissez-faire, robber baron–style American capitalism. He was equally wrong about the incoherence of a policy of encouraging employment by offering the inducement of a decent profit to investors who create jobs. The evidence is that any other method of job creation is hopeless.

Although Roosevelt's political success doomed the prospects of a third party, Dewey remained intransigent in 1936 as well. In answer to the *New Republic*'s inquiry about his voting intentions, he wrote: "I intend to vote for

Norman Thomas. It was a disappointment that no genuine mass third party was organized, especially in view of the fact that the so-called Union Party is a union of inflationists and semi-fascist elements. I realize that fear of reactionary Republicanism will lead many to vote for Roosevelt who have no faith in the Democratic Party; but I do not believe that the actual difference between the policies of the old parties will be great, whoever is elected. I think the Republican Party is conducting a campaign under false pretences."[19] The Republicans were arguing that Roosevelt was pushing through something close to socialism; they claimed that they would return to the old ways of sound money and limited government. Dewey's view that the Republicans were quite insincere in this seems right. If a Republican had, *per impossible,* got back into the White House, he would have had to continue a program of low interest rates, massive public works, and whatever measures of pump priming offered a chance to turn the economy around.

To that extent Dewey was right. His hostility to Roosevelt casts a somewhat bleak light on the basis of his semisocialism, however. Most of those of us who think of ourselves as socialists of some stripe do so out of a sense that the people who do most of the work have lower incomes, less education, less power, and less security than they should have. Justice for working people is an elementary principle. So is a measure of sympathy, but Dewey had an inadequate sense of the value of a president who was sympathetic to organized labor, or at least more sympathetic than any predecessor. Anyone with a prejudice against a philosophically based socialism would find his prejudice reinforced by reading Dewey. For all his stress on the needs of the consumer and his emphasis on the need of ordinary working people for stable and secure employment, Dewey had no clue about factory life or the extent to which labor relations were relations of bargaining power. He was an ardent unionist; he did his best to save his own teachers' union local from a Communist takeover in the early thirties, and he had a passionate dislike of the reactionary and oppressive behavior of school boards. But the positive side of his passion for the teachers' union was so wound up in a picture of the *teacher*'s role in society that it colored everything else. The teacher was doing God's work; the teacher was a social leader; the teacher was in the vanguard of those trying to create a new and more meaningful social order. Because of his obsession with the meaningfulness of experience, Dewey's detestation of the capitalist order had a semireligious quality, and so, therefore, did his vision of socialism.

The translation from education to the assembly line was not entirely convincing. It was hard to believe that the workers in the Ford plant in Dearborn, Michigan, were doing God's work and it was not easy to sympathize with their fight in such terms. It was easy to see that teachers were struggling to be allowed to use their own judgment about the education of the nation's children, but a lot less easy to see in the Ford workers' 1930s fights with the bosses a struggle for the right to use their professional judgment about American democracy's transportation preferences. I choose auto workers deliberately because after World War II Dewey had very close and friendly relations with the leadership of the United Auto Workers; he admired Walter Reuther, who returned the compliment and spoke at Dewey's ninetieth birthday celebrations.[20] During the 1950s indeed the UAW began to show a very Deweyan aspiration to close the gap between manual and managerial labor. But all this was built on very rough foundations during the 1930s, when the union had to fight for recognition with its members' fists. It was the role of brute power in political life that Dewey could never quite reconcile himself to. So when the Wagner Act gave the workers bargaining power they had previously lacked, Dewey did not give the Democratic party credit for its good deed and did not look forward to the unions' winning a few more battles but complained that it all fell short of the full social democratic agenda.

Teachers and Revolutionaries

Before we take a more analytical look at Dewey's agenda, it remains to see him in action in two other contexts. Much of his time was spent supporting teachers against their employers, arguing against assorted misguided educational policies, and trying to prevent the hard left from taking control of the New York teachers' organizations. And in 1937 Dewey chaired the extraordinary quasi trial in Mexico City that cleared Trotsky of the charges brought against him by Stalin and Vyshinsky during the Moscow show trials of 1936.

Dewey made innumerable speeches about the need for teachers to be unionized; they were more or less identical in tone and content and had been so for some thirty years. They were also entirely rational and persuasive, and one can readily understand his feeling that there was not much to be done other than keep on repeating himself until such time as a wider audience understood what was being said. One little radio talk might stand for almost all of his speeches on behalf of the American Federation of Teachers. Its theme was "Who is a worker? Are teachers workers? Do workers have common ties to unite them?" Having pushed his fellow teachers into the AFL as long ago as 1915, he knew the answer to those questions. Still, the answer was philosophically colored: Not all activity is work—to call a burglar a "second-story worker" is to make a bad joke—and more to the point, the exploitative activities of the rentier were parasitism, not work. Work was what produced something socially valuable; doctors produced good health, and successful teachers produced "a higher standard of intelligence in the community. . . ." Dewey went on to explain what this meant: "Skill, ability to act wisely and effectively in a great variety of occupations and situations, is a sign and a criterion of the degree of civilization that a society has reached. It is the business of teachers to help in producing the many kinds of skill needed in contemporary life. If teachers are up to their work they also aid in production of character, and I hope I do not need to say anything about the social value of character."[21]

The immediate problems faced by teachers, however, were ones the depression had worsened. With the economy in a bad way, taxpayers were unwilling to pay for education, and the result was not only a great retrenchment of anything that could remotely be considered a luxury—art, drama, music, kindergarten classes, and so on—but unemployment, too. "If something striking, striking home, was necessary to demonstrate to teachers that they are workers in the same sense in which farmers, factory employees, clerks, engineers, etc., are workers, that demonstration has been provided."[22] Although Dewey was not in the Marxist sense an enthusiast for class warfare, he had the old populist inclination to divide the world into the privileged and the people, and in this little broadcast he simply let fly at the privileged. Responding to an imaginary questioner who might wonder how society was, according to Dewey, still run in anything but an intelligent fashion even after a century of public education, he ascribed the failure of public education "to the excessive control of legislation and administration exercised by the small and powerful class that is economically privileged. Position, promotion, security of the tenure of teachers has depended largely upon conformity with the desires and plans of this class. Even now teachers who show independence of thought and willingness to have fair discussion of social and economic questions in school are being dismissed, and there is a movement, sponsored by men of wealth to label bolsheviks, reds and subversives all those who wish to develop a higher standard of economic intelligence in the community."[23] Only in a union, and in a union allied to other trade unions, could teachers combat "the state of servility, of undemocratic administration, adherence to tradition, and unresponsiveness to the needs of the community" that marked American education.[24]

It is no wonder that Dewey was much disliked by conservatives, the religious-minded, and traditionalists of all sorts. The readiness with which he talked in such aggressive terms about traditionalists and conservatives makes it implausible to close the gap between him and his opponents and critics. He was not an advocate of either the child-centered curriculum and classroom or "activity" for its own sake, but he was unabashedly an advocate of education with a political purpose, and he was unabashed about blaming resistance to it on the greed and selfishness of those who had much to lose from change. He did not want to "politicize the classroom" in the sense in which radical teachers in the 1960s and afterward wanted to; like many intellectuals, he wanted to have his cake and eat it: to claim that "intelligence" was on his side, that he advocated democracy and liberty, not the triumph of a particular ideology, and thus in a sense that his politics was not politics so much as the modern world in motion. This was why he could also say that he advocated not "progressive education" but education for a progressive society. Nonetheless, this was a decidedly political conception of education, and there is no point blinking the fact.

At the same time that he thought of the teachers' federation as an organization dedicated to promoting teaching as a professional activity and conducted by lively, forward-looking teachers of a center-left persuasion, Dewey defended the union against Communist take-over. This was a depressing and ultimately unsuccessful business. A representative, not to say deeply gloom-inducing, document in the case is the "Report of the Grievance Committee of Teachers Union Local No. 5 of the American Federation of Teachers."[25] By the middle of 1932 the local found itself in the familiar position of other union branches with a substantial Communist presence: Two leftist factions set out to make life intolerable for the middle-of-the-road elected leadership of the branch. They proposed motions for debate that were manifestly out of order and, when they were so ruled, distributed leaflets maintaining that the leadership was hostile to whatever good cause the motion was supporting; they claimed that any attempt to discipline them was another instance of "Red-baiting"; and they were as personally offensive as they knew how to be. The local set out to reorganize itself to curb the disruption, and Dewey chaired a committee that charged a group of members with disruptive behavior. One of their number was Bertram D. Wolfe, whose books *Strange Communists I Have Known* and *Three Who Made a Revolution* later educated generations of grateful students in the theory and practice of Communist insurrection. Local No. 5 failed in its attempt to have a new charter approved by the American Federation of Teachers and as a result split off into an independent Teachers Guild to which Dewey and some seven hundred members belonged thereafter, while the Communist members took over the rump organization. It was a familiar result, not only in the United States, and it confirmed the unfortunate truth that any organization that fell into the hands of the far left did so at the point where it had ceased to be able to do anything useful, though not before it had ceased to be able to make a nuisance of itself.

Because Dewey was so much encouraged in his anticommunism by Sidney Hook, it is easy to get the impression from Hook's autobiography and his many books and essays on Dewey that anticommunism was the central political passion of Dewey's life in the 1930s and 1940s.[26] It was nothing of the sort. In the 1940s Dewey became more aggressively hostile to Stalinism and the Soviet Union, but this was a wholly understandable reaction to the starry-eyed view of Russia that many people took during the Second World War. The American public, like the British public, rather excusably took the view that the gallantry and endurance of the Red Army not only had saved Western Europe from the Nazis—as indeed, it had, as a brief inspection of the casualty figures on the western and eastern fronts reveals—but showed that there was something fundamentally right with the Soviet Union. Dewey would have none of it. For once he abandoned his criticism of separations and distinctions and took the eminently sensible line that whatever assistance the United States might or might not get from the Soviet Union should not affect Americans' attitude to Stalinism. The lesson was simple: "People's democracy" was not democracy; Stalin was a despot who ruled by terror and manipulation, and he could not be trusted one inch. Hook, who had been a Communist in his youth, reckoned himself an expert on Communist duplicity and general wickedness and tried to keep Dewey in the same frame of mind as himself. Dewey suffered a good deal of abuse at the hands of American Communists and fellow travelers in the thirties and was therefore receptive to Hook's message, but he was nothing like as monomaniacal about the Communist threat as his mentor. Nor was he as ready as Hook to fight fire with fire. The fear that bad means corrupt good ends was one of Dewey's main reasons for disliking Marxism in theory and communism in practice, and he understood that it was a reason for being extremely careful about the way a democracy defended itself against subversion.

During the thirties the great bulk of Dewey's writings on academic freedom and the rights of teachers was concerned with the incursions of the right rather than the left. He himself was accused of Communist sympathies after his report of his visit to the Soviet Union in 1928, and the accusation rankled. In 1929 he got into a full-fledged row with one of the vice-presidents of the AFL, Matthew Woll. The AFL had censured Brookwood Labor College, claiming that Brookwood taught communism; Dewey said this was AFL smear tactics. Woll then claimed that Dewey "went to New York City for the purpose of planting the germ of Communism in our educational institutions."[27] Dewey denounced this as more of the AFL's usual reaction to any kind of liberalism in its ranks. In the thirties politics became increasingly polarized, and Dewey turned to defending teachers against loyalty oaths, Red-baiting, and attempts to dictate teachers' political activities. Already in 1929 he had written an acerbic little comment on the curious understanding of the notion of "freedom" prevalent in American politics. To the Wall Street banker it meant that the owners of property should be free to do whatever they chose with their assets, untouched by government; to Dewey it meant pursuing the life of democratic equality, in which each member of American society was encouraged to contribute his own individuality to the development of the individuality of others.[28] Dewey had nothing against requiring every American to pledge allegiance to the constitution of the country he lived in; voters were required to do so already. What he thought beneath contempt was the Wall Street banker and his friends imposing extra restrictions on teachers in the name of freedom. In the mid-thirties a new journal, *Social Frontier,* was set up to explore the conditions of educators in the depression and the prospects for progressive education. Dewey had an editorial page—"John Dewey's Page"—in the magazine, and there, as well as in *Common Sense* and a variety of educational journals, he wrote brisk little essays defending civil liberties, liberalism, democracy, and unflinching middle-of-the-road radicalism.

A vivid defense of his views was "The Social Significance of Academic Freedom," written in March 1936. It starts with a typical Deweyism: "I am not especially fond of the phrase academic freedom as far as the word *academic* is concerned. It suggests something that is rather remote and technical. . . .

Freedom of *education* is the thing at issue—I was about to say at stake."[29] Freedom of education meant the freedom of students to learn what they needed to know to become good citizens, and they could not learn that unless their teachers were free to teach them what they needed. Americans had long been passionate for "free schools," but they mostly meant schools that charged no fees for the teaching they offered and, on occasion, the meals they provided and the health and dental care they threw in. Their grasp of the deeper point—that these freedoms were only "tributary" to a wider social freedom—was not strong. Indeed, they had recently begun to try to "close the minds, mouths, and ears of students and teachers alike to all that is not consonant with the practices and beliefs of the privileged class that represents the economic and political status quo." For a man who so deplored the class war, Dewey could fight it with some flair.

He produced a delicious argument for the acceptability of pledges of allegiance to the Constitution. The Constitution itself provided the means of its own change, and among the rights it reserved to the people was "the right of revolution when conditions become intolerable—as both Jefferson and Lincoln have pointed out. . . ." No teacher should feel his or her freedom was abridged by loyalty to such a constitution. The sinister implication of the movement to impose loyalty tests on teachers but nobody else was that teachers were to be muzzled in the classroom, while those who did the muzzling enjoyed a monopoly of access to newspapers and radio. Dewey's argument against all this was not based on an appeal to First Amendment free speech rights, as it would be today. As always, he argued that freedom was social rather than individual and was instrumental to social growth and the increase of democracy. He had by this time published *Liberalism and Social Action,* in which he argued that society was controlled by the three forces of habit, force, and intelligence and that in times of change like the present, the answer to the question of what methods to employ to bring about change lay between violence and intelligence. Freedom of education was essential if intelligence rather than force was to prevail. The danger was that reactionaries would mindlessly obstruct social change by whatever coercive and duplicitous means they could lay hold of and that their victims, having themselves been deprived of the chance to exercise their intelligence, would resort to brute force to throw off their yoke. The Hearst press, said Dewey, blamed industrial violence and the spread of insurrectionary notions on the "teachers' imposition of subversive ideas under the camouflage of academic freedom."[30] The Hearst press was therefore talking nonsense. It was the *absence* of freedom in schools that did the damage; students never learned to exercise their intelligences in considering how to face the processes of change and social disruption and had no faith in anything but brute force.

The generally left-wing tone of Dewey's defense of free discussion did not mean any great sympathy with the Marxists. Their confidence that violent revolution would usher in universal brotherhood struck Dewey as superstitious in the highest degree, perhaps a hangover from the Hegelian dialectic, perhaps mere wishful thinking, but certainly incredible. A slender but famous volume, *The Meaning of Marx,* reprinted a symposium organized by Sidney Hook in the *Modern Monthly* of April 1934. Dewey, Russell, and Morris Cohen set out their reasons for not being Communists, and Hook offered his response. *The Meaning of Marx* was justly successful; Hook's account of why he was a Marxist but not a Communist was as intelligent and articulate an account of the intellectual dynamics of Marxism as any American produced in those years or for many years after.[31] From our point of view, Hook's account is illuminating because he makes Marx so Deweyan—a "naturalist" rather than a "materialist" and the dialectic not a Hegelian hangover but a commitment to scientific method—that it shows why Hook never quite gave up hope of converting his teacher to his own faith.

Three years later Dewey published *Logic: The Theory of Inquiry*. In Hook's view, it was just what Marx might have written: "Marx died before he could carry through his plan to write a dialectical logic. If he had been able to do it, it would have been a treatise on the fundamental concepts of scientific method, for that is all that dialectical logic is."[32] Hook's Marxism was both unorthodox and un-Deweyan in one crucial respect, however. He separated out the scientific treatment of social matters and the employment of this treatment to advance the interests of the proletariat in a way Dewey (and Marx) would not have done. Hook thought it was in principle possible to take Marx's social analysis absolutely seriously and then to employ it to hold off the revolution. This is not an implausible view. It is the view most people take of the relationship between natural science and ethics. Toxicology will teach doctors how to save the lives of poisoned patients *and* teach murderers how to poison people more effectively. One might even think that the history of the past 150 years suggests that capitalists have been better Marxists than the workers since they have ensured by a combination of threats and bribes that working people will think that the existing order is not so bad that it has to be destroyed and that its defenders are so well armed that any attempt to change it dramatically will be met with such resistance that it is unlikely to work. The owners of capital have maintained a degree of solidarity behind this program that no working class has matched.[33]

However tempting this line may be, it is un-Marxian and un-Deweyan. Although Marx and Dewey separated science and ethics, because they saw that we could, so to speak, stand back from our practical concerns when investigating the world, neither drew so sharp a line between analysis and commitment, fact and value as Hook's account suggests. Marx thought that once people understood their situation, they would side with the transformations that he believed society would have to undergo, and Dewey wrote as if he supposed that when intelligent analysis revealed how things were, it also revealed what we ought to do. Hook admired Dewey, Cohen, and Russell almost equally, and it is not unreasonable to think that this was because he had a strong sense of how plausible the empiricist separation of fact and value was and a greater attachment to the scientific than to the ethical aspects of social analysis. Dewey, on the other hand, was very much the embodiment of his own theory; there is little in his writings that suggests a wholly disinterested curiosity about how the world works, and at the point where one might expect him to defend disinterested curiosity—namely, where he points out the aesthetic aspects of scientific explanation and insists on the aesthetic quality of a great many things beside works of art—he takes back what he gives by turning aesthetic enjoyment into a moral attitude. Russell and Cohen were much closer to Hook's view on the separability of science and ethics both generally and in Marx.

Dewey, Russell, and Cohen concurred with Hook on something even more important, and that was their estimate of the extent to which Marx*ism*—as opposed to whatever Marx himself may have thought—had become a lay religion. Russell had observed this forty years earlier in his *German Social Democracy,* and Hook was at pains to insist that anyone who thought the rights of the proletariat were inscribed in Marxist science was "really asserting that Marxism is a religion according to which the nature of the world is such that 'the good'—socialism—*must* come to pass."[34] Dewey's objections to communism—that is, to communism in the sense in which the Communist party of the Soviet Union and its Western friends espoused it—were very like Russell's; Cohen, who had escaped from Russia and knew what it was like to live under czarist despotism, wrote a longer and more elaborate essay and said a good deal more about the resources of liberalism as well as about the failings of Third International Marxism. But little separated the three.

Dewey thought, in essence, that Communists held a simpleminded, monistic theory of history and had altogether too little sense of the specific and local features of the society in which they were actually operating. Marxism had succeeded in czarist Russia only because it was a repressive, undemocratic state that was vulnerable to revolution but not much else. In the United States Communist theory and practice were inapplicable, sure to be unsuccessful, and a distraction from the real task of repairing a wrecked social and economic system. "The autocratic background of the Russian church and state, the fact that every progressive movement in Russia had its origin in some foreign source and has been imposed from above on the Russian people, explain much about the form Communism has taken in that country. It is therefore nothing short of fantastic to transfer the ideology of Russian Communism to a country which is so profoundly different in its economic, political and cultural history."[35]

Three central propositions encapsulated Dewey's revulsion against the Communist program. The first was its hostility to liberal individualism; Dewey had recently published *Individualism Old and New* to explain what sorts of individualism were and what sorts were not to be fostered in a liberal democracy—roughly, those associated with laissez-faire and "rugged" individualism were not, while those associated with the equal cultural and intellectual development of all citizens were—and here he simply observed that the absence of a tradition of moral individualism in Russia explained the nature of Soviet communism and its entire unsuitability to the United States. The second was the theory of class war. Dewey had two simultaneous objections to the politics of class warfare. One was that fomenting class war was more likely to produce fascism than socialism and was thus more nearly suicidal than scientific; the other was that the politics of class war were indistinguishable from the politics of fascism. Depriving everyone bar the chosen few of their civil rights and winning arguments by breaking heads were liberticide. Lastly, the idea of launching a revolution in the United States was absurd. "Were a large scale revolution to break out in highly industrialized America, where the middle class is stronger, more militant, and better prepared than anywhere else in the world, it would either be abortive, drowned in a blood bath, or if it were victorious, would win only a Pyrrhic victory. The two sides would destroy the country and each other."[36] For good measure Dewey threw in the complaint that the argumentative manners of the American Communists left much to be desired; calling everyone who disagreed in the slightest a social fascist or worse was not calculated to achieve the solidarity they talked of with such passion.

Hook's reply was curious. He began by complaining that Russell, Dewey, and Cohen had nothing very constructive to say about what *else* there was to support in place of Marxism. Even the friendliest reader might think this foolish in the circumstances of a symposium in which three distinguished philosophers offered their reasons for being hostile to communism, not their blueprints for social reconstruction. One might want to complain that Dewey in particular did not have a strong sense of what policies a radical might espouse in the United States of 1934, but that complaint would better have been focused on other essays than "Why I Am Not a Communist." Almost as though he realized this, Hook then spent most of his reply to his friends savaging the philosophical ineptness of the official Soviet ideologists whose job it was to promote the dogmas of Marxism-Leninism-Stalinism rather than fill the gap he complained they had left.

The intellectual temper of those mid-thirties years is harder to summarize than much of the literature on it suggests. It was not true that the entire intelligentsia stampeded into the Communist party and assorted fellow-traveling outfits. Certainly there were many intellectuals who joined the party, though most came and went in a matter of months; the Communists' literary mouthpiece, *New Masses,* made a great deal of noise, though the violence of its prose cost it more converts than it made. Nonetheless, confusion, uncertainty, skepticism, and an overwhelming sense of simply not knowing where the world was headed were more common reactions than an ideological consensus. Representative samples of high-intellectual attitudes in collections of the "what I believe" variety more often display an emphasis on private happiness than on political revolution, more often bewilderment than a conviction that the revolution is at hand. Dewey was out of the mainstream, not so much in not being a Communist as in not having despaired of the modern world. It was not that he thought all was well. Capitalism had been shown to be a disastrous mode of economic organization, capable of providing neither prosperity for the mass of the population nor satisfaction in work even for those whom it enriched. Still, it was a failure only by modern standards; only recently had we been able to contemplate rebuilding a social and economic order in a rational way. The world's irrationalities struck modern observers painfully, but that was a tribute to the spread of rational ideals. Nor did Dewey exaggerate the problems of the United States. The Soviet Union had breadlines and famines, and most of the world was far worse off than America. Nor was the modern world in Dewey's eyes the spiritual wasteland that its conservative and literary critics alleged. People who thought that it was such a wasteland were suffering from self-inflicted wounds.

The Trotsky "Trial"

Considering Dewey's contempt for Soviet communism and for its American supporters, it is surprising that he so readily yielded to the idea that he should chair the commission of inquiry that spent much of 1937 looking into the charges of sabotage and treason on which Trotsky had been convicted in absentia in the fall of 1936 during the Moscow show trials. The trials defy rational analysis even now. It is hardly plausible to suppose that Stalin needed to engage in the judicial murder of the Old Bolsheviks merely to secure his own position; he had been unchallengeable for a decade. Nor did it make sense to murder his colleagues at just the moment he decided to open a popular front policy to secure the assistance of non-Communist Western political parties as allies against Nazi Germany. To cap the trials by going on to destroy the entire officer corps of the Red Army—one reason Hitler so nearly succeeded in defeating the Soviet Union in 1941—was to depart from the realm of rational political action entirely.

Nor were the trials calculated to persuade any unprejudiced observer that there had indeed been plots against the Soviet economy and national security. Most of the accusations were fantastic, the crimes alleged were impossible, the people against whom the accusations were made had plainly been tortured into confessing, and the accused were to a man people who had given their entire adult lives to the ideals of the Communist society. It is therefore hard to understand why the American liberal press, particularly papers like the *New Republic* and the *Nation,* was so ready to believe that the defendants were guilty. The American ambassador to Moscow, Joseph Davies, was thoroughly taken in by the trials, but nobody was taken in by Ambassador Davies, whose entire mission to Moscow was an exercise in patching up the ill feelings caused by William Bullitt. Bullitt had begun by being friendly to the revolution, had come to despair of it, and ended by seeing that Stalin was a tyrant of the same stamp as Hitler. Davies's remit was to say nothing that suggested he shared Bullitt's views. Since he knew nothing about Russia and took care to learn nothing, he found it easy to follow these instructions and probably never knew it was at the price of becoming an object of contempt to his better-instructed aides such as Charles ("Chip") Bohlen.

At this distance in time it is impossible to recapture the atmosphere in which Americans liberals found it so easy to swallow the party line. The obvious explanation may be the simplest: Americans were so unused to the truly Big Lie that they thought that what looked like a court of law must be a court of law and that the defendants must have done something to account for their presence in the dock. It was only after World War II, when a flood of memoirs from people caught up in the purges reached the West, that it became clear that most of the many millions who died had done so for no particular reason at all, and that was one of the truly horrible features of the purges. Of course, that was not true of the Old Bolsheviks and Trotsky. Their elimination was at any rate intelligible as part of a policy of removing everyone whose standing in the party might challenge Stalin's own. Dewey's lesson in the gullibility of the American left and the nastiness of the Stalinists came when he was prevailed on to join the American Committee (later Commission) for the Defense of Leon Trotsky and then to chair his "trial" in Mexico.

The American Committee for the Defense of Leon Trotsky was an extraordinary body. Much of the work was done by George Novack, perhaps the leading light among Trotsky's American supporters, and Dewey was recruited as chairman by Sidney Hook. There were several Trotskyists on the committee, including the writers Max Eastman, Dwight Macdonald, James Burnham, James Farrell, and John Dos Passos, but nonaffiliated liberals and leftists such as Reinhold Niebuhr, Lionel Trilling, Horace Kallen, Edmund Wilson, and Mary McCarthy swelled its ranks. Kallen and Dewey issued a statement insisting on the defense committee's liberal rather than partisan credentials; they particularly insisted that they did not start from any presumption that Trotsky was innocent. "This Committee does not affirm Trotsky's innocence or guilt. It does affirm that he has not been convicted or even tried." Dewey thought that Trotsky might well be guilty of one of the charges, that of trying to have Stalin assassinated. Just as the committee for the defense of Sacco and Vanzetti in 1925 had taken no stand on their guilt or innocence but only on their right to a fair trial, so the committee for the defense of Trotsky took no stand on whether he was guilty or innocent, only on the fact that he was entitled to a hearing. "Membership of such committees does not, of course, imply anything more than the belief that the accused is entitled to a fair trial."[37] This did no good, and Dewey was so annoyed by the *New Republic*'s accusation that merely by taking part in the inquiry, he had sided with the forces of reaction that he broke off all relations and brought to an end a writing career in its pages that had lasted almost a quarter of a century.

Dewey, chairman of the American committee, decided that he ought to join the small commission of inquiry that proposed to go to Mexico to take evidence from Trotsky himself. Dewey's family feared he would be made ill by traveling to Mexico for the inquiry and tried to get Hook, whom they blamed for the whole business, to persuade Dewey not to go. Being by now so furious with the lies of the Communists and the silliness of fellow-traveling liberals that it would have taken force majeure to stop him, Dewey brushed all opposition aside. The inquiry took place in Diego Rivera's house in Coyoacán, where Trotsky was living, and lasted a week, from April 10 to 17, 1937. The full account of the commission's activities occupies a four-hundred-page book, and it issued its final report clearing Trotsky and denouncing the show trials as a "frame-up" only in December 1937. The week in Mexico was, however, long enough to show conclusively that Trotsky simply could not have committed most of the crimes with which he was charged—either he was in the wrong place at the material time, or the people with whom he was supposed to have plotted were in the wrong place—and it became increasingly hard to understand why the Soviet prosecutors had not been more concerned than they were to bring charges that had at least a semblance of credibility.[38]

The final report unequivocally cleared Trotsky but even more unequivocally denounced the trials. It began:

> Independent of extrinsic evidence, the Commission finds:
>
> 1. That the conduct of the Moscow trials was such as to convince any unprejudiced person that no effort was made to ascertain the truth.
>
> 2. While confessions are necessarily entitled to the most serious consideration, the confessions themselves contain such inherent improbabilities as to convince the Commission that they do not represent the truth, irrespective of any means used to obtain them.[39]

And it ended:

> 20. On the basis of all the evidence we find that Trotsky never recommended, plotted, or attempted the restoration of capitalism in the U.S.S.R. On the contrary, he has always uncompromisingly opposed the restoration of capitalism in the Soviet Union and its existence anywhere else.
>
> 21. We find that the Prosecutor fantastically falsified Trotsky's role before, during and after the October Revolution.[40]

One spin-off from Dewey's and Trotsky's encounter in Mexico was a famous pamphlet, *Their Morals and Ours,* which set out in a particularly stark form the different moral perspectives that animated Dewey and Trotsky. Dewey had drawn some sharp lessons from the inquiry; his first report, immediately after the subcommittee's return from Mexico, had criticized liberals who refused to face the fact that they had either to believe the accusations against the Bolshevik Old Guard or else to accept that the Soviet Union was a terrorist state. This time the "apart" quality of the world was too clear to smooth over, and it was time for the politics of "either-or." Immediately after the final report was issued, Dewey gave a long interview to Agnes Meyer for the *Washington Post.* "The great lesson to be derived from these amazing revelations is the complete breakdown of revolutionary Marxianism *[sic]*. Nor do I think that a confirmed communist is going to get anywhere by concluding that because he can longer believe in Stalin, he must now pin his faith on Trotsky. The great lesson for all American radicals and for all sympathizers with the U.S.S.R. is that they must go back and reconsider the whole question of means of bringing about social changes and truly democratic methods of approach to social progress."[41]

The conclusion he drew was familiar, but no less cogent for its lack of novelty: "[W]hen violence is used to bring about economic and social reform, the method of force must be employed to keep the new government in power."[42] He went on to say that he saw less and less difference between Stalinism and Hitlerism; to people who still supported a popular front, he retorted that "if the methods used by the Soviet Union are merging more and more with those of Hitlerism, how can we rely on them? The essence of fascism is no sweeter if called by some other name," and in one of his rare moments of real political prescience he forecast the rapprochement that resulted in the Ribbentrop-Molotov pact of August 1939. "We may expect a gradual approach of the two nations toward each other. The policy of an alliance with Russia is an old policy of Bismarck's and of the German general staff. If war is delayed for a few years, it is not inconceivable that Russia and Germany will again be allies. We have to face this possibility."[43] The contamination of the socialist goal by violent methods was the burden of his contribution to the argument of *Their Morals and Ours.* This was a wonderfully clear-cut opposition of two different attitudes to the question of whether the end always justifies the means.

By this time Dewey not only thought ill of Marxism as a political practice but had come to see it as combining the worst deficiencies of messianic Christianity with the worst deficiencies of abstract deductive metaphysical rationalism. Trotsky's article—a variation on the familiar Leninist theme that we cannot make omelets without breaking eggs—appeared in the *New International.* It was written in February 1938 and published in June; Dewey's essay appeared two months later.[44] Dewey and Trotsky were genuinely at odds, but they were also at cross-purposes. Dewey was defending a liberal fastidiousness about violence against what he thought was a theologically based unconcern. Trotsky was struggling with demons rather than with Dewey. More prosaically he was responding to a renewed outbreak of the criticism that had haunted him for the previous seventeen years. The tragedy of Trotsky's life was the Kronshtadt uprising of 1921, when the sailors of the Kronshtadt naval base in Leningrad revolted in the name of giving the party back to the workers and fighters who had made the revolution of October 1917. As commissar for war Trotsky had the task of suppressing his own supporters. Kronshtadt was thus Trotsky's Achilles' heel; the sailors of Kronshtadt had been the fiercest and most loyal supporters of the revolution from its inception, and when they turned against the Bolsheviks, they did so from the left, from the direction from which Trotsky had criticized Lenin before the 1917 revolutions. To preserve the revolution, Trotsky ruthlessly crushed the revolt and executed its leaders. Anarchists like Victor Serge and Emma Goldman never forgave him for crushing the last sparks of spontaneous working-class revolutionary energy, and whenever his followers in later years had qualms about Trotsky, Kronshtadt came up again.

Trotsky was a genuinely tragic figure; his revolution had failed—it had, in his view, been betrayed—but he could not let go of it. To justify his past, he fell back on the thought that whatever assisted the revolution was acceptable, whatever did not was unacceptable. The crucial point was that *in*action was impossible. Not to act in defense of the revolution allowed the enemy to gain the upper hand merely because we were squeamish. Morally this was no better than a surgeon's suddenly deciding he could not stand the sight of blood. A surgeon should have no such qualms; he was not a butcher, let alone a murderer. He cut where necessary to save life. By the same token, revolutionary terror was permissible, counterrevolutionary terror not. Individual murder was disgusting, class warfare inevitable.

Philosophically Dewey got the better of the argument. He objected that Trotsky's belief in the absolute moral value of the revolution was nonempirical and not justified by the "scientific" stand he allegedly took. All Trotsky's talk of "deducing" the necessity of violent insurrection from "the law of the class-struggle" led Dewey to conclude that "Orthodox Marxism shares with orthodox religionism and with traditional idealism the belief that human ends are interwoven into the very texture and structure of experience. . . ."[45] As for Trotsky's claim that the only alternative to his views lay in "some form of absolutistic ethics based on the supposed deliverances of conscience, or a moral sense, or some brand of eternal truths, I wish to say," wrote Dewey, "that I write from a standpoint that rejects all such doctrines as definitely as does Mr. Trotsky himself. . . ." Indeed, the absolutist was Trotsky rather than Dewey, for "in avoiding one kind of absolutism Mr. Trotsky has plunged into another kind of absolutism."[46] Trotsky made no attempt to canvass the possibility of nonviolent ways of acting, before jumping to the conclusion that violent means would be needed. What Trotsky had done was swallow a vision of the world that brought everything else in its train. This was less like science than religion, and it must be simply unpersuasive to anyone who had not undergone the same conversion. Although Dewey sympathized with Trotsky's declaration that not *every* means was legitimate, only such means as were consistent with the promotion of human flourishing, he was surely right that Trotsky had not seriously canvassed all the alternatives to violent revolution, even in the Russian context. It is less clear that Dewey got the better of the argument as a political encounter. Trotsky felt the sheer fatality of politics on his pulses, and Dewey did not; Trotsky intuited when a situation would fall out one way rather than another if only a decisive and dramatic stroke were made but had no ready way of explaining this ability even to himself. It was Trotsky who had shown Lenin how to seize power by acting boldly when a sober calculation of the odds would have indicated that the Bolsheviks were too few, too demoralized, and too unpopular to take the Winter Palace, let alone govern. He had almost overthrown a government by sheer charismatic power during the 1905 revolution. It is hard to complain that thereafter he was prone to see the world in such terms. We would breathe more easily in a world where Dewey's politics were the rule, but if it came to a fight, it might be better to ride into battle behind Trotsky.

Before turning to Dewey's 1930s theoretical labors on behalf of liberal democracy, we should pause to acknowledge one more of his efforts on behalf of the persecuted. This was the famous episode in the spring of 1940 when Bertrand Russell's appointment as professor of philosophy at the City College of New York was overturned in the courts. Russell had been appointed to teach philosophical logic at City College from the fall of 1940. A Democratic hack, Judge McGeehan, annulled Russell's appointment on the petition of a Mrs. Jean Kay; she had complained that Russell's teaching of logic would subvert her daughter's morals and her intellect. Not only would it be "lecherous, salacious, libidinous, lustful, venerous, erotomaniac and aphrodisiac," but it would be "unscholarly," too. Horace Kallen edited an account of the affair, *The Bertrand Russell Case,* which contains many comic offerings, including the decision rendered by Judge McGeehan. This owed less than nothing to the law and a great deal more than it ought to the Catholic interests in the Bronx Democratic party who had secured McGeehan's appointment.

The whole business was less than comical for Russell since he had given up a position in California on the assurance of the job in New York and now found himself unemployed in a foreign country, unable to get back to Britain across a U-boat–infested Atlantic, and wondering how he might support a wife and three children. Dewey wrote a savage little piece entitled "Social Realities *versus* Police Court Fictions" for Kallen's volume, in which he pointed out just what a sober little book Russell's *Marriage and Morals*—published in 1929—actually was.[47] Dewey rightly noted that Russell was opposed to conventional morality for rather high-minded reasons.[48] More usefully Dewey prevailed on Albert Barnes to hire Russell to lecture on philosophy at the Barnes Foundation. The battle between Russell and Barnes that broke out almost as soon as Russell started giving his lectures has been described innumerable times elsewhere and did not involve Dewey.[49] Russell's lectures on the history of philosophy were high-spirited and amusing and less full of moral uplift than Barnes had hoped; Barnes took against Russell's new, third wife, Patricia, and tried to ban her from the lecture room where Russell was speaking. On a more commercial note Barnes claimed that Russell's contract forbade him to lecture anywhere else while he was engaged at the Barnes Foundation, and Russell was giving lectures at the Rand School in New York.

Barnes sacked Russell, and Russell sued for breach of contract. Russell had no difficulty getting a court to find in his favor, after which he was able to go home with twenty thousand dollars toward his retirement and the much more valuable manuscript of *A History of Western Philosophy* in his baggage. Dewey's good deed was not entirely spontaneous, for it is said that he had to be urged to it by Hook and Kallen. In light of the malice and rudeness of much of the criticism that Russell had leveled at Dewey's work on logic, it was noble enough that Dewey should do it at all. It showed a certain saintliness to labor on behalf of Trotsky on the one hand and the man whom Trotsky had once called a "moth-eaten aristocrat" on the other.

Advanced Liberalism

During the last decades of his life Dewey did not add much to his political philosophy in the strict sense of the term. His energies went into elaborating his thoughts on art and religion, into connecting his ideas on education with his new concern for "experience," and into the vast and somewhat baffling *Logic: The Theory of Inquiry,* which he published in 1938. But he spent a good deal of time and effort reiterating his fundamental ideas about liberty and democracy, about the relationship between politics and economics, and about the relationship between the individual and society. Dewey's liberalism remained elusive even when popularized; his philosophy of law, for instance, trod a narrow line between a regard for individual rights and an insistence that law was essentially driven by policy considerations. The law was sometimes said to be the expression of a society's better self, as if it were always what it ought to be, and at other times said to be a device for using collective opinion to enforce cooperation with social goals and therefore always open to scrutiny by anyone who wondered whether the goals were wisely chosen and whether the coercion involved in the operation of the law was a minimum.[50] One's inclination to complain about such ambivalence is diminished by the reflection that both views have much to be said for them: If law was not fairly close to an embodiment of the moral outlook of the community, it would not secure obedience as something we *ought* to obey, while it can hardly be reformed if it is not also seen instrumentally, as a coercive mechanism to be analyzed in the light of its effectiveness in securing democratically agreed-on goals.

In the thirties and early forties Dewey set out to sum up his views in ways that the plain man could grasp. The essays written in these years are short, rarely much more than sixty pages long, made up of short chapters, each of which was itself made up of brisk paragraphs that might almost be the numbered paragraphs of a lawyer's pleading. They defend a centrist social democracy, in terms that English writers such as L. T. Hobhouse and D. G. Ritchie would have found familiar and natural. All the same, they were not "old-fashioned"; on the contrary, they were emphatically forward-looking. They suffer one familiar, incessantly commented-on, obtrusive, and undeniable vice. Like Hobhouse and Green before him, though not wholly like G. D. H. Cole and H. J. Laski, Dewey had rather thin ideas about how to *institutionalize* social and economic democracy. A sympathetic reader feels in two minds about complaining. The obvious virtues of "non-Marxist naturalized-Left Hegelianism" make one reluctant to criticize what Dewey does *not* do, but the persuasiveness of the general outlook on social, economic, and political matters is such that the absence of specific institutional recipes is all the more frustrating. It is the same frustration that innumerable admirers of Marx have felt. Marx's vision of the socialist future is so compelling that we very much want to know *how* industry will be organized, *what* will replace the state once it has withered away, *why* new classes will not arise. Dewey's social philosophy was essentially the liberal counterpart to Marx's; both steered a delicate line between Hegel's emphasis on "the Whole" and the individualism of Bentham, Ricardo, and Mill. Both wanted to preserve Hegel's emphasis on collective and holistic features of social, political, and economic life, but without Hegel's metaphysical baggage. It is not surprising that Sidney Hook tried to use Dewey to remedy Marx's deficiencies; in the United States Marx and Dewey represented two possibilities open to progressive-minded people who wanted to preserve the merits of Hegel's vision of the world while advancing a liberal or a more radical politics.

It is this allegiance to progress that makes us want to know *how* the institutions of our society would be different if Dewey (or Marx) were to win out. Conservative defenders of the status quo have an operating social system to point to that satisfies at least some of our needs and holds at least some of our allegiances. They also have a story about how it works. It is a fairly well-understood system, successfully, if partially, analyzed by orthodox economics and sociology. Orthodox social science offers a plausible account of what motivates people to keep that society going, and that account in turns provides a picture of a liberal-conservative politics. It is, for instance, a persuasive thought, one on which orthodox economics depends, that economic transactions work efficiently if all participants have clear property rights over all usable resources, whether this be their labor or funds for investment, or trees to be cut down, or water to be dammed for a hydroelectric scheme. Governments exist to specify people's property rights, to provide courts to adjudicate disputes and police to ensure that the law is respected, and otherwise to facilitate their making all the private, mutually profitable bargains they wish to make. Such a vision of government and law has animated the American judiciary and the American public for long periods since the founding of the country.[51] It is famously articulated in Adam Smith's *Wealth of Nations* with its defense of "the simple system of natural liberty"; it is the core of the laissez-faire vision of government.

To combat the view of capitalism and its associated politics that his opponents defended, Dewey had both to argue that those systems were irreparably damaged and to supply an account of what might replace them. Dewey was more aggressive in doing the first than imaginative in doing the second. His view was that capitalism had failed in three dimensions simultaneously. As an economic system it had by the early 1930s failed to secure the livelihoods of ordinary people. In the way it employed the technological advances produced by modern science, it failed to give people work in which a normal person could take any pleasure or interest. Socially and politically it was a threat to democracy. One reason why Dewey argued that a third party ought to aim at a "bourgeois" audience was that Americans were passionately committed to the ideal of equal opportunity. This was an individual ideal rather than a class ideal; it was a very *American* ideal, based on an American hostility to inherited privilege and to the class prejudice that Americans associated with their colonial British masters. Long after 1945 equality of opportunity was seen as the moral basis of distinctively American institutions like state universities and other institutions of mass higher education that had no counterpart elsewhere. Conversely, the British view that democratic politics was a polite form of class warfare struck no chord in American hearts.

So when Dewey argued for social democracy as a solution to American ailments, it was deliberately distinguished from the *labor*-based reformism of the British Labour party. Its great weakness was the obverse of its strength. Its strength lay in its hostility to state socialism and a command economy; Dewey sought a "planning society" rather than a "planned society." This is all of a piece with his emphasis on participatory democracy, but to say this is unilluminating because it does not touch the central puzzle. What does participatory democracy look like? Dewey did not suppose that the American public was longing for a world in which the average worker would come home from work at six in the evening, grab a sandwich, and rush off to a town meeting to decide whether his block should purchase its electricity from Con Edison or brew its own. Oscar Wilde had complained that socialism was all very well but would eat rather painfully into one's evenings, and Dewey was not so attached to head-in-the-air abstraction that he could not see the point. But what is it to be like? Every clear answer is a negative answer. It is not to be one-party rule; it is not to be the dictatorship of the proletariat. Dewey shared Russell's view that the dictatorship of the proletariat meant the dictatorship of ex-proletarians over their rank-and-file fellows. It is not to be the imposition of an elite vision; it is not to be the manipulation of the humble many by the sophisticated few. Dewey believed that the advance of the social sciences allowed a degree of rationally organized planning in a way that had not been possible before; to that extent he shared in the New Deal and Progressive optimism about the usefulness of expertise. He did not, however, have any wish to see modern America turn into the sort of utopia that Huxley mocked in *Brave New World*, with everything engineered by an unelected and legally unanswerable directorate.

It is no small thing that Dewey knew what to avoid. Many theoretical socialists in the thirties were unconcerned about the dangers to freedom posed by the society they hoped to bring into existence. Others, such as the practical-minded supporters of the British Labour party, were quietly pleased that a party *officially* committed to securing the fruits of their labors to workers by hand and brain through the public ownership of the means of production would in practice take into public ownership only the parts of the infrastructure that any government would have regulated regardless of their ownership: power, iron and steel, docks, airports, and railroads. Their position was a good deal less honest than Dewey's. Dewey had a clear vision of the dangers to be avoided, primarily the substitution of one privileged class for another and the substitution of ideologically driven terrorism for the more unobtrusive maintenance of the position of the privileged classes through the courts and Congress.

Dewey plainly had some views about how the world would look if his side triumphed. He had read and admired the work of G. D. H. Cole, the British guild socialist; Cole's socialism changed a good deal over his lifetime, and the guild socialism he preached in 1915 was modified as he rethought it in the 1930s, but Cole thought a great deal about how to institutionalize guild socialism and wrote at length about forms of government based on representing producers rather than citizens in the abstract.[52] It is unlikely, therefore, that Dewey had given no thought to the mechanics of guild socialism. But he thought two rather different things: the first that other people had been thinking out the institutional detail, and he had little to add; the other that people would design and build social democratic arrangements as they went, and he could not preempt them. This is on all fours with his discussion of education. There, too, he was concerned with the politics of education rather than the delivery of instruction, and usually in a negative way, trying to remove obstructive, conservative, and oppressive forms of management rather than designing a school board for utopia. (Since there were to be no schools in utopia, it was unlikely that there would be school boards either.)

Dewey clearly liked the rough outline of Cole's account of a guild socialist society. Much of life would be regulated by industrial councils, and these in turn would be checked and controlled by a sovereign authority much like an existing Parliament or Congress. This was an idea much in vogue between 1880 and 1930, and not only on the left; the corporatism taken over and abused by Mussolini's fascism was based on functional representation, though the more Fascist it became, the more this meant in practice that the councils represented owners rather than workers. Nor is a broadly corporatist view old hat even now. Orthodox political science analysis of the functioning of parties and pressure groups in postwar liberal democracies like France, Britain, and the United States suggested that these countries were well governed because each had a system of representation that was corporatist in practice, though not in theory.

The idea of corporatism has been so tainted by its association with the fascism of the 1920s and 1930s that it is hard to say plainly that one could envision a society in which the familiar liberal civil rights were firmly entrenched and universally respected but in which much of the apparatus of political and economic representation was explicitly functional and thus corporatist. Yet it could be done, and perhaps it has been done. It has been argued that the British government functioned effectively during and immediately after World War II—from 1940 to about 1960—because a tripartite alliance of government, business, and trade unions pursued a vision of the national interest without regard to the ideological differences between the major political parties.[53] J. K. Galbraith's 1950s account of contemporary capitalism and its relationship to government was not dissimilar: Modern businesses were too large to be subject to the disorganization of the marketplace, and workers were an established part of the economic order whose interests could not be left out of the making of policy. Government had to be conducted by the same tripartite leadership.[54]

Dewey and Cole were not prescribing the "managed capitalism" of the post-1945 world. Modern accounts of functional or corporate representation see society as an economic-cum-political system and discuss its effectiveness in ascertaining the needs and wishes of important elements and responding to them. It is an assessment from the manager's perspective. Dewey and Cole started from the other end; they wanted society to be *felt* to be democratic by its inhabitants. It was an assessment from the citizen's perspective. Saying only this, however, may give the impression that Dewey and Cole were more individualist in their orientation than in fact they were. Cole was deeply influenced by J. J. Rousseau and his idea that a legitimate government was one governed by a general will rather than merely by the aggregate wills of many citizens. In Rousseau's own hands, this could have alarming implications; it was always possible that a dictatorially inclined person might decide that his will was the general will, while that of everyone else was no more than the "will of all" and of no moral weight. Indeed, Robespierre was accused of doing just this under the influence of his reading of Rousseau.[55]

There was no danger of Cole or Dewey's embracing collectivism or dictatorship. Dewey was not even as tempted as Cole was by talk of the general will. His experimentalism implied something else. Dewey thought of democratic processes as a search procedure in which we look for policies, laws, and administrative techniques that will allow us to continue a common life in a way that all of us can find fruitful and fulfilling. The idea that they should eventuate in the discovery of a general will is thus shut out of consideration. It is very like the way Dewey shut out the thought that what scientific investigation does is uncover the truth. There is no truth legitimating the observations and experiments of scientists and no will legitimating democratic decision making. Dewey's informality of ethical and political argument led him to throw out the deductive and hierarchical apparatus of justification employed by every political thinker before and after him. He eschewed any suggestion that "democracy" was uniquely legitimate either because it was government by the general will or because it was uniquely apt to uncover the truth. The nearest he got to a single account of democracy's virtues was that they were like those of science: It excluded the fewest alternatives, allowed all ideas a fair shot at being tried out, encouraged progress, and did not rely on authority. Democracy offered no guarantees, any more than science; science may destroy the human race and may make us stupider than we need be, and democracy may not work either. All Dewey thought he could do was keep on spelling out what a commitment to democracy amounted to. His growing obsession with the concept of "experience" made some difference to how he did this in the twenties and thirties, as his emphasis fell less on the *moral* equality of all members of a democratic community and more on the idea of an experience of "associated living" open to everyone on equal terms. The basic message was recognizably the same.

Is it enough to say that Dewey had much to say about the "spirit" of democracy and less to say about the "letter" of its arrangements? We do not complain of the New Testament that it encourages faith, hope, and charity without spelling out how much of each we ought to display and when. This won't quite do as a defense of Dewey. However one turns the argument around, he was too insouciant about things we worry about acutely. His was a "moral" socialism, but it is difficult to motivate workers to do a good job by presenting them with moral incentives; public spirit and revolutionary zeal can accomplish things that self-interest cannot, but over a long haul they are inferior to self-interest as motivating forces. Dewey seems to have had no real inkling of this.

Again, planning in anything but the broadest and most "indicative" fashion has turned out to be extremely difficult. The Soviet economy turned out to be not a miracle of effective central direction but a shambles kept going by an unofficial, illegal—and not infrequently lethal to those who ran it—market system run by "facilitators" who spirited materials and goods from places where they weren't needed to places where they were. Dewey feared the dangers of dividing society into planners and planned but had no doubts about the planners' getting things right. This is not a wholly damning complaint; during the 1930s it was only a few unfashionably free market–oriented figures such as Hayek and von Mises who tried to demonstrate a priori and in pure theory that planning was impossible, and since they suggested that modest forms of government intervention were as bad as a Stalinist five-year plan, they were not persuasive to middle-ground opinion. The enemies of planning whom Dewey encountered were libertarians like Albert Jay Nock, whose objection was to the way government intervention violated the natural rights of the owners of property rather than to the impossibility of the calculative tasks officials were setting themselves. If the complaints are not damning, they are nonetheless serious. They set someone who wishes to take Dewey seriously but not reverently a difficult task. The thought that animates this book, after all, is that although Dewey was in intention the Voice of Modernity, he was also and as a result the Voice of America or, to put it more cautiously, that it is no accident that he was the most highly regarded liberal of his day and has lately come back into high regard as someone who can speak to his countrymen at the very end of "the American century." If he was as careless as I have suggested about the way a society of the kind he wanted was to be built and sustained, what makes him worth our attention?

The answer is that he did what a modernizing liberal had to do in the 1920s and 1930s, and most of what he did had considerable staying power. Part of the staying power lay in what separated him from another of his British contemporaries, Bertrand Russell. Russell had been one of the most important of the creators of modern analytical philosophy; it was in aspiration a technical discipline, held to the standards current in mathematics and formal logic, and employing modern formal logic wherever it was helpful. It was by the same token a discipline detached from the affairs of everyday life. It could be understood only by experts, and its interests were esoteric. Hence Russell was up to a point right to say that his political views were detachable from his philosophical views. Dewey's philosophical career was much more of a piece with his political allegiances.

One might argue that the fact that Russell and Dewey held similar views about politics and economics while disagreeing so sharply about logic showed that Russell was right. One might, on the other hand, think it showed that Russell was wrong about the implications of his philosophy and that there was a closer connection between his philosophy and his politics than he imagined. From a rhetorical point of view, the advantage lay with Dewey. If one wanted to know why one should take an interest in Russell's politics, the answer was that he was a very clever man. If one asked the same question of Dewey, the answer was that his politics were one aspect of a deeply pondered view of the modern world and of human experience within it, ranging from the role of logic in human thought at one end of the spectrum to the utility of murals on United States Post Office buildings at the other.[56] The risk that Dewey ran was that confusion in one area implied trouble everywhere; having a system is a two-edged business. But there was always something to learn from Dewey besides what a clever man happened to think.

Nor was this merely a rhetorical matter, not that rhetorical matters are "merely" rhetorical either. It was a question of the capacity of Dewey's system of ideas to sustain exploration and to keep Dewey himself at work. I have mentioned his astonishing stamina. Some part of this was plainly physical and physiological and psychological; some people are born with large curiosities and much energy to sustain them, and other people are not. There was more to it than that, however. The academic world is full of clever and energetic people who have become bored by their own ideas and can hardly bring themselves to write them down or think them through except under compulsion or on the offer of large sums of money. Dewey was entirely unlike that. Thinking came more naturally to him even than eating. "One of the conditions of happiness," he remarked when replying to the speeches at his seventieth birthday celebrations, "is the opportunity of a calling, a career which somehow is congenial to one's own temperament. And I have had the sheer luck or fortune to be engaged in the occupation of thinking; and while I am quite regular at my meals I think I may say that I had rather work—and perhaps even more play—with ideas and with thinking than eat. That chance has been given me."[57]

Moreover, Dewey's loathing of traditional religion went along with a temperament that caught one of the major concerns of the religiously minded. He had intimations of a deep unity in the world quite at odds with his equally powerful intimations of the deeply ragged quality of everyday life, and he spent a great deal of time working his way through these oppositions: individuality and community, the is and the ought, ownership and public spirit, variety and unity in a painting. The homeliness of his prose meant that readers could join in the brooding; nobody thought the author knew all the answers and was simply hiding them, while the seriousness of his attention meant that no one need ever fear he or she was being palmed off with something he did not believe.

As a theorist of liberalism Dewey could properly and decently offer his liberal views as something larger and more enduring than a local political doctrine. It was a lay faith, a faith in the common man, and perhaps even more a faith in the common man's capacity for uncommon experience. It was a faith in the possibility of assimilating everyday work and ordinary duty to the creative efforts of the artist, of turning social life into an experience to be *had* in the way aesthetic experience is had. That is why it is not a devastating complaint to say that Dewey was more concerned with the spirit in which institutions were built than with the mechanisms by which they were to operate. Nor did it result in a "wishy-washy" or "preachy" liberalism. The liberalism that Dewey set out was a decidedly advanced liberalism. Sidney Hook might have wished that after he had turned Marx into a pragmatist, Dewey would do the decent thing and turn himself into a Marxist, but by American standards Dewey was quite Red enough. He detached liberalism from any connection with private property or with laissez-faire, made it possible to think of other enemies to freedom than government, possible to think of government as an aid to liberty under appropriate conditions. If he had been a young assistant professor in the 1930s, he would have been fired from half the schools and colleges in the country. It was in a rebellious spirit that Dewey spent so much time defending the right of such professors and schoolteachers to teach dangerous subjects—such as nonclassical economics and unorthodox sociology and history—in the classroom and to broach dangerous questions about social reform. It was this advanced liberalism that his short, crisp, and aggressive essays of the decade defended.

The first and best of them, *Individualism Old and New,* began life as a series of essays in the *New Republic* in 1929. It is fascinating in several respects. One is that it was written during the weeks leading up the great crash of October

1929,and there is never a mention of Black Thursday and the events of the few days that shook the capitalist world to its foundations. Another is that it is in spirit extraordinarily close to Marx's *Economic and Philosophical Manuscripts,* known at the time to a handful of scholars and not widely known until the 1960s. Dewey's complaint against the industrial society created in the United States in the previous century was not that it could not feed, clothe, or house its working people—the complaint most socialists leveled against capitalism from *The Communist Manifesto* on—but that it debases the culture of work and consumption. Dewey follows Marx (without ever having read his thoughts on the subject) even to the extent of arguing that the capitalist or rentier is more deprived than the worker. The worker is at least doing something useful, and his activities are, so to speak, debased versions of a proper human activity. Living off the proceeds of other men's work is not a human activity at all. In Marx's early essays this view was developed from the theory of alienation that Marx had inherited from Hegel and the Young Hegelians and had modified to suit his own purposes. In Dewey's reflections on the meaning of human existence in the advanced industrial societies it was developed from the pragmatist vision of human nature. As problem-solving creatures human beings build the world they inhabit; they find meaning in it, and they create meaningful structures to shape their social lives and to make their efforts to get a living from the world more effective. Capitalism evacuates the meaning of work from the activity of capitalists and workers alike. That makes it morally intolerable and psychologically unsatisfying.

It is an obvious complaint against Dewey that even when he is saying that the industrial order of the past two centuries is emotionally, morally, politically, and organizationally bankrupt, he does so in abstract terms. The gruesome details of the workers' everyday lives that Marx used to fuel the indignation of the readers of *Capital* are absent from Dewey's writings. When Dewey talked about the "problems of associated living," what he meant was boring work, unhappy marriages, crime, poverty, wholesale failure in the educational system, the folly of covering the countryside in concrete rather than build efficient public transport systems, and much else beside. There was something other than fastidiousness that explained why Dewey did not set out to rub his readers' noses in the horrors. Dewey was a critical and radical writer, but one way in which he was wholly unlike Marx was that he was always more eager to tell his readers of the good that might be born than of the evil it would be born from. Thus *Individualism Old and New* ends on a note of almost religious affirmation. "New" individualism could be achieved only in a new society; such a society's raison d'être would be the "new" individuals it created.

Dewey always insisted that individuality was not a brute fact but an achievement; the individuality we should admire is not "a mannerism" but something "original and creative; something formed in the very process of creation of other things."[58] We can only become individuals, only find self-realization, by moving *outward* into the world. "Ideals, including that of a new and effective individuality, must themselves be formed out of existing conditions, even if these be the conditions that constitute a corporate and industrial age. The ideals take shape and gain a content as they operate in remaking conditions."[59] Appealing to Emerson's injunction to "accept the place the divine providence has found for you, the society of your contemporaries, the connection of events," Dewey ends with this thought: "To gain an integrated individuality, each of us needs to cultivate his own garden. But there is no fence about this garden: it is no sharply marked off enclosure. Our garden is the world, in the angle at which it touches our own manner of being. By accepting the corporate and industrial world in which we live, and by thus fulfilling the precondition for interaction with it, we, who are also parts of the moving present, create ourselves as we create an unknown future."[60]

This affirmative ending was not the pollyannaish claim that all was well with American society. The book very largely said exactly the reverse. Dewey was much struck by the phenomena of social and individual disintegration; he was struck by the bewildered condition of the inhabitants of Muncie, Indiana, chronicled in the Lynds' *Middletown* study, and by the fear and anxiety of European observers when they looked at a society that struck them as materialistic and addicted to quantitative standards rather than to more sophisticated and qualitative standards of consumption, leisure, and culture. Dewey had been appalled by the outbreaks of nativist nationalism that swept the United States after the First World War, and he found paradoxical the growth of corporate organization in every area of the economy except where it was most needed—that is, in some kind of overall national control of economic activity.

Dewey thought, as did many of his contemporaries, that modern man had got lost; he could not make sense of his surroundings because these surroundings did not make sense. But Dewey was sharply critical of the innumerable observers who had noticed the same facts and left it at that. Waldo Frank's *Rediscovery of America,* for instance, seemed to Dewey to be simply feeble. Frank had looked to some sort of individual, spiritual rebirth for salvation. But the idea that individuals could first rebuild their own characters and then get together to rebuild an organically successful society was pure fantasy. "It marks a manner of yearning and not a principle of construction."[61] Modern man could recover his psychological poise only by living in a society that had recovered unity and order. This was a matter of extending to social organization generally the technical intelligence so far applied only to the narrow field of production, and the corporate organization so far applied only in industrial and commercial settings.

This could not be done by fiat or legislative say-so since law itself was only the expression of a society's inner commitments and convictions. If those commitments and convictions were not coherent, there was no point in trying to legislate them into order. As nobody needed telling in 1930, the United States Congress had imposed Prohibition on the public and had even persuaded the public to enshrine it in a constitutional amendment, but it had not changed the drinking habits of the American people. As Marx had done, but with none of the rhetorical bluster of the dialectic, Dewey argued that the only hope was to bring out the *latent* order and reasonableness of modern society, corporate and industrial as it was. What held things up was not a deep and worsening crisis—here Dewey was poles apart from Marx and his successors—but the clogging effect of traditional values and traditional ways of working. Blind tradition and a lack of "intelligence" were what stood in the way of a more integrated society.

The difficulty that *Individualism Old and New* poses is not Dewey's claim that everything is a matter of "intelligent action"; we may accept or reject that claim when we accept or reject Dewey's account of science. The task is rather to dispel the fog surrounding Dewey's view of individual freedom. Dewey agreed with virtually every other liberal from John Locke down to the present that liberalism must be built around the defense of individual liberty. The problem was to attach that thought to Dewey's ultrasocial conception of individuality. A few years later Dewey said he feared he had not properly emphasized the role of the individual in social affairs, and this suggests that "new" individualism had problems even in Dewey's own eyes. Discovering what they were is not easy. As always, Dewey's negative case is easy to understand: "New" individualism was opposed to old-fashioned, traditional laissez-faire individualism. Old-fashioned individualism was negative, and its concept of liberty was negative. In one of his surprising imaginative strokes, Dewey went on to declare that old-fashioned individualism was "irritable"; its vision of the world was that of the young man determined to "go west." The young man wanted to be free to go away, to seek adventure, and to carve out a life unimpeded by traditional ties and authorities. What Dewey wanted to preserve of this was the ideal of equal opportunity. The rest—the dislike of authority and organization especially—was outmoded.

Dewey was casual about his own view of freedom because he could turn against the defenders of old-fashioned individualism the complaint they themselves leveled against government intervention in the economy. They complained of "regimentation." Dewey maintained that laissez-faire produced it. Regimentation was a genuine evil, but it permeated the existing social and economic order. Regimentation was universal in the workplace, in ordinary people's leisure activities, and in popular taste. If society was to operate intelligently, it had to achieve a certain unity in production and consumption, as distinct from total chaos. The regimentation of mass production and mass consumption produced a *false* unity, however, as a sort of compensation for an absence of organic unity. Real unity is flexible, not rigid; spontaneous, not imposed. Dewey guessed his emphasis on the need for social unity would surprise his *New Republic* readers. "There are, I suppose, those who fancy that the emphasis which I put upon the corporateness of existing society in the United States is in effect, even if not in the writer's conscious intent, a plea for greater conformity than now exists. Nothing could be further from the truth."[62] It truly was. What Dewey thought was that Americans were not so much free as isolated, and when they did things together, they were not so much united as "massed." Individual freedom was yet to be achieved.

Dewey thus anticipated a view later made famous by David Riesman's best-selling book of 1950 *The Lonely Crowd*. Like Tocqueville, Riesman argued that Americans do not suffer from governmental tyranny, military brutality, and similar oppressions. They suffer at the hands of public opinion and even more at the hands of their own inner censors. They are "other-directed," seeking reassurance about their own worth by desperately trying to be like everyone else. This was essentially Dewey's view. Americans were other-directed because they lacked inner resources, but they could acquire strength of character only in a society that fostered it.

Dewey never suggested a debt to the picture of American life that Riesman found such a surprising precursor of his anxieties—namely, Tocqueville's terrifying vision of an America in which individuals had retreated to a private world in which their sympathies and interests were bounded by home and family and nothing further. But Dewey was as fierce as Tocqueville about the falseness of American sociability. "We should not be so averse to solitude if we had, when we were alone, the companionship of communal thought built into our mental habits. In the absence of this communion, there is the need for reinforcement by external contact. Our sociability is largely an effort to find substitutes for that normal consciousness of connection and union that proceeds from being a sustained and sustaining member of a social whole."[63]

Still, that claim itself raises an old anxiety. It is a familiar complaint against writers of a Hegelian persuasion that they confuse freedom with membership in a community.[64] Liberals who think we need rights *against* the community flinch at the idea that freedom stems from identification *with* the community. Dewey defused such anxieties with an indirect but deft response. Indeed, anyone looking for reasons to think well of *Individualism Old and New* could do worse than consider how he handles these familiar liberal anxieties. Dewey was enough of a materialist to believe that the root of America's troubles was economic but enough of an idealist to believe that freedom was cultural. Thus the traditional political liberties remain firmly in place in *Individualism Old and New,* but not because they are "natural rights"—there are no natural rights—or because there is a chronic problem of defending each individual in a democracy from the potential ill will of a majority. They remain in place as part of the machinery that allows a truly democratic public to form. In a democracy there is no chronic problem of defending the individual against collective ill will, but there is a chronic problem of finding a public and articulating its best conception of what its goals are. The diehard rights-obsessed liberal will not be persuaded by this, but Dewey would not be persuaded by him. Nor does this matter as much as it may seem. Dewey was quite ready to agree that the full battery of *legal* rights that the liberal traditionally demands are the indispensable way to institutionalize the ground rules of a democratic community. Whatever system of legal rights one may institute, the question then arises whether these rights will be *effectively* enjoyed by the population. Here Dewey's late 1920s anxieties run into those of the 1990s.

Effectiveness is the rub. We are used to thinking of effectiveness in egalitarian rather than pluralistic terms; this is surely right when it is a question of the way poor defendants suffer because of inadequate representation in criminal cases. For First Amendment issues, poverty is less of a problem than eccentricity. Thus the separation of church and state is so fastidiously enforced by American courts that a complainant can readily prevent a local government from erecting a creche at Christmas and can keep prayer out of public school ceremonies. But no school student would be well advised to declare complete unbelief at school or elsewhere. The social pressure to profess some religion or other is strong enough to negate the freedom the First Amendment is meant to protect. The record of the enforcement of First Amendment freedoms suggests that the courts follow public sentiment more often than they resist it. Nor is it only a matter of what happens in court; most damage is done unofficially and is not contested by the victims. In short, there is much to be said for Dewey; he was deeply opposed to intolerance, discrimination, and political oppression, and said so in innumerable forums, while his social, nonlegalistic view of how freedom might be achieved is far more plausible than its opposite.

As to how a "new" individualism was to spring from the emerging economic and social order, his ideas were large but abstract. Their interest is not in their detail, but in the way Dewey straddled the line between two very different ways of looking at the world with no great emphasis on the fact, though he was perfectly conscious of having done it. The penultimate chapter of *Individualism Old and New* was called "The Crisis in Culture." It is a very pure specimen of Dewey's mixed hopes and fears, for it paints a grim picture of existing cultural life while urging the possibility of democratizing Periclean Athens, Augustan Rome, and Elizabethan England. It does even more. One of Dewey's numerous sociological asides was the conjecture that previous "golden ages" had been such brief episodes in their originating nations' histories because they were the achievement of isolated individuals in societies dominated by the rich and powerful few and not reaching down to the poor many. Dewey sought the answer to what he termed "a qualitative question." This was not the question of whether America was capable of producing a number of poets, painters, novelists, and scientists; that, thought Dewey, was the easy task. The qualitative question was harder. "Can a mechanical, industrial civilization be converted into a distinctive agency for liberating the minds and refining the emotions of all who take part in it?"[65] It was, he thought, no good just urging a return to some previous or alternative culture. "Some flee to Paris or Florence; others take flight in their imagination to India, Athens, the Middle Ages, or the American age of Emerson, Thoreau and Melville. Flight is solution by evasion."[66] This is the voice of the man who complained that the pacifists of the First World War were escapist and unserious. Much as then, Dewey's thought was not that their aspirations were contemptible or worthless but that their ideas about how to realize them were childish, too much driven by fear of the present miseries they deplored, and too little informed by an intelligent appraisal of how their goals might be achieved.

The goal was to realize an integrated culture in an industrial society. Another of Dewey's elegant sociological sideswipes was the observation that modern society had achieved something that philosophers had always hankered after, a "complete separation of mind and body" such that industrial workers took to work only their hands and bodies, leaving their hearts and minds at home.[67] The elegance of the gibe is the way it neatly reverses the view that Dewey ordinarily took of the origins of philosophical dualism: In classical Athens manual labor had been the province of women, slaves, and noncitizens, and it had thus been tainted with their lowly status. Conversely, thought, argument, and appreciation had been the province of independent male citizens, and this association had established the familiar ranking of "higher" and "lower." Now, however, we had allowed the technology of the machine age to interact with the pecuniary drive of capitalism, and the result was that intelligence was embodied in the machine and mindlessness in the worker. This was not, however, the inevitable result of scientific progress. "The alleged fatalism of science is in reality the fatalism of the pecuniary system in which science is employed."[68] Pace some of Dewey's later remarks about the valuable role that decoration might serve in such humble places as the nation's post offices, here he argued very ferociously against any idea that we could make much difference by pressing art upon workers who went to work in hideous factories, traveled in hideous trains and buses, and otherwise dwelt, all their lives among ugliness.

It thus emerged that liberalism of a Deweyan kind aimed at something not unlike the Christian socialism of John Ruskin and F. D. Maurice, in which the central thought was the need to reverse the reversal of means and ends, consumption and profit, work and enjoyment that had taken place under capitalism. Herbert Croly had two decades earlier argued in *The Promise of American Life* that the American task was to pursue Jeffersonian goals by Hamiltonian means—that is, to employ all possible governmental and national means to promote individual liberty, equality of opportunity, a strong sense of the equal moral worth of all citizens, and the moral importance of the American experiment. Now Dewey argued that a socialist transformation of American society was needed if Americans were to achieve the individuality that liberalism had always aimed at. Like Croly, Dewey also aimed to set out the conditions for achieving a genuinely American individuality. Readers from the other side of the North Atlantic may flinch a little at the number of times Dewey employs "European" as a term of condemnation, but his underlying inclination was not cultural nationalism. His passion was for cultural diversity in the anthropologist's sense; cultures as the anthropologist understood the term were vitally interesting because they were the expression and embodiment of the varieties of the human spirit. If American culture was to be vital and to sustain Americans, it must have a character of its own and not be something hung on museum walls after being looted from elsewhere.

Liberalism and Social Action, the better-known defense of "advanced liberalism" that Dewey wrote some five years later, is less intriguing than *Individualism Old and New*. The latter is faintly maddening in the way it gestures at large issues without telling us quite what to do about them. Who, even now, has a clear idea how far a firm can make work more fulfilling without threatening its commercial survival, or how far a firm can ignore what Dewey calls "the pecuniary system" without risking the livelihood of its employees? And there are endless further questions one might ask. Nonetheless, Dewey weaves social, political, intellectual, and artistic considerations together in his account of why we are presently "lost" and what we are striving toward in a fashion that for all its clumsiness is both moving and inspiring. *Liberalism and Social Action* is clear, rational, straightforward, and persuasive, and therefore less engrossing. It is less continuously engaged with the idea of a society built around the goal of individual and social self-creation. It is, for that very reason, a more elegantly executed defense of the idea that a "new" liberalism must break with "old" or laissez-faire liberalism. Dewey had already quipped that "rugged" individualism had become "ragged" individualism as Hoover and the Republican administration he headed were discredited by the depression. Now Dewey offered to show, by way of a short history of the liberal idea, how this process had to be taken to its conclusion and then reversed, how the "social action" that liberals advocated would restore a new individuality.

He was, as his opening lines suggest, more deeply aware by 1935 that liberals were not attacked only from the standpat right. They were attacked from their left by a more radical Marxist and Communist left. Dewey's response was to offer an account of liberalism that traced its history to the need for emancipation from governmental and political oppression, through its blending of political, spiritual, and economic emancipation, and on to a twentieth century when the old threats mattered less than new ones.[69] The common thread in liberal aspirations was not provided by a purely "let alone" conception of freedom—what later became known as "negative liberty." Liberalism rested on a more positive conception of liberty, an ideal of rational, fulfilling control of self and environment; the serious question was what such ideals meant in the actual conditions of present-day society, not in the abstract and in some ahistorical vacuum. Dewey argued this case more fiercely in a long review of his old bête noire Walter Lippmann. Lippmann's latest book, *The Good Society,* was a signpost pointing rightward. *The Good Society* was a frightened book; it marked Lippmann's fear that the New Deal would end in complete governmental control of the economy and Lippmann's gradual move toward the espousal of natural law after World War II. Dewey's judgment was that "in spite of its criticism of *laissez-faire* and of the doctrines of the Liberty Leaguers its net effect is to give encouragement and practical support to reactionaries. . . ."[70] Lippmann offered only two alternatives: the administered state and a free market society. Given that the first looked very much like fascism or Stalinist communism, the latter was obviously destined to win in a canter.

For once Dewey said quite clearly what he thought the real choices were. He was all in favor of the free market and thought that in a free society there would be a free market for consumers. What he denied was the claim that the free market was what existed under capitalism. Indeed, it was inconsistent with capitalism. Lippmann was a good target for Dewey to aim at since many of Lippmann's aspirations were Dewey's. He had slid a long way from the days when he was assistant to the socialist mayor of Schenectady, but Lippmann was a reformist liberal still, and Dewey had no difficulty in convicting him of self-contradiction inasmuch as Lippmann first complained that the New Deal was a long step toward bureaucratic tyranny and then admitted that New Deal–style measures would be needed to sustain the good society and defend its weaker members against their stronger fellows.

The difference between Lippmann and Dewey was that Dewey believed that the technological and organizational realities that had caused disorder could be brought under a form of control other than private profit without falling into the hands of government. This allowed Dewey to complain that the New Deal was an incoherent hotchpotch of remedies for particular evils unsustained by a vision of the transformation to be wrought by "intelligent social action." The New Deal did too little, and what it did it did in an "external" and bureaucratic fashion that Dewey deplored. "External" change must involve either violent transformation or the violent repression of the would-be transformers of the world, while a Deweyan liberal socialism would be the expression of the demands of modern technique and organization in the service of modern ideals of individual fulfilment. Readers of Dewey and readers of this book need no further telling that he never spelled out just what it meant on the ground.

There is no rabbit to be pulled out of the hat. There is nothing in Dewey's later essays and reviews that reveals what he had in mind. I suspect that the answer is not complicated. He almost certainly thought that most existing American institutions would play an essential part; Dewey was a natural pluralist and federalist and a natural believer in civil liberties and individual rights. Pure old-fashioned individualism was doubly dead, both intellectually discredited and swept away by more powerful social forces, whether patriotic in wartime or commercial in peacetime; but the answer was to give our liberal aims a rational social basis, not to abandon them. The progressives on the Supreme Court had understood that. "Holmes and Brandeis are notable not only for their sturdy defense of civil liberties but even more for the fact that they based their defense on the indispensable value of free inquiry and free discussion to the normal development of public welfare, not upon anything inherent in the individual as such."[71] Dewey's references to the need to "abolish" the profit motive could have been met in institutional practice not by Marx's recipe of expropriating the expropriators but by a system of social audit that allowed the community to judge whether an enterprise's profit and loss accounts reflect its value to the wider society. Any government that chose to do so could tax and subsidize firms or more probably whole industries to reflect the costs they imposed or the benefits they conferred that weren't reflected in their accounts. Beyond that anyone's guess is as good as anyone else's.

Dewey's last extended venture into this field was *Freedom and Culture,* the work that Sidney Hook hoped would rival *The Communist Manifesto* in its appeal and impact.[72] That seems the hope of a man who had no idea what political prose should sound like since *Freedom and Culture* has all Dewey's usual stylistic and expository vices, while it buries its sharpest observations in the middle of long paragraphs on quite other topics. What is worse, its virtues would dish its chances in such a competition even more thoroughly than its vices: The Manifesto expounds a simple, monistic view of history, society, and human nature, and it gets its rhetorical power from that fact. *Freedom and Culture* is dedicated to the thought that the defense of democracy must rest on an inclusive account of a democratic culture and that we cannot give priority to a single causal factor. The unpredictability and uncontrollability of social affairs are what provides our problem. This is clearly right, but it makes a bad slogan. The interest of *Freedom and Culture* lies in its self-consciousness about the distinctively American aspects of a democratic culture, in its obsession with the concept of *culture* in the first place, and in Dewey's own account of why he here sets out the democratic (or liberal) vision in contrast with the Marxian—and occasionally the fascist—view of the world.

Dewey thought, and here we encounter the ghost of Herbert Croly once more, that Jefferson was the embodiment of the American vision. Jefferson was the great practitioner of the unity of theory and practice that Marx made so much of. But in this context it was Jefferson's insistence that "Nothing is unchangeable but inherent and inalienable rights of man" that Dewey wanted to embroider; not that Dewey wanted to talk of inherent rights, but he did want Jefferson's conclusions.[73] Institutions are not sacred and immutable, and Dewey went on to quote Jefferson's famous observation "As new discoveries are made, new truths disclosed, and manners and opinions change with the change of circumstances, institutions must change also and keep pace with the times. We might as well require a man to wear the coat which fitted him when a boy, as civilized society to remain ever under the regime of their barbarous ancestors."[74] That had obvious implications: It suggested that superstitious attachment to the Constitution itself was un-Jeffersonian, and in the spirit of the liberal corporatism that I sketched a little earlier, Dewey went on to question even the current system of voting rights and to wonder whether "some functional organization would not serve to formulate and manifest public opinion better than the existing methods."[75]

This again sounds like G. D. H. Cole and English guild socialism. Britain, however, was a centralized country, and its institutions were no model for the United States. Dewey knew this. Jefferson's un-English contribution to democracy was his passion for localism and federalism. On this Dewey could content himself with quoting the remark he had made a dozen years earlier in *The Public and Its Problems:* "Democracy must begin at home, and its home is the neighborly community,"[76] though here, too, Dewey made a nod toward updating Jefferson in the light of the theory of functional representation. A new *kind* of localism was needed where "groups having a functional basis will probably have to replace those based on physical contiguity."[77]

Dewey understood well enough that one attraction of both fascism and Marxism was their bustling quality; they did not throw up their hands in the face of the chaos of the world but set out to master events brutally and strenuously. They also got something right that liberals often failed to. They appealed to every aspect of a person's cultural attachments. They saw more clearly than liberals had that art was not a decoration to be stuck on to the social order after it had been assembled and that a society's artistic expression of itself was one of the features of its common life that allowed individuals to become attached to it and to find fulfillment in it. As Dewey also saw, but offered no further analysis of, the liberal and the democrat must try to understand the potentially political quality of art without in the negative sense "politicizing" it. Dewey's point was a solid one. If the older liberalism and the older democracy had been largely struggles against feudalism, class privilege, and governmental oppression, art could largely be left to take care of itself. It ought to be free from censorship, there ought not to be a market rigged by academies under royal patronage, and "equal opportunity" for those who chose to starve in garrets ought to be secured. The new liberalism needed a more self-conscious, social-scientific, organized confrontation with a capitalist economy's inherent tendency to chaos, depression, and cyclical instability; modern liberalism had to face the tendency of democracies to succumb to public folly and ungovernability. Education for democracy had to be taken seriously, and aesthetic education was part of it, and governments thus had a duty to think about culture. Mere laissez-faire was no good as a cultural policy, but what positive policy toward the arts a democratic government ought to pursue was a matter to be settled by experiment.

In arguing for this last version of radical liberalism or social democracy, Dewey paid homage to his old inspiration William James. James had a visceral hatred of monistic theories. He hated determinism, and the block universe in which everything was deterministically linked to everything else, was his favorite target. Dewey had a harder time of it because he felt the appeal of monistic theories in a way James did not. In *Freedom and Culture* he spent a few pages explaining what he did and did not believe about the Marxist view of the world, and his disbelief took a Jamesian turn. Economic arrangements *are* exceedingly important in determining the workability of all other social arrangements. They are everywhere constraints, and sometimes more than that. This can be taken in two ways. The historian—he probably had Charles Beard in mind—may treat materialism as a practical maxim; constitution builders ought to bear in mind the economic arrangements to encourage if their constitution is to "take." The Marxist elevates it to a monocausal theory of the social world. Marxism produces a block universe, an implausible, excessively deterministic picture of the social world.

The prospect Dewey offers is daunting. We are encouraged to seek a multicausal, culturally and historically sensitive recipe for a liberal-democratic society built on a socialized economy, but we are told it will be exceedingly difficult. We are told we shall be tempted by monocausal individualism or laissez-faire, or by monocausal collectivism of either a Marxist or Fascist kind, but we must resist. Then we are left to work out for ourselves how to build a revived Jeffersonian democracy in the complex situation thus outlined. Marx ended the *Manifesto* with the cry "Workers of the world, unite!" The last sentence of *Freedom and Culture* reads: "At the end as at the beginning the democratic method is as fundamentally simple and as immensely difficult as is the energetic, unflagging, unceasing creation of an ever-present new road upon which we can walk together."[78] It may be childish to wish that Dewey had raised his voice to the pitch of Marx's, but with the next war barely a year away, readers in 1938 must have hoped for more guidance than they could find here on *how* to build that road.

Nine

DEATH AND RESURRECTION

THIS CHAPTER IS A STORY of death and resurrection. In the literal sense I round off the story of Dewey's life as briefly as decently possible. I then do three things: first, gather together some criticism of his work to explain why Dewey's reputation sank upon his death, not in everyone's eyes and not universally, but very generally; second, say something about why his reputation has since recovered and whether his recent admirers have admired what is actually most admirable in his work; and finally, trail my coat with an estimate of Dewey's place as an American moralist.

Unity and Plurality

This is not a detective story, and I will give away my punch line. My sense of the world is that the tensions we experience between many of the dualities that Dewey tried to remove—the need for privacy versus the need to belong, the need for dispassionate and instrumental behavior at work, and the need for passionate involvement in play versus the enjoyment of culture and more—are irreducible. We can be rid of them only at a price not worth paying. Both sides of the tension have proper claims on us, and we cannot collapse the virtues of different activities and spheres of life into one another. What goes for commitments goes for ideas. We are plural creatures, not only in our commitments but in the intellectual and moral equipment we bring to our daily lives; we switch roles, outlooks, and moral universes in a thoroughly situational way. But Dewey was right to think that this breeds an unease on which modern writers, dramatists, social and political critics have dwelt at length and that we hanker for a more unified sense of self and a stronger sense of knowing our own minds than we usually have.

How far Dewey supposed he could satisfy that urge is unclear, but my own view is that the modern self is less an ego than a committee of strong-willed members; the best we can do is make it a tolerably harmonious committee.[1] Dewey's own account of personality is hospitable to such a view, but his aspirations were not. The same goes for "the religious"; Dewey gave a persuasive account of the needs that religion satisfies and what it is that survives disbelief in the literal truth of traditional Christianity. But he was too confident that a *secular,* nonsupernatural successor to the traditional theistic picture of the universe will do for those who subscribe to it *everything* traditional religion does for those who swallow its claims. Wholly secular societies can certainly flourish, and a Deweyan "creed" could help them to do so; but Dewey was wrong to suggest that they can flourish in just the same way as communities committed to the Judeo-Christian world view.

Others of Dewey's reconciliations run into similar difficulties: Building "the great community" in which the qualities of the face-to-face interaction of the village are replicated across a continent may not be a wholly intelligible project, and the vagueness of Dewey's account of the "planning not the planned society" may well reflect this implausibility in the project itself. But Dewey was right about the impossibility of leaving matters there; he was right about the importance of the experimental approach to social reconstruction; he was rightly sympathetic to the pluralism of the modern mind and rightly unwilling to suppress it; he had a proper sense that such unity in thought and action as we possess is an achievement, not the gift of a prior unity in the world around us; and he was right to insist that we must acquire the ability to live with uncertainty. In terms of the implications of his views for everyday politics, he was right at a more down-to-earth level to maintain that American politics is obstructed by a superstitious reverence toward the Constitution, by an excessively individualist understanding of the place of rights in human affairs, and by an unwillingness to think seriously about the relations between national and local authority.

In short, where his views gratify a familiar American longing to unify opposites, his fame is easy to explain, but I remain skeptical about the project. Where he argues for an antitraditionalist, antilegalistic liberalism, for an experimental politics that looks for ways of recasting existing economic arrangements in the interests of wider opportunities, more interesting work, and a heightening of the intellectual level of political discussion, I think well of him, but I am not surprised that he was in a minority in his lifetime and that his hopes have not been fulfilled. The area in which he was best known and most criticized, that of education, illustrates the point. His practical educational interventions were mostly admirable; his defense of teachers against their employers, of school expenditure against taxpayers, and of a rational syllabus against bigotry and prejudice was much needed. Since Dewey's practical influence was on the side of liveliness and interest, without encouraging sentimentality and mere anarchy, it was almost entirely to the good; I say "almost" to appease those who think that he cannot escape responsibility for the exaggeration and politicization of his ideas by his admirers at Teachers College and for some resulting neglect of the traditional scholarly virtues.

Dewey's practical activities could be justified on many grounds besides those that he put forward and could be supported by liberals of any philosophical stripe or none. Dewey's own philosophy of education, on the other hand, was most interesting when he struggled to give a picture of the way the school related to the world outside and found himself resorting to strange diagrams to show how it could relate more fruitfully.[2] Interest is not credibility, and I doubt whether the philosophical project makes complete sense. *How* the reproduction within the school of aspects of the larger social whole will make school more intelligible and the wider world eventually more amenable to rational control remains mysterious. One might unkindly call it a form of magical thinking, as though control over a symbolic representation of the outside world inside the classroom will give us control over the world itself. Even on the practical level, respect for the good things he achieved in liberalizing education must be tempered by the recognition that Dewey's emphasis on practicality and his dislike of the concept of "high culture" cannot have done much for the content of education in a country already overcommitted to a narrowly utilitarian view of education and something of a joke to the rest of the world for its dismissal of everything non-American. These, dogmatically stated, are the conclusions I steer toward.

Last Battles

After September 1939 and the outbreak of war in Europe, Dewey did not sit quietly, but he wrote almost nothing directly on the war. Several months earlier, in the spring of 1939, he and Hook were prime movers in establishing the Committee (later Congress) for Cultural Freedom, an anti-Communist, social democratic group of writers and others that swiftly gained the support of large numbers of intellectuals who had previously been members of one or other of the cultural front organizations set up by the Communist party, such as the League of American Writers. Some had long before been alienated by the name-calling and ideological rigidity displayed by Earl Browder, the general secretary of the CPUSA, and especially by his cultural commissar, Mike Gold, the ineffable editor of the *New Masses*.[3] Others had more recently become disillusioned by the way Communist party policy on everything from cooperation with the socialists to the form of the novel changed according to the whims of the Comintern. People like the writers and critics Waldo Frank and Van Wyck Brooks soon forgot they had been fellow travelers, and even Malcolm Crowley, who had staunchly defended the Popular Front in the *New Republic,* saw daylight when the Nazi-Soviet Pact was announced in August 1939. The party obediently abandoned the policy of the popular front for defeatism and an attack on the "second imperialist war" and those whose antifascism was stronger than their faith in Stalin left the party.

The Congress for Cultural Freedom's early history was very different from its postwar cold war history.[4] It was genuinely independent and genuinely social democratic. When it issued its founding statement, the *New Republic* was quick to sneer at it as a refuge for Trotskyites and for a pollyannaish gang that believed "that we have entire liberty in America and none at all in Germany, Italy and Russia." Dewey, who had resigned as a contributing editor of the *New Republic* two years earlier over the Trotsky inquiry, wrote an angry letter pointing out that it was the dangers to *American* cultural freedom that the committee was founded to combat.[5] Dewey was equally angry at the paper's suggestion that the committee was an antisocialist organization and demanded to know whether Norman Thomas was a likely member of any such enterprise. The degree to which Dewey's concerns were with American liberties emerged later that year, a month after war had broken out in Europe. In one of his few remarks that bore directly on American involvement in the war, and the committee's attitude toward it, he renewed his insistence that the United States should steer clear of military involvement in the affairs of Europe. "Resort to military force is a first sure sign that we are giving up the struggle for the democratic way of life, and that the Old World has conquered morally as well as geographically."[6] It was, of course, not from the left that a threat to civil liberties would come if the United States went to war. Dewey was frightened of the threat to American democracy posed by right-wing American nationalism and reactionary Catholicism, and the committee was not the drearily anti-Communist enterprise it became in the 1950s.

Nor was it the cultural arm of the CIA that it became during the cold war, and not only because the CIA was yet to be created; there is every reason to think Dewey would have left any organization that had become such. Hook, who stuck with the congress to the bitter end, when it was revealed that it had long been taking CIA money out of various secret funds, was ready to fight fire with fire; Dewey was not. A readiness to be duped by one's own government was the sort of thing that his criticism of Trotsky's political ethics was written to denounce.[7]

During the first two years of the war in Europe Dewey hardly discussed it publicly. His attitude was a very awkward one, and he must have felt it fairly uncomfortably himself. Westbrook catches the tone nicely when he writes of Dewey's being "perched" between isolationism and intervention.[8] Dewey was not in the strict and narrow sense an isolationist; he was in favor of lend-lease and of American economic assistance for the British Commonwealth, which after June 1940 was fighting Germany single-handedly; he did not believe in a policy of evenhanded abstention from assisting either side or of evenhanded assistance on strictly commercial terms. This was consistent with his view of American neutrality during the Spanish Civil War, and it was in line with Roosevelt's policy.

Nonetheless, Dewey was opposed to military involvement in the war. His reasons were entirely domestic, though one may suspect that a more than residual suspicion of British and French imperialism also played an undeclared part. The only statement he gave the public was a three-paragraph declaration in *Common Sense* in March 1939; the title, "No Matter What Happens—Stay Out," conveys its conclusions well enough but suggests little of its content.

Dewey offered two distinctive reasons why America should stay out. The first was "if the United States is drawn into the next war, we shall have in effect if not in name a fascist government in this country."[9] It was not merely the loss of civil liberties that he feared. He thought that all social progress would come to a halt. "We are forgetting that the years before the last war were a time of growth for a strong and genuine progressivism in this country, and that if its career had not been interrupted we should have made whatever gains have been accomplished in the New Deal much earlier and in a much less costly way."[10] The second was that the United States could not save Europe by fighting, only by strengthening American democratic institutions and habits. To go to war would "destroy the means by which we can be of use to a stricken Europe after the end of its attempt at suicide."[11] It is hard in retrospect not to think that Dewey was silly to argue in this vein, given the sheer horror of what Nazi occupation meant for much of Europe. All the same, we should remember that only after the United States was pitched into the war by the Japanese attack on Pearl Harbor and the German declaration of war that followed did it become clear just how vile Hitler's regime was, that it was bent on exterminating European Jewry and millions of Slavs and Gypsies with them as an act of settled policy.

Dewey was not wholly unrealistic about the prospects for military intervention in 1939 and 1940. Until the German invasion of Russia in June 1941, it was implausible to intervene in Europe: Stalin and Hitler were allies. They had cooperated in dividing Poland between themselves, while Stalin had taken advantage of the opening of the war to snap up the Baltic states and make an unprovoked war on Finland. It seemed to many dispassionate observers that the British would have to sue for what terms they could get and that the United States could not do much about it. This can only have led Dewey to conclude that the situation on the European mainland was beyond rescue and that the best the United States could do was keep out.

Dewey never thought that America should consider a policy of nonresistance. Unlike Russell, who took his consequentialism to the length of arguing that wars of self-defense were often *un*justified and wars of conquest justified, Dewey took the commonsensical view that self-defense was an unchallengeable right, if only because there was no point in telling people not to defend themselves when they would do so regardless. Once the Japanese had attacked Pearl Harbor on December 7, 1941, Dewey took it for granted that America had to see the war through to the end. Even then, there is something faintly absurd about the fact that when he delivered a speech entitled "Lessons from the War—in Philosophy" on the evening of December 7, he plowed ahead with the talk he had written and said of the events of that day only, "I hardly need say that when the arrangements were made for my speaking this evening, and when I prepared my remarks, I need not say that at neither of these dates did I have any idea of what would happen on the day of the evening that I was going to speak. I have nothing, had nothing, and have nothing now to say directly about the war."[12]

John Diggins gives a dramatic account of Dewey's comportment that evening, writing of a distraught and haggard Dewey,[13] but other eyewitnesses suggest that the more surprising thing was Dewey's ability to ignore almost completely the fact that America was now at war. The talk itself reiterated what Dewey had said twenty-five years before in *German Philosophy and Politics:* Americans who thought democracy must return to "spiritual" values in the face of nazism were wrong to contrast the realms of spirit and matter. This was what had infected the Germans, and the result was a ruthless exploitation of technique in the name of the "higher" value of the state and the race. Once America had been attacked, Dewey took it for granted that the country was now a full participant in the war, but he remained silent about its conduct and goals and said nothing about its evolution into a war to make the world safe for democracy—again.

Dewey was still working hard during the war years—that is, from 1942 to 1945, the years of American involvement. He was, for one thing, working with Arthur Bentley on what came out as *Knowing and the Known*. Still, he published almost nothing on politics during the war, and little thereafter. Not all of what he did publish was addressed to matters of the day; for instance, one energetic piece he wrote for *Commentary* in 1948 was concerned to defend the good name of pragmatism generally and of William James in particular against the misguided criticism of Julien Benda.[14] If he had nothing to say about the war itself, he was alert to issues of freedom in the classroom and the university. At the beginning of the war in Europe he wrote a savage little letter attacking Nicholas Murray Butler's suggestion that during wartime students had no right to "academic freedom" and that the university was serving a higher freedom than that of students and faculty. And he wrote another, faintly depressing in tone, to the American Association of University Professors arguing that the overwhelming interest that academics had in the war was an interest in preserving academic freedom.

> There are plenty of persons who will present and who will urge with vigor nationalistic, political, economic and ideological interests of different kinds. It is our business to stand up with at least equal vigor and aggressiveness for the cause of freedom and objectivity of mind to which our profession commits us. These remarks may seem to some aloof from the actual and practical world-scene. But it is this feeling against which these remarks are directed, since they are actuated by the belief that as teachers and scholars we too are soldiers in a cause which is as definitely ours as that of any nation at war in Europe is that of the soldiers who are fighting in its special behalf.[15]

Once again we have to remember that this was in December 1939, when Poland had been swallowed up but the world otherwise experienced a period of "phony war." Dewey must have thought that it was 1915 all over again, not that something new and nastier than before was abroad in the world. It was not so unreasonable to concentrate so hard on the local scene as he did. He took the same line on matters other than the impact of the war. Thus he insisted that it was in order to defend American intellectual life rather than Bertrand Russell in particular that he defended Russell against his Catholic and judicial detractors.

When the war came to America, there was no successor to "What Are We Fighting For?" and the other *New Republic* essays of 1917–19. Dewey's only contribution to clear thinking about the war lay in trying to curb American enthusiasm for Stalin and Stalin's Russia. His view on the alliance with the Soviet Union was simple. The United States had to ally itself with the Soviet Union to defeat Germany—the USSR joined the war against Japan only after the war in Europe was over—but it was unnecessary to fool oneself about the nature of the Soviet regime. It was a vile, totalitarian tyranny, led by a man whose hands were covered with the blood of those who had been his loyal allies for twenty and thirty years before he turned on them and had them judicially murdered.

Having endured the insults and abuse of Communists and fellow travelers throughout 1937 and afterward, when he served on the commission for the defense of Trotsky, Dewey was in no mood to be polite to them in 1942. When the former ambassador to Moscow, Joseph Davies, published his best-selling *Mission to Moscow*, Dewey wrote a long letter to the *New York Times* denouncing it as Stalinist propaganda. He took particular exception to Davies's account of the liquidation of the Old Bolsheviks as a necessary measure of self-defense against Nazi fifth columnists. Dewey's anxiety that casualness about the civil liberties of Russians would make it easier for those who wanted to use the war as an excuse for a curb on *American* civil liberties emerged when he wrote, "To justify the Soviet blood purge to the American people is to justify government actions diametrically opposed to the judicial processes of democracy, with their careful safeguards of the rights of accused persons. To excuse a government terror on any basis is to condone by implication the abolition of all those civil rights which protect the citizens of our democracy from persecution by those in power. It is the most dangerous kind of argument in these times, when democracy is in grave peril, and when Americans are defending it with their treasure and their lives."[16] One of Dewey's better lines was the observation that Stalin had a better appreciation of the limits of cooperation between democracy and totalitarianism than his American admirers did. "Our future would be much more secure than it now appears if we were to emulate his circumspection instead of indulging in the fatuous one-sided love feasts now going on in this country, of which Mr. Davies's book is merely one manifestation among many."[17]

Much as Dewey disliked the book, he hated the film of *Mission to Moscow* a lot worse. He fired off another letter to the *Times*, denouncing its inaccuracies and follies. Several observations scored direct hits. It was, for instance, hard to understand why Davies now said that when he was in Moscow as the U.S. ambassador and could see the trials at first hand, he believed they were simply a way for Stalin to kill off his potential rivals and had only understood them as a legitimate purge of fifth columnists and Nazi sympathizers in June 1941, when he was living in Wisconsin.[18] Dewey also had an easy target when he contrasted Davies's official reports to the State Department describing a cowed and terrified country with the film's picture of Russia as "gay, even festive." One plausible explanation is that the reports were written by Chip Bohlen, who understood the Soviet Union rather well and thought his ambassador was both feeble and ignorant.

The film was defended by Arthur Upham Pope, a noted fellow traveler; Pope made the familiar case for going easy on Stalin: There really had been attempts to bring down the revolution, Stalin really had been insecure, he had been driven to ally himself with Hitler because of the unwillingness of the West to help him earlier, and anyway, films weren't to be held to the standard of strict veracity. More fatally, he observed that in time of war freedom of speech had to be curbed and urged the *Times'* readers to hold their tongues about Stalin's imperfections in order to preserve the alliance against Hitler. Pope's enthusiasm for American restraint in criticizing Russia was, as Dewey dryly observed, not matched by any corresponding restraint in Pope's abuse of Britain and France, which were blamed for everything from Japanese aggression in China to the Moscow trials.[19] Even on the issue where Dewey guessed wrong—he doubted that Stalin meant to join the war against Japan when Hitler had been defeated—Dewey could have claimed a success, since even in 1943 Stalin was putting out peace feelers to Hitler and would have ditched his new allies if he had been able to.

Dewey's political views became steadily more centrist as the war progressed. He wrote less and less on such matters, however. By the war's end he was eighty-six, and even he was getting more tired, if not much less combative. His health had been astonishingly robust until he was eighty; he had then had prostate trouble, cured by surgery in 1943. Eventually, what John Aubrey in describing Hobbes's last years called "great age and naturall decay" began to overtake him.[20] Flu and bronchitis struck more often and were harder to shake off. Traveling became difficult and was confined to two long holidays: Summer vacations were spent in Nova Scotia, where he had had a house at Hubbards ever since the sale of his Long Island farm at the end of the 1920s, and the winter was spent in Key West.

If Dewey drifted gently toward the middle of the political road, he did not quite become a cold war liberal. He never thought the Soviet menace demanded a circling of the wagons around the American status quo. He was solidly anti-Stalinist, but he did not recant the views he had expressed in 1928 and 1929, when he had looked at Soviet education and thought that something vital and novel would grow from the energy and experimental spirit he had seen then. There had been green shoots in those years, and it was Stalin who had blighted them. Once he had taken Stalin's measure, he looked for no progress until death or revolution removed the tyrant. He had always said, and he continued to think, that it would be absurd to expect cooperation with the Soviet Union in postwar Europe, and events proved him right. On the other hand, he was not infected by the postwar American fear of the domestic threat posed by Communists, ex-Communists, fellow travelers, and spies. Unlike Sidney Hook, Dewey saw no reason why Communists should be forbidden to teach in colleges, and he remained as hostile to loyalty oaths as he had been before the war. He was more anxious about the threats to intellectual freedom posed by the cold warriors themselves.

Dewey's objection to totalitarianisms of the left was always a double objection: that they were disgusting in themselves and that they allowed totalitarianisms of the right to thrive. His old antipathies remained firmly in place. The Catholic Church still struck Dewey as a threat to human intelligence and social reform, and he still complained that its emphasis on supernaturalism was a threat to science, and its emphasis on authority a threat to individual liberty.[21] The church's leaders and rank-and-file Catholic intellectuals returned his distaste, as we shall see. Dewey remained an archetypical middle-of-the-road liberal, fighting off enemies to right and left.

In domestic politics this meant that Dewey finally slid into the embrace of the Democratic party. He thought Henry Wallace was virtually a fellow traveler and urged Democrats to vote for Truman in 1948.[22] He defended the American intervention in Korea, stood up for Dean Acheson, and at the same time made it clear that he thought the House Un-American Activities Committee was more of a menace to American civil liberties than to any Communist or ex-Communist who could lie with a straight face. None of this involved deep or complicated argument and was not hard work. Indeed, Dewey spent much of the last dozen years of his life writing prefaces for other people's work and attending or sending messages to dinners arranged in his honor as he passed his eightieth and ninetieth birthdays, collected honorary degrees, or was the guest of honor at celebrations for elderly colleagues, collaborators, and pupils. In fact, he moved gently out of the public eye in these years. It was his philosophical interests that remained undiminished; when he read Russell's *History of Western Philosophy* in 1948, with its slighting account of his work, he was moved to write to his old friend and fellow educationalist Boyd Bode, to tell him how inept a philosopher Russell really was.[23] More constructively he and Arthur Bentley published their curious joint work *Knowing and the Known,* to push along their project for a new way of talking about the world more adequate to the way the world really is.[24]

The book caught the eye of many of the next generation of philosophers partly because of its ideas about semantics, partly because it defended the views about truth that Dewey had advanced in *Logic: The Theory of Inquiry*. Dewey had come to think two scandalous things: One was that truth in the common or garden-variety factual sense was less important than generally thought.

Since the result to be sought was the enrichment of human experience, propositions ought to be assessed for their success in forwarding that end, and this would not always be a matter of their "truth." The other was that the *concept* of truth was unhelpful; it suggested, falsely, that we can peel our thoughts about the world away from the world itself to see whether our thoughts "correspond" to "facts." Dewey thought "warranted assertibility" was a more helpful concept. The two ideas run happily together; "my love is like a red, red rose" and "a carbon atom has twelve electrons" are high on warranted assertibility, but on the strength of very different sorts of warrant. Many of the unpublished typescripts he left when he died show that his thoughts were still running on philosophical first principles rather than everyday politics.

One representative item was a long consideration of Morton White's criticism of his moral philosophy.[25] Dewey, said White, had committed the same mistake as Mill and had confused the *desired* with the *desirable*. Dewey thought the "data" of ethics were our likings and wishings and longings and seemed to be reducing ethical argument to the discussion of what we desired rather than what we *ought* to desire. Dewey's typescript clarifies his theory but offers no novelties—that is, it reiterates the view that *Ethics* laid out as long ago as 1908 and that he elaborated first in *Human Nature and Conduct* and then in *Experience and Nature,* but it sets it out as determinedly and carefully as ever. Dewey thought his critics failed to see how firmly he believed that moral judgment involved *judgment;* moral judgment was not the expression of liking and disliking, or the description of a want, but the expression of considered, reflective, fully informed, and to a degree impersonal liking and disliking.[26] So far removed were moral approval and disapproval from the desires in which they were grounded that it was a mistake to assimilate them. Wholly to detach the desirable from the desired, on the other hand, was equally wrong; we point out the desirable features of whatever we are appraising in order that people should come to desire them, and in so doing can build only on existing desires. This is infinitely far from *collapsing* the desirable into the desired. Such a view has gained increasing favor over the past ten years; Dewey's defense of it, so late in life, showed how unimpaired by the passage of time his ruminative philosophical technique was.

Anyone who expects to see a sudden late flowering of incisiveness will be disappointed. The astonishing thing is how much the same Dewey remained. Some caution is needed in saying this, however, since the way in which he remained the same was in continuing to explore the themes he had started with *Experience and Nature* twenty years before. He thought of rewriting *Experience and Nature* and at the age of ninety-one wrote a new introduction in which he suggested that it was all the same if the word "experience" was replaced with the word "culture." Most people would be startled by the suggestion. It was not so surprising in Dewey. The honorific status that "experience" has in his work means that nobody *has* what Dewey thought of as *an* experience without bringing to bear on the raw materials of an encounter with the world the cultural resources that allow him to turn it into *an* experience. So it was, up to a point, much the same whether we concentrated on how individuals drew on their cultural resources in their encounters with the world or on what the resources were on which individuals could draw.

Domestically Dewey's last few years were quiet and happy. He and Roberta Lowitz Grant married in 1946 and adopted two young Belgian refugees, John, Jr., and Adrienne, who were said to chant, "I have a *good* mother, I have a *good* brother / sister, I have a *good* . . . grandpa." It is perhaps not an irrelevance that Dewey was unusual among educational theorists in liking children so much: Plato had no sympathy for childhood, Locke was unmarried and childless, Rousseau sent his five children to the foundling hospital, where they almost certainly died in infancy, Mill was childless and unkind to his siblings, Russell's advice to parents was that they should take care what sorts of servants they hired to look after their children, and Mme. Montessori had an illegitimate child she had to place for adoption. In such company Dewey comes out rather well. It was while playing with the children in the fall of 1951 that he slipped and broke his hip. He had elaborate pins put in to help it knit; but it refused to mend properly, and after some nine months he suffered an attack of pneumonia that resulted in his death on June 1, 1952. It was appropriate that his funeral took place at the Unitarian Community Church in Manhattan, a church dedicated to a metaphysically uncommitted faith in community.

It is more common than not for a thinker's reputation to collapse after his death; when someone lives as long as Dewey, there is often a sense by the time he dies that he belonged to an older epoch and has become redundant. Dewey's reputation did dwindle, but not quite in that way. Explaining what happened in any detail would be the work of a longer book than this, but there are four aspects of what happened that can be dealt with briefly, and they will serve to open the question of why there has been such a revival of interest in his work. Two of these aspects are the dislike felt for Dewey on the political right, especially on the Catholic right, and the dislike felt on the political left, especially on the Communist or "anti-anti-Communist" left. The two others are the peculiar reputation of progressive education even among liberals and social democrats and the sharp contrast between Dewey's style of philosophy and what became professional philosophy after 1945. These topics interconnect at one obvious place, the hostility of Catholics to Dewey's views on education, but even there we find some curious disconnections: Robert Hutchins pursued to the bitter end his campaign against Dewey's views on education and his own defense of a curriculum of great books and traditional attitudes, while fighting with great courage for the right of a secular, lay, liberal college or university to conduct its own intellectual life unmolested by the censorship of the decaying and drunken Joseph McCarthy on the one hand or the sprightly infant William Buckley on the other.[27] Since conservatives and Catholics hated Dewey across the spectrum, so to speak, we may risk a little repetition of his critics' views on education, especially since the most damaging—that is, the most widely read and most widely believed—charge against Dewey's educational views was laid by an impeccable liberal, the Columbia historian Richard Hofstadter.[28]

Catholic Anathemas

Dewey's battles with the Catholic Church went back to World War I and earlier. He had always opposed state aid to parochial schools and had opposed allowing religious groups to have any part in the public education system, for instance by giving students released time for religious instruction. Dewey's reasons were from the beginning those he always gave: Public education was supposed to concentrate on what united American students, not on what divided them, and to attend to what was rational and empirical, not to what demanded faith in and intuition of the supernatural. His later writings were more offensive. Although the criticism was latent from the beginning, it was once he started thinking in terms of a sharp contrast between the modern, scientific world and all its various antitheses—the ancient world, the medieval world, the world of other and more primitive cultures—that Catholicism as such came to stand for what was most obnoxious in Dewey's eyes. Thus, when he fought one last round of the battle with Robert Hutchins over the condition of higher education, it was as a battle with "medievalism." He regarded Mortimer Adler and Robert Hutchins as fellow travelers working in the interests of Catholic authoritarianism and superstition. This seems decidedly unfair to Hutchins, if not to Adler. Still, when Hutchins and Adler urged the study of classical Greece, Dewey agreed wholeheartedly that a knowledge of intellectual history was an essential part of a liberal education and that modern man needed to know whence he had come—and then refused to draw the conclusions his opponents drew.

Dewey launched two thoughts at his opponents. The first was that we needed to know *about* classical Greece, not to emulate classical Greek education. *It* had been elitist, snobbish, confined to upper-class males whose ability to spend time and energy in intellectual pursuits had depended on the drudgery of women, slaves, and the banausic class. *Our* conception of liberal education was that it must be open to everyone. The second of Dewey's thoughts was that classical Greece had achieved more in philosophy than in its social practice; it had set out ideals of free inquiry, the rational appraisal of evidence, an unconcern with mass opinion, and a distaste for superstition that had been thoroughly lost in medieval Europe. The so-called Dark Ages really were dark ages in Dewey's eyes, and they lasted until Descartes and Galileo liberated science from the toils of superstition. Dewey offered an olive branch to his opponents but promptly snatched it away. Observing that it was common coin that the educational system was overstretched, courses were unintegrated, and the whole process was lacking a persuasive rationale, he went on. "We agree as to absence of unity. We differ profoundly from the belief that the evils and defects of our system spring from excessive attention to what is modern in human civilization—science, technology, contemporary social issues and problems."[29] Of course, Dewey was almost equally anxious to fend off any suggestion that what he wanted was narrowly vocational and in that sense instrumental; his view was that only if science and its achievements were placed at the center of a humanist education would they cease to be "technical and relatively illiberal. . . ."[30]

Dewey was not indulging in unprovoked aggression. New York Catholics had long detested Teachers College and the "Dewey group" of professors there. Later commentators have gone to all lengths to separate Dewey from W. H. Kilpatrick, E. L. Thorndike, and Harold Rugg, but Dewey himself was ready enough to treat an attack on one as an attack on all. He did so, for instance, when Rugg's social science textbooks were pulled out of the Binghamton, New York, schools after a campaign by a combination of forces including the National Association of Manufacturers and the Daughters of the American Revolution, locally aided by Merwin K. Hart, chairman of the New York State Economic Council.[31] Dewey wrote indignantly to the *New York Times,* complaining that schools were to be forbidden to teach anything but a rose-colored picture of the United States; Hart wrote back to insist that the textbooks were biased attempts to propagandize in favor of Soviet economics. All this took place in the spring of 1940 at the height of the row over Russell's appointment at City College, when Dewey was thoroughly fired up against social and economic bigotry.

In the fall of 1940, while tempers were as high as ever, the *Wall Street Journal* and the Catholic University of America joined hands to denounce Teachers College in general and Dewey in particular as promulgators of atheism, communism, a lack of respect for one's elders and betters, and much else besides.[32] One curious feature of the attack was the way American Catholicism, even though church members were overwhelmingly lower-class, mostly recent immigrants, and Democrats into the bargain, had allied itself with the American business world and the ethos of capitalism, free enterprise, and an economic conservatism that in Europe the church had been more wary of. Father James O'Connell, from the Catholic University, announced that Dewey and his friends "for more than three decades have made Teachers College their point of vantage in their attempted destruction of Christian aims and ideals in American education."

It was all Dewey's fault. It was he who "ignores God, the supernatural, religion, the Ten Commandments, the eternal moral law, the soul, immortality, everything, in fact, which is above and beyond the purely empirical realm of existence." Dewey would have had to plead guilty to denying the supernatural; it was a central feature of *A Common Faith* that it did just that. On immortality he made only one remark in 1929 in answer to a newspaper inquiry into the beliefs of assorted thinkers and writers. As a matter of "continued existence," he said, the question of immortality belonged to science and presumably to psychical research. What he had so far seen of psychical research was not impressive.[33] It was an odd answer for Dewey to give; one might have expected him to fall back on Spinoza's claim in his *Ethics* that "the free man thinks of nothing less than death" and admit that this was the only triumph over death that reason can afford us.

It was not only Dewey's atheism that came under fire but his patriotism that was impugned as well. Thomas Woodlock of the *Wall Street Journal* gave a quick sketch of Dewey's un-Americanism. He and his allies "deny God the Creator; they deny the special dignity of human personality. They deny the equality of man in the possessions of that personality. They deny liberty as the right of the human person. They deny the first purpose of government to be the protection of human rights. They affirm the absolute supremacy of 'society' over the person. And they do all this in the name of 'democracy.' " In short, their views were incompatible "with the fundamental tenets on which American liberties are founded."[34] This was all part of the knockabout of politics, and Dewey does not seem to have been unduly bothered—or inclined to turn the other cheek. The intellectual level of such attacks was low, and their interest is only that they make one wonder why that particular set of complaints seemed plausible. After all, Dewey was simultaneously attacked by the friends of the Communist party because he was so hostile to the "Sovietization" of American social and intellectual life, denounced by his own friends for being too accommodating to the religiously minded, and denounced by assorted fellow travelers because he was so rigid about the priority of human rights over convenient alliances.

Among Dewey's traditionalist critics Robert Hutchins was one of the few who managed to say something intellectually to the point, before he lost his temper and slid off into silliness. In an essay in the *Christian Century* Hutchins resurrected Randolph Bourne's complaint that pragmatism was a philosophy of means and bereft of a philosophy of ends: Dewey's appeals to "scientific method" would make sense *if* there were already substantial agreement on ends and the only question were how to achieve them. But Dewey himself, said Hutchins, said there was no such agreement. What Dewey did not see was that science could not produce that agreement. That was the task of religion and moral philosophy. Science, philosophy, democracy, and the expansion of the human psyche were certainly great goods; what Hutchins denied was that science could show this to be true. "The difference between us and Mr. Dewey is that we can defend Mr. Dewey's goals and Mr. Dewey cannot. All he can do is say he is for them. He cannot say why, because he can appeal only to science, and science cannot tell him why he should be for science or for democracy or for human ends."[35] This was a real consideration, if not very novel. But by the end of his essay Hutchins had succumbed once more to irritation: "Men can hardly be blamed if they prefer the faith of their fathers to the monstrous faith of John Dewey."[36] "Monstrous" is very odd.

Hutchins was on safer ground when he complained that Dewey's obsession with the removal of dualisms hindered clear thought; to see science and philosophy as distinct disciplines did not in the least mean that one ought not to teach both in a university or that they should be taught without reference to each other. It only meant they tackled different questions in different ways. Hutchins was right that Dewey never *quite* explained what was wrong with that view. One crux lay in a buried premise. Hutchins thought philosophy was an authoritative body of truths, to be approached reverently by the student and teacher alike. Philosophy had to partition the universe with science, each getting its share. Dewey thought of philosophy as methodology and as "the criticism of social criticisms," and it is less clear that the division of labor Hutchins has in mind makes sense in such an account. They saw science differently, too. Hutchins thought of it as the body of authoritative truths that scientists at any given time declare their discipline to have established; Dewey thought of it as a way of life, a procedure, a method of investigating consequences. A "scientific ethics" for Dewey was no more than an approach to ethics that took consequences seriously, as well as the possibility of looking to other consequences than those we began with. It did not mean what Hutchins thought it met: that we could somehow derive our ethics from physics and chemistry.

Deeper than their visible disagreements was a temperamental disagreement that Dewey's *Quest for Certainty* had set out years before. Dewey urged his readers to learn to live with uncertainty and without a premature desire for finality; Hutchins's slogan "[T]eaching implies knowledge, knowledge implies Truth, and Truth is One" was appropriate for the opposite camp. After Dewey's death, and the election of Dwight D. Eisenhower to preside over a decade of unparalleled American self-satisfaction, the fight died down. Not everyone wished to let things rest. One representative item is Paul Crosser's exercise in misunderstanding *The Nihilism of John Dewey;* it has little intellectual interest but shows quite neatly how rapidly philosophical attacks on Dewey slid into political complaint. Crosser's avowed objections were to the slipperiness of Dewey's key concepts—"experience," "situation," and so on—objections that are not novel but are fair enough. Crosser then complains that slipperiness begets an intolerable relativism, a far less plausible objection. The charge of relativism in turn leads to a denunciation of Dewey's dislike of traditional education, and the familiar foolishness breaks out.

Crosser concluded that Dewey's "outcry 'How many students, for example, were rendered callous to ideas, and how many lost the impetus to learn because of the way in which learning was experienced by them?' was really a proposal to have ideas banned from the classroom. . . ."[37] To reach that position, one has to believe that "ideas" are what Hutchins thought they were—namely, the authoritatively enforced teachings of a church or a culture. Dewey's view was that it was rote learning that drove ideas out of the classroom and that if we wanted ideas, we ought to teach children how to think. It is significant that Crosser believed that Dewey's failings resulted from an attachment to John Stuart Mill's empiricism; as a view of Dewey's allegiances it is perfectly mad, but it suggests the extent to which Dewey's critics saw his vices as those of secular, humanist, empiricist liberalism in general, and they could not distinguish the tree from the wood.

More Conservative Complaints

The prize for wild misunderstanding from the religiously minded right goes to that astonishing book Russell Kirk's *The Conservative Mind.* Kirk may or may not have read Dewey, but the two pages of vituperation dedicated to Dewey's memory make about as many mistakes about Dewey's ideas as could well be crammed into the space. Their interest once more lies not so much in their erroneous character as in their revelation of what Dewey had come to stand for.

The belligerent expansive and naturalistic tendencies of the era found their philosophical apologist in John Dewey. No philosopher's style is more turgid; but Dewey's postulates, for all that, are simple and quite comprehensive. He commenced with a thoroughgoing naturalism, like Diderot's and Holbach's, denying the whole realm of spiritual values: nothing exists but physical sensation, and life has no aims but physical satisfaction. He proceeded to a utilitarianism which carried Benthamite ideas to their logical culmination, making material production the goal and standard of human endeavor; the past is trash, the future unknowable, and the present the only concern of the moralist. He propounded a theory of education derived from Rousseau, declaring that the child is born with 'a *natural* desire to do, to give out, to serve,' and should be encouraged to follow his own bent, teaching being simply the opening of paths. He advocated a sentimental egalitarian collectivism with a social dead-level its ideal; and he capped this structure with Marxist economics, looking forward to a future devoted to efficient material production for the satisfaction of the masses, a planners' state. Every radicalism since 1789 found its place in John Dewey's system; and this destructive intellectual compound became prodigiously popular, in short order, among that distraught crowd of the semi-educated and among people of more serious pretensions who found themselves in a withered world that Darwin and Faraday had severed from its roots. Intensely flattering to the presumptuousness of the modern mind, thoroughly contemptuous of authority, Dewey's works were a mirror of twentieth-century discontent; and the picture of the Utilitarian future toward which Dewey led the rising generation was not immediately repellent to a people who had subjected themselves to the lordship of sensation. Veneration was dead in Dewey's universe; indiscriminate emancipation was cock of the walk. This was the imperialistic craving of America and the twentieth century given a philosophic mask.[38]

It is not very interesting that this is wrong in every philosophical particular: that Dewey was antiutilitarian, hostile to Marxist economics, a naturalist but *not* a materialist in the fashion of Holbach, the promoter rather than the destroyer of spiritual values, and so on indefinitely. It is more interesting that Dewey was so much the emblem of an ideal of progress for which American conservatives had a visceral loathing. There *is* a great divide between the consciousness of a writer like Dewey and that of a sentimental conservative imbued with a real hatred of the modern world like Russell Kirk. Nor is the difference wholly in Dewey's favor. And perhaps that matters more than a pedantic accuracy.

The conflict between those who believe that the phenomenal world is self-sufficient and those who believe it is radically incomplete cuts across political divisions. For example, Dewey was sharply criticized by Reinhold Niebuhr for not taking the doctrine of original sin seriously enough. This irritated him a great deal. He and Niebuhr were politically on the same side; they both were members of the Congress for Cultural Freedom, and Niebuhr had joined in the defense of Trotsky. Niebuhr held, however, just those views that Dewey had described as the cause of the "inward laceration" of his youth. Human beings were radically sinful. Their motives were so mixed that few of us could ever be sure whether we had acted well for bad reasons, whether kindness masked pride and contempt, and so on. Politics was essentially a realm of impure motives, and Niebuhr's *Moral Man and Immoral Society* preached a spectacularly deflationary kind of progressivism: We must struggle to achieve justice while not fooling ourselves about the likelihood of achieving much of it. Dewey struck Niebuhr as shallow, unable to confront the depth of evil in the world, unwilling to face the doubleness of the human heart. Dewey could hardly see what Niebuhr was talking about. It seemed to him that Niebuhr clung to a Protestant obsession with sin that he had no need of and in whose intellectual foundations he had long ceased to believe.[39]

This was where Dewey and his opponents ceased to communicate. Dewey thought the world was self-sufficient; it posed no cosmic problem, other than that of emancipating ourselves from the habit of thinking it did. There is in Dewey a strain of cosmic optimism, a confidence that the world we live in needs no further support and no further justification than it receives as we live our everyday lives. C. E. Ayres described Dewey as the "Master of the Commonplace" in an admiring 1938 article in the *New Republic*. He remarked on Dewey's success in banishing "Awful Powers" from his mind. "[W]e might argue that whenever science does penetrate the unknown the newly discovered territory always turns out to be exactly like our own backyard. But for some reason we never do. That takes genius, Dewey's kind of genius, a special affinity for the commonplace. Most people are still sure, in spite of a thousand contrary demonstrations, that Mystery lies just beyond the latest scientific fence."[40] The "commonplace" here is an interesting idea since it does not mean "what everyone already knows"; rather the thought is that Dewey—for all his talk of "natural piety" and his fondness for Coleridge, Wordsworth, and Emerson—wanted to say, as others had before him, that appearances do not deceive, that the world is as it seems to be, and that there is no deep mystery at the heart of existence. It does not take much imagination on the part of anyone deeply committed to a traditional religious perspective to see Dewey's attitude as a hubris inviting retaliation from the "Awful Powers" so slighted. Anyone who thought that modern American society displayed an extreme cultural arrogance, a feeble sense of the limitations of human nature, and few resources to deal with the inevitable disappointments of human life might well think Dewey was both a symptom and a cause of the trouble.

An amusing feature of Kirk's complaints is that they so mirror those of the far left. The orthodox Communist view was that pragmatism was American capitalism and imperialism reduced to ideological disguise. George Novack wrote *Pragmatism versus Marxism* as late as the early 1970s to argue one last time that pragmatism was the ideology of bourgeois capitalist liberal democracy.[41] It was not only orthodox Marxists who said as much. We have already seen that as far back as 1925 Dewey was irritably defending himself, Peirce, and James against Russell's cheap gibes about pragmatism and American capitalism. We cannot *entirely* blame Russell; when writers who were commonly thought of as fellow-traveling pragmatists, such as Justice Holmes, defended freedom of speech in the idiom of "the marketplace of ideas," it was not just the critics of pragmatism who thought that the philosophers' ideal of truth had been sacrificed to the pragmatists' concept of "success" in a pretty down-to-earth sense. After Dewey's decisive swing away from the sympathy with the Soviet Union that he had felt after his visit of 1928, he was always condemned by Marxists as a bourgeois lackey and an apologist for the Americanization of the world.

Dewey's emphasis on the connection of the world of work and the world of the school has also continued to be assailed by the left in much the same way as it is by the conservatives. Dewey was accused of reducing working education to a crude vocational training designed to turn out docile workers in capitalist enterprises. What is curious is how few critics made the more plausible and in many ways more damning complaint that although Dewey insisted every time he discussed the subject that this was exactly what he did not have in mind and that the object of vocational education in his account of it was to *humanize* the subjects that people needed to know in order to fit into the working world, he never said how it was to be done and never understood how easily his views would be vulgarized into the utilitarian doctrines he deplored. Critics were not quick to point out that Dewey accepted the common assumption—itself very challengeable—that there were many children who were not intellectually inclined and for whom "book learning" was unattractive—and thus himself seemed to accept the familiar division between vocational and nonvocational education while protesting that he did not accept it in its present form.

Leftish Objections

The middle-of-the-road American left largely forgot Dewey until the 1960s. Then the most interesting criticism of his views was offered by Christopher Lasch in *The New Radicalism in America* and a little later in *The Agony of the*

American Left.[42] Lasch got Dewey in the right place in the political spectrum, seeing him as a liberal of the same stripe as Herbert Croly and Richard T. Ely, though not with *exactly* their allegiances.[43] However, Lasch accused the whole group of espousing a politics that would make the world safe for the emerging corporation. The key notion that Lasch seized on was that of social control through education. "[T]he new liberalism advocated by Edward A. Ross, Herbert Croly, Richard T. Ely, Newton D. Baker, and even by Jane Addams and John Dewey sought not so much to democratize the industrial system as to make it run more efficiently." The conclusion Lasch came to would have astonished both Dewey and his antagonists on the right: "Manipulative and managerial, twentieth century liberalism has adapted itself without difficulty to the corporation's need to soften conflicts and to reconcile the apparently irreconcilable forces—capital and labor, bureaucratic efficiency and personal intimacy, the life of the production line and the life of the spirit—to which it has given rise."[44] The obvious objection to this is that it is too sweeping to be plausible, and in the case of Jane Addams, whose allegiances were more Tolstoyan than Taylorist, just silly.

Dewey's case is less clear-cut than Jane Addams's, but Lasch's critique is a nice example of how Dewey looks when he is read with certain preconceptions. The 1950s and 1960s were the years of David Riesman's *The Lonely Crowd* and William H. Whyte's *The Organization Man*. Those of us who got our education from such sources all believed that Americans were "other-directed," manipulated by social forces which they did not understand, conformists with no inner resources with which to lead their own lives. It was easy to believe that the ideology of "social control" had triumphed. These were also the years of a search for consensus—or "The End of Ideology"—when it was easy to imagine that everyone who talked the language of social efficiency must have meant that democracy should be supplanted by the bureaucratic management of a capitalist welfare state. Critics would have had a case if they had only complained that Dewey was so unclear about what he was after that the manipulators, indoctrinators, and inegalitarians who were intent on subverting his vision of education and replacing it by the production of a docile work force had an easier time than they ought. That is a plausible objection. But the idea that Dewey set out to provide an ideology for the modern capitalist corporation boggles the mind, and the idea that he sacrificed democracy for the sake of efficiency is bizarre.

The criticisms we have considered thus far rest on a detestation of Dewey's entire world view. Dewey's atheistic and destructive philosophy entailed for one class of critic that Dewey's educational theories are wickedly atheistic and destructive; his supposed advocacy of an ethics and politics of "control" entailed for another class of critic that Dewey must have intended education to mold the passive beneficiaries of "corporate liberalism." The supposed educational disasters attendant on "Deweyism" are explained in terms of a defective underlying philosophy, and in both cases the obvious retort is that the critic is wrong about both the philosophy and the theory of education.

It is worth turning briefly to one last complaint against Dewey's educational views from a friendlier direction and from a critic who does not call into question Dewey's philosophical views. Indeed, this is a critique that captures very well the anxiety that Dewey's ideas can induce in a friendly reader. Richard Hofstadter's *Anti-intellectualism in America* argues at length that Dewey's contribution to education in the United States was to render it anti-intellectual. I have some sympathy with this complaint. There is a view of education that is "intellectualist" in a tough sense; what it values is the promotion of sheer cleverness and the inculcation of enough factual and theoretical raw material for a developing student to employ his cleverness on, and it is quite true that Dewey was wholly hostile to this view of education. I am not, though I would not wish to impose it on everyone. To wish for such education to be offered even to some children means that we must reject at least some of Dewey's moral and social vision, perhaps rather a lot. We shall find ourselves differing from Dewey over the goods and bads of a more competitive classroom or a more selective higher education system. We may also quarrel over the possibility of a wholly democratic culture. A taste for intellectual fierceness is likely to coincide with a belief in an elite culture—not a belief in snobbery but at least a readiness to recognize a cultural aristocracy. Dewey's antipathy to the distinction between high and low culture thus comes under threat, as I think it must and as Dewey very much thought it ought not.

This does not threaten social democratic politics, though it may well alter our view of their value. If we are anxious about how to maintain a distinctively "high" culture in a modern industrial society without creating an educational and cultural class system defined by the different esteem in which different cultural allegiances are held, we must be anxious about how to reconcile classlessness and high culture. We need not sit paralyzed before this tension; one way out is to give government—not "the state" but public agencies of many different kinds—resources for promoting high culture so that its enjoyment does not depend on high income, high managerial status, years of higher education, and access to corporate entertainment budgets. In this respect every European country save Great Britain does much better than the United States, and even Great Britain does better.

All this is to run ahead of the argument that *Anti-intellectualism in America* made when it was published in 1962. Hofstadter's book is a wonderfully enlightening and entertaining essay in social and intellectual history. Its concern was with the way an appeal to "democracy" has resulted in what others have called "the dumbing down of America" in religion, politics, and education. Hofstadter's account of American education at all levels complains of the neglect of the academic side of education in favor of practical training on the one hand and "life adjustment" on the other. Dewey, of course, talked much of practical training and much of adjustment and thus seems squarely in Hofstadter's sights. It is ironic that the emblematic figure on the other side of the divide is Dewey's friend and mentor William T. Harris; Harris, who was both a Hegelian philosopher and a school superintendent, fought a losing battle both in St. Louis and as U.S. commissioner for education for "mind culture"—that is to say, for the creation and strengthening of an academic high school curriculum.[45] As Hofstadter observed, the terms of the argument between Harris and his opponents were the same a century ago as they were in 1962. Nor has much changed since 1962. On the one hand stood those who thought the aim of education was to get the child to master an intellectual discipline; on the other, those who thought of the "needs" of the child. Hofstadter's enthusiasm for what came to be called life adjustment as an educational goal can be gauged from his quip "Life adjustment educators would do anything in the name of science except encourage children to study it."[46]

Unlike the complaints from the right, Hofstadter's complaints against Dewey are delicately and carefully put. They are not that Dewey set out to encourage the expulsion of academic subjects from the high school curriculum—Dewey had almost nothing to say about high schools—or that Dewey was himself an anti-intellectualist. Rather Dewey made the first fatal step by putting into circulation a romantic and Rousseauist conception of the child and the child's growth as the be-all and end-all of education and then more fatally by erecting a framework—the obsessive harping on "growth" that we saw earlier—that other people would clothe with the ideas of "life adjustment." Lawrence Cremin had already argued that the standard complaints against Dewey ought rather to have been directed against W. H. Kilpatrick, but even Cremin had admitted that "however tortuous the intellectual line from *Democracy and Education* to the pronouncements of the Commission on Life Adjustment, that line can be drawn." Hofstadter went on to say, "That it is fact an unduly tortuous line one may be permitted to doubt."[47] Hofstadter saw what others also observed: that the awkwardness of Dewey's exposition of his ideas suggests some real gaps and difficulties in the ideas themselves. When these gaps had been filled by people with clearer, if cruder, ideas than Dewey's, the direction in which what one might call the theory-as-received was pushed was toward the view that the task of education was to elicit from the child the naturally valuable characteristics that traditional education cramped but that progressive education would turn to social use.

There is a problem even with this view, however. It implies two rather contradictory complaints. The complaint against life adjustment is a complaint against a manipulative conception of education; the complaint against Rousseauian romanticism is a complaint against an excessively liberationist conception. Of course, Dewey might have held two firmly opposed views; people often do. Yet it seems unlikely, considering his emphatic distancing of himself from both. Life adjustment was a movement that proposed, as the name suggested, to send children into the world ready to fit in with the mores of

1950s American middle-class life. Hence the proliferation of high school classes in how to get on with other people and the obsession with personal hygiene and conventional political loyalties that marked classes in health and civics.[48] Nobody thought Dewey wanted to promote that sort of thing. It was politically bland, if not in an orthodox sense conservative, and its democratic pretensions were nil. Indeed, it was a plausible target for Christopher Lasch's complaints against education as a means of social control since it took the status quo for granted and thought of education as a way of teaching children to "go along to get along"; its values are consumer-oriented, and its occupational aspirations limited. The romantic, Rousseauist vision was quite different. It protected the child against society and tried—at any rate Rousseau's imaginary experiment in *Émile* tried—to produce a child who would be a good citizen of an ideal state but otherwise entirely self-reliant. It was, so far as Rousseau was concerned, an education of counteradjustment. There is much to be said against Rousseau's project, too, but the only point that matters is that even Dewey was unlikely to have subscribed simultaneously to the extreme versions of the oversocialized and antisocialized visions of education.

What is the underlying difficulty? It is that Dewey relied on something much too like the idea of a preexisting harmony between human nature and democracy. "To believe that Dewey's synthesis was successful required a certain credulity about the pre-established harmony between child nature and democratic culture which not everyone could share."[49] That seems to me to be almost right. Only to the extent that it attributes to Dewey an excessively fixed picture of "human nature" as displayed in the child is it not right. Dewey did not share the sentimental enthusiasm for childish innocence that his Chicago colleague Francis Parker did, nor did he share the much more interesting liking for all stages of child development that his teacher Stanley Hall possessed; Hall was years ahead of his time in thinking that the adolescent preoccupation with sex was wonderful and ought to be encouraged rather than subdued. Dewey was more nearly vulnerable to the charge that he was always looking to the ends or goals of education and left little room for the pleasures of any particular stage of it. Even the passages from *The School and Society* that Hofstadter rightly cites to show how ready Dewey was to let the child's *social* development go on for a very long time before particular academic subjects were taught to him do not emphasize a *child*-centered education so much as a *social*-centered child.

It is, then, a fair complaint against Dewey that when he wrote *Democracy and Education,* he allowed "democracy" to act as an all-inclusive goal of the educational process and "growth" to act as an all-inclusive moral end in such a way as to blur serious and difficult problems—such as how much mathematics we can teach the average child, and how painlessly, or how we can trade the benefits of early specialization against a broad curriculum, and so generally on. Was this anti-intellectual? In the sense that as between the defenders of the mastery of an existing discipline as a first educational requirement and their opponents Dewey is with the opponents, yes. In other ways it is a harder call. Hofstadter cites Dewey's student and colleague John Herman Randall, Jr., as the author of the complaint that Dewey's attitude to history and to the history of philosophy was philistine, and it is true that Dewey treats anything describable as "past thought" with a certain coldness.

The explanation is not hard to find, however. In the first place, Dewey's rhetoric was always situational. He wrote against what he supposed was the contemporary exaggeration that most needed to be combated. It was not the ideas of Thomas Aquinas that he deplored but Robert Hutchins's attempt to fix them once and for all as the touchstone of higher education in Chicago and everywhere else. It was not in defense of the view that children came "trailing clouds of glory" that he wrote but against an extreme reliance on rote learning. Considering the extent to which his opponents treated traditional philosophy as a form of Holy Writ, it was not surprising that Dewey comes across as an iconoclast, even though a look at the syllabuses of the courses he taught shows the extent to which he also taught out of a tradition. The second crucial point is that Dewey always emphasized the *present* use of materials that might be past, present, future, or entirely hypothetical. Plato was important not as a repository of fixed, dead truth but as a living interlocutor. Dewey's intellectual style is "antimonumental" rather than "presentist" or "antipast."

One might plausibly compare Dewey's views on the history of philosophy to his views on art: In both fields he was hostile to what one might call museum culture. Ideas were not to be hung on the walls, mummified, set apart to be approached with a reverence that most spectators would have to fake. Paintings were to be enjoyed; ideas were to be rethought. It remains true that Dewey was not good at simply *displaying* the kind of disinterested pleasure in high culture that critics like Hofstadter and myself would like to encourage in the young, and it remains true that he did not possess the intellectual high spirits that make reading Russell such a pleasure, no matter how abstract the topic, and whose absence leaves Dewey relying entirely on the reader's sympathy with what he is saying. But one may be more inhibited than Dewey and a very much less sprightly writer than he without having to plead guilty to charges of anti-intellectualism.

The Collapse of His Philosophical Influence

Dewey's philosophical style became unfashionable some years before he died. In Britain, Russell and Moore had made idealism unfashionable before World War I; pragmatism was represented by the lone figure of F. C. S. Schiller, who eventually moved to the United States.[50] The impact of Ludwig Wittgenstein after the war was yet another influence that strengthened the analytical strain in British philosophy, and when philosophers took an interest in the history of their subject, it was commonly in writers like Hume or in Aristotle's delicate analysis of the beliefs of commonsensical people. In the United States this process lagged by about thirty years. It was not until the émigré philosophers who had been driven out of Germany and Austria reached the United States in the 1930s that the analytical strain began to dominate the scene. "Dominate" is the crucial term. Americans educated in the graduate schools of the 1920s had already come to think that the new formal logic was an indispensable tool of analysis and that the philosophy of science and semantic analysis were the two central subjects in philosophy.

From the beginning, Americans contributed disproportionately to the development of logic. They were reinforced when the former members of the Vienna Circle arrive in the United States, in exile from Germany and Austria. Once Rudolfh Carnap and Hans Reichenbach, along with Herbert Feigl, and Carl Hempel were installed in the United States, the philosophical profession turned toward the logical empiricism that dominated postwar philosophy. The history of American philosophy is not our topic here. The fact that until the end of the 1930s "process philosophies" like Dewey's and Whitehead's remained part of the mainstream, however, does something to explain how Dewey had a much longer career than one can imagine him having had in Britain and why he was not earlier demolished by analytically minded Young Turks.[51]

After he died, his influence waned. One reason was purely professional. Dewey's philosophy is unsuitable for graduate education. It is very difficult to tell whether someone is doing good and interesting work in the Deweyan mode, but once philosophy became a subject that was taught in graduate schools to would-be professional philosophers, it was essential that it was gradable by teachers in some more or less objective fashion. Dewey himself observed that postwar philosophy seemed to be concerned only with technique or its own history. He thought this was part of a general failure of intellectual nerve, but it may also have reflected the fact that it is much easier to evaluate students as technicians or historians than as purveyors of the hard-to-characterize wisdom that Dewey offered.

The thought that what Dewey did was not "professional philosophy" has been challenged. One of the liveliest of recent commentators, Cornel West, argues in *The American Evasion of Philosophy* that Dewey cannot be invoked as an ally against the "professionalization" of philosophy. Dewey never spoke out against the tenure system, the proliferation of learned journals, or any other elements of the apparatus of academic philosophy. James, on the other hand, often expressed his doubts about the university as a factory for the manufacture of disciplines.[52] This is a low blow and anyway misses the point. Dewey never had much to say about universities at all, other than to fear that if the foundations were laid in a bad system of primary and secondary education, "higher" education would hardly be an impressive undertaking either. (He was not alone in this; Russell said the same.) The question is not whether Dewey found himself happily at home in a university like Columbia—considering his dislike of President Nicholas Murray Butler, it is hard to believe that he was strongly attached to Columbia qua Columbia—but whether his conception of philosophy lent itself to the characteristic enterprise of graduate education, the transmission of the technical skills that are the arcana of a discipline. The decisive point remains that Dewey practiced in the nineteenth-century mode of philosopher-as-sage, not philosopher-as-technician.

By the time he died, that style was obsolete. The work of the later Wittgenstein had been transmitted mostly by oral tradition but was increasingly the object of passionate attention. Students who wanted a philosophy more "relevant" than the diet provided by analytical philosophy took up mainland Europe rather than their own inheritance: Sartre's and Heidegger's existentialism attracted some; the Frankfurt School's mix of Hegelian philosophy and Marxist cultural analysis attracted others. Indeed, a fascinating aspect of the United States viewed from the other side of the Atlantic was the way in which "Continental philosophy" made little or no headway among philosophers in Britain, but a great deal in the United States. British theologians were more interested than their secular colleagues, however, and in the United States also it was what one might indifferently call its theological or its antitheological cast of mind that was so attractive. The combination of forces from the analytical and disengaged side with forces from the engaged and antianalytical side exposed an obvious weakness in pragmatism. As Richard Rorty has said, it was "neither hard enough for the atheists nor soft enough for the aesthetes, neither atheistical enough for descendants of Tom Paine nor transcendental enough for descendants of Emerson, a philosophy for trimmers." Speaking of the sudden decline of pragmatism in general, Rorty goes on to say, "It was as if pragmatism had been crushed between Tillich and Carnap, the upper and the nether millstones."[53] What happened within and without the academy was very different; academic philosophy became increasingly technical and analytic, while the politically engaged audience that would before the war have read *Art as Experience* or *Freedom and Culture* now turned to Sartre or Adorno or Marcuse.

His Reputation Revived

The revival of Dewey's reputation over the past fifteen years has been uneven. It has not been a revival of one thing only or of one aspect of Dewey's work, and this is not the place for a full-scale survey. This book's attention to Dewey has been highly selective, and so is this conspectus of what his admirers admire. In any event, admiration of Dewey's work is less important than the revival of a "Deweyan" style of philosophy (I shall not say "moral" or "social" or "political" philosophy, just because what comes with the revival is a refusal to draw lines between subdisciplines in the places where they have been drawn for forty years). One cause of both the revival of an interest in Dewey and a revival of a Deweyan style of philosophy has been the failure of the logical empiricist program and the petering out of the cognate program of "linguistic analysis."

As Rorty has remarked, at the end of every blind alley we seem to find Dewey. I turn my attention first to Dewey's reputation among academic philosophers, then to his adoption as a hero of postmodernist cultural analysis. This is no narrowly academic subject. During the "culture wars" of the 1980s, it seemed that every Republican politician had suddenly acquired an opinion on deconstruction, the role of a literary canon in political life, and the destruction of traditional virtue that would follow the dissemination of French and German social and cultural theory. Secondly, I take up what has been called the communitarian turn in recent political argument; here Dewey has often been invoked as a critic of a narrowly individualist and self-centered obsession with individual rights and even more often lurks in the background of arguments that are decidedly "Deweyan." Once more, these are anything but narrowly academic; President Clinton presented himself to the American people as a "New Democrat," but New Democrats strikingly resemble old Deweyan Democrats. Thirdly, I say something about recent attempts to give religion a proper place in a secular politics, not in the sense of attempts by fundamentalist Christians to stir up opposition to abortion, or to reinstate prayer in schools, but in the sense of attempts by nonsectarians to persuade us that a decent politics must rest on a religious faith of some kind. Lastly, I say a very little about the state of educational debate forty years after Dewey's death and end with what I think the strengths and weaknesses of Dewey's "American Creed" to be.

Even in fields where Dewey's reputation faded quickest, such as the philosophy of science, something closer to his naturalism has returned. When Dewey died, philosophers wanted to use the techniques of formal logic to analyze the nature of scientific laws, in the hope of giving a formal account of how evidence supports a theory and how observations verify or falsify a hypothesis. This program has increasingly been abandoned, and when not abandoned, it has been supplemented by a more sociological or "naturalistic" account of the practice of scientists. Philosophers have increasingly left it to scientists to set their own standards of respectability and have turned, as Dewey did, to discussing scientific practice as a way of life. There have been some interestingly "un-Deweyan" results. The work of T. S. Kuhn, by self-description a historian of science but one whose work has been taken up with a vengeance by philosophers and social scientists, suggested that Dewey was quite right to emphasize the *social* character of the natural sciences; but the argument of Kuhn's short bombshell of an essay *The Structure of Scientific Revolutions* appeared to be that the scientific community behaved more like a totalitarian society or a particularly intolerant church than anything one would want to set standards in everyday life. Young scientists were socialized into seeing the world in the light of what Kuhn called a dominant "paradigm," not by dispassionate argument but by brainwashing and intimidation. When scientists changed any substantial theory, they did so by lurching irrationally into a new world view in a process more akin to religious conversion than to anything Dewey would have cared for.[54] Kuhn subsequently insisted that he had meant nothing of the sort and that his rhetorical flourishes had been misunderstood; all he had meant—in a more nearly Deweyan spirit—was that there is no such thing as an unmediated, asocial encounter with nature or reality and that theorists of the scientific process should do justice to the social factors in the creation and testing of large and striking theories.[55]

This move is "Deweyan" rather than much influenced by Dewey himself, but it is part of the movement of ideas that he contributed to. The view that philosophy provides, or at least seeks, the "foundations" of knowledge, which is perhaps the oldest view of the discipline, cannot withstand the unkind question of whether we must wait for the philosopher to endorse what the physicist or chemist (or historian or classicist) has done. If I were to condemn the physics of my colleagues in the physics department, I should rightly be ignored. It is then hard to say quite what the philosopher is supposed to be doing. He can hardly be in the business of telling people in *less* contentious disciplines than his own how to do their job. Dewey's conception of philosophy as cultural criticism then becomes attractive. It is not one of the physicist's professional concerns to step back and reflect on the place of physics in modern culture, but somebody ought to do it. The same thought animates the discussion of the relations between almost any special discipline and its exploration by philosophers. Philosophy does not award certificates of intellectual respectability but explores the way different kinds of encounter with the world relate to one another.

In yet more technical fields of philosophy, such as the analysis of meaning and of the way our mental states relate to the world, more nearly Deweyan views have reappeared. Donald Davidson and those he has influenced deny that it is the task of sentences to "correspond" to facts, while agreeing that the point of speaking at all is to say something about the world. Our thinking as a whole is constrained by the world, but not in a point-to-point fashion. Modern "holism" is informed by formal logic and relies on the formalization of ordinary language to make it amenable to theoretical explication—all more nearly in the analytical tradition than in that of Dewey. As a thoroughly technical subject it meets the need for teachability and susceptibility to objective assessment that made Dewey's ideas less congenial to a profession so involved in graduate education. Yet it is naturalistic in the Deweyan mode and oddly reminiscent of its buried ancestor.

W. V. O. Quine took a similarly "holistic" view of meaning as early as the 1950s without turning away from formalism and modern logical theory. Like Dewey, he abandoned the idea that thoughts picture or represent the world, and he loosened the idea of truth, so that what became important was the utility of a whole skein of ideas, not one sentence's worth of truth or falsity at a time, and he has more recently acknowledged the similarity. The difference from Dewey is just as striking; Dewey was unwilling to saddle philosophers with any one story about what the fundamental constituents of the world might be, while Quine said they are what physics says they are. All the same, there is an interesting and curious affinity in the way Quine attacked the "dogmas of empiricism" from an empiricist standpoint, as Dewey had done years before.

Showing affinities between Dewey's work and recent technical philosophy makes Dewey respectable but not exciting. Making him exciting has been the project of Richard Rorty, who has recruited Dewey as one of the prophets of postmodernism. To find Dewey in the company of Ludwig Wittgenstein and Martin Heidegger, which is where Rorty puts him, gives many readers a jolt, but it is surprisingly plausible. It is at least true that all three rejected the idea that philosophy was in the business of providing foundations for knowledge, art, morality, or politics.

Unlike those philosophers who frequently produce rather Deweyan arguments without mentioning Dewey himself, Rorty writes in a strikingly un-Deweyan style, even while invoking Dewey's name. One illustration is Rorty's view of the relationship of philosophy and democracy, a Deweyan topic if there ever was one. Rorty detaches the defense of democracy from the search for a philosophical deduction of its virtues; democracy, says Rorty, may benefit from philosophical elaboration but does not stand in need of philosophical foundations. Dewey observed that we always begin in the middle of things, and Rorty invokes that observation for his own use. We find ourselves in a democratic society and then try to understand it. The title of Rorty's essay "The Priority of Democracy over Philosophy" does not reveal the way Rorty argues his case, but it summarizes the stance well enough.[56] A way of life and a set of institutions to which we become attached come first; *then* we think of ways of explaining to ourselves the nature of that attachment.

This makes political argument situational or, as Rorty provocatively has said, "ethnocentric." There is not, and could not be, a general philosophical theory that would persuade all rational beings of the merits of democracy. The search for one is more likely to hamper democratic practice than to improve it. Dewey thought the search for a general technique of social progress got in the way of progress, and like Dewey, Rorty is happy to say farewell to philosophy construed as such a general theory. Not only is philosophy not the Queen of the Sciences, but it is not in the usual sense a subject at all. The philosopher's role in public life is to be an unusually fluent citizen, pundit, or high-grade journalist. Philosophers have no political authority as philosophers, but they may have some useful skills as rhetoricians.

In a companion essay, "Post-modern Bourgeois Liberalism," Rorty continues the theme. The postmodern condition is one of disillusion but not hopelessness. We have rightly ceased to believe that nature, human nature, history, or the dialectic will hand us democracy on a plate or guarantee social progress. Nor can philosophy do anything to show that the antidemocrats of the past century were in any obvious way *mistaken;* Nietzsche, Sorel, Michel Foucault, enthusiasts for violence and cruelty, misogynists, and misanthropes know as much about the world as we do. All we can do is tell them that they are "mad."[57] As liberals we know that our private imaginings may match the public world only rather badly, but all we need to demand from one another is public good behavior and public decency. Postmodernist bourgeois liberalism has nothing to say to someone entertaining sadomasochistic fantasies other than that he or she must leave them behind when going into the polling booth.

It is not surprising that Robert Westbrook is one of those who find Rorty's account of Dewey irritating. Rorty's deflationary observations about the role of the philosopher strike Westbrook as flippant and insufficiently respectful of the philosophical seriousness with which Dewey stood up for his kind of liberal socialism.[58] It is not enough to say that what alienates Westbrook is the jocular *tone* in which Rorty praises Dewey. It goes deeper than that. Westbrook's objections to the grounds on which Rorty praises Dewey are worth considering on their own terms. What Westbrook objects to is what Rorty makes almost definitive of liberalism: the separation of private visions and public or political arrangements. Westbrook greatly admires Dewey's emphasis on the way we can find self-realization in the service of the "Great Community"; Rorty silently throws it out.

> Refusing to accept the ethical postulate conjoining self-realization and the social good which was at the heart of Dewey's ethics throughout his career, Rorty has argued for a 'liberal utopia' in which there prevails a rigid division between a rich, autonomous private sphere that will enable elite 'ironists' like himself to create freely the self they wish—even if that be a cruel, antidemocratic self—and a lean, egalitarian, 'democratic' public life confined to the task of preventing cruelty (including that of elite ironists). For Dewey, of course, democracy was a 'way of life' not merely a way of public life—an ideal that 'must affect all modes of human association'—and he would not have accepted Rorty's contention that 'there is no way to bring self-creation together with justice at the level of theory' for that would have required him to give up a principle *[sic]* article of his democratic faith. Rorty contends that the belief that 'the springs of private fulfillment and of human solidarity are the same' is a bothersome Platonic or Christian hangover. If so, Dewey suffered from it.[59]

This is right as an account of Dewey's allegiances and of what Dewey shared with T. H. Green and Josiah Royce, as well as with Randolph Bourne and the Young America movement. "All our idealisms must be those of future social goals in which all can participate, the good life of personality lived in the environment of the Beloved Community," wrote Bourne in "Transnational America."[60] The style is florid, but the thought is Deweyan. Whether the aspiration itself is plausible is another matter entirely. Part of Dewey's later acknowledgment that he ought to have taken the individual more seriously was his increased acceptance of the distance between our private view of the world and our acceptance of our public responsibilities. It is hard to escape the thought that both sides exaggerate: that Rorty ought to acknowledge the unlikelihood that many people will be Nietzscheans in private and good liberal democrats in public and that Westbrook ought to acknowledge that a commitment to participatory democracy implies rather little for one's tastes in opera, poetry, and mathematics.

One may doubt whether the term "postmodernism" has any very definite meaning outside literary criticism. In any case, it is clear enough that Dewey was a self-conscious defender of modernity, and it is impossible to believe that he would have been unsettled by any of the criticisms of modernity that have lately appeared. Of contemporary social theorists, the most "Deweyan" is the German thinker Jürgen Habermas, for all that he has written enthusiastically about Peirce rather than Dewey. There are many connections between Habermas's ideas about emancipatory forms of social theory and Dewey's conception of philosophy as social criticism; there is a clear affinity between the way Dewey's *Democracy and Education* links human communication and democracy and the way Habermas develops an account of democracy in communicative terms in his enormous *Theory of Communicative Action*. Lighthearted critics of both might even say there is something apt in the fact that Dewey and Habermas have themselves found it so hard to communicate with their readers and make themselves unequivocally understood.

The affinity is not hard to understand. Both Dewey and Habermas want to explore the resources of "Left Hegelianism." Habermas has worked his way away from Marx, while Dewey refused to embrace him at all, but both offer a holistic, communicative account of liberal democracy. Both to some degree dissolve the opposition between individual and society while retaining it in other ways. What goes is the thought that we are by nature rational, self-interested individuals who must bargain or contract with our fellows to build a liberal society, such a society always being more or less a compromise for each individual member of it. What remains is the idea that as we *become* individuals, we see that we are none too clear about ourselves, or about our relations to others, and that neither we nor our society can become transparent to us until it is in no one's interest to deceive or be deceived. This has social, political, and economic consequences. Only when people can communicate on free and equal terms can they achieve the deep self-understanding that we have hankered after since the Enlightenment. If freedom and equality are absent, what can be said and thus what can be thought will be limited.[61] How this translates into a concern for democracy in the usual, institutional sense, complete with voters and ballot boxes and average venal politicians may be hard to say. But the central ideas of *Democracy and Education* can without exaggeration be said to be alive and well seventy-five years later.

The Communitarian Turn

Dewey wrote on ethics in opposition both to Kant's emphasis on the subordination of the individual will to rational maxims that Kant supposed to be deliverances of the noumenal self and to the utilitarianism of Mill and Bentham. Both were unacceptably individualist; Kant put the entire burden of the moral life on isolated individuals who had to legislate to and for themselves, while utilitarianism held that the good that ethical behavior should aim at consisted in a mathematical sum of the pleasures of individuals. Dewey was in contrast a communitarian. The moral life was something we learned how to live in a community, and our ideals, however much they might go beyond current standards, were learned in and developed out of such a common life. Dewey's revolt against Kant and utilitarianism has been matched by a similar revolt in the past decade.

Many critics, both academic and in the hurly-burly of politics and public administration, have argued that the past twenty-five years saw too great an emphasis on individual rights and not enough on our duties to the public, too much emphasis on self-expression and not enough on responsibility, too much stress on doing our own thing and too little on other people's claims. One of the things that President Clinton took pains to emphasize during his election campaign in 1992 was that the Democratic party under his leadership would be devoted to the "responsible society," not to the expansion of individual rights with no corresponding attention to the duties that went with them.

This doubtless reflected a sense that in the party struggle the Republican party stood to gain by denouncing the Democratic party as the party that had recklessly expanded individual rights and had forgotten that every right imposes a duty on somebody else. But the Republican party was itself vulnerable to such a complaint, not that it emphasized the rights of just the same people as the Democrats had done but that its turn to a more laissez-faire economic policy amounted to saying that the owners of capital, the purveyors of junk bonds, and all those with imaginative schemes of self-enrichment had every right to enrich themselves with no thought of the social consequences of what they did. It hardly needs saying that to the extent that such criticisms were justified, they would have been endorsed to the letter by Dewey.

The party battle is conducted at a pretty low intellectual level. It is easy enough to imagine Dewey's denouncing the excesses of junk bond dealers and young women who have illegitimate children on welfare, but impossible to imagine that he would have thought that either could be dealt without more far-reaching changes than party politicians are willing to contemplate. In any event, arguments about the overextension of rights or the extension of rights to the wrong people or on the wrong terms do not quite pick up Dewey's point. After all, both Kant and Mill were quite fierce about our duties, and it was not for moral laxity that Dewey reproached them. The argument is rather that the overemphasis on rights reflects a mistaken way of looking at our moral situation.

A representative statement of the case was made a few years ago by Michael Sandel, a political theorist from Harvard. His *Liberalism and the Limits of Justice* was directed at John Rawls's great essay *A Theory of Justice*.[62] Rawls's book derived an elaborate account of the principles that should govern the constitution, the economy, and the public life of a liberal democracy by asking a seemingly simple question—namely, what rules we would choose to govern ourselves by if we had to make the choice by contracting with one another under conditions carefully set up so that none of us could rig the rules in our own favor. This is an individualistic device in many ways; it assumes that our concern for ourselves is more basic and more natural than our concern for others, it represents public life as a system of mutual bargaining, and it adopts a view of rational behavior modeled on the one we find in classical economics. Sandel argued, much as Dewey had done seventy years before, that the model misrepresents our actual experience and our actual relations to others. It exaggerates the importance of choice and understates the way our identities are embedded in our relations with others. If Sandel is correct, it is not so much that we have too many rights as that rights occupy too much of our attention, not so much that justice does not matter as that its place in the moral universe has been exaggerated. This, too, is a recurrence to what Dewey argued.

Nobody arguing in this style supposes that exaggerated individualism is to be demolished by pure thought. As Dewey knew and said, intellectual exaggerations reflect social dislocations. What is needed is not so much more and better philosophy as a society that does justice both to our individuality and to our need for social connection. This is the great modern need, and nowhere more so than in the United States. All modern societies are characterized by geographical mobility and job mobility, but the United States more than any. Americans who change their houses every four and a half years on average are simultaneously pursuing the individualist American dream of a better house, a better job, and individual happiness and are looking for communities to join, groups of like-minded people to spend time with, for other people to join with in churches, clubs, fire departments, and volunteer groups.

Recent sociological literature is full of anxious speculation about the inner loneliness of Americans for whom the pursuit of individual advancement has proved unsatisfying. Robert Bellah and his colleagues have published two best-selling investigations—*Habits of the Heart* and *The Good Society*—whose message is the insufficiency of the search for individual fulfillment and the need for attachment to a wider community that will anchor us, shape us, discipline us, and assure us that what we find fulfillment in is what we *ought* to find fulfillment in. This communitarian strain is often thought to be anti-individualist and antiliberal, even by its own supporters. It is not. It is not a reversion to a nineteenth-century conservative or backward-looking emphasis on *Gemeinschaft;* it is much more nearly a rehearsal of Durkheim and Dewey. Individuals need communities, and liberal communities consist of associated individuals. Modern individuals need flexible, forward-looking, tolerant communities to live in, and such communities can be sustained only by modern individuals who are looking for a meaningful existence in association with similarly autonomous people.

Piety and Deity

The reason for Dewey's resurrection is thus not difficult to see in outline. Americans especially, but almost everyone who lives in the advanced industrial societies of the North Atlantic, need a picture of the world and of their place in it that satisfies some not obviously compatible demands. It must be secular enough to allow us to use science and technology effectively and not resist innovation, but it must satisfy our wish for an answer to large questions about the meaning of life that technology cannot answer. It is a cliché of public opinion surveys that the American people are astonishingly religious, churchgoers on a scale unknown elsewhere, but that they are theologically and scripturally ignorant.

An unkind thought would be that the American public is deeply confused; people say they believe in God but do not know what they believe. This was Sidney Hook's view; he had a simpler, more Russellian view of the opposition of science and religion than Dewey. Physics was true, there was no God, and that was that. The sympathetic answer is that the thinness of popular theological and scriptural knowledge shows that people are looking not for a theologically certified competitor to the scientific view of the world but for an emotionally and morally sustaining vision—"religious" in Dewey's sense rather than St. Thomas Aquinas's. This is Richard Rorty's interpretation of American religiosity; science provides one thing we need—that is to say, control over the world and some understanding of how that control works—while religion supplies another—namely, a sense that the world is on our side, that we belong in it and it belongs to us. This is squarely in the mold of *A Common Faith.*

Skeptics will complain that this view, whether in Dewey's more decorous or Rorty's less decorous version, is just a license for wishful thinking. It may be true that a sufficient skill in self-deception allows us to evade the fact that the most important factual claims made by traditional religion are false, but it is morally deplorable to live in bad faith. The morality of the modern world is an ethic of authenticity, and this demands that we face the grim truth about the world—particularly the grim truth that it cares nothing for us and our purposes.

Sartre, the best-known exponent of this view, claimed that what we discover when we look hard at the world is that it is meaningless. And when we look at the social world, we discover that it is a field of forces in which the powerful bamboozle and destroy the less powerful, often without knowing or intending to do so. If that were the end of the story, we should be forced to conclude—as Sartre famously did—that the price of authenticity was cosmic anxiety, homelessness, rootlessness, and estrangement from the world. Richard Rorty's nice phrase about Dewey's being ground between Tillich and Carnap would be right. An irrational faith is the price we must pay for psychological security, and those who will not pay the price cannot have the benefits of faith. The political implications would be alarming, too; moderate secular liberalism appears to be entirely ill adapted to the needs of modern man. It is not surprising that Sartre and Heidegger seemed to take a perverse satisfaction in regimes built on pure terror.

Dewey thought the project of authenticity did not lead us into an arid void. Man is a cultural creature who learns to interpret the world by living in a community that teaches him how to interpret it. There may be many such communities, though not all of them are consistent with the world of advanced technology and the modern nation-state. Charles Taylor is the most distinguished of recent writers to defend the same view, as he does in *The Ethics of Authenticity*. It leads us to the crux between Dewey and his religious critics. Although we learn our understanding of the world in a community and employing the resources of a culture, we cannot help asking whether our interpretation of the world is *right*. Are sunsets "really" beautiful or "really" just light shining through dust and cloud onto which we project sentiments that we just happen to have? The fact that we learn to interpret the world by belonging to a community does not answer the question of whether what we say about the world is *mass* projection of our hopes, fears, and whatever else rather than an account of how the world really is.

Like Dewey before him, Charles Taylor tries to shut off this line of questioning. Like Dewey in *Experience and Nature,* Taylor denies that we can peel our account of the world away from the world and assign so much to the way the world is and so much to the expression of our psyches. The meaningfulness of the world possesses a "soft" objectivity—what Taylor himself refers to as "objectivity not in a *Ding an Sich* sense."[63] The qualities that give meaning to the world are independent of what any of us think about them, though they are not qualities needed by forms of inquiry, such as chemistry or physics, that prescind from the full richness of the world for their own particular purposes. Now we reach the decisive point. Many people suppose that the world loses its meaningfulness if the religious basis of its meaning is undermined; Dewey's naturalistic, cultural analysis denies this. On the face of it, Dewey was right; anthropologists agree that there are innumerable societies whose elaborate systems of ritual, taboo, and moral symbolism are wholly secular.[64] The difficulty arises when we ask whether one society's understanding of the world is, if not nearer the *truth,* more adequate to the way the world and human nature really are.

Charles Taylor, who is for the most part a Deweyan without knowing it, believes that philosophy must be supplemented by faith. Here we run into the difficulty that haunts Hegel's philosophy and therefore Dewey's as well as Taylor's. To see world as replete with *meaning* is to see it as a kind of text. Discussions of this topic often appeal to the medieval doctrine of "signatures"—the idea that plants have the shape they do because they are good for healing particular ailments or as a warning that they cause particular kinds of poisoning. We "read" the plants by understanding the code. This doctrine is more credible if God tells us whatever it is that he wishes us to know by inscribing it in the plant's appearance. When we read a letter, we read the meaning our correspondent put there; it is easier to look for a meaning in events if someone has put a meaning there. The alternative is that our imagination does all the work. A secular view seems to be trapped between an account of meaning that is credible but entirely subjective and a view that is objective but unacceptably nonsecular. And the trouble with the wholly secular view is that even if it understands the subjective contribution not as the work of the individual but as that of the culture, we still wish to know if the culture sees what is really there. That is why the contrast between science and religion haunts us.

Consider the thirsty man who finds a stream; the stream "means" the end of his thirst. This is Dewey's standard case of a meaningful event, and his account makes perfect sense. Dewey draws a plausible inference: A thirsty man will pick out the stream because of its significance; he does not experience individual sense data that he somehow assembles into "stream here," but a totality bearing the significance of a solution to his problem of getting a drink. We can also agree that to the man to whom the stream is an obstacle to cross on his way home, the encounter bears a different meaning and may decently be said to be a different experience.

None of this dissolves the problem. Suppose I see the stream and think that it would be fun to pollute it, or even that I think it would be fun to empty filth into it but have no conception of "pollution." We are tempted to say that I am abusing the stream, misusing it when I use it as a dump, that I am blind to something when I do not see that this is *pollution*. What water is *for* is drinking, not polluting, we might say. A picture of the world as divinely created for the satisfaction of "normal" and "proper" human needs will underpin this sentiment; it holds together ideas of normality and propriety and allows us to say that a person who fails to see what he is doing is perverse, psychologically obtuse, or morally blind.

Can we preserve such sentiments without such a sense of a divine source of the world's meaning? Dewey was sure we could; Taylor seems uncertain. Sometimes he suggests that religious belief is a bonus, sometimes a necessity.[65] Both thoughts are tempting. Dewey might say that it is only because the world naturally exhibits orderliness, beauty, awe-inspiring grandeur, and the like that we reach for the thought of a divine creator that built these qualities into it. The qualities need no divine support; they are divine aspects of the world. The perfection of Mozart's music makes us wish a deity could enjoy it, so talk of "divine inspiration" reverses what we really think. Great music inspires thoughts of divinity; the gods do not infuse our souls with music.

The supernaturalist like Taylor might say that unless the significance in our lives of art, music, personal affections, a tenderness toward the natural environment, and admiration for the achievements of human culture is underwritten by something higher, deeper, eternal, and providential, it remains insecure. Human culture is not enough of a guarantee; an entire culture might lose touch with the deep meaning of the world, and if there was nothing but human culture to give the world meaning, we have no way of preferring one understanding to another. We should be at the mercy of our culture and its vicissitudes—not too alarming a prospect if we face nothing worse than the difficulty of explaining the virtues of European high culture to Southern Californians but infinitely more alarming if we want to explain the evils of tribalism to anti-Semites, Zulus attacking Indian shopkeepers, and so endlessly on. Taylor in essence supposes that we are in the hands of a liberal providence; Dewey supposed that the evolutionary advantages of liberal cultures would see them home.[66] Those of us who are terrified by assorted tribalisms, fundamentalisms, and nationalisms at the end of the twentieth century can side with Dewey only with our fingers crossed. Dewey's confidence in "progress" was dismissed sixty years ago by Reinhold Niebuhr and a few years ago by Christopher Lasch as mere foolish optimism.[67]

Dewey's reply, which is perhaps the reply that Rorty would give if he were pressed, is that it is just a fact about human beings that at a certain point in human evolution they erect intellectual frameworks in terms of which they understand their own lives and their relations to the nonhuman world and then explore what one might call the intellectual and affective "built environment." It grows out of our interaction with the rest of nature but is in crucial ways objectively "there." This is the "Third World" that Karl Popper's later philosophy of science discussed, the world created by the interaction of the other two worlds of mind and matter.[68] It is a world that contains theories, musical styles, and traditions but also constitutions, houses, birds' nests, and whatever else can only be understood as an embodiment of intelligence. Is there progress in the "Third World"? There is no cosmic guarantee of the survival of a humane, nonviolent, imaginative culture that allows its members freedom to explore its resources and create more, and recent discussions of the "end of history" have not persuaded many participants that the triumph of liberal democracy is indeed the meaning of history.[69]

The fundamentalist panic in the face of secular society has lately focused on public education, something that also strikes many secular critics as a disaster area, and not always for very different reasons. Dewey remains a bugbear to educational conservatives; his supposed antipathy to discipline in the classroom, his lack of respect for intellectual tradition, and his overemphasis on developing the child's social skills rather than his or her moral character still cloud his reputation. Bizarrely, some of the evidence of the shortcomings of American education has suggested that it is a shortage of Deweyan influence that presents the problem. The familiar contrast between the mathematical competence of Japanese schoolchildren and American schoolchildren and between Asian-American students and black and Hispanic students turns out not to have much to do with their race or even with their family backgrounds. Rather the Japanese schools absorbed the Deweyan lesson that students who work together in a cooperative and mutually reinforcing fashion learn a great deal, and some recent California research showed that what seemed to make all the difference between successful Asian students and their peers was the way the former worked as a focused group, while their fellow students had got it into their heads that they were forbidden to do so.

By the same token, recent rows over "multiculturalism" raise questions that Dewey answered quite decisively eighty years ago. In "Nationalizing Education," Dewey defended multicultural education in simple terms; the peculiarity of the United States was, as it remains today, that it is a nation of nations, both one and many. Like Horace Kallen and Randolph Bourne, Dewey was unafraid of conservatives who wanted "one hundred percent Americanism" and proposed to deport all those "hyphenated Americans" who would not abandon the cultural attachments that stood to the left of the hyphen. But he was emphatic that what stood to the right of the hyphen must have its due. "Good" hyphens attach; "bad" hyphens separate.[70] The hysteria that marks today's debates would not have surprised Dewey, who wrote about the issue in the heat of war. Nor would it have surprised him to find himself in the position of saying, "A plague on both your houses," to the warring parties.

For Dewey's view was that a liberal culture is a plural culture; liberal-minded people cannot but be interested in the variety of human cultural achievements. A liberal education, therefore, had to be one in which children from different backgrounds could talk about the achievements of their own traditions and their contribution to American life.[71] This was the only way of achieving mutual respect and an unforced national unity. To the familiar and divisive question, What makes a real American? Dewey's response was to turn away from issues of national and cultural identity toward forward-looking questions. The real question was not *who* was a real American but *what* was the American project. A public education system was one of the places where that had to be worked out, and children given the resources to promote it.

Although Dewey was a philosopher of education and a strikingly absent-minded professor, he was anything but a fool. Much of his polemical writing on education was concerned with an issue whose importance puts that of ideological conflict in the shade: taxation. In his day the situation was not that we have reached by now, when American expenditure on higher education is enormous but elementary and secondary education is starved of funds.[72] It was for all that as true then as now that the American system of local taxation ensured that schools with the greatest needs had the fewest resources and that the quality of education was always under threat from the penchant of school boards for cutting out what they called "frills"—that is to say art, music, and drama—but rarely football.[73]

As to the vexed issue of the rights of localities to have their schools reflect the moral and religious enthusiasms of the area, Dewey's conception of local democracy was indeed as hostile to all such interventions as his conservative critics suspect. It is, to be strictly honest, not entirely clear how he could square his enthusiasm for community vitality with his adamant insistence on a secular and liberal approach to schooling. I do not mean that he had *no* resources for the purpose, but his ordinary arguments are not conclusive.

The great complaint against religion in school was that it was a force for separation, not unity.[74] This was fair enough as a complaint against either the enforcement of one creed on a diverse school community or the proposed practice of taking children out of school for a number of classes per week in order that they could have sectarian instruction. It cuts less ice against monolithic communities in which the children side with their parents and they all belong to one church or at any rate to congregations that are variants on one church. Current campaigns for the restoration of school prayer seem mostly to have sprung up in such communities, rather than in ones where there is much internal dissension. Nor have they evidenced any great desire to impose school prayer on other communities; the impression such campaigns give is that their protagonists feel beleaguered in a secular world. This is the kind of issue on which social and political pluralists divide among themselves, some thinking that all such movements are really oppressive, others thinking that they are not and that the oppression lies in preventing their adherents from expressing themselves. It is clear that Dewey would himself have been intransigently behind the Supreme Court decision that religion had to be kept out of schools, and school prayer with it. One may suspect that this has less to do with pluralism than his dislike of the Congregationalism in which he was brought up and with his insistence that the common faith of the common school is a faith in the democratic community. Since that faith needed no external props and assistance, they were to be left outside the schoolroom.

An American Creed

The confidence in the viability of everyday life distinguishes Dewey from the supernaturalists and transcendentalists on his "spiritual" flank and from despairing Sartrean existentialists on his antispiritual flank. It was his gift to his contemporaries, and the fact that we still hanker for such a vision of our place in the natural and social world explains why at the end of the twentieth century so many philosophers and social critics have been rereading him with renewed appreciation. We are not, in Heidegger's phrase, "thrown into the world," and we are not doomed to cosmic loneliness. We may find ourselves as individuals disappointed in all sorts of ways, may find ourselves lonely and frustrated, bored in our work, and much worse, but these are *problems,* not fate, and they may be coped with by searching for solutions, not drowned in narcotics or dealt with only by gritted teeth and a stiff upper lip. Dewey's characteristic literary product was well described by Lewis Feuer as the "lay sermon."[75] The lay sermon was a late-nineteenth-century English invention, an art form practiced to perfection by Dewey's hero T. H. Huxley and years earlier in the United States by Ralph Waldo Emerson; it was institutionalized in Britain in the addresses given by heads of colleges to their young men, and the art was acquired by Dewey in his Sunday morning talks to the students at Michigan. Once he had the style, he never lost it.

Is the lay sermon an apt style for a modern liberal? More nearly than one might think. A great deal of recent social and political writing has operated at one or the other of two extremes: a concentration on the legal framework of politics or a narrow focus on policy. This has left a substantial hole in the middle ground where Dewey operated. The lay sermon is at home in this middle ground; between pure philosophy and a policy paper lies the terrain of intelligent persuasion. Consider the extremes. John Rawls, whose ideas have quite rightly dominated American political philosophy for the past quarter of a century, has argued that liberalism must be a doctrine about the basis of just political and economic institutions and must avoid contentious arguments about the nature of the good life.[76]

Narrowing the scope of liberal commitment reflects a desire for a very rigid account of fundamental constitutional rights; the state is seen as a coercive mechanism, good to the degree that it protects those rights, dangerous where its power is not constrained by the same rights. This rights obsession has produced some astonishing results in free speech jurisprudence and is one reason why abortion law reform has been so contentious. But rights-obsessed liberalism is only one liberalism, and not the most persuasive. Never to think about persuading people not to do what they have a right to do or to do it with discretion, sympathy, charity, concern for the opinions of others, and so on is both implausible in itself and not calculated to reconcile liberals to their opponents.

Where we have not had a political philosophy devoted to elaborating rights that constrain any possible government, we have been offered policy fixes. To pick a representative sample is impossible and beside the point. What is worth noticing is how far liberals and conservatives have looked for technical solutions with little thought to whether the "problem" has been properly identified in the first place. Like the narrower liberalism, "fix"-oriented politics reflects a despair at the fate of public discussion of political principles. Recipes for the repair of education, the family, the falling rate of productivity growth have abounded; imagination in rethinking what the problem is has not. As Dewey might have feared, the longing for technical fixes has spread into the private world. A concern for what he called "the problems of men" has become an all too literal interest in "problems" and has spawned a vast self-help literature, whose effect in increasing the already excessive self-absorption of modern Americans can only be guessed at.

Dewey's interest in problem solving was unlike that of "how to" writing. He was skeptical of technical fixes because he supposed that what most needed fixing was people's attitudes to themselves and one another, and he was uninterested in either his own or other people's private miseries. He would have detested what Christopher Lasch has aptly described as the culture of narcissism and the New Age self-help and the psychobabble in which it trades.[77] It would have seemed a retreat from the world, doomed from the outset because it separated people from one another rather than helped them live more interestingly with one another.

Deweyan liberalism is different. It is a genuine liberalism, unequivocally committed to progress and the expansion of human tastes, needs, and interests; its focus is on the self-development and autonomy of the individual; it is, if not rationalist in outlook, certainly committed to the rule of intelligence. Nonetheless, it comes complete with a contentious world view and a contentious view of what constitutes a good life; it takes sides on questions of religion, and it is not obsessed with the defense of rights. What makes it an optimistic and expansive liberalism is its insistence that the individual whom liberalism wants to encourage is neither the rip-off artist favored by the economic changes of the 1980s nor the narcissist bewailing (or for that matter celebrating) the state of his or her psyche. The individual it celebrates is someone who is thoroughly engaged with his or her work, family, local community and its politics, who has not been coerced, bullied, or dragged into these interests but sees them as fields for a self-expression quite consistent with losing himself or herself in the task at hand.

In practical politics, such a liberalism has little use for the idea of the state at all but is happy to think about the positive contributions of government. It is a politics sensitive to the mild but continuous repressiveness of everyday social life that Mill and Tocqueville feared in the nineteenth century and David Riesman wrote of in our own. It is a politics that never had to be reminded of the existence of "civil society" because it never forgot it.

This is the only viable kind of argument a modern liberal can use. Whether we call it liberalism or social democracy is not particularly important; what is important is that it is not a property rights-based liberalism—individual personality is sacred, but few forms of ownership are—nor is it friendly to the command economy. This is the *via media* that advanced liberals sought in the 1890s, when Dewey found his own voice, and after a chastening century of totalitarian experiment we now know how easy is it to do much worse than follow the middle-of-the-road course. This is not to say that Dewey supplies all we need. He fails in many small ways and in two large ones. The small ways have been discussed. The unclarity of his educational views leaves room for excesses: the reduction of work to mere play; the reduction of moral training to mere manipulation; the reduction of vocational education to job training for the untalented. The vagueness of his view of "the great community" leaves us wondering whether his view of participatory democracy is that of the student insurgents of the 1960s or that of the Quaker meetinghouse and anyway not sure we can run a country of 280 million on either basis.

The large failures occur at the opposite ends of the spectrum. The first is Dewey's unconcern with the private world. For all his infatuation with Anzia Yezierska, he had nothing to say about sex, neither about its emancipatory possibilities nor about the difficulties that sexual passion, sexual jealousy, and sexual boredom pose for the progressive. Mill at least knew that there was a problem; Russell wrote a great deal about it. Dewey did not. I do not mean that he ought to have written *Sex as Experience* as a companion volume to *Art as Experience,* only that an acknowledgment of one of the twentieth century's more obvious preoccupations is needed to fill out the picture of the individual whose self-development and emancipation from merely superstitious and coercive ties liberalism is to achieve. Dewey was oddly untouched by Freud and oddly uninterested in either the anxieties or the possibilities of emancipation that Freud brought the twentieth century.

Dewey's silence on sex is part of a larger problem. The individual in Dewey always seems to be going outward into the world; "the bliss of solitude" is not a Deweyan thought, even though Wordsworth was one of his favorite poets. He did not have to say that we can find all our resources within ourselves or that all our problems are problems of the inner self, but he ought to have acknowledged that a new kind of self-consciousness was abroad in the world, and a new resource for both happiness and misery. Most of the time Dewey's steadiness, patience, and reliability are much more admirable than anything in Russell, Santayana, or Dewey's "cultural" critics, but every so often one longs for Russell's or James's—or Randolph Bourne's—passion for the quirky, idiosyncratic, and self-centered. It is not only the *vie intérieure* that gets shortchanged; one result of this lack of interest in the private, the intimate, and the sexually charged is that family life gets shortchanged as well, and at a time when we are terribly puzzled about how to get the benefits of stable family life without unduly interfering with the pursuit of happiness, this is rather a loud silence.

Conversely, Dewey underestimated the obduracy of large institutions, as well as the unpredictability of institutional change. By the time this paragraph is published, the illustration I am about to use will be old hat—itself an indication of the problem. The planners of European economic and political integration aim to have a unified monetary system in place by the year 2000. Some years ago they concluded that if a free market economy was to operate over the entire European continent, a common currency was needed and that in the meantime, a set of fixed exchange rates was required to get the benefits of a common currency before it was instituted. Liberalizing governments had abandoned exchange controls and had ceased trying to interfere with the actions of foreign exchange traders; large firms need to buy and sell enormous quantities of foreign currency to trade across national borders, and the fewer impediments they face, the better. This set up a situation in which it would take only one country to pursue a monetary policy at odds with the needs of other countries in the system to allow foreign exchange dealers a field day; when German reunification took place, the country with the strongest currency in Europe dealt with the inflationary consequences by raising its interest rates to levels that were bound to force a devaluation by almost every other country in the mechanism. Nobody wanted such a result, but it was a surefire consequence of the way things turned out.

Could anyone have predicted it? Only up to a point. Nobody knew that the Berlin Wall was going to fall, or that the West German government would redeem East German marks at a specially generous rate, or that the government would squeeze inflation by monetary rather than fiscal means, or . . . How could anyone have known any of this? Dewey rightly praised the scientific attitude but took for granted a malleability and predictability in institutional arrangements that all experience refutes. It is this that allowed him to stop a little book like *Liberalism and Social Action* just where it ought to have begun, urging us to be intelligent but not acknowledging how readily intelligent people trip each other up. Of course, we want intelligent social action rather than mere blind habit or brutal insurrection and repression; but Dewey's revolutionary opponents would have observed that insurrection was intelligent social action under the circumstances, and his conservative opponents would have reminded him that *Human Nature and Conduct* had explained at some length that habit could be more intelligent than intelligence. What we need to think about is what intelligence can and cannot do. Many liberals have therefore defined the tasks of government in negative terms: not the pursuit of happiness, but the minimization of misery, oppression, and despair. We know more about how to stop the latter than about how to achieve the former. We can build institutional bulwarks and dikes, but we have no idea how to build utopia. Dewey would undoubtedly have agreed with the last thought, but would have drawn different conclusions. We must pursue the positive goals of human emancipation and human happiness, but with whatever information and intelligence we can acquire. We may be chastened, but we cannot content ourselves with merely reducing misery. He was right, but he made it sound too simple.

Dewey was a visionary.[78] That was his appeal. He was a curious visionary, because he did not speak of a distant goal or a city not built with hands. He was a visionary about the here and now, about the potentiality of the modern world, modern society, modern man, and thus, as it happened, America and Americans in the twentieth century. It was his ability to infuse the here and now with a kind of transcendent glow that overcame the denseness and awkwardness of his prose and the vagueness of his message and secured such widespread conviction. Unlike so many of the country's leaders, he was not a "preacher's kid" with all that implied about a combination of arrogance and rebelliousness, self-confidence, and a taste for raising hell; but he became the century's most influential preacher of a creed for liberals, reformers, schoolteachers, and democrats. He addressed public concerns and avowable interests more adequately than he addressed the secrets of the heart and our unavowable private interests; but he will remain for the foreseeable future a rich source of intellectual nourishment for anyone not absolutely locked within the anxieties of his or her own heart and not absolutely despondent about the prospects of the modern world.

Notes

Preface and Overview

1. Robert Westbrook, *John Dewey and American Democracy* (Ithaca, 1991).
2. Steven Rockefeller, *John Dewey* (New York, 1991).
3. On Green, the best biographical study remains Melvin Richter, *The Politics of Conscience* (London, 1963).
4. Westbrook, *Dewey and Democracy,* p. 556.
5. Henry Commager, *The American Mind* (New Haven, 1950), p. 100.
6. *A Common Faith* [1934], *John Dewey, The Later Works,* (Carbondale, Ill., 1989) vol. 9. Hereafter cited as *LW.*
7. Sidney Hook, *Pragmatism and the Tragic Sense of Life* (New York, 1974), pp. 112–15.
8. *Liberalism and Social Action* [1935], *LW,* vol. 11.
9. Max Lerner, *America as a Civilization* (New York, 1949), p. 724.
10. Richard Bernstein, *John Dewey* (New York, 1967).
11. "Search for the Great Community" is the title of the penultimate chapter of *The Public and Its Problems, LW,* vol. 2, 325ff.
12. Even Professor Westbrook rather plaintively describes himself as "painfully aware" that he is "likely to find an audience mostly made up of professors." *Dewey and Democracy,* p. 552.
13. Christopher Lasch, *The True and Only Heaven* (New York, 1992).
14. ———. "Politics as Social Control," *The New Radicalism in America* (New York, 1965), ch. 5.
15. "The Ethics of Democracy" [1887], vol. 1, *John Dewey, The Early Works* vol. 1, p. 246. Hereafter cited as *EW.*
16. Reinhold Niebuhr was perhaps the most famous of these critics; his *Moral Man and Immoral Society* (New York, 1932) takes Dewey as the representative figure who epitomizes the liberal incapacity to understand just how deeply flawed human nature will always be.
17. "From Absolutism to Experimentalism," *LW,* vol. 5, p. 155.
18. There are counterexamples; an amusing one is the way his hatred of the American party system bubbles to the surface in his *Ethics,* when he denounces "party-politicians, whose least knowledge is of the scientific questions involved, just as their least interest is for the human issues at stake." *John Dewey, the Middle Works* (Carbondale, Ill., 1876–83), vol. 5, p. 423. Hereafter cited as *MW.*
19. Corliss Lamont, ed., *Dialogue on John Dewey* (New York, 1960), p. 15.
20. This, too, I hesitate over. The "communitarianism" of President Clinton's administration and the quick resort of so many of his supporters to talk of "a politics of meaning" are very Deweyan. Yet Dewey's understanding of a "problem" and its resolution remains light-years away from the concerns of so-called policy wonks.

1. Starting Out

1. Charles Forcey, *The Crossroads of Liberalism* (New York, 1961) is excellent as a guide to *New Republic* liberalism, but there is nothing comparable for the 1920s and 1930s.

2. But it was Lippmann, not Dewey, who wrote a best seller *called The Public Philosophy*.
3. E.g., Paul Crosser, *The Nihilism of John Dewey* (New York, 1958); John Blewett, S. J., ed., *John Dewey: His Thought and Influence* (New York, 1964).
4. Nietzsche, in fact, said something more elaborate: "We philosophers and 'free spirits' feel ourselves to be shone upon by a new dawn with the news that God is dead. . . . Finally! Our ships can embark again, and go forth to every danger. Every hazard is again permitted the inquirer. Perhaps there never was so open a sea." Arthur Danto, *Nietzsche as Philosopher* (New York, 1965), pp. 193–194.
5. Commager, *American Mind,* p. 165.
6. Lamont, *Dialogue,* p. 15.
7. Sidney Hook, *Out of Step* (New York, 1987), pp. 82–83.
8. *Reconstruction in Philosophy, MW,* vol. 12, p. 94.
9. See below, pp. 350–52.
10. Like all writers on Dewey, I draw heavily on George Dykhuizen, *The Life and Mind of John Dewey* (Carbondale, Ill., 1974) for this account; it is the only reliable source and was written over such a long period that Dykhuizen was able while working on it to talk to people who had known Dewey as a child. It is unexciting and unanalytical but indispensable.
11. Ibid., p. 7.
12. Arthur Schilpp, ed., *The Philosophy of John Dewey* (New York, 1938), p. 6.
13. Ibid., p. 5.
14. Dykhuizen, *Life and Mind,* p. 329.
15. Ibid., ch. 1, is quite sharp with the legend mongers and notes that Irwin Edman had Dewey born on a farm. . . .
16. Matthew Buckham, quoted ibid., p. 3.
17. Horace Kallen, "Dewey and Pragmatism," *John Dewey, Philosopher of Science and Freedom,* ed. Sidney Hook (New York, 1949), pp. 3–46; "As for me, I here stand with James" is his comment on James's greater insistence on a negative, idiosyncratic liberty than Dewey defended. See pp. 38–39.
18. Dewey preferred the account of socialism in Bellamy's less widely read *Equality,* the book devoted to showing that *Looking Backward* described a possible reality, not a utopia.
19. John L. Thomas, *Alternative America* (Cambridge, Mass., 1985), gives an excellent account of Bellamy's career and ideas; perhaps the best commentary on *Looking Backward,* however, is William Morris's *News from Nowhere* (Kelmscott, England, 1891), a book written in a blaze of indignation at the "unartistic" vision of Bellamy's "cockney utopia."
20. Quoted in Dykhuizen, *Life and Mind,* p. 6.
21. "From Absolutism to Experimentalism," *LW,* vol. 5, p. 153.
22. Schilpp, *Philosophy of Dewey,* p. 9.
23. "When their father was asked what the boys were going to do, he usually replied that he hoped at least one of them would become a mechanic." Ibid., p. 6.
24. Jane Dewey writes as though this were an affliction only of early childhood, but Dewey's bashfulness as a graduate student was marked enough for the president of Johns Hopkins to encourage him to take up some profession other than teaching. There is a famous essay by Max Eastman in which he claims that Dewey told him that in his early twenties he has tried to start an affair with a cousin, but "I was too bashful. I was abnormally bashful. I was abnormal." Max Eastman, "John Dewey," *Atlantic* (December 1941), pp. 672–73. Like the report of Dewey's "mystical experience" that Eastman reports in that article, this recollection may need to be taken with a pinch of salt.
25. Morton and Lucia White, *Intellectuals and the City* (New York, 1980) make more of his antipathy to the city than strikes me as plausible; a man who lives for forty-eight years in Manhattan when he could have lived almost anywhere he chose is not a man with a deep hostility to the city.
26. Save perhaps in his poetry, which is in an awkward way quite affecting. It is collected in Jo Ann Boydston, ed., *The Poems of John Dewey* (Carbondale, Ill., 1977).
27. Neil Coughlan, *Young John Dewey* (Chicago, 1974), pp. 3–6, speculates on this, but beyond suggesting that Mrs. Dewey's self-reliance may have been exaggerated by these differences and by the long separation during the Civil War, he sensibly comes to no very definite view.
28. "From Absolutism to Experimentalism," *LW,* vol. 5, p. 148.
29. Bruce Kuklick, *Churchmen and Philosophers: From Jonathan Edwards to John Dewey* (New Haven, 1985).
30. "From Absolutism to Experimentalism," *LW,* vol. 5, p. 149.
31. Lamont, *Dialogue,* pp. 15, 16.
32. Indeed, Dewey suggests in "From Absolutism to Experimentalism" that in the United States there was decided opposition between "the Germanizing rationaliz-

ers and the orthodox representatives of the Scottish school of thought through the representatives of the latter at Princeton." *LW,* vol. 5, p. 148.

33. "Intuitionalism" from *Johnson's Universal Cyclopedia, EW,* vol. 4, pp. 123–31.
34. "From Absolutism to Experimentalism," *LW,* vol. 5, p. 149.
35. Coughlan, *Young John Dewey,* ch. 3 and 4; Coughlan thinks Dewey's essays on psychology in the early 1880s and his *Psychology* of 1886 rest on the "dynamic intuitionalism" of Newman Smyth. I am not sure that they do not, but Dewey's teacher and guru G. S. Morris preached "dynamic idealism," and it is surely more plausible that Dewey's emphasis on the dynamism of the mind is a neo-Hegelian trope borrowed from his teacher rather than a new departure in intuitionalism.
36. "James Marsh and American Philosophy," *LW,* vol. 5, pp. 178–96.
37. "From Absolutism to Experimentalism," *LW,* vol. 5, pp. 147–48.
38. Ibid., p. 149.
39. Dykhuizen, *Life and Mind,* p. 14; "From Absolutism to Experimentalism," *LW,* vol. 5, p. 148.
40. Dykhuizen, *Life and Mind,* p. 23.
41. Ibid., p. 22; Eastman, "John Dewey," pp. 672–73.
42. Dykhuizen, *Life and Mind,* p. 25.
43. Ibid., p. 23.

2. PASTORS AND MASTERS

1. "From Absolutism to Experimentalism," *LW,* vol. 5, p. 154.
2. The best account remains Lawrence Veysey, *The Emergence of the American University* (Chicago, 1965) on the religious life of American universities and colleges, George Marsden, *The Soul of the American University* (New York, 1994) is unrivaled.
3. Dykhuizen, *Life and Mind,* p. 29.
4. Morton White gives an interesting, if hostile, account of Morris in *The Origins of Dewey's Instrumentalism* (New York, 1943), ch. 2; Coughlan, *Young John Dewey* also provides an interesting sketch of Morris's career; the main source is R. M. Wenley, *The Life and Work of George Sylvester Morris* (New York, 1917). Wenley was a sympathetic biographer, an idealist himself, but the book is not uncritical and gives some sense of what it was like to be an American philosopher looking to Europe for inspiration and recognition.
5. Wenley, *Life and Work,* p. 57.
6. White, *Origins,* pp. 13–25, gives a deft and elegant account of what Morris objected to in British empiricism.
7. Wenley, *Life and Work,* p. 59.
8. Coughlan, *Young John Dewey,* p. 20; Coughlan is unfair to the Reverend B. F. Cocker, a Yorkshireman of some energy who had been an accountant and a trader in the South Pacific; it was shipwreck and a too close encounter with cannibalism on Fiji that had urged him ashore and into the pulpit; Wenley, *Life and Work,* p. 135ff.
9. Wenley, *Life and Work,* p. 135.
10. Marsden, *Soul of the American University,* pp. 150–64, sheds some light on the subject; he takes the piety of both Gilman and Hall quite straightforwardly.
11. This view was expressed in the *Three Essays on Religion* that he wrote toward the end of his life but allowed to be published only after his death.
12. These were remarks Dewey supplied for inclusion in Wenley, *Life and Work,* pp. 315–16. With part of Morris's judgment it is easy to concur; being James Mill's son was obviously very hard work. Mill's greatest personal misfortune, however, was his marrying Harriet Taylor rather than, say, George Eliot.
13. Hall wrote an engrossing but self-serving and unreliable autobiography, *Life and Confessions of a Psychologist* (New York, 1923); Dorothy Ross, *G. Stanley Hall* (Chicago, 1973) is a serious but readable study not only of Hall but of the growth of American empirical psychology; Coughlan, *Young John Dewey,* pp. 33–36, has a vivid few pages on his career but makes too much of his manipulative qualities and too little of the extent to which he and Morris shared a concern to square the growth of science with Christian spirituality. This is treated in detail in Marsden, *Soul of the American University,* pp. 159–64.
14. Ross, *Hall,* p. 79.
15. Coughlan, *Young John Dewey,* p. 35, writes of his "impious detachment from what was being preached at Union Theological Seminary" and the "coolness with which he watched the giants of German theology and philosophy parade before him." Ross more plausibly suggests a deep ambiva-

lence in Hall: He wanted to kick over the traces but not to upset the cart.
16. Dykhuizen, *Life and Mind,* p. 35.
17. Ross, *Hall,* p. 113.
18. On all this, Ross, *Hall,* pp. 116–33, is fascinating.
19. Ibid., p. 138.
20. Ibid., pp. 144–46.
21. Dykhuizen, *Life and Mind,* pp. 31–32.
22. Schilpp, *Philosophy of Dewey,* p. 18.
23. "The Sphere of Application of the Excluded Middle," *LW,* vol. 5, pp. 197–202. Dewey's logic has now found a defender: Thomas Burke, *Dewey's New Logic* (Chicago, 1995).
24. "From Absolutism to Experimentalism," *LW,* vol. 5, pp. 156–57.
25. That this is how his employers at Johns Hopkins also thought of Peirce is confirmed by Joseph Brent, *Charles Sanders Peirce* (Bloomington, Ind., 1993), p. 133.
26. Quoted in Dykhuizen, *Life and Mind,* pp. 30–31.
27. Ibid., p. 31.
28. For Hall's lecture, Ross, *G. S. Hall,* pp. 139–41; for Dewey's paper, Dykhuizen, *Life and Mind,* pp. 37–38. Both were published in *Andover Review* (1885). Dewey's essay is discussed by Lewis Hahn, "Introduction" to *EW,* vol. 1, p. xiv; and the essay itself is in *EW,* vol. 1, pp. 48–60.
29. "The New Psychology," *EW,* vol. 1, p. 60.
30. R. L. Nettleship, ed., *The Works of Thomas Hill Green* (London, 1883).
31. David Hume, *A Treatise on Human Nature,* ed. T. H. Green and T. H. Grose (London, 1884).
32. "From Absolutism to Experimentalism," *LW,* vol. 5, p. 152.
33. Schilpp, *Philosophy of Dewey,* p. 17.
34. Coughlan, *Young John Dewey,* pp. 37–39.
35. Dykhuizen, *Life and Mind,* p. 39.
36. Ibid., p. 40.
37. Ibid., p. 45.
38. Schilpp, *Philosophy of Dewey,* p. 18.
39. "Education and the Health of Women," *EW,* vol. 1, pp. 64–68, reprinted from *Science* (October 1885); "Health and Sex in Higher Education," *EW,* vol. 1, pp. 69–80, reprinted from *Popular Science Monthly* (March 1886); "Psychology in High-Schools," *EW,* vol. 1, pp. 81–89, a paper read to the Michigan School-Masters' Club, 1886.
40. Rockefeller, *John Dewey,* pp. 145–51, finds more in Dewey's love letters than I have managed to do; as I said earlier, they strike me as touchingly inarticulate, but their inarticulacy is their most striking feature. It is unfair to compare them with the correspondence between Mill and Harriet Taylor; the illicitness of their love and the cosmic significance they attached to it made them put more on paper than Dewey and his "Chippie" had to. It is even more unfair to compare the correspondence of Dewey and Alice Chipman with Russell's letters to Ottoline Morrell. Still, I would not want Dewey's letters to be taken as representative of the way philosophers in love write.
41. "From Absolutism to Experimentalism," *LW,* vol. 5, pp. 150–51.
42. "Our Duty to Knowledge of God," *EW,* vol. 1, p. 61.

3. FINDING A VOICE

1. Rockefeller, *John Dewey,* pp. 98–205, provides a longer and more detailed account of this period; Coughlan, *Young John Dewey,* ch. 5 and 6, is briskly done, and full of interesting insights; Westbrook, *John Dewey and American Democracy* is unique in taking Franklin Ford's side against Dewey but is too eager for Dewey to get over Hegelian metaphysics and get on with participatory democracy to have much to say about the philosophical interest of his work.
2. Randolph Bourne, "Transnational America," *The Radical Will,* ed. Olaf Hansen (New York, 1977), p. 256.
3. The best-known philosophical defense of the existence of "non-natural" moral values is G. E. Moore, *Principa Ethica* (Cambridge, England, 1903), a work that Bertrand Russell and Maynard Keynes described as the Bible of Bloomsbury.
4. It is often argued that Green was in many ways even more indebted to Kant and Fichte than to Hegel. We need not engage that argument; Dewey was drawn to the Hegelian elements in Green's ethics and political philosophy and rejected the Kantian, dualistic elements.
5. E. M. Butler, *The Tyranny of Greece over Germany* (Cambridge, England, 1933).
6. G. W. F. Hegel, *The Philosophy of History* (New York, 1956), p. 21.
7. Westbrook, *Dewey and Democracy,* pp. 197–212; Bourne, "A Twilight of Idols"

and "The War and the Intellectuals," *Radical Will,* pp. 336–47, 307–18.

8. "Christianity and Democracy," *EW,* vol. 4, pp. 3–10.
9. Lasch, *New Radicalism,* pp. 158–60.
10. Ibid., p. 161.
11. Lamont, *Dialogue,* p. 30.
12. This is a difficult matter to get exactly right; the British philosophers, social workers, clergymen, and others who started the settlement movement in the East End slums in London were eager both to integrate immigrants from eastern Europe and to integrate the "outcast" poor into respectable society. See Gertrude Himmelfarb, *Poverty and Compassion* (New York, 1992).
13. Lords Balfour and Haldane respectively. Isaac Kramnick and Barry Shearman, *Harold Laski* (London, 1993), describe Haldane as "the author, also, of books on Dewey's philosophy and Einstein's theory of relativity," but I have found no trace of a book on Dewey.
14. James Kloppenburg, *Uncertain Victory* (New York, 1986), is one of the few commentators who has wholly taken the measure of the community of interests and intellectual allegiances on both sides of the Atlantic; his account is too crammed with information to be accessible to anyone who does not know quite a lot about his subject already, but anyone skeptical of my claim that Dewey was part of an international movement of ideas may find Kloppenburg reassuring.
15. Melvin Richter, *The Politics of Conscience* (London, 1963); Green's political ideas are treated in more detail in Peter Nicholson, *The Political Philosophy of the British Idealists* (Cambridge, England, 1990).
16. "The Philosophy of Thomas Hill Green," *Andover Review* (1889), in *EW,* vol. 3, p. 15.
17. J. S. Mill, "Utilitarianism," in John Stuart Mill and Jeremy Bentham, *Utilitarianism and Other Essays* (Harmondsworth, England, 1987), pp. 278–79.
18. Charles Taylor, "What Is Human Agency?," *Philosophical Papers* (Cambridge, England, 1985), vol. 1, pp. 16–44.
19. "Philosophy of Thomas Hill Green," *EW,* vol. 3, p. 17.
20. Rockefeller, *John Dewey,* p. 110ff, is kinder to the whole project and nicely catches the underlying sentiment; I remain more sympathetic to the sentiment than the argument.
21. "Philosophy of Green," *EW,* vol. 3, p. 24.
22. Ibid.
23. Ibid., pp. 32–33.
24. James Q. Wilson, *The Moral Sense* (New York, 1993) is the most recent example of such an attempt.
25. John Rawls, *A Theory of Justice* (Cambridge, Mass., 1971).
26. E.g., Michael Sandel, *Liberalism and the Limits of Justice* (Cambridge, England, 1981).
27. F. H. Bradley, "My Station and Its Duties," *Ethical Studies* (Oxford, 1924), p. 112ff.
28. G. W. F. Hegel, *The Phenomenology of Spirit,* tr. A. V. Miller (Oxford, 1977), pp. 111–19.
29. G. W. F. Hegel, *The Philosophy of Right,* tr. Allen Wood (Cambridge, England, 1991), pp. 360–64; the hussars appear at p. 362.
30. We know that he taught these courses; he describes the content in a general way in "Ethics in the University of Michigan," an account of all the moral and political philosophy courses the department put on in 1889. *EW,* vol. 3, p. 50.
31. Ibid.
32. Schilpp, *Philosophy of Dewey,* p. 18.
33. "From Absolutism to Experimentalism," *MW,* vol. 5, p. 151.
34. "Christianity and Democracy," *EW,* vol. 4, p. 9.
35. Ibid.
36. Hilary Putnam, *Renewing Philosophy* (Cambridge, Mass., 1992), ch. 9, "A Reconsideration of Deweyan Democracy."
37. The theory of the "open society" stems from Karl Popper, *The Open Society and Its Enemies* (London, 1945).
38. "Christianity and Democracy," *EW,* vol. 4, p. 10.
39. Richard Hofstadter, *Anti-intellectualism in American Life* (New York, 1963), part 2, "The Religion of the Heart."
40. Hofstadter, loc. cit, provides chapter and verse.
41. Reinhold Niebuhr, *Moral Man and Immoral Society* (New York, 1932); *The Children of Light and the Children of Darkness* (New York, 1944).
42. James Fallows, *Looking at the Sun* (New York, 1994).
43. "The Ethics of Democracy," *EW,* vol. 1, p. 235.
44. Ibid.
45. "Two Phases of Renan's Life," *EW,* vol. 3, pp. 174–79; "Renan's Loss of Faith in Science," *EW,* vol. 4, pp. 11–18.
46. "Poetry and Philosophy," *EW,* vol. 3, pp. 123–24.
47. Marsden, *Soul of the American University,*

ch. 10, pp. 167–80, is devoted to the religious aspects of James Angell's presidency at Michigan.

48. Coughlan, *Young John Dewey,* pp. 110–11.
49. Rockefeller, *John Dewey,* pp. 172–98; Westbrook, *Dewey and Democracy,* pp. 51–58.
50. Westbrook, *Dewey and Democracy,* p. 58.
51. For a gripping account, see Paul Avrich, *The Haymarket Tragedy* (Princeton, 1984).
52. Corydon Ford, *Child of Democracy* (New York, 1893); Coughlan, *Young John Dewey,* pp. 96–108, gives a wonderfully funny account of the disaster.
53. Dewey to Henry Carter Adams, April 29, 1899, quoted in Coughlan, *Young John Dewey,* p. 98.
54. *Michigan Daily,* March 16, 1892, in Coughlan, *Young John Dewey,* p. 102.
55. Ibid., p. 105.
56. Ibid., p. 107.
57. As later did his enthusiasm for F. M. Alexander and the Alexander Technique" and his (unique) ability to get along with the irascible Albert Barnes over a period of thirty-six years. Coughlan, *Young John Dewey* writes of Dewey's "lifelong weakness for quacks." p. 96.
58. Debs's recently published letters may suggest another meaning to that proposition; I mean only that historians of socialism and late-twentieth-century social democrats find his energy, courage, and warmheartedness irresistible.
59. Page Smith, *The Rise of Industrial America* (New York, 1990 [1984]), ch. 29, gives a briskly partisan view of the Pullman strike that is both informative in itself and takes much the view of events that Dewey took.
60. Georges Sorel, *Reflections on Violence* (New York 1961 [1917]).
61. "Ethics of Democracy," *EW,* vol. 1, p. 246.
62. Ibid., p. 248.
63. John L. Thomas, *Alternative America* (Cambridge, Mass., 1983) is now the standard work on George.
64. Henry George, *Progress and Poverty* (San Francisco, 1879); Bertrand Russell thought George a more useful economic theorist than Marx; absent the obsession with land, George's concern with monopoly persisted in the Fabians and other unutopian socialists.
65. Professor Westbrook claims that Dewey became a serious *American* thinker only when he moved to Chicago in 1894 and that his work at Ann Arbor was derivative and secondhand because he was too far removed from American life. Dewey's work certainly becomes more original in the later 1890s, but his intellectual universe is less *American* than secular, modern, and focused on economic and social issues: in some ways this makes it less American and more cosmopolitan. His attachment to Jane Addams illustrates this.
66. See, for instance, the works of Paul Avrich, including *The Haymarket Tragedy,* loc. cit., *The Modern School Movement* (Princeton, 1980), and *Anarchist Portraits* (Princeton, 1988).
67. Coughlan, *Young John Dewey,* pp. 109–12.
68. Westbrook, *Dewey and American Democracy,* p. 91.
69. See Bertrand Russell, *Roads to Freedom* (London, 1918), p. 138ff, for just that argument.

4. THE PEDAGOGUE AS PROPHET

1. I put it so by way of provocation; the relationship of Dewey to "progressive education" is wonderfully confused. The simplest plausible view is that he was *not* an enthusiast for progressive education, that he became a guru to those who were, and that he unfairly became an obvious target of criticism for those who disapproved of all educational change whatever.
2. Dykhuizen, *Life and Mind,* p. 85.
3. Schilpp, *Philosophy of Dewey,* p. 33.
4. Forcey, *Crossroads of Liberalism,* ch. 6.
5. Lawrence Cremin, *Teachers College* (New York, 1954), pp. 99–113.
6. Dykhuizen, *Life and Mind,* ch. 6, gives a restrained account of all this; Westbrook, *Dewey and American Democracy,* pp. 86–92, is hostile to Harper and John D. Rockefeller, but not wholly sympathetic to Dewey. Westbrook's doubts are not mine, however. Westbrook's position is that Rockefeller was a capitalist; the university was thus a capitalist university; Dewey was an anticapitalist; therefore, Dewey ought to have waged war against his employers but did not. My sympathies are not wholly different, but Dewey had no particular reason to fight anticapitalist battles at that point and was anyway preoccupied by his family, department, and school. So far as the Lab School is concerned, it would have looked like a luxury to any university president, and Dewey would have looked like a headline grabber to anyone trying to orga-

nize more orthodox and utilitarian activities in the teacher training field. Dewey fought all his life against the suggestion that the education he proposed was one of "fads" and "frills." "Frills"—such as education in art and music—were of the essence.

7. This is, of course, the main argument of Karl Popper's *The Logic of Scientific Discovery* (London, 1957), a work that argues, somewhat at odds with its own title, that there is *no* logic of discovery. It may be of some psychological interest how people come to think up scientific hypotheses, and it is surely of great socioological interest to know what cultures foster scientific inquiry and what cultures do not, but what gives the hypotheses scientific value is their success in withstanding the public process of criticism. Because Dewey held on to the nineteenth-century faith in the possibility of a "real logic," there was for him, as there cannot be for Popper, a *logic* to the process of thinking up hypotheses. All the same, in Dewey's work also, it is verification and falsification that count.
8. Since I argue later that Dewey's philosophy is a much more successful philosophy of public life than insightful into the inner life, I say a very little more about this weakness in my conclusion, below, pp. 367–68.
9. Brent, *Peirce,* pp. 151–52.
10. Dykhuizen, *Life and Mind,* p. 74ff.
11. Schilpp, *Philosophy of Dewey,* p. 24.
12. Dewey Papers, Southern Illinois University, Carbondale.
13. "The Reflex Arc Concept in Psychology," *EW,* vol. 5, pp. 96–109.
14. This is perhaps unfair to Charles Taylor, *The Explanation of Behaviour* (London, 1964), itself a rather Deweyan treatment of the shortcomings of a purely mechanistic analysis of behavior.
15. "Reflex Arc Concept," *EW,* vol. 5, p. 96.
16. Neil Coughlan is much taken with the image of this child, whom he visualizes as a rather stolid figure in a Dutch interior, and Dewey's taste for folksy pictorial examples is indeed engaging. Coughlan, *Young John Dewey,* pp. 138–42.
17. "Reflex Arc Concept," *EW,* vol. 5, p. 105.
18. *Human Nature and Conduct, MW,* vol. 14, p. 228.
19. Review of Josiah Royce's *Nature, Man and the Moral Order, MW,* vol. 2, pp. 120–37.
20. Particularly in *A Common Faith* and *Art as Experience,* discussed at length in ch. 7 below.
21. Lamont, *Dialogue,* pp. 15–18.
22. "The Evolutionary Method as Applied to Ethics: I Its Scientific Necessity; The Evolutionary Method as Applied to Ethics: II Its Significance for Conduct," *MW,* vol. 2, pp. 3–19; pp. 20–38.
23. Among interesting attempts to provide an evolutionary account of everyday morality, Robert Frank, *Passions within Reason* (New York, 1988) is strikingly clear and sensible.
24. T. H. Huxley, *Evolution and Ethics,* (Oxford, 1895).
25. William Graham Sumner, *What Social Classes Owe to Each Other* (Caldwell, Idaho, 1978 [1883]); Dorothy Ross, *The Origins of American Social Science* (Cambridge, England, 1991), pp. 85–90.
26. Ross, *Origins,* pp. 240–46.
27. "Evolution and Ethics," *EW,* vol. 5, p. 53.
28. "My Pedagogic Creed," *EW,* vol. 5, pp. 84–95.
29. I am not the first commentator to have had that sensation. "One is tempted to continue indefinitely quoting from this *Creed,*" wrote William H. Kilpatrick, when discussing "Dewey's Influence on Education," *Schilpp, Philosophy of Dewey,* p. 463.
30. "My Pedagogic Creed," *EW,* vol. 5, p. 95.
31. Lawrence A. Cremin, *The Transformation of the School* (New York, 1961), p. 100.
32. "My Pedagogic Creed," *EW,* vol. 5, p. 86.
33. Ibid.
34. S. J. Curtis and M. A. E. Boultwood, *A Short History of Educational Ideas* (London, 1953), pp. 377–81.
35. Rita Kramer, *Maria Montessori* (London, 1991), pp. 227–32.
36. The best account is still Katherine Camp Mayhew and Anna Camp Edwards, *The Dewey School* (New York, 1936); Cremin gives a nice account of the school's work, *Transformation,* pp. 115–26; *Middle Works,* vol. 1, contains Dewey's *The School and Society* and a great deal of informative material besides.
37. For an engaging account of Neill, though it incidentally gets Dewey quite wrong, see Robert Skidelsky, *English Progressive Schools* (Harmondsworth, England, 1968), part 3; for the observation that Dewey thought that "[t]he task of the educator was simply to provide educational experiences," see p. 148, as also for the entirely implausible claim that "Dewey never made clear what the difference was between an educational and a non-educational experience." Dewey, of course, had at least two answers to this latter claim: In the first place, schools are places "set apart" and organized in order to provide a sequence of experiences geared to the child's intellectual development, and in the second place, there

was all the difference in the world between experiences that had no particular shape or logic to them, or that consisted of the mere accumulation of unsorted data, and those that enabled the child to master, organize, and, as Dewey always put it, ascertain the "value" of what he was confronted with.

38. *The School and Society, MW,* vol. 1, p. 8.
39. Ibid., p. 9.
40. Ibid.
41. The latter was Christopher Lasch's criticism in *New Radicalism,* ch. 5, and provides the target of Westbrook's discussion, *Dewey and Democracy,* pp. 167–82.
42. This is a point I take up more aggressively in the last chapter.
43. *School and Society, MW,* vol. 1, p. 10.
44. Ibid., p. 39.
45. Ibid., p. 81.
46. Ibid.
47. Ibid.
48. The Prussian government banned the establishment of kindergartens in 1851; this seems to have been the result not of an authoritarian government's suspicion of all forms of freedom but of the Ministry of Education's confusing the apolitical, mystical Friedrich Froebel with his nephew Karl, a socialist. Harry G. Good and James D. Teller, *A History of Western Education* (New York, 1969), p. 287.
49. Bertrand Russell's two short books *On Education* and *Education and the Social Order* do not go off on long metaphysical excursions, but there is much to be said for the thought that Russell's attachment to Froebel and Montessori teaching methods was part of a desire to protect children *from* society rather than a desire to integrate the child *into* society.
50. E.g., "Interpretation of Savage Mind," *MW,* vol. 2, pp. 39–52.
51. Cremin, *Transformation,* p. 141.
52. *Interest in Relation to Training of the Will* [1895], *EW,* vol. 5, pp. 111–50.
53. *How We Think, MW,* vol. 6, pp. 177–355.
54. Ibid., p. 208.
55. Ibid., pp. 208–09.
56. Ibid., p. 215.
57. Ibid., p. 338.
58. Ibid., p. 339.
59. Ibid., p. 237.
60. I do not mean that Kilpatrick was *not* in intention, and perhaps to a large extent in fact, a disciple; rather that he pushed one side of Dewey's program in a way that Dewey would not have done.
61. Randolph Bourne, *The Gary Schools* (Cambridge, Mass., 1970 [1916]; Cremin, *Transformation,* pp. 155–56.
62. Westbrook, *Dewey and Democracy,* pp. 180–81; Cremin, *Transformation,* pp. 153–60.
63. Westbrook, *Dewey and Democracy,* ch. 6, "Democracy and Education."
64. Arnold Toynbee was a fellow of Balliol, famous above all for his saintly character and early death. He was the uncle of the historian, who was named after him but shared little else with him.
65. On the connection between the settlement movement and progressive education, Cremin, *Transformation,* pp. 59–64.
66. Jane Addams, *Twenty Years at Hull-House* (New York, 1910); Robert Merton, "Manifest and Latent Functions," *Social Theory and Social Structure* (New York, 1968), pp. 126–30.
67. Jane Addams, *A Modern Lear,* reprinted in Christopher Lasch, ed., *The Social Thought of Jane Addams,* 1965.
68. "The School as Social Centre," *MW,* vol. 2, p. 85.
69. Westbrook, *Dewey and Democracy,* pp. 80–81.

5. PRAGMATISM AT WAR

1. Schilpp, *Philosophy of Dewey,* p. 35.
2. It is a typical result of Dewey's success in burying his private life that the only source for the suggestion that Alice Dewey made his life miserable during the last twenty years of her life is Max Eastman. Dewey's children protested that he was quite wrong, but Dewey's headaches, backaches, and general depression during the war suggest that Eastman may have been right. One may draw much the same conclusion from Dewey's poetry.
3. Quoted in Caroline Moorehead, *Bertrand Russell* (New York, 1993), p. 199.
4. Thomas Bender, *New York Intellectuals* (New York, 1988), p. 227.
5. On all this, see Forcey, *Crossroads of Liberalism;* Christopher Lasch, *New Radicalism,* ch. 6, "The New Republic and the War."
6. Smith, *America Enters the World,* p. 849, reacts in a way that has tempted many critics; of Dewey's work in general, he observes: "That Dewey's philosophical views were in the main shallow was far less im-

portant than the fact that their practical consequences were on the whole exemplary." The war being a far from exemplary business, we then have a shallowness with no redeeming social merit.

7. Bourne was the most philosophically deft critic, and the most embittered as having been such an admirer of Dewey's work, but Harold Stearns, Lewis Mumford, Waldo Frank, and many others saw Dewey's support for American involvement in World War I as revealing some fatal flaw in pragmatism. The conflict between the demands of culture and the demands of state is the running theme of Casey Nelson Blake, *Beloved Community* (Chapel Hill, N.C., 1990), and Dewey was caught squarely in the middle of the fight. See especially Blake's chs. 5 and 6, pp. 157–228.
8. Thorstein Veblen, *The Theory of the Leisure Class* (New York, 1973 [1901]); Morton White, *Social Thought in America* (New York, 1976 [1947]), chs. X, XI.
9. Ray Stannard Baker, quoted in Smith, *America Enters the World*, p. 472.
10. The degree of self-control Dewey managed is suggested by James Farrell's recollection that the worst Dewey ever said of Russell was "You know, he gets me sore." That seems a very calm response to Russell's constant teasing and jabbing. Russell's criticisms caused particular irritation. One problem was that they contained jokes that Dewey did not see, but the greater difficulty was that Russell had a near-religious detestation of the pragmatist conception of truth. Although he often parodied it as the doctrine that we could believe anything that made us feel good and joined the throng of critics who held that it was a characteristically American idea that the truth is "whatever works," Russell's deeper objection was that in a cold and Godless world the only objective value mankind had left was the belief that what is true is true because of the way the world is, whether we believe it or not, and whether we are helped by it or not. This difference in outlook is one of the things that underlies the contrast between Dewey's essay *A Common Faith* and Russell's "A Free Man's Worship." Lamont, *Dialogue*, p. 35. Dewey could be nastier than Farrell recalled in the *Dialogue;* in a letter to Farrell he explained Walter Lippmann's turn toward the political philosophy of the classical world as "another case of Jewish inferiority compensatory reaction." Quoted in J. P. Diggins, *The Promise of Pragmatism* (Chicago, 1994), p. 349.
11. Dykhuizen, *Life and Mind*, p. 149.
12. Max Eastman thought she was "impossible except for saints to live with," but Dewey was, after all, widely thought to be a saint. Eastman, "John Dewey," pp. 80–81.
13. Lamont, *Dialogue*, pp. 82–83.
14. Ibid., p. 136.
15. Eastman, "John Dewey," pp. 680–81.
16. See Dewey's introduction to the Henry Street Settlement's guide to vocational education in New York City, *MW*, vol. 8, pp. 205–06.
17. Dykhuizen, *Life and Mind*, pp. 149–50.
18. Cremin, *Teachers College*, p. 47.
19. Ibid., p. 144.
20. William H. Kilpatrick, "Dewey's Influence on Education," Schilpp, *Philosophy of Dewey*, pp. 447–72.
21. Cremin, *Teachers College*, pp. 249–50.
22. J. H. Randall, Jr., "The Department of Philosophy," *The Faculty of Philosophy* (New York, 1954), p. 126.
23. Ibid.
24. Ibid., pp. 127–28.
25. Randall writes of Dewey's and Adler's engaging in many practical activities together, but Dykhuizen says that they "failed to develop the close ties that each would have welcomed and from which each could have profited." Dykhuizen, *Life and Mind*, p. 121.
26. "Biography of John Dewey," Schilpp, *Philosophy of Dewey*, pp. 35–36; other colleagues recall Dewey's being personally friendly with Montague but philosophically distant. Lamont, *Dialogue*, p. 98.
27. Randall, "The Department of Philosophy," pp. 116–17.
28. The best account of these movements of persons and thoughts alike is Dorothy Ross's *Origins*.
29. White, *Social Thought in America* remains the best general account of "the revolt against formalism."
30. Lamont, *Dialogue*, pp. 55–56.
31. Morton Horwitz, *The Transformation of American Law, 1870–1960* (New York, 1992), pp. 169–73.
32. White, *Social Thought in America*, ch. 12.
33. *German Philosophy and Culture* [1915], *MW*, vol. 8, pp. 135–204; the little book was reprinted during World War II with an introduction that maintained the existence of an "essential continuity" between the culture of Wilhelmine Germany and that of the Third Reich.

34. Alan Ryan, *Bertrand Russell: A Political Life* (New York, 1988), pp. 65–66.
35. Smith, *America Enters the World*, p. 471.
36. It is not a question susceptible of a naïve answer, of course, but many readers of *Democracy and Education* must have come away with a strong sense of Dewey's general orientation but with no clear view of what education *for* democracy and education *as* democracy were.
37. Horace Kallen, "Democracy versus the Melting Pot," *Nation* (1915); Horace Kallen, *Democracy and Culture* (Boston, 1924); Bourne, "Transnational America," pp. 248–60.
38. "A Key to the New World," *LW*, vol. 2, pp. 226–30.
39. Kramer, *Maria Montessori*, pp. 227–32; the villain of the piece was W. H. Kilpatrick, who published a savagely critical account of her work in *The Montessori System Examined* in 1914.
40. "Introduction," *MW*, vol. 8, p. 99.
41. See above, ch. 4, p. 149–50.
42. Interestingly enough, this idea has been making a comeback recently; Deborah Meier, the principal of the Central Park East school in New York City, has raised funds to create schools in which pupils will spend their entire school careers. *New York Times*, July 14, 1993, B 7.
43. *Schools of Tomorrow*, *MW*, vol. 8, p. 320.
44. In this, of course, I am at odds with Westbrook, *Dewey and Democracy*, pp. 167–82.
45. "A Policy of Industrial Education," *MW*, vol. 7, pp. 94–95.
46. Ibid., p. 95.
47. Lasch, *New Radicalism*, ch. 5.
48. Thus William Appleman Williams, *An Outline of American History* (New York, 1990), pp. 310–12, complains of Dewey's obscure and vacillating political style; the complaint is sharper because Williams assumes that Dewey's criticisms of industrial capitalism were derived from Marx and should have had Marx's clarity—but they weren't and couldn't.
49. How many traces of Comte is a subject of some controversy; Forcey, *Crossroads*, offers a more "Comtist" reading, Howard Stettner, *Herbert Croly and the Making of Modern Liberalism* (Lawrence, Kan., 1993) brings Croly into the 1920s as a proto–New Deal Liberal and thus as a "maker of modern liberalism."
50. "Some Dangers in the Present Movement for Industrial Democracy," *EW*, vol. 7, p. 99.
51. Ibid.
52. Hardheaded political scientists such as Robert Dahl continue to speculate about just how we might achieve this community control without destroying the efficiency of companies so managed; Dahl shares Dewey's conviction that a democracy confined to the political sphere is only half a democracy and is so unsure how far participation can be achieved in the political sphere that they naturally turn to its possibilities in the workplace. R. A. Dahl, *After the Revolution?* (New Haven, 1972).
53. "From Absolutism to Experimentalism," *LW*, vol. 5, p. 150.
54. Woodbridge (but not Randall) thought *Quest for Certainty* was the best single statement of Dewey's thinking. Lamont, *Dialogue*, p. 53.
55. "Introduction," *MW*, vol. 8, p. ix.
56. Ibid., p. xix.
57. "From Absolutism to Experimentalism," *LW*, vol. 5, pp. 150–52.
58. *Democracy and Education*, *MW*, vol. 8, p. 87.
59. Ibid.
60. Ibid., p. 88.
61. Ibid., p. 89.
62. Ibid., p. 105.
63. *German Philosophy and Politics*, *MW*, vol. 8, pp. 198–99.
64. Lamont, *Dialogue*, pp. 24–25; Rockefeller, *John Dewey*, pp. 333–44, gives a kindly account.
65. On all of which the introduction to Jo Ann Boydston, *The Poems of John Dewey* is admirably cool, sensible, and good-natured, and the story of how Dewey's poetry from this period came to be acquired by Herbert Schneider and Milton Halsey Thomas, then by Roberta Dewey, finally to be published by Professor Boydston is extremely gratifying. Steven Rockefeller discusses the not-quite affair from what seems to me an excessively sentimental perspective, but with a wonderful selection from Dewey's letters and poems (*(John Dewey*, pp. 344–56). Norma Rosen's *John and Anzia* (New York, 1989) is a novelized version of events, but readers may prefer Yezierska's own version, *All That I Could Never Be* (New York, 1932), and her autobiography, *Red Ribbon on a White Horse* (New York, 1950).
66. Louise Henricksen, *Anzia Yezierska*, pp. 181–87 (New York, 1990).
67. I take it that this is why Steven Rockefeller, *John Dewey*, pp. 344–56, devotes so much attention to the poems; in their own right they would not warrant it. Jo Ann Boydston, *Poems*, pp. lii–lxvii, gives a deft and delicate account of the relationship be-

tween the poems, Dewey's views on art, and Dewey's "religious" view of the natural world.

68. Ronald Steel, *Walter Lippmann and the American Century* (Boston, 1980) is a stunningly good account of a man about whom Steel must have felt the greatest ambivalence during the many years in which he was working on the book.
69. Lippmann was something of a fire-eater from the beginning, but he was also twenty years younger than his fellow editors.
70. Blake, *Beloved Community,* pp. 157–70, is not entirely sympathetic to Bourne; Westbrook, *Dewey and Democracy,* pp. 202–12, is, and is surely persuasive that Dewey was wrong, whether or not Bourne was right.
71. There is some evidence that Dewey was stung by Bourne's mockery of F. M. Alexander and the Alexander Technique, Lamont, *Dialogue,* p. 25.
72. Ray Ginger, *Debs: A Life* (Chicago, 1948), pp. 220–25.
73. See Dewey's reply to William Hocking's criticism of this view, *MW,* vol. 8, pp. 418–19 (from *New Republic* [1915], p. 236).
74. Hegel, *Philosophy of Right,* §256 addition.
75. *German Philosophy and Politics, MW,* vol. 8, pp. 166–67.
76. Ibid., pp. 201–02.
77. Ibid., p. 203.
78. Bourne, "Transnational America," pp. 248–64.
79. "The Principle of Nationality," *MW,* vol. 8, p. 289, from *Menorah Journal* (1917).
80. Bourne, "Transnational America," p. 255.
81. Ibid., p. 254.
82. 'Force, Violence and Law," *MW,* vol. 10, pp. 211–15; "The Future of Pacifism," *MW,* vol. 10, pp. 265–70.
83. "In a Time of National Hesitation," *MW,* vol. 10, pp. 256–59.
84. "In Explanation of Our Lapse," *MW,* vol. 10, pp. 290–95.
85. See Walter Feinberg's review of Westbrook, *Dewey and Democracy, Educational Theory* (1993) pp. 195–216.

6. Political Narrowness and Philosophical Breadth

1. This was one reason why he was so hostile to Marxism; Dewey thought that violent means poisoned the socialist end and that evil means, so to speak, polluted the goals for whose sake they were used. This was the crux of the famous debate with Trotsky reprinted in George Novack, ed., *Their Morals and Ours* (New York, 1965).
2. Even his close friends were not unanimous on this point, however; James Farrell's "high regard" was not shared by Horace Kallen and Herbert Schneider, for instance. Lamont, *Dialogue,* pp. 86–88.
3. Westbrook, *Dewey and American Democracy,* pp. 232–35, gives a long and detailed account of the maneuvring by which the *Dial* was transferred to a proprietor who would assemble a prowar board.
4. Lamont, *Dialogue,* p. 30.
5. Blake, *Beloved Community,* pp. 224–27.
6. Westbrook, *Dewey and Democracy,* pp. 231–40, 260–74; he gives an interesting account of Dewey's switch from believing in the (relative) virtuousness of American policy to his acceptance of the more radical view that the United States was an imperialist power much like the rest at pp. 252–60.
7. Westbrook thinks Dewey was ready to abandon hope in early 1919, but this strikes me as a little premature; an air of "hope against hope" pervades his essays on American involvement, but I suspect that he was so emotionally invested in the line he had taken that he did his best to persuade himself that matters might turn out well.
8. Steel, *Walter Lippmann and the American Century,* pp. 158–66, 252–54.
9. Dykhuizen, *Life and Mind,* pp. 290–91, is wrong to suggest that Dewey was anything but an isolationist from 1939 to 1941; he supported lend-lease and was in favor of the U.S. government's supplying Britain with war materials on easy terms, but his best-known remarks on the subject of American intervention were published under the heading "Whatever Happens, Stay Out."
10. Dykhuizen, *Life and Mind,* pp. 198–99; this contradicts Horace Kallen's recollection in Lamont, *Dialogue,* p. 36, but Dykhuizen's version sounds more plausible. Alice Dewey may well have disliked both Russell and Miss Black, but she would have rebelled against any attempt to discriminate against Dora.
11. Quoted in Dykhuizen, *Life and Mind,* p. 198.
12. "Pragmatic America," *MW,* vol. 13, p. 307.
13. It was also more attractive than Mrs. Dewey's rather fiercer radicalism; Russell used to tell the story of how she demanded

that the provincial governor of Hunan should set about instituting coeducation in the local schools. Dykhuizen, *Life and Mind,* p. 198. There are several accounts of Dewey's visit and impact; the best is generally agreed to be Barry Keenan, *The Dewey Experiment in China: Educational Power and Political Reform in the Early Republic* (Cambridge, Mass., 1977).

14. Howard Greenfield, *The Devil and Dr. Barnes* (New York, 1987).
15. Ibid., Dykhuizen, *Life and Mind,* pp. 222–23; Westbrook, *Dewey and Democracy,* pp. 387–89.
16. Sidney Hook, *Pragmatism and the Tragic Sense of Life* (New York, 1974), p. 108.
17. One of the unnerving features of Dewey's philosophical writings was his slipperiness about just what was and was not part of pragmatism; late in life he claimed that pragmatism was a theory of truth, art was not a matter of truth, so his theory of art was not a pragmatist theory. It would be hard to argue that it was anything but continuous with the rest of his philosophy, however.
18. One recent exception is Alasdair MacIntyre's *Three Rival Versions of Moral Inquiry* (London, 1991).
19. "The Need for a Recovery of Philosophy," *MW,* vol. 11, p. 1.
20. "Morals and the Conduct of States." *MW,* vol. 11, pp. 122–23.
21. "The Discrediting of Idealism," *MW,* vol. 11, pp. 181–82.
22. "Our National Dilemma," *MW,* vol. 12, pp. 4, 7.
23. Dykhuizen, *Life and Mind,* pp. 218–21.
24. Lippmann's attack is reprinted as an appendix to *MW,* vol. 15, p. 406.
25. "Ethics and International Relations," *MW,* vol. 15, p. 63.
26. "Shall We Join the League?," *MW,* vol. 15, p. 78ff.
27. Ibid., p. 79.
28. David B. Truman, *The Governmental Process* (New York, 1958).
29. Joseph Schumpeter, *Capitalism, Socialism and Democracy* (London, 1942), ch. XXII–XXIV.
30. Dewey's review of *The Phantom Public, LW,* vol. 2, pp. 211–20.
31. *The Public and Its Problems, LW,* vol. 2, pp. 245–46.
32. Ibid., p. 303.
33. Ibid., p. 300.
34. For a vivid image of what he was after, Dewey quoted a famous passage from W. D. Hudson's *A Traveller in Little Things* (New York, 1921), in which Hudson describes the way in which the news that someone had injured himself would fly from one end to another of the Wiltshire village he was describing, in such a way that not merely the *fact* of the accident was carried, but its whole emotional and psychological import as well. *The Public and Its Problems, LW,* vol. 2, p. 261. Passages like this explain why so many critics have thought of Dewey as a theorist of social nostalgia, hankering after a return to the rural values and environments of his childhood.
35. Of whom Jürgen Habermas is the best known. See below, ch. 9, pp. 356–57.
36. "Japan and America," *MW,* vol. 11, pp. 150–55; "Liberalism in Japan," *MW,* vol. 11, pp. 156–73.
37. "Japan and America," loc. cit., pp. 152–53.
38. Ibid., p. 152.
39. Ibid., p. 161.
40. Ibid., p. 160.
41. Ibid., pp. 160–61.
42. Ibid., p. 161.
43. Francis Fukuyama, *The End of History* (New York, 1992) is an inadvertent illustration of the difficulties of making a coherent case for this kind of convergence.
44. *MW,* vol. 13, p. 256.
45. "The Problem of China," *MW,* vol. 15, pp. 215–18.
46. "Chinese National Sentiment," *MW,* vol. 11, p. 215ff.
47. Ibid., p. 216.
48. "Is China a Nation?," *MW,* vol. 13, p. 72ff.
49. "Social Absolutism," *MW,* vol. 13, pp. 313–16.
50. "The Problem of China," *MW,* vol. 15, p. 218.
51. Carl Cohen, "Introduction," to *MW,* vol. 15, pp. xix–xxiii.
52. "Report," *MW,* vol. 15, p. 275.
53. Ibid., p. 276.
54. "Impressions of Soviet Russia," *LW,* vol. 3, p. 213.
55. Ibid.
56. Sidney Hook, "Introduction," *LW,* vol. 1, pp. xiv–xv.
57. Ibid.
58. *Reconstruction in Philosophy* 2d ed. (New York, 1948), ch. V.
59. Ibid., pp. 125–26.
60. Ibid., p. 126.
61. Ibid., p. 127.
62. Rawls, *A Theory of Justice.*
63. *Human Nature and Conduct, MW,* vol. 14, pp. 228–29.
64. Ibid., pp. 169–70.

65. Ibid., p. 226.
66. Ibid.
67. Ibid., pp. 226–27.
68. Ibid., p. 227.
69. *Experience and Nature, LW,* vol. 1, pp. 268–69.
70. Ibid., p. 273.
71. Ibid., p. 295.
72. Ibid., p. 307.
73. Ibid.
74. *The Quest for Certainty, LW,* vol. 4, p. 204.
75. Ibid., p. 209.
76. Ibid., p. 212, Dewey's italics.
77. Ibid., p. 224.
78. Ibid., p. 225.
79. Ibid., p. 244.

7. GOD, BEAUTY, AND THE HIGHER LEARNING

1. Dykhuizen has the story the other way about, that Dewey decided in 1939 that he wished no longer to continue as "Emeritus Professor in Residence" and so informed Columbia in the knowledge that this would involve a substantial reduction in his income. *Life and Mind,* p. 300.
2. Ibid., p. 313.
3. An engaging and scholarly, if somewhat overcrowded, picture of the New York background of Dewey's life in the thirties and forties is given in Alan M. Wald, *The New York Intellectuals* (Chapel Hill, N.C.: 1987).
4. Dykhuizen, *Life and Mind,* p. 313.
5. Putnam, *Renewing Philosophy,* especially ch. 9.
6. Karl Popper, *Conjectures and Refutations* (London, 1963).
7. The exception, as always, is Robert Westbrook, who thinks that Dewey's nonproletarian radicalism, expressed here and in his work for the People's Lobby made excellent sense. As I argue more aggressively in the next chapter, this strikes me as true in the negative sense that it would have been mad for Dewey to turn to Marxist insurrectionary ideas, but otherwise false. It is one thing to believe that the American two-party system chronically fails to produce national policies that address the country's problems in a serious fashion—itself an accusation I would not entirely endorse—and another to believe that attacks by radical loners such as the leaders of third-party insurgencies usually are will do much to improve matters. *Dewey and Democracy,* pp. 441–52.
8. "No Half-Way House for America," *LW,* vol. 9, pp. 289–90.
9. His obituary in the *New York Times* cited his presidency of the People's Lobby and his work for the league as notable aspects of his political liberalism, however. *New York Times,* June 2, 1952, p. A1. It is, of course, true that just as we may display gallantry in a skirmish that has no impact on the major battle in which our fellows are engaged, so we can display our political characters in the same sort of affair.
10. Wald, *New York Intellectuals,* pp. 130–39.
11. Lamont, *Dialogue,* pp. 13–15.
12. As in *Theory of Valuation, LW,* vol. 13, pp. 190–241.
13. John Goldthorpe and David Lockwood, *The Affluent Worker* (Cambridge, England, 1964–68).
14. *The Wit and Wisdom of John Dewey* (New York, 1949).
15. Benedetto Croce, "On the Aesthetics of Dewey," reprinted in *LW,* vol. 15, pp. 438–44.
16. As of this writing, the collection is closed while its French paintings are on tour; a visit to the collection is wonderfully disconcerting, not least because of the near invisibility of some wonderful things and the mind-boggling juxtapositions that Barnes's wall arrangement sometimes produces.
17. *Art as Experience, LW,* vol. 10, p. 10.
18. Ibid.
19. Ibid., p. 16.
20. Ibid., p. 115.
21. Ibid.
22. Ibid., pp. 10–11; incidentally, passages like this must do something to modify the view of Morton and Lucia White that Dewey was fundamentally driven by nostalgia for rural life and that he found the bustle and noise of the city too much for comfort. *The Intellectual versus the City,* pp. 171–79.
23. *Art as Experience, LW,* vol. 10, p. 11; the echoes of Ruskin and William Morris are not accidental.
24. Ibid., p. 18.
25. Ibid., p. 12.
26. In this, at least, Dewey would be seconded by the most interesting of contemporary writers on his subject; Richard Wollheim's *Painting as an Art* (Princeton, 1988) finds the roots of esthetic enjoyment in the in-

fant psyche rather than in an animal pleasure in the expenditure of energy in a task, but it shares with Dewey an essentially genetic approach to the explanation of what makes paintings so engrossing.

27. *Art as Experience, LW,* vol. 10, p. 20.
28. Ibid., p. 115.
29. Ibid., p. 55.
30. Ibid., p. 140.
31. Ibid., p. 141.
32. Ibid., p. 142, Dewey's italics.
33. Ibid., p. 275.
34. Ibid., p. 344.
35. Ibid., p. 345–46.
36. There is a sense in which Dewey did not entirely mean that; he was accused by Santayana of slighting the background and of "foregrounding" everything—that is to say, of emphasizing what was visible, clear-cut, graspable, and lying ready to human hands. This is a natural reading of him, but not right, or at least not what he intended. *Art as Experience* happily quotes Santayana on the mysterious of experience and the importance of what lies at the edges of the known and understood.
37. "Dr. Dewey Replies," *LW,* vol. 9, pp. 223–28.
38. "A God or the God?," *LW,* vol. 9, pp. 213–22.
39. "Dr. Dewey Replies," *LW,* vol. 9, p. 224, Dewey's italics.
40. "From Absolutism to Experimentalism," *LW,* vol. 5, p. 153.
41. "Dr. Dewey Replies," *LW,* vol. 9, pp. 227–28.
42. Ibid., p. 225.
43. "From Absolutism to Experimentalism," *LW,* vol. 5, p. 154.
44. Commager, *The American Mind,* p. 165.
45. *A Common Faith, LW,* vol. 9, pp. 5–8.
46. Ibid., p. 4.
47. Ibid., p. 5.
48. Ibid., pp. 5–6.
49. Ibid., p. 8.
50. *"Religion and Science," LW,* vol. 11, pp. 454–63.
51. Quoted in *Common Faith, LW,* vol. 9, p. 10.
52. Ibid., p. 11.
53. Ibid., p. 14.
54. Ibid., p. 36.
55. It seems that Dewey got the question at one remove from Haeckel: "In his fascinating book, *The Dawn of Conscience,* James Henry Breasted refers to Haeckel as saying that the question he would most wish to have answered is this: Is the universe friendly to man?" Ibid., p. 37.
56. Ibid., p. 15.
57. Ibid., pp. 16, 17.
58. Ibid., p. 19.
59. That is one reason why Steven Rockefeller, himself sympathetic toward a Buddhist view of the universe, finds Dewey's "religious humanism" so congenial. None of the strictures against an obsession with the existence of an individuated God, an intellectualized theology, and the authority of priests would hold against Buddhism.
60. Hook, *Pragmatism and the Tragic Sense of Life,* pp. 110–15; *Common Faith, LW,* vol. 9, p. 9.
61. *Common Faith,* loc. cit., p. 36.
62. Ibid.
63. Ibid., p. 41.
64. Ibid., pp. 48–49.
65. Ibid., p. 136.
66. As suggested above, ch. 5, pp. 000.
67. William H. McNeill, *Hutchins' University* (Chicago, 1992.)
68. *The Higher Learning in America* (New York, 1936), p. 66.
69. Ibid., pp. 66–67.
70. Mortimer Adler and Milton Mayer, *The Revolution in Education* (Chicago, 1958), p. 157ff.
71. *Experience and Education, LW,* vol. 13, p. 6.
72. Cremin, *Transformation of the School,* pp. 3–5.

8. Liberal Politics in Theory and in Practice

1. Dykhuizen, *Life and Mind,* pp. 231–32.
2. "Justice and Psychology," *LW,* vol. 3, pp. 186–89.
3. Dykhuizen, *Life and Mind,* pp. 290–91, argues that Dewey was not an isolationist inasmuch as he supported policies such as lend-lease, whereby American resources were supplied to the British during the eighteen months in which the British Commonwealth faced Germany and Italy alone; it is true that Dewey was not an isolationist *pur sang* and never thought that the opponents of the Nazis and their allies were no better than the Nazis. Still, it is clear enough that had it not been for Pearl Harbor, he would have argued for American

neutrality even if that had meant a British defeat and the subjugation of Europe by Hitler and Mussolini.

4. Ibid., pp. 228–30; Westbrook, *Dewey and Democracy,* pp. 446–50.
5. "The Need for a New Radical Party," *LW,* vol. 5, p. 442.
6. "Dewey Asks Norris to Lead New Party," *LW,* vol. 5, p. 445.
7. "Insurgents Back Norris in Refusing to Quit Republicans," *LW,* vol. 5, p. 505.
8. "The Need for a New Party," *LW,* vol. 6, p. 160.
9. Mancur Olson, *The Logic of Collective Action* (New York, 1962) is the classical account of why small well-placed groups do well.
10. "The Need for a New Party," *LW,* vol. 6, p. 160.
11. Ibid., p. 169.
12. Ibid., p. 170.
13. Ibid., p. 171.
14. Ibid.
15. Ibid., p. 172.
16. Ibid., p. 179.
17. Robert Skidelsky, *The Life of J. M. Keynes* (London, 1993), vol. 2, pp. 489–94.
18. "There Is No Halfway House," *LW,* vol. 6, pp. 289–90.
19. *LW,* vol. 11, p. 526 (*New Republic,* October 7, 1936).
20. Lamont, *Dialogue,* pp. 76–77.
21. "The Teacher and the Public," *LW,* vol. 11, p. 159.
22. Ibid., p. 160.
23. Ibid., p. 161.
24. Ibid.
25. *LW,* vol. 9, pp. 313–20.
26. Westbrook, *Dewey and Democracy,* pp. 476–95, gives a usefully anxious account of how hard Dewey struggled to keep his balance between a lack of vigilance against the infiltrators and totalitarians on the one side and uncritical support for the status quo on the other.
27. "Mr. Woll as a Communist Catcher," *LW,* vol. 5, p. 392.
28. He wrote in exactly the same terms in 1936; businessmen would press for laissez-faire and claim that the freedom to use their property as they chose was one of their civil liberties but would never think that free speech for their opponents was an even more important one. "Liberalism and Civil Liberties," *LW,* vol. 11, p. 374.
29. Ibid., p. 376.
30. Ibid., p. 378.
31. This is not to impugn Edmund Wilson's classical account of the journey from utopian socialism to the Bolshevik Revolution in *To the Finland Station;* I mean rather that Hook wrote *philosophically* better sense about Marx's early, "Hegelian" work than anyone in the English-speaking world at that time.
32. Sidney Hook et al., *The Meaning of Marx* (New York, 1935), p. 52.
33. I mean this at least half-seriously; the Labour party in Britain has always had some difficulty in capturing more than some 55 to 65 percent of the working-class vote, while the Conservative party has often had over 80 percent of the middle- and upper-class vote.
34. Hook, *Meaning of Marx,* p. 53.
35. Ibid., p. 86.
36. Ibid., p. 90.
37. "Declaration of Purpose," *LW,* vol. 11, p. 305; "Preliminary Statement," *LW,* vol. 11, pp. 306–07.
38. There is an amusing account of the proceedings in Mexico in Wald, *New York Intellectuals,* pp. 130–39.
39. "Summary of Findings," *LW,* vol. 11, p. 321.
40. Ibid., p. 323.
41. "Significance of the Trotsky Inquiry," *LW,* vol. 11, p. 331.
42. Ibid.
43. Ibid., p. 332.
44. Both, and a third on the same theme by the editor, are reprinted in Novack, *Their Morals and Ours;* Dewey's contribution, "Means and Ends," is in *LW,* vol. 13, pp. 349–54.
45. "Means and Ends," loc. cit., p. 354.
46. Ibid., pp. 350, 354.
47. "Social Realities *versus* Police Court Fictions," *LW,* vol. 14, pp. 235–48.
48. A judgment shared by the committee that gave Russell the Nobel Prize for Literature in 1951 on the strength of that book.
49. Greenfield, *Devil and Dr. Barnes,* pp. 199–230.
50. "My Philosophy of Law," *LW,* vol. 14, pp. 115–22.
51. Horwitz, *Transformation of American Law,* ch. 1.
52. Anthony Wright, *G. D. H. Cole and Socialist Democracy* (Oxford, 1979).
53. Keith Middelmas, *The Politics of Industrial Society* (London, 1975).
54. J. K. Galbraith, *American Capitalism* (New York, 1966).
55. The most famous attack on the potentially dictatorial implications of Rousseau's conception of democracy was J. L. Talmon's

The Origins of Totalitarian Democracy (London, 1956).

56. "Art as Our Heritage," *LW,* vol. 14, p. 256.
57. "In Response," Henry Homes, ed., *John Dewey: The Man and His Philosophy* (Cambridge, Mass., 1930), p. 177.
58. *Individualism Old and New, LW,* vol. 5, p. 122.
59. Ibid.
60. Ibid., pp. 122–23.
61. Ibid., p. 72.
62. Ibid., p. 82.
63. Ibid., p. 83.
64. Among other famous expressions of the anxiety, see L. T. Hobhouse, *The Metaphysical Theory of the State* (London, 1918) and Isaiah Berlin, "Two Concepts of Liberty," *Four Essays on Liberty* (Oxford, 1971).
65. *Individualism Old and New, LW,* vol. 5, p. 100.
66. Ibid., p. 101.
67. Ibid., p. 104.
68. Ibid., p. 105.
69. *Liberalism and Social Action* thus has something in common with T. H. Marshall, *Citizenship and Social Class* (Cambridge, England, 1948).
70. "Liberalism in a Vacuum," *LW,* vol. 11, p. 488.
71. "Liberalism and Civil Liberties" *LW,* vol. 11, p. 374.
72. *Freedom and Culture, LW,* vol. 13, pp. 63–188.
73. Ibid., p. 173.
74. Ibid., p. 174.
75. Ibid., p. 175.
76. Ibid., p. 176, quoting *Public and Its Problems, LW,* vol. 2, p. 368.
77. *Freedom and Culture, LW,* vol. 13, p. 177.
78. Ibid., p. 188.

9. DEATH AND RESURRECTION

1. Daniel Bell, *The Cultural Contradictions of Capitalism* (New York, 1974) is a particularly plangent account of what I have in mind. Bell worries that capitalism was launched by people with a strong sense of identity, of being "one and the same" in all they thought and did and that modern affluence has rotted that strong and morally serious ego. I think that we are better at doing without a fixed identity than Bell supposes. We adjust our behavior and attitudes to different audiences and their demands without suffering incipient schizophrenia.
2. *The School and Society, MW,* vol. 1, pp. 58–59.
3. On Gold and his baneful effects, see Daniel Aaron, *Writers on the Left* (New York, 1969); for a good general account of the relations of intellectuals to the Communist party, see Harvey Klehr, *The Heyday of Communism* (New Brunswick, N.J., 1985). The careers of a representative selection of intellectuals who came and went are engagingly recounted in Jack Diggins, *Up from Communism* (New York, 1973).
4. On the latter, Christopher Lasch, *Agony of the American Left* (New York, 1969), ch. 3, remains indispensable.
5. "The Committee for Cultural Freedom," *LW,* vol. 14, p. 365.
6. "Democratic Ends Need Democratic Methods for Their Realization," *LW,* vol. 14, p. 367.
7. "Means and Ends," *LW,* vol. 13, pp. 349–54.
8. Westbrook, *Dewey and Democracy,* p. 511.
9. "No Matter What Happens—Stay Out," *LW,* vol. 14, p. 364.
10. Ibid.
11. Ibid.
12. "Lessons from the War—in Philosophy," *LW,* vol. 14, pp. 325–26.
13. John P. Diggins, *Promise of Pragmatism* (Chicago, 1994), p. 1.
14. E.g., "William James' Morals and Julien Benda's," *LW,* vol. 15, pp. 19–26.
15. "Higher Learning and War," *LW,* vol. 14, p. 274.
16. "Russia's Position," *LW,* vol. 15, pp. 340–41.
17. Ibid., p. 341.
18. "Several Faults Are Found in *Mission to Moscow* Film," *LW,* vol. 15, p. 347. The heading from *New York Times,* May 9, 1943, p. 8, understates the ferocity of Dewey's views to a degree remarkable even in the *Times.*
19. "*Mission to Moscow* Film Viewed as Historical Realism," letter from Arthur Upham Pope, *LW,* vol. 15, pp. 492–501; Dewey's reply to Pope is at *LW,* vol. 15, pp. 351–55.
20. John Aubrey, *Brief Lives* (London, 1949) p. 154.

21. "Anti-naturalism in Extremis," *LW,* vol. 15, pp. 46–62, first published in *Partisan Review* in 1943.
22. "Henry Wallace and the 1948 Elections" and "American Youth, Beware of Wallace Bearing Gifts," *LW,* vol. 15, pp. 239–41, 242–47.
23. "I've not gotten over being sorry that I let B. Russell down so easily as I did. I have never been able to take him seriously enough intellectually to do him justice. If any evidence of the dam low estate of philosophy at present were needed, his inflated rep would be enough—he may or may not be an authority on the formalization of mathematics. I'm suspicious about that on the authority of A. F. Bentley, but even so it is pitiful that should give him a rep in philosophy." Quoted by L. S. Feuer, "Introduction,"*LW,* vol. 15, p. xiin.
24. *Knowing and the Known, LW,* vol. 16.
25. "Comment on Some Points in Recent Moral and Logical Theory," *LW,* vol. 17, pp. 480–82.
26. Mary Warnock gives a good brief account of the issue in *Ethics since 1900* (Oxford, 1962), pp. 109–16.
27. R. M. Hutchins, *Observations on Education* (London, 1953).
28. Hofstadter, *Anti-intellectualism in American Life,* ch. IX, pp. 359–90.
29. "Challenge to Liberal Thought," *LW,* vol. 15, p. 262.
30. Ibid.
31. Dykhuizen, *Life and Mind,* pp. 303–04; Dewey's and Hart's letters are in *LW,* vol. 14, pp. 370–73, 427–09.
32. The conference was reported in *New York Times,* October 27, 1940.
33. Rockefeller, *John Dewey,* pp. 488–89; Rockefeller points out that Dewey was, when pressed, ready to admit that he did not believe in the literal survival of death.
34. *New York Times,* October 27, 1940, p. 14.
35. "Education for Freedom," *Christian Century* (November 15, 1944), p. 1315.
36. Ibid., p. 1316.
37. Paul Crosser, *The Nihilism of John Dewey* (New York, 1958), p. 178.
38. Russell Kirk, *The Conservative Mind* (New York, 1952), pp. 418–19.
39. This is Westbrook's view, *Dewey and Democracy,* pp. 523–32.
40. C. E. Ayres, "Dewey: Master of the Commonplace," *New Republic* (1938), p. 303.
41. George Novack, *Pragmatism versus Marxism* (New York, 1975).
42. Lasch, *New Radicalism,* ch. 5; *The Agony of the American Left,* ch. 1.
43. Lasch, *Agony,* p. 11.
44. Ibid., pp. 11–12.
45. Hofstadter, *Anti-intellectualism,* pp. 329–30.
46. Ibid., p. 345.
47. Ibid., p. 361, quoting Cremin, *Transformation,* p. 239.
48. Among the skills taught to young women was the art of climbing into low-slung sports cars without displaying their underwear.
49. Hofstadter, *Anti-intellectualism,* pp. 386–87.
50. It is of some significance that every review of Dewey's work in the British periodical *Mind* was written by Schiller.
51. Reichenbach's contribution to *The Philosophy of John Dewey* comes close to deploring Dewey's attempt to cover the entire philosophical landscape as an essentially old-fashioned way of doing philosophy. "Dewey's Theory of Science," in Schilpp, *Philosophy of Dewey,* p. 192.
52. Cornel West, *The American Evasion of Philosophy* (Minneapolis, 1988), pp. 86–88.
53. Richard Rorty, *Philosophical Papers* (Cambridge, England, 1990), vol. 1, p. 64.
54. T. S. Kuhn, *The Structure of Scientific Revolutions* (Chicago, 1962).
55. See Imre Lakatos and David Musgrave, *Criticism and the Growth of Knowledge* (Cambridge, England, 1965) for a representative (and representatively intemperate) account of all this by Kuhn, Karl Popper, Paul Feyerabend, and others.
56. Rorty, *Papers,* vol. 1, pp. 175–96.
57. Rorty, "Post-Modernist Bourgeois Liberalism," *Papers,* vol. 1, pp. 197–202.
58. Westbrook, *Dewey and Democracy,* pp. 539–42.
59. Ibid., p. 541.
60. Bourne, "Transnational America," p. 263.
61. Westbrook notes that Habermas counts American pragmatism as "the third productive reply to Hegel" and invaluable as a democratic corrective to Marxism. *Dewey and American Democracy,* p. 539n. I was amused to learn (at second hand) that Habermas had for years urged his German students to take an interest in Dewey as I had urged my students in Oxford—and with the same lack of success.
62. Michael Sandel, *Liberalism and the Limits of Justice* (Cambridge, England, 1981); Charles Taylor, "Cross-Purposes," in *Liberalism and the Moral Life,* ed. Nancy Ro-

senblum (Cambridge, Mass., 1990), pp. 183–200.

63. Charles Taylor, *Sources of the Self* (Cambridge, Mass., 1988), pp. 59–60; *The Ethics of Authenticity* (Cambridge, Mass., 1992).
64. Mary Douglas, *Natural Symbols* (London, 1968).
65. Taylor, *Sources of the Self*, pp. 517–21.
66. I have never seen this set out in print. I have heard Professor Taylor suggest it in a seminar; it would not be easy to infer it from *Sources of the Self*, pp. 495–521, but it is not impossible to see that it might underlie the argument there. Richard Rorty is perhaps the leading theorist of the faith that the secular advantages of liberal societies will see them through.
67. Niebuhr, *Moral Man and Immoral Society;* Christopher Lasch, *The True and Only Heaven* (New York, 1991).
68. Karl Popper, *Objective Knowledge* (Oxford, 1972), particularly ch. 4, "On the Theory of the Objective Mind," pp. 153–61.
69. Fukuyama, *The End of History*.
70. "Nationalizing Education," *MW*, vol. 10, p. 204.
71. Ibid., pp. 205–06.
72. Conservatives often claim that since the United States spends as high a proportion of GNP on education as countries like Germany, France, and Japan, the problems of American education cannot be financial, but this ignores the question of distribution.
73. "Shall We Abolish School Frills? No," *LW*, vol. 9, pp. 141–46.
74. His last published essay was "Implications of S.2499," *LW*, vol. 15, pp. 281–85, attacking a Senate bill to afford protection for religious teaching in schools.
75. Feuer, "Introduction," *LW*, vol. 15, p. xxiii.
76. John Rawls, *Political Liberalism* (New York, 1993).
77. Christopher Lasch, *The Culture of Narcissism* (New York, 1978).
78. This is spelled out with great elegance and persuasiveness in J. H. Randall, Jr.'s obituary of Dewey, "John Dewey 1859–1952," *Journal of Philosophy* (1953), pp. 5–13.

Bibliography

Works by Dewey Referred to in the Text
(in order of appearance in *Middle Works [MW]* and *Later Works [LW]*)

Books

The School and Society, MW, vol. 1, pp. 1–109.
Ethics (with James H. Tufts), *MW,* vol. 5.
How We Think, MW, vol. 6, pp. 177–356.
German Philosophy and Politics, MW, vol. 8, pp. 135–204.
Schools of Tomorrow (with Evelyn Dewey), *MW,* vol. 8, pp. 205–404.
Democracy and Education, MW, vol. 9.
Reconstruction in Philosophy, MW, vol. 12, pp. 77–201.
Human Nature and Conduct, MW, vol. 14.
Experience and Nature, LW, vol. 1.
The Public and Its Problems, LW, vol. 2, pp. 253–372.
The Quest for Certainty, LW, vol. 4.
Individualism Old and New, LW, vol. 5, pp. 41–123.
A Common Faith, LW, vol. 9, pp. 1–58.
Art as Experience, LW, vol. 10.
Liberalism and Social Action, LW, vol. 11, pp. 1–65.
Experience and Education, LW, vol. 13, pp. 1–62.
Freedom and Culture, LW, vol. 13, pp. 63–188.
Theory of Valuation, LW, vol. 13, pp. 189–252.
Knowing and the Known (with A. F. Bentley), *LW,* vol. 16.

Essays, et cetera
(in order of appearance in *Early Works [EW], Middle Works [MW],* and *Later Works [LW]*)

This list omits some very insubstantial items, such as letters to newspapers, but it includes the reports of the 1937 commission of inquiry into the charges against Trotsky that Dewey chaired in Mexico.

"The New Psychology," *EW,* vol. 1, pp. 48–60.
"The Obligation to Knowledge of God," *EW,* vol. 1, pp. 61–63.
"Education and the Health of Women," *EW,* vol. 1, pp. 64–68.
"Health and Sex in Higher Education," *EW,* vol. 1, pp. 69–80.
"Psychology in High-Schools from the Standpoint of the College," *EW,* vol. 1, pp. 81–89.
"The Ethics of Democracy," *EW,* vol. 1, pp. 227–49.
"The Philosophy of Thomas Hill Green," *EW,* vol. 3, pp. 14–35.

"Ethics in the University of Michigan," *EW,* vol. 3, pp. 48–50.
"Outlines of a Critical Theory of Ethics," EW, vol. 3, pp. 239–388.
"Poetry and Philosophy," *EW,* vol. 3, pp. 110–24.
"Two Phases of Renan's Life," *EW,* vol. 3, pp. 174–79.
"Christianity and Democracy," *EW,* vol. 4, pp. 3–10.
"Renan's Loss of Faith in Science," *EW,* vol. 4, pp. 11–18.
"Intuitionalism," *EW,* vol. 4, pp. 123–31.
"The Study of Ethics: A Syllabus (1894), EW, vol. 4, pp. 221–362.
"Evolution and Ethics," *EW,* vol. 5, pp. 34–53.
"My Pedagogic Creed," *EW,* vol. 5, pp. 84–95.
"The Reflex Arc Concept in Psychology," *EW,* vol. 5, pp. 96–110.
"The Evolutionary Method as Applied to Ethics: I Its Scientific Necessity; The Evolutionary Method as Applied to Ethics: II Its Significance for Conduct," *MW,* vol. 2, pp. 1–38.
"Interpretation of Savage Mind," *MW,* vol. 2, pp. 39–53.
"The School as Social Centre," *MW,* vol. 2, pp. 80–93.
"Review of Josiah Royce's *Nature, Man and the Moral Order,*" *MW,* vol. 2, pp. 120–37.
"A Policy of Industrial Education," *MW,* vol. 7, pp. 93–97.
"Some Dangers in the Present Movement for Industrial Democracy," *MW,* vol. 7, pp. 98–103.
"Nationalizing Education," *MW,* vol. 10, pp. 202–10.
"Force, Violence and Law," *MW,* vol. 10, pp. 211–15.
"The Future of Pacifism," *MW,* vol. 10, pp. 265–70.
"In a Time of National Hesitation," *MW,* vol. 10, pp. 256–59.
"In Explanation of Our Lapse," *MW,* vol. 10, pp. 292–95.
"The Need for a Recovery of Philosophy," *MW,* vol. 10, pp. 3–48.
"Morals and the Conduct of States." *MW,* vol. 11, pp. 122–26.
"Japan and America," *MW,* vol. 11, pp. 150–55.
"Liberalism in Japan," *MW,* vol. 11, pp. 156–73.
"The Discrediting of Idealism," *MW,* vol. 11, pp. 180–85.
"Chinese National Sentiment," *MW,* vol. 11, pp. 215–27.
"Our National Dilemma," *MW,* vol. 12, pp. 3–7.
"Pragmatic America," *MW,* vol. 13, pp. 306–10.
"Is China a Nation?," *MW,* vol. 13, pp. 72–78.
"Social Absolutism," *MW,* vol. 13, pp. 311–16.
"Ethics and International Relations," *MW,* vol. 15, pp. 53–64.
"Shall We Join the League?," *MW,* vol. 15, pp. 78–82.
Review of Bertrand Russell's *The Problem of China, MW,* vol. 15, pp. 215–18.
"A Key to the New World," *LW,* vol. 2, pp. 226–30.
"Psychology and Justice," *LW,* vol. 3, pp. 186–95.
"Impressions of Soviet Russia," *LW,* vol. 3, pp. 203–50.
"From Absolutism to Experimentalism," *LW,* vol. 5, pp. 147–60.
"James Marsh and American Philosophy," *LW,* vol. 5, pp. 178–96.
"The Sphere of Application of the Excluded Middle," *LW,* vol. 5, pp. 197–202.
"The Need for a New Party," *LW,* vol. 6, pp. 156–81.
"Imperative Need: A New Radical Party," *LW,* vol. 9, pp. 76–80.
"Shall We Abolish School Frills? No," *LW,* vol. 9, pp. 141–46.
"The Teacher and the Public," *LW,* vol. 11, pp. 158–61.
"No Half-Way House for America," *LW,* vol. 9, pp. 289–90.
"A God or the God?" *LW,* vol. 9, pp. 213–22.
"Dr. Dewey Replies," *LW,* vol. 9, pp. 223–28.
"Liberalism and Civil Liberties," *LW,* vol. 11, pp. 372–75.
"Liberalism in a Vacuum," *LW,* vol. 11, pp. 489–95.
"Declaration of Purposes," *LW,* vol. 11, pp. 303–05.
"Preliminary Statement," *LW,* vol. 11, pp. 306–09.
"Summary of Findings," *LW,* vol. 11, pp. 321–25.
"Significance of the Trotsky Inquiry," *LW,* vol. 11, pp. 330–35.
"Review of *Religion and Science,*" *LW,* vol. 11, pp. 454–63.
"Means and Ends," *LW,* vol. 13, pp. 349–54.

"My Philosophy of Law," *LW,* vol. 14, pp. 115–22.
"Social Realities versus Police Court Fictions," *LW,* vol. 14, pp. 235–48.
"Art as Our Heritage," *LW,* vol. 14, pp. 255–57.
"Higher Learning and War," *LW,* vol. 14, pp. 273–74.
"Lessons from the War—in Philosophy," *LW,* vol. 14, pp. 312–33.
"No Matter What Happens—Stay Out," *LW,* vol. 14, p. 364.
"The Committee for Cultural Freedom," *LW,* vol. 14, pp. 365–66.
"Democratic Ends Need Democratic Methods for their Realization," *LW,* vol. 14, pp. 367–68.
"William James' Morals and Julien Benda's," *LW,* vol. 15, pp. 19–26.
"Implications of S.2499," *LW,* vol. 15, pp. 281–85.
"Russia's Position," *LW,* vol. 15, pp. 338–41.
"Several Faults Are Found in *Mission to Moscow* Film," *LW,* vol. 15, pp. 345–50.
"Anti-naturalism *in Extremis,*" *LW,* vol. 15, pp. 46–62.
"Henry Wallace and the 1948 Elections," *LW,* vol. 15, pp. 239–41.
"American Youth, Beware of Wallace Bearing Gifts," *LW,* vol. 15, pp. 242–247.
"Challenge to Liberal Thought," *LW,* vol. 15, pp. 261–75.
"Comment on Recent Criticisms of Some Points in Recent Moral and Logical Theory," *LW,* vol. 17, pp. 480–84.

SECONDARY SOURCES

Aaron, Daniel. *Writers on the Left*. New York, 1969.
Addams, Jane. *A Modern Lear*. In *The Social Thought of Jane Addams,* ed. Christopher Lasch. New York, 1965.
———. *Twenty Years at Hull-House*. New York, 1910.
Adler, Mortimer, and Milton Mayer. *The Revolution in Education*. Chicago, 1958.
Avrich, Paul. *Anarchist Portraits*. Princeton, 1988.
———. *The Haymarket Tragedy*. Princeton, 1984.
———. *The Modern School Movement*. Princeton, 1980.
Bell, Daniel. *The Cultural Contradictions of Capitalism*. New York, 1974.
Bender, Thomas. *New York Intellectuals*. New York, 1988.
Berlin, Isaiah. "Two Concepts of Liberty," *Four Essays on Liberty*. Oxford, England, 1971.
Bernstein, Richard. *John Dewey*. New York, 1967.
Blake, Casey Nelson. *Beloved Community*. Chapel Hill, N.C., 1990.
Blewett, Father John, S. J., ed. *John Dewey: His Thought and Influence*. New York, 1964.
Bourne, Randolph. *The Gary Schools*. Cambridge, Mass., 1970 [1916].
———. *The Radical Will,* ed. Olaf Hansen. New York, 1977.
———. "Transnational America." *The Radical Will,* ed. Olaf Hansen. New York, 1977.
Boydston, Jo Ann, ed., *The Poems of John Dewey*. Carbondale, Ill., 1977.
Bradley, F. H. *Ethical Studies*. Oxford, England, 1924.
Brent, Joseph. *Charles Sanders Peirce*. Bloomington, Ind., 1993.
Burke, Thomas. *Dewey's New Logic*. Chicago, 1995.
Butler, Mrs. E. M. *The Tyranny of Greece over Germany*. Cambridge, England, 1933.
Commager, Henry S. *The American Mind*. New Haven, 1950.
Coughlan, Neil. *Young John Dewey*. Chicago, 1974.
Cremin, Lawrence A. *Teachers College*. New York, 1954.
———. *The Transformation of the School*. New York, 1961.
Crosser, Paul. *The Nihilism of John Dewey*. New York, 1958.
Curtis, S. J., and M. A. E. Boultwood. *A Short History of Educational Ideas*. London, 1953.
Dahl, Robert A. *After the Revolution?* New Haven, 1972.
Danto, Arthur. *Nietzsche as Philosopher*. New York, 1965.
Diggins, John P. *The Promise of Pragmatism*. Chicago, 1994.
———. *Up from Communism*. New York, 1973.
Douglas, Mary. *Natural Symbols*. London, 1968.
Dykhuizen, George. *The Life and Mind of John Dewey*. Carbondale, Ill., 1974.
Eastman, Max. "John Dewey." *Atlantic* (December 1941).

Forcey, Charles. *The Crossroads of Liberalism*. New York, 1961.
Ford, Corydon. *Child of Democracy*. New York, 1893.
Frank, Robert. *Passions within Reason*. New York, 1988.
Fukuyama, Francis. *The End of History*. New York, 1992.
Galbraith, John Kenneth. *American Capitalism*. New York, 1966.
George, Henry. *Progress and Poverty*. San Francisco, 1879.
Ginger, Ray. *Debs: A Life*. Chicago, 1948.
Goldthorpe, John, and David Lockwood. *The Affluent Worker*. Cambridge, England, 1964–68.
Good, Harry G., and James D. Teller. *A History of Western Education*. New York, 1969.
Greenfield, Howard. *The Devil and Dr. Barnes,* New York, 1987.
Hall, G. Stanley. *Life and Confessions of a Psychologist*. New York, 1923.
Hegel, G. W. F. *The Phenomenology of Spirit,* tr. A. V. Miller. Oxford, England, 1977.
———. *The Philosophy of History*. New York, 1956.
———. *The Philosophy of Right,* tr. Allen Wood. Cambridge, England, 1991.
Henricksen, Louise. *Anzia Yezierska*. New York, 1990.
Himmelfarb, Gertrude. *Poverty and Compassion*. New York, 1992.
Hobhouse, L. T. *The Metaphysical Theory of the State*. London, 1918.
Hofstadter, Richard. *Anti-intellectualism in American Life*. New York, 1963.
Homes, Henry, ed. *John Dewey: The Man and His Philosophy*. Cambridge, Mass., 1930.
Hook, Sidney, ed. *The Meaning of Marx*. New York, 1935.
———, ed., *John Dewey, Philosopher of Science and Freedom*. New York, 1949.
———. *Pragmatism and the Tragic Sense of Life*. New York, 1974.
Horwitz, Morton. *The Transformation of American Law, 1870–1960*. New York, 1992.
Hume, David. *A Treatise on Human Nature,* ed. T. H. Green and T. H. Grose. London, 1884.
Hutchins, Robert M. *The Higher Learning in America*. New York, 1936.
———. *Observations on Education*. London, 1953.
Huxley, T. H. *Evolution and Ethics, The Romanes Lecture*. Oxford, England, 1895.
Johnson, A. H., ed. *The Wit and Wisdom of John Dewey*. Boston, 1949.
Kallen, Horace, *Democracy and Culture*. Boston, 1924.
———. "Democracy versus the Melting Pot." *Nation* (1915).
———. "Dewey and Pragmatism." In *John Dewey, Philosopher of Science and Freedom,* ed. Sidney Hook. New York, 1949.
Keenan, Barry. *The Dewey Experiment in China: Educational Power and Political Reform in the Early Republic*. Cambridge, Mass., 1977.
Kirk, Russell. *The Conservative Mind*. New York, 1952.
Klehr, Harvey. *The Heyday of Communism*. New Brunswick, N.J., 1985.
Kloppenburg, James. *Uncertain Victory*. New York, 1986.
Kramer, Rita. *Maria Montessori*. London, 1991.
Kramnick, Isaac, and Barry Shearman. *Harold Laski*. London, 1993.
Kuhn, Thomas S. *The Structure of Scientific Revolutions*. Chicago, 1962.
Kuklick, Bruce. *Churchmen and Philosophers: From Jonathan Edwards to John Dewey*. New Haven, 1985.
Lakatos, Imre, and David Musgrave. *Criticism and the Growth of Knowledge*. Cambridge, England, 1965.
Lamont, Corliss, ed. *Dialogue on John Dewey*. New York, 1960.
Lasch, Christopher. *The Agony of the American Left*. New York, 1969.
———. *The New Radicalism in America*. New York, 1965.
———, ed. *The Social Thought of Jane Addams*. New York, 1965.
———. *The True and Only Heaven*. New York, 1992.
Lawson-Dick, Oliver, ed. *Aubrey's Brief Lives*. London, 1949.
Lerner, Max. *America as a Civilization*. New York, 1949.
MacIntyre, Alasdair. *Three Rival Versions of Moral Inquiry*. London, 1991.
Marsden, George. *The Soul of the American University*. New York, 1994.
Marshall, T. H. *Citizenship and Social Class*. Cambridge, England, 1948.
Mayhew, Katherine Camp, and Anna Camp Edwards. *The Dewey School*. New York, 1936.
McNeill, William H. *Hutchins' University*. Chicago, 1992.
Merton, Robert. *Social Theory and Social Structure*. New York, 1968.
Middelmas, Keith. *The Politics of Industrial Society*. London, 1975.
Mill, J. S., and Jeremy Bentham. *Utilitarianism and Other Essays*. Harmondsworth, England, 1987.

Moorehead, Caroline. *Bertrand Russell*. New York, 1993.
Nettleship, Richard L., ed. *The Works of Thomas Hill Green*. London, 1883.
Nicholson, Peter. *The Political Philosophy of the British Idealists*. Cambridge, England, 1990.
Niebuhr, Reinhold. *The Children of Light and the Children of Darkness*. New York, 1944.
———. *Moral Man and Immoral Society*. New York, 1932.
Novack, George. *Pragmatism versus Marxism*. New York, 1975.
———, ed. *Their Morals and Ours* by Leon Trotsky/John Dewey. Pathfinder Press. New York, 1973.
Olson, Mancur. *The Logic of Collective Action*. New York, 1962.
Popper, Karl. *Conjectures and Refutations*. London, 1963.
———. *The Open Society and Its Enemies*. London, 1945.
Popper, Karl Raimund. *The Logic of Scientific Discovery*. London, 1957.
———. *Objective Knowledge*. Oxford, England, 1972.
Putnam, Hilary. *Renewing Philosophy*. Cambridge, Mass., 1992.
Randall, John Herman, Jr. "The Department of Philosophy," *The Faculty of Philosophy*. New York, 1954.
Rawls, John. *Political Liberalism*. New York, 1993.
———. *A Theory of Justice*. Cambridge, Mass., 1971.
Richter, Melvin. *The Politics of Conscience*. London, 1963.
Rockefeller, Steven. *John Dewey*. New York, 1991.
Rorty, Richard. *Philosophical Papers*. Cambridge, England, 1990.
Rosen, Norma. *John and Anzia*. New York, 1989.
Ross, Dorothy. *The Origins of American Social Science*. Cambridge, England, 1991.
———. *G. Stanley Hall*. Chicago, 1973.
Russell, Bertrand. *Roads to Freedom*. London, 1918.
Ryan, Alan. *Bertrand Russell: A Political Life*. New York, 1988.
Sandel, Michael. *Liberalism and the Limits of Justice*. Cambridge, England, 1981.
Schilpp, Arthur, ed. *The Philosophy of John Dewey*. New York, 1938.
Schumpeter, Joseph. *Capitalism, Socialism and Democracy*. London, 1942.
Skidelsky, Robert. *English Progressive Schools*. Harmondsworth, England, 1968.
———. *The Life of J. M. Keynes*, vol. II. London, 1993.
Smith, Page. *The Rise of Industrial America*. New York, 1990.
Sorel, Georges. *Reflections on Violence*. New York, 1961.
Steel, Ronald. *Walter Lippmann and the American Century*. Boston, 1980.
Stettner, Howard. *Herbert Croly and the Making of Modern Liberalism*. Lawrence, Kan., 1993.
Sumner, William Graham. *What Social Classes Owe to Each Other*. Caldwell, Ida., 1978 [1883].
Talmon, Jacob L. *The Origins of Totalitarian Democracy*. London, 1956.
Taylor, Charles. "Cross-Purposes," In *Liberalism and the Moral Life*, ed. Nancy Rosenblum. Cambridge, Mass., 1990.
Taylor, Charles. *The Ethics of Authenticity*. Cambridge, Mass., 1992.
———. *The Explanation of Behaviour*. London, 1964.
———. *Sources of the Self*. Cambridge, Mass., 1988.
Thomas, John L. *Alternative America*. Cambridge, Mass., 1985.
Truman, David B. *The Governmental Process*. New York, 1958.
Veblen, Thorstein. *The Theory of the Leisure Class*. New York, 1973.
Veysey, Lawrence. *The Emergence of the American University*. Chicago, 1965.
Wald, Alan W. *The New York Intellectuals*. Chapel Hill, N.C., 1987.
Warnock, Mary. *Ethics since 1900*. Oxford, England,
Wenley, R. M. *The Life and Work of George Sylvester Morris*. New York, 1917.
West, Cornel. *The American Evasion of Philosophy*. Minneapolis, 1988.
Westbrook, Robert. *John Dewey and American Democracy*. Ithaca, N.Y., 1991.
White, Morton. *The Origins of Dewey's Instrumentalism*. New York, 1943.
———, and Lucia White. *Intellectuals and the City*. New York, 1980.
———. *Social Thought in America*. New York, 1976 [1947].
Williams, William Appleman. *An Outline of American History*. New York, 1990.
Wilson, James Q. *The Moral Sense*. New York, 1993.
Wollheim, Richard. *Painting as an Art*. Princeton, 1988.
Wright, Anthony. *G. D. H. Cole and Socialist Democracy*. Oxford, England, 1979.
Yezierska, Anzia. *All That I Could Never Be*. New York, 1932.
———. *Red Ribbon on a White Horse*. New York, 1950.

INDEX